Reviews

"Hills of Sacrifice *is a magnificent history of 'Hawaii's own', the 5th RCT during the Korean War. It will be widely read, and deserves to be."*

Governor Benjamin J. Cayetano,
State of Hawaii

"At last, after 49 years, the best and most definitive book on infantry combat at the bayonet level in Korea. It grips the reader into the firestorm, fury, terror and grief of it all.

Hills of Sacrifice *is deeply researched, grimly detailed, personalized histo-riography of battlefield infantry action by American 'grunts' fighting determined North Korean and Chinese soldiers.*
This superb book is not for the faint-hearted. Graphic descriptions of the bloody details of close-in grunt infantry battle and the love of soldiers for one another."

LTGEN Harold G. Moore

"A hell of a read! Hills of Sacrifice, *explodes like a hand grenade and is riveting combat reportage. It's the most detailed account of the bloody Korean War that I have read.*
The reader is there in the trenches, with the Grunts, stopping massed attacks or storming enemy held hills. The 5th RCT was a great regiment, with top leaders, brave warriors, and this remarkable book captures their gallantry and sacrifice dead on a target. A must read for anyone wanting to know the Grunt's heroic story form the Korean War and how a gallant regiment became the Fire Brigade of the Korean War."

COL David H. Hackworth

Master Sergeant Frank Chandler comforts a grief-stricken infantryman from the 1st Battalion 5th RCT, whose buddy was KIA on 18 August 50. Corporal Joseph Villaflor, a medic from Eleele, Kauai, is filling out casualty tags in the background. This Al Chang photo was nominated for the Pulitzer Prize. (source: Chang)

Hills of Sacrifice
The 5th RCT in Korea

TURNER PUBLISHING COMPANY

Michael Slater

Turner Publishing Company

Turner Publishing Company Staff:
Editor: Lisa K. Thompson
Project Coordinator: Herbert C. Banks II
Designers: Heather R. Warren/Herbert C. Banks II

Copyright © 2000 Michael P. Slater
Publishing Rights: Turner Publishing Company

ISBN: 978-1-68162-440-2 (pbk.)
Library of Congress Catalog Card No: 00-101691

Additional copies may be purchased directly from the Publisher.

On the cover: *SGT Herbert Ohia from Hilo, Hawaii, views dead
NKPA soldiers on Hill 268, 19 September 1950. One of the dead
NKPA is wearing a Russian helmet. (source: Chang)*

ISBN 978-1-56311-588-2 (hc)

*An artillery officer directs United Nations troops as they drop white phos-
phorous on a communist-held post, while soldiers of Companies A and K,
5th RCT, 25th Infantry Division, keep a sharp lookout for enemy movement, 1 February 1951. (source: 25th ID Museum)*

TABLE OF CONTENTS

This book is dedicated to

the soldiers who served

in the 5th Regimental Combat Team,

and especially to the families

of those men

who fell on the Hills of Sacrifice

in the Korean War.

Mahalo

(source: National Archives [NA])

FOREWORD

The Korean conflict has been variously ascribed over the years as a "limited war" or "police action." To the soldiers in close combat on the front lines, that "war" was anything but limited.

To them, living from day to day with each day and night bringing the possibility of death or serious wounds, their war was very real. In addition to the ever-present personal dangers were the lack of comforts that are normally taken for granted. Hot meals, cool drinks, and uninterrupted sleep were comforts of which the front-line warriors could only dream.

The author's thorough research into detailed actions of the 5th Regimental Combat Team, and adjacent units in the early actions of the Korean War, are so real that the reader can feel a part of the fears, uncommon bravery, devotion to comrades, and the daily discomforts of life on the field of battle. Liberal but carefully chosen excerpts from personal letters of both the participants and their families provide a human touch and insight not often found in the literature of war.

This book brings to life the story of an individual soldier, and his part in the conflict that should never have been labeled "The Forgotten War."

Lt. Gen. A.L. Bowser
United States Marine Corps
Retired

Able Company climbs a Hill of Sacrifice.
(sources: NA/Chang)

PROLOGUE

Human sacrifices were drowned in Kewalo, then brought to the heiau of Kane-laau, situated at the Robert Louis Stevenson School and extending west to Kehehuna, then taken to the top of Puuowaina to an altar on the little prominence where the cross was set up at the time of the Missionary Centennial . . .
Sterling and Summers, Sites of Oahu

Under the shadow of the Koolau Mountains lies Honolulu's Punchbowl Crater, site of the National Memorial Cemetery of the Pacific. The ancient Hawaiians called this place Puuowaina, the Hill of Sacrifice. In the distant past, a violator of a kapu, or law, would be led by a priest, known as a kahuna, to the Kewalo fish pond and drowned. There was no appeal — Hawaiian law was understood by all.[1]

When the sacrifice reached Kewalo, the kahuna would begin to chant, *"Moe malie i ke kai o ko haku,"* which translates as, "Lie still in the waters of your superior." The sacrifice cooperated in his death and entered the water willingly. As the sacrifice's head receded beneath the surface, the kahuna would lean over and gently, but firmly, help in holding his head under the water. There was no struggle. Death was mercifully swift.

The unblemished body of the drowned man was then taken to the large stone heiau, or temple, of Kane-laau nearby. After a solemn ceremony, a group of priests would carry the body up the steep slopes of Puuowaina, an extinct volcanic tuff cone that geologists say was formed in a single day during a cataclysmic explosion a quarter of a million years ago.

The priests would walk in unison, bearing their load in regal silence. When the kahunas reached the caldera's rim, they would place the body on a large rock that served as an altar stone overlooking Honolulu Bay. Upon this altar, the priests often burnt the body. Occasionally, the body was left for relatives to collect; others were abandoned on the Hill of Sacrifice, never to be touched again by the hand of man.

Puuowaina is known as the Punchbowl today because of its shape. The manicured green lawn on the floor of the crater provides a pleasant contrast to the thousands of flat granite headstones standing in formation, row upon row, awaiting roll call on Judgment Day. The National Memorial Cemetery was selected as a permanent burial site after World War II when objections were raised against leaving the bodies of those fallen in the war against Japan in temporary cemeteries located on central and south Pacific islands.[2] Construction began in August 1948, and the first remains were interred on 4 January 1949. Seven hundred and seventy-six casualties from Pearl Harbor were among the first to be interred here. Thousands followed as the fallen were retrieved from World War II battlefields and America's wars in Asia continued.

The Honolulu Memorial sits high on the wall of Puuowaina crater overlooking the headstones in the National Memorial Cemetery far below. This unique memorial honors those men declared missing in action (MIA), or who were buried at sea, in World War II, Korea and Vietnam. All 1,102 men who lie entombed in the USS *Arizona* are listed here. The names of 18,093 people who were never recovered from central and south Pacific battlefields in World War II; 8,195 from the Korean War; and 2,489 from the Vietnam War are inscribed on the cool marble walls.

While some people visit the Punchbowl to pay their respects to fallen friends and relatives, others come solely to enjoy the view of the bustling city of Honolulu and the pristine blue Pacific Ocean far below. Few visitors depart Puuowaina untouched by the sacrifice this place represents. Even a victorious nation counts its dead, and Puuowaina provides a rare opportunity for the living to see firsthand the tragic human cost of war. The names etched in stone here represent people like you and me — Coast Guardsmen, soldiers, sailors, airmen and Marines, who fell fighting our Nation's wars. Listen closely, for the men and women interred at Puuowaina have tales to tell — tales of love, hope, courage, fear, grief, triumph and despair. There are tales of sailors who perished in the burning, exploding hell of Battleship Row one Sunday morning in December long ago and of submarine crews who vanished in the Sea of Japan; Marines who died in the blue lagoon of Tarawa and amid the blasted rubble of Hue City; soldiers who fell on frozen ridge lines in Korea and in the dense, steaming jungles of Vietnam; B-29 crews shot down in flames over Tokyo and F-105 pilots who never returned from missions over Hanoi. They are all honored here at Puuowaina, the Hill of Sacrifice.

Sergeant Ernest Malcolm Calhau, Jr., United States Army, my wife's uncle, is buried on the crater floor. Born and reared on the island of Oahu in the days when Hawaii was a United States Territory, he, too, has a tale to tell. Early one July morning in 1950, Sonny, as he was known to friends and family, hugged his parents good-bye on the porch of their home in Lanikai, which in Hawaiian means "Heavenly Waters." His unit, the 5th Regimental Combat Team (RCT), would sail within a few days to fight in the Korean War. Nine months later Sonny was killed in action while leading a rifle squad in a desperate firefight near the crest of Hill 814, a few miles south of the 38th Parallel in the Republic of Korea. The United States Army returned the soldier from Lanikai to his family and home. Sonny lies in state today, shoulder-to-shoulder with others like him on the floor of Puuowaina crater, brave men all. This is the story of Sonny and his comrades in the 5th RCT, who dreamed, laughed, fought and bled together in the terrible years of the Korean War.

CHAPTER ONE

LANIKAI

*Mrs. Alona told us that the old name for Lanikai was Kaohao.
Lanikai is its "real estate name" and not its true name at all.*
Sterling and Summers, *Sites of Oahu*

Ernest Medeiros Calhau, the deputy sheriff and bailiff of Honolulu, had one passion in life. He loved to fish, a hobby he had shared with his deceased father, Manuel, the creator and former owner of the Honolulu Civic Auditorium. Born and reared on Oahu, Ernest was tired of living in Honolulu and wanted to buy a beach house where he could relax with his family and fish on his free time. In

early 1941 Ernest bought his dream home in Lanikai, on Oahu's windward side, where he could stand in his yard and cast a fishing line into the roaring surf of the mighty Pacific Ocean.

Ernest and his wife, Theresa, reared three sons on Oahu. Ernest Malcolm Calhau, Jr. (Sonny) was born on 15 December 1930. Sonny's two younger brothers, Leroy James Calhau (Buddy) and Manuel George Calhau (Manley), were born on 12 January 1932 and 27 December 1933, respectively. The three brothers spent their idyllic days playing on the beach, swimming in the emerald green waters offshore, and sailing their father's small boat in Kailua Bay. On his free time, Ernest taught his boys how to fish, and together they reaped a good harvest from the bountiful sea.

A deeply religious couple, Theresa and Ernest attended Mass every Sunday morning at Saint Anthony Church in Kailua. One Sunday in December 1941, the sound of explosions emanating from the direction of Kaneohe Naval Air Station momentarily stunned the congregation. After Mass, Ernest saw smoke and flames billowing skyward from the direction of the Naval Air Station as he drove his family home.

Ernest M. Calhau and Theresa Lauber Calhau honeymoon photo. (source: Calhau family)

Ernest thought an unannounced tactical exercise was underway as he occasionally glimpsed low-flying aircraft from behind the windshield of the family car. He left Theresa inside the car to watch the boys when he stopped at a fruit stand in Kailua to purchase fresh-papaya for the family's breakfast. While waiting in line to purchase his fruit, a truck full of armed soldiers slammed on its brakes in front of the startled civilians. The soldiers were clearly upset as they yelled at everyone to get off the road. One bellicose sergeant shouted, "The Japanese are attacking and this isn't any damn drill!" Ernest remained skeptical until an aircraft roared low overhead. He could clearly see the rising sun insignia of Imperial Japan painted under the wings. America was at war.

Ernest forgot about his papaya and drove home as quickly as he could. Once he had his family inside the dubious safety of their home, he fiddled with the radio to hear the news. Theresa, innocently enough, asked him what the Deputy Sheriff of Honolulu was going to do. While Ernest explained to his nervous wife that, frankly, he did not know, Sonny led his brothers outside unnoticed to see the show.

Lanikai lay between Bellows Army Airfield and Kaneohe Naval Air Station. The U.S. Pacific Fleet based its long-range maritime patrol aircraft at Kaneohe, and the Army used Bellows as an auxiliary airfield for its P-40 fighters. Both bases attracted the unwanted attention of the Imperial Japanese Naval Air Arm on 7 December 1941.

The U.S. Army and Navy had conducted large aerial maneuvers over Lanikai several times before the war, but the three Calhau boys had never seen anything so awesome or terrifying as the sight now unfolding. The second wave of Japanese bombers and fighters to attack Oahu that morning had arrived over their targets. Sleek Zero fighters streaked low overhead, strafing targets of opportunity as they flew a race course pattern be-

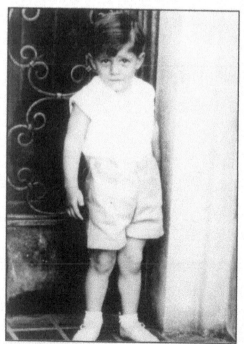

Sonny, age 3, standing in front of the Honolulu Advertiser *building. (source: Calhau family)*

8

tween Kaneohe and Bellows that took the planes, one after another, right over the roof of the Calhau home.

Sonny ran back inside the house, to emerge a few seconds later with his Red Ryder BB gun clutched firmly in hand. As the Japanese fighters made their strafing runs, the horrified boys witnessed a tragic event. They stood transfixed as an Army P-40 flew overhead in pursuit of two Zeros. The badly outnumbered American pilot was flying at low altitude where the nimble Zero fighters were in their element. Both Zeros whipped around in tight turns to engage the P-40. Japanese cannon fire struck home, and with the engine of his P-40 on fire, the intrepid aviator bailed out offshore, not far from the beach house. One Japanese pilot had not completed his business that morning and bored on in with his machine guns firing to finish the kill. The American pilot's bullet-ridden, lifeless body hung suspended from his parachute harness, drifting with the wind over the heads of the shocked boys to land in the hills behind the house. Long after the war, when the pilot's son visited the Calhau home, he heard for the first time how his brave father had died that day.

Sonny, Buddy, and Manley reenact the Battle of Lanikai Beach with their mom. Note the barbed-wire obstacles on the beach. (source: Calhau family)

In a righteous rage, Sonny started taking potshots with his BB gun at the Zero fighters flying fifty feet overhead. Manley thinks Sonny hit the canopy of a Zero. The enemy pilot did not appreciate this display of defiance and returned on a strafing run that thankfully missed the boys, but shot up the side of the family garage. An angry Ernest rushed outside, shaking his fist and shouting Portuguese insults at the Japanese aviators for attacking his home. When Ernest discovered Sonny blazing away with his BB gun, common sense prevailed, and he hustled his sons into the dubious shelter of the living room. So

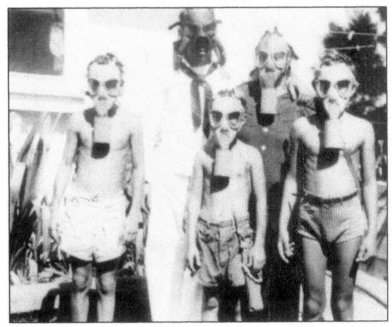

A family photo. The sailor is a visiting relative. (source: Calhau family)

ended the "Battle of Lanikai Beach," the Calhau family's contribution to the defense of Hawaii that terrible, frightening day.[1]

The family remained in Lanikai throughout the war. The boys had school to attend, and their father had business to conduct in court. They were all too young or too old to fight in this war.

When not at school, the boys earned pocket money working at the Benny Bourgess Riding Stable in Kailua where servicemen rented horses at the exorbitant rate of five dollars an hour. Nearer to home, the three entrepreneurs shined shoes and sold newspapers to the large influx of servicemen who frequented the Kailua Beach USO during the war. Their hard-earned nickels kept the boys in ice cream which they purchased and consumed on the steps of the Kalapawai Market in Kailua.

The boys also helped their father fish. Immediately after Pearl Harbor, Oahu's defenders strung swaths of barbed wire obstacles along the island's beautiful beaches to help defeat the dreaded Japanese invasion force that thankfully never appeared. Lanikai Beach was no exception; civilians were forbidden to swim or fish on the beach. Ernest evaded this rule by casting his line from the roof of his house over the defensive obstacles into the surf. Whenever Ernest hooked a fish, one of the boys would run to a nearby machine gun position and ask the soldiers to help lift his father's catch over the barbed wire. The friendly soldiers happily cooperated in this endeavor during their otherwise tedious hours of guard duty. Ernest and the boys spent many pleasurable hours on the roof casting their lines into the Heavenly Waters.

Later in the war, the Army allowed civilians to fish on the beach during the day. Due to rationing, fresh meat was at a premium, and fishing ceased to be a hobby and became a means to assuage the family's hunger. Ernest and the boys often ran a fishing net from a point just below the Lanikai

Sonny departs for Basic Training. (source: Calhau family)

Monument to Flat Island, a small, pancake-shaped speck of coral in Kailua Bay. While Ernest kept a wary eye out for the large sharks that patrolled the reef, the boys pulled the catch in at sunset each day.

When the war ended on 15 August 1945, the Calhaus felt lucky to have survived the global inferno unscathed. Shortly after V-J Day, the family sailed on the S.S. *Matsonia* to the Mainland for a long overdue vacation. Ernest drove his freshly overhauled and repainted blue Buick to all the major tourist sites. The boys stood on the rim of the Grand Canyon, collected petrified wood in Arizona, ate hot dogs on Coney Island, and viewed New York's skyline from the top of the Empire State Building. This was Sonny's only visit to the United States, the country he would die for in Korea a few years later.

When the S.S. *Matsonia* returned the family to Oahu, the boys resumed their studies. They attended Roosevelt High School together in Honolulu, not far from where their father worked. Ernest drove his sons over the Pali every morning to Honolulu. Usually, the boys hitched a ride home from school.

Sonny was a handsome young man of medium height, with dark complexion and hair, and sparkling, mischievous brown eyes. His slender athletic build, ready smile, and sense of humor made him especially popular with the ladies. The one who stole Sonny's heart was Lona Mladinich, a lovely young woman of Hawaiian-German descent who lived in Lanikai and attended Roosevelt High School. If Sonny had survived the Korean War, they probably would have married.

An indifferent student at best, Sonny repeated his sophomore year twice, a humiliating experience for any lad, especially one with younger brothers. Worse, Sonny experienced several brushes with the law that upset his parents. One pastime was to steal a car and go joyriding with his friends from school. Sonny returned the cars after each joyride, but his antics deeply troubled Ernest, a man of the law.

Ernest's stern counseling sessions with Sonny failed to influence his son. After Sonny was caught painting rival Ponahou School's elite walls with Roosevelt's red and gold colors, Sonny's exasperated principal finally tired of his shenanigans and expelled him. Ernest believed Sonny needed discipline and thought the Army was the place to instill it. Encouraged by his father, Sonny enlisted in the Army in May 1949.

CHAPTER TWO

SOLDIERING

It was not their fault that no one had told them that the real function of an army is to fight and that the soldier's destiny — which few escape — is to suffer, and if need be, to die.
T. R. Fehrenbach, This Kind of War

Sonny attended fourteen weeks of basic training at Schofield Barracks, Oahu, in the 3rd Platoon of an unidentified training company. Of the twenty-two recruits who formed this platoon, E. Bettencourt, J. Horino, A. Oshiro, James Kawamura, J. Garcia, Lang Lorenzo, H. Bukoshi, "Speed," "China," "Aku," and "Eight Ball" wrote their names or nicknames on Sonny's graduation photograph. That Sonny acquired the additional nickname of "Rosy" is attested to on this photograph.

Private Joseph Gonzales, from Kula, Hawaii, recalled, "Ernest and I attended basic training together in the same platoon. He was a very good soldier. He did what he was supposed to do, and he did it well …. [Later] I went to George Company and he went to Fox, so we were in the same battalion. We lost about three or four of our basic platoon members in the Korean War and, of course, Ernest was one of them. In basic I was an acting squad leader, and we never had any problems with Ernest. He was a doggoned good soldier. I looked to him to be a twenty-year man or more. We both had plans to stay in, but he got killed and I stepped on a mine and blew off my leg …. I'm trying not even to think about the Korean Conflict any longer."[1]

One of Sonny's drill sergeants was Sergeant (SGT) Alfred S. Los Banos, a tough, no-nonsense, combat veteran of World War II. Another one of his drill sergeants was Sergeant First Class (SFC) Samuel L. Kealoha, an experienced soldier who taught his teenage recruits the fundamentals of soldiering. Working together, the two noncommissioned officers would ensure that their recruits had a fighting chance to survive the war.[2]

A great fire consumed Sonny's service records in St. Louis over twenty years ago. Therefore, his exact duties after graduation from recruit training

Sonny after Basic Training. (source: Calhau family)

Sonny's Basic Training Platoon. Seated (L to R): Kalei, unknown, Ernest Calhau, unknown, CPL Wilfred Lincoln, unknown, LT William Willis, SGT Samuel Kealoha, SGT Alfred Los Banos, Sylvester Garcia, Frank Wills, unknown, Pestana. Standing (L to R): Kamai, unknown, George Matsunaga, Joseph Gonzales, Bukoski, Lorenzo, Wilson Park, unknown, unknown, unknown, James Kausamura, Higa, John Hosino, Bettencourt. (Last names used when only one name is listed.) (source: Calhau family and Mr. Joseph Gonzales, Sr.)

are obscure today. Sonny did serve in a U.S. Army Pacific Color Guard. He marched in funeral processions at Puuowaina in honor of men returning from distant battlefields to their final resting place at the National Memorial Cemetery of the Pacific. The Color Guard was a crack ceremonial unit, and its members wore their khaki dress uniforms with pride at the funeral ceremonies.[3]

Private Calhau's Army buddies often accompanied him home on weekend pass. The youthful, exuberant soldiers would sit on the beach drinking Coca-Cola and Primo Beer, and engaging in soldier talk through the long, pleasant hours of the night.

One of Sonny's best friends was Private First Class (PFC) John W. Kenawell, otherwise known as Johnnie. Born on 14 December 1929, the Army cook was exactly one year and a day older than Sonny. He was from Burnham, Pennsylvania, where his father, Brady, was a steelworker for Standard Steel, and his mother, Dorothy, a seamstress.[4]

Johnnie was a frequent guest at the Calhau home. A serious young man, neither loud nor boisterous, Johnnie was in many ways the opposite of Sonny. Perhaps their differences were what drew the two soldiers together. We'll never know; a dreadful war was coming, and the two young lions had little time left to live.

America's possession of the atomic bomb implied there never would be a major ground war again, or so most civilians and professional military people thought in 1949. Sonny's mother thought differently, or at least in retrospect she said she did. After Sonny was killed in action, Theresa never forgave her husband for convincing their oldest son to sign the enlistment papers that in her eyes proved to be Sonny's death warrant in Korea.

CPL Joseph Gonzales after recovering from wounds in Korea. (source: Joseph Gonzales)

SGT Alfred Los Banos after WWII. (source: Los Banos family)

CHAPTER THREE

I'LL TRY, SIR

Here we come marching 'neath the flag we love,
Always on forward with the stars above;
Never to turn back,
Either stand or fall — for liberty,
At our country's call.
"5th Infantry March," Kurt Freier

While Sonny mastered the soldier's trade, the U.S. Army's 5th Regimental Combat Team (RCT) defended a series of outposts in South Korea along the 38th Parallel, an arbitrary line that divided the troubled peninsula into two hostile countries. The core of the 5th RCT was the 5th Infantry Regiment, the third oldest regiment in the U.S. Army.

According to tradition, the 5th Infantry's motto, "I'll try, Sir," dates to the War of 1812. As the story goes, at 2200 on 25 July 1814, Major General Jacob Brown asked Colonel (COL) James Miller, the regimental commander, if he thought his regiment could charge and seize a battery of British guns during the Battle of Lundy's Lane. Several other American regiments had tried to storm the guns in the daylight hours, but had failed in the face of heavy fire. Not given to brash statements that might prove beyond the capabilities of his men, COL Miller first surveyed the ground and devised a plan before reporting back to Major General Brown with the words that became this illustrious regiment's motto. The regimental crest is adorned with the seven cannons COL Miller's soldiers seized that night.[1]

Afterwards, the 5th Infantry fought the Seminole Indians in the swamps of Florida and Santa Anna's legions under a blazing Mexican sun. The regiment skirmished with Indians, rather than Confederates, out West during the Civil War. In 1898 the 5th Infantry fought Spaniards in Cuba and, later, Filipino guerrillas during the occupation of the Philippines. Much to the disgust of the long-service regular soldiers, the 5th Infantry guarded the Panama Canal while their comrades fought in France during World War I. The regiment sailed to Europe in 1918 where it was billeted near Andernach on the Rhine with the Allied occupation forces in Germany.[2]

In World War II, the 5th Infantry served with the 71st Light Division, an outfit trained and equipped for combat in mountainous terrain. While the soldiers struggled to master their cantankerous mules, the 71st Light Division was not in demand overseas where theater commanders appreciated the manpower, mobility, and firepower advantages of traditional infantry divisions.

The 71st was eventually reorganized as a traditional infantry division and entered combat in Europe during the closing days of the war. Its 5th Infantry Regiment fought its way across the Rhine, advanced into Austria, and made contact with our Russian allies on the Danube. A few months after V-E Day, the Army deactivated the 5th Infantry in Salzburg, but events unfolding in Asia would ensure a brief sleep.

In September 1945, on the other side of the globe, the Red Army and U.S. Army troops linked-up at Sond Do Kaijo, Korea, a village located on the 38th Parallel.[3] In arrangements agreed to at Potsdam at the close of World War II, the Soviets accepted the surrender of all Japanese forces north of the 38th Parallel, while American forces accepted the surrender of Japanese units south of that line. Thus Korea was bisected by a controversial, imaginary line, one Joseph Stalin soon incorporated into an Asiatic segment of his Iron Curtain. When the early unification of Korea by peaceful means did not occur, North Korea, under Kim Il Sung, and South Korea, under Syngman Rhee, mobilized for war. The Cold War was starting to simmer.

The United States Government had little interest in Korea. President Harry S. Truman wanted to reduce the military budget, not expand it, and neither he nor the Joint Chiefs of Staff (JCS) believed the defense of South Korea was in our vital interests. Truman did order the Army to assist President Rhee form a small defense force known as the Republic of Korea (ROK) Constabulary to expedite the withdrawal of American troops from Korea. To prevent President Rhee from initiating a war to reunify the country, the United States provided the Constabulary with a minimum of defensive armament that did not include armor, heavy artillery, or aircraft.[4]

The Soviets had no such qualms and equipped the North Korea People's Army (NKPA) with tanks, self-propelled and towed artillery, and aircraft. Joseph Stalin ensured a return on his modest investment by dispatching a tough group of Red Army advisors to kick the NKPA into shape. Mao Tse-tung, on his own initiative, released tens of thousands of combat-hardened Korean troops from his Chinese Peoples Liberation Army (PLA) following the Communist victory over Chiang Kai-shek's Nationalist Forces in 1949. These Korean veterans of the Chinese Civil War formed the cadre of the NKPA.[5]

As Kim Il Sung's combat-hardened ideological shock troops prepared for war, the Truman Administration slashed the defense budget following the victorious conclusion of World War II. For example, when the Army's Ordnance Department requested $750,000,000 in Fiscal Year 1948 to cover the procurement of essential ammunition and equipment, storage and distribution of ordnance material, maintenance of stand-by plants and arsenals, training, research and development, the Bureau of the Budget reduced this figure to $275,000,000. Congress sliced the final appropriation to $245,532,000.[6] The politicians saved money by reducing the Armed Forces to a dangerously low level of operational readiness. One immediate consequence was a dramatic decrease in the number of serviceable weapons and equipment.[7]

Americans believed that the nuclear armed, long-range, strategic bomber had rendered conventional warfare obsolete. The public, a budget-conscious Administration, Air Force bomber generals, and a growing number of influential think tanks shared this wishful thinking. The Army had no role in Armageddon; consequently, its fighting power was ignored. Unfortunately, no one informed the North Koreans that conventional warfare was passe.

Most American soldiers serving in Korea were pleased to hear in March 1948 that the President was going to withdraw them to Japan at the earliest possible date. They had no qualms about leaving this destitute country of extreme climatic variations. In winter they froze; in summer they baked. The nauseating stench of rice paddies fertilized with human feces did not sit well with the men. On the other hand, the Koreans had a deep-seated fear that Uncle Sam was going to colonize their country. Consequently, the relationship between Americans and Koreans was often strained.[8] Few Americans or South Koreans shed any tears when the JCS ordered General Douglas MacArthur, Supreme Commander for the Allied Powers in Japan and Commander-in-Chief, Far East (CINCFE), to commence the withdrawal of American forces in January 1949.

The 7th Infantry Division, commanded by Major General William F. Dean, who would earn the Medal of Honor eighteen months later leading the 24th Infantry Division's doomed defense of Taejon, garrisoned South Korea. General Dean's three infantry regiments manned a series of twenty-five isolated outposts (OPs) along the 38th Parallel to deter Communist aggression.

Second Lieutenant Henry E. Emerson was one of a large number of West Pointers to serve in the 7th Infantry Division. The son of an Army doctor, LT "Hank" Emerson was no stranger to Army life. Upon graduation with the Class of 1947, the last of the U.S. Military Academy's three-year emergency classes, LT Emerson requested assignment to Korea. "In those days," he recalled, "that was considered about the most adventurous place you could go in the Army. We had little skirmishes back and forth across the 38th Parallel and the North Koreans would infiltrate down and cause problems here and there."[9]

The platoon leader commanded OP 25 on the extreme east coast of Korea. Outpost 25 was so isolated that it did not even have a road leading to the compound. Lieutenant Emerson was in command of a sixty-man detachment from the 31st Infantry, which he described as "a good learning experience."[10] Sergeant First Class Karpinski, a highly decorated World War II veteran, trained his lieutenant well and kept him out of trouble. A C-47 touched down a couple of times a month bringing supplies and the mail to the garrison.

A few miles to the west, a reinforced rifle platoon from K Company, 32nd Infantry, garrisoned OP 23. Few units in Korea were up to strength, and this platoon amounted to just twenty-six men. The OP boasted one Quonset Hut reserved for a barracks and another divided in half to form a combination barracks and chow hall. Barbed wire surrounded the perimeter of the two-acre outpost. A nearby concrete bridge spanned a dry streambed that delineated the border in this part of Korea. Swaths of concertina wire blocked the bridge, but otherwise the border was obstacle free. Civilians often crossed the border to visit relatives, and to conduct an illicit, yet flourishing trade.[11]

Outpost 23 dispatched a patrol every morning to a nearby ridgeline to observe the actions of the North Korean and Russian soldiers on the other side of the border. The OP also dispatched contact patrols every three days to the nearest adjacent units. The North Koreans occasionally sniped at these patrols, but no one from OP 23 was ever hit by their fire.

The soldiers were not authorized to return fire, but the ROK Constabulary could and often did. Wild firefights between South and North Korean units erupted with deadly frequency. Whenever the South Koreans carried a wounded comrade to the OP, an Army medic would provide first aid outside the perimeter gate. The treatment of wounded South Koreans was not authorized on the grounds of the compound, as this could have been construed as unauthorized military assistance.[12]

Outpost 23 had a machine gun position on the ridge overlooking the camp. From here the men enjoyed unobstructed observation far into North Korea. Two soldiers manned this machine gun in an endless succession of two-hour shifts. As Private First Class Horace Anderson dozed one sunny morning behind the machine gun, a rifle discharged next to his ear. His buddy, PFC Donald K. Burton, had fired his M-1 into North Korea. "Oh man," thought PFC Anderson. "They're going to hang us now!"[13]

Koreans eat dogs, animals most Americans regard as "man's best friend." Private First Class Burton probably loved dogs, for that morning, as he gazed across the border into North Korea, he witnessed a sight that tore at his soul. The dastardly North Koreans were stringing up a live dog from a tree limb in the best traditions of America's Wild West. If the North Koreans had simply shot the poor canine, or dispatched it with a blow to the head, the potential for World War III would have been averted. Perhaps dog tastes better if it is hung first and eaten later. Maybe any other form of execution wastes too much meat. These were things the Koreans understood and the Americans did not. All PFC Burton saw was a group of bloodthirsty Commies lynching a dog, and he was not going to let the bastards get away with it. In fact PFC Burton decided on his course of action so fast that he did not bother to awaken his buddy, PFC Anderson, before he raised the stock of his M-1 rifle to his shoulder, aimed in, and squeezed the trigger. We will never know for sure whether PFC Burton was aiming at the lynch mob or the dog. Armageddon may have been averted that day because PFC Burton's bullet did not kill one of the Commies. Rather, it hit and killed the dog.

Within moments of the bullet's impact, frantic North Korean border guards reported to their Russian advisors that a fanatical American Imperialist had fired a bullet across the border. The Soviet Embassy in Pyongyang is alleged to have flashed a message to Moscow where Red Army Marshals studied the capitalist provocation before it was handed off to the Soviet Embassy in Washington. The Soviet ambassador is reputed to have lodged a protest with the State Department, which in turn demanded an explanation from the Pentagon that exasperated staff officers handed off to General MacArthur's Headquarters in Tokyo. At the far end of the food chain, General Dean was finally notified. He fired off a terse message to OP 23, asking platoon leader SFC Greenly, "Just what the hell was going on?" Shortly thereafter, 1st LT Jerry Collins, the Commanding Officer (CO) of K Company, whose father was Chief of Staff of the Army, drove up in a jeep to learn the details of the incident that was subsequently put to rest. The North Koreans learned their lesson and never killed another dog in front of OP 23.

The North Koreans took their anger out on OP 10. Manned by a platoon from E Company, 32nd Infantry, relations along this part of the Iron Curtain had remained pleasant and professional until the Russians withdrew their combat units. No fraternization had been allowed between the American and Russian soldiers, but the men had often exchanged waves and smiles across the ideological gulf that divided the Hermit Kingdom.

Things changed when North Korean soldiers replaced the Russians. Friendly waves were replaced by rude gestures, and smiles by scowls as Kim Il-Sung's ideological shock troopers expressed their undisguised hatred. Sometimes the North Koreans exchanged more than scowls. After guerrillas knifed an American sentry to death, the mood of the American soldiers turned justifiably ugly. When the North Koreans opened up on OP 10 with a machine gun one night just before Christmas in 1948, the soldiers returned a devastating barrage of machine gun and rifle fire that probably made the North Koreans wish for the good old days of mere scowls and rude gestures. The Americans quickly gained fire superiority and raked the North Korean positions for several minutes. No American soldiers were hit. North Korean casualties remain unknown, but they never fired on OP 10 again.[14]

While the U.S. Army guarded South Korea, President Truman was working on an exit strategy. He decided to assist South Korea in forming an indigenous military force capable of defending the country from North Korean aggression. The JCS directed General MacArthur, Commander in Chief, Far East, to organize and equip a regimental combat team (RCT) from the 7th Infantry Division. This RCT would remain in Korea to help defend the country and to assist in the training of the ROK Army after the 7th Infantry Division was withdrawn to reinforce the Eighth Army occupation forces in Japan. When the infant ROK Army was operational, the RCT would be withdrawn and not replaced.

Augmented by units from other combat arms and service sup-

SGT Robert H. Middleton, Baker Company, Silver Star March 1951, poses with children in 1949. (source: Robert Middleton)

PFC Worth presents COL Simpson a check in support of the March of Dimes campaign. (source: NA)

port organizations, an RCT was capable of operating more independently in combat than a conventional infantry regiment and could sustain itself longer because it was less dependent upon higher organizations for support. Doctrinally, an independent RCT was viewed as a shock unit, one trained and equipped to execute a forced river crossing or a breakthrough of a fortified position. One suspects, however, that the activation of an RCT in Korea was viewed primarily as an economical way of showing American resolve in Asia.

On 1 January 1949, the 5th RCT was activated in Seoul using personnel and equipment provided by the 7th Infantry Division to flesh out its component units. Most of the soldiers serving in the 32nd Infantry Regiment, 48th Field Artillery Battalion (FAB), the 7th Cavalry Reconnaissance Troop, and B Company, 13th Combat Engineer Battalion, were transferred en masse to the rolls of the 5th RCT. The combat team consisted of the reactivated 5th Infantry Regiment, 555th FAB (Triple Nickel), 72nd Engineer Company, 58th Cavalry Reconnaissance Troop Mechanized, and combat support and service support units. To round out the 5th RCT, the 282nd Army Band was included to provide the pomp and circumstance at official ceremonies.[15]

General Dean took the necessary steps to ensure his subordinates transferred their best soldiers to the 5th RCT. For example, when the former CO of the 32nd Infantry, COL James R. Simpson, a giant of a man whom the soldiers referred to as "Jungle Jim," assumed command of the 5th RCT, General Dean gave him wide latitude to select his officers and men. Soldiers with previous courts martial convictions or company punishments were not transferred.[16] Some men from the 31st Infantry were transferred to the 5th RCT, too. Due to the overall grim personnel situation affecting all Army units in Asia, however, the 5th RCT did not reach its authorized strength. The infantry companies consisted of two rifle platoons, rather than three. A token number of crew-served machine guns and light mortars rounded out each company's firepower.[17]

Upon activation, the 5th RCT was the only Army combat unit remaining in Korea, but its stay was destined to be brief. The Korean Military Assistance Group (KMAG) was already preparing to assume the mission of training the ROK Army. Meanwhile, the security of the 38th Parallel remained the combat team's primary mission. A secondary mission required the 5th RCT to assist the KMAG in training the ROK Army. Until its withdrawal from Korea, the 5th RCT trained the ROK Army in squad-to-battalion tactical problems. Republic of Korea Army observers served for short periods of time with regimental units.

The 5th RCT's mission changed two weeks after it was activated. Border security was turned over to the ROK Army when the regiment withdrew from its forward positions on the night of 14-15 January 1949. One soldier was killed when a truck flipped over on an icy road.

Colonel Simpson initiated daily patrols on 16 January from Seoul and Uijongbu to visit former OPs on the 38th Parallel. These patrols kept the 5th RCT in touch with the Korean people and the police. When fighting broke out between ROK and NKPA troops during the week of 23-29 January, COL Simpson directed reconnaissance flights along the border. That week, NKPA raiders burned down the South Korean police station at Paekchon.[18]

The unpredictable and dangerous situation in Korea kept American patrols on their guard. Private First Class Ronald Denton served in the 58th Cavalry Reconnaissance Troop Mechanized, a unit equipped with M-8 armored cars, jeeps and trucks.[19] He explained, "The 58th Cavalry Reconnaissance Troop Mechanized was constantly on the go. We ran patrols up to the border all the time. The North Koreans often shot at us with small arms. Occasionally they hit one of our vehicles, but thankfully they were lousy shots and we never lost a man. We were not allowed to return fire, so we never did. I think it had something to do with the United Nations Commission."[20]

First Lieutenant Dick J. Oostenink, Jr., a Protestant chaplain assigned to 1st Battalion provided religious services to the soldiers. North Korean border guards often shot at the chaplain as he drove on a road running parallel to the border.[21] Yet, Communist gunfire never delayed one of his sermons.

North Korean sabotage teams attempted to wreak havoc on South Korea's fragile economy. Second Lieutenant Keith W. Whitham, a recent Officer Candidate School graduate assigned to the 58th Cavalry Reconnaissance Troop Mechanized, led motorized patrols to intercept North Korean saboteurs operating in the vicinity of the dams near Seoul. He said, "I don't recall the North Koreans ever inflicting any major damage, but there was apparently a fear that they could. So we stayed busy, coordinating our patrols with the South Koreans."[22]

The North Koreans fired on two 5th RCT patrols during the second week of February. Although bullets hit a radio and jeep, no one was killed or wounded. The following week heavy machine gun fire wounded the pilot of an L-5 reconnaissance aircraft north of Kaesong. Second Lieutenant Frank B. Brooks, Jr., a platoon leader in F Company, investigated the incident and concluded the culprits were probably trigger-happy South Korean Constabulary.[23]

During the last half of February, the situation in Korea was tense. A patrol from 2nd Battalion was shot at in the vicinity of OP 10. The situation calmed down when a "reported invasion by North Koreans was investigated by aerial reconnaissance but found to be groundless."[24]

In March, two ROK soldiers accompanied a 3rd Battalion patrol and fired into North Korea against the orders of the patrol leader. North Korean border guards retaliated by engaging a 1st Battalion patrol the following week. Another patrol was engaged in April, but no one was hit.

Basketball, not patrolling, was the regiment's passion that winter. The regimental basketball team, coached by LT Hank Emerson, won the championship in Korea and the Army Far East championship in Japan. Air Force beat the 5th RCT in the final game of the Far East Championship. Undaunted by this defeat, the team competed at an Army-wide tournament at Fort Dix, New Jersey, where it finished a respectable second place.[25]

In addition to basketball, the soldiers actively raised funds for charity. After a March of Dimes campaign waged in February, Private Paul E. Worth, L Company, presented COL Simpson with a check for $5994.45. Love Company was the single largest contributor with $448.

Ceremonial duties kept the regiment busy, too. When Major General Coulter, Commanding General XXIV Corps departed Korea for Japan, 3rd Battalion provided the honor guard. The 282nd Army Band led the regiment and attached units on a Washington's Birthday parade through the streets of downtown Seoul. An honor guard from the 3rd Battalion greeted the Secretary of the Army, the Honorable Mr. Kenneth C. Royall, during his visit to Korea. Army Day was celebrated with a regimental parade observed by members of the United Nations Commission in Seoul and the South Korean Government. Finally, L Company represented the regiment at Memorial Day services held in front of the regimental headquarters.[26]

Few soldiers enjoyed serving in Korea. A deep cultural chasm separated Americans from Kore-

Washington's Birthday Parade in Seoul, 1949. The 282nd Army Band is behind COL Simpson and his staff. (source: NA)

17

ans, and lasting friendships rarely formed. Korean men ostracized women who associated with the Americans. Thugs preyed on soldiers in the vicinity of the 32nd Street Circle.[27] Koreans often stripped military vehicles of their tires, tools, and fuel cans. Soldiers joked that the Koreans thought the only thing dishonorable about stealing was to get caught.

First Lieutenant James A. Johnson, from Stoughton, Wisconsin, West Point Class of 1947, served as a platoon leader in the 72nd Engineers. He remarked, "The people were very friendly, but extremely poor. They didn't have any wherewithal. I can remember working out on the roads and little kids would come up, without coats, and they would be absolutely blue because of the cold. As a result they would steal you blind."[28]

When KMAG announced it was seeking volunteers to extend their tours in Korea to train the ROK Army, a deluge of soldiers did not pound down the doors. Though it had an authorized strength of 182 officers, four warrant officers, one nurse, and 293 enlisted men, KMAG possessed just 92 officers and 148 enlisted men in April 1949. Enlisted volunteers did not prove as difficult to obtain as officers. When officers did not volunteer in sufficient numbers, the qualification standards were slashed once, and yet again.

A newly promoted 1st LT Frank Brooks escaped the KMAG draft because Fox Company was demonstrating platoon-level offensive and defensive tactics to the ROK Army. A small number of extremely disgruntled officers were finally ordered to volunteer, hardly the enthusiastic men KMAG needed to train the ROK Army.[29]

First Lieutenant Wilbur G. Jones, Jr., West Point Class of 1947, volunteered for duty with KMAG on his own volition.[30] He served as an advisor to the ROK 2nd Infantry, 6th Division until captured by the Chinese in October 1950. He died of wounds the following May after months of maltreatment and neglect. He is remembered here as a soldier of the Korean War.

An element of 1st Platoon, 72nd Engineer Company, near Kapyong in 1949. Charles Carroll (KIA 26 September 1950), who earned the Distinguished Service Cross posthumously, stands 2nd from left. Camp Carroll in the present-day ROK is named after him. On the right is Platoon Sergeant Thomas. (source: James Johnson)

In April morale soared when the men learned the 5th RCT was going to be transferred to Hawaii. Not everyone was going to Paradise. The Eighth Army had directed the 5th RCT to transfer several hundred men to units in Japan. Soldiers with enlistments due to expire were transferred to the States.

The combat team deployed to Hawaii severely under strength. Lieutenant Hank Emerson was placed in temporary command of C Company for the movement. He recalled, "That was a big thrill. I'd only been commissioned for a short while. But it was just for the move. I brought the company guidon, the morning report, and maybe thirty guys to Hawaii."[31]

While planning was in progress for the combat team's imminent transfer to Hawaii, on 5 May, an estimated force of 1,000 NKPA soldiers mounted a surprise attack in the vicinity of Kaesong, fifty miles north of Seoul.[32] After a furious engagement, the ROK Army succeeded in repulsing the NKPA. Five days later, an American reporter noted that several lives were being lost every day in the undeclared war waged on the 38th Parallel. After accompanying a 5th RCT patrol to the border, the reporter concluded that, although the South Korean soldiers were probably superior to the North Koreans, the most pressing concern was the position of American troops if the Russians and North Koreans should mount a combined invasion of South Korea. He need not have worried.[33] The Russians had no intention of invading South Korea — they had trained and equipped the NKPA to perform that task.

After the last Army reconnaissance flight was flown over the border on 31 May without incident, the 5th RCT commenced its redeployment. One after another, Army transport ships sailed from Inchon for Hawaii in June 1949. The departure of the Americans did not go unnoticed. While many Koreans may have regretted the departure of the soldiers, others showed their lack of appreciation and respect by screaming insults, throwing rotten fruit, and spitting at the men.[34] Ironically, the truck convoys drove to Inchon on the reverse of the route the Marines and soldiers would take the following year to liberate Seoul from Kim Il-Sung's murder squads.

We will never know if Kim Il-Sung would have dared to invade South Korea if the Truman Administration had kept the 5th RCT in Korea. Perhaps Stalin would never have authorized the invasion. In any event, few Americans would have predicted that the 5th RCT would return to Korea in thirteen months to fight in the Forgotten War.

Privates Parker (left) and Carl Ade (right) pose next to their first company sign at Uijongbu, February 1949. (source: Arlen Russell)

CHAPTER FOUR

ALOHA

Welcome Soldier
Hawaii welcomes the 5th Regimental Combat Team, which will make its home here after service in Korea.
The organization was the advance guard of more than 4,000 troops to be stationed here after occupation
duty in the orient. Honolulu doesn't seem like Honolulu without khaki-clad men on the streets in large
numbers, without white-garbed sailors roaming Waikiki. We have been short of both in recent months. All of
Hawaii extends a warm greeting to the men of the 5th RCT, hopes to make their stay a pleasant one.
The Honolulu Advertiser, *12 June 1949*

The 5th RCT arrived in Honolulu aboard three transport ships in June and July 1949. A paralyzing dock strike had most of the local populace in turmoil, but the strike did not affect the military, and the men disembarked without difficulty. Young ladies from the Hawaiian Visitors Bureau draped colorful leis around the necks of grateful soldiers, who in turn were astonished by the sight of beautiful Hula girls dancing on the piers to the sound of blaring music from an Army band.[1]

The 5th RCT's new home was Schofield Barracks, soon to be immortalized in the James Jones' novel *From Here to Eternity*. The Post Commander, Brigadier General Claude B. Ferenbaugh, had working parties "GI" the concrete quadrangle barracks, known as "Quads," before the combat team's arrival. Vacant since the close of World War II, the Quads were overgrown with foliage. Garden tools were initially unavailable when the 5th RCT moved into its quarters. The men had to use their bayonets to trim the shrubbery.[2] Nevertheless, the soldiers enjoyed their barracks so much that many joked that they had died and gone to heaven. Billeted in large open squad bays, every man had a wall locker and foot locker to stow his clothes and equipment. Soldiers never thought to lock up their gear when they left the barracks. Thievery was virtually unknown.[3]

The Army authorized soldiers to have their families join them on Oahu. In August and September wives and children arrived on steamships from California. A family atmosphere began to pervade the lush tropical surroundings of Schofield Barracks.

Army regulations authorized soldiers serving in infantry divisions to wear a divisional shoulder patch on their uniforms. The 5th RCT was an independent combat team, however, and its soldiers wore the U.S. Army Pacific shoulder patch instead. The 5th RCT had adopted a scarlet pentagon with a white border as its unofficial crest after a combat team-wide competition held in Korea. The five-sides of the pentagon design stood for the 5th Infantry's three infantry battalions, the 555th FAB, and the 72nd Engineer Company. The soldiers painted this design on the sides of the polished helmet liners they worn in garrison.[4]

Colonel Simpson pushed his men hard and achieved noteworthy results. His first task was to prepare the 5th RCT to serve as an aggressor force during Exercise MIKI, a massive joint exercise scheduled to culminate with an Army infantry division conducting an amphibious landing on Oahu in October. That the JCS assigned an Army, rather than a Marine, division this mission was largely due to the machination of Secretary of Defense Louis A. Johnson who was determined to emasculate the Corps.[5]

Meanwhile, the 5th RCT prepared to defend Oahu from the 2nd Infantry Division, which was sailing in a large convoy from Fort Lewis, Washington, to "liberate" Oahu. Lieutenant General Henry S. Aurand, Commanding General, U.S. Army Pacific, was the senior commander of the aggressor forces. To his credit, General Aurand provided enthusiastic and detailed briefings to the press while wearing full aggressor uniform regalia and using his assigned sobriquet, Bocquet, for the exercise.[6]

Colonel Simpson hiked his troops all over northern Oahu to familiarize them

Element of the 5th RCT receives a true Aloha welcome upon arrival at Honolulu. This is the first photo that Al Chang, then a SFC assigned to the 8295th Service Unit, took of the 5th RCT. (sources: NA/Chang)

with the terrain and to physically toughen the combat team's newly assigned soldiers. Everyone went to the rifle range to qualify with the M-1 service rifle. Crew-served weapons gun drill and range firing brought the 5th RCT's machine gun and mortar crews up to a high state of technical efficiency. The training regimen had the desired results. By October, the combat team enjoyed a strong sense of pride in self and unit.

Peacetime training on Schofield's limited maneuver areas and ranges presented problems for the combat team. "I think we trained reasonably well and hard," recalled Lieutenant General Hank Emerson long after the Korean War. "But we really didn't have good training facilities at Schofield Barracks. We used to go to the Kahukus and to a field area near Kailua Beach, but to the best that I can recall, there were no areas we could do really serious live-fire training, especially with the artillery. Some of the other infantry units may have gone over to the other islands for training, but mine never did. It was a typical peacetime Army

COL Simpson receives a silver plaque from the ROK Army on 3 November 1949. Note the early use of the 5th RCT emblem worn on his helmet liner. Lieutenant General Aurand, CG ARPAC, is wearing sunglasses. Brigadier General Ferenbaugh is second from the right. (source: NA)

thing. If you've ever seen the movie or read the book *From Here to Eternity*, it really wasn't too far from that .... Kind of laid back .... The main firing we did with weapons was kind of an annual thing, old style Army and Marine Corps known distance ranges and competitions.... I don't ever recall going out and using overhead machine gun fire in a training exercise, even with peacetime constraints and safety regulations. We weren't able to do that."[7]

According to MIKI's exercise scenario, the 5th RCT soldiers were the enemy, and the tough young soldiers enjoyed the role immensely. The men received a special dark green aggressor uniform with red and blue caps, and a helmet that looked like those worn in antiquity, to distinguish the 5th RCT from the 2nd Infantry Division. Inflatable pneumatic artillery pieces, tanks, and mortars were employed as decoys. Soldiers armed with the tape-recorded sounds of machine gun, mortar, and artillery fire, accompanied the units to the field. Umpires carried flash-bang artillery simulators.[8]

The 5th RCT acquitted itself with distinction in Exercise MIKI. When the 2nd Infantry Division stormed ashore at Waianae, the combat team greeted them with the sounds of blank bullets, sonic blasts, and flash-bangs. Army umpires expressed favorable comments about the combat team's tactical performance, but the script called for the enemy to lose, and the 5th RCT was overwhelmed on schedule.[9] Colonel Simpson received accolades from several general officers for his unit's high level of professionalism, tactical prowess, and overall fine performance in the exercise.

What residents later described as the "second invasion" of Oahu commenced on 26 October when the troops stormed downtown Honolulu on pass. For the first time in many years, hordes of soldiers and airmen "on pass," and sailors and Marines "on liberty" jammed the streets. Ecstatic merchants anticipated the promise of a forthcoming military payday with advertisements designed to entice servicemen to shed their hard-earned dollars.[10] The soldiers dressed for the occasion wearing brightly colored Aloha shirts, regulation khaki trousers, and brown shoes.[11] The Army blessed this deviation from uniform regulations in honor of the traditional Aloha Week celebrations.

General Aurand expressed his pleasure with the results of Exercise MIKI. He stressed the necessity to train all Army combat units in airborne and amphibious forcible entry operations.[12] One consequence was that he instructed COL Simpson to train the 5th RCT in the art of amphibious and gliderborne operations. General Aurand said that he could get gliders any time he asked for them, and he personally believed that Barber's Point Naval Air Station was a good site for glider training.[13] Colonel Simpson saluted and inaugurated a 30-week training schedule after MIKI designed to culminate in amphibious landings, glider training and RCT field exercises.[14]

There was time for pomp and circumstance, too. On 3 November, Mr. Beum Foo Yun, the First Secretary to the Republic of Korea Consul General in Honolulu, presented the 5th RCT with a silver plaque from the officers and men of the ROK Army. The inscription praised the 5th RCT's exceptionally meritorious service in training the ROK Army. The following week, the 5th Infantry Regiment stood erect on the parade field where in a solemn ceremony, the regiment was presented its colors.[15]

New soldiers continued to join the combat team. Private Arlen S. Russell, a fifteen-year-old soldier, arrived in Honolulu aboard a troop transport in April 1949. Private Russell hailed from Columbus, Ohio, where, after dropping out of high school, he had altered his birth certificate to join the Army. When his first crude attempt failed to pass the rigors of the recruiting sergeant's scrutiny, he asked his mother to pretend his real birth certificate was lost, and to request a new one from the hospital. All she had to do, he told her, was to provide the hospital with a 1932 date of birth that would make him the required seventeen years of age to join the Army. Perhaps fearful that her son might run away forever if she did not acquiesce to his wishes, she acquired the false birth certificate for her son. "You have to remember," he recalled after the war, "this was peacetime. She had no idea that I would wind up in Korea!"[16]

Private Russell joined Headquarters Battery, 555th FAB, and was billeted in Quad K. The idealistic wireman couldn't believe he had such good fortune to be assigned right out of Basic Training to Schofield Barracks in Hawaii. One of his proudest moments was riding in the back of a truck towing a howitzer through downtown Honolulu during the Memorial Day parade in 1950.[17]

The 555th FAB trained every week in the field practicing for a war few men believed would ever come. Arlen Russell recalls, "They kept us very physically fit in everyday training. And the morale of the people was very high. The artillery gun sections used to brag that they could drop a projectile in a rabbit hole, they were that good. And they were almost that good."

The Triple Nickel often trained near Kaiena Point, on Oahu's north shore, where the 105-mm howitzers would hammer away for hours at a target barge towed by the Navy. While the gun crews fired their howitzers, the rest of the men conducted .50-caliber machine gun live-fire training from ring mounts on their trucks, shooting at drones flying offshore.

The Triple Nickel's NCOs were an experienced lot, well versed in the intricacies of their artillery

Able Company conducts a route march through the Kahuku Training Area north of Schofield, 29 July 1949. (sources: NA/Chang)

trade. Sergeant First Class Earl J. Law, for example, the Chief of Firing Battery for B Battery, had served in the horse-drawn artillery before World War II. He had fought in the Northwest Europe Campaign with the 18th FAB, seeing almost continuous action from Utah Beach to the Elbe River. Released from active duty following V-J Day, he returned to the Army he knew and loved less than a year later. After he initially refused to apply for a reserve commission in 1947, the crusty Sergeant Major of the 48th FAB ordered SGT Law to take the written commissioning exam in Seoul. Sergeant Law passed the exam and received an appointment as a 2nd lieutenant in the Army Reserve, but he retained his NCO rank on active duty. He aspired to be a master sergeant (MSGT), not an officer, and promptly forgot about his reserve commission.[18]

Dog Company was one of the 5th Infantry's heavy weapons companies. Billeted in Quad E, exactly 7.2 miles from Kole Kole Pass, the company could often be found out in the field training or hiking to the top of the pass in full combat gear.[19] The intense, physically demanding training regime caused morale to soar in Dog Company.

Private George "Kenny" Freedman, from Kahuku, Oahu, reported to Dog Company's 81-mm Mortar Platoon just before Christmas, after graduating from recruit training at Schofield Barracks. His father was the Superintendent at The Boys School in the Kahuku, on Oahu's north shore. Prior to accepting that position, the family had lived in China, the Philippines

Private Arlen S. Russell. (source: Arlen Russell)

and Japan before returning to Oahu just before Pearl Harbor. The McKinley High School graduate enjoyed the experience of soldiering. He recalled, "It seemed to me that we developed a certain pride that we were members of a damn good unit."[20]

Dog Company's soldiers carried their crew-served weapons on all tactical evolutions.[21] Noncommissioned Officers taught their soldiers how to tactically employ their weapons, respond to an ambush, and dig in silently in the middle of the night. Private Freedman declared, "Some of us learned to move around 'enemy' 12-gauge rock salt shot! Some received sore 'Okoles' [butts] for their heroics."[22]

Dog Company's intensive training regime probably saved Private Freedman's life in Korea. "I can still remember my 81-mm [mortar's] forty-four-pound base plate digging into my shoulder or back. If it wasn't a base plate, it was the tube or bipod. Thank God for all that suffering, because it no doubt saved my life at a later time …. What about the march on the Burma Road all the way to KTA? It was twenty-one miles of what we thought was pure hell… little did we know what was in store for us in a few months."[23]

When the 58th Cavalry Reconnaissance Troop Mechanized was deactivated shortly after the 5th RCT arrived at Schofield, two new units were born: Tank Company and the Heavy Mortar Company. Corporal Ronald Denton transferred to the Heavy Mortar Company. "We were always out on the range firing live ammunition, and learning the intricacies of the 4.2-inch mortar," he said. "We were a physically hard, well trained unit. It saved my life when we had to go to war. The only problem was our ammunition. Some of the mortar rounds had not been properly stored or maintained after World War II. Sometimes a round would explode in a tube. Thank God we never lost anyone that way."[24]

Colonel Simpson established an NCO Leaders Course at Schofield Barracks and sent a large number of men to the three-week course. One of the instructors was 1st LT James Johnson from the 72nd Engineers.[25] Sergeant First Class Carl H. Dodd, a tough and extremely competent NCO, was an assistant instructor who tolerated no nonsense from his students. Graduates returned to their units cognizant of their duties as small unit leaders.

Private First Class Robert H. Middleton, from Hatfield, Indiana, served in B Company and credits the training he received at Schofield Barracks with saving his life later in Korea. "We trained, and we trained hard," he recalled. "It was the bayonet training in particular that I credit with saving my life, and I did use the bayonet a lot in Korea. After awhile it just comes natural."[26]

There was time for play, too. In the Spring of 1950, training was reserved for the morning hours only, the afternoons being reserved for team sports.[27] In hindsight, the soldiers would have been better served spending all of their hours training, but America was at peace and no one had foreseen the coming war. A number of soldiers did enjoy their training to the extent that they continued it on weekends, hiking with full combat loads through the mountains or conducting crew-served weapons gun drill unsupervised by NCOs in the courtyards of the company Quads.[28]

The soldiers looked forward to payday on the last day of the month.[29] Privates earned $75. Generals earned approximately $800, hardly a princely sum even in 1950. Servicemen did enjoy certain advantages over the civilian community. On the practical side, the beaches were free, and four of them were reserved for the Army's use on Oahu alone. Schofield Barracks offered sporting facilities, a movie theater, swimming pool, and an NCO and Enlisted Club where a man could enjoy a cold beer or chocolate milkshake along with his hamburger and fries. Private David Eckert, F Company, enjoyed his free time on Schofield Barracks so much he never left the base on pass.[30]

For adventurous souls, Honolulu was a wonderful place to blow off steam. Private Arlen Russell mailed home a $25 bond each payday. The rest of his salary could easily be spent in one night in Honolulu. "We spent a lot of time on River Street," said Russell. "They still had a dime-a-dance place there. I looked so young, it was hard for me to get into the bars. But I did every now and then."[31]

Private First Class Robert Middleton found Honolulu to be "paradise after Korea."[32] He spent one paycheck for the opportunity to be spoiled for a weekend at the Royal Hawaiian Hotel.

The relationship between soldier and civilian was friendly. A few sharks prowled the streets, but most Honolulu residents treated the soldiers with courtesy and respect. The Aloha Spirit was partially accounted for by the large number of soldiers from Hawaii who served in the 5th RCT. The 5th Provisional Training Company provided Basic Training at Schofield Barracks for local recruits. Graduates were given two duty choices — occupation duty in Japan or service in the 5th RCT.[33]

Lieutenant Keith Whitham shared a small Bachelor Officers Quarters with five other officers, among them Hank Emerson, Gordon M. Strong, and Donald Krause.[34] Like many of the bachelors, LT Whitham visited the night spots on Waikiki or the Officer Club at Pearl Harbor when not in the field.[35]

Second Lieutenant D. Randall Beirne, West Point Class of 1948, joined K Company at Schofield Barracks after graduation from The Infantry School. The native of Baltimore, Maryland, found social life to revolve around the Officers Club, largely because officers found it difficult to break into Honolulu's tightly knit social circle. Parents found the Officers Club provided a wonderful opportunity for their daughters to meet the right young men, and a lot of matches were made.[36]

Lieutenant Keith Whitham thought the Officers Club was the social hub for the regiment's officers, too. When COL Simpson retired from the Army in the Spring of 1950, the 5th RCT's new Commanding Officer, COL Godwin L. Ordway, Jr., took great delight in hosting regimental officer calls at the club. He required every officer to maintain a glass at the bar with his name etched upon it. What happened to all those glasses after the combat team deployed to Korea is a mystery.[37]

Enlisted men had little day-to-day contact with their officers before the Korean War. Noncommissioned Officers saw to the daily training and supervision of the men. Many of the NCOs were combat veterans, stellar soldiers in peace or war. Lieutenant Randall Beirne attended the Marine Corps Embarkation School at Coronado, California, with one of the Army's finest NCOs, Master Sergeant Melvin O. Handrich, who was destined to earn the Medal of Honor, posthumously, for heroic actions one desperate night on a hotly contested ridgeline in the early days of the Korean War. Lieutenant Beirne said, "Master Sergeant Handrich was a soldier's soldier, sharp in bearing and crisp in military appearance. He was a bright and articulate professional NCO who displayed a strong sense of self-confidence to those around him. We sent some of our best NCOs to that school in Coronado, and by any man's measure, MSGT Handrich was one of the best. Even the Marines were extremely impressed with him."[38]

A handful of combat veterans found it difficult to adjust to a peacetime garrison routine. Several NCOs lost their stripes as a result of brawls in private establishments, or for some infraction of military discipline. Alcohol abuse was common. One drunken NCO was busted to private after a court martial convicted him of urinating on the grounds of the Post Chapel. In Korea he redeemed himself in combat. A handful of soldiers got drunk one night, grabbed their rifles, jumped in a car and drove to Hickam Air Force Base where they proceeded to demonstrate their individual marksmanship prowess by

LT Hank Emerson and LT Ed Lange, Schofield Barracks, 1950. (source: Arlen Russell)

shooting out the street lights. This incident did not sit well with either the Air Force or the Army, and the busted soldiers were languishing in the stockade when the war broke out. These renegades were released for duty in time for the combat team's deployment to Korea. While en route to the war zone, they regained their stripes, and of those who survived, a few earned battlefield commissions.[39]

Sergeant First Class Kermit Jackson, from West Virginia, was "a twenty-eight-day soldier." He had received a severe head wound while earning a Silver Star at Anzio. The combat veteran joined K Company at Schofield Barracks where everyone stood in awe of his extensive knowledge of weapons and tactics, military bearing, command presence, and the combat decorations that adorned his massive chest. Sergeant First Class Jackson's appearance in uniform was always immaculate, and he expected his men to look that way too. In short, everyone respected him. His performance was exemplary for the first twenty-eight days each month, but everyone cringed when payday approached.

Sergeant First Class Jackson had a drinking problem. He claimed that the metal plate in his skull expanded when he had too much to drink. The intense pain caused him to lose both his judgment and temper in Wahiawa's bars. His fistfights were legendary. Usually, it took several men to knock the enraged NCO senseless. Sometimes SFC Jackson did not recover in time to escape being reported as Absent Without Leave (AWOL) when his weekend pass expired.[40]

Following one particularly nasty fight, SFC Jackson was reported AWOL after being hit over the head with a chair in one of Wahiawa's nightclubs. Lieutenant Randall Beirne was ordered to investigate the incident with the admonishment: "Take some money from him if you have too, but don't you dare bust him." After visiting SFC Jackson in the hospital, LT Beirne went to the nightclub in Wahiawa where the fight had taken place. He said, "All these women were in there sweeping the floor the next morning. They didn't know anything. 'Fight?' they said. 'I don't know what you are talking about. What fight?' They had never heard of anything going on that night. Dear old Wahiawa was a real Army town I'll tell you. Jackson went to Korea as the company First Sergeant. Later, when we received someone senior to him, Jackson reverted to platoon sergeant. In Korea, of course, Jackson was an outstanding soldier. For his bravery on Hill 268 near Waegwan he was recommended for the Distinguished Service Cross."[41]

While the soldiers trained and played hard on Oahu, Korea exploded in a firestorm of shot and shell. Long-simmering hostilities reached critical mass at 0400, on 25 June 1950, when NKPA artillery and mortars opened fire on the ROK Army's defensive positions along the 38th Parallel. The South Korean officers and enlisted men who had presented the 5th RCT its lovely silver plaque died by the thousands as NKPA infantry, supported by T-34 tanks and SU-76 self-propelled guns, crushed the defenders who futilely attempted to bar their path. Few ROK soldiers survived the tornado of artillery fire and the onrushing wave of armor.[42]

Private Arlen Russell was watching a movie one evening in the Base Theater at Schofield Barracks when the film suddenly stopped. The projectionist displayed a note on the silver screen that informed all soldiers to report to their units. After he returned to Headquarters Battery, an NCO informed the men that the 5th RCT had to be prepared to move out on a moment's notice because a war had broken out in Korea.[43]

While out on pass with friends, PFC Kenny Freedman realized something was out of the ordinary. He explained, "Every Saturday night there would be a live band dance at the Maluhia Service Club at Fort De Russy in Waikiki. We used to get free food and soft drinks there. It was staffed with the Girls Service Organization. The ladies were all volunteers and were very gracious hostesses. Many of us enjoyed their company and friendship. One Saturday night in the middle of a dance, a Marine Master Sergeant stopped the band in the middle of 'Blue Moon' and told us to report back to our duty stations. He stated that free transportation would be provided by Hawaiian Rapid Transit. We left the club not knowing what was going on and went out to Kalakaua Avenue looking for a ride back to Schofield. Taxies, buses and even civilians were driving around picking up servicemen. A civilian picked us up. He had heard that South Korea had been invaded by the North. Soon as we returned to the company area, 1st SGT George La Fountain ordered us to pack all civilian clothes and take the bags to the supply room. We complied and then watched all the 'Brass' coming to battalion headquarters."[44]

Sergeant First Class Earl Law was at Camp Stoneman, California, after enjoying a sixty-day reenlistment leave. A transportation clerk put him on the next plane to Hawaii rather than assign him to a berth on a slow troop ship.

The Triple Nickel was desperately short of officers. When the personnel officer informed LTC John H. Daly, the battalion commander, that SFC Law was one of three reserve officers serving in the outfit, he replied, "Good, have them report to me first thing in the morning." Regrettably, no one informed SFC Law of his pending appointment. He went out that evening with his best friend, MSGT McKinley G. Buckner, "to tie one on in Honolulu." The next morning, LTC Daly informed a hung-

Private Calhau and PFC Johnnie Kenawell at Lanikai.
(source: Calhau family)

over SFC Law that the paperwork had been placed in motion to get him his commission. In the meantime, he assigned SFC Laws to FO duty with Captain England's E Company.[45]

While the 5th RCT awaited developments on Oahu, President Truman ordered General Douglas MacArthur to stop the North Korean invasion. As CINCFE, General MacArthur commanded all Army, Air Force, and Navy units operating in the Far East. The strongest ground combat formation available for immediate commitment to Korea was Lieutenant General Walton H. Walker's Eighth Army in Japan. Unfortunately, the Eighth Army was in poor shape. General Walker commanded four infantry divisions (1st Cavalry, 7th, 24th and 25th) but these units were not staffed, trained or equipped for sustained ground combat. Few training areas existed in Japan to support realistic training. Moreover, and unlike the 5th RCT's experience at Schofield Barracks, the lack of suitable ranges prevented the field firing of most artillery and infantry heavy weapons. Limited training areas, the wide geographical dispersion of Eighth Army units, a high annual personnel turnover, and worn out weapons, vehicles, and communications equipment all hampered the implementation of an effective training program.

A relaxed atmosphere pervaded the occupation forces assigned to plush duty in Japan. Many of the Eighth Army's soldiers had never fully comprehended the harsh reality that their function was to fight and, if need be, to die. General George B. Barth, the Artillery Commander in the 25th Infantry Division, later wrote, "The realization that many of our men lacked the will to fight came as a great shock to me in the early days of Korea." He blamed this situation on pre-war recruiting practices that failed to emphasize it was a soldier's duty to fight, and on the lack of psychological preparation the soldiers had received from their commanders prior to being committed to combat.[46]

For the first time in our Nation's modern history, the opportunity did not exist to properly train and equip the American soldiers bound for war. In General MacArthur's own words, "The Korean War meant entry into action 'as is.' No time for recruiting rallies or to build up and get ready. It was move in — and shoot. This put the bulk of the burden on the GI."[47]

It was an onerous burden the GIs carried, but to their everlasting, glorious credit, the meagerly trained and inadequately equipped soldiers followed their orders and marched to war. The bulk of the Eighth Army's trucks and tanks had been salvaged from Pacific battlefields and repaired in Japanese factories. Quite often, the soldiers were issued ammunition so corroded with age that it failed to function as designed. In too many units, rifles, mortars and machine guns malfunctioned in combat due to worn and broken parts. Of the weapons that did fire, men with little training in their tactical employment manned an inordinate number.

On 5 July 1950, the battle-hardened, superbly equipped, and well-trained NKPA severely mauled Task Force Smith in a sharp engagement that sent shock waves rippling up the chain of command.[48] More disasters followed, as inexperienced American soldiers struggled to come to grips with the enemy. Battalion after battalion was smashed in the whirlwind. Driven back by NKPA tanks, infantry, and self-propelled artillery, the shattered remnants of the 24th Infantry Division attempted a stand at Taejon. It was a forlorn hope. The NKPA wrested control of the city in bitter and sustained close combat. With losses soaring, the Eighth Army urgently required an influx of fresh units and equipment to plug the yawning gaps in shattered defensive lines.

The JCS was initially reluctant to send General MacArthur reinforcements. No one knew if the Korean War would remain an isolated event on the periphery of Asia, or whether it was the prelude to a global war incited and directed by Stalin. A decision to reinforce the Eighth Army had to be made, and the President had to make it soon. Leaving a wary eye on the tense situation in Europe, the President ordered the JCS to take a calculated risk and alert specific units for deployment to Korea.

On 1 July, Major General Charles L. Bolte, the G-3 Operations Officer, Department of the Army, suggested to Lieutenant General Matthew B. Ridgway, Chief of Staff for Administration, that the 5th RCT be sent to Korea. Nine days later, the Chief of Staff of the Army, General J. Lawton Collins, passed through Hawaii on his way to visit General MacArthur in Japan. In the course of a telephone conversation with General Ridgway, General Collins asked him to query key Army staff officers for their opinions on whether the 5th RCT should deploy to Korea as a unit or as battalion-sized cadres to bring other outfits already in combat up to strength. It was subsequently decided to deploy the 5th

RCT as a unit, and on 13 July, the JCS directed General Aurand to dispatch the 5th RCT to Korea.[49]

The alert order arrived as the 5th RCT was conducting a live-fire weapons demonstration for a group of reserve and National Guard officers. Colonel Ordway directed 2,000 of the combat team's soldiers to observe the demonstration from the bleachers. Every regimental weapon except the tank-mounted 76-mm gun was fired to the cheers of the soldiers in the stands.[50] Following an ear-splitting "mad minute," during which every weapon was fired simultaneously, a lieutenant moved smartly to the center of the firing line with a carbine in hand and announced it was time to demonstrate the newest secret weapon in America's arsenal of freedom, the atomic carbine round. Over in the impact area stood a small shack, perhaps the size of an outhouse that the engineers had secretly rigged for demolition. According to Private Arlen Russell, "The officer sighted in on the house, fired, and that building exploded into a jillion toothpicks. There was nothing left of it. And you could hear all the 'Ohs' and 'Ahs' from the gullible such as me who actually believed we had an atomic carbine round. Of course, that was the only time I ever saw the atomic carbine round used."[51]

While the 5th RCT was on alert, its battalions received last-minute fillers from soldiers serving in the U.S. Army Pacific. Private Ernest Calhau and PFC Johnnie Kenawell were transferred to the 5th RCT where they both joined 1st Squad, 1st Platoon, F Company. The fillers conducted familiarization fire with their newly issued M-1 rifles, and threw one hand grenade apiece before boarding the transport ships bound for Korea.[52]

(source: Calhau family)

Sonny had not been a model soldier up to this time. There is reason to believe that he had been busted to Private for an infraction of military discipline.[53] Moreover, he had been drinking heavily when he wrecked his 1932 Ford Sport Roadster after falling asleep at the wheel in June 1950. Manley, his youngest brother, was thrown from the car and almost killed. When Sonny left for Korea, his father paid the large repair bill for the car.

Sonny and Johnnie were young and immortal soldiers in the Summer of 1950. Sonny was nineteen years old; Johnnie just a year older. Like soldiers before and since, they took advantage of their last overnight pass before shipping out. On 18 July, Johnnie accompanied Sonny home for a short visit. Wearing their combat fatigues, the two soldiers posed for photographs on the lawn. One photo shows the two friends clowning around, their fatigue caps worn backwards, all smiles for the camera. Sonny posed in one photo with his mother and father. Theresa is clearly worried in the photo; Ernest appears solemn.

Sonny left with Johnnie later that afternoon to visit friends and relatives and to enjoy one last night on the town. While Sonny was out, the Officer of the Day called and informed Ernest that his son had to report to Schofield Barracks the next morning. Implicit in this phone call was the warning that Private Calhau had better not be late. Ernest stayed awake all night, hoping Sonny would return so he could inform him of the news. When an inebriated Sonny arrived home early the next morning, Ernest told him that he had to report to his unit.

Sonny's youngest brother, Manley, was awakened to the sound of voices speaking in hushed tones outside on the porch. Manley overheard Sonny say to his parents that he wanted to leave quietly, so as not to awaken his sleeping brothers. Manley desperately wishes today that he had gone outside and said good-by. He did not want to intrude on Sonny's privacy, so he lay in bed listening to his brother say farewell to their mother who gave her son a last tearful hug.

Ernest drove Sonny over the Pali to Schofield Barracks where Fox Company was assembling for morning formation. After Ernest shook hands and hugged his oldest son, he drove home alone, deep in thought, completely oblivious to the natural beauty around him. No one in the family ever saw Sonny again.

CHAPTER FIVE

RIFLES AND MEN

The enemy expects no quarter and gives none. The Americans entered the Korean War with polished bright crosses on their ambulances and flags flying from their litter jeeps. The corpsmen who attended the wounded wore arm bands and carried no weapons. "What a bunch of innocents we were," PFC Edward Wilson, Chico, Calif., said today.
The Honolulu Advertiser, *19 July 1950*

Headlines in *The Honolulu Advertiser* screamed, "Reds Near Taejon." Adjoining photos featured soldiers cleaning their rifles at Schofield Barracks. Meanwhile, working parties hammered shut wooden packing crates and loaded them onto vehicles heading down to the waterfront.[1]

"With all that going on," said PFC Kenny Freedman, "we still found a few minutes here and there to sneak to Kemoo Farm across the main gate for a few drinks and a great steak. Most of us were too young to legally drink in the Territory of Hawaii. However, the bartenders said, 'If you're old enough to go and die for your country, you are old enough to drink!'"[2]

New men joined the combat team until it sailed. The 5th Provisional Training Company's recruits fleshed out the combat team's thin ranks. At least 100 soldiers from the 8292nd Post Engineers, a grounds maintenance unit, traded their rakes and shovels for rifles and bayonets when they suddenly found themselves transferred to the infantry.[3]

Newly commissioned 2nd Lieutenant Herbert H. Ikeda approached Captain Vaugn Evans, the S-1, 5th Infantry, with the news that several reserve officers from the Territory of Hawaii, including himself, wanted to volunteer for active service. After the Army blessed the idea, 2nd LTs Ikeda, Thomas P. Bartow, Oliver King, Carl F. Knobloch, Vernon Jernigan, Clifford Coleman, Roy T. Nakashima, Leonard K. Warner, Vance B. McWhorter, and Antonio Ventura joined the 5th RCT. Few of these exuberant yet sadly inexperienced lieutenants survived the war.[4]

Chaplain Dick Oostenink received thirty-six hours notice from Tripler Hospital that he would be deploying with the 3rd Battalion. His pregnant wife accepted the news with good grace, and their neighbors at Fort Kamehameha took excellent care of her while he was gone.[5]

The former commanding officer of 1st Battalion in Korea, LTC Thomas B. Roelofs, requested a transfer from the U.S. Army Pacific to accompany the combat team. Permission granted, LTC Roelofs served on the combat team's staff as the Intelligence Officer. In reality he was a battalion commander in waiting.

On 22 July, the combat team held a final formation before moving out. As the convoys pulled out of the main gate, the soldiers saw groups of civilians lining the route cheering, waving, and, in a few cases, standing silently beside the road with streams of tears rolling down their cheeks. Shouts of "Aloha! Good Luck, and God's speed" were heard along with quite a few "Give 'em Hells!" Several pineapple-truck drivers drove slowly alongside the Army vehicles so the grateful soldiers could reach out and grab a pineapple, or two, and taste Hawaii's bounty for the last time.[6]

Four transports were dispersed between the Army Pier on the Honolulu waterfront and the piers at Naval Station, Pearl Harbor: the USNS *General Hugh G. Gaffey*, the USNS *General W. A. Mann*, the USS *Ventura* and the USS *Merrill*. The deep holds of the USS *Ventura* swallowed the bulk of the combat team's vehicles, and tons of urgently needed ammunition and supplies, while the USS *Merrill* took onboard the tanks, liaison aircraft, and howitzers. Sonny boarded the USNS *Gaffey* with the 2nd Battalion, the 72nd Engineer Company, the Heavy Mortar Company, most of Medical Company, and Headquarters and Headquarters Company, 5th Infantry. When the 1st Battalion, 3rd Battalion, the 555th FAB, Tank Company and the rest of Medical Company reached the Army Pier in Honolulu, an Army band from Fort Shafter serenaded the men with "Now is the Hour" as they walked up the brow of the *General Mann*.[7] It was an emotional scene, for hundreds of tearful relatives and friends had gathered behind a fenced-off portion of the pier to witness the departure of their loved ones.

The embarked 178 officers and 3,319 men stood at the rails waving goodbye to their families and friends as the ships slipped anchor and headed for open sea.[8] Quite naturally, the married soldiers were thinking about their families. Of the 5th RCT's 1,127 dependent wives and children, 600 had elected to leave Hawaii for the Mainland, including the wife of Colonel Godwin Ordway, Jr. Two hundred and eleven dependents were residents of the Territory of Hawaii, and, therefore, had no reason to leave Schofield Barracks. The remaining 316 dependents decided to remain at Schofield Barracks when the combat team shipped out. General Aurand told reporters that he would do everything in his power to look after the families who remained behind. He kept his promise.[9]

SFC Andrew Book, George Company, (KIA 3 September 1950) awaits the order to mount the trucks at Schofield Barracks. Awarded the Silver Star posthumously. (source: Ray Warner)

The USNS Hugh G. Gaffey *departs Honolulu. (source: Chang)*

The 5th RCT mounts up. (source: Chang)

Now is the hour. (source: Chang)

With the 5th RCT's departure, Schofield Barracks reverted to a near ghost town in population and appearance. When LTC John L. Throckmorton deployed to Korea in command of the 2nd Battalion, his oldest son, Thomas, continued to serve the base community as a paperboy. Thomas' paper route took him past boarded-up houses to the handful of households that remained on otherwise empty streets.[10] The grass, plants, and trees grew unchecked across the base, increasing the sense of isolation and anxiety for the wives and children who remained behind. Civilian morale would plummet later that summer when hardly a day would pass without one or more families receiving the tragic news that a loved one had been reported killed, wounded, or missing.

The sudden departure of the married men often caused financial hardship for their families. Warrant Officer Sal Bosco, Headquarters Battery, 555th FAB, decided to send his wife and their two children to the States. The Army was willing to provide transportation for his family, but not for his car. Given the choice of either selling the car or leaving it parked on the parade field, he sold it for a loss.[11]

For many soldiers, the voyage marked the beginning of a thrilling adventure. Sonny's morale was high. He received his shots on the voyage over, played cards, and watched movies in the evening while becoming acquainted with the other soldiers in his new unit. Sonny's comrades conversed in small groups, ate and slept when they could.

It was difficult to conduct realistic combat training aboard ship. One enthusiastic lieutenant in the Triple Nickel trained his soldiers to adjust indirect fire with binoculars while he moved orange peels on the deck to simulate shell bursts.[12] The Executive Officer (XO) of Fox Company, 1st LT Frank Brooks, received permission to conduct live-fire weapons training from the fantail of the USNS *General Gaffey*. The men threw boxes overboard and received some last-minute training shooting at the targets.[13] The other companies, to include those embarked on the USNS *General Mann*, followed suit.

Many soldiers slept on deck to escape the cramped holds. They stretched out where the air was cool and the view of the star filled heavens was indescribably beautiful. Fifteen-year-old Private Arlen Russell carved out a personal niche on deck and watched the mighty blue Pacific Ocean roll by.[14] Private Gene McClure, on the other hand, spent the voyage below deck, assigned against his will to the never ending drudgery of K.P. Duty, peeling potatoes in the kitchen and scrubbing pots in the scullery.[15]

First Lieutenant Hank Emerson felt cheated. Due to his seniority, he had been kicked upstairs shortly before the war to become 1st Battalion's assistant operations officer. This prestigious peacetime job was not to LT Emerson's liking. He understandably wanted to be in a rifle company when the shooting started. As luck would have it, a rifle platoon leader in A Company fell down a ladder well a few days out from Pusan, and LT Emerson took over this officer's platoon. Lieutenant Emerson's friends jested that he had pushed his way into the job.[16]

Rumors spread rapidly. The combat team's destination, though guessed by many, had not been officially announced. A handful of men heard scuttlebutt that the combat team was sailing to the Philippines where they would receive additional training before going on to Korea. Another rumor had the 5th RCT sailing to Japan to replace the units now fighting in Korea. Still others believed they were going to Okinawa. Lieutenant Martin L. Pitts, a rifle platoon leader in B Company and a graduate of The Citadel, believed there might be an element of truth to the rumors and packed a tuxedo in his duffel bag just in case.[17] The mighty steel hulls were not swayed by rumors and maintained a steady course toward Korea.

Colonel Ordway finally squashed the rumors in an official announcement that declared their destination was Pusan, Korea. Chaplain Oostenink no-

PFC Namoru Imimura (left) from Honolulu, Hawaii, fires into enemy positions while CPL Chuck Bitgreaves from Los Angeles, California, inserts a new clip into his M-1 on 31 January 1951. Note the flash suppressor and scope on PFC Imimura's M-1. (sources: NA/Chang)

ticed an increased attendance at religious services after the announcement.[18]

The 5th RCT enjoyed numerous strengths. A large number of officers were West Pointers, superbly trained professional leaders from the Long Gray Line. With few exceptions, the soldiers were all volunteers, Regular Army to a man. Combat veterans served in many of the key officer and NCO positions, including soldiers who had fought in the highly decorated, all-volunteer, Japanese-American "Go for Broke" 442nd Infantry Regiment and the equally illustrious 100th Battalion.[19] Many soldiers called Hawaii home, and the combat team's future exploits would be closely followed in the Honolulu newspapers, a morale factor of immense importance. Most small-unit leaders had an appreciation for Korea's difficult terrain and harsh weather conditions, and possessed a rudimentary knowledge of the Korean people, their language and culture. A long period of mutual association had cemented the relationships between the 5th Infantry, 555th FAB, and the 72nd Engineer Company, an advantage not enjoyed by the so-called regimental combat teams the Eighth Army had hastily scraped together from Army occupation forces in Japan. Finally, the squads, platoons, companies and batteries that formed the 5th RCT were near their authorized personnel strengths, unlike the sadly under strength units that had deployed from Japan.

A 555th FAB FO teams observes an airtstrike. Note the P-51 pulling up above the smoke. (source: Chang)

Unfortunately, the 5th RCT's numerous advantages would be nullified to a certain extent by an unsound tactical organization inherent to all Army infantry formations during the Korean War. All infantry tactics focus on the last 100 yards. Artillery barrages and air strikes alone never take ground. Tanks can overrun ground, but they can not hold it without infantry. The infantry can take and hold ground, but only if it can cross the last 100 yards, the loneliest, most terrifying place on the battlefield.

The rifle squad was both the Army's smallest tactical organization during the Korean War and its weakest link on the battlefield. This situation was not the squad leader's fault. He did the best job possible with the men and equipment assigned to him. One has to contrast the different organizational approaches taken by the Army and the Marine Corps to traverse the last 100 yards to understand the fundamental weakness of the Army rifle squad in the Korean War. Both the Army and the Marine Corps maintained three rifle squads in each rifle platoon, and three rifle platoons and one weapons platoon in each rifle company. Thus, on the surface, Army and Marine platoons and companies looked the same. The difference lay in the organization and armament of their respective squads.

A Marine rifle squad consisted of a squad leader and three four-man fire teams. Each fire team was built around a M1918A2 Browning Automatic Rifle (BAR), a light machine gun carried by an automatic rifleman trained in its tactical employment.[20] The fire team leader controlled the fires of his automatic rifleman and detailed a second rifleman to assist the BAR man in action. The fourth Marine served as a basic rifleman. With the exception of the three automatic riflemen, everyone else in the Marine rifle squad carried the M-1 Garand Rifle, a semi-automatic weapon of immense hitting power, yet one that was no match for an automatic weapon.[21] The Marine rifle squad leader directed his three fire team leaders to employ their respective BARs to suppress the enemy's defensive fire in order to gain and maintain fire superiority, a prerequisite in offensive combat, which in turn facili-

1st LT Norman Cooper, 2nd Battalion's P&A Platoon Leader, hugs his son, Gregory, goodbye at Schofield Barracks. (source: Norman Cooper)

tated tactical maneuver across the battlefield. The flexible triangular organization of the Marine rifle squad facilitated mutual support between the fire teams. One or more fire teams could maneuver while the other fire team(s) suppressed the opponent with BAR fire. In defensive combat, the Marine squad leader had three BARs to employ across the width of his squad's assigned frontage. Finally, it was easier for a single rifle squad leader to control three fire team leaders, rather than to control twelve men all at once.

An Army rifle squad did not enjoy these advantages. After World War II, the Army concluded that it was easier for a rifle squad leader to control fewer men, but rather than sub-divide the squad into fire teams of equal size and firepower, the Army reduced the size of the squad. An Army rifle squad in 1950 consisted of nine men: a squad leader, an assistant squad leader, an automatic rifleman armed with a BAR, an assistant automatic rifleman, and five riflemen. In theory, the assistant squad leader, automatic rifleman, and assistant automatic rifleman, formed a BAR team, which supported the advance of the squad with automatic weapons fire. If this BAR jammed, or was put out of action by enemy fire, a second or third BAR did not exist to continue firing. Moreover, while a Marine rifle squad would retain its effectiveness even after three or four casualties, an Army rifle squad would be rendered rapidly ineffective. Finally, during defensive combat, the Army squad had just one BAR to cover its frontage. In the final analysis, the Army committed its rifle squads to combat with one-third of the automatic weapons firepower and three-quarters the personnel of a Marine rifle squad.[22]

The Army addressed the paucity of automatic weapons in its rifle squads by adding an M1919A4 or A6 machine gun team to the 4th squad, or weapons squad, of each rifle platoon. The platoon's 2.36-inch, and later its 3.5-inch, bazooka team was found in this squad, too. If the machine gun was put out of action through malfunction or enemy fire, or if the gun team had to change barrels or position, a second machine gun team did not exist to maintain a high rate of automatic weapons fire.[23]

In contrast, a Marine rifle company had a machine gun platoon equipped with six machine guns organized into three machine gun squads.[24] A machine gun squad with two machine guns was often attached to a Marine rifle platoon to accomplish a specific tactical mission. If one of the machine gun squad's Brownings was silenced due to enemy action, malfunction, change of barrel or position, the second machine gun could increase its rate of fire. On other occasions, the massed firepower of the platoon's six machine guns could be employed either in direct support of a specific rifle platoon's mission or in general support of the entire company.

In summary a Marine rifle company was equipped with twenty-seven BARs to an Army rifle company's nine, and six machine guns to the Army's three. A Marine rifle platoon reinforced with a squad of two machine guns had nearly the same weight of automatic weapons firepower as an Army rifle company.[25]

There were other differences, too. The Marines enjoyed superb close air support (CAS) in the form of Marine aviation. The Air Force, on the other hand, having neglected CAS in favor of strategic bombing and battlefield interdiction after World War II, had to relearn how to provide CAS to the Army in Korea.

Even after the Air Force began to provide effective CAS, Army officers continued to look with undisguised envy at the Marines who enjoyed the benefit of an integrated air-ground team. The Marines, for example, assigned a tactical air control party (TACP) to the headquarters of each division, infantry regiment, and infantry battalion for the express purpose of controlling CAS. A single TACP could direct a hellish combination of rockets, bombs, napalm, and cannon fire to support the forces in contact at the focal point of the battlefield. The Marines had thoroughly tested their CAS doctrine in numerous field exercises before the war and were adept at integrating precise, air-delivered supporting fires into the scheme of maneuver.[26]

To Marines, CAS meant delivering fires as close as 50-200 yards in front of friendly units in contact. Marines viewed Naval Aviation (Marine and Navy aircraft) as flying artillery and used it as such with devastating effect. In contrast, Air Force doctrine stressed that targets located within 1,000 yards of friendly troops would be more profitably engaged by artillery. The Air Force preferred to conduct interdiction strikes against an enemy's logistical network. In all fairness to the Air Force, interdiction strikes played a crucial role in preventing a North Korean victory. Nevertheless, CAS had its place on the Korean battlefield, too. The interdiction effort, though important, would have proven meaningless if the NKPA had overrun the Eighth Army and captured Pusan in August 1950.

The Air Force's doctrinal reluctance to attack close in targets before the war saw drastically fewer

TACPs assigned to Army maneuver units in comparison to the Marines. Initially, the Air Force assigned just one TACP to each Army infantry division, quite a difference from the Marines who enjoyed a TACP in every infantry battalion. As the struggle intensified, the Air Force began to provide a TACP to each infantry regiment. This took time, and the 5th RCT, for example, would not receive its TACP until long after the summer crisis had peaked. At no time during the Korean War did the Air Force routinely assign TACPs to Army infantry battalions. The single TACP assigned to an Army infantry regiment could not hope to provide the same level of effectiveness and coverage as the four TACPs assigned to a Marine regiment. Moreover, the Air Force initially rotated its pilots in and out of TACP duty at twelve-day intervals. Although the Air Force, at the Army's urgent request, eventually increased this period of duty to fifteen days, and later yet again to twenty-one days, the resultant gap in experience was never satisfactorily resolved. An Air Force officer assigned to a TACP rarely had time to master the intricate technical and tactical details associated with his job before another inexperienced officer replaced him.[27]

To counterbalance the handful of TACPs the Air Force assigned to Army ground combat units, it fielded an airborne system consisting of a two-man crew, pilot and controller, flying in the venerable AT-6 Texan trainer aircraft to control supporting arms. Known as "Mosquitoes", these airborne communications platforms enabled a controller in the back seat of the AT-6 to coordinate air strikes, artillery fire, and naval gun fire with the infantry's maneuver. As one veteran recalls, "Many of us in the 5th RCT called the Mosquitoes 'Angels' because it was like talking to Heaven and getting an answer — an air strike or even Big Mo [USS *Missouri*'s 16-inch naval rifles]."[28]

Yet even this method of controlling CAS had its disadvantages. Prior to the summer of 1951, for example, when the Mosquitoes were belatedly fitted with rockets to mark enemy positions with white phosphorous, the airborne controllers had to rely on "talking" aircraft onto their targets.[29]

The official history of the U.S. Air Force in the Korean War characterized the Marine method of providing CAS to ground troops a wasteful employment of trained pilots and equipment. "Since it cost far more to deliver aerial bombs than to fire artillery shells," it states, "the routine use of airpower as flying artillery constituted a severe expense to American taxpayers."[30] One has to wonder if the taxpayers would have felt differently if NKPA T-34 tanks had suddenly appeared in their neighborhoods.

On a positive note, the 5th Infantry deployed to Korea with three organic infantry battalions. Most of the infantry regiments from Japan had gone into combat with only two, one battalion in each regiment having been disbanded prior to the war for fiscal economy.[31] Regiments with two battalions had been called upon to perform missions normally assigned to regiments with three, often with disastrous consequences for the men. The presence of a third battalion in the 5th RCT made it easier for the combat team to field a strong reserve that could exploit a tactical success or counter an enemy move.

The 5th Infantry was organized along standard Army lines with an organic Headquarters and Headquarters Company, Tank Company, Heavy Mortar Company, Service Company, Medical Company, and three infantry battalions. Headquarters and Headquarters Company provided the combat team's command and control together with all associated functions. Carried on the rolls of the company were the commanding officer and his staff composed of personnel (S-1), intelligence (S-2), operations (S-3), and logistics (S-4). The company included a regimental headquarters section, a counterfire platoon, a communications platoon, an intelligence and reconnaissance (I&R) platoon, an antitank mine platoon, and a security platoon to protect the command post.[32]

An Easy Eight from Tank Company 5th RCT, in action. (source: Chang)

Service Company's soldiers were the jacks-of-all-trades who labored in personnel, supply, and graves registration sections. The company also provided organizational maintenance for motor transport, in addition to supplying the combat team with ammunition, food, clothing, equipment, and fuel.[33]

Medical Company cared for sick and wounded soldiers. The company included a headquarters, a collecting platoon, and three medical platoons. The medical platoons were normally attached to a specific battalion within the RCT. In his dual capacity as a surgeon, the medical platoon leader also advised the battalion commander on medical and sanitation matters pertaining to the accomplishment of assigned tactical missions. Each of the platoons had two medical officers and thirty-five enlisted men assigned who provided emergency medical treatment, operated an aid station, and evacuated casualties from the front lines.[34]

Organized around a small headquarters element and three firing platoons, the Heavy Mortar Company provided long range, indirect fires in support of the infantry in all stages of the attack, defense, and counterattack. The 4.2-inch mortar shell weighed approximately twenty-five pounds and could be fired a maximum range of 4,397 yards.[35] The mortar's rifled tube helped to make accurate gunnery possible even at maximum range.

The crews attached various types of fuses to the shells to accomplish specific missions. For example, the "Time-Super-quick" fuse attached to a high explosive round was deadly against troops in the open, while the "Delay" fuse proved most effective against dug-in troops with overhead protection.

Twenty-five and one-half propellant increments came attached to each shell. Removing increments from the shell and adjusting the elevation of the tube attained the desired range. Additional increments could be attached to a shell to attain a range out to 6,000 yards, but this procedure was not recommended due to the possibility of bursting a tube.[36]

Four 4.2-inch mortar squads, of eight men each, comprised a platoon. Four members of each mortar squad were transferred shortly after the 5th RCT reached Korea to replace losses in the rifle companies. South Korean soldiers replaced these men to bring the mortar squads back up to strength. Weighing in at 639 pounds, the M30 4.2-inch mortar was normally broken down into component parts for transport on trucks. For this purpose, a 3/4-ton truck usually sufficed to carry both weapon and ammunition.

The company headquarters included a fire direction center (FDC), which in theory received and monitored calls for fire, assigned fire missions to the platoons, maintained the regimental commander's targeting priorities, and kept careful watch of safety features built into the scheme of maneuver to include unit boundaries and patrol overlays. In reality, the 5th RCT's three 4.2-inch mortar platoons usually operated independently in Korea, one attached to each infantry battalion. Though 1st Mortar Platoon, as one might expect, supported 1st Battalion, oddly enough, the 2nd Platoon supported the 3rd Battalion while the 3rd Platoon supported the 2nd Battalion.[37] Every mortar platoon maintained its own FDC and provided one 4.2-inch mortar FO Team of two men to the infantry battalion it supported.

A weakness associated with the 4.2-inch mortar was its inability to traverse beyond 180-degrees, unlike the Soviet manufactured 120-mm mortar the NKPA employed that could traverse a full circle. A 4.2-inch gun crew had to physically move the heavy weapon whenever the azimuth to the target exceeded the mortar's traverse, a disadvantage in a gunnery duel.

Tank Company was the one distinct advantage an Army infantry regiment enjoyed over the Marines

B Battery 105 in firing position, 1952. The muzzle cap confirms this is a simulated action shot. (source: 5th RCT Association)

Corps in the Korean War. The Army and Marine infantry division structure included a battalion of tanks, but a regimental tank company was not organic to Marine infantry regiments.[38] The 5th Infantry's Tank Company consisted of seventeen M-4 A3E8 "General Sherman" tanks, referred to by their crews as "Easy Eights" or "Shermans." A small company headquarters equipped with two tanks and a tank retriever, and three tank platoons with five Easy Eights apiece, rounded out Tank Company.[39] Due to a combination of battle damage and maintenance problems, the tank platoons often operated with just three or four tanks in Korea, and the company headquarters consistently released its two assigned tanks to replace losses in the platoons.

A tank platoon was further subdivided into two sections: a heavy section of three tanks, and a light section of two. The sections provided mutual support to one another in combat. The

A How Company 81-mm Mortar crew in action, Spring 1951. Keith Krepps is in the foreground. (source: Arlen Russell)

platoon leader commanded the heavy section, while the platoon sergeant commanded the light section.

Tank platoons were usually attached to the infantry battalion with a corresponding number and employed in an infantry support role. For example, 1st Tank Platoon was normally attached to 1st Battalion. This was not a hard and fast rule, and over time a tank platoon found itself supporting every battalion, to include the artillery, in the combat team.

An M-4 A3E8 tank had a crew of five men: a commander, gunner, loader, driver and bow gunner. Armament consisted of a 76-mm high velocity cannon capable of defeating the frontal armor of NKPA tanks, a co-axial .30-caliber machine gun, and a second .30-caliber machine gun mounted in a ball socket on the bow of the tank. A .50-caliber anti-aircraft machine gun rounded out an Easy Eight's formidable firepower. Mounted on the rear of the turret, the .50-caliber machine gun could only be employed by a soldier brave or fatalistic enough to stand on top of the engine deck while in full view of the enemy.

Tank commanders rarely "buttoned up," meaning their heads and shoulders were exposed to small arms fire and shrapnel. To "button up" meant to abandon all-around vision and place sole reliance on the crew's narrow vision blocks for a view of the battlefield. As a result of not "buttoning up," Tank Company would lose many soldiers to serious, and often fatal, head wounds.

Due to a lack of suitable training areas on Oahu for armored vehicles, the level of training in Tank Company was not high. Only a handful of NCOs had served in armored units in World War II. The men would learn their trade the hard way in Korea.[40]

The 5th Infantry Regiment's three infantry battalions were the backbone of the combat team. An infantry battalion consisted of a Headquarters and Headquarters company, three rifle companies and one heavy weapons company. Headquarters and Headquarters Company included a battalion staff section that manned the battalion's command post, an intelligence section, an I&R platoon, a communications platoon, and a pioneer and ammunition (P&A) platoon.

The I&R Platoon in the 2nd Battalion consisted of a lieutenant platoon leader, who doubled as the battalion intelligence officer, and fifteen to sixteen enlisted men. The primary mission of the I&R Platoon was to conduct patrols behind enemy lines to gather information on the terrain and the enemy. Occasionally, the I&R Platoon was specifically tasked to capture prisoners. This exceedingly hazardous duty called for a special kind of soldier, one who possessed extraordinary self-discipline and initiative. "We were the dirty guys, the ones who got the dirty jobs in my opinion," explained Sergeant Bud Throne, from Tulsa, Oklahoma, who joined the 5th RCT a few days before the outfit sailed to Korea.[41] Casualties in the I&R Platoons were correspondingly heavy.

The P&A Platoon's mission was to lay mines, set booby traps, sweep for mines with mine detectors, construct foot bridges, emplace barbed wire, provide security for the battalion command post, and transport ammunition forward to front line combat units. It had a secondary engineering mission for tasks that did not require technical training.[42]

An infantry battalion's rifle and heavy weapons companies were also known as "line" or "letter" companies. A specific letter from a phonetic military alphabet designated each line company to avoid confusion when speaking on the radio net.

1st Battalion	2nd Battalion
Headquarters and Headquarters Company	Headquarters and Headquarters Company
A Company / Able	E Company / Easy
B Company / Baker	F Company / Fox
C Company / Charlie	G Company / George
D Company / Dog (Heavy Weapons)	H Company / How (Heavy Weapons)

3rd Battalion
Headquarters and Headquarters Company
I Company / Item
K Company / King
L Company / Love
M Company / Mike (Heavy Weapons)

A rifle company consisted of three rifle platoons, organized as previously described, and a weapons platoon equipped with three 60-mm mortars and three 57-mm recoilless rifles.[43]

Korea would prove to be an infantryman's war, and although artillery and armor would play their own important roles, the infantry was destined to suffer the heaviest casualties. Those who survived the ordeal would wear the Combat Infantryman's Badge with pride.

Radio communication equipment for each rifle company appeared adequate on paper. A rifle company possessed two SCR-300 FM radios to communicate with its battalion headquarters and its sister companies. One SCR-300 usually remained in the company command post, while the second accompanied the company commander wherever he went. A simple change of frequencies allowed the company commander to communicate with the regiment or another battalion if so required. Artillery and mortar FOs carried the SCR-300 radio, too, and the existence of these extra radios in the company command group provided an alternate means of communication if one of the SCR-300s was destroyed. Unfortunately, the SCR-300 radios were old and worn pieces of equipment that often failed to operate as designed in the harsh weather conditions and mountainous terrain of Korea. Weighing in at thirty-eight pounds with the larger of the two batteries available for its use, the SCR-300 was also extremely heavy to carry, particularly for a radio operator already encumbered with a weapon, ammunition, rations, water and equipment.[44]

Twelve shorter range PRC-526 AM radios, or "Walkie Talkies," rounded out a rifle company's radio communications equipment. Regrettably, the five-pound PRC-526 was an extremely unreliable piece of equipment. Men would perish when frustrated company commanders found themselves unable to communicate their orders to rifle platoons locked in combat.[45]

An infantry battalion's heavy weapons were found in either Dog, How or Mike Companies. A heavy weapons company was organized around a headquarters element and three platoons: heavy machine gun, mortar and recoilless rifle.

The heavy machine gun platoon was equipped with four .30-caliber M1917A1 water-cooled heavy machine guns and four .30-caliber M1919A6 light machine guns.[46] At the outbreak of the Korean War, the platoon was organized into a headquarters and two machine gun sections. Two machine gun teams, with one machine gun per team, comprised a section. Although the platoon could man its eight machine guns in the defense, during offensive combat it had only enough men to physically carry four weapons. As the war progressed, and the deficiency in automatic weapons firepower became acutely felt, the combat team's battalions added more manpower to form a third machine gun section in each platoon, which facilitated fire support for all three infantry companies.[47] Moreover, the large number of surplus M2 .50-caliber machine guns lying around in Korea did not escape the notice of the machine gunners, who often used these excellent heavy weapons to augment their organic firepower.

The 75-mm Recoilless Rifle Platoon was organized around a headquarters and two sections. Two recoilless rifles comprised a section. The 75-mm recoilless rifle, though it had seen limited combat service in the closing days of World War II, had yet to be produced in sufficient numbers to fully equip the regiment's three 75-mm Recoilless Rifle Platoons when the 5th RCT was alerted for movement.[48] At the last minute, the Hawaiian National Guard transferred additional recoilless rifles from its stocks to remedy the shortfalls.

It was not unusual for the 75-mm Recoilless Rifle Platoons to exchange their recoilless rifles for excess .50-caliber machine guns whenever the tactical situation demanded it. Private Gene McClure served on one of How Company's 75-mm Recoilless Rifle Squads. He explains, "What we needed most was an automatic weapon that would fire bullets by the hundreds per minute, killing at close range, instead of a gun that fired two or three times per minute killing at long range such as the 75-

mm gun. Also the machine gun was lighter and much easier to carry up and down the endless hills and valleys."[49]

The 81-mm Mortar Platoon served as a battalion commander's hip-pocket artillery. The platoon was organized around a headquarters, which included an FDC, and two mortar sections of two squads each. A squad manned one smooth-bore 81-mm mortar. The versatile high-angle fire weapons fired a variety of ammunition that could be fused to explode in a combination of fiendish ways. Maximum range varied with the type of ammunition fired: high explosive light, 3,200 yards; high explosive heavy, 2,560 yards; smoke (white phosphorous) 2,465 yards; smoke (FS), 2,430 yards; and illumination, 2,200 yards. The smoke (FS) round was rarely used in Korea because it did not cause casualties. Like the 60-mm and 4.2-inch mortars, range was determined through the removal of increments, or charges, and the elevation of the barrel.

The 81-mm Mortar Platoon attached one FO Team to each of its battalion's three rifle companies. The platoon FDC monitored their calls for fire and assigned fire missions to the sections.

A Korean War vintage 81-mm mortar weighed 136 pounds and was usually hand carried across rough terrain by its squad. To increase the combat team's firepower, more 81-mm mortars were acquired in Korea. First Battalion, for example, quickly integrated two additional 81-mm mortars to form a six-tube platoon in the Pusan Perimeter. Reducing the size of the twelve-man squads formed the manpower for the two additional gun crews.[50]

The 72nd Engineer Company performed combat engineering tasks in support of the infantry. It consisted of a headquarters element and three combat engineer platoons. An SCR-300 radio was assigned to each engineer platoon, which enabled the platoon leader to stay abreast of the regiment's tactical situation and respond as required. Combat engineers performed a multitude of tasks, including the construction and repair of bridges, improving roads, clearing and laying minefields, and blasting tunnels and bunkers with satchel charges and field demolitions. Heavy equipment included a roadgrader for the company and one D-7 bulldozer per platoon. Armament consisted of small arms, rocket launchers, and vehicular mounted .50-caliber machine guns. In tactical emergencies the combat engineers doubled as infantry. The platoons were often attached to the infantry battalion that shared their number.

The quality of the combat engineer personnel was superb. The Commanding Officer (CO) of the 72nd Engineers was Captain Lester P. Gayhart who had won a battlefield commission in World War II. His three platoon leaders were West Pointers, professional soldiers to a man. First Lieutenant James A. Johnson, the 1st Platoon Leader, explained, "In our company we had seven or eight former combat engineer first sergeants. My platoon sergeant, Emitt D. Parrish, who was not the ranking sergeant, had been the sergeant major of the 39th Combat Engineer Regiment that had fought in Italy. That was a very famous organization — a good combat outfit. My squad leaders were all ex-first sergeants. We had those kinds of people. I could tell anyone in my platoon to 'go on out and build a bridge,' and they would get it done. It was that kind of an organization."[51]

The 555th FAB provided sustained fire support to the infantry in all phases of the attack, defense and counterattack. The Triple Nickel was organized along standard Army lines with a Headquarters Battery, Service Battery, and three firing batteries — A Battery, B Battery and C Battery. Headquarters Battery functioned as the field artillery battalion's nerve center. It contained an instrument and survey section, and communications, maintenance, supply and medical personnel. Headquarters Battery assigned an artillery liaison section to the 5th Infantry's command post to plan, coordinate, and integrate artillery fire support into the infantry's scheme of maneuver. An FDC manned by Headquarters Battery personnel responded to calls for fire from FOs who usually transmitted their requests over the artillery conduct of fire radio net. The FDC analyzed each request, and assigned a firing battery, or sometimes batteries, the mission of engaging the target with a designated type or combination of munitions and fuses.

Four 105-mm howitzers capable of firing at a rapid rate and with great accuracy to 12,000

555th FAB officers aboard the USS General Mann *en route to Pusan. LTC Daly stands third from the left. Perry Graves, the CO of B Battery, stands fifth from the left. LT Stoll and LT Mercer, both KIA on 8 August 1950, stand second and third from the right respectively. CAPT Vincent Marchesselli, Artillery Liaison Officer, stands sixth from right. (source: Dick Lewis)*

1st LT Clarence H. Jackson, Texas, returning to Kimpo Airfield after going on R&R in Japan with LT D. Randall Beirne. As a rifle platoon leader and XO in Easy Company, he was awarded the Silver Star. (source: D. Randall Beirne)

yards equipped each firing battery. A 105-mm howitzer fired high explosive, smoke, and white phosphorous ammunition armed with either delay, point detonating or variable timed fuses. A high-explosive antitank round existed for direct fire over open sights at enemy tanks, but quantities were few. Ammunition, maintenance, communication, motor transport and medical personnel pitched in to protect their battery from infantry and air attack with personal weapons and ring-mounted .50-caliber machine guns mounted on their trucks and weapons carriers.

A firing battery assigned one artillery liaison section and three FO teams to the infantry battalion it supported. Normally, A Battery provided FOs and a liaison section to 1st Battalion, B Battery to 2nd Battalion, and C Battery to 3rd Battalion. When the tactical situation demanded it, an FO Team could be attached to Tank Company or to the 72nd Engineers.

A peacetime FO Team consisted of one officer and an enlisted radio operator, but as casualties mounted in Korea, FO Teams often consisted of one man: either an officer or NCO who carried his own radio. Forward observers, encumbered as they were with an SCR-300 radio, map case, and binoculars, made conspicuous targets as they roamed the forward edges of the battlefield, adjusting artillery fires in support of the infantry. As a consequence, FO (mortar and artillery) casualties were heavy.

Service Battery kept the firing batteries supplied with ammunition, fuel, and rations. It was a vital job that had to be smartly performed or the firing batteries could not effectively support the infantry. Service Battery was destined to experience a savage awakening near a small village with a strange name on the combat team's twelfth day in Korea.

Although the 555th FAB was an integral element of the 5th RCT, in combat it took orders from the division artillery commander. This officer, usually a brigadier general, was responsible for the training, equipment, maintenance, resupply, and personnel of the division's organic field artillery battalions. One element of his staff manned the division's fire support coordination center (FSCC), an agency responsible for the planning, coordination, and execution of the divisional commander's fire support plan which included CAS, naval gunfire, and artillery fires.

The FSCC was capable of rapidly massing and shifting the weight of all organic and attached artillery fires. As a result, the 555th FAB was often tasked with firing missions in support of infantry units other than the 5th Infantry. On the other hand, the 5th Infantry often received fire support from field artillery battalions other than, and in addition to, the Triple Nickel.

The 555th FAB, often erroneously described as an African-American outfit, was nothing of the sort.[52] Perhaps seventy-five percent of the soldiers serving in the Triple Nickel were Caucasian, though in some of the batteries this percentage was considerably reduced.[53] The remaining soldiers were Hawaiian, Samoan, Filipino, Chinese, Portuguese, Korean and Japanese, with a handful of Mexican-American and American Indians included. No Black enlisted men served in the 5th RCT until later in the war.

Second Lieutenant Clarence H. Jackson, a platoon leader in E Company, was the combat team's sole Black soldier. While a student at The Infantry School's first racially integrated officer training course in 1949, the Army selected 2nd LT Jackson to become the first Black officer to command Caucasian troops.[54] He was highly respected by his men and fellow officers for his physical and moral courage. Thrust into an experimental role in a premier Army combat unit, LT Jackson was destined to survive the coming inferno with honor and dignity intact, thus proving once and for all that the color of a man's blood transcends such nonsense as racism in all human endeavors.

Colonel Godwin Ordway, Jr., "a noted disciplinarian and paper work demon," was the CO of the 5th RCT.[55] A West Pointer, Class of 1925, COL Ordway had initially served as a War Department public relations officer in World War II. When COL Ordway reported for duty in the 29th Infantry Division, he served as the division's Chief of Staff. All accounts state he was a hard-working, talented staff officer who cracked the whip to help prepare the division for its starring role in Normandy.

Six days after the 29th Infantry Division stormed ashore at Bloody Omaha Beach, the executive officer of 2nd Battalion, 116th Infantry encountered COL Ordway near the front lines. Years later, he wrote, "... the divisional chief of staff, a colonel, appeared striding down the road from the front.... The colonel, a big, square man, acknowledged my report and, looking us over thoughtfully, began a fatherly talk on the experience of combat. I recall him saying that entering a firefight eased nervousness — something like the first action of a football game. We listened respectfully, but we had been under fire for the past six days, and I doubt that he convinced anyone that this was a sporting event or obscured its terminal probabilities. His calm and obvious good intent were more impressive than his logic.... The colonel wished us luck, which we returned, and he continued down the white, dusty road. Inspired by his presence, if not by his exposition on combat, we gathered the map board and field telephone to move closer to the battle."[56]

Colonel Ordway's good spirits that day may have been bolstered by the knowledge that he was finally going to receive the field command he desired above all else. The 115th Infantry Regiment was stalled in the Normandy hedgegrows when COL Ordway assumed command. The divisional commander ordered the 115th Infantry's new commander to get the regiment moving — or else. As the ferocious battle raging for St. Lo unfolded, COL Ordway discovered that war had absolutely nothing in common with football or organized athletics. He could not get his regiment moving fast enough to please the divisional commander and, on some days, he could not get his soldiers to move at all. As his superiors grew more impatient and vocal with their displeasure, COL Ordway succumbed to his fears. On one occasion he refused a direct order from the Assistant Divisional Commander to leave the protection of a slit trench located near his command post (CP) which was not under fire at the time.[57] Evacuated for combat fatigue, COL Ordway recovered and later served in the G-3 Operations Section of General Omar Bradley's Twelfth Army Group. After the war, COL Ordway earned the respect and praise of Lieutenant General Ridgway, while working the Latin American desk at the Pentagon. When General Ridgway recommended that COL Ordway be promoted to brigadier general, General Dwight Eisenhower rejected the recommendation.[58]

Colonel Ordway assumed command of the 5th RCT in the spring of 1950. His assignment to Schofield Barracks was no accident. He had favorably impressed no less a personality than Lieutenant General Ridgway. That COL Ordway was a personal friend of the Chief of Staff of the U.S. Army, General J. Lawton Collins, probably did not hurt either.[59] Colonel Ordway was thus given a rare second chance to succeed in a prestigious assignment as commanding officer of one of the Army's premiere combat units. As a peace time commander there was no cause for concern. When war erupted in Korea, however, COL Ordway was thrust into a role he was ill-suited by personality and temperament to fulfill.

Colonel Ordway's four battalion commanders as a group lacked extensive command and combat experience, too. The Army had instituted a policy before the Korean War that provided a large number of officers who had reached their present grade as staff officers in World War II an opportunity to command infantry battalions and regiments. Many of these officers had commanded nothing larger than platoons in their careers, and that experience had not been in combat. The Army wanted to give these men the command opportunities they needed to compete for promotion with their peers, many of whom had led battalions and regiments in action against the Germans and Japanese. Some of the newly assigned battalion and regimental commanders rose to the occasion under fire. Others, regrettably, did not measure up, and their soldiers suffered on the harsh altars of fairness and equality the Army had instituted before the war. The 5th RCT was no exception to this rule.

Lieutenant Colonel John P. Jones, Jr. assumed command of 1st Battalion shortly before the combat team was alerted for movement. Prior to this assignment, he had commanded a provisional battalion of sorts that included the combat team's 4.2-inch Mortar, Tank- and Service-related companies.[60] He had little opportunity to establish a mark as the commander of a maneuver battalion before his unit went to war.

Lieutenant Colonel John L. Throckmorton, the CO of 2nd Battalion, Sonny's outfit, was affectionately known as "the Rock." The Rock entered the Infantry Branch after graduating high in his West Point class of 1935. Two years later, the crack shot with the service rifle and pistol led the Army Rifle Team to victory in the 1937 National Matches held at Camp Perry, Ohio. He was awarded the Distinguished Marksman Medal and savored the Army's first triumph over the Marines after a thirty-year hiatus.[61] During this period, he married Regina "Gina" Higgens of Long Island, New York.

Lieutenant Colonel Throckmorton had earned a superb reputation as the Assistant G-3 for Operations for the First Army in the European Theater during World War II where he reached the temporary rank of colonel. Much to his chagrin, the Rock did not receive an opportunity to command troops in combat.[62]

After the war, he served in a prestigious position as the Regimental Tactical Officer at West Point where he reverted to his permanent grade of lieutenant colonel.[63] Very much aware that he had not earned the Combat Infantryman's Badge worn by so many of his friends and peers, the Rock knew that certain paths would remain blocked until he had successfully completed a command tour. When the opportunity arose in 1949 to command a battalion in Hawaii, he eagerly accepted.

Lieutenant Colonel Throckmorton took Gina and their sons to Schofield Barracks where he assumed command of the 2nd Battalion in late 1949. A competent tactician, he was always well organized and extremely calm under intense pressure. He quickly earned the trust and respect of his officers and men, who admired his quiet dignity, penetrating mind, and direct approach to tackling difficult problems. If he gave the appearance of favoring the West Pointers over the other officers serving in the 2nd Battalion, this was understandable, for as a general rule graduates of the Long Gray Line were better educated and trained than their peers. He did not suffer fools gladly, rarely joked or smiled, and cracked the whip on subordinate officers regardless of commissioning source when required. Colonel Simpson, and later COL Ordway, relied heavily on LTC Throckmorton's ability to get the tough jobs done right the first time in peacetime. Combat would prove no exception.

The CO of the 3rd Battalion, LTC Benjamin W. Heckemeyer, was a close friend and West Point classmate of LTC Throckmorton's. A brilliant man, LTC Heckemeyer had earned a masters degree at Harvard before World War II. He reached the temporary grade of colonel while serving as an intelligence officer in Europe during the war. New to troop command, LTC Heckemeyer was often found leading from the rear in the relative comfort and safety of his command post. He was known to sit back and watch the other infantry battalion commanders volunteer for the tough jobs in the peace time Army. Combat in his case, too, would prove no exception.

His officers and men admired LTC John H. Daly, the CO of the 555th FAB. The Texan had served with the horse artillery in a cavalry division following his graduation from West Point in 1936. During World War II, he served in the 42nd Infantry Division Artillery from 1943 through 1944. He spent the rest of the war as the S-2 intelligence officer for X Corps artillery. Following a tour as the Regular Army Instructor assigned to the Hawaiian National Guard's 487th FAB, he assumed command of the Triple Nickel in August 1949.[64] "He was a Prince"[65] and a "crackerjack artillery officer."[66]

Corporal Samuel L. Lewis, a soldier serving in the FDC, Headquarters Battery, said, "When COL Daly gave an order he knew it was going to be obeyed. He had no trouble delegating responsibility and trusted the men. Colonel Daly was a pleasure to work for. He tolerated no slackness and looked every inch the part of a battalion commander."[67]

With a prevailing overconfidence that bordered on arrogance, the 5th RCT was sailing to war. Mars was ascendant as the troop transports entered the war zone. Those who believed they would quickly destroy the impudent NKPA and return to Hawaii as conquering heroes would receive a brutal awakening. Nearly one-third of the combat team's soldiers would be killed, wounded, missing, or non-battle casualties within the next six weeks. One man's Police Action, another man's war. And this war would last three years.

LTC Heckemeyer is welcomed to Schofield Barracks by General Ferenbaugh in 1949.
(source: Ray Warner)

CHAPTER SIX

THE PUSAN PERIMETER

Comrades, the enemy is demoralized. The task given to us is the liberation of Masan and Chinju and the annihilation of the remnants of the enemy. We have liberated Mokpu, Kwangju and Yosu and have thereby accelerated the liberation of all Korea. However, the liberation of Chinju and Masan means the final battle to cut off the windpipe of the enemy. Comrades, this glorious task has fallen to our division! Men of the 6th Division, let us annihilate the enemy and distinguish ourselves!
Major General Pang Ho-san, CG NKPA 6th Division,
United States Marine Operations in Korea 1950-53. Vol. 1.

Late on the night of 31 July, the transports carrying the embarked 5th RCT entered Pusan's harbor. A nauseating aroma of human waste and mounds of garbage assaulted the senses of the soldiers as they debarked early the next morning under a sweltering sun. Asia's Perfume: honey buckets, kimchee, and fish sauce. After the soldiers had mustered on the piers, they route-stepped in a column-of-twos toward distant bivouacs. Thousands of destitute refugees observed their arrival.

Pusan was the Eighth Army's jugular. All supplies and reinforcements had to be unloaded at the modest port. Moreover, if the decision was made to evacuate Korea, Pusan was the only way out. In short, the Eighth Army's survival was dependent on holding the Pusan Perimeter.

On 1 August 1950, the Pusan Perimeter began at Chindong-ni, on the south coast of Korea, and ran due north to Naktong-ni. From here it curved eastward to P'o-hang on the Sea of Japan. By this date, the ROK Army had suffered an appalling 70,000 casualties, and the three U.S. Army infantry divisions rushed to Korea from mundane occupation duties in Japan had incurred a shocking 1,884 dead, 2,695 wounded, 523 missing and 901 captured in just four weeks of combat.[1] As the battered remnants of the Eighth Army dug in on the Pusan Perimeter, General Walker and his staff were heartened by the arrival of the fresh 5th RCT, the first ground combat reinforcement to reach Korea from an area outside of Japan.

Additional U.S. Army reinforcements, to include the 2nd Infantry Division, would soon arrive from the States to confront the advancing NKPA. The powerful 1st Provisional Marine Brigade was scheduled to arrive within a few days, too. Yet, even with these reinforcements, the Eighth Army's situation remained precarious. The scent of fear and defeat lingered in the air.

In the face of mounting casualties and ferocious air attacks, elements of ten NKPA divisions were advancing on all fronts and victory appeared to be within North Korea's grasp. Caught off guard by the unanticipated entrance of American combat units, however, the NKPA High Command realized it had to rapidly seize Pusan to win the war.

At this critical moment, the NKPA High Command directed its 4th and 6th Divisions, reputedly its two best formations, to commence a time-consuming envelopment of the Eighth Army's western flank. Of the two NKPA divisions, the 6th Division received the toughest mission, a wide and deep envelopment through Chinju and Masan to seize Pusan.

The NKPA High Command exploited an opportunity when it committed its 6th Division into the undefended southwestern sector. In the words of the Army official history, the NKPA 6th Division's "maneuver was one of the most successful of either Army in the Korean War. It compelled the redisposition of Eighth Army at the end of July and caused Tokyo and Washington to alter their plans for the conduct of the war."[2] Overcast skies concealed the NKPA 6th Division's advance until 23 July, when aerial reconnaissance informed General Walker that he had a major crisis on his hands.[3] During the desperate days ahead, General Walker used his advantage of interior lines to shift his slender reserves to check the enemy's advance.

It is necessary at this juncture to introduce the NKPA 6th Division, the combat team's principal opponent in the early days of the war. The large Korean contingent serving in the CCF 166th Division, 56th Army, had fought for the Communists during the Chinese Civil War. After Mao's victory, he transferred this division en masse to North Korea where it formed the cadre for the newly raised NKPA 6th Division. Although the NKPA 6th Division had captured the industrial section of Seoul in the first days of the war and, subsequently, stormed Kumchon following a forced crossing of the Kum River while under heavy

A troopship with embarked elements of the 5th RCT enters Pusan. One-third of the combat team's soldiers would be casualties in the next six weeks. (source: NA)

fire, it had not, in contrast to other NKPA formations, participated in much hard fighting. The division had incurred approximately 400 casualties in these actions, rather trivial losses by NKPA standards. Commanded by Major General Pang Ho-san, the 6th Division spearheaded the main effort in a determined bid to capture Pusan by 15 August, the fifth anniversary of the liberation of Korea from the Japanese.[4]

Reinforced with the NKPA 83rd Mechanized Regiment, the 6th Division was pounding down the road toward Masan after wresting control of Hadong from the remnants of the 24th Infantry Division. When the 5th RCT commenced unloading operations, the situation on the dusty coastal road had turned critical.[5]

The NKPA 6th Division was organized and equipped along Red Army lines with the soldiers

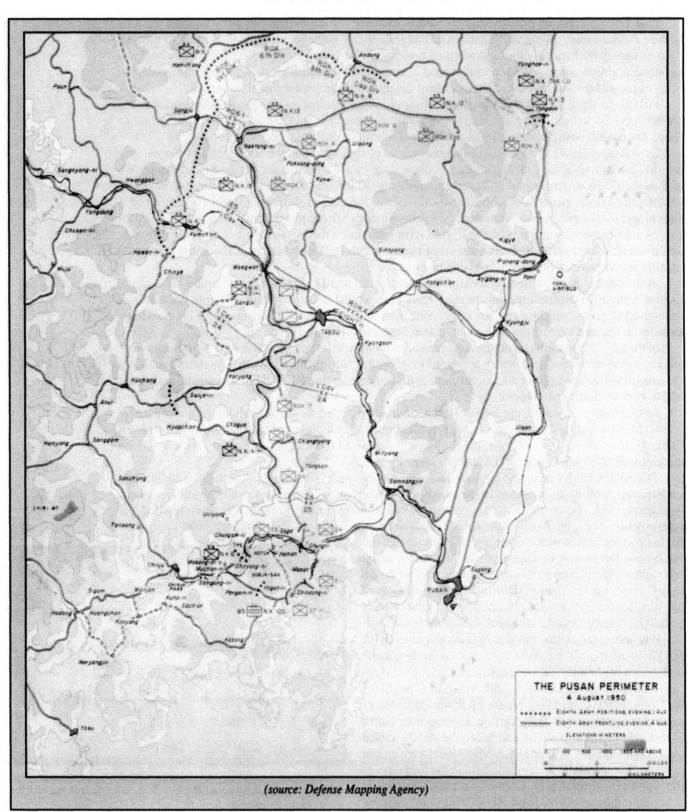

(source: Defense Mapping Agency)

enjoying a quantity and quality of Soviet manufactured weapons and equipment unavailable when they were in the service of Mao Tse Tung. The divisional structure included a headquarters, three infantry regiments, an artillery regiment, a signals battalion, an antitank battalion, a reconnaissance company, a training battalion, and medical, supply, transport, and veterinary units.[6]

An NKPA infantry regiment had a strength of 2,500 men, organized into three battalions and supporting artillery in the form of 76-mm field guns or 120-mm mortars. Infantry battalions had a strength of 650 men, and consisted of three rifle companies, a heavy machine gun company, an 82-mm mortar company, an antitank platoon equipped with 45-mm high velocity antitank guns, and an antitank rifle platoon equipped with 14.5-mm antitank rifles.

Soviet weapons were simple to maintain and operate. The 82-mm mortar, for example, had the advantage of being able to fire American 81-mm ammunition. The reverse was not true. At ranges under 1000 yards, the dual-purpose 45-mm antitank gun was a dangerous opponent for the M-4 A3E8 tank. The 14.5-mm antitank rifle, though ineffective against American tanks, proved itself as a long range sniper rifle. American troops dubbed the long-barreled weapon the "elephant gun."

An NKPA rifle company consisted of approximately 150 men organized around a headquarters, three rifle platoons, and a heavy machine gun section. Rifle platoons were subdivided into three squads and armed with weapons of Soviet manufacture to include the PPSH-41 submachine gun, otherwise known as the "burp gun", the M1891/30 bolt action rifle, and the light 7.62-mm DP machine gun. Old models of Imperial Japanese Army weapons partially equipped some NKPA units. Captured stocks of American weapons and ammunition were now being used against their former owners. Liberally supplied quantities of hand grenades remained the classic Communist close combat weapon throughout the war.

An NKPA artillery regiment possessed two 76-mm field gun battalions, and a 122-mm howitzer battalion. Artillery battalions were further subdivided into a headquarters battery, and three firing batteries with four guns each. One self-propelled gun battalion, equipped with sixteen SU-76s, rounded out the artillery firepower. This tracked armored vehicle mounted a 76-mm field gun behind thin gun shields on an open-topped compartment.

General Pang had at least twenty-five T-34 tanks temporarily attached to his command.[7] This formidable armored fighting vehicle, which mounted two machine guns and an 85-mm cannon, was difficult to knock out, due to the thickness and slope of its armor plate.

The NKPA fielded a superbly trained soldier, physically and mentally toughened by years of arduous training and combat against the Japanese and Chinese Nationalists. Courageous in battle to the point of fanaticism, he believed in the righteousness of his cause, the unification of Korea under the Red Star. He esteemed subterfuge and routinely dressed in civilian clothing to penetrate American lines. Often, he deliberately herded masses of civilians in front of his advance to serve as human shields. Terror was a weapon; mercy was an alien concept. The murder of noncombatants and prisoners of war was common.

Political officers served as deputy commanders down to the company level and enjoyed the power of life and death over officers and men. Discipline was swift and brutal. Summary executions cured disciplinary infractions.

Strangely enough, the typical NKPA soldier's iron combat discipline often broke down when confronted by American interrogators. For instance, when the 1st Cavalry Division captured the operations officer of the NKPA 19th Infantry Regiment on 2 September, he voluntarily disclosed that his outfit planned to mount an attack at dusk. When the assault went in on schedule, the alerted Americans successfully repulsed it.[8]

In summary the NKPA soldier was a well-trained, adequately equipped, and competently led opponent who viewed his American counterpart as a physically soft, pampered, road-bound mercenary, who panicked if flanked or enveloped and was unwilling to engage in close range combat. On the other hand, the NKPA soldier respected American artillery fire and dreaded air strikes, particularly napalm.

CHAPTER SEVEN

Fox Hill

"Oh Sulley, they got you...Sulley, what a damn shame," he murmured. Then the boy slipped a few inches down in the grass, turned his head to one side. We looked away as he died there, wondering why the over-worked medics and their life-saving plasma couldn't have been a few hundred yards closer to our little hill.
Charles and Eugene Jones, The Face of War.

The arrival of the 5th RCT and the 1st Provisional Marine Brigade provided General Walker a powerful reserve. He assigned Major General William B. Kean, the Commanding General of the 25th Infantry Division, the mission of organizing a task force built around both units, and elements of his division, to mount an offensive designed to disrupt the NKPA's advance on Pusan.[1]

There was a clash of personalities, and it had nothing to do with the arrival of the Marines. As the former Chief of Staff of the First Army in Normandy, to which the 29th Infantry Division had belonged, General Kean knew the details surrounding COL Ordway's relief as CO of the 115th Infantry. General Kean probably worried that Korea was neither the time nor place for a replay, and he was perfectly prepared to relieve COL Ordway of his command at the first sign of trouble. For his part, COL Ordway had no illusions. His personal reputation and military career were on the line.[2]

Colonel Ordway's personal problems aside, many Oriental soldiers serving in the 5th RCT faced the rude possibility of mistaken identity and becoming friendly fire casualties. One soldier of Korean descent, SFC Chong C. Kim, of Lanai City, Lanai, quipped, "I'd hate to have two armies shooting at me at once."[3] The combat team's novel solution paired off its Oriental soldiers with Caucasians. No group of non-Caucasians would go on patrol unless a Caucasian soldier accompanied them.

Meanwhile, the ownership of vehicles and equipment was up for grabs down at the pier. In the midst of this scene of confusion, a cable on a ship's hoist snapped while lowering one of Tank Company's Easy Eights. The battered pier fared better than the demolished Sherman.[4]

Not everyone found his vehicle. After Private Gene McClure failed to find his How Company jeep, he was ordered to report to the 75-mm Recoilless Rifle Platoon as an ammunition bearer.[5] A newly promoted PFC Arlen Russell, Headquarters Battery, 555th FAB, looked in frustration up and down the docks for his Wire Section's weapons carrier. "Everybody in my outfit was gone, and I still hadn't found my truck," explained PFC Russell. "A sergeant from Service Battery told me he needed a driver for a GMC 6x6 truck which was loaded with artillery ammunition. For the next three days I drove between the dock and Service Battery hauling ammunition." On PFC Russell's third day in Korea, his Headquarters Battery commander found the hapless lad unloading a truck at Service Battery. The devastated fifteen-year old soldier was busted to private and returned to the Wire Section where he belonged.[6]

The soldiers had little time to ponder their situation. Sergeant Horace Anderson, a 57-mm recoilless rifle squad leader in E Company, said, "After getting off the ship in Pusan, we were assembled in a bean field where we were told to leave our personal bags. We were instructed to make a light pack with a change of socks, underwear and an extra pair of pants and shirt. Our bags were to catch up with us later and, of course, that's the last we ever saw of them."[7]

As Private First Class William J. Straney, F Company, prepared his field equipment in the bivouac, he noticed, "All of a sudden, starting at one end, the entire battalion started falling to the ground as if they were domi-

SFC Robert Muramoto, Honolulu; SFC Castro Corpuz, Waipahu, Oahu; and SFC David Kauanui, Honolulu, enjoy a rare moment of relaxation. Note the canned Poi, dried squid, and ukulele, M-1 rifle and Thompson SMG. (source: Chang)

noes stacked on end and then knocked over. I grabbed my rifle and hit the ground. The only thing I saw to get behind was my pack. One platoon thought we were being attacked by guerrillas and moved off to the flank. It seems one soldier had dropped a hand grenade, starting the mass falling. Embarrassed, I looked around to see if anyone had seen me fall behind my combat pack. My embarrassment was nothing compared to one of our Major's. He had dived into a slit trench and from then on he was known as the s...y Major."[8]

There was precious little time left for jokes or embarrassment. On 2 August, the 2nd Battalion departed Pusan and traveled first by train, and later by trucks, to oppose the NKPA 6th Division's relentless advance on Chindong-ni.

First Lieutenant Frank Brooks remained behind in Pusan for a couple of hours to gather Fox Company's ammunition, rations and equipment. He had just received an order to replace all of Fox Company's 2.36-inch bazookas with the new 3.5-inch ones, a marvelous weapon

Marine M-26 tank crews load ammunition at Pusan prior to commencing offensive operations. (source: NA)

that out performed its predecessor in range, accuracy and hitting power. Lieutenant Brooks was not happy to receive this order because no 3.5-inch rockets were provided for the new bazookas. While 2.36-inch rockets lay stacked in crates near the port, rockets for the 3.5-inch bazookas were in critically short supply. Fox Company's bazooka teams were going into action for the first time with a new weapon, and one for which they had no ammunition. One of LT Brook's men was subsequently KIA near Chindong-ni with a 3.5-inch bazooka cradled in his arms, without ever having received a round of ammunition for the weapon.[9]

Chindong-ni was a coastal village situated on an important road junction eight miles west of Masan. Here the unpaved, tree-lined coastal road intersects with the road to Haman, a north-south road that hugs the eastern slopes of the Sobuk-san mountain chain. By 2 August 1950, the advance guard of General Pang's NKPA 6th Division was beginning to climb the Sobuk-san mountains. Rice paddies covered the low land, and corn grew part way up Hills 342 and 255, two key terrain features. Beyond the final row of corn, little grew in the way of shrubs or trees.

Whoever occupied Hills 342 and 255 controlled Chindong-ni and the assembly area Task Force Kean intended to use for its forthcoming offensive. After the 2nd Battalion reached Chindong-ni late on 2 August, Lieutenant Colonel John Throckmorton ordered George and Easy Companies to dig in on an arc facing generally north and northwest around the dusty little village. Fox Company was in reserve.[10]

On the morning of 3 August, a sizeable NKPA force repulsed George Company when it attempted to seize the crest of Hill 342.[11] Fox Company witnessed the combat team's first firefight in Korea from positions near the coastal road. According to PFC Straney, "The weather was well over a 100 degrees so I believe that was a factor in their failure as well as the enemy. Although some distance away, we had a good view, and being green troops it hardly seemed real."[12]

The repulse did not herald an auspicious beginning for the combat team. An incensed LTC John Throckmorton ordered CAPT Stanley Howarth, the CO of Fox Company, to take the hill. An assault up the steep hill in broad daylight under a merciless sun would probably have failed with a heavy losses, so LTC Throckmorton sensibly directed CAPT Howarth to mount a night attack.

Meanwhile, the NKPA 6th Division's advance was checked further west and northwest of Chindong-ni in a bloody engagement won by the 27th Infantry "Wolfhounds," commanded by LTC John H. Michaelis. Lieutenant Colonel Throckmorton's mission to secure the hills in an arc to the north of Chindong-ni remained unchanged after the 2nd Battalion, 5th Infantry was attached to the 27th Infantry at 1600 that day. The Rock's battalion faced an enraged opponent who up to this time had largely had his own way in this bitter war.

That day, 1st LT James Johnson returned to his combat engineer platoon after a scouting trip to locate some construction materials when he discovered that somebody had "scarfed up one of my squads and was going to have them run ammunition to the 27th Wolfhounds Regiment."[13] After a brief argument with the regimental S-3, MAJ Elmer G. Owens, who did not want LT Johnson to go with the convoy, he finally received permission from COL Ordway to accompany his squad. On the way to the "Wolfhounds," the convoy was hit by NKPA small arms fire from the hillsides as the drivers negotiated the narrow mountain road. After delivering the ammunition, one of the trucks failed to negotiate a turn on the return trip while under heavy fire and ran off the road. At least four

General Kean (standing) confers with LTG Walker. (source: NA)

CPL Imo Alo, Laie, Oahu, receives a haircut from SGT William Tamanaha, Lanikai, Oahu, while SGT Rosalino Gallios from Waialua, Oahu, looks on. (sources: 25th ID Museum/Chang)

A 5th RCT machine gun team covers medics carrying a wounded soldier in the vicinity of Fox Hill. (sources: NA/Chang)

men from the 72nd Engineers were killed: PFC Robert W. Labar, Jack Rosselli, Harold D. Woodbury, and CPL Rosalio J. Torres. Nine more men were injured.[14] Lieutenant Johnson secured the crash site and extracted the killed and wounded.

"I lost some top-notch people," LT Johnson explained. "The squad leader was a fellow by the name of CPL Torres. He was outstanding. Before he died, he turned to one of the men and said, 'Take care of LT Johnson.' You know, to this day it still clutches me up. When we got back … I went to see COL Ordway, and I told him… 'When the regiment moves take the high ground. Don't go down those valleys because that's where these ambushes were.'"[15]

Night attacks are difficult to control and require well-trained troops. Sonny and his comrades in Fox Company were up to the job and commenced what may have been the Army's first night attack of the Korean War. Two rifle platoons, supported by the company's heavy weapons, participated in the assault on Hill 342 while a third rifle platoon remained in reserve. The physically fit soldiers sweated profusely under the exertion of the climb, but the relative coolness of the evening air spared the men from the worst of the day's oppressive heat. When the company neared the crest, the muzzles of numerous NKPA rifles and machine guns erupted in flame. Tracers lashed the assault platoons, and mortar rounds exploded in their ranks. Men fell screaming in agony on the desolate ground, their tortured flesh pierced by burning tracers and white-hot shell fragments.

Fox Company returned a hot and heavy fire, the tracers from their machine guns and BARs converging on the muzzle flashes of enemy gun emplacements. Platoon and squad leaders shouted orders and exhorted their soldiers to rush forward across the fire-swept ground. Forward Observers requested 81-mm and 4.2-inch mortar fires to support the advance, and the mortars were soon pounding away at targets on and beyond the crest. The crump of grenade explosions heralded Fox Company's final assault and, within a few bloody minutes, the soldiers reached the summit in time to witness a rare event at that stage of the war — North Korean soldiers running away in panic from the scene. After the victorious soldiers finished shooting their opponents down under the light of parachute flares, they christened their objective Fox Hill.[16]

The true cost in blood spilled that night may never be told in full. We know that Private Freedman Wadsworth was shot in half by machine gun fire while advancing next to Private David Eckert during the assault.[17] Private Wadsworth and Miss Norma Casaba had been planning their wedding on Oahu just a few short weeks before. The war interrupted their plans in this world forever.

Private First Class David C. Joseph, from Oahu, had left his wife Barbara Joseph in Honolulu when he went to war with Fox Company. He was KIA during the assault and is buried today at Puuowaina. Barbara Joseph received her husband's Silver Star at a solemn ceremony held at Schofield Barracks on 3 April 1951. Her photograph appeared in a Honolulu newspaper on the day she received her husband's award for valor. The caption states that PFC Joseph remained in an exposed position under concentrated enemy fire as he fought a personal duel with an enemy automatic weapon. Tracers sought out and killed the valiant soldier as his comrades enveloped and destroyed the NKPA machine gun crew. Mrs. Joseph was the combat team's first widow. She would not be the last.[18]

While the Rock's soldiers settled down for a protracted defense in the hills north of Chindong-ni, the NKPA remained a deadly opponent and American casualties mounted at a steady rate, draining the life blood from the 2nd Battalion. Corporal John W. Fain, Jr., a World War II veteran, was the first soldier in E Company to die in Korea.[19]

From the moment Fox Company seized the crest of Hill 342, the NKPA had subjected the soldiers to near continuous small arms and automatic weapons fire, with an occasional mortar barrage thrown in. Men started to go down, killed and wounded, a few every day, as NKPA marksmen scored hits from firing positions located across a wide saddle on even higher ground to the north of Fox Hill. The soldiers persevered and held their ground in the face of searing 110-degree temperatures and intense enemy fire. Swarms of flies and mosquitoes, combined with a shortage of water, added to everyone's misery.

Mortar fire knocked out Fox Company's land lines on the outfit's first morning on the hill. Attempts to splice the lines failed with casualties under heavy fire. Fox Company had to rely on one SCR-300 radio and a handful of exceptionally fit runners to maintain communications with the 2nd Battalion.

On 5 August, as Fox Company struggled to maintain its tenuous hold on Hill 342, General Walker outlined his plan for Task Force Kean at the CP of General Kean's 25th Infantry Division. In forceful terms he declared that the Eighth Army had been pushed around for too long. Now, with NKPA supply lines stretched to the limits, Task Force Kean was going to strike back hard. In the parlance of the *Official Marine Corps History of the Korean War*: "To the 25th Division, 1st Provisional Marine Brigade, and 5th RCT would go the honor of launching the counterattack from Chindong-ni."[20]

Activated on 6 August, Task Force Kean's mission was to mount a counteroffensive at 0630 the next day to seize and hold Line Z at Chinju.[21] The plan called for the 5th RCT to seize a road junction a few miles to the west of Chindong-ni located next to the village of Tosan. Once this road junction was secured, the 5th RCT would continue the attack to the northwest, destroying enemy forces in zone, and link up with the 35th Infantry at Much'on-ni, which was attacking due west from an assembly area near Haman. After the 5th RCT had cleared the Tosan road junction, the 5th Marines would pass through the combat team's lines and commence a southerly sweep, destroying NKPA forces in zone. The intent was for the 5th RCT, the 35th Infantry, and the 5th Marines to link up at a mountain pass near Chinju. General Kean envisioned a pincher movement designed to surround and destroy the NKPA 6th Division. He demanded speed and aggressiveness from his subordinate commanders to make the plan work.

General Walker required the services of the 27th Infantry "Wolfhounds" to reconstitute his reserve now that the Eighth Army had committed the 5th RCT and 1st Provisional Marine Brigade to combat. On 6 August, General Kean ordered the 5th RCT to conduct a relief in place with the 27th Infantry on the Main Line of Resistance (MLR).[22]

Colonel Ordway had little time to move his units into position, brief his commanders, and prepare for the assault the next morning. He assigned his 1st Battalion the mission of securing the road junction and continuing the attack to the north to seize a ridgeline that dominated the road to Much'on-ni. His 2nd Battalion was ordered to support the 1st Battalion's attack, while the 3rd Battalion remained in reserve. Colonel Ordway does not appear to have taken into consideration that the 2nd Battalion was under heavy pressure from the north when he issued his orders.

Trucks carrying the main body of the 5th RCT closed on Chindong-ni at 2230, on 6 August, where the soldiers dismounted in the darkness and began the relief in place with the "Wolfhounds." Until the relief was complete, the CO of the 27th Infantry retained immediate tactical control over all Army and Marine units converging on Chindong-ni.

The first Marine unit to reach Chindong-ni was LTCOL Robert D. Taplett's 3rd Battalion, 5th Marines.[23] While the Marine infantry companies were digging in, LTCOL Ransom M. Wood's 1st Battalion, 11th Marines (artillery), arrived on the scene and established firing positions in the vicinity of Chindong-ni after relieving an Army FAB that was pulling out to support the "Wolfhounds" in Eighth Army reserve. As the Marines were positioning their 105-mm howitzers, an NKPA high velocity, flat trajectory, high explosive shell hit one of the guns, killing the entire crew.[24]

Shortly after midnight, LTC John Michaelis, CO of the 27th Infantry, directed LTCOL Robert Taplett to relieve Fox Company from its defensive responsibilities on Hill 342. This task had to be accomplished so the 2nd Battalion, 5th RCT could concentrate its three rifle companies prior to crossing the LD the next morning to participate in the assault. Probably due to his own shortages, LTCOL Taplett protested his orders until LTC Michaelis informed him that the soldiers fighting on Yaban-san were being chewed to pieces, and that General Kean wanted Hill 342 held at all costs. Taplett acknowledged the order and did his best to execute it. If the crest of Yaban-san fell to the NKPA, the enemy would be able to rake the LD with automatic weapons fire and bring observed indirect mortar and artillery fire crashing down on the ranks of the assault units. Task Force Kean's success initially hinged on the dogged defense of Hill 342.

Lieutenant Colonel Taplett assigned 2nd LT John H. Cahill's 1st Platoon, Company G, 3rd Battalion, 5th Marines, the mission of relieving the soldiers on Fox Hill. The Marine battalion commander had just two rifle companies, for a total of six rifle platoons, and expected to go into action the next morning when his battalion crossed the LD. This may explain why a larger force was not dispatched to Fox Hill. Reinforced with a machine gun squad equipped with two machine guns, LT Cahill's platoon had as many BARs, and almost as many machine guns, as Fox Company.

The Marines departed their assembly area in the darkness and arrived at the CP of the 27th Infantry. A "Wolfhound" guide led the Marine platoon to the CP of the 2nd Battalion, 5th Infantry where LT Cahill received a short tactical briefing and yet another guide to lead his platoon to Fox Company's perimeter. Along the way, the column

A group of Easy Company soldiers pose at Schofield Barracks. L to R: Ed Murphy, Charles Santi (WIA 16 September 1950), Frank Valvo (WIA 16 September 1950), Bob Noneman (KIA 22 March 1951), and Manual Munaz (WIA 16 September 1950) (source: Frank Valvo)

advanced under sporadic artillery fire until approximately 0500, when two Marines were wounded by small arms fire.[25] The sweat-soaked Marines had marched three miles from their assembly area.

At first light, the Marine platoon began to climb Hill 342 under a brutal sun. As canteens emptied, Marines started to go down from heat exhaustion. Near the crest, LT Cahill ordered his men to take cover, as bullets kicked up dust around their feet, and await his return. He walked the remaining seventy-five yards to the crest. Here 1st LT Frank Brooks, the new CO of Fox Company, greeted him.

Fox Company was in bad shape. "We were so low on ammunition," said PFC William Straney, "that the men were throwing clips of M-1 ammunition from hole to hole. And some were completely out."[26] The soldiers had repulsed a series of sharp enemy attacks throughout the night. Hand-to-hand fighting had raged at first light. Captain Howarth and 1st LT Kenneth S. Hino were both wounded by mortar fire. Private David Eckert had dropped his empty M-1 rifle and grabbed LT Hino's carbine from the dirt at his feet, flipping the selector switch to automatic, to fire at the enemy soldiers running up the hill. The NKPA retreated after considerable losses to higher ground north of Fox Hill.[27]

Captain Howarth knew the details of the forthcoming relief, but LT Brooks was on the reverse slope with his mortars when the wounded company commander was carried down the hill. When LT Brooks reached the CP, he heard that the company was supposed to be relieved by another unit so it could participate in an offensive. He knew neither the time nor the place of the offensive, and the source and size of the relieving force remained a mystery until the Marine platoon closed on the company's perimeter.

Radio communications with the company's old SCR-300 radio had proven difficult in the mountainous terrain and in the extreme heat of the day. Now it was impossible, because the radio had been destroyed. Private First Class William Straney had been using the radio's long whip antenna when MSGT Gant pulled it down saying it was drawing too much fire. Communications with the shorter tape antenna proved possible after PFC Straney changed his position to a small knoll farther down the slope where he finally regained radio contact with the battalion. Second Lieutenant Roy T. Nakashima, an FO from B Battery, 555th FAB, used PFC Straney's radio to commence calls for fire on NKPA positions. Everything was fine until an artillery observation aircraft flew low overhead and dropped a crate of urgently needed M-1 rifle ammunition on top of the radio.[28] It happened so fast that neither PFC Straney nor LT Nakashima knew which way to turn as the heavy crate fell towards them from the pale blue sky.

With his radio reduced to a pile of rubble, LT Brooks was forced to rely on a small group of incredibly brave runners to maintain a tenuous communications link with his battalion. The NKPA shot and killed two of these runners, including CPL Jack R. Starkey, who died guiding the Marines up Fox Hill.[29]

Lieutenant Brooks was a brave man in a bad spot, and that morning, before the arrival of the Marines, he made one of the toughest decisions of his career. He dispatched a rifle platoon and the 60-mm Mortar Section from his hard-pressed perimeter to the 2nd Battalion's CP to participate in the forthcoming offensive. Until Fox Company's relief arrived, he intended to remain on the hill with the rest of his men. Thus, LT Brooks was startled to discover that the Marines intended to relieve his company with one rifle platoon.[30]

There was no time for second thoughts or to change the fact that one of his rifle platoons and most of his heavy weapons were already down at the base of the hill. Lieutenant Brooks concluded that LT Cahill's platoon alone could not hold the hill and resolved to stay. As he briefed LT Cahill on the situation, the Marine platoon came under NKPA automatic weapons fire that killed and wounded several men. The Marines returned fire, advancing by ragged leaps and bounds, until they reached a covered position on the reverse slope. Just thirty-seven of the original fifty-two Marines were still in action.

As the Marines consolidated, the NKPA raked Fox Company's perimeter with another hail of automatic weapons fire. A handful of soldiers

A platoon of Easy Eights on the march in the Pusan Perimeter. (source: Keith Whitham)

panicked, but LT Brooks and his NCOs restored order. Lieutenant Brooks sent the Marine platoon three guides who led the unit into three different locations. Two more Marines were KIA while moving into their positions. Although mixing the Marines between the soldiers reduced the tactical efficiency of the Marine platoon, it proved to be a sound psychological move. Neither soldier nor Marine wanted to appear less brave than the other on the firing line. Lieutenant Cahill's nine BARs and two machine guns more than doubled F Company's firepower and provided a moral boost to the weary soldiers.

Lieutenant Cahill kept LTCOL Taplett informed of his tactical situation over his SCR-300 radio. His request for an emergency resupply of ammunition and water was relayed to the Brigade Air Section. An Air Force R4D transport made the first resupply drop, but most of its precious cargo fell into NKPA hands. The next airdrop was attempted by VMO-2, a Marine observation squadron equipped with OY-2 aircraft. After loading as many five-gallon water cans as their plane could carry, the crew braved intense enemy small arms fire before releasing their cargo within the perimeter. Most of the water cans unfortunately burst on impact. A few drops were recovered, enough for everyone to fill half a canteen. An airdrop of Red Cross parcels was less welcome. Salted peanuts, chewing gum, and Red Cross stationery were not in demand. Seconds later, a mortar round scattered the peanuts, gum, and shredded stationery across the hill.[31]

By noon, Fox Company had suffered several more casualties, while a sniper had shot and killed a Marine. When LT Brooks appraised LTC John Throckmorton of the worsening tactical situation, presumably over LT Cahill's radio, the Rock directed him to remain in place.

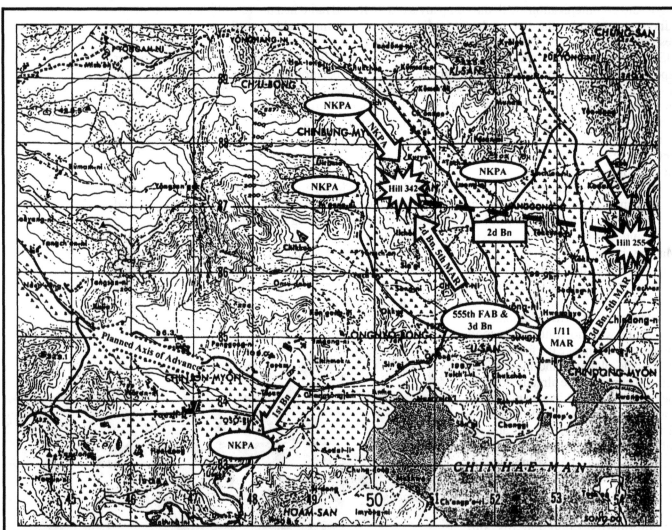

TASK FORCE KEAN, 7 AUGUST 1950. This map, and those that follow, are copies of maps used in the Korean War. The top of each map is North. The distance between the vertical and horizontal gridlines is 1,000 meters (1 km). Contour interval is 20 meters. The unit positions depicted on this map, and those that follow, are approximate. During the early days of the war, many men carried inaccurate maps made by Imperial Japanese Army surveyors. This map, made by US surveyors, was not available at this stage of the war. On 7 August 1950, the 2nd Battalion is occupying defensive positions from Hill 342 to Hill 255 (dotted line). While the NKPA assaults Fox Company and a platoon of Marines on Hill 342, another NKPA assault overruns Hill 255. Meanwhile, the 5th RCT has crossed the LD in the first phase of the Task Force Kean offensive. The 1st Battalion turns south instead of north at the Tosan road junction, and the assault bogs down. General Kean assigns General Craig command of all Army and Marine units on the scene. General Craig commits two of his Marine battalions to clear up the situation on Hills 342 and 255. (source for maps: NA)

The Rock had other problems, too. A series of audacious enemy assaults had inflicted heavy losses on other elements of his battalion.

Easy Company's 1st Platoon was spread thinly across the crest of Hill 255 north of Chindong-ni. The platoon leader, 1st LT Gordon M. Strong, had established his CP near an attached machine gun from How Company's Machine Gun Platoon. This machine gun was poorly positioned on a finger. The gun crew was clearly skylined. Corporal Frank Valvo, the platoon's 4th Squad Leader, manned the rifle platoon's organic M1919A6 machine gun. His principle direction of fire covered a draw to the north.[32]

Suddenly, NKPA infantry emerged from a freak early morning fog and commenced their assault. A series of grenade explosions knocked out the water-cooled machine gun, killing nineteen-year-old PFC Bobby W. McDonald, from Dallas, Texas, and two other men on the gun team. Private Glenn R. Hurst, from California, though severely wounded, managed to stagger down the hill to safety. The NKPA quickly overran the foxholes nearest the machine gun and killed the startled occupants. Lieutenant Strong was shot in the head as he tried to run to another position. The NKPA quickly turned the machine gun on its former owners, firing down on the Americans crouching in their foxholes. With heavy enemy pressure to their direct front, and plunging machine gun fire from their right flank, the 1st Platoon was on the verge of being destroyed.

Corporal Frank Valvo returned fire with his M1919A6, holding the stock tightly in his shoulder as he fired from the prone position using the bipod for support. His rounds tore into the NKPA, hitting several to his direct front and pinning the rest down. Sergeant Robert P. Noneman threw hand grenades toward their former CP to keep the pressure off their flank. Private First Class James Kawamura, from Eleele, Kauai, kept screaming in Japanese to "come and get it" as he emptied BAR magazines into the NKPA, killing forty-one, and earning the Distinguished Service Cross.[33] Sergeant First Class Carl H. Dodd, the platoon sergeant, was wounded in this engagement, earning both the Purple Heart and the Silver Star. His personal appointment with destiny lay in the near future, on another fire-swept ridgeline where he would earn the Medal of Honor.

During a brief lull in the action, SFC Dodd withdrew the remnants of his platoon. Ten soldiers had fallen, including 1st LT Strong, C.L. Johnson, Private William D. Amberger, Private Jerome C. Crocker, and a couple of new men no one ever got to know.

Lieutenant Strong's parents had named their son after a former Chief of Staff of the U.S. Army. His best friend was 1st LT Donald Krause, a rifle platoon leader in George Company. They had known each other since their first days at West Point. After graduating with the Class of 1947, both officers had attended The Infantry School before reporting together to Schofield Barracks. Lieutenant Krause discovered LT Strong's body a week later while leading a patrol. He removed his friend's class ring and returned it to LT Strong's parents.[34]

The CO of E Company, Captain England, was severely wounded about the time his 1st Platoon was being assaulted.[35] First Lieutenant William E. Conger, Jr., West Point Class of 1947, assumed command of Easy Company.

While the 2nd Battalion weathered heavy NKPA assaults, the Task Force Kean offensive bogged down. Fog prevented the air strike planned to proceed the 1st Battalion's assault and interfered with the artillery preparation. Twenty minutes of largely unobserved artillery fire made little impression on the NKPA.[36]

At 0720 the 1st Battalion crossed the LD. A few moments into the assault, an Easy Eight received a direct hit from an antitank shell fired by an SU-76.[37] Sergeant Easter's crew bailed out as their tank exploded in flames. Revenge was swift. Another Easy Eight destroyed the self-propelled gun, killing the crew.

The 1st Battalion secured the Tosan road junction without difficulty when everything went wrong at once. The lead rifle company turned south instead of north, advancing down the road slated for the Marines. Everyone followed. Suddenly, NKPA resistance stiffened dramatically, which prevented the rifle companies from conducting a rapid change of direction. Meanwhile, the 1st Battalion's objective, a ridgeline overlooking the northern fork of the road, remained unoccupied by either side.

In fairness to the 1st Battalion, the maps in use were incredibly inaccurate ones produced by the Japanese prior to World War II.[38] The point remains that the 5th RCT did not achieve its assigned objectives that day. General Kean was not happy with COL Ordway, who in turn did not rise to the occasion. The combat team's wire land lines had been carelessly laid by inexperienced troops in the path of an advancing platoon of tanks which promptly tore them to shreds.[39] With wire communications down, the unreliable SCR-300 radios overheating, and COL Ordway's unwillingness to lead from the front, the assault bogged down.

Captain Claude Baker, from Saranac, Michigan, commanded D Company, 1st Battalion. He was not impressed with the combat team's tactics. Captain Baker explained, "We had heard coming over on the ship about the dangers of staying on the low ground and being hit from hills and ridges. I was quite concerned that we were doing the same thing. We marched down the road in a column of twos with no flank security which bothered me from my experiences as an infantry platoon leader and company commander in World War II."[40]

With 1st Battalion bogged down, and 2nd Battalion pinned down, COL Ordway could have committed his 3rd Battalion to an advance up the right fork of the Tosan road junction to maintain the momentum. Colonel Ordway, however, kept his 3rd Battalion in the rear of the road-bound combat team to protect the artillery, a course of action that reflects poorly on either COL Ordway's judgment or his opinion of LTC Benjamin Heckemeyer's ability, and perhaps both.

After the NKPA overran Lieutenant Gordon Strong's positions, they established a fireblock on Hill 255, northeast of Chindong-ni. From this position, their weapons dominated the main supply route (MSR) behind the LD.[41] The 3rd Battalion, 5th Marines fought a fruitless battle throughout the day attempting to clear this fireblock. The Army's 159th FAB fired 1,600 rounds in support of the Marine attack, but the NKPA held on. Even the weight of the Triple Nickel's fires failed to impress the enemy, who fired at anything that moved on the road below. It took two days of heavy fighting before the 3rd Battalion, 5th Marines finally cleared Hill 255 with the aid of two battalions from the 24th Infantry.[42] The confused tactical situation forced the 1st Battalion, 11th Marines to lay its three batteries on different azimuths: north, east and west, as the gun crews responded to frantic requests for fire support.[43]

Meanwhile, the main body of the 5th Marines, expecting to advance down the left fork of the Tosan road junction, stalled behind the 5th RCT's vehicles crowding the road at Chindong-ni. A number of Marine vehicles left the road only to become stuck in the mud. Artillery impacted around the long column of vehicles, causing casualties and much confusion in the ranks. Disgusted with the lack of progress, General Kean took an extreme step at 1130, when he placed the Marine brigade commander, Brigadier General Edward A. Craig, in command of all forces around Chindong-ni.[44]

General Craig toured the front lines and determined through personal observation that enemy resistance was light in the west. He decided to employ one of his Marine battalions to attack the NKPA forces nibbling away at the defenders on Fox Hill so the 2nd Battalion, 5th Infantry could disengage and support the offensive.[45]

The 2nd Battalion, 5th Marines, commanded by LTCOL Harold S. Rosie, reached Chindong-ni later that day with the mission of relieving the men on Fox Hill. Lieutenant Colonel Rosie was under the mistaken impression that his battalion's ascent would be unopposed. He received a rude shock when his Marines were raked by NKPA automatic weapons fire as they began the long, hard climb.

Lieutenant Frank Brooks received a message from CAPT John Finn, Jr., the CO of Company D, just before the Marines began their ascent. Captain Finn informed him of the pending assault and requested to know where he should place his Marines when they reached the crest. Lieutenant Brooks recommended

SFC Richard F. Lewis on the Naktong River. (source: Dick Lewis)

An aerial view of Fox Hill, 7 August 1950. Note the men marching on the road. The smoke is from Hap Easter's burning Easy Eight. (source: Roy E. Appleman, South to the Naktong*)*

that CAPT Finn wait for darkness, because intense automatic weapons fire was sweeping his position. Moreover, a night ascent would spare the Marines from the deadly heat.

Captain Finn was in no position to wait. General Kean wanted the situation on Hill 342 cleaned up, and General Craig was brokering no delays. Company D attacked up the southern spur in the searing 112-degree heat, while Company E tackled the western spur, but neither company made it to the crest that day. Although sniper and automatic weapons fire killed and wounded several Marines, the intense heat played the key role in delaying the advance up the rugged hill.

When Company D's exhausted Marines bogged down near the summit, a Marine platoon leader climbed the remaining distance to announce their arrival. Lieutenants Brooks and Cahill followed this officer down the slope for a conference with CAPT Finn. They informed CAPT Finn that their soldiers and Marines could hold the hill through the night. Captain Finn decided to hold his present position and conduct the relief at dawn.

The North Koreans had plans of their own. Shortly before dawn, the NKPA struck the perimeter on Fox Hill from three sides. Close range fighting dominated this action. One Marine died from multiple gunshot and bayonet wounds. Private David Eckert's arm was shattered by automatic weapons fire as he attempted to give first aid to another soldier dying from a chest wound.[46] An exploding white phosphorous grenade severely burnt LT Brooks' wrists. A fusillade of small arms fire stopped the NKPA assault, however, and the enemy withdrew leaving a score of dead.

Private David Eckert recovering from his wounds at the Nagoya Army Hospital, Japan. (source: David Eckert)

Captain Finn moved out at daybreak and reached the crest a few minutes later. Company D had lost eight Marines KIA, including three officers, and twenty-eight men WIA, in the two-day battle to relieve Fox Hill. Estimated NKPA losses ranged from a low of 150 to a high of 400.[47]

Once the relief was underway, LT Brooks directed his men to carry the dead and seriously wounded to a covered position. A handful of Marines started an ugly rumor that the Army was bugging out when they saw Fox Company's survivors moving towards the reverse slope. "Hell," said LT Brooks. "We weren't bugging out. We knew better than they did that there wasn't anywhere to go, and that we would be better off staying in our holes than trying to run down that hill."[48]

When CAPT Finn was badly wounded attempting to retrieve the body of a Marine lieutenant, LT Brooks decided to keep his men on the hill a little longer. An hour later the shattered remnants of F Company trudged down the hill after giving the last drops of their precious water to the parched Marines who were about to experience their own purgatory on Hill 342. Fox Company's total casualties on Hill 342 are estimated at fifteen KIA, thirty WIA and one MIA.[49] One of the survivors, Private Gerald Pack, from Wayne, West Virginia, recalled, "If we'd known what to do, then we'd never have held that hill. As it was, we didn't know enough to be really scared. That may sound crazy to some people, but if you had been there, you would understand."[50]

A Navy Corpsman injected Private David Eckert with two shots of morphine before he walked down the hill cradling his shattered arm. After climbing into an ambulance at the bottom of the hill, an NKPA patrol took the weaponless and wounded men under fire. Two of Tank Company's Easy Eights roared to the rescue with guns blazing in the best traditions of the U.S. Cavalry.[51] Private Eckert's eight-day war in Korea was finally over.

Lieutenant Brooks found LTC John Throckmorton at the 2nd Battalion CP and reported for duty. The Rock took one look at LT Brooks' burnt wrists, poured his subordinate a stiff drink, and told him to "put your platoon in reserve and get your butt to the hospital." Captain Alexander Kahapea assumed command of Fox Company.[52]

Lieutenant John Cahill's battered platoon followed Fox Company down the hill. One of the Marines gave Sonny an envelope on Fox Hill. This envelope, with its distinctive Marine Corps emblem, arrived in Lanikai a few weeks later. It was the first letter Sonny mailed home. Later that evening, other Marine units commenced a relief in place with the 2nd Battalion to free that unit up for tomorrow's assault.

Sergeant Horace Anderson was sitting on a knoll with his 57-mm Recoilless Rifle Squad watching the Marines arrive. He was angry for two reasons. First, he did not have a single round of 57-mm recoilless rifle ammunition to reply to the NKPA fire that occasionally hit his position. Second, a Marine lieutenant had refused to listen to his advice. As regular as clock work, the NKPA had seen fit to fire three mortar rounds at sunset into his position for the past few days, and the bunched up Marine platoon had not started to dig in. Sergeant Anderson said, "It was getting late in the evening, but when I told the lieutenant about the mortar rounds, the lieutenant told me he had everything under control. I told my buddy McCoy, and he replied, 'Well, that was all we could do.' In a little while, three mortar rounds came in. We heard a lot of screaming, and, when it was safe to come out of our hole, we saw that one poor Marine had lost his leg and several more were wounded. The rest were digging in. Sometime after dark, hot chow was brought up the ridgeline and we all shared it, Army and Marines. About midnight E Company moved off the ridge."[53]

Colonel Ordway knew his career was on the line and ordered LTC Throckmorton, his favorite thoroughbred, to seize the ridge north of Tosan. Of the 2nd Battalion's three rifle companies, two were still combat effective. Fox Company required time to rest and reorganize after its harrowing ordeal on Hill 342. The 2nd Battalion moved out at 0930, 8 August, to seize the ridge. Heavy enemy fire, combined with the inability of the supporting artillery to adjust on target, and the critical absence of recoilless rifle ammunition, caused LTC Throckmorton's attack to breakdown by 1150.

During the 2nd Battalion's attack, the 555th FAB was seriously mauled by NKPA fire. The battalion's Fire Direction Center (FDC) had dug in immediately behind B Battery, and was processing fire missions in support of the 2nd Battalion's attack. The Survey Section, Headquarters Battery, was established in a large hole off to the flank of B Battery, learning how to perform as an alternate FDC in the event the primary FDC was knocked out.

Sergeant First Class Richard F. Lewis, a surveyor, sat in the alternate FDC when recoilless rifle rounds impacted on B Battery and the primary FDC. Within seconds, NKPA indirect fire weapons, either artillery or 120-mm mortar, plastered B Battery, adding to the carnage. The battery's Operations Center took a direct hit, killing 1st LT John A. Mercer, 1st LT James W. Stoll, the battery first sergeant, and the operations sergeant.[54] Warrant Officer George D. Gillispi, Jr., a World War II com-

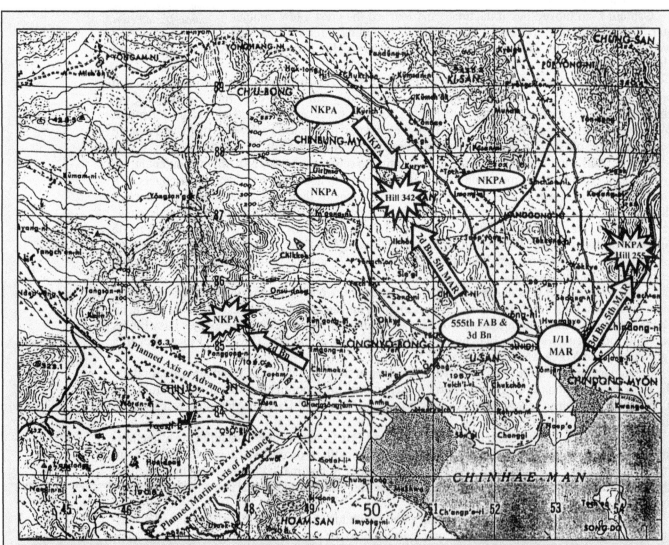

TASK FORCE KEAN, 8 AUGUST 1950. The 2nd Battalion, 5th Marines relieves Fox Company on Hill 342. Fighting continues for control of Hill 255. NKPA fire mauls the 555th FAB and prevents the 2nd Battalion, 5th RCT from overrunning its objective in daylight. A night atttack is successful and, after the 2nd Battalion consolidates on its objective, the 3rd Battalion moves up on its left flank.

bat veteran, was Tank Company's personnel officer. He had often joked at Schofield Barracks that he planned to fight the next war with a pen. After his foxhole took a direct hit, there was little left of him to bury.[55]

Two of the B Battery's four 105-mm howitzers were destroyed.[56] The battery limbered up its two remaining howitzers and moved forward to C Battery's firing position where LTC Daly temporarily combined the two units to create the first six-gun battery in the battalion. One of these guns went into a position where it could employ direct fire into the hillsides to the north. The other howitzer joined C Battery's configuration. Brigadier General Barth, the 25th Infantry Division's artillery commander, witnessed the shelling and concluded that "The 'Triple Nickel,' as they called themselves, were to receive one of the

8 August 1950. The displeased GEN Kean (center) receives 5th RCT briefing with COL Ordway, who is kneeling to the General's front. MAJ Owens, the S-3, is seated to the General's right. (source: NA)

toughest baptisms of fire experienced by any artillery unit in Korea on this and the four following days."[57]

General Kean was in an ugly mood when he departed on a personal tour to the front lines to see for himself the cause of the delay. Earlier that day, he had distributed a letter to all units directing that "action be taken to punish all men guilty of misconduct before the enemy. Cowardice and shirking of duty would not be tolerated."[58] An uncomfortable COL Ordway escorted General Kean to the 2nd Battalion's CP where the task force commander gruffly informed LTC Throckmorton, "I want that hill tonight."[59]

General Kean had been the Rock's mentor throughout much of the battalion commander's career. For starters, Captain Kean had been 2nd LT Throckmorton's company commander, and the person who had encouraged the Rock to cultivate his shooting skills. In World War II Major General Kean had personally drafted LTC Throckmorton to serve in the First Army's G-3 Operations Section. The Rock's competence in this billet forced General Kean to deny his friend's repeated requests to command a combat unit. Past friendship aside, General Kean demanded results from the grim battalion commander. In response the Rock prepared a meticulous night attack plan supported by the fires of three tanks, the battalion's 81-mm mortars, and an attached platoon of 4.2-inch mortars.[60]

At 2000 the 2nd Battalion crossed the LD and assaulted its objective in a sharply contested firefight under the stars. The Rock's tactical acumen, and his skillful integration of supporting fires, served his men well. The battalion routed the NKPA defenders at little cost in blood. Following this success, the 3rd Battalion moved up on the 2nd Battalion's left flank.[61]

A smiling General Kean congratulated LTC Throckmorton the next morning. When CPL Lorrin Thurston, the CO's driver, arrived after a harrowing drive through NKPA sniper fire with hot food, the Rock took a short break to eat and express his thoughts to a reporter from *The Honolulu Advertiser*. "This is the first so-called hot meal I've had in three days," he commented. "Things are going damn good. I hate to say it because we may be kicked back tomorrow, but we've got the enemy rolling. He is losing his communications and we are pressing him."[62]

CHAPTER EIGHT

BLOODY GULCH

Infantry, cavalry, and artillery are nothing without each other.
They should always be so disposed in cantonments to assist each other in case of surprise.
Napoleon

The 1st Provisional Marine Brigade's rapid advance south of the 5th RCT inflicted excruciating punishment on the NKPA. On 11 August, Marine F4U Corsairs from VMF-323, supported by a handful of Air Force P-51 fighter-bombers, obliterated the unsuspecting NKPA 83rd Mechanized Regiment caught napping on the side of a road. The 5th Marines, ably supported by Marine aviation, mopped up scattered NKPA die-hards in a series of brisk firefights.

Meanwhile, the 5th RCT advanced at a slow, cautious pace toward Much'on-ni. Many soldiers wore their rubber gas masks as they marched under the glaring sun through the choking, billowing clouds of dust-filled air.[2] Late-afternoon rain showers brought welcome relief from the heat of the day. Flies and mosquitoes plagued the soldiers, however, and men were going down with malaria and dysentery.

Sniper fire and small unit ambushes killed or wounded several men. On 9 August, the 25th Infantry Division's War Diary stated, "Snipers were active wherever United States forces were moving." A document found on the body of a North Korean cultural advisor stated, "Although the puppet regime relies on U.S. forces in the fight against us, we alone can conquer them. And, although the American Imperialists are proud of their atom bomb, do not forget that we have prepared poison gas."[3]

During a visit to the 5th RCT's CP on 9 August, General Barth witnessed yet another NKPA attack bubbling out of the hills to the north. The soldiers defended the CP with small arms fire as the North Koreans pressed home their assault. A nearby Triple Nickel battery depressed its howitzers for direct fire into the NKPA assault formations. Luckily, three Marine Corsairs swooped down unannounced and wreaked havoc on the NKPA infantry with the multiple strafing runs. Leaving a score of dead littering the hillsides, the NKPA withdrew into the rugged hills.

General Kean demanded that the 1st Provisional Marine Brigade and the 5th RCT continue their advance through the night. The combat team's axis of advance was northwest, toward Much'on-ni, astride a narrow country lane.[4]

Colonel Ordway ordered the 2nd Battalion to lead the advance. The Rock complied, but his soldiers were nearing mental and physical exhaustion after much hard fighting. Why COL Ordway did not commit the unblooded 3rd Battalion remains a mystery. In any event, 1st LT Keith Whitham's 2nd Tank Platoon and Captain Alexander Kahapea's Fox Company formed the advance guard.

Captain Kahapea was a muscular, athletic soldier who had coached the 5th RCT football team at Schofield Barracks. He had earned an admirable combat record during World War II, earning the DSC while serving with the 442nd RCT. This was a new war, and while Fox Company was a good outfit, something snapped that night.

Part of the problem lay with CAPT Kahapea, a genuine war hero who unfortunately never stopped telling people about it. The combat weary soldiers were not enamored with their new CO's superior attitude and loud talk. Furthermore, Fox Company had lost most of its officers and NCOs in the vicinity of Fox Hill. Several of the soldiers who marched into the unknown that evening were walking wounded and not up to a hard fight. Lieutenant Kenneth Hino had just returned to the company after being treated for shrapnel wounds when the word was passed to move out.

The going was deceptively easy at first. Then the tanks crossed a dry streambed spanned by a concrete bridge. Here the narrow road took a sharp turn into the mouth of a mountain pass. The Easy Eights

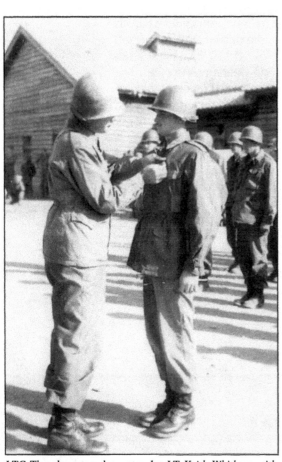

LTC Throckmorton decorates 1st LT Keith Whitham with the Silver Star. (source: Chang)

were about midway up the steep incline, with engines growling in low gear, when a 45-mm antitank gun cracked once, then twice, at point-blank range. One shell penetrated LT Keith Whitham's tank and the crew bailed out. The men took cover beneath an embankment where NKPA soldiers stood, taunting the Americans with shouts of "Hey Joe! Hey Joe!" in between bursts of burp gun fire.[5]

The NKPA held the high ground on both sides of the road and swept Fox Company with automatic weapons fire. Most of the men broke, the panic stricken troops running past CAPT Kahapea who stood in the middle of the road with arms outstretched trying to stop the fleeing men. Lieutenant Hino was hit, fell down in a ditch, and was left behind in the confusion.

Fox Company's disintegration made it perilous for the tanks to remain unescorted on the narrow road. Lieutenant Whitham raced to the second tank in the column and attempted to get it turned around. The road gave way and the tank flipped completely over into a deep ravine landing on its tracks. Miraculously, no one was seriously hurt.

He loaded his two dismounted tank crews and about fifty Fox Company soldiers onto the three remaining tanks and did not stop until he reached the 2nd Battalion's main body that was moving up the road.[6]

Lieutenant Colonel John Throckmorton was near exhaustion himself when word reached him of the reverse. He had little time to sleep, for at 0400 the NKPA, following a night of considerable infiltration, struck the 2nd and 1st Battalions. Two hours later, after heavy losses on both sides, the NKPA broke off the attack.

Midway between Chindong-ni and Much'on-ni lay the twin villages of Pongam-ni and Taejong-ni, which sat on the eastern end of the mountain pass that Fox Company had failed to force the night before. A narrow north-south trail intersected the main road near the center of Taejong-ni. This trail wandered through a valley to the north that was infested with NKPA soldiers.

On the afternoon of 10 August, LTC John P. Jones' 1st Battalion was advancing on the right (north) side of the road, while LTC Throckmorton's 2nd Battalion moved up on the left (south) side. In the face of light resistance the 1st Battalion quickly seized Pongam-ni and began to consolidate on the high ground on the northern side of the pass.

Regrettably, LTC Jones' standing with his company commanders was tenuous at best. Moreover, his battalion XO had developed a "knee problem" during the first days of the advance and had been evacuated to rear. He was presumably evacuated from Korea, or transferred to another unit, for no one in the battalion ever saw him again. Lieutenant Colonel Jones asked CAPT Claude Baker, the CO of Dog Company, to double as battalion XO. This was a fortunate choice. Captain Baker was a brave and capable soldier who was highly regarded by the battalion's officers and men.

A serious leadership crisis erupted in the 1st Battalion as the soldiers climbed the steep ridge to their objective. That afternoon, B Company, commanded by CAPT Ed Walsh, advanced uphill across rugged terrain along the northern ridgeline running parallel to the road. Charlie Company followed, while Able Company remained on the low ground in reserve. With the exception of the 81-mm Mortar Platoon, Dog Company's heavy weapons were attached to the rifle companies.

First Lieutenant Stanley W. Crosby, West Point Class of 1947, had served in Korea before the war. The soldiers in Baker Company adored the young rifle platoon leader, who by all accounts was a competent, likeable officer, who took care of his men. Lieutenant Crosby was on emergency leave when the 5th RCT deployed to Korea and had therefore missed the first few days of fighting. He reached Pusan in time to join his company near Pongam-ni. Lieutenant Crosby felt badly about having missed the first few days of combat and volunteered his rifle platoon to lead the advance. The platoon encountered a reverse slope defense on the other side of the ridge and came under heavy NKPA fire. Several men were hit. Lieutenant Crosby was KIA.

Captain Ed Walsh withdrew his battered company down the hill without orders. Some say he withdrew without attempting to aid LT Crosby's embattled rifle platoon. Baker Company's remaining two rifle platoons dutifull followed their commander down the hill. They were subsequently joined by the remnants of LT Crosby's shattered platoon. Captain Walsh blamed LTC Jones for LT Crosby's death. Corporal Middleton believes CAPT Walsh was upset because he had lost several men to friendly mortar fire.[7] In any event, an enraged CAPT Walsh walked up to LTC Jones and threatened to shoot his battalion commander in the presence of witnesses.[8]

While this bizarre argument ran its course, the CO of C Company saw the activity around the CP and decided to pull his men off the hill without orders. A surprised and angry LTC Jones understandably relieved CAPT Walsh on the spot and replaced him with 1st LT Kermit "Pappy" Young, from Arab, Alabama. Lieutenant Young was probably the oldest, most laid-back, and popular officer in the 1st Battalion. "He was the bravest man I ever saw," said CPL Middleton.[9] With that particular problem solved, LTC Jones turned to the CO of Charlie Company and ordered him to take his men back up the hill.

Meanwhile, the 2nd Battalion dug in on the high ground south of the pass without incident. The NKPA retained control of the western side of the pass and were suspected to be present in force north of Pongam-ni. The 555th FAB and the 90th FAB, minus one battery, established firing positions a few hundred yards farther to the east in the vicinity of Taejong-ni. Organic to the 25th Infantry Division, the 90th FAB reinforced the Triple Nickel with a battery of 155-mm howitzers.[10]

In keeping with his commander's intent, COL Ordway ordered LTC Benjamin Heckemeyer's 3rd Battalion to punch through the pass and continue the advance on Much'on-ni. As the soldiers boarded trucks and moved out on the road, 1st LT Randall Beirne noticed LTC John Throckmorton standing in the open, pumping his fist up and down, and shouting "Hurry up! Hurry up!" as he directed the trucks through his battalion's lines. Off to the side of the road, he saw COL Ordway standing in a deep hole, flanked on either side by two military policemen. Lieutenant Beirne said, "The men wondered, and I wondered too, what he was so nervous about that he was standing in a hole with two MPs guarding him while all the rest of us were exposed."[11]

The 3rd Battalion barreled through the pass, taking occasional small arms fire from the ridgelines on either side of the road. With the exception of two shot-out tires, the enemy fire inflicted no casualties or damage. Lieutenant Colonel Heckemeyer's battalion dug in on the far side of the pass and hunkered down for the rest of the night before pressing on early the next morning.

During the advance, the 3rd Battalion recovered LT Kenneth Hino and evacuated the wounded officer to an aid station.[12] Lieutenant Hino's oriental features had saved him from being summarily executed by the NKPA. The North Koreans had apparently mistaken him for one of their own dead and had left him lying in the ditch undisturbed. Other Americans recovered that day had been less fortunate.

The Sobuk-san mountain chain was dotted with abandoned mine shafts that the NKPA used to shield their men from air strikes and reconnaissance aircraft. Thus, as the 5th RCT marched through this desolate region, large elements of the NKPA 6th Division awaited nightfall from their lairs beneath the ground. That evening, thousands of NKPA soldiers emerged from the mine shafts and assembled in the darkness, weapons ready, grimly determined to make the hated Americans pay for their meager territorial gains.

A totally unexpected and extremely powerful NKPA night attack materialized out of the predawn darkness and crashed into the main body of the 5th RCT still occupying positions on the eastern side of the pass.[13] By 0400 the regimental CP was under fire. The 1st Battalion and the artillery positions were badly hit, the soldiers fighting at close range for their lives. Veteran NKPA soldiers drove hard into the 5th RCT's flank, inflicting considerable losses on the Americans. Charlie Battery, 555th FAB, defended its positions near Taejong-ni with every weapon at its disposal and held the NKPA marauders at bay. When communications with A Battery, 555th FAB, were lost, LTCs John Daly and John Jones organized a scratch counterattack force of infantrymen and cannoneers to relieve the hard-pressed battery. Both battalion commanders were wounded in the attempt to fight through to the battery. Later, as LTC Jones was being evacuated to the rear, he directed CAPT Claude Baker to assume command of 1st Battalion and this was done. Lieutenant Colonel Daly's wounds were less serious, and he remained in command of his artillery battalion.[14] The 1st Battalion's Logistics Officer (S-4), 1st LT Howard Stephenson, was badly wounded in this engagement and evacuated to Japan.[15]

LTC Roelofs shaving in the Pusan Perimeter. (source: NA)

North Korean infantry assaulted LTC John Throckmorton's CP at dawn. The Rock clutched his .45-caliber pistol firmly in hand as he directed the defense of the command post. "We were on the verge of being annihilated," said 1st LT Norman Cooper whose P&A Platoon was in the thick of the engagement. The Rock dispatched LT Cooper to bring E Company to the CP. The P&A platoon leader went on foot to explain the Rock's plight to 1st LT William Conger, the company commander. "Easy Company was instrumental in helping repulse the attack," said LT Cooper, "but one man in particular, a SFC Napier, was more instrumental in repulsing the attack than anybody in the whole battalion. He got up on a 3/4 ton truck and manned a .50-caliber machine gun and fired eighteen to twenty boxes of ammunition into the attacking forces. I think that's what repulsed the attack, though, of course, everyone was firing."[16]

Sergeant Horace Anderson's 57-mm Recoilless Rifle Squad participated in the fighting with their personal weapons. The disgusted soldiers still had no ammunition for their recoilless rifle, which explains why their platoon leader had looked the other way when they discarded the heavy and cumbersome tripod during the previous afternoon's march.[17]

After the fighting died down, 1st LT Keith Whitham fell into a trance-like sleep on the ground next to his tank. Captain Robert W. Ecoff, the 2nd Battalion S-3, woke him up with a couple of swift kicks to his feet. The tank platoon leader was instructed to intercept and escort a convoy of ammunition trucks coming up the road from Chindong-ni.[18]

Sergeant Adrian J. K. Sylva's rifle squad from A Company volunteered to accompany the tanks and climbed up on the engine decks to provide infantry protection. The modest armor-infantry task force roared off down the road, leaving a trail of choking dust in its wake. After driving about two miles, LT Whitham's three tanks reached the stalled truck convoy, which was under heavy NKPA fire from all sides. Two burning trucks marked the scene as a handful of survivors returned fire from the protection of the roadside ditches.

Sergeant Sylva, from Honolulu, was a brave and fatalistic soldier. He stood behind LT Whitham on the engine deck firing the turret-mounted .50-caliber machine gun. Meanwhile, LT Whitham maneuvered his tanks to bring their formidable firepower to bear.

North Korean return fire started to concentrate on the tanks. Lieutenant Whitham received a light head wound. A few minutes later, his right arm suffered an agonizing jolt when the recoil of his tank's main gun struck it. No bones were broken, and the intense pain did not interfere with his satisfaction of witnessing the North Koreans being shot down when they tried to flee.

Lieutenant Whitham directed the remnants of the convoy to follow his tanks as he led the column down the road. The NKPA was still pressing the 5th RCT CP hard when the convoy reached the scene. The Regimental S-2, LTC Thomas Roelofs, was standing in the open on a little knoll observing

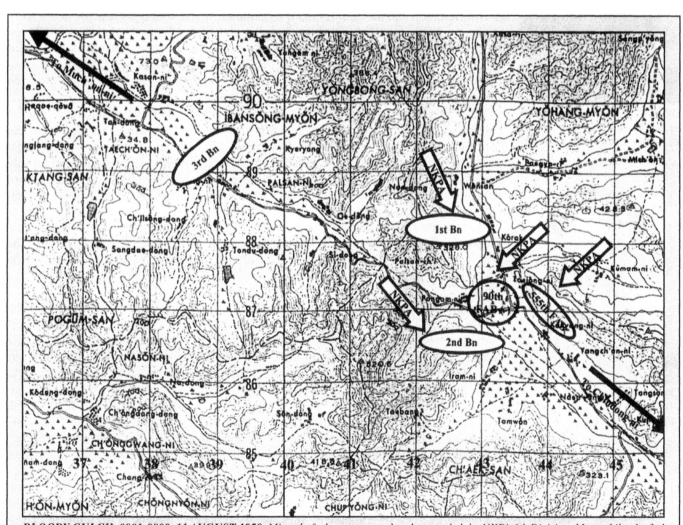

BLOODY GULCH, 0001-0800, 11 AUGUST 1950. Mine shafts have protected and concealed the NKPA 6th Division. Meanwhile, the 3rd Battalion, having punched through the pass on 10 August, is preparing to move out to link up with the 35th Infantry at Much'on-ni. In the early morning hours of 11 August, the NKPA strikes the 5th RCT units still on the eastern side of the pass. Heavy losses are inflicted on both sides, but the NKPA withdraws. They will return.

PFC Albert Semasko on R&R in Tokyo, February 51. (source: Al Semasko)

LTC Claude Baker in Germany after the Korean War. Note his 5th RCT patch. (source: Claude Baker)

Gene McClure in the 11th Airborne Division after his tour in Korea. (source: Gene McClure)

the fall of each shot from Tank Company's single 81-mm mortar manned by the tank vehicle retriever's crew. After the fall of each shot, LTC Roelofs would run down the knoll to within hollering distance of the gun crew to give the necessary range and deflection adjustments. While this was going on, COL Ordway was "sitting in a gully, shaking his head, obviously out of it."[49] The ever-defiant NKPA eventually broke contact on their own accord, the decision hastened by the timely arrival of Marine Corsairs roaring in on strafing runs at tree top level. Lieutenant Whitham returned to the 2nd Battalion with his platoon, SGT Sylva's rifle squad, and a single truckload of ammunition. It had been a busy morning, and the tank platoon leader's battered head and bruised arm hurt like hell.

Dog Company's 81-mm Mortar Platoon was swamped with requests for fire support during the fighting. The mortar platoon's basic load of ammunition included 150 high explosive (light), 60 high explosive (heavy), and 60 white phosphorous shells. The men had dispensed with carrying the smoke round, because it did not inflict casualties or damage on the enemy. Rather, they fired white phosphorous ammunition when the infantry requested screening or obscuration fires.

After expending their basic load of ammunition, a truck dropped off a resupply of 81-mm rounds at dawn. When they broke open the wooden ammunition crates, the shocked men discovered badly rusted shells and pitted compressor rings from a lot of ammunition manufactured in 1940 and 1941. They had no choice but to load and fire the aged and badly deteriorated ammunition. Quite often, the assistant gunners had to sand globs of rust off a shell before it would fit down a mortar tube.[20]

The 555th and 90th FABs had felt the lack of infantry support in the fighting. When COL Ordway recovered his composure, he saw no need to adjust the tactical layout of his infantry battalions. It was still his plan to force the pass in daylight and link up with his 3rd Battalion and the 35th Infantry. In the interim, the 90th FAB was protected from enemy direct fire by a low ridgeline, but the guns of the Triple Nickel were deployed next to Taejong-ni in a dry stream bed near a concrete bridge in an area otherwise devoid of cover. When COL Ordway's plan to force the pass in daylight on 11 August failed to materialize, the artillery did not alter the tactical layout of its firing positions. Nor was infantry protection provided. These oversights would cost the Red Legs dearly.[21]

Colonel Ordway directed LTC Thomas B. Roelofs to assume command of the 1st Battalion. This officer's excellent reputation was based on his prewar assignment as the CO of the 1st Battalion in 1948-49. One of his officers believed his level of intellect approached that of a genius. A skilled map reader, he possessed the ability to rapidly devise solid tactical plans based on his keen eye for ground. Although he had commanded 1st Battalion before the war, he was actually a professional intelligence officer, and time would tell if he could lead men in battle.

Lieutenant Colonel Roelofs' mission was to seize the northernmost ridgeline that dominated the pass. Once this objective was secured, COL Ordway planned to push the 2nd Battalion, the regimental trains, and the artillery in that order through the pass. The 1st Battalion would peel off the ridgeline and bring up the rear after the main body had cleared.

Lieutenant Colonel Roelofs reached his CP at approximately 1400 where LTC John Daly and CAPT Claude Baker greeted him. He asked CAPT Baker to continue to perform the dual functions of battalion XO and Dog Company Commander. Captain Baker agreed.[22] After a brief conversation, LTC Roelofs departed the CP to make a short personal reconnaissance. He issued his orders to his company commanders upon his return. After much time consuming delay, Baker and Charlie Companies jumped off in the attack late that afternoon. Fire support from the battalion's heavy weapons and the 555th FAB facilitated the infantry's advance along the rugged terrain. By nightfall, Baker and Charlie Companies were digging in on their objectives. One platoon from A Company, reinforced with a platoon of tanks, screened the trail running through the valley north of Taejong-ni. The rest of Able Company remained in reserve.

Meanwhile, the 3rd Battalion, unaware of the opposition encountered by the rest of the combat team, continued to advance down a railroad track. The advance guard discovered an arms cache located inside a tunnel guarded by a couple of very surprised NKPA soldiers. A detachment of soldiers destroyed the arms cache as the foot-sore battalion marched on Chinju.

Many of the 3rd Battalion's soldiers believed they were dangerously far in front of the main body. Chaplain Dick Oostenink was riding in his jeep near the rear of the battalion trains with the medical detachment when an NKPA volley of long range rifle fire struck the column. One Hawaiian sergeant was hit in the mouth and knocked off his feet. To the chaplain's amazement, the soldier stood up, spit out a couple of bloody teeth along with the spent round, and continued to march.[23] The weary soldiers reached a hill overlooking Chinju where the 3rd Battalion dug in for the night.

Colonel Ordway was probably unaware of the 3rd Battalion's remarkable progress. After the 1st Battalion seized its objective, he changed his mind and decided to march through the pass at night under the cover of darkness. General Kean was not pleased with the delay and, in a lengthy radio conversation late that afternoon, he urged COL Ordway to advance. The task force commander did not believe the enemy was present in great force. General Kean promised to provide COL Ordway a battalion from the 24th Infantry to support the advance, but he reluctantly concurred with COL Ordway's plan.[24]

With LTC Throckmorton's 2nd Battalion serving as advance guard, C Battery and the regimental trains got on the road that night.[25] The 2nd Tank Platoon, minus Lieutenant Keith Whitham who was nursing his wounds in his jeep, moved out with 2nd Battalion at 2100. Charlie Battery followed with LTC John Daly traveling behind the howitzers with his Artillery Survey Section. Once over the rim, LTC Throckmorton's command lost radio communications with COL Ordway.

Shortly after moving out, the NKPA raked the 2nd Battalion from firing positions located further to the west on both sides of the pass. Lieutenant Norman Cooper's P&A Platoon led the advance, sweeping on foot for mines, and bore the brunt of the enemy's intense fire. "We hadn't gone 500 yards before every man in my platoon, except myself, was wounded," explained LT Cooper.[26] The wounded were placed aboard trucks as the column fought its way through the pass.

Private Gene McClure, How Company, 75-mm Recoilless Rifle Platoon, recalled, "This was one of the heaviest walls of small arms fire I was ever to pass through during the war…. Machine gun tracers coming from the hills bounced all over the place. The vehicle I was riding in was hit several times and a bullet ripped through one man's leg who was riding in the cab…. We returned fire into the hills on either side of the road but never stopped our forward movement for very long at any time until we cleared the pass, which took an hour for my own truck and three hours for the whole battalion."[27]

The 2nd Battalion and C Battery fought their way clear of the enemy fire. At first light, the battalion's advance guard halted short of a roadblock on the far side of the pass.

The Artillery Survey Section was less fortunate. When the NKPA succeeded in cutting the road behind C Battery, the Artillery Survey Section exited their vehicles to take cover. Private Arlen Russell said, "An NKPA ambush stopped the convoy in short order. I could hear heavy machine gun as well as small arms fire from the right side of the road and the hills to the right. Word filtered down the column that LTC Daly had been hit by machine gun fire. A sergeant crawled up and down the ditch urging us all to stay awake. Troop movement over the hill behind us could be heard, but no one was sure whose troops they were, so we were told to hold our positions."[28]

Sergeant First Class Richard Lewis crawled up and down the road urging the men to stay awake. Much to SFC Lewis' disgust, he found two soldiers asleep in their vehicle. He shook the culprits awake. Later, SFC Lewis led six men in a grueling climb to high ground overlooking the road to cover the convoy from the heights with their individual weapons until first light.[29]

Colonel Ordway was out of radio contact with 2nd Battalion and unaware of LTC Daly's plight. General Kean intervened at this moment with an order for COL Ordway to halt his advance. General Walker wanted General Kean to detach a portion of his task force to another threatened sector of the Pusan Perimeter, and the 5th RCT was the most likely candidate. Two of COL Ordway's three infantry battalions were now west of the pass, along with one battery of artillery. The regimental trains were lined up on the road, sitting ducks when daylight arrived. The NKPA was pressing the combat team hard, particularly from the north. At dawn, the 5th RCT would be poorly deployed to repulse yet another NKPA attack.

Colonel Ordway attempted to explain his situation to General Kean, but radio communications with the 25th Infantry Division's CP failed at the critical moment. Colonel Ordway did not possess a strong enough personality to disregard the orders of a general officer, even when he knew those orders probably spelled disaster for his command. Moreover, he took no steps to alter the combat team's tactical layout when faced with the changed situation. His fear of personal failure, and probable fear of injury or death, paralyzed him into a curious state of inaction as he sat alone that long August night at the bottom of a deep hole that had been dug for his own personal protection.

Meanwhile, CAPT Claude Baker stayed on the field phones in the 1st Battalion CP throughout the night talking to his company commanders. He had not slept in the previous forty-eight hours and was annoyed that LTC Thomas Roelofs had disappeared earlier in the evening to find a place to sleep. No one knew where to find him. The hours passed slowly as CAPT Baker tried to reassure his company commanders over the landlines with calm words. The company commanders believed the NKPA would hit them in force that night. Captain Baker agreed and felt the 1st Battalion alone could not withstand the fury of an all out NKPA assault. He found it all the more disconcerting that the 5th RCT CP had not started to push the regimental trains and the remaining artillery batteries through the pass while there was still time to take advantage of the darkness to conceal the movement.[30]

Annoyed that LTC Roelofs could not to be found, CAPT Baker walked to the 5th RCT CP on his own initiative to explain his battalion's perilous situation to COL Ordway. A soldier at the CP directed CAPT Baker to a hole that must have been eight feet deep and appeared big enough to park a jeep in. Captain Baker stood on the edge of the hole and started to tell COL Ordway about the necessity to get the trains moving through the pass when the regimental commander interrupted, saying, "Don't talk to me. Go talk to Wes [LTC Wes Blanchard, the XO of the 5th RCT]."[31]

A disgusted Captain Baker departed to find LTC Blanchard who in turn directed him to see Major Elmer G. Owens, the S-3 Operations Officer of the 5th RCT. It was either during CAPT Baker's meeting with MAJ Owens, or shortly thereafter, that the NKPA assaulted Charlie Company in force and cut its landlines to the 1st Battalion's CP. The sounds of grenade explosions and gunfire could be heard from Charlie Company's positions, but since radio communications were down, it could only be assumed that the rifle company was being overrun.

Major Owens agreed with CAPT Baker that it was time to get the combat team's trains rolling. As CAPT Baker returned to the 1st Battalion CP, COL Ordway heard his operations officer explain just why it was necessary to disregard General Kean's orders, and soon, before the NKPA attacked in force. Before COL Ordway would issue the necessary orders, he made one last futile attempt to reestablish contact with General Kean. Radio communications with the 25th Infantry Division were still down when COL Ordway finally issued orders at 0400 for the trains and artillery to push through the pass. With Charlie Company's apparent collapse, the NKPA would soon be in position to fire on the road.

Confusion reigned. Some units misunderstood COL Ordway's orders, still others did not get the word. March discipline broke down when vehicles attempted to cut in front of one another, and a traffic jam soon succeeded in blocking the narrow entrance to the pass. At first light, NKPA small arms fire from the ridge formerly occupied by C Company began to impact on the column, causing casualties and even more confusion. After strenuous efforts, MAJ James P. Alcorn, the Regimental Adjutant, regained a semblance of control and managed to get the trains moving. Colonel Ordway drove at their head to the 2nd Battalion, which he found digging in after overrunning the enemy road block that had temporarily barred its path.

Lieutenant Keith Whitham's injuries prevented him from accompanying his tank platoon that night. He was riding in a jeep in the middle of the regimental trains when the column began to snake slowly through the pass. The column jolted to a halt near the summit and remained stationary for what seemed like hours. Lieutenant Whitham finally jumped out of his jeep and trudged to the head of the column to see what was causing the delay. He found a truck driver asleep in his cab. The vehicles ahead of him had moved on. He said, "I am sure had this not happened many of the men and vehicles who were caught in the gulch would have been clear of the pass when the North Koreans struck at dawn."[32]

A rifle platoon from A Company, reinforced with the 1st Tank Platoon, had been assigned the mission of blocking the trail leading north from Taejong-ni. Neither platoon wanted to be left behind in the confusion when the soldiers saw the combat team's trains pulling out. Without orders, the infantry mounted the tanks and both platoons withdrew. Tragically, NKPA tanks and infantry exploited this opportunity, and daybreak found the enemy attacking in great force down the uncovered trail.

At first light, PFC Albert Semasko was on guard duty with a couple of other soldiers from B Battery. They were awaiting orders to limber up the 105-mm howitzers and move out. The soldiers had placed trip flares to their front, but "who knows, maybe not far enough."[33] The tired men were looking forward to a hot meal after a quiet, tedious night of guard duty, when suddenly, PFC Semasko noticed sparks shooting off some rocks a few feet away. "It took me

LT James Johnson just before Bloody Gulch. In the background is 1st SGT Ralph Loefflor. (source: James Johnson)

about one tenth of a second to figure out that bullets were causing those sparks," said PFC Semasko. "That's when all hell broke loose." The sentries dove into their foxholes, which PFC Semasko suddenly thought resembled individual graves. When the 105-mm howitzers started to return fire, the sentries fell back to a stone wall that surrounded Taejong-ni where the battery's soldiers had gathered to take cover and return fire with their rifles and carbines. A few NKPA soldiers were shot down in a nearby rice paddie, but most of the enemy soldiers remained on the ridgeline firing down at the exposed cannoneers in the gun positions. Private Michael A. Gbur, from Russeltown, Pennsylvania, was shot in the head. A helicopter evacuated him shortly thereafter, but he died of his wounds on an operating table. The Army returned his personal effects to his grief-stricken family — a pair of dog tags and seventy- five cents in change.[34]

Dawn found LT James Johnson's combat engineer platoon driving slowly down the road when it was struck by a whirlwind of small arms fire. The men dismounted and started blasting the hillsides with their rifles and cab mounted .50-caliber machine guns. Lieutenant Johnson fired his carbine from behind his jeep at fleeting targets. Suddenly, Warrant Officer Bradley, the 72nd Engineers' Maintenance Officer, knocked his lieutenant to the ground just as a burst of burp gun fire shot out the jeep's tires. One slug ripped through the meaty part of one of the LT Johnson's legs. The two men swore at each other before breaking into laughter. The platoon remounted their vehicles and, with guns blazing, escaped through the pass.[35]

The FDC section, Headquarters Battery, was not so lucky. It, too, had been driving toward the pass when the NKPA opened fire. The FDC section turned around and returned to Taejong-ni where the men dismounted and took cover behind the stone wall. Officers and NCOs walked the line, directing the return fire of their soldiers.[36]

Captain Perry H. Graves, the CO of B Battery, took cover behind a water trailer that was spouting water from multiple bullet holes. He managed to reach the protection of the stone wall during a short lull in the firing.[37] Events suddenly worsened.

The 13th Regiment, NKPA 6th Division, supported by T34s and SU-76 self-propelled guns, struck the 555th and 90th FABs that morning from three sides. The gun crews fought a courageous duel with the T-34s, firing over open sights. But the 90th FAB could not depress its 155-mm muzzles far enough to hit the tanks, and the 105-mm high explosive rounds fired by the 555th FAB had no effect on the T-34s.[38] A couple of howitzers took direct hits from the T-34s, killing the gun crews. Prime movers were smashed by tank fire and exploded in blazing balls of fire. The surviving gun crews fought it out as infantry, often hand-to-hand, as the NKPA closed on the firing positions with burp guns, grenades and bayonets. Deployed in the open, without cover, the cannoneers were shot down by a merciless enemy.

Near the mouth of the pass, NKPA infantry fired from the ridge overlooking Pongam-ni and shot up a 4.2-inch mortar platoon emplaced below. Dog Company's Heavy Machine Gun Platoon returned fire from positions below the ridge, killing scores of the enemy silhouetted on the heights.[39]

Lieutenant Colonel Thomas Roelofs returned to his CP and did what he personally could to keep the trains moving through the intense small arms and automatic weapons fire. The bulk of the 5th RCT's trains made it through the pass before the T-34s put an end to LTC Roelofs' efforts. Trucks exploded, and burning drivers and passengers fell screaming to the ground, as the T-34s raked the column from point-blank range. The battalion commander ordered the 4.2-inch mortar platoon to disengage, and Dog Company's Heavy Machine Gun Platoon followed. Chaplain Francis A. Kapica's overloaded jeep filled with wounded soldiers brought up the rear.

After the 1st Battalion had assembled near the summit of the pass, CAPT Claude Baker urged LTC Roelofs to mount a counterattack.[40] Able and Baker Companies were relatively unscathed, and with the support of the 1st Tank Platoon, and the 4.2-inch Mortar Platoon, a counterattack might have succeeded. The artillery batteries were putting up considerable resistance, and defeat was by no means in sight. Lieutenant Colonel Roelofs disagreed, and the 1st Battalion broke contact on his orders. By 1000, the battered battalion was clear of the pass.

The situation facing the Triple Nickel was rapidly deteriorating. A handful of 105-mm howitzers returned fire for a couple of hours. The gun crews served their howitzers, praying for relief from their infantry comrades, while soldiers from Headquarters and Service batteries fought back with small arms and vehicular mounted .50-caliber machine guns.

North Korean infantry pressed home a pitiless assault and overran the gun positions in brutal close quarters fighting. Many of the cannoneers died where they stood. Master Sergeant Bertram F. Emerson, the first sergeant of Service Battery, was killed by burp gun fire.[41]

Further to the east, the NKPA ambushed a platoon from the 72nd Engineer Company. The NKPA struck the 159th FAB in turn and destroyed several ammunition trucks. The fury of the NKPA's massive assault was as awesome as it was deadly.

Master Sergeant Robert A. Tedford from the 25th Infantry Division's Reconnaissance Company

SGT Henry Awohi, Honolulu, was one of Service Battery's survivors during the engagement at Bloody Gulch. (sources: NA/Chang)

Sal Bosco. (source: Bosco family)

earned the Distinguished Service Cross, posthumously, attempting to rescue the embattled cannoneers. He boldly counterattacked with just two light tanks and died a soldier.[42]

Sergeant First Class Harry L. Chang, Territory of Hawaii, the Mess Sergeant for Headquarters Battery, 555th FAB, drove a truck mounting a .50-caliber machine gun above the cab into the open where he could engage the enemy with clear fields of fire. His automatic weapons fire forced the NKPA to flee in his sector.[43] Sergeant Chang's resolute stand saved the lives of many of his comrades and earned him the Bronze Star for valor.

Master Sergeant Rayburn M. Emrick, Tank Company's maintenance sergeant, loaded everyone he could cram into his armored recovery vehicle. This intrepid group shot their way through the NKPA and drove at high speed for Chindong-ni. Two mechanics, CPL Herbert C. Schuman and CPL Marshall Vanhoesen, perished in the fighting.[44]

Warrant Officer Sal Bosco, the Administrative Officer for Headquarters Battery, 555th FAB, took cover near an impromptu aid station under the concrete bridge that spanned the dry riverbed near Pongam-ni. A Marine helicopter landed at the height of the battle, bringing four boxes of the blood plasma to the beleaguered soldiers. Warrant Officer Bosco braved the intense automatic weapons fire to retrieve the plasma, an action that earned him a Bronze Star for valor.

As the medics treated the wounded, everyone knew the end was near. Warrant Officer Sal Bosco said, "We were pinned down under a bridge, some wounded including myself. My supply sergeant, SFC William A. Cooke, Jr., was very badly wounded. He had been machine gunned across the chest. He asked that we place sandbags across his chest to relieve the pain. This was done. About twenty-five of us were pinned down. We waited until dark and broke out down the river-bed heading south. We moved only at night and remained hidden during the day. It took us five nights to reach friendly lines, approximately twenty-five miles. Only five of us got back. The rest either were lost while traveling at night or were captured.[45]

The FDC section escaped in a truck that drove down a dry creek bed. Corporal Samuel Lewis was shot in the buttocks by a burp gun as he scrambled aboard the truck. After reaching Chindong-ni, CPL Lewis was evacuated to Japan.[46]

Most Triple Nickel survivors made it to safety on foot. Marine and Air Force fighter-bombers covered those survivors who avoided capture. Regretably, the NKPA captured fifty-five unfortunate souls from Headquarters, Service, and Able Batteries. After binding their arms and hands with wire, the NKPA murdered their captives.[47]

Meanwhile, back in the pass, SFC Richard F. Lewis led his six soldiers down the slope of the ridgeline at first light when they heard the convoy's engines crank over.[48] They reached the convoy in time to jump aboard their respective vehicles as the column moved out.

American automotive engineering saved Private Arlen Russell's life. The Artillery Survey Section withstood the NKPA's fire throughout the long night lying in a ditch beside the road. At daybreak, orders to mount up and drive clear of the ambush were given. Private Russell said, "The wire section 3/4 ton was driven by a wireman I remember as 'Okie.' I rode in the right seat firing at the hills and ditches on the right side of the road. I recall Okie had put the truck in four-wheel drive since both rear tires were flat. A rider who had jumped in the back of the truck as we started the run was not there when we caught up with the infantry. No one had any idea what happened to him. We assembled on the road with the infantry and tanks as the story of our comrades trapped in the dry riverbed began to filter among us. It was soon obvious that we survived the ambush because the NKPA was determined to destroy the gun batteries."[49]

When the extent of the disaster at Pongam-ni was finally understood at the 5th RCT CP, COL Ordway ordered the fatigued 2nd Battalion to retrace its steps and attack back into the pass. This was not an easy task because the 2nd Battalion was under heavy attack at the time. After the Rock's soldiers repulsed the NKPA assault, they moved out to rescue the beleaguered artillery. At 1500 LTC Throckmorton observed a large NKPA force infiltrating through the hills to attack the 5th RCT CP in his rear. He broke off the attack and established a perimeter defense around the regimental CP for the night.

The 25th Infantry Division War Diary stated, "Enemy activity which had been continuous and vigorous, exploded…. The 555th FAB (minus C Battery) and the 90th FAB (minus C Battery) were ambushed in the rear of the 1st Battalion 5th RCT positions at 120330 August 1950, in what appears to be an all out attack. Automatic weapons, mortars, selfpropelled guns, small arms, grenades and anti-tank rifles were used with devastating effect. These Field Artillery Battalions were also badly damaged by direct enemy artillery fire. Positions were overrun. Batteries were unable to displace or move part of the vehicles and equipment due to congestion on the road. All elements moved to the 2nd Battalion 5th RCT and Headquarters 5th RCT for local protection." The entry concluded with the wildly optimistic statement: "The enemy is encircled, expect to attack and destroy them on the morning of 13 August 1950."[50]

The 555th FAB lost between 75-100 soldiers KIA, 80 WIA, and virtually all its vehicles and six 105-mm howitzers at the battle the troops came to know as Bloody Gulch.[51] On the day following the massacre, the 555th FAB could muster just twenty percent of its soldiers.[52] The 90th FAB suffered heavy losses, too, losing 10 KIA, 60 WIA, 30 MIA, and six 155-mm howitzers.[53] The 1st Battalion had lost heavily, with C Company reduced in a single night from 180 to twenty-three men.[54]

The only bright spot in an otherwise abysmal day occurred early on the morning of 12 August when the 3rd Battalion shot to pieces an NKPA infantry company near Chinju. Lieutenant Randall Beirne woke up to the sight of a forest of bushes and trees advancing up the hill defended by Item Company on his flank. The enemy had tied small trees and bunches of leaves to their backs and was using this camouflage in hopes of advancing up the hillside undetected. Lieutenant Beirne explained, "This incident reminded me of the Birnam Woods in Shakespeare's 'Macbeth.' The 'woods' was rapidly moving up on I Company located on our flank. We called them up and informed them. Everyone opened fire like mad. No matter what that 'great military expert' said about the American soldier never firing his weapons, well that's a lot of baloney. Because our men certainly did. Our problem was keeping them from firing too much. We drove the NKPA company back, and that was our real introduction to combat."[55]

For the next couple of days, the 1st and 2nd Battalions, in cooperation with the 24th Infantry, attempted to regain control of the pass to destroy the "surrounded" enemy. A secondary mission to recover the large number of abandoned vehicles and guns, and the bodies of soldiers listed as missing in action (MIA), proved equally unattainable. Air strikes later destroyed much of this equipment. Most of the bodies were recovered in late September when the 25th Infantry Division broke out of the Pusan Perimeter.

The 3rd Battalion withdrew on order from its precarious positions near Chinju through the 35th Infantry and returned to Chindong-ni by way of Haman. The rest of the combat team followed on the same circuitous northern route to the original LD. Sonny's former drill sergeant, SFC Alfred S. Los Banos, was struck in the spine by gunfire during I Company's long march back to Chindong-ni. The brave man survived his wounds and represented all of Hawaii's veterans at ceremonial functions on the National and International scene, until he passed away.[56]

During the withdrawal, K Company marched past a 5th RCT communications vehicle that had been ambushed the night before. Dead American soldiers lay sprawled nearby in eternal sleep on the blood-soaked ground. From the position of the driver's body, and the damage inflicted on the burnt-out truck, LT Beirne surmised that he had hurled a white phosphorous grenade into the engine to prevent its capture before a burst of burp gun fire cut him down.[57]

Seoul City Sue, a North Korean radio an-

Charlie Company was given no time to lick its wounds. On 15 August it was in action in this burning town. (source: NA)

nouncer provided a rare moment of comic relief a few days after the battle, when she announced that the American soldiers defending the Pusan Perimeter were digging their own graves. She proceeded to illustrate her point by reading the names of the men killed at Bloody Gulch. Private First Class Albert Semasko, B Battery, 555th FAB, sat listening to her propaganda show with a couple of friends when she rattled off his name, too. It took a lot of good-natured argument before PFC Semasko convinced everyone that he was not a ghost. He had lost all his belongings when B Battery was overrun, including his dog tags, which explains how Seoul City Sue came to read his name off a list that hot August night so long ago. As for Seoul City Sue, she high-tailed it to Pyongyang when the Marines landed at Inchon.[58]

General Kean blamed the 5th RCT's losses at Bloody Gulch on COL Ordway. In COL Ordway's defense, the promised battalion from the 24th Infantry did not advance to the sound of the guns when the artillery came under heavy attack at Bloody Gulch. Rather, the infantry battalion retreated when it made contact with the NKPA.[59] On the other hand, LTC Roelofs' decision to break contact with the enemy was largely ignored. Still, COL Ordway's lapses in leadership played a significant role in the debacle. If the regimental commander realized his days were numbered, he did little to improve his stature.

On 15 August, MAJ Elmer Owens instructed 1st LT James Johnson to construct the regimental CP near the front lines. The combat engineers went to work building an access road and excavating the CP position on the reverse slope of a hill. Lieutenant Johnson took one squad to locate some timber for use as overhead protection. When he returned, the two squads left at the CP site had disappeared. He finally found SGT Parrish, with the two remaining squads, five miles farther east and a considerable distance from the front lines. The platoon sergeant informed LT Johnson that COL Ordway had personally ordered the platoon to construct the CP at the new site. The platoon had no

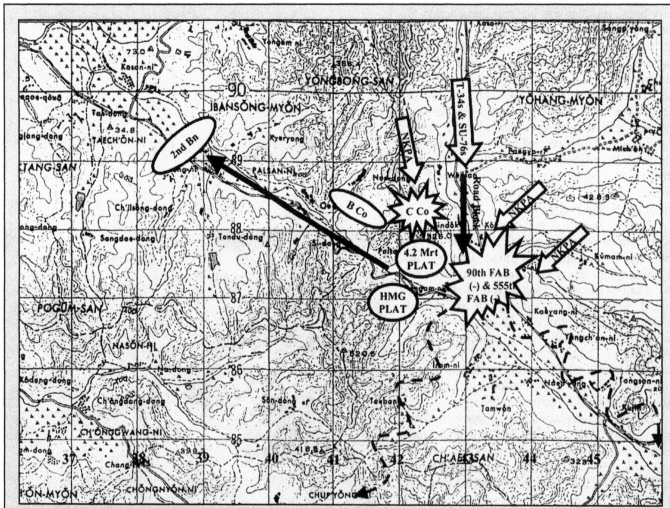

BLOODY GULCH, 12 AUGUST 1950. On the night of 11 August, the 2nd Battalion and C Battery punch through the pass. The NKPA strikes the poorly deployed 5th RCT elements still east of the pass before dawn on 12 August. C Company is overrun. Small arms fire hits the 5th RCT trains as they roll through the pass. A 5th RCT roadblock positioned north of the artillery disengages without orders. NKPA tanks and self-propelled guns attack down this road with considerable infantry support. The 1st Battalion moves out to join the 2nd Battalion (black line), but the artillery is cut off and unable to follow. Survivors break out in small groups (dotted lines).

sooner started working again, when MAJ Owens happened by and ordered LT Johnson to return to the original site.

The thoroughly bewildered soldiers returned to the original site and went back to work. All of a sudden, the Assistant Divisional Commander, Brigadier General Vennard Wilson, drove up and asked LT Johnson what he was doing. Lieutenant Johnson, who knew General Wilson from a previous assignment, replied, "Sir, I don't know." He proceeded to explain the day's bizarre turn of events to the general, who responded by directing the platoon leader to get into his jeep. They sped off to the 5th RCT's temporary CP where, on arrival, General Wilson stalked into the tent and demanded to know, "Where's COL Ordway?"

When one of the captains announced that COL Ordway was shaving, General Wilson icily replied, "Get him." Lieutenant Johnson recalled, "Colonel Ordway came running out. General Wilson said, 'Johnson, tell COL Ordway what you told me.' So I said, 'Sir, I don't know where you want that command post built. I keep getting conflicting orders.' He pointed at a map and said he wanted it built in the back location. Wilson looked at Ordway and said, 'I'll be God damned. Johnson, you build it where I saw you building it.' Then he said, 'You know, since I've been in the Army, normally there are two ways to do things, the right way and the wrong way.... Now there's the Ordway, and that's no damn good. You're relieved.'"[60]

The Eighth Army disbanded Task Force Kean on 16 August 1950.[61] General Walker's counteroffensive had achieved mixed results. The NKPA had clearly won a tactical victory at Bloody Gulch. On the operational level, however, Task Force Kean's blood sacrifice had temporarily blocked the North Korean offensive toward Pusan and had inflicted tremendous losses on the NKPA 6th Division and the 83rd Mechanized Regiment.

Of the combat team's three infantry battalions, the 1st was badly shaken, the 2nd a proven performer, while the 3rd remained relatively untested. Lieutenant Colonel John Throckmorton's daring night attacks had proven that, given aggressive leadership, the American soldier could beat the North Korean soldier on his own terms. Morale had suffered across the board, however, under the hammer blows of merciless NKPA assaults. The recent reverses and heavy losses had shaken everyone's faith in a quick and glorious victory. Harry Truman's "Police Action" was turning out to be quite a war.

CHAPTER NINE

SOBUK-SAN

Time and again, the hill changed hands and often different parts of the slopes were occupied by the 5th Infantry and the enemy. All three battalions of the 5th took their turn in the fight, allowing the exhausted attackers to withdraw to more quiet parts of the front to rest and reorganize. There were no reserves available due to the long front to be held. The 5th's fight at Sobuk-san was one of the outstanding performances of the Korean campaign. Ably led by Colonel Throckmorton, a cool-headed, courageous leader, the regiment made a proud record of itself. I saw a good deal of the 5th in those days and its three battalion commanders, Lieutenant Colonel Albert N. Ward, Jr., Benjamin W. Heckemeyer and Thomas B. Rollof [sic] were among the best the Army had.
Brigadier General G. B. Barth, Tropic Lightning and Taro Leaf in Korea: July '50 - May '51

To the probable annoyance of several ambitious colonels, General Kean personally selected LTC John Throckmorton to command the 5th RCT. The divisional commander viewed the Rock as a known quantity, an extremely competent leader who would get results out of the battered combat team. General Kean probably viewed the Rock's elevation to regimental commander as an opportunity to repay an old debt, for he had played the primary role in preventing LTC Throckmorton from commanding a battalion in World War II.

General Kean's choice elated the men. Private First Class Donald L. Gottschall, from Trenton, New Jersey, and an assistant gunner on a 4.2-inch mortar claims, "Colonel Throckmorton was the best regimental commander we ever had for the simple reason that he was all for the men."[1]

First Lieutenant Hank Emerson recalled a succinct leadership lecture LTC Throckmorton gave his officers after taking command. "Hey, listen up!" the Rock said. "You can not afford to ever, ever, let your men see you cold, hungry, tired, or afraid. You may feel and be all those things, but you must never let your men see you down. They are watching you and looking up to you. It is your duty never to let them down."[2]

The Rock had his hands full when he took command of the dispirited combat team as it reformed in a dry riverbed near Chindong-ni. Most of the men had not eaten a hot meal or slept more than a few hours a night over the last couple of weeks. Lieutenant Randall Beirne said, "You talk about disorganization and confusion. That was the 5th RCT at this time. Third Battalion had not taken many losses, but 1st and 2nd Battalions and the Triple Nickel had taken a lot of losses. As time went on, and LTC Throckmorton became known as 'the Rock,' the men developed a tremendous respect for him."[3] Lieutenant Keith Whitham noted that LTC Throckmorton was always up front, with map in hand, at the focal point of the battlefield.[4]

The 5th RCT staff at Sobuk-san. Seated (L to R): LTC Throckmorton and his XO, LTC Wes Blanchard. Standing (L to R): MAJ James Alcorn (S-1), CAPT James Pleasant (S-2), MAJ Elmer Owens (S-3). (source: Chang)

Lieutenant Colonel Albert N. Ward, Jr., assumed command of the 2nd Battalion. "As I recall," said 1st LT Norman Cooper, "he had fought in an armored infantry unit in Europe during World War II, either part of the 14th or 4th Armored. He knew how to fight the armor. If he told a tank platoon leader to do something, and that officer responded by saying, 'It can't be done,' he'd hop on the tank and say, 'I'll show you how.'"[5]

Lieutenant Colonel Ward was a consummate fighter. One of his brothers, a war correspondent with the *Baltimore Sun*, visited the battalion quite often in the early days of the war, which resulted in good press for the outfit. In combat, LTC Ward led from the front. "It wasn't unusual to see him on top of a tank giving the crew orders and making his own personal reconnaissance," said 1st LT Cooper. If he had a weakness, it was his fondness for the bottle. He would offer visiting senior officers a drink, an act one straight-laced general later failed to appreciate.

Lieutenant Colonel Ward immediately began to visit his companies to meet his officers and men. Whenever he visited a unit, LTC Ward invariably asked the soldiers to state their names. When the NCOs jokingly asked if he was trying to imitate LTC Throckmorton's gift for remembering names, the battalion commander would reply, "Well it wouldn't hurt."[6] He quickly gained the respect and confidence of his soldiers.

Lieutenant Colonel Throckmorton's hands were tied on some matters. Equipment, ammunition, and replacements remained in short supply. Heavy Mortar Company received a lousy "ten rounds per gun per day, and when it was fired we got no more ammo," recalled PFC Donald L. Gottschall.[7] Sergeant Anderson finally received six 57-mm high explosive rounds for his recoilless rifle. He was anxious to slam a high explosive round through the embrasure of a North Korean bunker.[8]

The 5th RCT quickly recovered from Bloody Gulch. The men demonstrated a remarkable resiliency that became the unit's hallmark in Korea. This resiliency had many fathers, which included LTC Throckmorton's assumption of command and the long period of mutual association that existed between the combat units. No matter how bad the situation, the 5th RCT's soldiers never lost confidence in the unit or in their leaders. Nowhere was this more evident than in the decimated ranks of the Triple Nickel.

Brigadier General Barth's artillery staff worked around the clock to repair the Triple Nickel to fighting trim. Guns, trucks, and radios originally destined for the ROK Army were redirected to Masan where the 555th FAB was in the process of rebuilding its shattered batteries.[9] Army reservists joined the 555th FAB in sufficient numbers to replace the brunt of the losses incurred during the brief Task Force Kean offensive.

Lieutenant Colonel Daly's wounds forced his evacuation to Tripler Hospital on Oahu, so Brigadier General Barth personally selected LTC Clarence E. Stuart to take command of the 555th FAB.[10] In Barth's words, "A heavy-set officer, Stuart was endowed with the highest qualities of leadership. He faced one of the toughest assignments that could befall a newcomer and, by his forceful manner, coupled with technical competence in artillery matters, quickly brought the 555th Field Artillery back to a state of high efficiency."

Lieutenant Colonel Stuart was a talkative man, who rarely used profanity. His favorite expression was "balls." He took the mission of supporting the infantry — or "my infantry" as he called them — very seriously.[11]

"Lieutenant Colonel Stuart was a real fine officer," said Master Sergeant Earl Law.[12] Like LTC Throckmorton, he was a sincere and energetic officer who favored his West Pointers in matters of assignments within the artillery battalion. Unlike the Rock, LTC Stuart was a former school teacher turned reserve officer who eventually transferred to the Regulars.

Many of the 555th FAB's officer replacements were inexperienced.[13] One officer, who did not join the 555th FAB until late October, described the Triple Nickel as an outfit that "could play beautiful music but couldn't read notes."[14] Very few of the replacement officers had been to the Artillery Advance Course, which resulted in an overall degradation of skill. The use of sophisticated meteorological messages and survey skills were rarely employed due to a lack of corporate knowledge in the unit.[15] One consequence was that the firing batteries became dependent on the artillery liaison spotter plane organic to the combat team to register fires. As soon as a battery went into position, the spotter plane would fly overhead, and the battery would adjust fire onto a prominent terrain feature. Subsequent fire missions were shifted from this known point — an archaic and time-consuming method. The 555th FAB's batteries adjusted onto a target by firing white phosphorous ammunition from the center platoon until an FO spotted the impact. Then the gun crews would switch over to high explosive ammunition to continue the adjustment.

Although the batteries practiced both low and high-angle fires in combat, LTC Stuart personally favored high-angle fire at a time when other artillery units in Korea refused to practice the technique, because it forced the artillery to fight from positions close behind the front lines. He believed the moral value of placing his guns within sight of the infantry outweighed the disadvantages.

Even a man of LTC Stuart's character had difficulties replacing LTC Daly who had been revered by his troops. Over time, LTC Stuart won their respect, but some of his idiosyncrasies often left their jaws flapping. One of these was his propensity to make quick personnel decisions. For instance, when Captain Walter H. Horton reported to the Triple Nickel, LTC Stuart assigned him to command Headquarters Battery without first checking the officer's qualifications in his personnel record. Thus CAPT Horton, who had been a gunnery instructor at Fort Sill, Oklahoma, was assigned to a post that failed to exploit his extensive gunnery skills at a time when the 555th FAB was desperately short of officers who possessed a similar high level of training.[16]

Self-propelled antiaircraft weapons reinforced the Triple Nickel

LTC Albert N. Ward, Jr. (right) and his radio operator in the Pusan Perimeter. (source: Chang)

at this time. These included M16 half-tracks armed with a power-driven turret mounting four .50-caliber machine guns, also known as the "Quad 50." A few of the older M15 A1 half-tracks, armed with a single 37-mm automatic cannon and two .50-caliber machine guns mounted in a revolving turret, rounded out the welcome increase in automatic weapons firepower.[17] Usually two M16s, or one M16 and one M15 A1, supported each firing battery. While few North Korean planes flew overhead at this stage of the war, the antiaircraft weapons were employed extensively in a fire support role. Their long-range automatic weapons firepower was highly esteemed by the infantry.

Service Battery quickly learned to obtain whatever the Triple Nickel required in the way of ammunition, vehicles, and equipment to get back into the fight. During this period, the firing batteries were enlarged to six guns apiece. Within days of the slaughter at Bloody Gulch, the Triple Nickel had three batteries laid on azimuths ready to prosecute fire missions.[18] "They didn't give us time to feel sorry for ourselves, which was good," said SFC Richard Lewis.[19]

Following the dissolution of Task Force Kean, the 25th Infantry Division transitioned to the defensive. The Tropic Lightning's sector of the MLR ran for twenty-five miles from Chindong-ni on the south coast, north to the junction of the Nam and Naktong rivers.[20] The 1st Provisional Marine Brigade was detached to serve as the Eighth Army's fire brigade along with the 27th Infantry "Wolfhounds." The Tropic Lightning, which retained just its organic 35th and 24th Infantry Regiments, was pleased to have both the 5th and 29th RCTs attached to its command. The NKPA, though badly bloodied, was pressing hard against the thin MLR. Retreat for the Americans was no longer an option. The Pusan Perimeter had to be held at all costs.

The 700-meter heights of the Pilbong and Sobuk-san mountains dominated the battlefield. The 24th Infantry Regiment was assigned the mission of defending the Pilbong Hills, known to the troops who fought there as "Battle Mountain." The 5th RCT defended farther south on an adjacent ridgeline. Sobuk-san, an even higher ridgeline that ran parallel to 5th RCT lines, remained in NKPA hands.

On 14 August, the 25th Infantry Division's weak regiments started to dig in on their defensive sectors. The 1st Battalion dug in on the combat team's right flank, along a ridgeline that in turn was overshadowed by the North Koreans who occupied Sobuk-san. There were too few men to occupy every meter of the MLR, so the rifle companies formed strong points on select pieces of high ground while doing their best to cover the numerous gaps with fire. The 2nd Battalion dug in on the central sector of the MLR, and the 3rd Battalion on the left. King Company held the left flank, its position anchored on low ground near the coast west of Chindong-ni.[21]

The Tropic Lightning's battalions were often forced by necessity to defend 8,000-yard frontages, contrary to the tactical tenet that a battalion front should not exceed 2,000 yards. A handful of ad hoc South Korean police units were inserted to fill a few of the gaps on the defensive line. Gun crews cleared fields of fire, and registered indirect fire weapons, while the infantry patrolled, and the engineers constructed obstacles, emplaced road blocks, and laid minefields to bolster the weak front lines. The Tropic Lightning war diarist recorded that "more than 1,200 miles of wire, 30,000 pickets and 350,000 sand bags would be required to prepare strong defensive positions over an area as large as the Division front."[22] The required engineer supplies were offloaded from ships at Masan and trucked to the front.

"There was never any linear defensive position ala World War II where you had tie in points and interlocking bands of fire between units," explained Lieutenant Hank Emerson. "There was too much space. So in effect what you had was a series of strong points right on the topographical crests that you could defend 360 degrees because it was so easy for the North Koreans to come through the gaps."[23]

The terrain in the 5th RCT's sector was devoid of roads. Ammunition, rations, water, and coils of barbed wire had to be hauled up the steep, craggy trails on strong backs. Conversely, wounded men had to be carried down the hills by teams of soldiers, usually at night, because NKPA fire often prevented medical evacuation during the day. As a result, even lightly wounded men occasionally succumbed to shock and died while awaiting evacuation.[24] The dead had to be rapidly evacuated, too, for in the harsh heat under the Korean sun, bodies

A Heavy Mortar Company gun crew in action near Sobuk-san, August 1950. (source: NA)

rapidly decompose. All forms of motorized transportation gave way to the stout backs and strong arms of the bone-weary soldiers.[25]

The Tropic Lightning authorized the 5th RCT to hire local civilians to carry supplies and equipment up the mountain, which helped to alleviate the physical demands made on the infantry. The soldiers had a lot of names for the Koreans who performed this vital logistical task, but the two that seemed to stick were "Chiggy trains" or "Chiggy bearers."

Reserves were few. First Lieutenant James Johnson's 1st Engineer Platoon, 72nd Engineers, was often LTC Throckmorton's sole hip-pocket reserve. Lieutenant Johnson recalled, "Many times my platoon was designated the regimental reserve, and I'd sit with LTC Throckmorton all night long waiting to be committed. And he would keep saying: 'I don't want to use you. I don't want to commit you.' Because if he committed me, that was it. He was a remarkable commander."[26]

Poor maps hindered the defensive effort, making it difficult for the FOs to direct accurate artillery and mortar fire. The Rock tackled the problem by sending LT Johnson to the top of the highest peak where he sketched the terrain in front of the companies. These maps, laboriously hand drawn with a pencil, were reproduced and proved remarkably effective.[27]

As the soldiers adjusted to the daily grind of battle, the men found time to write an occasional letter home.

Sonny wrote his first letter on 18 August from his fighting position near Chindong-ni.[28] "Dear Mom and Dad, I'm sorry I did not write sooner. Well hello. Are you folks all fine and in good health? I'm doing fine, although it's plenty rough at times. I miss Honolulu very much, but we'll be back soon. The boat ride was pretty good, and they gave me my shots on the ship. They showed a movie every night, and we played cards every day. They put out good food on the boat, and I gained six pounds. It took us nine days to get to Korea where we landed at Pusan. Korea is a funny place, lots of mountains and rice fields. Well to get on with the letter, after we hit Pusan, we spent the night there and one day. The next night we caught a train and it took us to Masan which is about 40 miles from Pusan. We spent the night there and half of the next day. We pulled out by truck and traveled about 40 miles to where there are guerrillas fighting. Our 5th Regiment joined the 27th [sic] Division. We helped them out. Oh. I forgot to mention that it is plenty hot, and I mean hot. All we do is drink water. We are eating rations three times a day. When we reached this point we had to climb the mountains, and it is hard climbing. We are now pushing them back, but slowly. We are now on the top of a mountain and have been up here for three days. I'm writing this letter on the mountain in my trench. Please excuse my handwriting and the dirty paper for my hands are plenty dirty. I haven't taken a bath in five days and I'm black like a Negro. Sunburn. Oh boy. This a good place to catch a tan, but the hard way. Well say hello to all my friends, and most of all to Lona, who I miss a heck of a lot. Tell her I said hello and that I'll write to her next time. There is a shortage of paper and each man gets only three pieces. Well goodby for now and don't worry about me. I'll be back soon."

A handful of infantry replacements trickled in to join the 5th RCT after Task Force Kean was disbanded. Their numbers were insufficient to bring the depleted rifle squads up to full strength. One replacement assigned to the 3rd Battalion was KIA on his first day on the line before his squad had a chance to even learn his name.[29]

The desperate manpower situation facing the Eighth Army called for a radical solution. On 19 August, General Walker sanctioned the Korean Augmentation to the U.S. Army (KATUSA) program to provide his depleted combat units desperately needed replacements. According to the Tropic Lightning, "Beginning immediately untrained Korean Army personnel will be assigned to each company or battery level unit until 100 are in each such units."[30] The intent was to pair each KATUSA with a U.S. Army soldier who was expected to assist the ROK soldier in his training.

A KATUSA soldier was the product of a government press gang. After being issued a uniform and a rifle, he found himself thrust into the midst of foreigners who ate strange food, spoke an incomprehensible language, and who knew little of Korean culture or history. Many KATUSA soldiers were under age by U.S. Army standards, mere boys in their teens. Few American soldiers could correctly pronounce the names of the KATUSAs assigned to their unit. Nicknames became the norm.

The first seventy-three KATUSAs reported to the 5th RCT on 20 August.[31] Over the course of the next three years, hundreds followed. Not surprisingly, a combination of cultural and linguistic difficulties impeded the effectiveness of the KATUSA program.[32] An American soldier had much to worry about in combat without the added burden of shepherding an untrained South Korean conscript who most likely did not speak English. A handful of KATUSA soldiers proved stellar performers, most did their jobs, and a few were a major headache for their American officers and NCOs. Sadly enough, this desperate expedient, which might have worked well in peacetime, proved an unmitigated disaster in most Eighth Army combat units at this early stage of the war. The 1st Cavalry Division war diarist explained, "The integrated Korean soldiers proved to be unsatisfactory. All CO's [sic] reported that most of these men break and run when attacked and that they cannot control them in battle due to language difficulties. It is also becoming evident that most of the casualties are GI's and when the stragglers are reorganized it is found that the companies are mainly South Korean. Many of our enlisted men have threatened to shoot the SKs."[33]

One KATUSA, SGT Kang Sin Kwan, served as an interpreter in George Company. Sergeant Kwan's military career began in 1941 when he was dragooned into the service of the Imperial Japanese Army while attending Seoul University. After service in Manchuria, he was sent to the Philippines where he was captured by American forces in August 1945. At the outbreak of the Korean War, he joined the ROK Army and was assigned to the 5th RCT. In September 1951, he played an instrumental role in the capture of 313 enemy soldiers.[34]

Sonny mailed another letter to his parents on 20 August to announce that he had been awarded the Combat Infantryman's Badge for his participation in Task Force Kean. On Red Cross stationery, Sonny wrote, "How are you getting along? Swell I hope. As for me I'm doing all right. I miss you folks very much. Buddy and Manley too. Well down here the Army is doing pretty good. I can't say very much because they might censor this letter. All we do is keep on the move, climbing mountains, making long marches and so on. It's very hot and there are plenty of mosquitoes. It's hard to sleep at night. Many a times I wish I was home in my own bed because it was so big and soft, and there was always that cool ocean breeze. We have to sleep out in the open on the ground, and if we are lucky we get a blanket. Most of the time we don't even sleep straight, it's on a hill or in a foxhole, which is very uncomfortable. Every night we pull guard duty, which is about two hours a night, and then everybody is up at 5 o'clock in the morning. We are now digging in on another hill, and the kitchens are only about a mile away, so that means we get hot food 2 times a day. I lost about 10 pounds, but don't worry, I'll gain it back. Well I don't know too much news about the war, and we don't even know the date sometimes. Do you folks get much news about the war there? I guess you know more about it than we do. Do you get any news about the 5th INF? All I can say is that I hate Korea, and I want to get home soon. Daddy, how is my car? Please don't sell it. I made PFC again, and we all went up for corporal, but I don't know if we'll make it right away. We get $5 more a day for combat duty, and $10 more a month for some kind of combat badge, which I will be wearing on my uniform when I get back. If I make corporal, I'll be making $147 a month. If I get paid during battle, I plan on sending it to you Daddy. I made out an allotment for $60 to you Dad. Tell Mommy to buy some clothes and Buddy and Manley some Levies. All the rest of the money is kept by the Army until we go back. They will pay it to us at one time. Who knows, I'll probably have enough to pay all my bills and still have enough to save for the future. Take care of yourselves. When I get back we'll throw a big party, and then Mommy will cook some good food and I'll get fat. Then I'll sleep for two weeks. Well, I'll be waiting to hear from you. God Bless you. Your son, Sonny."

First Lieutenant Norman W. Cooper assumed command of Fox Company on 19 August.[35] He relieved CAPT Alexander Kahapea who had fallen ill with dysentery during the Task Force Kean offensive. Captain Kahapea served as the combat team's Grave Registration Officer when he recovered, a thankless but necessary task.

Lieutenant Cooper saw things he did not like and immediately took corrective action. Henceforth, he ordered Fox Company to keep their bayonets fixed at all times. He taught his men several tricks he had learned in the previous war. NKPA infiltrators had often succeeded in drawing Fox Company's fire at night. The resulting muzzle flashes betrayed the location of Fox Company's weapons, providing excellent targets for NKPA mortars. Fox Company learned to reply to infiltration attempts with grenades, rather than rifle fire.

The 2nd Battalion was thinly stretched across the mountainous terrain. "Easy Company was on the left and George Company on the right," said LT Cooper.[36] "Fox Company was in reserve when I took over the company." The next day, Fox Company moved up on George Company's right flank where LT Cooper's machine gun training as an enlisted man in World War II was useful. Fox Company's prime defensive position enabled it to bring flanking fire to bear when the NKPA attacked George Company. A detachment from the Constabulary Police was dug in on Fox Company's right flank. Everyone was relieved when A Company moved up a couple of days later and replaced the South Koreans.

C Battery soldier inserts fuses. (source: NA)

Second Lieutenant James C. Anguay, from Oahu, was Sonny's platoon leader. He and LT Cooper were the only officers left in Fox Company. Like Sonny, LT Anguay was a last-minute filler. "He was a fine officer and an aggressive combat leader," said LT Cooper of his 1st Platoon Leader.[37]

A replacement officer, who joined Fox Company a few days later on its defensive positions, did not receive a rave review. "I can't take this," said the officer. "I cracked up in World War II."

Lieutenant Cooper replied, "I'm not running a nursery. I'm trying to fight a war here, and I don't have any choice but to assign you to a rifle platoon."[38] So this officer, a psychological cripple from the previous war, took over the 2nd Rifle Platoon.

Fox Company quickly adjusted to the war fought in the rugged mountains, a jumbled mass of rocky terrain that contained other terrors besides North Korean soldiers. One evening, Private Gerald Pack, a BAR man in Fox Company's 2nd Platoon, witnessed a soldier who jumped

Able Company, August 1950. (sources: NA/Chang)

into a foxhole only to encounter some kind of wild animal. After much snarling and roaring on the part of the animal, and screaming and cursing on the part of the hapless soldier, they both jumped out of the hole and ran in opposite directions. People swear to this day that the animal was a mountain lion. Private Pack believes this incident caused more firing than an NKPA attack.[39]

The front opposite the 5th RCT remained relatively quiet until 20 August when its 1st Battalion conducted an attack to seize the crest of Sobuk-san. From this vantage, the NKPA enjoyed unlimited observation into American lines. The Rock was determined to do something about it.

The 1st Battalion, minus A Company, reached the crest after encountering light resistance. Later that afternoon the NKPA reacted violently to this success and conducted a furious counterattack with two battalions. The Triple Nickel fired 1,093 rounds in support of the 1st Battalion on Sobuk-san, but the NKPA regained the mountain crest.[40]

General Kean ordered LTC Throckmorton to seize Sobuk-san. Lieutenant Colonel Roelofs' 1st Battalion crossed the LD shortly after noon the next day. Once again Able Company remained in reserve. An estimated 1,000 NKPA defenders put up a terrific fight as the sweat-drenched, dust-covered American infantry clawed their way up the rocky slopes.[41] The North Korean defenders had to be beaten down with artillery, mortar and small arms fire.[42] Desperate fighting raged across the last 100 yards of fire-swept ground as squad leaders employed their BARs to suppress the enemy's defenses. The soldiers advanced in short rushes, panting from the heat and exertion, their parched throats choked from dust and fear, firing their rifles at fleeting targets. Once the soldiers reached the crest, platoon leaders had their men consolidate on the position. The men could not dig in on the rocky ground, so they piled up boulders for protection in anticipation of the inevitable North Korean counterattack.[43]

Five 5th RCT soldiers were buried in the Masan Cemetery as the fighting raged that day on Sobuk-san. PFC Johnny D. Light, B Company; Private Clifford A. Barber, E Company; Corporal Edward T. Weaver, company unknown; Corporal Samuel Keomaka, I Company; and "Unknown X-26," were laid to rest in temporary graves.[44] During the first twenty-two days of August, the 5th Infantry had incurred 57 KIA, 346 WIA, 115 MIA, and 281 non-battle casualties.[45]

American and North Korean lines were intermingled on the long, narrow, and jagged crest of Sobuk-san, well within grenade range of one another. Incessant fighting raged for possession of Sobuk-san throughout August and into September.[46] Platoon leaders and company commanders encountered tactical dilemmas never discussed in the hallowed halls of Fort Benning.

First Lieutenant Randall Beirne, a platoon leader in K Company, wrote home on 22 August, "We've been on defense for about a week awaiting an attack. Thus have had time to write a few letters. We've been lucky and only had four casualties. One company today on assault had thirty-nine. This was nine killed including two officers, one an old buddy of mine. This company was trying to take a position attempted by C Company the other day. C Company reached the top and came on the bodies of two companies of Negroes of 24th RCT who slept one night and were overrun. They'd been there a week. C Company's CO went out of his head and ran down the hill. All the company followed. They carried seventy bodies down that night. The moral is you can't sleep in your foxhole at night. All is not beautiful."[47]

By luck, the 3rd Battalion's war was easier than that experienced by her sister battalions embroiled in the struggle for Sobuk-san. Destroyers patrolled off the coast, and the first sailors soon came ashore looking for souvenirs. The soldiers were willing to trade and an informal pact was quickly made on the beach. In return for gallons of ice cream, the soldiers supplied the sailors captured enemy equipment, particularly burp guns. What the sailors did with their burp guns is yet another lesser mystery of the Korean War.[48]

The Navy's real mission here had little to do with either ice cream or burp guns. A destroyer's 5-inch guns were capable of extremely accurate, high volume, flat trajectory gunfire support. On several occasions the destroyers intervened in the fighting on Sobuk-san with excellent results. Unfortunately, the command and control apparatus for Naval gunfire was deficient. Unlike the Marines, who had Naval gunfire spot teams equipped with communications gear compatible with that mounted on the ships, the 5th RCT could not communicate directly with the destroyers. Requests for Naval gunfire had to be processed through the Tropic Lightning's FSCC, which in turn maintained a Naval gunfire liaison section equipped with the appropriate communications equipment to relay targeting information to the destroyers. At best this was a time-consuming, cumbersome arrangement. At worst, it led to an unexpected and tragic incident when an over-ambitious destroyer mistakenly opened fire one day on a 3rd Battalion patrol, slamming round after round into the hapless men. Frantic radio calls to the 25th Infantry Division finally halted the shelling, but not before several men had been killed and wounded.[49]

American air power saw to it that the front opposite the 3rd Battalion remained quiet in the day. In the heat of the afternoon, it was not unusual for small groups of soldiers to move forward of the MLR to partake in a cool bath in one of the wells commonly found in the abandoned villages. The greatest challenge facing small unit leaders was simply keeping their tired men alert at night. When the men were not improving the battalion's defensive positions, they were out patrolling day and

Baker Company in action on Sobuk-san.
(source: 25th ID Museum/Chang)

night. Sleep was a precious commodity, an essential body function usually performed in daylight. Those who failed to remain alert at night often paid the price. North Korean soldiers were extremely adept with their sharp knives.

In the NKPA's arsenal of weapons, the one the soldiers feared the most was the Soviet manufactured 120-mm mortar. Every NKPA infantry regiment had a battery of these deadly, versatile weapons. Corporal Ronald Denton, who served in the Heavy Mortar Company, explained, "You could usually hear North Korean artillery shells coming at you and take cover. Not so with their 120s. We'd get a few 4.2-inch rounds out of our tubes, and BLAM! BLAM! BLAM! the 120s would come down our throat. The North Korean gunners were good, too damn good. And you never heard the incoming. We lost a lot of boys to the 120s."[50]

Counterbattery fire was the best antidote for the 120-mm mortars, but the Eighth Army's supply of artillery ammunition was rapidly dwindling. On 23 August, the Eighth Army informed 25th Infantry Division that the supply of 105-mm howitzer ammunition had turned critical. Every round had to count.[51]

As the fighting raged on Sobuk-san, commanders attempted to take care of their men. Whenever possible, the soldiers were served hot meals. Beer breweries in the United States pitched in to help, distributing tens of thousands of cases of free beer to the troops. Lieutenant Randall Beirne said, "The men usually received a hot ration and a hot can of beer in the afternoon. After eating their meal, the men would place their can of beer near their foxhole. In the morning, when the can of beer had cooled, it was enjoyable to drink. That hot meal and cool beer were important to the men. Real morale builders."[52]

On 23 August, Sonny wrote, "It's hot during the day here and very cold during the night. We are now on another hill. We had a little rain the other night, and everything was damp and cold, but the sun came out bright the next day and everything got dry. You see, all we have is a blanket. That is I do, but some boys have a shelter half. They feed us hot chow now twice a day and rations in between. We get pretty good food - steaks, chicken, and pancakes for breakfast. We get fruit such as mixed fruit, peaches and cherries. Then we get fruit juices such as tomato, V8 and grapefruit juices. We get candy, cigarettes and beer, two cans per man about every other day. So they take pretty good care of us. The other day me and Kenawell took a hot shower and then a swim in fresh water. We get a bath only once a week, although we can wash our face about every day. I had a long beard, but I shaved it off."

While Sonny was writing home, the 1st Battalion fought a ferocious duel with the NKPA for control of Sobuk-san. That morning, LTC Thomas Roelofs directed A Company, commanded by CAPT Robert L. Timmons, to conduct a reconnaissance in force three miles in front of friendly lines to locate the North Korean positions on Sobuk-san, and so they did.

First Lieutenant Charles L. Worley had fought in the Pacific with the Marines in World War II. He was from Valdosta, Georgia. After the war, he graduated from North Georgia University and accepted a commission in the Army. He led a rifle platoon in A Company and was best friends with LT Hank Emerson, another rifle platoon leader. Neither officer was particularly happy with the idea of being used as bait. That the NKPA was present in great force on Sobuk-san was obvious to all the men who saw no need to walk into a trap waiting to be sprung. Both platoon leaders voiced their reservations to CAPT Timmons in a dry river bed before the company moved out. He agreed with his platoon leaders and attempted to convince LTC Roelofs to change his mind — to no avail.

When CAPT Timmons returned with the grim news, the rifle platoons prepared to move out. Shortly before they crossed the LD, the company administrator, Warrant Officer Junior Grade Carl E. Sabo, approached the two lieutenants to wish them good luck.[53] Lieutenant Worley gave him his wallet and a few items from his pocket, and said, "Please send these to my family. I'm going to get killed today."

"Oh come on Chuck," interjected LT Emerson. "I don't want to hear this shit!"

"No really, I am," replied his fatalistic friend.[54]

The platoons moved out, with LTs Emerson's and Worley's in the lead. Able Company's final objective was a high peak on a jagged ridgeline. After a hard uphill march under the fierce August sun, the company reached an intermediate objective, a small knoll that had a few scraggly trees growing on it. This in itself was a rather odd sight on the scorched brown slopes of Sobuk-san, because the Japanese had cut down most of the trees to produce charcoal before World War II. The soldiers did not have time to appreciate the beauty of nature or to contemplate Korean history, for when A Company reached the inviting shade of the trees, the NKPA opened fire.

"We were just getting reorganized when sure as shit here it comes from all directions," said LT Emerson. "They had us zeroed in. Criss-crossing fire and 120-mm mortar rounds crunching in. We were right in their kill zone."

Captain Timmons ran up and joined LTs Emerson and Worley who lay crouched behind the crest of the knoll. Tracers ricocheted off nearby rocks, and shrapnel whizzed through billowing clouds of oily smoke and choking dust, as the three officers tried to locate the enemy gun positions.

SFC David K. Broad, Laie, Oahu. (source: Chang)

"What do you think we should do?" asked CAPT Timmons.

"Jesus Christ we got to get out of here!" LT Emerson shouted above the roar. "Let's take the whole company and attack towards the hill on the right. Right now we're in a kill zone." Lieutenant Worley agreed with his friend. An NKPA machine gun team must have seen the three officers crouched together, pointing and gesticulating with their hands, for right about then, a burst of automatic weapons fire raked the position. One round ripped through LT Worley's heart and killed him instantly. "Sir, let's take the company and attack the hill on the right," implored LT Emerson as he gazed at the body of his friend.

Captain Timmons responded, "We have so many casualties that I think I have to protect them. Will you take your platoon?"

"Hell yes, Sir!" replied LT Emerson. He turned and yelled down the slope to his platoon sergeant that the platoon was moving out. Sergeant Robert L. Lyons, a nineteen-year-old professional soldier who had enlisted at the age of fifteen, understood and passed the word to the men. Meanwhile, LT Emerson dashed about forty yards, running from cover to cover, until he took shelter in a shell hole near his platoon. He yelled to SGT Lyons that they were going to move out and take the hill. A soldier sharing the shell hole with LT Emerson died about this time, his back shredded by shrapnel.[55]

Lieutenant Emerson was about to lead the attack when another soldier shouted that CAPT Timmons was hit. The platoon leader ran back up the knoll where he found the company commander lying on the ground with a gaping, bloody hole in his side, big enough to stick a fist into, obviously a mortal wound. Captain Timmons was still trying to command the company, ashen faced, calling on the radio for fire support, when he mercifully drifted into unconsciousness. After LT Emerson gave his company commander a shot of morphine and dressed the wound, he eased the radio mike out of his company commander's grasp and was startled to hear the calm, soothing, voice of his regimental commander, LTC Throckmorton, on the other end of the line.

"What's the situation?" asked the Rock.

"Well, I can't count how many casualties we have," replied LT Emerson. "Captain Timmons is down."

"What do you think you should do?" asked LTC Throckmorton.

"I think we should take the whole company and attack the hill on the right," answered LT Emerson.

"Well, you take what you can get and attack that hill on the right, but leave enough men behind to protect the wounded and the bodies," instructed LTC Throckmorton.

The company XO was a World War II infantry combat veteran whom the men called "Cactus Jack." He ran up to see what was going on, but before LT Emerson could explain the tactical situation Cactus Jack blurted out, "I can't handle this shit!" and took off running. In the confusion, five or six soldiers followed him, running for their lives down the hill.[56]

Lieutenant Emerson stopped the rout and mounted an attack against an NKPA position located on a small rise to his right front. After bitter fighting, Able Company overran the NKPA position later that afternoon. The artillery FO helped LT Emerson to control the situation. Captain Timmons perished about this time, having succumbed to his wounds. Able Company's soldiers had expended most of their ammunition in the fighting, an uncomfortable predicament, because the situation was deemed ripe for an NKPA counterattack. Worse, an NKPA assault troop had cut behind LT Emerson and succeeded in overrunning the men detailed to protect the casualties on the tree-covered knoll.

Lieutenant Emerson was informed that 200 Chiggy bearers were on the way up the hill to resupply his company with water and ammunition. They never arrived. The NKPA overran the unarmed, overloaded South Korean porters, who fell shrieking and pleading to the ground as the North Koreans emptied their burp guns and tossed grenades into the screaming mass of helpless souls.

Lieutenant Emerson withdrew his decimated company and led the men down the hill by a circuitous route until the soldiers reached the morning's LD where the exhausted men bivouacked for the night. The next morning, LT Emerson, now confirmed as the CO of A Company, led his men back up another hill that they captured in a brisk firefight. For the next nineteen days, Able Company repulsed assault after assault as the enraged NKPA attempted to wrest control of the hill. In two days of fighting, the 5th Infantry reported the loss of 9 KIA, 55 WIA, and 11 MIA.[57] The mind numbing paper work that accompanies modern armies to the field had yet to record A Company's casualties incurred on the bitter slopes of Sobuk-san.

Baker Company was shaping up into a superb combat outfit on Sobuk-san under 1st LT Pappy Young's sure hand. Sergeant Robert Middleton said, "I want to say one thing about Kermit Young. I don't know where it was at, or what hill it was on. But they told us to attack a hill, and we didn't get to the top of it before it got dark. We started to dig in and we got hit all night long. And all through this Banzai, Kermit Young was up walking, telling us to keep calm, keep firing. We lost a lot of men up there that night. Dead plus casualties. I'd say, out of Baker Company, very few men walked off that hill the next morning."[58]

On 23 August, the NKPA struck Baker Company in daylight as the two opposing sides grappled for control of a disputed ridgeline. Sergeant Middleton, the platoon sergeant of 2nd LT Martin L. Pitts' 1st Platoon, answered a ringing field phone in the middle of the firefight. From the far end of the line, a BAR man dug in on the tip of a finger shouted that he was nearly out of ammunition. Sergeant Middleton dispatched his runner, who ran down the finger with an armful of bandoleers. An NKPA machine gun took the lad under fire, and a burst from this weapon knocked him down in a bloody heap on the rocky ground well short of the BAR position.

The platoon sergeant jumped out of his hole with ammunition for the BAR and ran down the finger as slugs from the enemy machine gun kicked up dust around his feet. He reached the BAR man, took the weapon out of his hand, loaded a magazine, aimed in, and killed the NKPA machine gun crew. His satisfaction was short lived. Almost immediately thereafter, another NKPA soldier off to his right emptied a burp gun magazine at SGT Middleton from close range. The platoon sergeant was evacuated down the hill, bleeding heavily from several bullet wounds, including one that penetrated his cheekbone and lodged behind an eye. Sergeant Middleton reached Osaka, Japan, where Army doctors operated successfully to save his eye. To this day, fine pieces of shrapnel continue to work their way out of his damaged eye.[59]

Throughout the day on 25 August, sporadic mortar and flat trajectory weapons fire slammed into the 5th RCT's defensive positions. Unknown to the American soldiers, the newly arrived NKPA 7th Division was registering its weapons prior to commencing an all-out assault. At 2130, the NKPA commenced a vicious pounding of the 1st Battalion's positions with direct fire artillery, recoilless rifles, antitank guns, and automatic weapons fire. For two hours, the North Koreans flailed the defenders, setting the stage for a determined infantry assault.[60]

Long lines of North Koreans advanced up the ridge, the shrill, eerie wailing of their bugles sending shivers of fear down many a defender's spine. Their path lit by parachute flares and burning brush, the NKPA assault formations materialized out of the darkness fifteen minutes before midnight. Screaming "Manzai!" the merciless North Koreans ran forward, hurling grenades and firing their burp guns from the hip.[61] The enemy directed his main effort at C Company, and the impact of the assault sent many American soldiers reeling in disorder down the slope. Others held their ground, defending their positions with resolute valor and grim determination. The battle raged throughout the night, as the North Koreans charged again and again, seeking an opening in the thin American lines.

Master Sergeant Melvin O. Handrich was one of a handful of men on whom the burden of victory or defeat rested that night. When an estimated force of 150 NKPA soldiers hit C Company during the initial assault, MSGT Handrich was in the thick of the fighting, calmly directing the defensive effort of his soldiers. Charlie Company had been skittish ever since its mauling at Bloody Gulch, and it took a great deal of effort on MSGT Handrich's part to keep his men glued to their fighting positions. After the soldiers repulsed the initial NKPA assault, a group of 100 North Koreans attempted to infiltrate Charlie Company's lines. Master Sergeant Handrich left the safety of his foxhole to crawl forward where he could direct artillery and mortar fires on the NKPA infiltrators. He remained there for the next eight hours directing fire on the enemy who approached to within fifty feet of his position. At dawn, a skirmish line of North Koreans advanced at a rush in yet another attempt to overrun Charlie Company, but they had not counted on one lone soldier who rose to his feet and fired from the off-hand position clip after clip of ammunition into the attackers. When MSGT Handrich ran out

MSGT Melvin O. Handrich as a SGT at Schofield Barracks. (source: Walter Woelper)

2nd Battalion soldiers enjoy mail call at a roadblock near Sobuk-san. (source: NA)

of targets, he continued to direct artillery and mortar fire onto suspected NKPA positions. At the height of this action, MSGT Handrich observed a group of soldiers who had abandoned their position without orders. With complete disregard for his own personal safety, he ran back across the fire-swept ground to the men. Through his forceful example, and probably a few well-deserved kicks in the butt, he reorganized the defenders and put the heart back into their fight. He returned to his position and recommenced calling in indirect fires on the enemy. Later that morning, the NKPA overran MSGT Handrich's position and mortally wounded the brave soldier. Charlie Company counterattacked and recovered MSGT Handrich, who died shortly thereafter. Over seventy dead NKPA were found on or near his position. Master Sergeant Handrich's comrades recommended him for the Medal of Honor, a posthumous award that was presented to his widow in April 1951.

Dog Company's 81-mm Mortar Platoon had established firing positions behind piles of stacked rocks on the reverse slope of the ridge behind Charlie Company. Near daylight, a large group of infantry broke under the relentless pressure and abandoned their positions on the contested ridgeline, running through the mortar pits as the astonished gun crews looked on.

Captain Carter D. Hilgard, who until recently had served as the battalion operations officer, had commanded C Company since his predecessor was wounded during the initial assault up Sobuk-san. Captain Claude Baker, the CO of Dog Company, came across CAPT Hilgard in the middle of the fight as both officers strove to turn Charlie Company's terrified soldiers around. Captain Baker told Captain Hilgard to run down the right side of the line to rally the men as he took off to do the same on the left side. As CAPT Hilgard attempted to regain control of his company, a burst of gunfire ended his life.[62]

Corporal Kenny Freedman was manning his 81-mm mortar when soldiers from Charlie Company ran past his position just before dawn graced the eastern sky. North Korean self-propelled guns and mortars had been pounding the 81s intermittently throughout the night. The dust-and-smoke-filled air added to the surreal, confusing situation. Corporal Freedman saw a soldier he recognized running by, grabbed him, and pulled the infantryman down, yelling, "Where are you going? Just where in the Hell do you think you're going?"

"I'm getting out of here! They're right behind us," exclaimed the soldier. "The gooks are coming! They're right behind me!"

"Get a hold of yourself!" shouted CPL Freedman.

"I'm shot damn it! I'm shot in the back," shouted the soldier. Corporal Freedman treated the soldier's wound and picked up his rifle to join the fight.[63]

Rifle and machine gun fire picked up in intensity as swarms of NKPA infantry spilled over the crest and started shooting at the mortar crews positioned behind their rock walls. The soldiers leveled their rifles and carbines over the rocks and returned a brisk fire into the thick dust and acrid smoke, aiming for the occasional muzzle flash that one could observe in the predawn darkness. The situation was one of noise, terror, and confusion - victory or defeat held by a slender thread.

Captain Claude Baker emerged out of the dust and darkness to rally his men. "Dog Company, let's go! Let's retake this damn hill!" he shouted above the din.[64] The mortar platoon followed their company commander up the hill, shooting their rifles from the hip, advancing over intermingled bodies of dead and wounded friends and foe alike. The NKPA broke before the fury of the unexpected counterattack and ran away.

Dog Company recovered the dead and wounded after the fighting finally subsided. Corporal Kenny Freedman searched the ground for Corporal Donald W. Mann, one of his friends in the Heavy Machine Gun Platoon who had been attached to Charlie Company before the fight. When CPL Mann's best friend, SGT William J. Poole, had been KIA two days before, CPL Freedman had attempted to cheer up the distraught machine gunner. Corporal Freedman reached CPL Mann's position and found his friend sprawled on the blood-soaked ground, both legs blown off below the knees, lying unconscious beside his demolished machine gun. He carried his friend down the ridge to the aid station. Along the way, CPL Mann regained consciousness and asked him what had happened. Corporal Freedman told his buddy, "Hang on. You'll be OK." When they reached the casualty collection point, CPL Mann was already dead. After lowering CPL Mann to the ground, CPL Freedman placed one of his friend's dog tags between the valiant machine gunner's teeth, just like he had been taught to do in one of his pre-war training lectures so long ago. "He had a gold front tooth. I remember that," recalled CPL Freedman.

The 1st Battalion's defensive victory had hinged on the skill and valor of its determined infantrymen and on the massed fires of the Tropic Lightning's divisional artillery. General Barth's batteries fired 129 missions and claimed the destruction of two artillery pieces, three machine guns, four mortars and three trucks. More importantly, "extremely heavy casualties were inflicted and assisted in stopping enemy attack in 5th RCT area."

Lieutenant Colonel Thomas Roelofs remained in his CP during the fighting that crucial day for Sobuk-san. Neither he, nor the newly reported XO, MAJ John K. Eney, appeared on the firing line apparently out of a belief that, in a defensive engagement, the battalion commander should remain in the CP where he could direct the battle. Lieutenant Colonel Roelofs' absence from the firing line resulted in a regrettable source of friction between himself and his company commanders.[65]

Just before the NKPA assault, as flares illuminated the darkness, and green and red tracers crisscrossed the disputed ridge, CAPT Claude Baker had submitted an urgent request for an ammunition resupply which, strangely enough, in view of the critical tactical situation, was denied. The battalion supply officer informed him that MAJ Eney had refused to let the Chiggy trains operate at night because they might get lost. Captain Baker got MAJ Eney on the line and told him that he needed ammunition immediately; and if the XO refused to send it, then the least he could do was "to get his ass up here and do some fighting if he couldn't do anything else!" Captain Baker got his ammunition.[66]

Second Lieutenant Vernon Jernigan was the first man in King Company to die in Korea. The Honolulu police officer had earned a commission in the reserves and was performing his annual stint on active duty when the war erupted. He heard the bugle calls and volunteered to accompany the 5th RCT to Korea. Lieutenant Jernigan paid the blood price for his patriotism.

On 27 August, LT Jernigan led his platoon on a daylight patrol into enemy territory. A Marine Graves Registration Team accompanied the patrol in the hopes of recovering the remains of Marines reported MIA a few weeks before in this area. A couple of 5th RCT ordnance sergeants went along to blow up a few abandoned NKPA 45-mm antitank guns a previous patrol had found.

Lieutenant Jernigan made two mistakes that played a role in his death. First, the gold bars he proudly wore on his collar glinted brilliantly in the light of a harsh, burning, remorseless sun. Second, he led his patrol down a well-traveled road just as if he was walking a beat in Honolulu. The soldiers and Marines walked in a column of twos, with their weapons pointed outboard, at the ready. Lieutenant Jernigan walked down the middle of the road between his men. An NKPA patrol spotted the column and set-up a hasty ambush in a nearby rice paddy. The astute North Koreans identified the leader of the American unit by observing his flashing rank insignia and position in the column. When LT Jernigan entered the killing zone, an NKPA soldier rose up from the rice paddy and emptied a burp gun into him at point-blank range. He died under a hail of 9-mm slugs before his body ever hit the ground. The surrounded platoon, under heavy fire from all sides, radioed a frantic appeal for help.

The CO of K Company never exposed himself to enemy fire if he could avoid it.[67] In fact he was the kind of man who would ransack his unit's rations in search for the prized cans of fruit that he grabbed for his own personal consumption, much to the annoyance of his men. He remained at his CP and directed LT Randall Beirne to lead the rescue effort.

"You never saw another officer who looked more like a private than I did," LT Beirne explained. He led his men on a circuitous route over rough terrain to reach the encircled platoon. Once in position, LT Beirne noted that while the infantry soldiers and Marines were returning fire, the ordnance sergeants were not. "The sergeant types were

Three Hawaiian soldiers after Sobuk-san. L to R: SGT Mitsuo Imai, Kohala, Hawaii; SFC Castro Corpuz, Ewa, Oahu; and CPL Arsanio Vendiola, Waipahu, Oahu. (source: Chang)

wailing away that they were cut off and were not doing anything," he said. "This was the beginning of my admiration for the Marines, for I quickly saw that they had been taught to be soldiers first and technicians second. The ordnance sergeants had forgotten they were soldiers, and it took a great deal of effort on my part to get them to act."

With the arrival of LT Beirne's platoon, the NKPA broke off the action and fled toward sanctuary in the hills to the west. The soldiers placed LT Jernigan's body on a poncho and carried their deceased platoon leader back to friendly lines.

The NKPA attempted to pierce the 3rd Battalion's lines a couple of hours after LT Jernigan died.[68] The soldiers were hunkered down in their deep entrenchments, protected by swaths of barbed wire, trip flares, and mines, when King Company's listening posts detected movement to their front. Officers and NCOs toured the front lines to ensure their soldiers were awake and prepared for action. On order, machine guns and BARs laced the darkness with red tracers, M-1s cracked, and mortars coughed 60-mm and 81-mm shells into deadly parabolas through the sky. So devastating was the American fire that the surprised North Koreans did not get off a single round. Like phantoms, the NKPA withdrew, dragging their dead and wounded behind.

On the morning of 28 August, an NKPA probe hit the 1st Battalion's positions on Sobuk-san, but this attack was repulsed with heavy enemy casualties.[69] The 5th RCT was gaining a reputation in the Pusan Perimeter as an outfit that held its ground.

The fighting for Sobuk-san settled into a deadly routine as the days went by. Elements of the NKPA 15th Regiment, 6th Division, and the independent 83rd Mechanized Regiment, invariably hit the 1st Battalion around 0500 each morning, only to be driven off by small arms fire and pre-planned defensive artillery concentrations.[70] Captain Claude Baker recalled that NKPA mortar fire was particularly effective during this stage of the fighting, and that B Company suffered heavily from it.[71]

On 31 August, the Eighth Army issued an order outlining the relief in place of the 5th RCT by the 27th Infantry. The relief was abruptly postponed when the "Wolfhounds" were diverted to mount a counterattack after the hard-pressed 24th Infantry's MLR was penetrated during a ferocious NKPA assault.[72] Meanwhile, the 5th Infantry's casualties for August had risen to 101 KIA, 494 WIA, 129 MIA, and 403 non-battle casualties.[73] Tank Company was down to ten operational Easy Eights. Two more tanks were in company maintenance.[74]

On the night of 1 September, the NKPA slammed into Fox Company — Sonny's outfit.[75] Private Gerald Pack saw the NKPA soldiers creeping up the hill from his listening post located 200 yards forward of the MLR. He pulled the pin from one of his grenades and rolled it down the hill where it exploded, throwing screaming North Koreans into the air and, regrettably, shrapnel into his own face. The NKPA rallied and rushed up the hill, firing their burp guns from the hip, hitting Private Pack in the left arm and leg. The NKPA leaped over his body and continued their assault, overrunning and inflicting heavy casualties on the 2nd Platoon.

First Lieutenant Norman Cooper had two rifle platoons, the company's heavy weapons, and an attached heavy machine gun squad, positioned on the MLR. Lieutenant James Anguay's 1st Platoon covered the left sector with Sonny and his comrades. Second Platoon defended the right sector. Third Platoon, led by MSGT Wheeler, was detached and resting in battalion reserve after conducting a long-range patrol behind NKPA lines.

"We had a large front to cover with just a few men and were at about fifty-percent strength," explained LT Cooper. No KATUSAs had joined Fox Company to date. When the NKPA assault struck the MLR, the lieutenant who had "cracked up" in World War II abandoned his 2nd Platoon and ran down the hill.[76] The NKPA knocked out one of Fox Company's machine guns, killing the crew, and overran the 2nd Platoon in furious close combat.

Lieutenant Cooper located MSGT Pierce, the Platoon Sergeant of the 2nd Platoon, in the confusion and, together, they reorganized the survivors. Meanwhile, Sonny's platoon refused its right flank and fought a grim close combat duel on the MLR. On his own initiative Master Sergeant Wheeler led his 3rd Rifle Platoon from its reserve position up the hill toward the fighting. Upon their arrival, LT Cooper gathered his 2nd and 3rd Platoons and mounted a counterattack that slowly gained ground in the face of intense NKPA return fire.

The NKPA resisted the counterattack until just before dawn, when they suddenly broke contact and withdrew, probably to evade the inevitable air strike. On their way down the ridge, a North Korean pumped four more bullets into Private Pack's motionless body just to make sure he was dead. The PPSH-41's low muzzle velocity slugs did not hit Private Pack's vital organs, and he survived the ordeal. Fox Company recovered Private Pack and rushed their desperately wounded comrade to a field hospital.[77]

The NKPA 83rd Mechanized Regiment conducted a series of battalion-sized attacks the next day. The focal point of the battle at 0500 was the 3rd Battalion's sector on the MLR near the coastal road. As artillery direct fire pounded Love Company's positions, NKPA infantry crept to within grenade range and commenced the assault. The fighting quickly spread up the ridgeline to the 2nd Battalion's positions where Fox Company's automatic weapons caught the NKPA in a cross fire during an attempt to overrun George Company's lines.[78] Lieutenant Norman Cooper's 60-mm Mortar Section fired 324 rounds of ammunition in support of George Company's defensive effort.[79]

In 3rd Battalion's sector, the NKPA advanced at a rush screaming "Banzai!" One platoon from L Company was hit hard, disintegrated, and abandoned its positions in panic. The NKPA exploited the penetration and, by daybreak, controlled most of the hill overlooking King Company's positions on the coastal road below. Seven Love Company soldiers remained on the crest, surrounded by the NKPA, fighting desperately. Fortunately, FEAF jets arrived, firing rockets and machine guns at the North Koreans, just before these men were overrun. Meanwhile, Love Company regained its composure and counterattacked, driving the enemy off the hill. One hundred NKPA corpses littered the battlefield.[80]

Three Honolulu members of the 5th RCT take a short rest on Sobuk-san. L to R: CPL Celestine Sun of Wailuku, Maui (KIA October 1950); PFC Adam W. C. Cho, and CPL Miguel Taoy. (sources: NA/Chang)

Close air support was America's decisive weapon in the Korean War. Lieutenant Randall Beirne explained in a letter home, "It's funny here. The days seem like normal days. We walk around in our positions in the open. We watch the 'gooks' walking around. We sleep, bathe and so do they. Then at night all hell breaks loose. The difference of course is the air. The enemy can move only at night. The air has also saved us many times by smashing up concentrations right before an attack. They are a wonderful arm, but they still can't do it alone."[81]

At midnight, the North Koreans came again, slamming into Able and Fox Companies. When these two companies held their ground, the NKPA shifted the weight of the attack into G Company's sector. George Company fell back, reorganized, counterattacked, and recaptured their former positions. On 3 September, the NKPA struck G Company at 0700 and, after fierce fighting, ejected the American soldiers from their positions. Following an air strike on the North Koreans, George Company counterattacked and regained the crest two hours later. The NKPA returned in force the next day, once again overrunning part of George Company's lines, only to be expelled by counterattack later that morning.

Throughout the fighting, SFC David K. Broad, from Laie, Oahu, was a source of strength on which his soldiers leaned. His selfless courage and resolute leadership played a decisive role in G Company's successful defensive effort against heavy odds. Corporal Joseph Gonzales recalled, "David Broad was highly respected by all the officers and men. He was a really great guy."[82]

On 5 September, the war diarist for the Tropic Lightning recorded, "The enemy made his routine attack against the 1st Battalion of the 5th RCT, rather later than usual."[83] The fighting on Sobuk-san had settled down into a stalemate of life and death, an inferno reduced to a boring routine for those not directly exposed to the action.

"There were twenty-seven major attacks against A Company in nineteen days," said Lieutenant Hank Emerson. "They usually attacked us twice a night. But the North Koreans were very inflexible and rigid. Had they been flexible, we would have been overrun, and the Pusan Perimeter would have fallen. By this I mean we were on a narrow ridgeline, and they attacked from the same direction every night. I got down finally to forty-one men. I had eight machine guns though because I kept asking for more and more. But they kept attacking from the same direction every night. So I started off with an egg-shaped defensive position with the mortars in the back. The perimeter was only, maybe, eighty yards long. We brought our 60-mm mortar rounds in close, shooting them straight up into the air. Since they came from the same direction every night, we shifted the perimeter into a horseshoe shape, leaving our rear open. If they'd had any sense, they would have come up behind us, and we would have been dead ducks."[84]

The low point came when A Company was down to forty-one men. Lieutenant Colonel Thomas Roelofs had already sent his cooks and bakers to fight as infantry when he offered LT Emerson a handful of KATUSAs as reinforcements. The desperate company commander agreed to take the ROK soldiers that night. Able Company's KATUSA replacements came up the hill with a column of Chiggy-bearers carrying rations and ammunition while it was still light. The NKPA seized the moment and poured mortar fire into the crowded position, killing scores of Chiggy-bearers and six or seven KATUSAs.

"We quickly discovered the ROK soldiers weren't soldiers at all," said LT Emerson. "They were guys who had been pressed into uniform off the streets of Pusan and handed an M-1 rifle. As you can imagine, they were scared shitless, and they weren't trained at all. They goddamn nearly cost me the hill. The first night they were there, an attack came in. Two of them bugged out and ran right at the hole occupied by SFC Earl Davis, my heavy weapons expert and a real stud. Earl tackled one and I knocked the other one over. 'Stay here,' I said. Just about then, here come two GIs. 'Stop!' I said. 'Just what in the hell do you think you're doing?' They answered, 'They said withdraw! They said withdraw!' Well they sure as hell didn't, because they couldn't speak English, but this is a good illustration of how easy it is for panic to spread in a defensive position at night under heavy pressure from the enemy. Fortunately I had a good platoon sergeant named Santiago Bunda, a Hawaiian and a great athlete, who ran over to a key machine gun the two GIs had abandoned right on the razor back top of the ridgeline. He arrived just in time to mow down a bunch of North Koreans.

"After this we spread the ROKs around and gave them a lot of on the job training," said the company commander. "They became pretty good fighters, but the way they were initially sent up to us was a pretty flawed decision. You're better off with no replacements at all than having a bunch of guys who are going to take off running on you. One of them almost killed me. Whenever an attack would start, I would go to one side of the perimeter and Davis to the other. This attack had just about petered out when I went over to this hole. I didn't notice that two ROKs were lying on their backs shooting straight up in the air until I looked over the rim. One of them almost shot my head off!"[85]

Corporal John Back, from Paragould, Arkansas, played a pivotal role in Able Company's successful defensive effort. LT Emerson had first met PFC Back aboard a ship en route to Korea. Back had impressed the lieutenant as being a confident, mature soldier, one the officer knew he could count on in the days ahead. That both soldiers had spent their teenage years hunting and fishing in Arkansas was icing on the cake. Upon assuming command of Able Company, LT Emerson promoted Back to CPL and made him a squad leader. The company commander valued CPL Back's leadership, maturity, and courage under fire. It never occurred to LT Emerson to ask Back his age.

The NKPA usually mounted two attacks every night against Able Company's perimeter. Before dawn one morning, CPL Back had taken cover in a foxhole with another soldier, when the NKPA commenced the second assault of the night. Together, the two soldiers manned one of the eight machine guns that LT Emerson had demanded to reinforce his hard-pressed perimeter. As the NKPA infantry rushed the barbed-wire obstacle strung around Able Company's perimeter, LT Emerson gave the order to commence firing. CPL Back and his comrade opened up with a Browning machine gun. Their fire was particularly effective and killed numerous NKPA infantry in the wire.

CPL John Back. (source: John Back)

Not everything went Able Company's way. One well-thrown hand grenade landed unnoticed in the foxhole CPL Back shared with his friend. The force of the explosion hurled CPL Back out of his hole and killed his friend.

CPL Back quickly discovered that shrapnel has almost completely severed one of his feet at the ankle. White-hot fragments had riddled his body. A lesser man would have quit. Not CPL Back. He knew the NKPA would take advantage of the hole they had knocked in Able Company's defensive line unless he returned to his foxhole and manned his machine gun. In agony he crawled toward the Browning. Just as the North Koreans burst through the barbed wire and rushed the company's foxholes, CPL Back opened up with the machine gun, killing over 30 NKPA at point-blank range. He shattered the NKPA assault.

Lieutenant Emerson wrote a recommendation to award CPL Back the Distinguished Service Cross. Much later, a rear-echelon staff officer downgraded CPL Back's award for valor to the Silver Star. It was not until long after the war that Lieutenant General Hank Emerson learned that CPL John Back was a seventeen-year-old squad leader the night he made his heroic stand.

On 7 September, the Tropic Lightning issued verbal instructions for the 5th RCT to prepare for a relief in place. General Walker intended to pull the 5th RCT out of the line and place it in reserve near Taegu.[86] The relief did not occur without incident. The NKPA took advantage of the overcast sky on the night of 9 September to attack the 2nd Battalion. As the North Koreans crawled up the hill, a listening post gave the warning, and the battle was joined. The Americans, hampered by poor visibility, could not bring effective small arms fire to bear.

The USS *Whiltsie*, a destroyer steaming off the coast, entered the fray, her searchlights trained on the low overcast skies, turning night into day. Caught in the glare of reflected light, the soldiers blasted the NKPA off the hill. The 2nd Battalion was relieved the following day, and for the weary infantrymen who survived the ordeal, the battle of Sobuk-san was finally over. The 5th Infantry had incurred 145 KIA, 586 WIA, 135 MIA, and 531 non-battle casualties, during its brief attachment to the Tropic Lightning.[87]

The soldiers realized they were gaining the upper hand over the North Koreans. The Americans, pushed around for too long, were ready to push back — hard. Tough fighting lay ahead, but the men were more confident now of a successful outcome. Moreover, the troops knew that a counteroffensive was being planned, one much stronger than the ill-fated counterattack mounted by Task Force Kean.

Mailed started to trickle in for the soldiers fighting on Sobuk-san near the close of August. Those fortunate enough to receive mail escaped the war for a few minutes while they relaxed and read their letters from home. When PFC Donald Gottschall noticed that everyone was receiving mail except his heavy mortar platoon, he brought the subject up with a chaplain who said he would look into it. The next day, the CO of Heavy Mortar Company drove up in a jeep with a sack of mail. It was commonly believed that this unpopular officer remained in the rear out of fear for his own personal safety. The officer confirmed everyone's suspicions when an NKPA mortar shell exploded nearby, and he took off in his jeep without delivering the mail.[88]

Sonny's morale was buoyed by the arrival of his first letters from home in early September. He thanked his mother on 7 September for the stationery she had included in her latest letter. He informed Theresa that F Company had more shelter-halves and blankets now, but the cold rain at night was making life difficult for the men.

In Sonny's absence, Ernest had been promoted to Chief Bailiff in Honolulu. On 8 September, Sonny wrote, "Well Dad, you asked if the hills are as big as ours in Honolulu. They are, and tougher climbing. We are now fighting in a different place called 'Death Valley.' But news came today that the 5th will move to Taegu. We're doing a good job though, holding our ground. You wanted to know if I was a rifleman. I am. I carry a carbine, which is an automatic rifle. It shoots from 15 to 30 rounds at a time."

Sonny informed his Grandmother that the weather in Korea was getting worse.[89] The foxhole he shared with Johnnie Kenawell often filled with rain that they had to bail out with their helmets. Sonny now wore a field jacket to cope with the cold nights. It was still blazing hot during the day, however. In another letter to his parents, he wrote, "Well we are now in Masan, where we spent one good night's rest. Then on 10 September we are going someplace between Pusan and Taegu where we will be in reserve for Eighth Army. We were attached to the 24th and 25th Divisions which is why you did not hear too much about the 5th INF. Daddy wants to know if I'm a sharp shooter. Well, I can say some Koreans won't be able to tell you that. You know what I mean, Pop? I take damn good care of my weapon and myself. So don't worry about me. I took a good hot shower today and put on some clean clothes. We're getting good food now, and I am gaining my weight back. I'm trying hard to keep up with the letters coming in. Tell Buddy and Manley to win that canoe race for me. They are in their last year of school, and I sure wish I was with them. Well Mom and Dad, I sure miss you a lot. I promise to be a good son to you from now on so you don't have to worry anymore."[90]

About this time, CAPT Perry Graves, the CO of B Battery, pulled MSGT Earl Law off FO duty.

DD716 USS Whiltsie. *(source: U.S. Naval Institute)*

When asked if he wanted to be an officer, MSGT Law replied, "Hell no! I'd rather be a master sergeant." Captain Graves said, "Good, because you would be more help to me as a master sergeant. I'll see what I can do."

A few days later, CAPT Graves informed MSGT Law, "I'm sorry. I've got to send you back out on FO duty." That night, MSGT Law placed a call through to battalion and told the personnel officer, "I'll take that damn promotion now. If I'm going to get shot at, I might as well get paid for it!"[91] On 10 September, 2nd LT Law received his commission in the Army Reserve.

Sonny wrote his mother on 11 September from an abandoned town near Taegu. "Things are now going pretty good for us. We are resting in a small town. I don't know the name of it. We are in reserve for Eighth Army. We'll have three days rest here and then move to some other place. We had been getting two hot meals a day. But here we are receiving three hot meals, and the food is very good. They give us PX rations such as candy, gum, cigarettes, beer and writing paper. We are resting in a peach grove. There are peaches, apples, grapes and even corn. We roast the corn at night over a fire. The first night we all made fires, and sang songs, drank beer, and had a swell time, just like camping out on Flat Island. Only I'm so far from it all."

In a short note to Buddy and Manley, Sonny told them to "study hard and don't worry Mom and Dad. Don't stay out late, because take it from me, I'm sorry now for staying out late and worrying Mom and Dad."[92]

After six days of rest, the 5th RCT moved to Taegu. The long awaited counteroffensive was about to commence. Sonny wrote his Mother, "We are now ready for the Big Push. The Army is gathering in Taegu. We have plenty of troops here. We are to go all the way to Seoul. I won't be able to write much now Mom, but please keep writing to me. We are to keep moving. There won't be much rest now. We've been getting good food, but now we'll have to eat rations. They gave us PX rations too. We got gum, beer, candy, toddy-milk, cokes and milk. So Mom they are taking pretty good care of us. I had a lot of sleep. I sure miss my bed. Well Mom, let's hope this push keeps those Koreans on the run. I sure would like to come home before Christmas."

A handful of Able Company soldiers on Sobuk-san. (source: NA)

CHAPTER TEN

THE BEER WAR

On the Taegu Front, Sept. 12. They were crying in their beer on this embattled front today, and it was weak enough — and hard enough to get — in the first place. It's the last day the GIs get their beer ration. Henceforth, by order of somebody in Washington, if a GI wants a beer he must buy it. When the Washingtonians are coming over to open Beer shops in the foxholes, nobody knows.
The Honolulu Advertiser, *13 September 1950.*

There is a saying: "Old soldiers never die. Young ones do." This was especially true during the blazing hot summer of 1950 on the blood-drenched Pusan Perimeter where thousands of young men were killed, wounded, or maimed in some of the most vicious close-combat fighting Americans have participated in since the Civil War. By 15 September American battle casualties had reached an appalling 19,165 men, including 4,280 KIA, 319 died of wounds, 12,377 WIA, 2,107 MIA, and 401 prisoners of war.[1]

While the soldiers fought, bled, and died in Korea, various religious, temperance, and social groups in America were raising a ruckus in opposition to the beer ration the Army was providing free of charge to the troops. The Army bought the beer with appropriated funds and issued it to the soldiers in the same manner as cigarettes and candy bars.

The beer's alcohol content was weak, a mere three-point-two brand of brew that few civilians would have bothered to purchase at home. In Korea, where the official ration was one can of warm beer per man per day, the soldiers appreciated their foamy brew. Beer was a morale builder, pure and simple. The soldiers therefore found it incomprehensible when their ration was abruptly terminated on 10 September 1950.

The soldiers had an ally in Washington, D.C., Representative John D. Dingell (Democrat, Michigan), who vowed to find and punish the guilty culprits who had turned off the taps. "It's not a question of free beer," Congressman Dingell thundered. "It's a matter of life and death. That Korean water is deadlier than bullets. If we want to up the casualty lists — just make those soldiers drink Korean water. The Koreans have sense to leave it alone, as they know it causes all sorts of things — cholera, dysentery and typhus. Somebody here doesn't have enough sense to stand behind the boys and furnish them a healthy food drink. Whoever issued this order should either be court martialed or impeached — depending on his status."[2]

The troops from general to private agreed. "If a man has enough stomach to watch his buddies getting killed it's strong enough to stand a beer a day," declared one general who chose to remain anonymous. Private First Class Albert E. Coker had nothing to lose by remaining anonymous except his beer. He opined, "We are doing the fighting over here and it gets pretty bad. One can of beer a day never hurt anyone."[3]

The Woman's Christian Temperance Union (WCTU) disagreed most vehemently with the sentiments of mere soldiers and mounted a coun-

After the WCTU won the Beer War, these George Company soldiers had to buy their beer. Left to right: Bill Welch, unknown, Joe Lang, and unknown. (source: Mrs. William Welch)

terattack in the popular press. The ladies claimed they were actually looking out for the boys when they turned off the taps. The President of the WCTU, Mrs. D. Leigh Colvin, explained, "We didn't say much until the boys over there in Korea said they needed reinforcements rather than toothpaste, Burma Shave and beer."[4] She hinted that her allies in the Pentagon had finally enforced a law on the books since 1901 that prohibited the "sale or dealing with any intoxicating liquor on any transport or territory under Army supervision."

The WCTU's determined assault on the beer ration was temporarily repulsed on 14 September when the Army once again authorized the distribution of free beer to the troops. As the WCTU vowed to continue its righteous struggle, The *Honolulu Advertiser* reported that five more soldiers from Hawaii had been KIA in Korea. Two more were missing.[5] That same day, a patrol from the 3rd Battalion, 7th Cavalry discovered the bodies of four American soldiers on Hill 314 near Waegwan. The 1st Cavalry Division's War Diary recorded, "The bodies bore evidence of having been bayoneted and shot while their hands were tied."[6] The next day, the NKPA threw an undisclosed number of wounded captives onto a raging bonfire.[7] None of these unfortunate young men would ever drink another can of beer.

Mrs. Colvin mounted a counteroffensive in the Beer War on 17 September with an absurd statement recorded in *The Honolulu Advertiser*: "Wet Washington is evidently ready, if unofficially, to add a department of beer to the army, navy and air force." If true, the irreverent boys on the firing line would have cheered. She denounced Blatz Brewing Company's recent gift of 600,000 cans of beer to the boys in Korea as a sinister ploy "to promote a new crop of drinkers among men in uniform as in the last war."[8] An adjoining article in *The Honolulu Advertiser* reported three more of Hawaii's sons wounded at the front.[9]

Word finally filtered down to the troops in the field that their beer ration had been restored. As the 1st Cavalry Division's War Diary recorded on 18 September, "The Division G-4 announced that beer was back as an item of gratuitous issue through Quartermaster channels for the front line combat elements. The beer was purchased through non-appropriated funds of higher headquarters and authorized by GHQ. It was welcomed by the men especially since they could not understand why it had been cut off originally."[10]

On 28 September, a grateful Army cheerfully accepted 1,200,000 cans of donated beer from the Schlitz and Blatz brewing companies of Wisconsin. The breweries hoped the beer would arrive in time for the men to celebrate victory in Korea.[11] The family of 1st LT John A. Mercer, B Battery, 555th FAB, received the deceased officer's Silver Star that same day in a solemn ceremony held at Schofield Barracks. On 8 August, 1st LT Mercer had continued to process fire missions for the hard-pressed infantry while NKPA artillery and direct fire weapons pounded his battery. The infantry needed fire support, and LT Mercer was doing his best to deliver it, when a high explosive shell burst directly overhead.[12] Lieutenant Mercer would never again raise a glass of cheer.

After an arduous, epic struggle, and an immense blood sacrifice in the Pusan Perimeter, the Eighth Army finally succeeded in defeating the NKPA. Mrs. Colvin prevailed in the Beer War, however, and thanks to her infamous victory, the sweat-soaked, filthy, dog-tired, hungry, and bitter young men serving in the war were deprived of the one luxury they had come to appreciate in Korea. Mrs. Colvin turned off the taps later in the year to the everlasting disgust of the fighting men. But we are getting ahead of ourselves. First there was Waegwan.

CHAPTER ELEVEN

WAEGWAN

The 5th Regimental Combat Team was attached to the 1st Cavalry Division on 14 September. It went into an assembly area west of Taegu along the east bank of the Naktong River six miles below Waegwan and prepared for action. On 16 September it moved out from its assembly area to begin an operation that was to prove of great importance to the Eighth Army breakout.
LTC Roy E. Appleman, USA South to the Naktong, North to the Yalu

On 15 September, the Korean War entered a new phase when the 1st Marine Division spearheaded the independent X Corps' amphibious assault at Inchon. General MacArthur ordered the Eighth Army to conduct a breakout from the Pusan Perimeter for the operational purpose of linking up with X Corps and destroying the NKPA in the vicinity of Seoul before the onset of winter. The Eighth Army was the hammer; X Corps, the anvil. The "Big Push" was on.

It was not going to be easy. The Eighth Army was desperately short of everything from ammunition to infantry replacements. To compensate for a severe shortage of 105-mm artillery ammunition, the assault battalions would have to move quickly under the artillery's suppressive fire. Every round would quite literally have to count. Engineering equipment, particularly bridging equipment, was in critically short supply, and the Eighth Army would have to fight its way across several water obstacles prior to reaching Seoul.[1] The first of these was the Naktong River.

The danger existed that skillful North Korean resistance might weaken the Eighth Army to the point where it would be unable to breakout and link-up with X Corps, thus disrupting General MacArthur's plans. The Eighth Army's assault battalions would have to hit hard and fast to penetrate the NKPA defensive line so that General Walker's armored units could rapidly exploit the breakthrough and begin the race to Seoul.

One day prior to the Inchon landing, the Eighth Army attached the 5th RCT to the 1st Cavalry Division, I Corps. Lieutenant Colonel John Throckmorton was assigned the mission of spearheading the tactical breakout from the Pusan Perimeter in the vicinity of Waegwan, a small town located on the Naktong River approximately fourteen miles northwest of Taegu.

There were other units preparing to break out of the Pusan Perimeter on different portions of the line. The difference was one of degree. If the Eighth Army succeeded elsewhere, but failed at Waegwan, General Walker could expect to win at most what Alfred Count von Schlieffen would have described fifty years previously as "an ordinary victory" — a victory without annihilation of the enemy.[2] The shortest route to Seoul led through Waegwan, and if the 5th RCT quickly punched through the enemy defensive belt here, the Eighth Army stood an excellent chance of destroying the NKPA in close cooperation with X Corps.

Looking north towards Hill 268 as 1st Cavalry Division artillery fire hits near the crest, early September 1950. (source: Roy Appleman, South to the Naktong*)*

General Walker had his reasons for assigning the 5th RCT this critical task. He appreciated the combat team's performance on Sobuk-san where the Rock's boys had acquired a reputation for holding their ground against the worst the NKPA could throw at them. Now it was time to see if the combat team had the fortitude to take ground as well.

The 5th RCT was not going to do it alone. The 1st Cavalry Division's three infantry regiments, the 5th Cavalry, 7th Cavalry, and 8th Cavalry, were going to conduct their respective assaults on the 5th RCT's right (east) flank.[3] Far Eastern Air Force B-29s were on alert for employment in a tactical role to smash NKPA troop concentrations near Waegwan. Assault boats

An aerial view of the highway and railroad bridges spanning the Naktong at Waegwan. The summit of Hill 303 is located in the lower right. (source: Roy Appleman, South to the Naktong*)*

A 1st Cavalry Division patrol discovers the bodies of murdered GIs in the vicinity of Hill 303, early September 1950. (source: NA)

LTC Throckmorton (left) confers with Major General Hobart R. Gay, CG 1st Cavalry Division, at Waegwan. (sources: NA/Chang)

were readied for the operation, but the 5th RCT would have to seize Waegwan before a crossing of the Naktong occurred.

The Naktong River was a natural barrier that flowed north-to-south on this portion of the front. It was spanned by a railroad and highway bridge at Waegwan, lines of communications leading north to Taejon and ultimately Seoul. The bridges had been blown in the recent fighting, but the North Koreans had repaired both of them to accommodate foot traffic. North of Waegwan the NKPA had built an underwater bridge made of sandbags where tanks and vehicles could cross. Hill 303, north of Waegwan on the east bank of the river, overlooked the bridges and the ford. It would have to be captured before the river was crossed.

Southeast of Waegwan lay Hill 268, the key to the enemy outer defensive belt. Hill 268, also known as "triangulation hill," commanded the railroad and highway leading south to Taegu, as well as the river bank south of Waegwan. From its heights, the NKPA could rake an American advance with automatic weapons fire and bring observed artillery barrages crashing down on an opponent's ranks. On the other hand, if the 5th RCT succeeded in gaining the crest of Hill 268, the North Korean defensive line would be flanked and the door to Waegwan kicked open for General Walker's armor to pass through and exploit.[4]

There was little room to maneuver. The 5th RCT would have to conduct a frontal attack on Waegwan, due north, into the teeth of the enemy defenses. Shell craters pockmarked the landscape, and the stench of half-buried corpses lingered over the ground where the 1st Cavalry Division had fought for the past several weeks. The fighting here had been protracted, brutal, and bloody beyond comprehension. Following one desperate counterattack mounted by the 5th Cavalry Regiment, the 1st Cavalry Division's War Diary recorded, "At times the attacks appeared almost hopeless. Particularly, when once during the day the 2nd Battalion, 5th Cavalry, reported having only 100 men remaining in the Battalion."[5]

Remnants of the NKPA 3rd Division blocked the path from inside deep bunkers with earthen covered logs piled overhead for protection. Narrow trench lines, protected by thick barbed wire entanglements, connected the NKPA positions. The North Korean commanders had registered their mortars and artillery on predesignated targets. Mines, liberally sown to reap a bloody harvest of shredded flesh and smashed bone, awaited the unwary. The hard-core NKPA defenders possessed high morale, were excellently armed and equipped, and enjoyed considerable artillery and mortar fire support.

Probably no more than one-third of the 3rd Division's original complement of men had survived the summer's ferocious fighting, but these were tactically adept soldiers, prepared to kill and die for the Red Star. The poorly trained and badly armed North and South Korean conscripts, however, who had recently arrived to flesh out the division's decimated combat units, were of dubious loyalty and questionable fighting power. Political officers watched these new arrivals closely. Signs of disloyalty and cowardice were quickly rectified with a bullet to the back of the head. All told, approximately 1,200 enemy troops, reinforced with tanks, artillery, guns and mortars defended the southern approaches to Waegwan.[7] The 5th RCT was in for one hell of a fight.

Waegwan possessed more than mere operational importance to the American soldiers fighting in Korea. On 17 August, a patrol from the 5th Cavalry Regiment had come across a grisly scene. Twenty-six soldiers from H Company, 2nd Battalion, 5th Cavalry had been captured on Hill 303 overlooking Waegwan during an NKPA attack. The patrol found the bodies "shoulder to shoulder, lying on their sides, curled like sleeping babies in the sun," hands tied behind their backs, shot in the back at point-blank range by NKPA automatic weapons.[8]

The Americans executed at Waegwan were not the first helpless people the NKPA murdered. Thousands had been murdered — soldiers and civilians alike. Prisoners had been inhumanly tortured — eyes gouged out, limbs severed, genitals mutilated, and often doused in gasoline and set afire. North Korean atrocities had done much to harden the soul of even the most faint-hearted soldier. Brigadier General Barth explained, "Strangely enough, the enemy handed us the psychological weapon that almost overnight changed the attitude of our men towards combat. In a counterattack by the 21st Infantry at Chichowan, the bodies of six American soldiers were recovered. Their hands were tied behind their backs and each had been shot through the head. This news traveled like wildfire and our men realized they were pitted against a ruthless foe who recognized no rules and gave no quarter. Our men now knew what they were up against and that they would have to fight to survive. The murder of our soldiers was the first and, probably, one of the greatest mistakes the Reds ever made."[9]

While President Truman and Congress argued and pontificated on the merits of the Police Action in Korea, the GIs had discovered first-hand the harsh, brutal reality of war. Waegwan, Chichowan, and other massacre sites had personalized the war for the American soldier, giving him what his government had proven incapable of providing, a reason to fight — even if that reason was revenge. After the debacle at Bloody Gulch and the agony of Sobuk-san, the 5th RCT was looking for vengeance at Waegwan.

At the time of the Inchon landing, the 5th RCT's personnel strength was 2,599 men, which reflected a shortage of 1,194 soldiers. Its three under strength assault battalions averaged 590 men each.[10] Personnel shortages were counterbalanced by the fact the men were experienced veterans now, no longer the green troops who had gone into action the previous August with Task Force Kean. Lieutenant Colonel Throckmorton had demonstrated superb leadership and brilliant tactical acumen during the previous month's fighting. The Rock's skill and the valor of his soldiers would be sorely

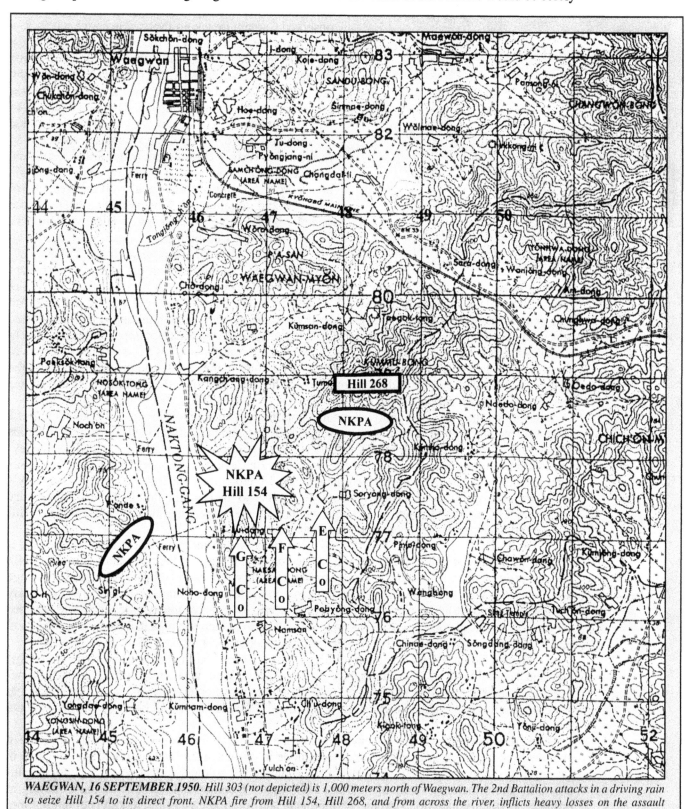

WAEGWAN, 16 SEPTEMBER 1950. Hill 303 (not depicted) is 1,000 meters north of Waegwan. The 2nd Battalion attacks in a driving rain to seize Hill 154 to its direct front. NKPA fire from Hill 154, Hill 268, and from across the river, inflicts heavy losses on the assault companies. By nightfall Hill 154 is secured.

Two Easy Company soldiers who earned their Purple Hearts on 16 September 1950: CPL Charles Santi (left) and CPL Frank Valvo (right). Frank earned the Silver Star for his actions on this date. (source: Frank Valvo)

tested in the next couple of days. Victory was going to depend on the courage and tenacity of a bunch of sixteen to twenty-year-old men.

The 2nd Battalion, 5th RCT closed on its forward assembly area at 1300 on 15 September. Farther to the rear, the 3rd Battalion reached the 1st Cavalry Division near 1800 and dug in for the night. Meanwhile, the 1st Battalion was still on the march from Sam-Wang Jin.[11]

Lieutenant Keith Whitham was sitting in the turret of his tank in the assembly area earlier in the day when he observed Captain Leuck go forward in a jeep with a few men from the 555th FAB to reconnoiter the ground. A short distance up the road, the jeep was ambushed. Three soldiers were KIA, four WIA, and two MIA in the firefight. An NKPA lieutenant was killed by return fire in the otherwise successful enemy ambush. The jeep returned to friendly lines on its shot-out tires with the wounded crammed on board. None of the wounded ever returned to the 555th FAB.[12] Things went badly in the rest of the 1st Cavalry Division's sector that day, too. A "Banzai" attack drove A Company, 7th Cavalry off the crest of Hill 312. The 2nd Battalion, 8th Cavalry was clobbered in the open by NKPA mortar fire during its attack on Hill 570, and suffered heavy casualties.

The 1st Cavalry Division was informed of the successful Inchon landing early on the morning of 16 September. In view of the fact that the Eighth Army planned to commence its breakout from the Pusan Perimeter two days after the Inchon landing, the 1st Cavalry Division ordered the 2nd Battalion, 5th RCT and the 5th Cavalry Regiment to clear enemy opposition from the high ground to their immediate front in anticipation of the main assault going in the next day. Overcast skies, accompanied by intermittent rainfall, forced an armada of eighty-two B-29s heading for Waegwan to divert to secondary targets in North Korea. A handful of FEAF fighter bombers found holes in the clouds and pounded targets in the vicinity of Waegwan, but, by midafternoon, the weather had deteriorated even further which led to a cessation of close air support.[13]

Thus, when the 5th Cavalry moved out in a pouring rain on the morning of 16 September after a short artillery preparation, and limited air support, it was immediately pinned down by murderous defensive fire from well dug in NKPA defenders who contested every inch of ground. The 1st Cavalry Division committed its reserve, the 2nd Battalion, 7th Cavalry, to support 5th Cavalry, but losses continued to mount and little ground was gained. By 18 September, the 2nd Battalion, 7th Cavalry's rifle companies would average fifty men apiece. Farther to the east, the 2nd Battalion, 8th Cavalry was hit hard by an NKPA counterattack and withdrew under heavy pressure down the slope of Hill 570, suffering severe casualties for the second day in a row.[14]

In the 5th RCT's sector, LTC Albert Ward's 2nd Battalion advanced against light resistance until it reached the vicinity of Hill 154, a small rise situated on the east bank of the river and southwest of Hill 268, where the soldiers came under heavy fire from automatic weapons and self-propelled guns. The three rifle companies were on line with George Company on the left, Fox Company in the center, and Easy Company on the right.[15] Sergeant Horace Anderson, whose 57-mm Recoilless Rifle Squad was attached out to the lead rifle platoon in Easy Company, was sitting in a ditch during a halt when LTC Ward and CAPT William Conger, the recently promoted company commander, walked up to the soldiers.

Lieutenant Colonel Ward asked the soldiers what they were waiting for, and someone replied that they had been told to wait. The battalion commander said, "Well, what are you waiting for?" Someone else chimed in, "We don't know. We were just told to move on up here and wait." Realizing that this conversation was leading nowhere, LTC Ward said, "Well let's not wait here any longer." And the men moved right out.[16]

The ground near the river was heavily forested, a death trap for many of the men. North Korean gunners fired high explosive shells fused to explode in mid-air from 76.2-mm field guns located in caves across the river. Air bursts showered the 2nd Battalion's soldiers with shrapnel and wood splinters, killing and maiming many men. Other NKPA guns hammered the 2nd Battalion from dug in positions astride the battalion's avenue of approach, and additional guns and mortars poured fire into the assault companies from the heights of Hill 268.

(Left) A camouflaged Easy Eight vicinity of Waegwan. L to R: SGT Herman Singleton, Gunner; SFC Charles Shepherd, Tank Commander; and PFC Raymond Fryer, Loader. (source: Chuck Shepherd) (Right) Waiting to move out. (source: Chang)

D. Randall Beirne. (source: D. Randall Beirne)

One of the T-34s knocked out at Waegwan. Hill 268 is in the background. (source: Chang)

Easy Company's field first sergeant was one of several men killed by tree bursts. First Lieutenant "Big Pete" Peterson, the CO of G Company, was badly hit by artillery fire and crippled for life. First Lieutenant Don Krause took command of the company.[17] Lieutenant Colonel Ward requested artillery support to silence the enemy guns. Meanwhile, the outnumbered NKPA fought on, tenaciously fighting from their caves, log-covered bunkers, and trench lines in a desperate bid to hold their ground.

The 1st Platoon, E Company, charged a nest of four 45-mm antitank guns that returned a rapid fire over open sights. An armor-piercing round ripped off SGT John W. Jeal's head. PFC William Richardson took another antitank round through the chest. PFC John R. Paradise and CPL Bobby L. Smith both died about this time, the latter in the course of a heroic action that saw him awarded the Distinguished Service Cross, posthumously.[18]

Corporal Frank Valvo at the age of twenty-one was the third oldest man in the 1st Platoon. He saw several of his close friends go down, killed and wounded, as he charged into the midst of the antitank nest, shouting and swearing in Italian as he fired the M1919A6 from the hip. The Browning machine gun jerked and roared in his hands, a belt of ammunition running smoothly through the breech, spitting bullets out at the cyclic rate. He stood in full view of the enemy, shooting down the NKPA gunners, until a bullet tore into the side of his chest, knocking him to the ground. As he fell, his platoon overran the enemy position and captured the three surviving NKPA soldiers.[19]

Though CPL Valvo's wound was not life threatening, CAPT Conger prudently ordered the wounded machine gunner to the rear. Corporal Valvo helped evacuate some of the wounded to the aid station, but his friends were still fighting and dying on the firing line, and he found it impossible to remain out of the fight. He rejoined his company where he jumped up on the engine deck of an Easy Eight, commanded by SFC Charles "Chuck" Shepherd, and commenced firing the turret mounted .50-caliber machine gun into the dug in NKPA positions located a few yards to his front. The tanks attracted intense North Korean return fire, and it was only a matter of time before he was hit again. Eyewitnesses disagree whether it was a fragment from a 45-mm antitank round that ricocheted off the tank's frontal armor, or shrapnel from a barrage of mortar rounds that impacted nearby. Either way, the results were tragic. Corporal Valvo received a terrible head wound and no one expected the blood-soaked soldier to live. He defied all predictions and survived two pain-filled years in various military hospitals before the doctors released this valiant soldier from their care. Corporal Valvo was awarded the Silver Star for gallantry.[20]

Sergeant First Class Chuck Shepherd, West Virginia, had seen considerable action fighting in Italy during World War II. In Korea he quickly welded an inexperienced tank crew into a formidable team. On 16 September they had their hands full as they fought a direct fire engagement with a deadly nest of antitank guns. Sergeant Herman Singleton, who had served as a Navy SEABEE in World War II, fought from the gunner's position. The tank's driver, PFC Dale Raymer, at the age of seventeen, impressed his tank commander with his coolness under fire. Eighteen-year-old PFC Warren Lange, a solid young soldier, manned the bow gun. The loader, PFC Raymond Fryer, had just turned seventeen. Six weeks ago, SFC Shepherd had harbored doubts about the competence of his green crew. No longer. On this critical day, the tank commander was proud of his men.

Off to the side, SFC Shepherd observed 1st LT Clarence H. Jackson, the only Black soldier assigned to the 5th RCT, calmly directing his platoon's assault on an NKPA bunker complex as bullets kicked up dust around the officer's feet. The tank commander admired LT Jackson's performance from afar, thinking, "That's one fine officer in my book."

A few minutes later, a battery of NKPA antitank guns took SFC Shepherd's Easy Eight under fire. The tank commander fought unbuttoned as his gunner and bow gunner raked the enemy position with 76-mm high explosive rounds and machine gun fire. After suppressing the enemy fire, SFC Shepherd supported the 1st Tank Platoon, led by 1st LT George H. Gaylord, as it advanced through the cornstalks toward the enemy. By this time, CPL Valvo was firing the tank's .50-caliber machine gun. When PFC Fryer stuck his head up through the loader's hatch on the top of the turret to catch a glimpse of the action, the tank commander bluntly told his loader to duck back inside the tank before he got his head blown off. A few seconds later, an NKPA mortar or antitank shell exploded on or near the turret. His crew helped evacuate the seriously wounded tank commander to the rear where the doctors patched him up as best they could and shipped him to the States for proper medical treatment.[21]

The Rock led from the front that day, with map in hand, as high explosive shells burst around his forward CP. In the evening, as the 2nd Battalion dug in for the night, he devised a change to his plan. He decided to commit the 3rd Battalion up the right fork in the road early the next morning to envelop Hill 268 from the east. The 2nd Battalion would continue its frontal assault and push north through Hill 140 and continue to drive on Waegwan. His 1st Battalion would remain in reserve to exploit success.

Intermittent shellfire slammed into the 2nd Battalion throughout the long night, killing and wounding more men. At daybreak, SGT Horace Anderson saw an appalling sight. Inside the bed of a 2 1/2 ton truck parked near his foxhole lay bodies, stacked like card board, in three layers, covered in ponchos with just their boots sticking out.[22]

On 17 September, the 1st Cavalry Division's war diary noted, "Today was D-Day for Operation Plan 19-50. The Inchon Plan having been successfully accomplished on 15 Sept, it was now the mission of 1st Cav Div to smash out of the Pusan Perimeter to the northwest, in an attempt to link-up with elements of X Corps and thereby trap the North Korean People's Army in southern Korea. However, the North Koreans, attaching little heed to the fact that their supply lines to the north had been severed; continued to defend stubbornly and in many cases launched strong attacks."[23]

Attempts to punch through the NKPA's iron ring in the 5th Cavalry's sector incurred heavy losses

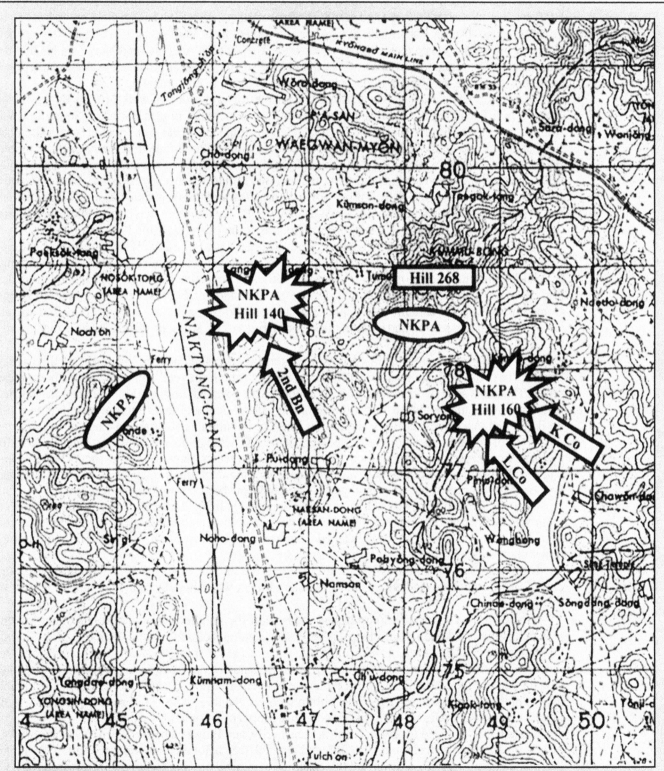

WAEGWAN, 17 SEPTEMBER 1950. The 2nd Battalion overruns Hill 140 after fierce fighting. NKPA fire from across the river continues to inflict losses on the 2nd Battalion. When the 3rd Battalion attempts to assault the eastern flank of Hill 268, it encounters an NKPA defensive position of Hill 160 that has to be reduced first.

and "continued throughout the day with little success." The 3rd Battalion, 7th Cavalry remained pinned down on the LD, caught in a murderous cross fire from a force of 300 heavily armed NKPA dug in on the steep, wooded slopes of Hill 371, and an undetermined number of NKPA on the heavily fortified Hill 203. Its sister outfit, the 2nd Battalion, 7th Cavalry advanced through intense fire, losing men for every yard gained. By nightfall, George and Fox Companies had lost radio contact with battalion in the midst of a furious NKPA counterattack. Their situation was known to be desperate, the FO team with Fox Company having been knocked out, and CAPT Fred P. DePalma, the CO of George Company, killed.[24]

The 2nd Battalion, 5th RCT crossed the LD early in the morning in a determined push to seize Hill 140's heavily defended crest. Easy Company advanced parallel to the river, with George Company on its left flank. Enemy mortar fire impacted near SGT Horace Anderson's squad, but not close enough at first to do any damage. During a short halt, SGT Anderson turned his head to speak to a friend when a shell fragment struck him square on the bridge of his nose. The act of turning his head had saved his life, for otherwise the shell fragment would have decapitated the soldier. Sergeant Anderson was evacuated to an aid station where he remained until healed sufficiently to return to his company.

Corporal Johnnie Kenawell's luck ran out on the forward slope of Hill 140. At daybreak, as Sonny's best friend led his squad into the firestorm, a sniper shot him in the head. Sonny reached Johnnie and started to give his friend first aid. He told Johnnie to "hang on" and helped a stretcher team carry him down the hill where they loaded their wounded comrade into the back of an ambulance. Another soldier who helped was Marvin L. Shildt, one of Johnnie's friends from Pennsylvania. Sonny clasped his friend's hands one last time and told him to write when he got to Japan, or better yet, Honolulu. "It will be OK. You'll see." With tears streaming down his face, Sonny climbed back up the hill to rejoin his company. Unknown to Sonny, CPL Johnnie Kenawell, the cook turned infantryman from Burnham, Pennsylvania, died of wounds on an operating table later that day.[25]

Meanwhile, George Company advanced into a hornet's nest of mutually supporting NKPA machine gun emplacements. When his comrades hit the ground in search of cover, CPL Arnold Ching, from Honolulu, did just the opposite and braved withering defensive fire as he hurled hand grenades into the enemy gun positions, knocking them out one after another. For his courageous role in George Company's successful assault, CPL Ching was awarded the Bronze Star for valor.[26] The 2nd Battalion pressed home its assault and overran the smoking ruins of the smashed NKPA bunkers that marred the crest.

The 3rd Battalion jumped off early in the morning, accompanied by a platoon of three Easy Eights. Three days of rain had transformed the deeply rutted dirt roads into ribbons of bottomless muck. The tanks soon broke through the shoulders of the road and bogged down in the adjacent rice paddies. The infantry plodded forward, the individual soldiers and their equipment caked in mud, until they began receiving artillery and mortar fire. The battalion had overshot a checkpoint, and was in danger of missing its objective altogether, when LTC Benjamin Heckemeyer received a radio message from regiment alerting him to that fact. First Lieutenant Randell Beirne, the XO of K Company, said, "No one was reluctant to turn around at that moment, but perhaps if we had known what lay ahead on our new route we would just as soon have pushed on into that artillery fire."[27]

Once the 3rd Battalion was reoriented and moving on Hill 268, the lead elements discovered that there was another piece of high ground between 3rd Battalion and Hill 268 that had to be captured first. This was Hill 160, a narrow E-shaped ridge running north to south with three fingers running downhill to the east.

King Company had the mission of attacking up the middle finger of Hill 160 and seizing the crest. Love Company would attack up the southern finger, while Item Company remained in reserve to exploit success.

King Company's skirmish line reached the base of the middle finger without encountering enemy opposition. Suddenly, North Koreans were seen running across the skyline on the crest. Shortly thereafter, the NKPA opened up with automatic weapons at the soldiers clambering up the slope. As the Americans searched for cover, their company commander, CAPT Joseph E. Lukitsch, sized up the situation and requested artillery fire. Lieutenant Randall Beirne's 60-mm mortars began dropping high explosive rounds on top of the hill. Within seconds, the three rifle platoons were in action, their machine guns and BARs stitching the crest with a chorus of automatic weapons fire.

Captain Lukitsch had fought in North Africa, Sicily, and Italy as a paratrooper during World War II. Later in that war, he had joined the OSS and jumped deep behind enemy lines to work with Italian partisans. Though CAPT Lukitsch had just assumed command of King Company the previous day, he was a skillful tactician, well versed in the intricacies of small unit infantry combat. He understandably wanted to coordinate his actions with Love Company's attack on his left flank when he assaulted up the ridge.

There was a problem. The enemy fire directed at Love Company appeared light from CAPT Lukitsch's vantage. Yet for some inexplicable reason, Love Company was pinned down near the crest and no longer moving. Captain Lukitsch attempted to contact CAPT Frank E. Hula, the CO of Love Company, but his temperamental SCR-300 radio had malfunctioned and contact could not be restored.

Turning to his XO, CAPT Lukitsch instructed LT Beirne to run over to Love Company and get the soldiers moving. As LT Beirne ran off to carry out the order, CAPT Lukitsch decided to hedge his bet. Just in case L Company failed to move, he ordered SGT William M. McCraine, the 3rd Platoon Leader, to swing to the left and attack through Love Company, thereby rolling up the NKPA defenders on Hill 160 from south to north.

Sergeant McCraine was an combat veteran of World War II who had run afoul of his officers for a disciplinary infraction at Schofield Barracks, losing his stripes in the process. On the way to Korea, it was recognized that Private McCraine was one of a small number of combat veterans in the unit and he regained his stripes. As officer casualties mounted in the Pusan Perimeter, SGT McCraine was elevated to lead a rifle platoon. What he lacked in education and cultural refinement had no bearing on his ability to lead men into battle. When SGT McCraine turned to his men and said, "Follow me!" — they followed. On 17 September 1950 this proved sufficient. The under strength rifle platoon moved out at the double time to take on the NKPA.

As LT Beirne ran toward Love Company, a bullet struck the ground near him and the young officer hit the dirt. Lieutenant Beirne explained, "As I went back down the hill there was a lone sniper who seemed to get enjoyment out of placing his rounds about a foot behind me. Fortunately my patience outlasted his. After he had finished firing, and there was a pause, I would dash across the open spots. Before he could react and take aim I would be under cover. By this method I got down our part of the hill and went back up to L Company."[28]

When LT Beirne reached Love Company, he saw groups of soldiers sitting on the ground. No one was moving or firing. He said, "One group of men was huddled around a prone figure. It turned out to be Captain Hula, the CO, who had a nasty head wound. He was still alive but the blood was flowing fast and covering the ground around him. His deathly pale head was in a medic's lap and his feet seemed to be uphill; why, I don't know. A helicopter was sent for by radio, but it arrived too late. It seems the company bogged down when one man was hit as they started up the hill. Captain Hula, to get them moving, rushed up and started to lead them up the hill. This sniper's round happened to be accurate."

While LT Beirne looked about, a soldier sitting nearby cracked up and started bawling and beating his fists on the ground shouting over and over again, "I'll get 'em. I'll kill em all. The dirty so and so's." His platoon leader knelt beside the man to comfort him, "a touching scene," but still no one was moving. Lieutenant Beirne found 2nd LT James U. Young, the senior officer left in Love Company, and told him to get his men moving up the hill. As LT Beirne quickly explained the tactical situation, SGT McCraine's platoon came barreling through the motionless men, weapons at the ready, closing for the kill on the North Korean defenders. By the time LT Young got Love Company moving again, SGT McCraine's soldiers were on top of the NKPA, hurling grenades into their foxholes and shooting the enemy who attempted to flee down the reverse slope toward Hill 268 and safety. Lieutenant Beirne said, "Sergeant McCraine did a wonderful job and knocked out five holes this way, killing six or eight of the enemy. He didn't take a single casualty."[29]

When CAPT Lukitsch saw his 3rd Platoon hit the flank of the enemy position, he led the 1st and 2nd Platoons in an assault up the finger into the enemy fire. Lieutenant Beirne watched the action from afar. "They were exposed quite a bit and took a number of casualties. Edward A. Queja was hit in the leg, SGT Kato in the arm and SGT Castro in the leg. Cecil V. Woodard was hit in the arm. As he turned over a round hit him directly between the eyes. He was a good, quiet soldier and had just received a package from home that day. It was hard to see one of your old men die."[30]

Street fighting in Waegwan. L to R: PFC Austin Dela Cruz, CPL William Purdy, PFC Alexander Domingo, and SGT Robert I. Muramoto, all from Honolulu. (source: Chang)

A .30-caliber machine gun team fires on NKPA soldiers from the crest of Hill 268. (sources: NA/Chang)

5th RCT soldiers shoot down NKPA soldiers attempting to escape across the Naktong. (sources: NA/Chang)

CAPT Fred Griffits, Cleveland, Ohio, and a KATUSA soldier rest in the ruins of Waegwan. (sources: NA/Chang)

Once 1st Platoon gained the crest, it swung to the right and rolled up the enemy dug in on the northern half of Hill 160. Sergeant Duval and CPL Clifford N. Fauss were laughing, joking, and tossing grenades into foxholes when a "dead" North Korean raked both soldiers in the back with his PPSH-41. Sergeant Duval, though shot several times, continued to protest that he was still fit to fight until he passed out from loss of blood. Corporal Fauss was hit in the legs.[31]

Lieutenant Beirne counted sixteen North Korean bodies on the crest of Hill 160. More enemy bodies lay farther down the slope. Love and King Companies split Hill 160 in half and started digging in for the night. As the men scratched out their holes, mortar fire began to impact nearby and a T-34 started to slam 85-mm shells in from long range. Sergeant Cooper was killed by the same shell that wounded "Pop" Davis and another man. "Pop" Davis had served as a machine gunner throughout his fifteen-year career. The shell severed both his legs, but he was still joking as a litter team carried him down the hill.[32]

Three soldiers were too badly wounded to walk. King Company requested litter teams from battalion to evacuate them from the hill. The litter teams never arrived. Just before dusk a helicopter landed to evacuate CAPT Hula, but since he had died, it was sent to King Company.[33]

Lieutenant Beirne explains, "Hannikiavi was hit in the stomach and Queja in the knee and both were losing a lot of blood. The pilot of the helicopter said he could take only one litter case, so Queja told Hannikiavi to go ahead. It was a very noble gesture. We left a squad down below where Queja was and carried Fauss to the same place. They stayed there all night. At 3 A.M. Queja died from exposure and shock. Fauss was not removed until noon the next day, and then he was carried down by our first sergeant and supply sergeant in a shelter half."[34]

North Korean mortar and tank fire pounded Hill 160 most of the night. Men took short naps during brief lulls in the shelling as they crouched in their holes sitting on piles of pine needles trying to stay dry. The NKPA blew whistles throughout the night, a psychological ploy that played on the frayed nerves of the American soldiers. Ammunition and rations finally arrived at first light, 18 September, along with orders to assault Hill 268.

On the morning of 18 September, the 5th RCT commenced its full regimental attack.[35] The 1st and 2nd Battalions attacked due north and parallel to the river. As the soldiers rushed through the billowing smoke and debris, half-choked with thirst and fear, they entered the NKPA's cunningly constructed defensive maze. The fighting was fierce, close and personal. Superbly camouflaged NKPA machine guns were usually not discovered until too late, after the weapon was already firing at point-blank range into an advancing group of soldiers. Squad and platoon leaders employed their automatic weapons to suppress each NKPA machine gun nest long enough for an infantryman to crawl forward and smother the emplacement with grenades, heralding the final assault. Quarter was rarely asked or given.

The NKPA fought back with skill and desperation, its soldiers urged on by Political Officers who were perfectly willing to shoot anyone who dared to attempt surrender. Of the handful of Prisoners of War (PWs) captured that day, some of them belonged to the 65th Regiment, 105th Mechanized Division, an indication that the NKPA was making an attempt to reinforce its 3rd Division. The NKPA counterattacked with tanks, but failed to regain ground or disrupt the cohesion of the 5th RCT.

The 1st Battalion encountered determined opposition from T-34s to its front as the soldiers advanced on their objective, Hill 178. The North Korean armor must have been low on high explosive main gun ammunition because most of the incoming rounds were solid-shot armor piercing and thus had little effect on the advancing infantry. Able Company knocked out one T-34 with a 3.5-inch Bazooka, but LTC Roelofs believed there were four more to his front.

"A T-34 had my company under fire," explained CAPT Hank Emerson.[36] "One of my soldiers, an incredibly brave man, crawled down a ditch to close with the tank. We hadn't had any goddamn experience with the bazooka. He was probably ten or fifteen feet away from the tank when he fired. He blew the crap out of that tank, but he was too damn close to it, and a lot of shrapnel blew back and killed him. I'll never forget how brave this guy was. We just didn't know that much about the 3.5. We were proud of ourselves for knocking out a tank, but it was a relatively easy kill because it lacked infantry support."[37]

The NKPA resisted the 2nd Battalion's assault on Hill 121 with small arms and light machine guns. Flanking, enfilade fire from antitank guns and T-34s located in caves on the western bank of the Naktong slowed the advancing infantry, but the combat team's attack never faltered. More importantly, help was on the way.

Forty-two B-29 bombers of the 92nd and 98th Bombardment Groups arrived in the clearing skies over Waegwan to neutralize the enemy fire pouring in from the western bank of the Naktong.[38] The four-engined silver birds of prey released their hellish load of 1,600 500-pound

Victory at Waegwan. NKPA PWs. Hill 268 is in the background. (source: NA)

bombs in a tight, concentrated pattern. The earth shook and the sky roared as a howling inferno of death and destruction pounded the NKPA gunners into submission. Concussions from the bomb bursts could be felt from miles away as astonished soldiers cheered the airmen from afar.

Private Gene McClure commented afterwards, "The mountains looked something like a checkerboard from the bomb pattern.... We all cheered this wonderful sight. We thought that every living thing in that bomb pattern was now dead. It was the only time I would see infantrymen jumping up and down weaving and shouting at the top of their voices cheering anything. I have since read that this particular bomber raid resulted in few casualties for the enemy, but I can tell you that it more than made up for that by the great boost in our morale. When you actually witness something like that you are aware that there is real power helping you. Prior to the raid we were receiving heavy fire from there, then after the raid everything got real quiet on that side of the river. I can testify that it was indeed worth every single bomb by producing a rejuvenated infantryman on the ground, which in turn translated into victory at Waegwan."[39]

The 2nd Battalion's assault on Hill 121 was executed right out of a tactical textbook. How Company's 75-mm Recoilless Rifle Platoon supported the final assault on the objective from a base of fire located on the side of a hill. The platoon manned every one of its recoilless rifles in addition to the bootleg .50-caliber machine guns it had acquired along the road. Recoilless rifles slammed high explosive rounds into the apertures of NKPA bunkers as .50-caliber machine guns stitched the enemy's trench lines. The assault company advanced in a long skirmish line, shooting their M-1s, BARs, and towel-wrapped Browning machine guns to their direct front as they walked up the hill.[40] From the battered crest of Hill 121, Sonny and his comrades could finally see the ruins of Waegwan.

The 3rd Battalion had the toughest objective, Hill 268. According to LT Randall Beirne, "Hill 268 looks like a caterpillar with a long thin body and feelers on both ends. These feelers are fingers. The top of the hill is long and narrow and the sides almost perpendicular except for the fingers. On the top are four knobs that we marked Two, Three, Four and Five on the map. Along the sides is a heavy growth of trees, but few trees were on top."[41]

The plan called for elements of B Company, 1st Battalion, and L Company, 3rd Battalion, to advance up the finger located on the southwestern side of the hill and seize the left half of Objective One. Meanwhile K Company would attack along the southeastern finger through the right half of Objective One to seize Knob Two. Once Knob Two was secured, I Company would attack due west up the steep slopes to seize Knob Three, and pivot to the north and seize Knobs Four and Five.[42]

The size of the NKPA unit that defended the crest is difficult to estimate. It was probably the remnants of one of the NKPA 3rd Division's regiments with a strength of at least 300 men. The NKPA soldiers awaited the assault with calm resignation. Political officers exhorted the men to fight to the death while grizzled NCOs kept a sharp eye on the recently arrived conscripts who fleshed out the Communist rifle squads. The veterans of the Chinese Civil War understood their mission and were prepared to sell their lives dearly for the Red Star.

When the 3rd Battalion's two assault companies crossed the LD at 0700, LT Beirne remained behind on Hill 160 to support King Company's attack with 60-mm mortar, 57-mm recoilless rifle, and overhead machine gun fire. From his vantage, he observed the rifle platoons moving briskly across the narrow valley and commence the assault on Hill 268. While he was watching, I Company started to occupy a reserve position on the reverse slope of Hill 160.

As Love and King Companies closed on Objective One, LT Beirne's 60-mm mortars began to lob shells onto the North Korean position. During this action, Item Company's Artillery FO, Lieutenant Dover, was wounded in a position LT Beirne had temporarily vacated to better observe the action.

The NKPA defenders waited until K Company was halfway up the slope of Hill 268 before they lashed out with an intense volume of automatic weapons fire that killed and wounded several soldiers. King Company went to ground and called for artillery fire. Meanwhile, the company's 60-mm mortars failed to knock out the stout NKPA emplacements. As K and L Companies fought to reach the crest, mail was delivered on Hill 160. Lieutenant Beirne noted the strange contrast of soldiers calmly reading their letters while others fought for their lives just a few hundred yards away.[43]

Triple Nickel shells soon impacted with a mighty roar. Captain Lukitsch took advantage of the suppressive fire to get King Company moving again, but the NKPA was still full of fight. The 3rd Platoon took ten casualties advancing up a draw covered by a Soviet Maxim heavy machine gun emplaced in a pillbox. Sergeant William McCraine and Corporal Caen, a squad leader, worked their way towards the left of the enemy emplacement. The two courageous soldiers crawled close enough to hurl a couple of grenades through the bunker's aperture. After the grenades and ammunition stored within exploded in a tremendous blast, SGT McCraine and CPL Caen jumped into the enemy position and shot to death the handful of survivors. The 3rd Platoon rushed forward to consolidate on the remnants of the destroyed bunker, with squads peeling off left and right to roll up NKPA defenders in foxholes nearby.[44]

Meanwhile, MSGT Kermit Jackson, the Anzio veteran with a steel plate in his skull, formed a skirmish line with a Sergeant James R. Jackson, Sergeant Troulius Adams, Sergeant Moran, Corporal Donald C. Henderson, and Private First Class Dennis E. Finn. They were joined by Corporal Gay, an unidentified BAR man, and a KATUSA, who came running downhill towards the skirmish line yelling that North Koreans were in foxholes to their immediate front. Corporal Gay was explaining that his rifle had jammed when, suddenly, grenades landed around the group of soldiers. Master Sergeant Kermit Jackson leaped into a draw and some of the men followed. A few were caught by the blasts and wounded. Shrapnel smashed PFC Finn's jaw. Sergeant Adams received light shrapnel wounds in the arms and legs. The KATUSA suffered a minor face wound.[45]

After hurling three grenades at the enemy foxholes, MSGT Kermit Jackson and his men rose to their feet and charged up the hill. The "twenty-eight-day soldier" led the way, leaping over a barbed wire entanglement and shooting to death the North Koreans who had survived the grenade explosions, thereby knocking a hole in the enemy defensive line. Using a tree line for concealment, the group of daredevils penetrated deeper into the NKPA position and commenced stalking their opponents from behind with bursts of gunfire and grenades. Perhaps MSGT Kermit Jackson did not enjoy shooting the enemy in the back, or maybe he savored revenge and the moment of the kill. Whatever his reason, the crack shot and expert woodsman from West Virginia crept up behind his opponents and yelled, "Turn around, you dirty S.O.B.!" before he blew their heads off, one by one, with his M-1 rifle.[46]

The intrepid soldiers worked their way into a group of empty foxholes located behind and overlooking Objective One. When the NKPA defenders on Objective One broke from the pressure of the combined assault by Love and King Companies, they ran into SGT James Jackson's raised M-1 rifle. He killed eight North Koreans in rapid succession within fifteen feet of his hole. Meanwhile, MSGT Kermit Jackson had overrun Knob Two. From this vantage, he began to hurl liberated NKPA grenades down into the enemy trench lines below, while SGT Moran and CPL Henderson blazed away at anything that moved. As the 1st and 2nd Platoons came huffing up the finger to reinforce MSGT Jackson's success, SGT Moran shot and killed a mortar ammunition bearer. The handful of North Koreans who survived the unexpected onslaught broke and ran towards Knobs Three, Four and Five.

King Company incurred forty casualties in the assault. Thirty NKPA dead were found on Objective One. Master Sergeant Kermit Jackson's gallant band of warriors had inflicted most of the damage on the enemy. In appreciation CAPT Lukitsch recommended MSGT Kermit Jackson for the Distin-

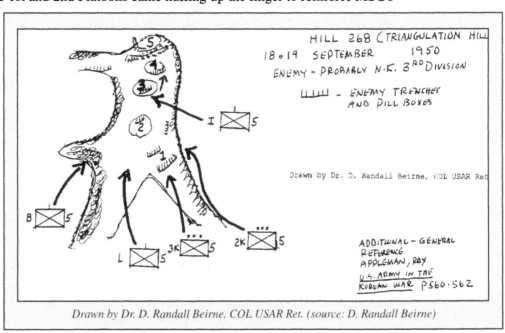

Drawn by Dr. D. Randall Beirne, COL USAR Ret. (source: D. Randall Beirne)

guished Service Cross. This award was not conferred and may have been downgraded to the Silver Star. If a greater force had been present to block the NKPA's retreat, the battle might have ended there, but such was not the case, and the fighting continued unabated.

Lieutenant Beirne climbed up to Objective One with the company's heavy weapons to support Item Company's pending assault on Knobs Three, Four and Five. Wounded men had to be evacuated, wire laid, and a resupply brought forward. Lieutenant Beirne carried a five-gallon water can because there was no one else to carry it. The walking wounded struggled downhill, supporting each other as they hobbled in pain toward a casualty-clearing center. Korean laborers carried the badly injured in litter teams organized by the executive officer. Quite a number of medics had fallen, killed or wounded, so volunteers administered morphine and gave first aid. Sergeant Neil K. Dorrion, a medic serving in the 3rd Platoon, patched up thirty-two men and administered plasma to many of the wounded on the spot.[47] Meanwhile, I Company had commenced its assault.

Item Company quickly overran the enemy defenses on Knob Three, but suffered heavy casualties capturing Knob Four. Intense automatic weapons fire and grenade explosions shot up the lead platoon while assaulting Knob Five. The platoon withdrew and called for artillery support. When the artillery began to impact, King Company's 60-mm mortars entered the fray, pounding the NKPA bunkers with high explosive fires.

Item Company rushed the position as the last rounds impacted on the objective, but the North Koreans were burrowed deep into the ground, with earthen-covered logs piled several feet thick for overhead cover, and they had weathered the bombardment in relative safety. The NKPA waited until Item Company reached point-blank range before they opened fire with machine guns, PPSH-41s, and rifles, as other troops hurled grenades. Twenty-five yards short of their objective, Item's advancing ranks exploded under a hail of grenades, the long skirmish line raked from end to end by automatic weapons. This fusillade of enemy fire killed ten soldiers and wounded many more.[48]

From LT Beirne's position, a couple of King Company's best marksmen fired at North Korean heads bobbing up and down in the enemy trench on Knob Five as enemy soldiers rose to fire a burp gun or hurl a grenade. King Company's rations arrived during Item Company's fight and were being distributed when a mortar round exploded wounding five men. A second round impacted in a foxhole, killing CPL Phillip B. Johnson and a KATUSA, and wounding two other men. Lieutenants Beirne and LeRoy Burk frantically dug a hole for themselves in anticipation of more rounds. The company dug deep, the men cursing their previous complacency.

Suddenly, a soldier ran up to CAPT Lukitsch yelling that a T-34 tank was moving down the road next to the hill. The company commander ordered a 57-mm recoilless rifle gun crew to get into position to engage the armored monster. Up to this stage of the war, the 57-mm was notorious for not knocking out T-34s, but the range was too great for the more potent 3.5-inch Bazookas, so the longer range recoilless rifle would have to do. The 57-mm started to bark, as the gun crew fired, reloaded, and fired again as fast as they could. One round hit the tank and, much to everyone's considerable surprise, the squat, heavily armored T-34 swerved into a ditch and moved no more. The jubilant gun crew claimed a kill, their success acknowledged by the company's hoarse cheers.[49]

When the shouting wore down, the men noticed the remnants of I Company staggering toward their lines. The 3rd Battalion had ordered Item Company to disengage and withdraw to more defensible ground. The NKPA defenders on Knob Five dominated Knobs Three and Four with their fires, and I Company was still taking casualties as it withdrew to the relative safety of Knob Two. As a great many wounded were lying exposed in the killing zone, CAPT Lukitsch told LT Beirne to collect some men and help Item Company retrieve their wounded comrades.

Lieutenant Beirne led his men through the concealment offered by the tree line. He personally crawled out into the open to retrieve two wounded men. Sergeant MacEenrue dashed across the crest of Knob Four and retrieved a wounded man in his arms as bullets licked around his feet. Four more soldiers braved the enemy fire and retrieved two badly wounded men they carried out on shelter halves. No more could be accomplished here, and LT Beirne's detail returned to King Company's position with the officer carrying a wounded man in his arms.[50]

The 81-mm Mortar and 75-mm Recoilless Rifle Platoons moved up that night to Knob Two to support the attack planned for the next day. While the heavy weapons were dug in, the company commanders wondered what had happened to their battalion commander. The entire battalion, minus LTC Heckemeyer and his staff, was crammed shoulder-to-shoulder on the hill, an inviting mortar target if there ever was one. "I won't ask where the CO was. I won't ask where the staff was. The senior company commander gave the orders," explained LT Beirne.[51] The company commanders established radio contact with their battalion and requested an air strike on Knob Five for the following morning. The night was strangely quiet, and those men not on watch caught a few hours of fitful sleep.

By nightfall, the capture of Waegwan appeared within sight. The 3rd Battalion had seized the crest of Hill 268 after bitter fighting, but a tough group of North Korean fighters continued their fanatical resistance from log-covered bunkers on Knob Five. Infantrymen from the 1st Battalion were pinned down 500 yards short of their objective, Hill 178, while those in the 2nd Battalion were dug in on Hill 121 overlooking Waegwan.

The Eighth Army's plan for the breakout from the Pusan Perimeter called for the 24th Infantry Division to spearhead the assault crossing of the Naktong River. Its 21st Regiment's mission was to force a crossing of the Naktong River south of the 5th RCT, and to advance northward on the river's western bank to link-up with LTC Throckmorton at Waegwan. Unfortunately, the plan broke down, and the 21st Infantry had yet to cross the river.[52] The 5th RCT was to be attached to the 24th Infantry Division once the crossing sites near Waegwan had been cleared of the enemy. This mission was judged sufficiently accomplished on the evening of 18 September, and at 1800, the 5th RCT was detached from the 1st Cavalry Division and attached to the 24th Infantry Division.[53]

Frank Brooks survived his wounds and earned his wings as an Army aviator after the War. (source: Frank Brooks)

Thus, at a critical moment of the campaign, the 5th RCT was attached to the 24th Infantry Division, where it filled in as the division's third infantry regiment. The combat team replaced the 34th Infantry, which had gone into action in July with 2,000 men. Eight weeks later the decimated regiment was deactivated. Its 184 survivors were parceled out to the Taro Leaf's remaining two regiments, the 19th and 21st Infantry.[54]

North Korean resistance slackened considerably on 19 September, perhaps in response to news of the Inchon landing finally reaching the lower ranking NKPA soldiers. The 5th RCT rapidly gained ground, its 1st and 2nd Battalions seizing Waegwan and overrunning an NKPA engineer unit attempting to lay a minefield in their path. The fighting was heavier in the 1st Cavalry Division's sector where, for instance, the 2nd Battalion, 7th Cavalry made four attempts to seize Hill 300 before it was finally secured in bitter, close quarters fighting. Artillery ammunition was in extremely short supply and only the center guns of each battery were authorized to conduct fire missions.[55]

The 2nd Battalion, 5th RCT continued its attack north of Waegwan and overran the southwestern slope of Hill 303, where the 1st Cavalry Division troopers had been murdered by their captors a few weeks before. Over 300 dead North Koreans were counted during the advance. Most NKPA casualties appeared to have been inflicted by artillery and air strikes on North Korean units attempting to withdraw on crowded roads. Much enemy equipment was captured, including an intact T-34 tank found by a 1st Battalion patrol.[56]

First Lieutenant Frank Brooks reported back to the 2nd Battalion that day after a spell in the hospital recovering from wounds received at Bloody Gulch. When he reached the CP, he was provided a jeep and driver to take him forward to Fox Company. As the jeep turned a corner near a low hill, it came face-to-face with an NKPA 45-mm antitank gun dug in on the road. The driver made a high-speed bootleg turn to get out of the line of fire as the 45-mm gun began to bark. Once they reached the cover afforded by the hill, LT Brooks told the surprised driver drop him off. He was determined to get that gun. Lieutenant Brooks climbed to the top of a low mound overlooking the NKPA position and shot both the loader and the gunner with his rifle. North Korean mortars searched for the American tormentor on the knoll, and the concussion caused by a near miss knocked LT Brooks unconscious. He awoke to find himself lying on a hospital bed in Japan. The cure was more deadly than his wounds. Lieutenant Brooks experienced an allergic reaction from an injection of penicillin that nearly killed him. He never returned to the 5th RCT. Thrice wounded was enough for any man, and LT Brooks' war was over.[57]

Sniper fire lashed Hill 268 at first light. In Mike Company a Puerto Rican soldier, PFC Julio Rodriguez was hit in the shoulder and died of shock. Two machine gunners were hit in the head and died instantly while sitting in their foxhole. Yet another soldier was shot in the stomach and died. The same expertly camouflaged sniper killed all these men.[58]

Item Company had the dubious honor of spearheading the attack on Knob Five that morning. As the grim ranks moved into their attack positions, a flight of P-51 ground attack aircraft struck the objective with rockets and napalm. Artillery picked up where the air strikes left off, pounding the enemy position with delay-fused shells. The battalion's 81mm mortars and 75mm recoilless rifles added their weight to the fires, reducing the objective to a churning mass of exploding soil.

During the preparatory barrage, Item Company's CO asked CAPT Lukitsch for the loan of a platoon to make good his losses from the previous day. A head count revealed that the 2nd Platoon was down to eighteen men. Captain Lukitsch quickly combined these soldiers with the seventeen left in 1st Platoon to form a thirty-five man composite unit. Serving as Item's "reserve platoon," the composite unit was directed to follow the company's lead elements when the order was given to move out.

As the last 105-mm and 81-mm shells impacted on the North Korean position, Item Company crossed the LD and advanced swiftly through Knob Three, meeting no resistance. When the skirmish line closed on Knob Four, however, the soldiers discovered that, napalm or no napalm, many of the holes on Knob Five were still manned by die-hard NKPA troopers who refused to quit. Automatic weapons fire forced I Company to hit the dirt short of their objective. The soldiers lay naked in the open, lashed by machine gun fire. Bullets struck flesh and bone, men died, and the wounded screamed for medics above the frightful din.

Sergeant First Class Cabral was a powerful man, a football player of some renown in the U.S. Army Pacific. Following a transfer to the 3rd Battalion at Schofield Barracks, SFC Cabral had discovered to his surprise that many of the NCOs did not respect him because he was not a combat veteran and, in their eyes, he owed his rank solely to athletic ability on the playing field. When his bluster failed to gain the respect of his platoon, he resorted to bullying the men, which only made his situation worse. Since SFC Cabral's arrival in Korea, he had been attempting to earn everyone's respect in combat by doing crazy and extraordinarily brave deeds.[59] Today was no exception.

Sergeant First Class Cabral was the platoon sergeant of the 2nd Platoon, K Company, which combined with 1st Platoon, was following in trace of Item Company when the enemy opened fire. Being something of a hothead to begin with, the NKPA's obstinate refusal to vacate Knob Five merely served to inflame SFC Cabral's passions. Shouting for his men to follow, he ran forward to Item's pinned-down infantry, where he stood upright in full view of the enemy, cursing the American soldiers, appealing to their manhood, and daring them to charge the enemy fire.

As SFC Cabral cursed and cajoled the pinned-down soldiers, stalking the length of the firing line as if he was walking the sidelines of a football game, an NKPA soldier rose out of a foxhole and opened up with a burp gun. The first burst shattered SFC Cabral's arm and killed another soldier in the line of fire. Yet SFC Cabral's heroic, if crazy, example had spurred Item into advancing, and the end on Hill 268 was finally in sight.

As Item Company shot to death, and blew apart with grenades, the remaining die-hards on Knob Five, litter bearers carried SFC Cabral through King Company's CP on the way down the hill. Tendons gleamed whitely through a bloody hole in SFC Cabral's arm large enough to stick a hand into. Even with a tourniquet, the blood flowed freely, and LT Beirne feared the brave man was going to die. Sergeant First Class Cabral thought so too, and grabbed the officer's hand with a weak clammy grasp. "Lieutenant," he said. "I was no good in Schofield. I caused you a lot of trouble." Then, his voice weakened from shock and loss of blood, he whispered, "Tell them I was a good soldier, Sir."[60]

By noon, Hill 268 was secure. The North Korean soldiers deserve credit for a courageous stand. Although a murderous, cruel and savage foe, the NKPA fought bravely, tenaciously, and with great skill. Outnumbered and outgunned, they fought to the death when overrun. Over fifty NKPA bodies were counted on the crest, unrecognizable masses of bloody flesh, most partially consumed by fire. More enemy dead lay outside the burned area in nearby foxholes. All told, an NKPA regimental commander (colonel) and 250 bodies were found dead on Hill 268. The 3rd Battalion's officers later presented LTC Throckmorton one of the dead colonel's epaulets.[61]

Lieutenant Beirne gazed upon the scene attempting to make sense out of the sacrifice. "There was no time for sentimentality. Perhaps if one had the time he might have gazed at the youth lying there, his blond hair blowing in the mountain breeze just like the blades of grass nearby, and thought of the kid's family, his past and what his girl might say. But soldiers usually are too busy and too tired. They must move on to another hill. So they pass by this kid and think to themselves, 'Tough luck old boy. Perhaps you're better off. Thank God it wasn't me.'"[62]

With the collapse of resistance on Hill 268, the NKPA defensive line was flanked and on the verge of being rolled up. The North Koreans began to vote with their feet, pulling out of their exposed positions and abandoning what equipment and supplies the tough peasant soldiers could not physically carry.[63]

Of the NKPA prisoners captured that day, one surrendered as the result of a safe conduct chit. Another PW reported that each man in his platoon had received only twelve rounds of rifle ammunition the day before to contest the American advance. Nevertheless, this prisoner said morale was very high among the NKPA regulars. The forcibly conscripted North and South Koreans, on the other hand, just wanted to return home alive.[64]

On 20 September, the 5th RCT killed over 100 North Koreans who attempted to swim the Naktong and flee the trap. The 3rd Battalion encountered a minefield and heavy NKPA artillery fire at mid-day that held up its advance for several hours. The 72nd Engineer Company performed magnificently that day, clearing a path through the mines and building bypasses at blown bridges, all the while under heavy fire. The combat team captured a total of nineteen PWs, three SU-76 self-propelled guns, and over 1,000 rounds of tank ammunition.[65]

Much to everyone's surprise, Fox Company reached the crest of Hill 303 without encountering any resistance.[66] Sonny stood on the wind-blown hill amid the bomb craters, empty foxholes and abandoned bunkers. Rotting, mangled, and partially buried corpses littered the hill, including those men from the 1st Cavalry Division who had fallen here in the previous weeks.

The combat team lost eighteen men KIA, 111 WIA and three MIA on 20 September while clearing out the last remaining nests of die-hard NKPA defenders.[67] In return, the 5th RCT received thirty-six enlisted infantry replacements for its understrength battalions and one officer replacement for the 555th FAB.[68] By nightfall, the 1st and 2nd Battalions were awaiting orders to cross the river, and the 5th RCT CP was established in Waegwan.

As LT Keith Whitham's Easy Eight negotiated the blasted rubble-strewn streets of Waegwan, he drove past a curious sight. A young NKPA officer in dress uniform, complete with Russian-type shoulder boards, was sitting upright on

The smile says it all. (sources: NA/Chang)

the steps of a public building near the center of the town. At first glance, one did not realize that the enemy officer was dead.[69]

Rifle companies and heavy weapon platoons gathered on the banks of the Naktong that evening for the next leg of the journey. Morale was high, for in spite of its grievous losses, the 5th RCT had successfully penetrated the enemy's iron ring to liberate Waegwan. Although headlines in the States would proclaim, "1st Cavalry Division Seizes Waegwan," LTC Throckmorton and his soldiers knew better.

So did Major General Hobart R. Gay, the Commanding General, 1st Cavalry Division, who described the 5th RCT's combat performance at Waegwan in a newspaper article published the following year. "I've never seen a battle command do better in this war or the last. We'd been fighting for forty days to hold the damn place. And it was rugged. The 5th RCT, under the command of Colonel John L. Throckmorton of Honolulu, was given the assignment of paving the way in that sector by capturing Waegwan and establishing a beach head across the Naktong River. Four days later, marked by a bloody battle to capture strategic 'triangulation hill,' the combat team was in Waegwan and had established the beach head across the Naktong. The 5th suffered quite severe losses, but the men never looked back over their shoulders. They just kept on."[70]

CHAPTER TWELVE

Go For Broke

At the present time, men of the 5th are spearheading the 8th Army's drive across the Naktong River.
The Honolulu Star-Bulletin, *27 September 1950*

On the night of 19 September, a patrol from the 2nd Battalion's I&R Platoon paddled across the Naktong to the western bank of the river near the railroad bridge. Their mission was to gather information on the enemy's defenses and to identify possible crossing sites. After accomplishing their mission, the soldiers were preparing to shove off in their boat when they heard a T-34 rumbling towards them in the darkness. Sergeant Bud Throne took cover in an empty foxhole with a couple of other men when the armored monster emerged into view. The tank drove directly over their hole and stopped. After an eternity of terror, the T-34's engine roared into life and the tank lumbered off in another direction. The patrol quickly paddled back across the river.[1]

At 2035 the following night, the 1st Battalion paddled across the Naktong River in assault boats manned by the 3rd Combat Engineer Battalion.[2] Their initial objective was the high ground located about one hundred yards south of the railroad bridge.

Charlie Company led the assault. A recent replacement, SGT Hibbert J. Manley, from Wahiawa, Oahu, had earned a Purple Heart while serving in a combat engineer battalion at the beginning of the war. His request to transfer to the 5th RCT was approved in September. On 20 September, he was a squad leader in the 1st Platoon, C Company.

Just before C Company shoved off, SGT Mingie, the platoon sergeant, said, "Manley, you used to be an engineer. Take the lead boat."

The 3rd Battalion crossed the Naktong on the morning of 21 September 1950. (source: Chang)

"So my squad," recalled SGT Manley, "loaded up. I asked the Beaver (3rd Engineer's nickname), 'Where are the burlap sacks to wrap around the paddles to muffle the sound if a paddle hits the boat?' He didn't know what I was talking about. Had to be a new man. The 3rd was a good outfit. When we pushed off to cross the Naktong, I expected the NKs to open up on us any second. But for the dipping of the paddles in the water, there was silence. I don't know which was worse, the silence or waiting for the gunfire. When we reached the other side, we jumped out of the boat and moved inland about 30-40 yards looking for the enemy. It was pitch black. As the company closed in our area, we were told to secure the slope on the high ground left of the main road and the railroad tunnel. A and B Company were to push through us and take the high ground just before first light. We set up on the lower slope, knowing someone was on top. So it was no noise, no smoking, no digging."[3]

Meanwhile, 1st LT James Johnson's combat engineer platoon crossed the river with A Company. When LT Johnson's assault boat struck what the men thought was the opposite shore, the soldiers piled over the sides and rushed inland. Having actually landed on a sand bar in the middle of the river, the men soon found themselves up to their waists in water again.

In the confusion, A and B Companies did not link up with C Company. Rather, they seized the high ground to their front. Lieutenant Johnson's engineers advanced down a road and encountered a minefield of wooden box mines.

"You don't clear mines with a mine detector at night," explained LT Johnson. "You do, but it's tedious, time consuming. I mean, hell, we would have been doing it yet if I had to do it that way.... We'd find the mine and just throw it off the side of the road. Just pick it up and throw it off."[4]

The 1st Battalion's lead elements captured twenty PWs without resistance on their first objective. As 1st Battalion consolidated on its second objective, SGT Manley saw two T-34s accompanied by infantry lumbering down the MSR toward the railroad tunnel, unaware that C Company was 30 yards away.

"The word was passed to lay low," recalled SGT Manley, "because we would be silhouetted by anyone up the hill if we engaged the tanks."[5]

The 3rd Combat Engineer Battalion ferried much of the 5th RCT's combat equipment and vehicles across the Naktong. This ferry was later destroyed by NKPA artillery fire. Note the B-29 bomb pattern on the hillsides. (source: NA)

Sergeant Robert L. Lyons led a rifle squad from A Company forward to ambush the tanks. He allowed the lead T-34 to approached to within twenty-feet before he fired a 3.5-inch Bazooka that blew a track off the tank. After several North Koreans fell killed and wounded under a hail of small arms fire, NKPA determination evaporated, and the enemy withdrew. About this time, an NKPA concussion grenade blinded 1st LT John G. Hayes, West Point Class of 1949. The 1st Battalion started digging in.[6]

Lieutenant Colonel Albert Ward's 2nd Battalion paddled across next and expanded the bridgehead north of the MSR. Sonny and his comrades in Fox Company moved out to secure the high ground on the regiment's right flank where they dug in for the night.

At dawn, LT Norman Cooper saw GIs wandering around to his front. It turned out that LTC Ward had accidentally established his CP three-quarters of a mile in front of the rest of the battalion. Thankfully, the NKPA was fully occupied in the 1st Battalion's sector and did not discover the error in time to overrun the battalion headquarters.[7]

Just before dawn, Charlie Company jumped off to seize the high ground on the combat team's left flank. Sergeant Manley explains, "It would be light soon and still no sign of A and B Companies. When it got light, the NKs up above us would be looking down our throats. It was time to take the hill by ourselves. So we jumped off without fire support. As soon as we started our assault, two machine guns just above us opened up and pinned down most of the company. We couldn't just lie there, so I took the one grenade I had and another from one of my riflemen. I had him pull the pins. Corporal Vincent Houten of Boston, Massachusetts moved left, laying down fire with his M-1. I ran straight up between the two machine guns

2nd LT Robert L. Lyons received a battlefield commission. (source: Lyons)

until I was close enough to drop the grenades in their holes. I kept thinking, 'Why am I not being hit?' I could feel the muzzle blast from the machine guns. I ran back and picked up my rifle and told my two-man squad (Houten was off to the left raising hell) and anyone else around, 'Let's Banzai 'em!' We started yelling 'Banzai!' The next thing I knew I was looking up at Ohara of Honolulu who was our platoon medic. He was giving me a shot and wrapping up my leg. He said, 'Manley, you lucky kanaka [Hawaiian]. It's a good wound; at least Japan.' I looked around and saw the machine gun nests. They were close together and no riflemen in between. Real dumb. But good for us. When I got back to the MASH in Pusan, they changed the bandage, turned my ass around, and I went back to 'Banzai Charlie' — the greatest collection of bad-asses I ever knew or would hope to know. All the Hawaiian guys had to say about what the 5th had done was 'Ain't no big ting [local talk for 'thing']. And the mainland guys would say, 'Y'all can say that again — Go for broke brah [brother].'"[8]

The haul in captured NKPA supplies and equipment grew throughout the day. Over 280,000 rounds of small arms ammunition, 2,500 rounds of 57-mm antitank ammunition, three 57-mm antitank guns, six heavy machine guns and 2,000 grenades were captured. To help maintain the momentum of the advance, the 3rd Combat Engineer Battalion started ferrying the combat team's vehicles across the Naktong.

Ground attack aircraft knocked out five T-34 tanks at daybreak, including the one SGT Lyons had damaged the night before. The 5th RCT reported, "The enemy is withdrawing in haste and abandoning equipment in large quantities in an effort to move north and northeast. He is very disorganized and is not capable at this time of effective, strong resistance."[9]

The 5th RCT suffered fifteen WIA crossing the Naktong and securing its objectives on the far side. On 22 September, the 5th RCT's mission changed. As I Corps pushed armor and motorized infantry through the breach made by LTC Throckmorton's soldiers, the 24th Infantry Division directed the 5th RCT to mop-up bypassed NKPA units in the hills astride the MSR. The 5th RCT conducted aggressive patrols and continued to accept the surrender of isolated groups of North Koreans. Casualties mounted as the day wore on. The 5th Infantry lost eight KIA and six WIA in scattered firefights with die-hard NKPA units.[10]

In the evening, Sonny wrote his parents, "I received your box that Mom made. And I want to thank you very much for it. I got it on September 20. I did not open it yet because we are moving very fast. I will open it today. Well things are going pretty good. We're pushing along fast. We take a hill in the evening and move along the next day. We got them on the run now. We hit Waegwan and headed for Taejon. I don't know how to spell them, but if you look on the map you will see where we are. By the time you get this letter we will be past that. We are to push to Seoul, where we will meet X Corps. We are attached to the 24th Division but are still called the 5th RCT. It is getting cold at night. I sure wish we had warm clothes. In every letter you write you want to know if I'm getting your mail. We'll I've got every one that you wrote. It takes about nine days for your letters to get here. Tell Miss Slattery thanks for the fudge. Tell Buddy and Manley to keep up the good work in school. Tell them I wish I was with them. I sure miss my brothers. But I'll be back soon. These North Koreans will give up soon. Kenawell got hit on the last hill we took. He went back to Japan or Tripler General. Why don't you find out if he is there in Tripler Hospital? I sure miss him a lot. There are now only two old timers left in our squad of seven men. All the rest of them are new replacements. We got a bunch of them today. The whole Army is moving in the Big Push. The planes blast the way for us. The big guns stay behind us and shoot over our heads. And do those shells come low! They blast the enemy right in front of us. We are now taking plenty of prisoners. They are coming out of the hills. Fifty or 70 a day. Yesterday we took 59 of them. Well I hope it won't be long now. I miss home and all of you very much. I'm getting tired of sleeping in foxholes. Well I guess that is all I have to say for now. I think we are going to move off the hill we're on and push on today."

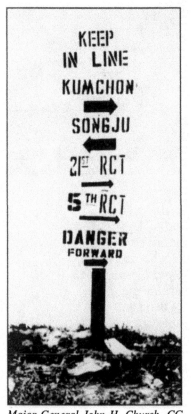

Major General John H. Church, CG 24th Infantry Division, was Danger Six. Danger Forward was the division's tactical CP. (source: Chang)

On the evening of 23 September, the Rock received orders to advance and seize Kumchon where remnants of the NKPA 105th Armored Division and the 1st Regiment, 9th Division had elected to make a stand. A spirited NKPA defense had succeeded in holding up the 21st Infantry's advance, which combined with a logistical crisis at the crossing sites, threatened the success of the Eighth Army's drive on Seoul.

North Korean long-range guns had searched out and destroyed the ferry at Waegwan the day before. Intense shelling had also damaged the two footbridges spanning the Naktong, which made it too hazardous to push supplies across the river during daylight. Though stout South Korean peasants carried fuel, ammunition, and rations on their backs across the footbridges at night, with the offensive at Kumchon apparently stalled, the situation was grim.[11]

The 1st Battalion conducted a passage of lines through the 21st Infantry at 2130, with 1st LT Pappy Young's Baker Company mounted on the engine decks of Tank Company's Shermans. North Korean mortars and machine guns opened up on the 1st Battalion, as T-34s and antitank guns took the Shermans under fire. Self-propelled guns entered the fray, firing over open sights. Baker Company quickly scrambled off the engine decks and took up positions on higher ground located on both sides of the road. Losses mounted and the infantry's advance slowed.

As the 1st Tank Platoon attempted to deploy off the road to bring its fires to bear, an antitank gun knocked out the lead Easy Eight in a narrow defile with one of its first shots. Sergeant John Pearce, who commanded the second tank in the column, directed his driver to press on to a firing position just ahead of the knocked out tank where he could cover its crew with his onboard weapons. His Sherman squeezed past the lead tank and brought its formidable armament into action, slamming 76-mm main gun high explosive shells down range as the bow and co-axial-mounted .30-caliber machine guns raked suspected NKPA positions.

An enterprising NKPA officer dispatched an antitank assault team to deal with the Easy Eight. The NKPA squad crept to within four feet of SGT Pearce's tank before they leaped into action with satchel charges, grenades, and small arms fire. Sergeant

Pearce fought a desperate, personal, close range battle throughout the night from his turret hatch with hand grenades and his .45-caliber automatic pistol to hold the marauders at bay.

Meanwhile, the rest of Tank Company remained stalled behind the 1st Platoon in a column formation, unable to deploy due to the steep hills on both sides of the road. As the night wore on, 1st LT Keith Whitham dismounted his tank to find the reason for the delay. He discovered a large and badly wounded soldier lying directly behind the tracks of the third tank from the head of the column. If this tank had to reverse for some reason, the soldier was going to be crushed, so LT Whitham attempted with little success at first to drag the large man out of the way. A

The infantry moves out. (source: Chang)

handful of infantrymen noticed his plight and, together, they managed to carry the heavy man to safety. Lieutenant Whitham then returned to his tank.[12]

A couple of hours later, LT Whitham dismounted his tank again to discern the cause of the delay. He reached SGT Pearce's Sherman at daybreak and discovered six NKPA corpses sprawled on the ground.[13] Lieutenant Whitham thanked his stars that he had stumbled across the wounded man earlier in the night. Otherwise he probably would have been killed by the NKPA unit attacking SGT Pearce's tank.

The NKPA High Command orchestrated the defense of Kumchon from inside deep bunkers constructed in the town. It ruthlessly sacrificed the remnants of decimated battalions and regiments to hold Hill 140, the key terrain feature south of Kumchon, to cover the withdrawal of the shattered divisions retreating from the Pusan Perimeter. The NKPA 849th Independent Antitank Regiment formed the backbone of the defense on Hill 140, and its T-34s and antitank guns fought a ferocious, skillful, and tenacious rearguard action to prevent the 5th RCT from breaking into the town that night and all the next day.

Dawn found LTC Throckmorton up front with his leading rifle companies and tank platoons, personally directing the assault and coordinating the combat team's supporting arms, while serving as an inspiration to his young soldiers. At one point, the Rock advanced 300 yards ahead of his lead rifle company to direct the fire of one of his tank platoons. Antitank fire struck two tanks as LTC Throckmorton stood calmly in the open, pointing out targets to his tank commanders.

Major Claude Baker, recently promoted and now serving as the XO of 1st Battalion, said, "LTC Throckmorton was an excellent combat leader. He was very concerned about the men. He was where he should be, when he was supposed be there. He was well liked by the people who got to know him. I recall that he was consulted quite frequently by the division staff and asked what they should do and how they should do it. He was a natural leader of men."[14]

An NKPA sniper shot 1st LT William B. Williams, the 1st Battalion S-2, West Point Class of 1947. Known to his friends as "Jughead" or just plain "Jug," LT Williams had served with the 5th RCT in Korea in 1949. Upon arrival in Hawaii, one of the company commanders had latched onto a lovely woman by the name of Frances at the Pearl Harbor Officers Club. The captain and Frances continued their affair until the former's wife arrived from the States. In the meantime, Jughead had become infatuated with Frances. A few weeks later Jughead was reported missing from duty at Schofield and was finally found shacked up with Frances. Being that Jughead's father was a colonel serving at Fort Sill, the son was loaded on the first plane from Hickam going to Oklahoma. Shortly thereafter, LT Williams reported for duty in Korea and pulled the necessary strings to get himself reassigned to the 5th RCT. The intelligence officer was waving a map in the breeze when the sniper shot him. He survived his wound but never returned to the 5th RCT.[15]

Supported by FEAF ground attack aircraft, the 5th RCT fought its way through successive enemy defensive lines. Of the eight T-34s that attempted to bar the advance, five were reduced to smoldering wreckage by FEAF napalm and rocket strikes. Bazooka teams knocked out three more.

Able Company, led by CAPT Hank Emerson, suffered heavy losses taking a hill to the left of the road. As enemy mortar rounds rained down on the soldiers, CAPT William C. Hedberg, the Regimental Surgeon, walked slowly amid the carnage, and calmly provided life-saving medical aid to the wounded.

A 5th RCT tank infantry team advances on Kumchon. (source: Chang)

The 5th Infantry advances at Kumchon under enemy fire. (sources: NA/Chang)

L to R: SGT Joseph Tupa, Anahole, Kauai, earned three Silver Stars, a Bronze Star, and four Purple Hearts before he was captured by the Chinese on 25 April 1951; LT Herbert Ikeda, Honolulu, led "Ikeda's Raiders" with valor and skill; CPL Homer K. Kuhns, another brave Charlie Company soldier, was KIA within hours of this photograph being taken. (source: Chang)

A Browning machine gun team in action at Kumchon. (source: Chang)

"One of my NCOs, SGT Adrian J. K. Sylva, a veteran of the 442nd and a super stud, was a platoon sergeant in one of my rifle platoons," recalled CAPT Emerson. "Sergeant Robert L. Lyons was Sylva's platoon leader. He fell wounded when NKPA mortar rounds hammered his platoon. I went with the left-hand platoon. The fire was too intense to make a stand-up assault, so we squiggled forward on our bellies, shooting our weapons and throwing grenades until we got to the top of the hill. From there, we could see North Koreans withdraw off to our right in front of Sylva's platoon. We opened up on them. I could still see one machine gun though that was covering their with-drawal. Sylva stood up and rushed the emplacement. The fucking inter-company radios never worked! It was too far for me to yell, 'Stop! Stop!' Sylva got right on top of the machine gun and threw a

SGT Adrian J. K. Sylva, Honolulu, on Sobuk-san. He was awarded the Silver Star, posthumously, for his actions at Kumchon. (sources: NA/Chang)

grenade. I saw him go down and knew he'd gone down hard. Bill Hedberg, our surgeon, was there and I screamed for him to follow me. Sylva had been right on top of the fucking machine gun. He'd taken five or six slugs right through his body. I cradled him in my arms and tried to buck him up. I said, 'God damn it Sylva, you just got yourself the million dollar wound and will be back in the States before you know it.' Sylva replied, 'Don't you shit me, Captain. I know I'm dying.' He was the best of the men we had who had been in the 442nd Infantry. He was a fatalistic guy, a real brave man. I'm haunted to this day because the radios didn't work, and I couldn't yell loud enough to make him stop. That machine gun had to fall, but we'd gotten behind them. Sylva was one of my all-time favorite soldiers ever, a real exceptional battle leader. Bill patched him up and we rushed him to the rear. He called me an hour later and told me that Sylva didn't make it. Our regiment's unofficial motto was 'Go for Broke' because we admired the 442nd so damn much."[16]

On the right side of the road, B Company, commanded by 1st LT Pappy Young, suffered terrible losses. The NKPA had dug in on the low ground for once and their grazing fire was extremely effective. Pappy, who was jokingly referred to as "the oldest 1st Lieutenant in the Army," had served as the regimental trial counsel at Schofield Barracks. A popular and courageous officer, Pappy paid the price for leading from the front. An NKPA machine gun zeroed in on the officer and severe wounds forced his evacuation.[17]

Elements from Dog Company were pinned down by automatic weapons fire, too. Master Sergeant Thomas T. Dunn, from Honolulu, boldly advanced through the enemy fire to an exposed position where he opened up with his M-1 and killed an enemy machine gun team.[18]

The 2nd Battalion came abreast of the 1st Battalion in the afternoon and attacked through heavy enemy fire toward Hill 140. When the NKPA pinned down George Company with automatic weapons fire, Fox Company attacked through them with 2nd LT James Anguay's 1st Platoon in the lead. After Sonny and his comrades gained a toe-hold on the objective, LT Anguay reported that he could hold it if the rest of Fox Company moved up to join him. Regrettably, 1st LT Norman Cooper had already received orders to withdraw the company and conduct a night assault on another hill located on the combat team's right flank that had been bypassed earlier in the day. The 1st Platoon retraced its steps to rejoin Fox Company in time to seize the new objective in a night attack.[19] The soldiers routed the NKPA and dug in on the hill where they spent a sleepless night dodging flat trajectory harassing fire.

On the evening of 24 September, LTC Roelofs returned from the front to his temporary CP located in a dry streambed and directed LT James Johnson to clear some mines that were holding up the advance. The combat engineer platoon, supported by a few tanks, started to clear a lane through a minefield that straddled the road leading to Kumchon. They had not completed the task when an expertly camouflaged NKPA machine gun located just a few feet away on the left side of the road opened up on the soldiers. Most of the men took cover in a ditch on the right side of the road. By mistake, Sergeant Suga jumped into a ditch on the left side, almost on top of the enemy machine gun crew. Within seconds the shaken NCO rejoined his comrades on the opposite side of the road, pursued by bursts of enemy fire.

CAPT William C. Hedberg, MD, treated the wounded under fire. He was awarded the Silver Star. (source: Chang)

As LT Johnson threw a grenade, a tank crew slammed their hatches shut and fired blindly into the engineers. It was a costly mistake. A slug that grazed LT Johnson's thigh blew off another soldier's head. Another bullet wounded SGT Suga.

Lieutenant Johnson rose to his feet and hobbled over to the Easy Eight where he grabbed the tank-infantry phone and yelled, "You son of a bitch! If you fire one more round on that side of the road, I will personally blow you to kingdom come."[20]

The engineers eliminated the machine gun and cleared the road of mines. Shortly thereafter, the Rock directed LT Johnson to take over B Company.

The 3rd Battalion remained in reserve on 24 September, its rifle companies far below their authorized strength. Having started the assault at Waegwan with 160 soldiers, K Company now had just seventy-eight men. Eighteen soldiers, on average, remained in each rifle platoon.

Soldiers can find humor even in the face of adversity. King Company was marching toward the sound of the guns beside a stream when the NKPA fired on the column from long range. Lieutenant Randall Beirne said, "From experience, by listening to the crack of the enemy rounds, we could tell they were not too dangerous. A new replacement, however, dove headfirst into the stream, rifle, helmet and all. I couldn't help laughing as he emerged with a dumb expression on his face."[21]

By the end of the day, the 5th RCT had killed an estimated 300 North Koreans, yet the NKPA fought on. The 5th RCT reported, "Throughout the period stubborn enemy resistance supported by heavy artillery, mortar fire and tanks slowed the attack."[22] The combat team captured just seven enemy soldiers in the bitter engagement, a strong indication that a hard-core NKPA unit barred the advance.

The 5th RCT renewed the attack in conjunction with the 21st Infantry the following morning, 25 September, to capture Kumchon and clear the road of North Korean forces and enemy mines. While the 2nd Battalion destroyed an NKPA detachment dug in on the reverse slope of Hill 140, the 1st Battalion was heavily engaged with the remnants of an enemy battalion that barred its path.

As Able and Baker Companies advanced under heavy fire, suffering grievous losses for every step of ground, LTC Thomas Roelofs lost patience and relieved CAPT George Walsh, the CO of C Company, for his inability to get his company moving.[23]

Lest there be any misunderstandings, there were plenty of fine soldiers in Charlie Company, too. Second Lieutenant Herbert H. Ikeda, for example, a rifle platoon leader from Honolulu, led "Ikeda's Raiders," a tough group of Charlie Company soldiers that included Corporal Joseph S. Tupa, from Anahola, Kauai, and Corporal Homer K. Kuhns, from Honolulu. Ikeda's Raiders patrolled day and night, gathering intelligence, ambushing NKPA units, and snatching an occasional enemy prisoner.[24]

"Tupa was a very compassionate person," recalled SGT Hibbert Manley. "He cared for everybody, but he was vicious when the shooting started. A hell of a fine soldier. He made you glad he was on your side."[25]

Corporal Tupa had prevailed in over ten close combat duels with NKPA soldiers in August and September. His courage was legendary in the combat team, and he would go on to earn the title "Most Decorated Soldier in the 5th RCT," receiving three Silver Stars, a Bronze Star, and four Purple Hearts in eight months of combat.[26]

"Homer Kuhns was a brave soldier who displayed great personal intitiative in combat," recalled SGT Hibbert Manley. Corporal Kuhns had carved a notch into the stock of his M-1 for every NKPA soldier he killed. A North Korean may have carved a notch on his stock on 24 September, the day CPL Kuhns was killed.

After CPL Kuhns was KIA, LTC Roelofs directed LT Ikeda to conduct a night attack with his platoon to seize a Y-shaped hill that was holding up A Company's advance. Lieutenant Ikeda explained, "I was supposed to take the hill without any fire support, by fixed bayonets under cover of darkness. The artillery liaison officer told me that this was a suicidal mission which I need not accept. He also commented that I was armed with only a burp gun [captured PPSH-41] and he wanted to give me his .45-caliber pistol and five clips of ammo. I thanked him for his concern but told him that I had the only automatic weapon [in his platoon] with three fully loaded drums (72 rounds) of ammo. I told him that I always went on the point on attack and I'd make out okay. We passed through Hank's A Company to jump off…. The enemy knew we were coming so they took off as I started up the hill.

When Hank saw us on the hill at daybreak [25 September], he said, 'Hey Ikeda, what the hell, you took my objective.' I told him, 'Hank, I didn't take your objective. The old man and I went to your hill to look for you but couldn't find you. He wanted to tell you that Ikeda's Raiders were going to chogi on up the hill and avenge the gooks for killing my best man Homer Kuhns.'"[27]

On 25 September, the 3rd Battalion penetrated into Kumchon where Love and King Companies fought it out house-to-house with die-hard NKPA soldiers in a ferocious close range gun battle. Lieutenant Colonel Benjamin Heckemeyer was awarded the Silver Star for this action.[28] The Triple Nickel provided excellent fire-support throughout the day, knocking out one T-34 and killing numerous North Koreans. Meanwhile, the 72nd Engineer Company earned its hazardous keep clearing the road of mines. By 1445, Kumchon was in friendly hands.[29]

About this time, CAPT Robert A. Kennedy, the CO of Tank Company, who often fortified his courage with grapefruit juice laced with medicinal alcohol, ordered LT Keith Whitham to "go out there and see what was going on."[30] As LT Whitham's tanks rolled forward, they passed Chaplain Francis Kapica who was administering the last rights to eight soldiers lying dead in a ditch.

Lieutenant Whitham's platoon had advanced a mile down the road when SGT Paeloa halted his Easy Eight and announced over the radio that he could see many troops to his front heading north toward Kumchon. Lieutenant Whitham assured him that these were "our boys" and took advantage of the halt to climb out of his turret to stretch his legs on the engine deck. Sergeant First Class MacMillan radioed from another tank that there were two NKPA soldiers sitting on a low hill on the left side of the road about 100 yards away. The platoon leader reassured him that these were friendlies. As LT Whitham stretched his legs, he noticed to his horror that the "friendlies" were in fact North Koreans who were traversing a machine gun in his direction. The tank's .50-caliber spoke first as LT Whitham opened fire on the NKPA, the heavy slugs causing the enemy soldiers to jerk in a bizarre death dance that remained fixed forevermore in the officer's mind. "We immediately backtracked to friendly lines," he said. "This incident only serves to emphasize the confusion, lack of information, and perhaps the lack of aggressiveness on my part. Had I realized that the troops to our front were withdrawing NKs my five tanks could probably have attacked down the road wiping out what was no doubt at least the remnants of an NK regiment."[31]

In two days of fighting, the combat team reported the loss of seventeen men KIA and ninety-two WIA.[32] The 6th Tank Battalion, which supported the 5th RCT's assault, lost ten M-46 Patton tanks to NKPA T-34s, antitank guns, and mines.[33]

The medics worked in the open on their wounded comrades under intense enemy fire. Captain William C. Hedberg, the combat team's surgeon, braved heavy fire to aid the wounded soldiers lying on the battlefield, thereby earning the undying admiration of the men and the Silver Star for gallantry.[34]

Corporal Joseph Villaflor, a medic from Kapaa, Kauai, used up his supply of bandages while treating the wounded early in the fighting. He found himself searching in vain for a bandage in his empty medical kit to treat yet another wounded soldier when a man lying nearby gave the medic one of his own. When CPL Villaflor finished applying first aid, he turned to thank the donor only to discover that this man was more seriously wounded than the soldier he had just finished treating.[35]

The NKPA suffered heavy losses at Kumchon. Several NKPA units fought to the last man, including the 849th Independent Antitank Regiment. Through this ruthless sacrifice of men and equipment, the NKPA High Command accomplished its delay mission at Kumchon. Thousands of hardcore NKPA troops escaped from the threat of imminent encirclement and certain destruction.

General Edward M. Almond's X Corps could still have intercepted and destroyed most of the fleeing NKPA. But the ill-advised decision to divert major elements of the 7th Infantry Division from its blocking positions south of Seoul to participate in the liberation of the city ensured that many NKPA soldiers would live to fight another day.[36]

Lieutenant Colonel Throckmorton would eventually receive the Distinguished Service Cross on 27 March 1951 for extreme gallantry in action during the fighting at Waegwan and Kumchon. The citation reads, "The 5th Infantry attacked the key cities of Waegwan and Kumchon, capturing them and succeeded in breaking the iron ring of the Pusan Perimeter. During the entire successful engagement, COL Throckmorton personally directed the assault of his forward battalion and front line companies. With utter disregard of his own safety, he moved from position to position along the entire front, exposing himself to heavy enemy small arms, mortar and direct tank fire in order to command his troops with utmost effectiveness. East of Kumchon, he assumed a position with the lead tank some 300 yards in advance of the foremost infantry. Despite intense enemy fire, which hit two friendly tanks in the immediate vicinity, he remained in his exposed position to personally supervise the movement of the leading tanks and infantry assault companies. His gallant leadership under the most adverse conditions inspired the men of his command to fight with an unconquerable will to succeed.

His conspicuous bravery and highly efficient combat skill, influenced greatly the capture of these most strategic objectives. The extraordinary heroic achievements of COL Throckmorton reflects great credit on himself and the military service."[37]

On 26 September, the 5th RCT conducted aggressive patrols against the remnants of NKPA units in the hills around Kumchon. Though badly beaten, the disciplined, hard-core NKPA soldiers were still full of fight. The combat team suffered lop-sided losses that day, losing six men KIA and twelve WIA in North Korean ambushes.[38] In return, the 5th RCT killed one NKPA soldier and captured twenty prisoners. One of the men killed was SFC Charles F. Carroll, who served in the 72nd Engineer Company. His family was subsequently awarded the Distinguished Service Cross he had earned leading from the front at Waegwan and Kumchon. Camp Carroll, near Waegwan, was named after him and is still used by the Army today.

Prisoner of War reports indicate that most of the PWs captured by the 5th RCT were deserters. The hard-core NKPA fighters were either dead or attempting to reach North Korea. Most of the PWs were recent inductees who possessed little training, poor armament, and no desire to die for the Communist unification of Korea. One PW claimed he was strongly influenced to desert after reading a UN safe conduct pass. He stated morale in his unit was very low and that the majority of the conscripted troops saw no chance to win the war. The prisoner also said NKPA troops were dreadfully afraid of American artillery and, especially, napalm bombs. Another PW said just the platoon leaders in his battalion had rifles. The other soldiers had been told they would receive weapons when they reached the Naktong. Another PW claimed only one man in his platoon carried a rifle. Moreover, this prisoner's battalion had lost 200 men before it arrived at Kumchon due to the poor physical condition of the recent draftees. Yet another PW had been drafted on 7 August in Kang Won Do, North Korea, where he had received only twelve days of training before being shipped to the front.[39]

While the 5th RCT continued to patrol and capture NKPA stragglers, Tank Company was temporarily attached to the 19th Infantry's drive on Taejon. Tank Company spearheaded the advance because the 6th Tank Battalion's M-46 Pattons were considered too heavy and cumbersome to lead a high speed dash across Korea's roads and bridges.

Numerous firefights erupted during Tank Company's rapid advance as it overran and shot up the fleeing remnants of the vaunted North Korean military machine. On the bright side, Tank Company inflicted considerable losses on the enemy and even freed a couple of American PWs from captivity. Regrettably, an ugly incident marred the advance when a soldier in the 3rd Combat Engineer Battalion shot and killed an old Korean man who was doing nothing more than waving at the onrushing column from the side of the road.

Throughout the day, flights of Australian and South African P-51 fighters supported the tanks, swooping down at tree-top level to strafe suspected ambush sites. The relentless advance continued into the early hours of the night until Tank Company exhausted its fuel supply near Okchon. After covering seventy dusty miles, the tank crews stopped for a short rest until the heavier Pattons and refuelers caught up with the column.

Lieutenant Keith Whitham kept an old Korean straw mat tied to the back of his turret to sleep on. That night, as he climbed down from his tank to get some much needed rest, he untied the mat and placed it on a pile of soft ground next to his tank. The exhausted platoon leader slept peacefully on this mat next to the tracks of his tank until 0200 when a pack of angry T-34s burst into the town from the north with every gun blazing. Lieutenant Whitham instinc-

South Koreans cheer the combat team's advance on Seoul. (source: Chang)

tively climbed back into his turret, throwing the mat onto the engine deck of his tank. The NKPA armor withdrew after a confusing firefight that witnessed one M-46 from the 6th Tank Battalion hit at point-blank range in the melee.

As LT Whitham sat in his turret searching for targets and awaiting orders, he noticed an awful stench. After the fighting died down, he investigated the source of the stench only to discover to his disgust that his sleeping mat was smeared with human excrement. Looking down beside his tank, he realized he had been sleeping on night soil piled high to fertilize a nearby rice paddy.

The 6th Tank Battalion led the advance the following morning as the armored column roared into Taejon. Tank Company went into bivouac to await the arrival of the 5th RCT. In a post operations critique, COL Ned D. Moore, the CO of the 19th Infantry, praised Tank Company for its "audacious tenacity." Captain Robert Kennedy, no doubt

A smoke break on the way to Seoul. One officer (center) is speaking on his SCR 300 radio. (source: Chang)

braced with grapefruit juice spiked with medicinal alcohol, stood up in the briefing and said, "Sir, will you put that in writing?" Colonel Moore never did.[40]

A few replacements arrived to flesh out the combat team's depleted ranks during a lull in the fighting. First Lieutenant William O. Perry, Jr., West Point Class of 1945, joined the combat team and took over the 81-mm Mortar Platoon in Dog Company. The native of Denver, Colorado had been stationed in Korea before and spoke the language fluently. While addressing his platoon, he noticed that a large portion of the soldiers were Asians. Lieutenant Perry wanted to make a good first impression on the KATUSAs, too, so he spoke to them in Korean. After his first couple of sentences, he realized to his dismay that everyone was looking at him strangely.

"Sir," one of the Asian soldiers interjected in perfect English, "we don't understand you." Lieutenant Perry had not realized up until that moment that his Asian soldiers were actually from Hawaii. "They were, of course, of Japanese descent. We got that straightened out real quick," he recalled long after the war.[41]

The 5th RCT received 232 replacements and sixty-nine returned to duty personnel in September. An additional 200 KATUSA joined the 5th RCT that month. The 5th Infantry carried on its rolls 2,492 men at the close of September, or 1,300 men below of its authorized strength of 3,792 men. The 555th FAB was in better shape, with 670 men on the rolls compared to its authorized strength of 678 men. The 72nd Engineers, with an authorized strength of 169 men, was down to 116 combat engineers. A total of 741 KATUSA soldiers were serving in the 5th RCT on this date.

A 5th RCT Personnel Periodic Report, dated 30 September 1950, states the combat team had incurred 153 battle casualties in September. With the exception of two engineer casualties, the other 151 losses were infantrymen. This report included 51 non-battle casualties in September, and 9 transfers out of the combat team. These personnel statistics are incorrect. Based on the casualty statistics listed in the 25th Infantry Division's Personnel Status Reports and the 5th RCT's Unit Reports from 18-30 September, the combat team had incurred at least 94 men KIA, 355 WIA, 9 MIA, and 188 non-battle casualties in September. A complete accounting will remain elusive, because soldiers who fell in the first two bloody days of the assault on Waegwan were listed as belonging to the 1st Cavalry Division rather than to the 5th RCT. Few of the men who perished at Kumchon are listed on the casualty rosters either. Years after the event, it remains nearly impossible to reconstruct the 5th RCT's total casualties from the surviving documents.[42]

Sonny mailed a handful of letters home at the close of September. These were some of his observations and comments:

"The going is rough and tough. I won't have much time to write now, but I'll try anyway. We are headed for Seoul, and we don't have much time to rest. We climb mountains at night now and move off at dawn. My feet are killing me. We do a lot of walking now. I'm tired and feel like I'm getting old. Oh, by the way, I work with the lieutenant now. I have to carry the radio on my back and it weighs about 40 pounds. Me and another guy take turns. It's not bad. You take the calls and all the information. We still get hot meals about twice a day. We had steak yesterday and it was good. I always eat two or three servings. I have to close now. We are ready to eat and are moving off of a hill."[43]

A couple of days later, Sonny wrote, "I'm having a hard time answering all the letters because we're on the move now. I don't hear too much about the 5th RCT. It might be because we're attached to the 24th Division. So when you hear about the 24th Division, that is probably us. We are making that Big Push you folks probably heard about. We are moving fast and don't stay in one place long. It's getting cold up here now, and they gave us each one blanket. I now have a field jacket, one blanket, and that is all. I don't know when they will give us winter clothes. I heard that we will get them next month. If we are lucky, we get two hot meals a day, if not, we get one. And if we are really under fire — battle —we get Army rations. The rations are not too bad, but they are cold, and there are no greens. All you get in the line of fruit is one can. Lots of times I go hungry. When you have to eat the same thing over and over again, it gets sickening. It's not like going down to the store and getting a sandwich, or going to the Chop-Suey house, or getting some Ice Cream and candy."[44]

Sonny did not know that Johnnie Kenawell had died of wounds. In a letter to his grandmother, he wrote, "Do you remember the other boy I brought over to Aunt Margaret's house that day before I left? Well, he was wounded about a week ago. He was with me when he got wounded, but he will be OK. I think he is in Japan now. I do a lot of praying, and it sure helps me. We don't have Mass too much because when we are fighting there is no time, and we have to keep moving. We don't get too much rest, for if we stop for a few days, that will give the North Koreans a chance to build up their forces. You see Granny, if we keep pushing them back, they won't have time to form their troops and

Mopping up on the way to Seoul. (source: Chang)

get ready for us. I did lose a few pounds climbing those hills, but I think I gained some of it back. When I get home I'm going to eat and sleep, but mostly sleep. We are now having pretty good weather, but it is cold at night. They are going to give us warm clothes next month."[45]

The 5th RCT took 123 PWs on 1 October alone, but a patrol from the 2nd Battalion incurred three WIA in an enemy ambush.[46] Three 5th RCT soldiers were killed the following day when their vehicle hit a mine. Two more soldiers were KIA in firefights with NKPA stragglers. The combat team captured 179 PWs on 2-4 October, as it advanced on Seoul. Two soldiers were KIA and two WIA in sporadic fighting on 7 October.[47]

Rumors that the 5th RCT would return to Hawaii buoyed the men. On 6 October, Sonny wrote his parents, "We got some warm underwear…. I am now assistant squad leader. We are now about 100 miles from Seoul. We will be next to the 38th Parallel. I hope we don't have to cross it. There is a rumor going around that we all might go back to Honolulu, but it's only a rumor. I still miss home and dream of the day when I can come home. Things look good. I hope it's all over soon."

From 9-13 October, the Rock had the 5th RCT conduct realistic combat training near Seoul.[48] Captain Hank Emerson recalled, "The whole personality of the regiment was a reflection of Throckmorton. He was tough. Every time we went into reserve, we didn't just lie around. We immediately went out and went through the whole field manual — attack, defense, withdrawal under pressure, attack of a fortified position. All with live fire. All with artillery… ignoring the peacetime safety regulations. I had a man or two killed doing that. But we practiced live fire. I wound up making a night attack in North Korea that was right out of the manual, but we had practiced it [in South Korea] about three times with live fire."[49]

Sergeant Horace Anderson, fresh from a short spell in the hospital, took over a rifle squad in one of E Company's rifle platoons. His nine-man squad included four KATUSAs, just one of whom could speak English.[50]

Each battalion established a boot camp for the KATUSAs to ensure they were properly trained and integrated into their units. The 1st Battalion, for instance, ran three separate 100-man classes during this period. One-third of the KATUSA soldiers from each class were integrated into the line companies. The remaining KATUSAs were transferred to the ROK Army.

Lieutenant James Johnson, the CO of B Company, recalled, "We were loaded with KATUSAs. Once they were integrated in the company that way they really did a masterful job. The biggest problem, of course, was language communication…. The KATUSAs did a hell of a good job. They really came through quite well… we had the good fortune of having time to train them because we weren't heavily engaged."[51]

On 14 October, Sonny wrote his parents, "I haven't had too much time to write. We have been training, just like in Basic. We are about sixty miles from the 38th Parallel. Tomorrow we move up to the 38th. We might move into quarters, but that is only a rumor. We have been hearing a lot of rumors about the 5th RCT lately. I'll tell you some of the ones I have heard. Number One. The people in Hawaii want the 5th RCT back in Hawaii. Number two. We are supposed to leave here and go to Japan to do a parade for General MacArthur. Number Three. We'll leave Korea on October 28, and head for Honolulu. Number Four. The bags that we left at Pusan are on a ship and ready for shipment. But these are only rumors. We still have to watch ourselves. We are about three miles from Seoul and four miles from Kimpo airfield. We have been getting three hot meals a day, and I'm getting a good rest. We have been getting PX rations. You know, candy, gum and so forth. We got a beer ration yesterday - 3 cans. One at every meal. We got more warm clothes. Just about everything. I sleep warm now and had a hot bath today, and I'm feeling fine. We haven't seen any fighting lately. I wish they would send some fresh troops here so we could go home. We got paid the other day, but I'm letting the Army hold my money. Next month I'll send the two pay checks home. They have been very busy and couldn't send it home until about the end of October…. That's about all the news I have. I will let you know if we have to cross the 38th Parallel."

CHAPTER THIRTEEN

NORTH TO THE YALU

Military Operations conducted by UN forces in Korea north of the 38th Parallel are primarily for the purpose of completing the destruction of North Korean forces... [and to] create conditions favorable to early unification of the area into one republic.
Annex One, Administrative Order One, 5th RCT, 20 October 1950

At 0900 on 9 October, the Eighth Army invaded North Korea. General MacArthur's race to the Yalu River was on. Severe logistical constraints precluded a role for the 5th RCT in the initial phases of the offensive, and the combat team was retained south of the 38th Parallel until sufficient motor transport and fuel could be found to bring it forward.

On 15 October, the 5th RCT rode on trucks to Tongjang-ni, where the infantry dismounted and, after a short rest, trudged on foot in the darkness under a pouring rain to Paekchon. One hundred and ninety-three bypassed NKPA stragglers surrendered during the advance.[1]

Sonny mailed a brief, mud-splattered letter to Dawn Mladinich, the sister of his girlfriend Lona, the following day. It read, "We are now about two miles from the 38th Parallel. There is not much fighting, but we still have to be on our guard. The weather is pretty bad, rain one day, sun the next. Last night we had to get up at 11:30 and walk about 7 miles in the rain. I tried to make the best of if, so I sang the song 'Rain.' You know the song, it was popular when I was still in Honolulu. It was very cold, and when I think about my warm bed, and blankets, I sure wish I was home. Well Dawn, say hello to the rest of the family and most of all to Lona."

Although the records are not specific, the 5th RCT probably crossed the 38th Parallel on 17 October 1950. Unknown to Generals MacArthur and Walker, the "Iron" troops of the Chinese Fourth Field Army crossed the Yalu River into North Korea at the same time.[2]

The next few days passed quietly for the men. On 18 October, Sonny wrote to his mother, "The candy was very good. I always give some to the boys, and when they get packages from home, they give us some things. The news here is still the same. We are now over the 38th Parallel, about 8 miles over. It's pretty cold during the day and cold at night. We are now sleeping in barracks that were used by the North Koreans. We sleep warm at night. All I do is pull guard duty. I don't carry the radio anymore. I don't know how long we'll stay here before going on further. I hope this war will get over soon. You asked if Kenawell was hurt bad. Well, he was shot by a sniper above his left eye. I was about 20 feet away from him when he was shot. I helped the medics carry him down the hill. That was the last I ever saw of him. I hope he will be all right. I don't think he will be back, because it was a bad wound."

The 5th RCT advanced deeper into North Korea, encountering little resistance. Much to the disgust of the combat team's soldiers, General Walker assigned their rival, the 1st Cavalry Division, the starring role during the drive on Pyongyang, the North Korean capital. The 5th RCT advanced on bad roads along the west coast of Korea. The weary troops marched through rain and mud or jarred their kidneys loose riding in the back of bouncing trucks over the deeply rutted dirt roads. Along

When the 5th RCT crossed the Han River and marched into North Korea, the fall rains had arrived and the weather was starting to turn cold. (sources: 25th ID Museum/Chang)

the way, North Korean civilians, who appeared very happy to meet their liberators from the Communist regime, waved small American flags from the side of the road. Where they acquired the flags remains a mystery.[3]

The 5th RCT received an issue of sleeping bags, but not enough to provide one for each man. The Rock sensibly gave the infantry first priority on what was rapidly becoming an essential piece of equipment. Everyone else relied on blankets and ponchos to stay warm. The nights had turned bitterly cold.

Lieutenant Colonel Throckmorton demanded strict noise and light discipline from his soldiers. He forbade warming fires within the perimeters of his units. The same could not be said for other Army combat units in Korea.

The Rock decorates SGT Flortino Romano, Honolulu, with the Bronze Star. (source: Chang)

"If you looked over at night to some of the other regiments nearby," recalled CAPT Hank Emerson, "hell, you could see right where their defensive positions were because you could see their damn fires. Everyone thought LTC Throckmorton was tough, mean, and hard, but that was the kind of discipline he inserted in the regiment."[4]

General MacArthur's plan for the invasion of North Korea called for X Corps to conduct an amphibious landing on the east coast at Wonsan while the Eighth Army attacked up the west coast. He directed the two converging forces to link up near Pyongyang to encircle and destroy the NKPA. It was the hammer and anvil all over again. The failure to destroy the NKPA south of the 38th Parallel was the driving force behind the invasion of North Korea.

Supplying the advance was causing the Eighth Army more problems than the feeble North Korean resistance it occasionally encountered. The Wonsan operation tied up the port of Inchon where the 1st Marine Division had to be laboriously back-loaded onto its amphibious assault ships. Due to the extreme tidal flow at Inchon, it soon proved impossible to load the 7th Infantry Division there in time to meet the 20 October deadline assigned to the Wonsan landing. Therefore, much of the Eighth Army's scarce motor transport and fuel was exhausted transporting 7th Infantry Division south to Pusan where its ships were waiting. As a consequence, the Eighth Army's advance into North Korea was subject to severe logistical constraints.[5]

Everyone agreed that Wonsan had to be captured for logistical reasons. In contrast to General MacArthur, however, the Navy, Marine and Army commanders involved in the Wonsan operation opposed the amphibious landing because it would take too much time and tie up too much logistical support. They favored a hot pursuit by X Corps across the 38th Parallel instead, leaving the capture of Wonsan to the ROK Army.[6] Yet after the dazzling success at Inchon, few chose to openly question General MacArthur's strategic view, and the Wonsan operation was mounted. General MacArthur's prestige was such, wrote General Ridgway after the war, that "had he suggested that one battalion walk on water to reach the port, there might have been someone ready to give it a try."[7]

When the invasion force arrived off Wonsan, the Navy discovered that the port was heavily mined. The Navy's mine sweeping units proved to be scandalously insufficient in numbers and equipment to clear the necessary lanes to land the amphibious force on schedule. As a result the ROK Army captured Wonsan in an overland advance while the Navy struggled to clear the harbor of mines. The Marines conducted an anti-climactic administrative landing after a lane through the mines was belatedly swept.[8]

The delay at Wonsan saved the NKPA from annihilation. There was no hammer or anvil. The Eighth Army's advance on Pyongyang merely pushed the NKPA into the rugged, bleak, and frozen mountains adjacent to Manchuria and Siberia. Tens of thousands of Kim Il-Sung's soldiers had died, and thousands more of his dejected followers were marching with bowed heads into captivity. But once the surviving Communist cadres reached the forbidding sanctuary of the northern mountains, all efforts to close with and destroy these fanatical zealots would be to no avail.[9]

When the Rock announced on 21 October that meals would henceforth be restricted to "two meals per day, or 3 meals per day at 2/3 quantity," he was not displaying a callous disregard for the welfare of his men.[10] Rather, LTC Throckmorton was facing the facts. The Wonsan operation had left little in the way of a logistical tail to support the Eighth Army's offensive, and the advance to the Yalu River required fuel, ammunition, and food in that order.

On 21 October, Sonny described the advance to his parents. "We are way over the 38th Parallel now. We move during the day on trucks and then find a place to stay for the night. We don't stay more than two nights in any one place. I think we are heading for the capital of North Korea. The other night I went on a patrol in a jeep. It was raining and very cold. We left at 10 o'clock in the night and got back at 12:30. The road was pretty rough. I'm writing this letter in the morning and it's very cold. I'm not used to this weather. I miss Honolulu. There is not much to say, but when we get where we're going, I'll let you know. Just say hello to the family and give my love to Granny. We are getting ready to move again, always on the move."

As the 5th RCT advanced deeper into North Korea, bypassed NKPA troops surrendered in droves. In one seven day period, 893 North Korean soldiers surrendered to the combat team.[11] The 5th RCT reached Anjong-ni on 22 October, capturing 84 more NKPA stragglers without a fight.[12] One soldier was wounded the next day during a brief skirmish that resulted in the capture of 36 more North Korean troops.[13] When the 5th RCT reached Sinanju on 25 October without encountering any resistance, the NKPA's disintegration appeared complete. The most pressing concern at the time was poor mail service.[14] Everyone thought the war was almost over.

CHAPTER FOURTEEN

TWO MOTHERS

The Lord is my light and my salvation; whom shall I fear? The Lord is the strength of my life;
of whom shall I be afraid? When the wicked, even mine enemies and my foes, came upon me to
eat up my flesh, they stumbled and fell. Though an host should encamp against me, my heart shall not fear:
though war should rise against me, in this I will be confident.
Psalm 27:1-3, Holy Bible (KJV)

While Sonny was fighting in Korea, Theresa and Ernest inquired at Tripler General Hospital on Oahu to locate their son's wounded friend, Johnnie Kenawell. After they discovered that Johnnie was not a patient in one the wards, Theresa wrote Mrs. Dorothy Kenawell a letter expressing her condolences that Johnnie had been wounded. She enclosed a couple of photographs taken of Sonny and Johnnie before the two soldiers shipped out to Korea. Theresa was shocked to hear from Dorothy a few days later that Johnnie was dead. A lively correspondence ensued between the two ladies that continued for many years after Sonny's death the following year. Here are excerpts from a couple of Dorothy's letters to Theresa.[1]

5 November 1950
Dear Mrs. Calhau:
I received your letter and was certainly glad to hear from someone who was a friend of Johnnie. I can not thank you enough for the pictures. But I have some bad news for you and your son. Johnnie died the day after he was wounded. I have never heard from the Army how it happened or how bad he was hurt. Words can never tell how much it means to me to know that he was taken care of by your son until they took him to the hospital. I am going to write your son and tell him how much I appreciate his kindness. Mrs. Calhau, about a week before Johnnie died he wrote and told me how he prayed and read his testament, also how he knew the Lord was watching over him or he would have been dead before that. He said that with everybody praying for him he would be home safe. He did go safely home to his Heavenly Father that wanted him for His own child. The Lord has given me the strength to go on and faith to believe. I feel that God only lends us His children and when He thinks we have had them long enough, He takes them back. Johnnie left so much happiness behind him everywhere he went. He gave us all here at home

so many nice things. Last Fall when he was home on furlough he traded the car we had then on a '47 Chevrolet because he wanted us to have something better. He was always trying to spread sunshine all around him. A friend in Honolulu wanted him to telephone home to us before he left for Korea, but he wouldn't do it because he thought we would worry more about him. He always told us not to worry about him. This war is a terrible thing. It has taken so many young boys. None of them have had a chance to enjoy their lives. The young boys haven't a thing to look forward to. Will you please forward Ernest's letter to him as I am not sure where to send it. Please read Psalms 27 & 46 for strength and believe in the Lord Jesus Christ and He will help us at all times. Anxiously awaiting an answer. Love and Prayers. Mrs. Brady Kenawell.

Some of the mothers and fathers who have donated to the ultimate sacrifice. The Gold Star Mothers Club, Windward, Oahu. Theresa is sitting, third from left. Ernest stands behind her. (source: Calhau family)

Theresa quickly posted a warm response, and Dorothy's next letter to Theresa soon followed.

19 November 1950

Dear Mrs. Calhau:

I'll try to answer your letter tonight. I have been so busy working this past week. Yesterday I put in 10 hours at the store where I work. I work as a seamstress, and when I came home last night I was almost dead on my feet. I have to work tomorrow, but I don't know how it's going to be, because I did not get much rest today. I guess part of my being tired is nerves more than anything. Mrs. Calhau, I just pray that Ernest gets through that mess in Korea safe. I hope and pray that you will never go through what we are going through. I just can't make up my mind that Johnnie will never come back to us again. How the boys from Hawaii can stand that cold over there is only something that God alone understands. If only our leaders would quit playing politics and get down on their knees and pray to God for deliverance out of this terrible mess and put our boys' lives ahead of their dumb, stupid selves. I hope that Ernest writes to me. I feel so close to all of the boys and all the people in Hawaii who have been so kind to Johnnie. I know that God has given me strength to go on, and I want to live as close to God as I can so we can be re-united in Heaven. You said you wanted to hear from me again if I cared to write. I enjoy your letters and want to continue hearing from you. Regardless of religion, or race, we are all looking to go to the same place — Heaven. We got the LIFE magazine you told us about. The one boy certainly does look like Johnnie. I want to send Ernest some gift for Xmas in remembrance of Johnnie, but I believe it would be better if I sent it to you instead of sending it to Korea. I sent Johnnie several boxes, but it is doubtful whether he got his first one for all his letters written from 5 September on came back although the boxes haven't, neither has his personal belongings. Love and prayers. Mrs. Kenawell.

CHAPTER FIFTEEN

ENTER THE DRAGON

This will be an infantryman's war.[1]
Peng Dehuai, Commander, Chinese People's Volunteers

On 25 October 1950, the Chinese People's Volunteers made their presence known in North Korea. The 3rd Battalion, 2nd Regiment, ROK 6th Division was advancing towards the Yalu when it was shot to pieces in a Chinese ambush a few miles east of Onjong. Of the battalion's 700 men, 350 were killed or captured. An American KMAG advisor, 1st LT Wilber G. Jones, Jr., West Point Class of 1947, was assigned to the ROK 2nd Regiment. He had served in the 5th RCT in 1949. Reported MIA on 27 October, he would perish in Chinese captivity.[2] The Chinese overran and destroyed the 2nd Regiment's remaining two battalions that night. More disasters followed and, by 1 November, the Chinese had crushed the ROK 6th Division and severely mauled one regiment from the ROK 8th Division.[3] General MacArthur, however, continued to discount the Chinese military presence in North Korea.

Of the 142 North Korean PWs the 5th RCT captured on 25 October, one claimed to have observed 2,500 - 3,000 Chinese troops in Yongsan, and 200-300 Chinese troops in the vicinity of Taechon. Clearly, the tactical situation was rapidly deteriorating.[4] This was particularly evident in the unexpected revival of the NKPA on the battlefield.

Much of the blame for the NKPA's resurgence can be attributed to General MacArthur and General Walker. The stated objective of the invasion of North Korea was to unify the peninsula under one republic. This objective implied the destruction of the NKPA, a task that should have been accomplished immediately following the Inchon invasion. When General MacArthur allowed X Corps to divert the 7th Infantry Division from its primary blocking mission so it could compete for headlines with the 1st Marine Division's attack on Seoul, much of the NKPA escaped and slipped across the 38th Parallel to sanctuary. General MacArthur compounded this error by not permitting X Corps to conduct a hot pursuit into North Korea to overrun and destroy the NKPA. As the battered, yet defiant, NKPA cadres withdrew into North Korea, General MacArthur insisted on conducting the amphibious operation at Wonsan, an operation of dubious value that tied up port facilities, motor transport, expended precious fuel, and wasted the most valuable military commodity of all — time.

While General Walker's Eighth Army laboriously concentrated men, equipment, and supplies along the 38th Parallel to invade North Korea, Kim Il-Sung commenced to ruthlessly rearm and reorganize his shattered forces in remote areas of the country adjacent to Manchuria. Once the Eighth Army invaded North Korea, General Walker compounded General MacArthur's mistakes by making Pyongyang his army's objective rather than concentrating his efforts on the destruction of the NKPA. Due to these serious errors in judgment and strategy, the battered and bruised NKPA escaped complete annihilation and commenced a remarkable recovery in the relative safety of its mountain strongholds. North Korean commanders were anxious for an opportunity to inflict punishment on the unsuspecting Eighth Army, and soon they would have their chance.

Meanwhile, supply problems continued to dog the combat team. Lieutenant Randall Beirne wrote home, "We are living off the country because supply is critical and we are down to two-thirds rations. Our company is well organized at robbing and we have eggs for breakfast (to order) and steaks for lunch and chicken for supper. This will last as long as the land can bear it, I suppose."[5]

King Company captured a Russian truck that they quickly placed in service. Unlike American trucks, this one's engine always turned over in the bitter cold of a North Korean morning.

On 25 October, Sonny wrote his parents, "We are now about fifty miles from the Manchurian border, and it is very cold. There is frost on the ground every morning. I think we are going up as far as the border and then stop. The British and Australian troops are in front of us about three miles. When they move, we move. They are paving the way for us. The 11 Airborne [187th Airborne RCT] made a parachute landing behind the enemy lines, and that helped us a lot. Yesterday, me and some of the boys from our platoon caught some chickens. We gave them to a lady and she fixed us some soup. It was very good. They only feed us two hot meals a day now. It's hard to get food supplies because we are always moving. In fact, I have not got any mail and none of the packages you sent yet. I asked the mail clerk when the mail will get here, and he said today or tomorrow. Well I hope so.

I don't have much time to write now. After we reach the border there is some talk about us going along the east coast line, and maybe to Japan. Some high officer said we would be home before Thanksgiving. I hope and pray that it is true."

First light, on 28 October, found the half-frozen soldiers riding on trucks. For security reasons the canvas tops were down. With weapons at the ready, the men huddled close to one another to block the bitterly cold wind and share their body warmth. As the combat team drove northward on the rutted roads, Sonny had time to write another brief letter to Dawn. "We are still moving, don't stay in one place long. Wish I was home with all of you. It will snow soon. It's very cold here now. It's even cold during the day. I'm writing this letter on a truck, and I'm having a hard time."

The 1st and 2nd Battalions had to dismount their trucks and force their way through an NKPA blocking force before the day was out. Fighter-bombers paved the way for the infantry's advance, blasting a path through the North Korean defenses with rockets, bombs and napalm. For the cost of one American casualty (records do not indicate whether the soldier was KIA or WIA), nine NKPA tanks, four self-propelled guns and eight trucks were destroyed and 78 PWs captured.[6]

Reports of Chinese forces in the 5th RCT's sector continued to flood LTC Throckmorton's Command Post. One report stated that 800 Chinese had passed northwards two days before.[7] At 2125, the 5th RCT S-2/S-3 Journal entry stated, "2nd Battalion is 5,000 yards short Check Point 6 (Taechon) and are stopping for the night. 300 enemy KIA on Objective C. Air and own tanks knocked out 8 enemy tanks and 2 SPs [self-propelled guns]. Air killed an additional 100 enemy… Civilians and prisoners continue to state there are Chinese Communists in vicinity (approx 200)."[8]

Taechon fell to the 5th RCT the next day. Two of the 89 PWs taken during the day's advance were from the Chinese Peoples Volunteers, otherwise known to American military intelligence circles as Chinese Communist Forces (CCF). One might think the capture of two CCF soldiers operating in

The Rock (right) confers with LTC Ward, the CO of 2nd Battalion, somewhere in North Korea. Note the 5th RCT insignia on the Rock's helmet, and the felt tabs worn on his epaulettes that identified him as a unit combat commander. (sources: NA/Chang)

North Korea would have raised considerable interest and excitement in higher headquarters. Indeed, LTC Throckmorton's men had captured the first Chinese troops to be taken prisoner in Korea. Higher Headquarters, much to the combat team's astonishment, refused to believe at first that the prisoners were Chinese.[9] The Rock explained, "We had interrogators who were part Chinese, who spoke Chinese. There was absolutely no question that these prisoners were Chinese. After we questioned them, we sent them to the rear - back to the division [24th] G-2 people for further interrogation. But nobody back at division, or higher echelons, believed they were Chinese."[10]

General MacArthur had staked his professional reputation on his firmly stated belief that Red China would not intervene in a lost cause. In his opinion Red China had missed its best opportunity to intervene when the Eighth Army was fighting in the Pusan Perimeter. He saw no purpose in Chinese intervention at this stage of the conflict and, therefore, discounted viewpoints to the contrary. Such was the force of General MacArthur's personality and reputation that subordinates rarely challenged his intellect or judgement. At this stage of the war, President Truman and the JCS deferred to General MacArthur, too. Reports from units in the field that indicated the presence of sizeable CCF ground combat units in Korea were either ignored or interpreted in such a way that they agreed with MacArthur's strategic view.[11]

The NKPA demonstrated its resurgence on the battlefield, offering unexpectedly stiff resistance as the 27th Commonwealth Brigade advanced a few miles northwest of Sinanju.[12] Twenty-four spanking new T-34 tanks, and large numbers of self-propelled guns and other heavy weapons, provided by the Soviet Union in return for cold, hard cash, opposed the brigade. Led by the Australian Battalion, the brigade advanced under heavy fire and seized Chonju on 29 October, only to be ejected by a vicious North Korean counterattack that killed the CO of the Australian Battalion.

Lieutenant James Johnson felt uneasy as he led Baker Company deeper into the frozen hills. He explained, "The closer we got to the Yalu River, the tougher it became. It was like pushing against a spring when the coils get tighter. The resistance against the spring is harder and harder."[13]

CHAPTER SIXTEEN

REVENGE

*Then said Samuel, Bring ye hither to me Agag the king of the Amalekites. And Agag came unto
him delicately. And Agag said, Surely the bitterness of death is past. And Samuel said, As
thy sword hath made women childless, so shall thy mother be childless among women.
And Samuel hewed Agag in pieces before the Lord in Gilgal.
1 Samuel 15:32-33, Holy Bible (KJV)*

During the advance on Taechon, Sonny discovered that Johnnie Kenawell was dead. He probably read about his friend's death in a letter his parents had forwarded to him from Dorothy Kenawell. Sonny had little time to grieve for his friend. Shortly thereafter, the 2nd Battalion was caught in a series of enemy ambushes in the vicinity of Pokhang. Fox Company committed a war crime in the heat of one of these engagements.

Sonny wrote, "Well we moved up again from the place where I wrote my last letter to you. We are in a small town someplace between Sinanju and Taechon. The name I think is Taifui-ni… about 30 miles from the border. We are traveling northwest near the coast line. I think tomorrow we will go west along the coast line. We have been meeting a little fighting, mostly small enemy road and bridge blocks. We had, rather our platoon had to take a small hill and had a tough time. We started up, and got about half way, when they fired at us. Everybody hit the ground. At first we thought it was from some other GIs, but found out later that there were a few enemy up there. Our lieutenant gave us the order to charge up the hill while our machine gun would cover the advance. We got almost to the top, when them damn guys started throwing grenades at us. They were landing only a few feet in front of us. We could not get to the top by firing our weapons, so we threw grenades back at them. We still could not get to the top, so we went down the hill, about half way. Our lieutenant had one of the tanks that was down below us fire [its] gun to the top. He fired about 5 or 6 rounds, and we started up again. The tank has a 90-mm gun on it, so I guess you know what that could do to them.[1] Well, the machine gun covered us again, and we made it this time. We got to the top, and then they started to come out with their weapons. We let them have it. The Lieutenant gave the order to take no prisoners, so we blasted anything that moved. I don't like to shoot a man that wants to give up, but when you stop to think what they did to our boys, plus my friends that they killed, I got mad and so did the rest of the boys. They hide in these holes, and when you get near they toss a grenade at you. So we shot every one that was on the hill, 20 of them. It was a hard day for our platoon. We have the smallest in Fox Company. Only 23 men now. My squad leader got wounded. Just a light wound, and [he] went back to the aid station. So I am squad leader now. Oh, I almost forgot to tell you… I made corporal a week ago on 26 October, so you will have to put corporal on the envelopes. Well Mom and Dad, I have heard that Kenawell died. I was very sorry to hear that, I'll miss him very much. Him and I was very good friends. I did not think the wound he got was too bad, but they said it was in his head. I sure was broken hearted to hear about him…. Don't worry about me, I'll be all right. I don't think it will be long now before we will come back home."[2]

War is a terrible thing that often brings out the worst in men. While there is no excuse for shooting men attempting to surrender, there is an explanation for why this happened one bitterly cold day on top of a barren, wind-swept hill in North Korea. Losses had taken a steady toll on the 5th RCT's small unit leadership, and although tactical leadership was in evidence that day, responsible, disciplined leadership during the final assault was not. Of the officers who had served in Fox Company in September, only one was left. The others had become casualties during the advance.[3]

The soldiers took revenge for murdered GIs. The NKPA tied this soldier's hands behind his back before they murdered him. (source: Chang)

No one wanted to die in a war that senior officers had declared almost over. Only days before, the NKPA had been a disorganized mob, fleeing in terror before the American advance. Yet suddenly the North Koreans were standing their ground, fighting and killing American soldiers. Thus, the initial feeling of fear experienced by Sonny's platoon was quickly replaced by one of rage. As General Ridgway later wrote, "the men were in no mood to accept the fact that there might be anybody left in North Korea capable of giving them a fight."[4]

Sonny and his comrades were fully aware that the NKPA had brutally murdered hundreds of captured American soldiers earlier in the war. It was well known that, just a few days before, NKPA guards had gunned down 80 defenseless American prisoners on a railroad siding near Pyongyang.[5] The bitter fact that Kim Il Sung's execution squads had murdered thousands of South Korean soldiers and civilians was no mystery either.[6]

That the South Koreans rarely took prisoners at this stage of the war is as understandable as it was deplorable. After all, it was their country that had been laid waste by the invaders, and their friends and loved ones who had been murdered by the North Koreans. People often forget that Korea was a Civil War, a passionate war, the most murderous form of conflict known to man.

On 22 August 1950, an intelligence officer serving in the Tropic Lightning set the tone for the war when he reported, "First Battalion, 35th RCT apprehended two suspected NK agents among refugees who were lepers. They were turned over to the South Korean police who are believed to have executed them. One leper suspected of being an enemy agent was held in the MASAN police station last week. There is the possibility that the enemy are using lepers as espionage agents under the belief that they will not be searched."[7]

That the NKPA exploited lepers for their objectives, and American soldiers handed their captives over to the South Koreans knowing that the latter were sure to execute them, is a succinct and despairing commentary on man's inhumanity to man, and paints a depressing picture for the entire Korean War.

In short, it can not be denied that some American soldiers were looking for revenge. A few days prior to the offensive at Waegwan, and as word of NKPA atrocities poured in, General Walker fanned the flames with a highly irregular speech that he gave to the 7th Cavalry Regiment: "General Walker expressed the hope that when the Regiment moved forward they would have only one thought in mind and that was to kill. 'No prisoners are needed now,' he said, according to the [7th Cavalry] Diary. General Walker further stated that he hoped that present members of the 7th Cav would be the equals of the killers of the 7th Cav history who served in the Regiment when General Custer commanded it. He said if the men did that, then they would have done what God placed them in the world for."[8]

In spite of General Walker's bombastic statement, a macho rhetoric deliberately designed to restore the flagging morale of a severely mauled infantry division, the 1st Cavalry Division's "killers" captured 389 NKPA soldiers during the first four days of bitter, casualty-intensive fighting that characterized the breakout from the Pusan Perimeter.[9] Tens of thousands of NKPA soldiers surrendered to the Eighth Army during the next couple of weeks, a strong indication that few Americans took General Walker's exhortation to heart.

It should be understood, however, that capturing North Korean soldiers often proved extremely dangerous for American soldiers even under ideal conditions. Standard operating procedures called for newly captured PWs to strip naked, precisely because the North Koreans often tried to kill American soldiers with concealed weapons even in captivity. Wounded prisoners were the worst offenders. Instances abounded where a wounded NKPA soldier had used his last grenade to blow up an unsuspecting American soldier attempting to apply first aid. During the fighting at Waegwan, Love Company had carried an unconscious NKPA prisoner swathed in bandages to an aid station. When the doctors checked the prisoner's bandages,

The 5th RCT captured these two NKPA soldiers wearing white civilian clothes in the Pusan Perimeter. (sources: NA/Chang)

they discovered that the NKPA soldier was not wounded. He had been deliberately doped up and left behind for the Americans to find. His instructions were to grab a weapon when he regained consciousness and shoot as many medics as possible before he too was killed.[10]

Nevertheless, wounded prisoners were taken and treated in Army medical facilities. Lieutenant Johnson recalled one horribly wounded NKPA soldier his men wanted to shoot simply to put the poor man out of his misery. "I believe he had been hit by white phosphorous or napalm. The back of his head was almost gone and maggots were growing in his wound…. My people were wondering what to do with him. I said, 'Put him on a jeep and take him to an aid station.' They said, 'Lieutenant, we're going to blow his brains out.' They felt he was in that bad of a condition. Whether or not he survived, I don't know, but we took him to an aid station."[11]

It is often said that revenge is a dish best served cold, and in October 1950, Fox Company took its revenge on the NKPA with cold steel. The soldiers took revenge for being yanked out of their peacetime existence and sent to fight in a war disparagingly described as a Police Action back home. Revenge was taken for American prisoners murdered by their North Korean captors and for the loss of comrades like Johnnie Kenawell, shot in the head by a sniper's bullet near Waegwan.

War is an ugly thing for it consumes not just life and property, but dignity and justice as well. Yet those who cast judgment on the wartime conduct of others from inside the peace and comfort of their own homes should think twice before they confine Sonny and his comrades to the moral dustbin of history. Those who have not experienced the combat soldier's lot, the endless fear, horror, filth, and privation they all endure, should temper their judgments with caution and pray that their own exposure to warfare remains limited to the television set and the printed page. Shooting men attempting to surrender was wrong. Such actions served only to erase what intelligence value the prisoners may have offered the command and encouraged other enemy soldiers to fight all that much harder. Sonny was sufficiently bothered by this incident to write home about it. This is judgement enough.

Lieutenant James Johnson departed the combat team in November after COL Throckmorton's recommendation to early promote the company commander was turned down. The Eighth Army had reversed its policy of promoting lieutenants to captain after they had commanded an infantry company for thirty days when a ship arrived at Pusan with over 700 captains crammed on board who eliminated the previous dire shortage of potential company commanders.

To rub salt into the CO of B Company's wounds, a rear echelon staff officer saw fit to turn down COL Throckmorton's recommendation that LT Johnson be awarded the Combat Infantryman's Badge. It mattered little to the staff officer that LT Johnson had commanded Baker Company with courage, skill, and distinction since Kumchon. Rather, the inflexible bureaucrat followed the administrative regulations. An engineer did not rate to wear the prestigious infantryman's award, or so thought the pen pusher who went about his daily business in a warm tent with a full belly while sitting behind a desk far from the front lines where LT Johnson had risked his life.

When COL Throckmorton asked LT Johnson what he wanted to do, he responded, "I may as well go back to the engineers." Colonel Throckmorton had LT Johnson transferred to the 3rd Combat Engineer Battalion, but the Rock refused to let the issue with the Combat Infantryman's Badge die, and LT Johnson eventually received the coveted award. He was also promoted to captain — and much later to major general.[12]

CAPT Hedberg treats a wounded NKPA prisoner while LT George Hong, Honolulu (kneeling to Hedberg's left), questions the PW. The 5th RCT had a large number of men who spoke fluent Korean, Chinese, and Japanese, an invaluable resource that LTC Throckmorton tapped. (source: Chang)

From Taechon, the 5th RCT attacked northwest towards Kusong. The 3rd Battalion led the advance on 30 October, its momentum slowed by 120-mm mortar barrages and self-propelled guns firing over open sights. Lieutenant Colonel Throckmorton committed the 1st Battalion to the fight, with orders to come up on the

3rd Battalion's left and envelop the stubborn NKPA defenders. The North Koreans gave ground reluctantly, contesting every step of the advance. The combat team reported two Americans and one KATUSA KIA, and twelve Americans and four KATUSAs WIA. Three more Americans died of their wounds at MASH units in the rear.[13]

The combat team's losses on 30 October may have been heavier. Lieutenant James Johnson recalled seeing a reconnaissance team of six men ambushed while driving down a road. There were no survivors. One of the six men killed was 2nd LT Elvin M. Lee, a soldier with long and faithful service in Dog Company, who had received a battlefield commission that very morning. His exemplary combat performance and superior leadership ability during the Chinju Offensive, and the fighting at Sobuk-san and Waegwan, had earned him a set of golden bars. Second Lieutenant Lee had little time to savor the moment. A few hours later, he was caught in an NKPA ambush and killed in the crossfire.[14]

Kusong fell after a stiff fight on Halloween Day. North Korean minefields, small arms fire, and mortar barrages slowed the advance considerably, but FEAF B-26 bombers pounded the defenders, and the 3rd Battalion finally overran the burning town. The combat team reported eight soldiers KIA and ten WIA before the close of the day.[15]

Kusong probably marked the first engagement between American and Chinese forces in Korea. The KATUSA soldiers serving in the combat team identified many of the enemy dead as Chinese.

LT James Johnson wearing the CIB in Sasebo, Japan, when he rotated home later in 1951. (source: James Johnson)

One North Korean PW captured near Kusong stated, "Morale was low, and the troops are deserting the unit at every opportunity. Troops are guarded even when urinating."[16] Nevertheless, NKPA resistance was clearly and surprisingly stiffening.

On 31 October, the combat team's operations officer wrote, "The 5th RCT will continue the attack to the northwest and seize final objective on the Yalu River."[17] An S-2/S-3 Journal entry countered the pervasive optimism later that evening with a civilian's statement who claimed to have seen fifteen truck loads of Chinese troops billeted in a village southeast of Kusong.[18]

From 29 September to the morning of 31 October 1950, the 5th Infantry had incurred 21 men KIA and 52 wounded in action. Non-battle casualties took a steady toll on the combat team in October, with 209 men evacuated due to injuries and sickness.[19]

Replacements arrived in time to participate in the final push to the Yalu. First Lieutenant Frank A. Athanason joined the 555th FAB in the last days of October. The Army had drafted him during his sophomore year at The Citadel in the closing weeks of World War II. Lieutenant Athanason arrived in Korea five years later determined to play his part in the war. When LTC Clarence Stuart decided against assigning him a specific job because the war would soon be over, the artillery officer was disappointed.[20] The CCF would soon solve this problem, and we will have cause to return to LT Athanason later.

On 1 November, the 1st Battalion attacked northwards up a narrow valley into fierce enemy automatic weapons and mortar fire. Their objective was a road junction a few miles north of Kusong where a combined force of approximately 5,000 CCF and NKPA soldiers had dug in to fight. Lieutenant Keith Whitham's 2nd Tank Platoon supported the advance, the long barrels of the 76-mm main guns slamming high explosive shells into the enemy positions. Captain Hank Emerson's Able Company executed a classic envelopment after a night infiltration through the hills to strike the rear of a Chinese infantry company dug in on the forward slope of a ridgeline. As the Chinese fired down into the valley at other elements of the 1st Battalion far below, Able's soldiers caught the enemy with his pants down and wiped out the terribly surprised CCF rifle company.

Lieutenant Whitham recalled, "We had reached a point ten to twelve miles north of Kusong when 1st Battalion executed what was probably the finest by the book small unit envelopment of the Korean War. In the confusion of the Chinese officially entering the Korean War that same night this action was never recognized or publicized… Hank Emerson's A Company achieved complete surprise and demolished the entire company of Chinese in their foxholes. When I joined Hank Emerson and his lieutenants on the hill they were counting Chinese casualties. Lieutenant Colonel Roelofs

(source: NA)

later told me that when he called in his company commanders to explain this mission, Hank Emerson kept saying 'let me go, let me go,' so A Company was given the mission."[21]

Regrettably, the new CO of Baker Company failed to cross the LD in support of Able Company. This was the second time in the past few days that this officer had failed to accomplish an assigned mission while under enemy fire. Captain Emerson was understandable angry that Able Company was not properly supported; Lieutenant Colonel Roelofs concurred and relieved this officer on the spot.

Long after the war, Lieutenant General Emerson explained, "I received a lot of credit for running a good company in Korea, but I had a bunch of outstanding NCOs. Two of them, Earl Davis and Robert Lyons, earned battlefield commissions. I was damned fortunate to have men like Lyons and Davis in my company," he recalled. "It's my personal opinion that men who earn battlefield commissions make the best leaders in combat. Whenever our country is thrust into a big shooting war, a lot of guys with West Point or ROTC commissions are killed and wounded. The Army has historically reached down into the ranks to commission some of its best NCOs to fill the gaps. We have not done a good job of taking care of these guys after our wars are over. I think the Army should pull out all the stops to help them get an education. Bob Lyons rose to the rank of lieutenant colonel on a Ninth Grade education. Just think how far he went, and how much further he might have gone, if the Army had done him right and given him a paid sabbatical so he could have earned a college degree."[22]

By sunset, the combat team had killed approximately 400 NKPA and CCF soldiers, destroyed two self-propelled guns, eight 76-mm field guns, eight mortars, and six anti-tank guns.[23] In one village, where all the huts were burning, the ammunition laboriously stored by the enemy had begun to cook off and explode.[24]

Late that afternoon, a courier plane dropped LTC Throckmorton a message that ordered him to halt the combat team's northward advance.[25] A few hours later, as enemy mortar shells burst around the 1st Battalion, the 5th RCT received another message to "How Able" and withdraw to the south.[26]

Lieutenant General Walker, concerned about the deteriorating situation in II ROK Corps' sector where the CCF had made their presence known with devastating results earlier in the week, had ordered I Corps to halt its advance. After conducting a near unopposed advance to the Yalu, the Eighth Army had unknowingly entered a massive, intricately planned, Chinese trap. Sensing that the inhospitable hills around him contained thousands of CCF troops, LTC Throckmorton was relieved to receive the order to withdraw. "By that time," he recalled, "I could feel the hair was standing up on the back of my neck."[27]

CHAPTER SEVENTEEN

KUNU-RI

A massive assault by Chinese Communists and North Koreans trapped an American regiment on the north-west front today. It was the first time U.S. and Chinese forces met in battle.
The Honolulu Advertiser, *2 November 1950*

Despite evidence to the contrary, General MacArthur refused to believe the Chinese had massively intervened in the Korean War. He could not have been more wrong. Strong elements of the CCF Fourth Field Army were present in great force, having skillfully eluded FEAF reconnaissance flights through a combination of arduous night marches, superb light discipline, and exemplary use of terrain and camouflage.[1]

A CCF field army consisted of two or more army groups. An army group was further subdivided into two or more armies of three divisions each.[2] Chinese infantry divisions averaged 10,000 men apiece divided into three infantry regiments and one artillery regiment. With few exceptions, the Chinese divisions that crossed the Yalu in October 1950 had left their artillery regiments behind in Manchuria, largely because the presence of heavy weapons would have slowed the advance of the infantry through the mountains.[3]

A CCF infantry regiment was organized in a traditional triangular pattern with three infantry battalions for a strength of approximately 2,500 men. Similarities with Western armies, and even between other CCF regiments, ended at the regimental level, because the CCF was armed with a hodgepodge of Soviet, Japanese, and even American weapons captured at the close of the Chinese Civil War. A distrustful Stalin had not bestowed the same largess on the CCF that he had expended on the NKPA before the Korean War.

Chinese equipment deficiencies were counterbalanced by the superb organizational skills of the Communist Party and the CCF's recent and extensive combat experience. Political officers combined their own unique leadership talents with those of hard-bitten, combat experienced officers and NCOs who thoroughly understood the brutal business of war.[4] Together, they formed the cadre, the backbone of the CCF combat units committed to Korea. The cadre ensured the CCF soldiers who crossed the Yalu in October 1950 were well-trained, highly motivated, and firm believers in the righteousness of their cause — "Resist America, Aid Korea." In briefings the cadre emphasized the CCF's vast numerical superiority over the Eighth Army in Korea. As one Chinese soldier was told, "Seeing that there are only 50,000 U.S. troops in Korea at present, and their weapons are not particularly excellent, our mere appearance in Korea will put them to rout as far as Pusan, only to flee away to Japan thereafter."[5]

Communist Party membership extended down to squad leaders, who never ceased to extol the gains made in China by Chairman Mao's revolution, and the danger posed by an American advance to the Manchurian border. Rifle squads were further subdivided into several "groups of three," a fireteam organization. These groups were led by a soldier the Party apparatus considered politically reliable. Indeed, the CCF leadership, in the words of one historian, had "very little tolerance for the development of comradely ties that were not cemented by mutually shared Communist convictions."[6] Most Chinese soldiers fought out of conviction rather than fear of punishment. In fact, CCF soldiers were serving in the first Asian army to have abolished the practice of beatings in the ranks.

Lightly armed CCF soldiers marched an average of eighteen miles a night toward a predetermined assembly area. By sunrise, the men and their equipment were thoroughly camouflaged and remained that way throughout the day. When an offensive was imminent, the CCF emphasized the rapid concentration of forces to conduct the assault, followed, if necessary, by an equally rapid disengagement. The Chinese practiced meticulous tactical reconnaissance, and were masters at locating and exploiting unit boundaries, gaps, and flaws in their opponent's defensive lines.[7]

Colonel Alpha L. Bowser, the G-3 of the 1st Marine Division, aptly described Chinese offensive tactics as "assembly on the objective."[8] Chinese commanders preferred to conduct night attacks to avoid artillery fire and air strikes. Units advanced in column formations, over rough terrain, until contact was made. Once engaged, the Chinese hit the ground, opened fire, and crawled forward to within grenade range of their opponents. As the fighting raged, Chinese commanders funneled an ever-growing number of combat troops into the action regardless of casualties in order to achieve short-range fire superiority over their opponent at the decisive point. Units advanced to force a penetration whenever their opponent's defensive fire slackened. Multiple penetrations were sought. Once the Chinese overran one position, unit commanders would immediately attack the flanks of opposing forces still defending the front lines. As described in the Marine Corps official history of the Korean War, "Each step of the assault was executed with practiced stealth and boldness, and the results of several such penetrations on a battalion front could be devastating."[9]

The CCF suffered from several major handicaps in November 1950 when Mao confronted the UN in Korea. First and foremost, the Chinese were in no position to contest American air superiority. As a consequence, the Chinese were vulnerable to air attack once battle was joined. In the mountains of North Korea, the CCF successfully employed passive air defense measures to limit damage from this form of attack. Nevertheless, the constant threat of air attack was a bitter reality faced by CCF commanders, and one much feared by Chinese soldiers who possessed few antiaircraft weapons at this time.

The further the CCF advanced into Korea, the more it became necessary to adopt Western logistical practices in the form of truck convoys and trains to carry food and ammunition forward to the combat units. Once this occurred, the FEAF exacted a steep price in destroyed supplies and equipment from Chinese and North Korean transportation units.

The inordinately weak CCF logistical tail made it difficult for the Chinese to supply their forces in an intensive war of maneuver. A Chinese soldier who crossed the Yalu in October 1950 carried a four-day supply of food. After this ran out, he was on his own. Hunger was common. Starvation and disease would savage the ranks of the CCF as the first year of the war progressed.

Limited organic infantry firepower, inadequate artillery and mortar fire support, and the virtual absence of radio communications below the regimental level all posed a severe handicap to CCF combat units. Only one out of every three or four CCF soldiers in the opening stages of the Chinese

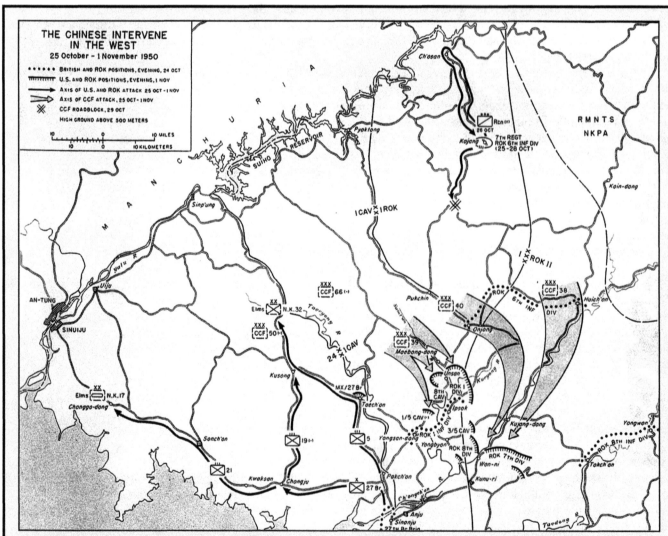

After seizing Kusong, the Eighth Army halted the 5th RCT's advance to the Yalu and redirected the combat team to Kunu-ri to hold this vital crossroads. (source: Center for Military History)

intervention actually carried a rifle or submachine gun. Crew-served weapons were few, and ammunition scarce. Most CCF infantry initially fought solely with grenades. Excellent leadership and a massive pool of manpower partially compensated for the CCF's poor logistics, limited communications and inadequate firepower.

Another handicap, one less remarked on than others, hindered the tactical employment of the CCF in Korea. United States Army and Marine Corps infantry generally displayed more tactical initiative at the small unit level than that found in CCF combat units. For instance, even if all the officers and NCOs in an Army or Marine platoon became casualties in the course of an engagement, there was invariably a private or PFC who took charge of his comrades and continued the fight.

The same level of tactical initiative on the part of the individual Chinese soldier remained rare throughout the Korean War. If the cadre was incapacitated by heavy losses, groups of CCF soldiers often succumbed to panic or laid down their arms and surrendered. In short, the fighting power of a CCF unit was proportional to the cadre's casualty ratio. In the case of a prolonged war, the danger existed that extensive losses in the cadre would threaten the political stability and combat effectiveness of the CCF. "Once their key men became casualties, Chinese units quickly collapsed," recalled one of the combat team's former battalion commanders.[10]

By November 1950, the CCF XIII Army Group had 180,000 men poised to strike an unsuspecting Eighth Army a devastating blow with a juggernaut of nineteen divisions. A further 120,000 CCF troops from the IX Army Group threatened X Corps in the vicinity of the Changjin Reservoir.[11] The dragon was prepared to strike.

Approximately 20 miles to the east of the 5th RCT, the 8th Cavalry Regiment paid a terrible price for their own, and General MacArthur's, arrogance. At dusk, on 1 November, strong elements of the CCF 116th and 115th Divisions hit the ROK 15th Regiment, and the 1st and 2nd Battalions, 8th Cavalry Regiment.[12] Within two hours the ROKs had completely collapsed. Intense CCF pressure forced a wedge between the 1st and 2nd Battalions, 8th Cavalry, and both units fell back on Unsan. By 2200, elements of the 1st and 2nd Battalions had expended their ammunition and, in places, the CCF had overrun the front lines. One hour later, the 3rd Battalion, 8th Cavalry was ordered to cover the withdrawal of the 1st and 2nd Battalions, but the plan rapidly fell apart.

Losses were heavy, with the 1st Battalion losing 265 of its 800 men, and the 99th FAB all 12 of its 105-mm howitzers during the withdrawal. A handful of survivors reached the dubious safety of the 3rd Battalion's lines before that unit, too, came under attack.

When a large force of CCF soldiers approached a bridge guarded by the 3rd Battalion's sentries, the American soldiers allowed the Chinese to cross without being challenged. These Chinese troops, probably mistaken for ROK soldiers by the sentries, attacked the CP and mortally wounded the battalion commander. The fighting increased in ferocity as the Chinese struck the 3rd Battalion's perimeter from all sides. At dawn, a devilish combination of fog, smoke, and haze protected the CCF from air strikes. With the guns of the 99th FAB out of action, the 3rd Battalion had to rely solely on organic weapons for its own defense. Ammunition was running low when the dazed survivors rallied around the ruins of the CP to make a stand.

At daybreak the 5th and 7th Cavalry regiments counterattacked to relieve the beleaguered defenders, but the CCF inflicted appalling casualties on both outfits and prevented a link up. With CCF forces swarming into the Eighth Army's vulnerable rear, I Corps ordered the 1st Cavalry Division to withdraw and abandon the 3rd Battalion, 8th Cavalry to its fate. Those unfortunate men too badly wounded to be moved were left behind when the battalion broke out in small groups. Only 200 of the battalion's 800 soldiers reached friendly lines.[13]

General Walker halted the offensive to the Yalu in order to extract units from his overextended front to plug the yawning gap on his right flank. As headlines in the United States screamed, "U.S. Suffers War's Worst Defeat," I Corps ordered the 24th Infantry Division, with 5th RCT attached, to withdraw to Sinanju on the Chongchon River line.[14] On the eastern edge of this line lay the obscure town of Kunu-ri.

Nestled in a valley surrounded by rugged mountains, Kunu-ri straddled an important road junction that had to be held at all costs to allow the battered ROK II Corps to extricate its men and equipment from the mountains to the north and east of the town. The north-south MSR that ran through Kunu-ri doubled as the boundary line between the ROK II Corps and I Corps. On 3 November, I Corps detached the 5th RCT from the 24th Infantry Division and rushed the combat team to Kunu-ri to backstop the remnants of the ROK 7th Division. A tank platoon from the 21st Infantry reinforced the combat team.

The CCF slammed into the ROK 7th Division the next morning, and kicked the ROK 5th Regiment off Hill 622, a key terrain feature overlooking the crossroads below. Captain Hank Emerson, the CO of A Company, halted and reorganized the fleeing ROK soldiers and ordered them to retake their former positions.[15] "We were tackling and holding them as they ran past our lines," recalled CAPT Emerson. "My company got strafed by two South Korean P-51s that thought we were Chinese. We got hit by rocket and machine gun fire and lost two men."[16]

The ROKs rallied and counterattacked, driving the CCF off the crest of Hill 622. The hill changed hands several times in bitter, brutal fighting throughout the day. Yet when the sun set, the battered and bloodied ROKs held the crest.[17]

Meanwhile, the CCF struck the 5th RCT a heavy blow. An overcast sky precluded effective air support throughout the day, while freezing rain soaked the miserable soldiers. The rifle companies had dug in on isolated hill masses, and were attempting to cover the large gaps between units with fire, when the CCF commenced the assault.

Screaming masses of Chinese infantry formed up in the open without fear from air attack to strike the 5th RCT's thin lines. With bugles blaring and whistles shrilling, the Chinese infantry ran forward firing burp guns and rifles from the hips and hurling grenades into the 5th RCT's shallow foxholes. The 555th FAB's batteries employed high angle fire, slamming hundreds of 105-mm high explosive shells into the enemy ranks. Still the Chinese came on, seeking a weak spot in the 5th RCT's line.

Private First Class Gene E. McClure's 75-mm Recoilless Rifle Squad had traded its recoilless rifle for an extra .50-caliber machine gun. The men had just arrived in their position, and had yet to dig in, when the fog lifted and exposed a mass of Chinese infantry advancing on the American lines.

The .50-caliber machine gun crew took the CCF infantry under fire at long range, knocking the Chinese down in piles of bloody rags. "There were so many that you simply could not miss," explained Private McClure. "The best part about it was that at this time we were receiving very little return fire, everything was going our way…. But still they came on, and on, and on, endless ranks of them…. Within 45 minutes to one hour the CCF were building up their firepower from positions they had reached — despite our best efforts — on the hill just opposite ours about 300 yards away. We simply could not kill them all, some were getting through…. During this time my squad had two casualties…. Chinese firepower had built up to such an extent that anyone who stuck his head up would get hit. The whisper of small arms bullets passing overhead sounded like a sewing machine near our ears as they began to put more automatic weapons fire on us. I remember watching as bullets hit some twigs and branches of a small bush just behind me… the enemy fire had built up to such an extent all along the line that Chinese infantry had been able to cause the rifle company on our right flank (perhaps E Company) to withdraw, leaving our own position exposed to an attack from that quarter… we were taking turns… standing up in full view of the enemy on the opposite hill, and firing our weapons while those who had just emptied theirs were reloading, and all the while our machine gun never let up…. Normally most of us never acted so foolishly as to stand up in full view, kind of showing off in front of each other, and it served no useful purpose other than being a good way to get hurt, nor did we usually joke back and forth with each other so much as we were doing this time, especially if we were on the verge of being overrun as in this case. But for some reason which I have never quite understood, our morale was exceptionally high at this particular moment, almost a state of euphoria, and we were joking and laughing a lot and throwing caution to the winds…. Eventually we received orders to fall back…. This was the only time I ever remember our unit giving up this much ground while a battle was in progress, but pressure generated by a massive Chinese attack of this type is very great…. We had continued to fire our machine gun until almost all the other infantrymen around us had quit the hill…. I had never felt so alone before. It goes without saying that a .50-caliber machine gun and its tripod is very heavy… so we simply unscrewed the barrel taking it with us... and placed a thermite grenade in the breach of the gun…. We just made it out by the most narrow of margins."[18]

Charlie Company drew considerable enemy fire as it defended a heavily wooded area. Soldiers who had survived the disaster at Bloody Gulch, and the severe mauling on Sobuk-san, found their nerves sorely tested as masses of mustard-clad Chinese infantry rushed their shallow foxholes.

First Lieutenant Morgan B. Hansel, a rifle platoon leader in Charlie Company, had until recently been serving in Headquarters and Headquarters Company, 5th RCT. Known as "Morgie" to his friends, the combat veteran from World War II had volunteered to take over a rifle platoon and was assigned to C Company.

That afternoon, as the CCF pressed Charlie Company hard, LT Hansel ran upright in front of his company's foxholes, carbine in hand, to close with a Chinese machine gun that was killing his soldiers. The company first sergeant followed LT Hansel, not to be outdone by the officer. Neither soldier reached the Chinese weapon — both died in a fusillade of enemy fire.[19]

Sergeant Hibbert Manley was the platoon sergeant for the 1st Platoon, Charlie Company at Kunuri. After the death of LT Hansel, his platoon withdrew under intense enemy fire a short distance. Here, they dug in and repulsed the Chinese. Corporal Jacob "Jake" B. Kahaihipuna stood upright with a towel-wrapped machine gun cradled in his massive arms, pouring automatic weapons fire into the Chinese. For his actions that day, CPL Kahaihipuna was awarded the Silver Star. "He was the best machine gunner I ever knew," said SGT Manley.[20]

After a long spell on FO duty, SGT Kenny Freedman had returned to Dog Company's 81-mm Mortar Platoon for a rest. "Some rest," he thought as he adjusted his mortar sight. The platoon's six 81-mm mortars fired as fast as the assistant gunners could drop rounds down their smoking tubes, and still the Chinese came on, in squad and platoon rushes, through a howling inferno of defensive fire. Sergeant Freedman raised the el-

Two 5th RCT soldiers watch for enemy activity. (source: Chang)

evation, leveled the sight's bubbles, and directed the assistant gunner to drop another round down the long, black tube. The high explosive shell hit the firing pin at the base of the tube, where the increments exploded and sent the projectile hurtling in a high parabola through the overcast sky until the shell came crashing down amidst the Chinese. Within an hour, the mortar platoon had consumed a basic load of ammunition, having killed and wounded scores of Chinese, their mangled, bloodied corpses sprawled in grotesque patterns across the frozen ground. Service Company's magnificent performance kept the mortars supplied with ammunition that day, much to the discomfort of the Chinese.[21]

Lieutenant Randall Beirne witnessed the death of a medic, SGT Neil K. Dorrion, who sacrificed his life to save a wounded comrade. "This medic came out of Tripler General Hospital," said LT Beirne. "He jumped forward to patch up a man who had been hit when they shot him, but he didn't bother and kept on working until they killed him. The bravery of some of those medics was unbelievable. Here was a man, a sergeant, who had worked in an operating room of a peacetime hospital. He knew exactly what to do to keep these guys alive, and his business came first, not his own personal safety. It was so cold that he had been keeping his morphine next to his body to keep it warm."[22]

The 5th RCT's stand at Kunu-ri temporarily stabilized the Eighth Army's hard-pressed lines. During the fighting, the combat team captured a handful of cold and hungry Chinese PWs. "They appeared to be extremely well dressed," said PFC Arlen Russell. "They were better equipped for the cold weather than we were with their quilted uniforms, good quilted hats and everything. The one thing that stuck out in my mind, however, was their feet. They were still wearing those rubber soled canvas tennis shoes and their feet had to be freezing in that weather. They were obviously different people than the ones we had been fighting, better dressed and better equipped. They did not have a defeatist attitude, that much was certain. When we found out for sure that they were really Chinese, it was disheartening, because we knew at that point that the war wasn't over. There wasn't any going home by Christmas."[23]

The following day, 5 November, SGT Hibbert Manley led a group of men from C Company to recover the bodies of LT Hansel and the first sergeant. They found eight dead CCF soldiers, too, including one who must have been a paymaster. This particular Chinese soldier was loaded down with paper currency and carried a large Mauser automatic pistol in a leather holster.[24]

The combat team's casualties soared with the active intervention of the Chinese. From 28 October to 4 November 1950, the 5th RCT had incurred ninety-seven battle losses, more casualties than during the first twenty-seven days of October combined.[25] American forces had incurred nearly 30,000 casualties in Korea since the war began, and most of these losses had been in the infantry.[26] General MacArthur's promise to have the boys home before Thanksgiving was turning into a cruel joke for the troops on the firing line.[27]

On 9 November, Sonny vented his frustration and weariness to in a letter his parents. "I'm really sick of Korea. I have not been writing much, because I don't have time. I am very busy now. I made corporal, and I am also a squad leader of the 1st Squad in my platoon. It's a big job now. I have to check all my men every time we go into battle, to see if they have all the right equipment, such as ammunition, [make sure] their rifles fire, and that they have warm clothes. I have nine men in my squad. There's me, my assistant and his assistant. You see the squad is composed of three GIs and six Koreans. We are short of GIs. It's hard to explain to them [KATUSA]. Well we still get along good anyway. We are seeing plenty of action, so I guess all those good rumors I told you about are really all rumors. Looks like we'll be home for Xmas. I still pray for this war to end. We were only 8 miles from the Manchurian border line, but were called back about 50 miles. I don't know where the heck we are now… I gave the boys some things from my last package, and they all liked the coconut candy best. I also got a package from Granny. It had Poi and fish in it. I sure liked that."

How Company's mess sergeant issued hot bouillon soup to the grateful soldiers who came down from their hillside positions a handful at a time late one freezing cold night to fill their canteen cups with the life-saving brew. As PFC Gene McClure stood off to one side of the line, he witnessed a never to be forgotten incident. "One of our Nisei soldiers came out of the darkness," he recalled, "and walked right up to me without going through the chow line… I noticed that he seemed to be clutching or holding something under his coat near his stomach, but I attributed this to him trying to keep… warm. He was holding a cigarette in one hand and said, 'Hi McClure, how are you doing?' I said, 'Well I'm trying to get warm right now,' and noting that he came from the direction from which the sounds of heavy firing were coming from, I asked him how things were going over there in his area. He said it was doing OK, and then asked me if I had a light. I fished around and found my matches and lighted his cigarette. He said 'thanks,' then without another word walked off into the night toward the rear. I soon found out that this man had been severely wounded in the abdomen and had several bullets in the gut and was walking out by himself. He had been with us since Hawaii, of course, but now for the life of me I can not remember if he lived or died from his wounds. I know he never returned to our unit."[28]

The wily CCF field commanders broke contact with the Eighth Army on their own accord. Chinese morale soared after the defeats they had inflicted on the vaunted Americans. They would strike again.

On 12 November, Sonny was promoted to sergeant.[29] He was a combat experienced infantry sergeant at the tender age of nineteen. Sonny did not find out about his promotion until the middle of January 1951 when he was a patient in the 35th Station Hospital in Kyoto, Japan.

CHAPTER EIGHTEEN

Aloha, From Across the Sea

Aloha! is a word always on the Hawaiian's tongue, and it is the most expressive word spoken by any
people, except when the superlative affix "nui" accompanies it. Aloha-nui! What does not the
expression carry with it! Extreme felicitation, and love, and hope, and sympathy
— all that is loveable and beautiful of thought and feeling.
William S. Bryan, Our Islands and Their People, Volume II

Corporal James Shaw, from Ogden, Utah, was a very sick man. Since his arrival in Korea, this veteran from Charlie Battery, 555th FAB, had been assigned to the FO Team supporting King Company. Deep inside North Korea, he fell prey to a disease as deadly as shrapnel and bullets. After much prodding from comrades and friends, an exhausted and nauseated CPL Shaw reported to a field medic. One look at the yellow whites of his eyes sufficed for a diagnosis — yellow jaundice. "You're in trouble," said the overworked medic. "We're shipping you to Japan."

Most of the cold, tired, and hungry soldiers serving in Korea would have relished the prospect of being evacuated to Japan. Captain Joseph Lukitsch, the CO of King Company, quite naturally exclaimed, "My God, you lucky cuss, you!"[1]

An ambulance transported CPL Shaw to Pyongyang where an Air Force transport flew him out that same night. Upon arrival at the 35th Station Hospital in Kyoto, Japan, he was billeted in a room with another soldier suffering from yellow jaundice, CPL Ernest "Sonny" Calhau, the soldier from Lanikai.

On 15 November, Sonny had been evacuated from Korea with yellow jaundice, an often fatal disease that plays havoc with one's liver. The treatment for American soldiers consisted of bed rest, plenty of wholesome food, and swallowing sixteen yeast pills twice a day. Once a week a patient had a dye injected into his bloodstream. An hour later, he had a blood sample taken. If the dye was gone, then the soldier's liver was considered fully functional, and he was granted seven days of convalescence leave in Japan before he returned to his unit. A few serious cases were returned to the States or Hawaii for further treatment.[2]

On 23 November 1950, Sonny wrote his first letter home from the hospital."Hello Mom and Dad. How are you? Fine I hope. Well I'm in Japan now. I'm in a hospital, but I'm not wounded. I have a sickness called yellow jaundice. I don't have a serious case. This sickness is in the liver.... I will stay in this hospital for about 1 or 2 months. This sickness I got requires a lot of rest and plenty of good food. After being in Korea, this place is like Heaven. I have a nice room. There are only two beds in this room. There is another boy in this room with me. He is from the same outfit I'm from, the 5th RCT. There is a lot of this type of sickness in this hospital. The bad cases have to stay in this hospital from 3 to 6 months. I have a nice soft bed and after sleeping in holes, I sleep like a log. And they give you the best food. I get three hot meals a day. I eat everything that they give me. They serve you right in bed. The nurses change the bed every morning. They give you a clean towel and wash rag every morning too. Now I can eat all I want, sleep all I want, and I can take a good bath every night. Mom this Hospital is Heaven. I hope the war is over before I ever get out of this hospital. I never want to go back to Korea. In fact Mom, I'm kind of glad I got this sickness. As I said before, it's not serious, so don't worry about me. I will probably be in here for my birthday, and Xmas. It's much better than being in Korea. When I left Korea it was snowing, and it was very cold. I'm not used to cold weather.... I should gain lots of weight now. I weighed myself today — 161 pounds — not bad. When I left Honolulu I weighed 170 pounds. Dad I don't have any money. Could you please send me about $10. You see, on paydays, I never took any money because I had no use for it in Korea. I've spent my last $5 since I've been in the hospital. You see Dad, they have a little snack bar, like a soda fountain, and I've been buying ice cream and hamburgers. I have not eaten any ice cream since I left Honolulu. So when I got to Japan and found out about the snack bar, I just had to eat ice cream and hamburgers. And I need money to buy stamps also. I am going to try and get a small partial pay through the Red Cross. But I don't know when I can get it. I miss you all very much. I dream about all of you every night. I hope when I'm all well that they ship me home. May God Bless you Mom and Dad. Love, Sonny."

Sonny slowly recovered his health, nurtured by dreams of home. He bore his nightmarish fear of returning to Korea with pride and dignity. Family and friends wrote Sonny and cheered him up with the local news from Oahu. He quickly made friends with the other hospitalized soldiers, particularly with CPL Shaw and other comrades from the 5th RCT. They passed the long, pleasant days exchanging experiences from home and Korea.

Sonny's menu cover. (source: Calhau family)

"Sonny was an exceptionally neat guy," said CPL Shaw. "He was probably the best friend I ever had in my life. He was congenial and tough at the same time. We'd go out into town and no one would mess with us. He was the kind of guy who would do anything for you. A true friend."[3]

Sonny wrote many letters to family and friends while he slowly recovered at the 35th Station Hospital. A few of his thoughts are presented below.

29 November
Dear Mom and Dad,

We had a nice Thanksgiving dinner. We get the best of food. I get milk and cereal for breakfast..... They are trying to build up my strength. I feel good now - plenty of sleep..... Everyone in this hospital is nice. The Red Cross nurses come by everyday to ask what you want or need. They give you soap, shaving things, and all the writing paper you need. Last night they put on a quiz show. I had a lot of fun, but we don't leave our beds..... We have a lot of library books to read. The other boy in my room has a radio. His name is Shaw, and he is from the same outfit. We listen to the news and radio programs. We heard some boxing and some good football games. Last night, I listened to Suspense. So don't worry about me. I'm fine and much happier here than in Korea. Shaw was in Honolulu when the 5th was there. He's been with the 5th a long time. He is a corporal too..... I still pray every night. Give my love to Granny. Tell Buddy and Manley to write. I sure miss them. Tell them I'll be with them soon, I hope. P.S. Tell Miss Slattery hello. Dear Dad, could you please send me the clipping of the Thanksgiving Day football game?

1 December
Dear Buddy and Manley,

How are you guys? How is school? Did Roosevelt finally make out in football this year? Buddy, did you fix your car yet? Did Manley ever buy that car he wanted? Well I'm in Japan taking life easy. I hope I don't have to go back to Korea. Don't ever go into the Army until they call you. This is your last year of school. Study hard and you will make it. I sure wish I did not fool around in school. How is the weather there? Do you still go out swimming and go out in the boat? When I left Korea, it was snowing and plenty cold too. Well this month is a birthday for Manley and me. I'll be twenty years old. I will probably be in bed on my 20th birthday. There is another boy in my room with me. He is from the 5th too. His birthday was yesterday, November 30. He is also 20 years old. He is about my size and has a nice build. Him and I hope to go to Honolulu together. Well Buddy and Manley, I'll say Aloha for now, and take care of the body. I miss you guys very much and hope to see you soon. P.S. Write to me and give me the dope on what is going on around Kailua and school.

4 December
Dearest Mom and Dad,

Well today I was happy to get your letter and the newspaper you sent me. I also got the money you sent me and the stamps. Believe me Dad, I want to thank you so much for the money and the stamps. So far I did not get paid yet, but I did put in for one. Now I will have plenty of stamps, and Dad you don't have to send me any writing paper, because the Red Cross gives us all we want. I got a package from Mom. It came from Korea..... Please don't send anymore because I can't eat certain foods. Anything with fat or lard is no good for me. I can not eat candy. Me and the other fellow in the room are eating the things you sent little-by-little. Mom I want to thank you for all the packages you sent me, I have enjoyed them very much. I will never forget the things you did for me and sent to me. You kept my morale high while I was in Korea... Well the news in Korea is very bad. I hate to think of going back there... I had a "Dream" the other night that I came home and everything was the same again.... when I woke-up I really felt like crying. Today I got mail from Aunt Lucille Gomes and a card from Pat and Allen. Aunt Lucille always wrote to me while I was in Korea. She even sent me a nice package... She is a darn good aunt to me. I will always remember her for that. Uncle Able sent me a small surf-board, about 5 inches long with my address on it.

5 December
Dearest Granny,

Hello Granny, how are you? I'm in the best of health..... I've been in Japan 3 weeks. I'm very glad to be here. In fact I'm glad I got sick. At least I'm not in Korea, although I kind of hated to leave my friends, because I came with them, and fought with them, and then I had to leave them. I'm always praying to God to protect them boys..... After being in Korea so long, and not sleeping on a bed, and not getting good food, and no good care, this hospital is like heaven, believe me..... All I do is sleep, read and eat. I would like to stay here till the war ended. I only wish it would end soon.

5 December

Dearest Mom,

Well Mom I got your letter today dated 29 November... You wanted to know what caused my yellow jaundice. When I was in Korea, the first thing was that my stomach hurt me, and I did not have any [desire] to eat anything. I got weak, and my eyeballs turned a yellowish color, also my skin. It was like that for about a week until I went to sick report. I did not know that I had yellow jaundice. I went to sick call because I had a cold. I can eat only special foods. I get the packages that you sent to Korea, and I give them to the Red Cross. They will send them to the boys that are in Korea still fighting for Xmas. That is the least I can do for them. I know how happy I was when I got a package from home. That will make them feel good. They are asking for things for the boys there..... I wish I could be shipped to a hospital in Honolulu near my family and friends. I sure miss Lanikai. One of these days God will answer my prayers, and I will be home. But I should not complain too much. This is much better than being in Korea.

7 December

Dear Mom,

Yesterday we had a Japanese magician here. He gave us a pretty good show. Today we had some Japanese actresses here. Not bad looking Japanese girls. They gave us flowers and cards. Tomorrow I get a blood test. They put some kind of fluid in one arm, and wait about one hour, and then take blood from the other arm. I have had several of them. That is to check if your liver is normal. Nothing to it. I got a hair cut the other day. Since I left Honolulu my hair grows slow. I got another letter from Lona today and was happy to hear from her.

10 December

Dearest Mom,

Yesterday they sent four boys who had yellow jaundice back to the States. Their cases will take more than two months to cure. I wish they would send me home..... I hope you folks keep writing me as I'm very lonely and mail means a lot to me..... I guess by the time you get this letter, I'll be 20 years old. I wish I was home with you on my birthday. We've been having good weather here in Japan. Most every night, I get some ice cream. Yesterday we had some Hawaiian music here. I got homesick when they played. Well looks like I will be here for Xmas. Better here than in Korea..... Say hello to Dad and the rest. God Bless you Mom.

11 December

Dearest Mom,

Today I got three packages, a bunch of mail, and two Star-Bulletin Newspapers. I was very happy to get the gifts. I got three sweaters, but what am I going to do with them? I can't wear them even when I get out of the hospital. Japan is not like Honolulu where you can wear civilian clothes. We have to wear Army clothes while in Japan. I'm still wondering what I am going to do with the clothes. Maybe I should send them back to Honolulu till I can come home..... Unfortunately, I got all the tags mixed-up. I don't know what is from whom. I know Miss Slattery sent me a pen. Will you thank her for me? I think one sweater is from you..... I am happy that everybody is trying to make it a Happy Birthday for me.

11 December

Dearest Granny,

I want to thank you so much for the sweater and also the money. It made me very happy to hear from you, and also to get these nice gifts..... I will never forget this as long as I live. Granny I also want to thank you for praying so hard for me and for lighting the Seven-Day Candle. Granny, you and the whole family have done a lot for me, and most of all, it was your prayers for me that really saw me through..... I am writing this letter with tears in my eyes, and praying this war ends, so all the boys will be able to come home. I will be much better off than them boys that are in Korea. They will not have half the Xmas that I will enjoy. So I will spend my time praying for those boys, because Granny, believe me, I know what it is like in Korea. You see Granny, I want to come home, but I'm not thinking about it too much, because so long as the war is still going on, I would rather go back there and help my buddies. Nobody likes Korea. I know I don't. But if I'm going to come home, I want to come home with everybody, all together... May God Bless you always. P.S. Aloha, from across the sea.

12 December

Dearest Mom,

Well here I am again. Today I got the box of Ellen Dyes candies you sent me..... I was very glad to get the candy, most of all because it is made in Honolulu. I opened it and passed it around to some of the boys. I told them it was from Honolulu. We ate half the box. There is one Japanese boy here. He also has yellow jaundice. He worked at Ellen Dyes candy store for two weeks. His name is Horace Nakamura.[4] He is also a corporal.....

16 December

Dearest Mom,

Hello Mom, I got the telegram you and Dad sent me on my Birthday. It came right on the morning of the 15th. I sure missed being home with all of you..... It was dead here. I stayed in bed as usual..... I got your letter the other day, and also one from Benny Silva. I was very surprised to hear from him. Mom, I'm very lonely here..... Looks like I will spend Xmas and New Years here..... Well Mom, I'm twenty now, getting old. But I still feel the same..... How is Dad making out in Real Estate? I wish him all the luck in the world.

19 December

Dear Mom and Dad,

I got a letter from Dad yesterday. Well it's nearing Xmas now, and I'm still in bed. Yesterday the Red Cross brought an Xmas tree for our room. We decorated it, and also put lights on it. All that is under it now are the gifts I got from home. I am in a room with four other boys, one from Honolulu, but who lives in Japan. The three others are from the States. Shaw is in the next room. On Xmas there will be a Santa Claus to come around and see us..... This will be my first time away from home on Xmas. I will be in the hospital for New Years too.... I will probably have to go back to Korea by the looks of things. I hope not. I wish they would send me home. At least I could help them train troops. I did hear that they sent some boys back.... But that is one of those rumors. Looks like Truman is going all out to build up UN forces. I hope Buddy don't get in it. Tell him to join the Navy if anything. But I sure hope the war doesn't get worse. Well looks like you're having bad weather. The ocean is rough too, and the sand is going out. But Mom and Dad, I still love the place. If I was there now, I'd go for a swim, rough or not. I miss home more than ever.... P.S. I heard some Hawaiian music the other day and was sure homesick.

27 December

Dearest Mom,

Well Mom, how was your Xmas? I had a pretty good one here, but had to stay in bed. The Red Cross gave us boys a little party. We also had a nice Xmas dinner. Buddy and Manley must be Confirmed by now.... I heard where the Lanikai Chop-Suey house burnt down. Lona sent me a clipping of it. Mom, I want to ask you, if Dad could drop sending me the paper? I'm not getting it very good, although I did get one yesterday.... I think it would be better, if anything important comes up, you just send me a few clippings with your letter.... It's alright if you stay in one place, but when I get out of the hospital, I don't know where I'm going.... The paper will never get to me.... You can save that much more money. Gee, Kailua is sure growing. Another Super Market! It seems that since I left, everything is happening. Today is Manley's birthday. I wish him a very Happy Birthday. He must be big now, probably as tall as I am.... The days seem to go by so fast. As soon as I get up, it's time to go back to bed. Do you know the boy that was in my room with me, James Shaw? Well he is out of the hospital, but is still in Japan. I don't really know if we have to go back to Korea.... I'm just hoping for the best. I only hope this New Years brings peace to the world so that all us boys can go back home to our families and loved ones. Things look pretty bad in Korea. Something has to pop sooner or later. I only hope for the good. I'll always hate the name of Korea as long as I live.... Dad said Buddy might join the Navy. Well if he likes it, I think it is better than the Army. And Manley wants to go to college. Well I think that would be swell. I know Dad wants one of us three to go to College. Of us three boys, I think Manley would be the one. He always was the best in school. I just hope everything turns out fine.... I will miss all of you this New Years.... May God Bless all of you.

3 January 1951
Dearest Mom and Dad,

I received a package from Mrs. Kenawell…. Gee Mom, I didn't expect Mrs. Kenawell to give me anything. But Mom, I'm really grateful, and I want to thank her very much. I don't have her address, but if you will send it to me, Mom, I will write to her and thank her. She sent me a nice wallet, a very nice one. I'm going to send it home, to keep. When I come home, I will use it to remember my old buddy Kenawell…. I'll try very hard to get a 30-day furlough, but can't promise you anything. I want to come home very badly, but the war is not over yet. I will probably have to go back to Korea. I won't like that one bit, but if I have to go, I'll have to go. They are sending some boys back to Korea and only a few of them home. That is, only if you have a very bad case of yellow jaundice. My case takes only about two months. By the time you get this letter, I might be out of the hospital. When we get out of the hospital, we go to a place called the Annex and stay there about two weeks. But before we go back to Korea, they give everyone a 7-day furlough…. I will go down to see the sergeant you talked about in your letter. But, Mom and Dad, I won't promise you… I think I will be going to the Annex next week. Dad, are Buddy and Manley giving you a bad time? Tell them I said they had better settle down. They better study hard and obey you and Mom more often. I know now. I learned it the hard way. There is only one in every family who has to learn it the hard way, and I had to be it. If only I could start all over again. But Mom and Dad, I'll be a real son to you when I get back. I'll pray for peace and happiness. I pray every night for the boys in Korea. Aloha.

5 January
Dearest Mom,

I got a package from you. It was mailed from Honolulu on November 8th and went all the way to Korea. It had Poi, Laulau and a box of crackers and one candy bar. I saw Johnnie Blyth today. We talked about home…. There were three other Island boys with him. One boy used to go to St. Louis College. I knew him…. I will be going out on pass soon and will see what Japan is like…. There is a boy stationed at this hospital who was in Fort Shafter. I knew him well and asked him about getting a furlough home. He said only on an emergency case. But I will keep on trying. I will phone you folks when I get out of the hospital. Don't worry about me Mom, I'll take care of myself. You and Dad should go out more often, like to the Ohio Club on a dance or party. Don't stay home all the time…. Mom, you wanted to know if I go back to Korea, will I go back to the 5th? Yes….

13 January
Dearest Mom,

Instead of going out on pass tonight, I thought I would write you a letter. Mom, I have some pretty good news. Your son is now a sergeant, better known as a staff sergeant.[5] The patch has three stripes on top and one on the bottom. My papers, or orders, just came from Korea. I made corporal sometime in September, but did not know till a month later. I made sergeant in November, but did not know about it. A squad leader is supposed to be a sergeant, but I was a squad leader when I was a corporal…. I wrote a letter to Mrs. Kenawell…. Oh Mom, tell Buddy I wish him a very Happy Birthday…. Does it still rain much? It is snowing here a little tonight…. It's pretty quiet around here. Tomorrow I think I will go to the show…. Love Sonny. P.S. Say hello to Granny.

Army rank insignia. (source: Center for Military History)

19 January
Dearest Granny,

Hello Granny, how are you? There are about five Island boys here with me. One boy is from Kailua. He lived only 5 blocks from me. His name is Johnnie Blyth. He is 24 years old. He had the same sickness I had. He has been stationed here in Japan 53 months now. He wants to go home now. There is a Hawaiian boy here. He lives in Kaimuki on 21st Ave. I told him I used to live on 19th Ave. I told him my Grand Ma lives on 15th Ave. He was wounded pretty bad.... Love Sonny.

20 January
Dear Mom and Dad,
I didn't take the pictures yet. Just found a place yesterday and will take some next week.... I have to get one more blood test before I know where I'm going. All I do now is go out on pass. I eat, maybe have a few beers, and then go to a show or shoot pool. We have a big Service Club here. Nice place. I might listen to the hit parade tonight.... Aloha.

22 January
Dear Buddy and Manley,
I got your letter today Manley. I was happy to hear from you.... We get very good Japanese food here.... When I get home, I'll be able to talk some Japanese.... Buddy why don't you join the Air Force? It's the best thing now.... You guys say everyone is souping up cars.... I don't think I should sell my car yet.... Does it still have a little soup? I think the old Smitty Mufflers leak.... I sure wish I was with you guys.... Try not to worry Mom and Dad. Most of all, don't worry Mommy. You guys, try and be good. You're getting old now.... Say hello to all my friends. I hope I'll be with you guys soon.

22 January
Dearest Mom,
Tonight I'm going to take some pictures of myself. Then I will mail them home. It's pretty cold now... I stopped this letter about three hours ago. I went out and had some pictures taken a little while ago. I will get them back in five days. I will send them to you right away Mom. Tomorrow, Johnnie Blyth, and Shaw and another Mexican boy are going to go out and have a big Suki-aki steak dinner. The Japanese food here is perfect. Boy do I eat.... Don't worry about me. I'm not even thinking about Korea. If I have to go back, I'll wait until the time comes.... Try and take a picture of my car. A side view of it would look nice....

26 January
Dearest Mom and Dad,
I was sure sorry to hear that Tweetie got out and was lost. I bet you folks miss him very much. How is Pooch, the hound? ... Last night, Johnnie, Shaw and me went out together. We had a pretty good time.... Dad, I'm really eating lots of Japanese food. Boy, is it number one. I've learned quiet a few words now. When I get back, I'll talk to you in Japanese only. Ha! Ha! Tonight Johnnie, Shaw and me are going to the show.... Mom, I stopped this letter, and I am starting it again the next day. It is 9:30 now. I just had a blood test, my last one. If I pass it, I'm on my way. And I hope it's not Korea. Last night, Johnnie, Shaw, me and two sailors went out. One of the sailors is a very good friend of Shaw. They grew up together. Both of the sailors are on the VALLEY FORGE. The ship that stays off Korea. I know you've heard of it. Also, both of the sailors were stationed in Pearl Harbor. We all went out, ate, talked about home and other things. We had a good time.... Say hello to Miss Slattery, and my love to Granny. Love Sonny.

29 January
Dear Mom and Dad,
I wish I was home now with all the nice weather. I still remember when the ocean used to be calm. I sure miss all those things, but I guess I have to make the best of it. I got my pictures back, and I'm sending you some of them. I had two pictures taken (that's two different ways), six for me and six for Shaw. Three of us together and three single. I'm going to send one single to Lona, one to Granny, and all the rest to you.

31 January
Dearest Mom,
Yes Mom, there are a lot of GIs here in Japan. There are more Marines here than anyone else. Most of us will have to go back to Korea.... Johnnie Blyth has left the Annex. He is on a 7-day furlough and then back to Korea. He said he wants to go to the 5th RCT. I might see him soon. Shaw is still with me. He will leave when I do. If we go back, we want to go together.... It's time for Chop-Chop, "chow".... Please do send me a picture of you and the family, and some of my car....

Sonny. Note his comments written on the photo's upper left and lower right corners. (source: Calhau family)

Sonny and his close friend, CPL James Shaw, Ogden, Utah. (source: Calhau family)

3 February

Dearest Mom,

I have a bad cold again. The doctor is giving me penicillin shots…. I guess I'm not used to this weather at all. This morning it was snowing outside…. Japan is a very pretty place. I don't think I will go out on pass today. I'll stay in and catch up on my writing and on my rest…. It won't be long now. I guess I will have to go back to Korea. I sure hope things will end soon…. You also say we are having beautiful weather there in Hawaii now. Boy, I sure miss the ocean…. I hope by now that you got my pictures. I did not get any negatives of them. The Army only paid me $50 for the month of January. I was supposed to get full pay, around $500…. I don't spend my money foolish now…. Every time you guys talk about Lanikai's weather, I get homesick…. Love Sonny. Aloha.

8 February

Dearest Mom and Dad,

Well I just got three more letters from you folks today. There is not another family in all the world that is better. You're tops…. I got a letter today from Mrs. and Mr. Kenawell. They sure are nice, always asking me if I need or want anything. I sure would like to meet them. Mrs. Kenawell says that you sent her a picture of John and me. I sent her one also. Last night Shaw, Tomas and I went out. This boy Tomas, he is a Filipino Island boy. We saw another Island boy. He is in the 2nd Division. His name is Paa. He knows Johnnie Blyth real well. He came to Japan in 1946, and has been here since. We talked about the Islands, and he sang a few Hawaiian songs. Boy can he sing…. I came back to camp early to catch up on my writing. Tomas is bringing me some Sushi when he comes in. I'm sure hungry. Always eating. I'll never be this fat in Honolulu. I'm glad that you liked my picture. I should have had more of them made. Now all I have to do is phone home. I want to hear your voices. I hope to get around to it soon…. Love Sonny.

The soldier from Lanikai had recovered his health. His doctors had repaired a valuable Army asset, a combat experienced rifle squad leader. Sonny had compared his stay at the 35th Field Hospital to being in heaven. Now it was time to return to hell.

"We really had a rip-roaring good time in that hospital," explained CPL Shaw. "When they'd let us go out, we'd go to the best restaurants and eat like kings. Sometimes when we were done eating, we'd go outside and borrow some poor guy's rickshaw and take turns pulling one another as fast as we could down the streets. But deep down, I don't think Sonny believed he was going to make it. I know I never did. It's a weird feeling, one that is impossible to explain. So all you can do is go out and live life to its fullest, and that's what we did."[6]

Sonny prayed hard every night before he returned to Korea, but he never made his promised phone call home.

CHAPTER NINETEEN

RANGER

On the northern front, Korea, Nov. 17. — A first sergeant described by his buddies as the most fearless soldier they ever knew was the only man killed when the 5th Regimental Combat Team of Hawaii advanced four miles yesterday without firing a shot.
The Honolulu Advertiser, *18 November 1950*

The 5th RCT sailed to Korea with an excellent cadre of competent NCOs, the backbone of the Army, including such men as MSGT Melvin O. Handrich, SFC Kermit Jackson, and SFC David Broad. Privates were quickly promoted to corporal and then sergeant to replace killed and wounded rifle, machine gun, and mortar squad leaders. Other NCOs like SFC Carl H. Dodd and SFC Robert L. Lyons received battlefield commissions to replace officer casualties. By November 1950, many of the bravest NCOs had fallen on the battlefield, much to the sorrow of those who knew them.

During the Task Force Kean offensive, Private Gene McClure rode in a convoy that drove into an NKPA ambush one hot August night. Tracers lashed the darkness as vehicles and men were hit in the killing zone. The first burst of enemy fire badly wounded the lieutenant in command of the convoy. When the lead truck exploded in flames, the column of vehicles halted abruptly on the road. Those soldiers who survived the first incredibly deadly and destructive seconds of time, hastily dismounted and began to return fire from the cover of road-side ditches.

The outnumbered American soldiers were also outgunned in the vicious close-range firefight. Unfortunately, a few of the motor pool personnel assigned to the convoy had forgotten they were soldiers first and mechanics second. One sergeant, for example, was not carrying his personal weapon. He paid for this lapse with his life.

Vehicles raked by machine gun fire began to burn, and then explode, much to the discomfort of the soldiers getting chewed to pieces in the killing zone. That one of the enemy's automatic weapons

The Rock decorates his officers and men.
(source: Chang)

was a captured Browning .30-caliber machine gun made the situation even more galling. The men could identify its distinctive sound in the darkness.

One determined sergeant, identity unknown, led a small group of soldiers forward into the rice paddies in a desperate attempt to outflank the enemy. Private McClure followed this sergeant to a point where everyone in the small group could clearly hear the NKPA soldiers speaking to one another in between bursts of automatic weapons fire. The sergeant hurled a couple of hand grenades at the North Koreans while the other Americans opened up with their rifles and carbines. When it became evident that there were just too many North Koreans for the small band of soldiers to over-run, the sergeant ordered the men to withdraw to the cover of a ditch.

A three-quarter ton truck stalled in the center of the convoy was one of two vehicles in the column not burning. The soldiers could clearly see a .50-caliber machine gun mounted above this vehicle's cab, but no one tried to man the weapon. A .50-caliber machine gun is one of the most devastatingly effective automatic weapons ever made, but, at that particular moment, whoever attempted to man the weapon from the exposed cab was a candidate for suicide. Tracers streaked through the night, right over the heads of the soldiers crowding the shallow ditches on both sides of the road. Known in soldier's parlance as "grazing fire," the trajectory of the enemy bullets did not rise above the height of an average man. Nevertheless, someone had to man that machine gun, and soon, for the Northern Koreans had clearly gained fire superiority and were preparing to rush the Americans with grenades, burp guns, and bayonets.

One may ask why the soldiers did not flee the carnage on foot, seeking safety in the darkness. The answer is simple. Several badly wounded American soldiers could not walk, much less run, from the killing zone, and no one thought to abandon these men to the NKPA. Even at this early stage of the war, word of North Korean atrocities had filtered down to the soldiers. Kim Il-Sung's boys were torturing virtually everyone who surrendered before dousing their captives in gasoline and setting them ablaze, or simply shooting them in the back of the head.

With surrender not an option, life and death boiled down to a .50-caliber machine gun mounted above the cab of a truck stalled in a column of burning vehicles. One man made a difference. To his comrades in G Company, 2nd Battalion, 5th RCT, SGT Albert Veenstra from Worchester, Massachusetts, was the bravest of the brave. His previous service in the elite Rangers during World War II had earned him the sobriquet "Ranger." That terrifying, blood-soaked night, while lying on the ground in a North Korean killing zone, Ranger chose life. More accurately, SGT Veenstra risked sacrificing his life to save those of his comrades.

Private McClure watched Ranger bound into the cab of the truck to unlimber the mighty .50-caliber voice of doom. North Korean tracers converged on Ranger as he pulled the charging handle back once, then twice, and let loose with a burst of return fire, the heavy slugs ripping into the dug in NKPA soldiers located just a hand grenade's throw away. Machine guns roared and rifles cracked as the North Koreans desperately tried to kill the arrogant American who was methodically shooting to pieces the densely packed NKPA assault platoon preparing to rush the ditch. With deadly accuracy the .50-caliber bullets streaked out of the barrel at a muzzle velocity in excess of 2,500 feet per second, tearing into the screaming, writhing bodies of dying North Koreans. Whenever the long barrel grew temporarily silent, the awe-struck American soldiers lying in the ditch would look up at Ranger, who stood upright under the moon and stars, silhouetted by the flames of burning trucks, cursing the jammed gun with words known but to God and combat-experienced NCOs.

Private McClure said, "Within a few minutes he had expended the first box of ammo with which the gun had been loaded in the first place and called for another soldier to get him some more ammunition, cursing this soldier, the gun, and the enemy all the while. Like a man gone mad, he went on raving and killing everything in front of him, and to this day I have never understood how he missed being killed then and there. Unlike the movies where the hero usually comes out alive, in real life it simply follows, if you continue to stick yourself up in front of oncoming bullets, you are bound to catch some of them sooner or later. There were no supermen in Korea — but Ranger was as close as any I ever saw."[1]

Ranger's devastating fire covered a group of soldiers who loaded their wounded comrades onto an undamaged jeep at the rear of the column. Under a hail of enemy fire, the gutsy jeep driver put the vehicle in gear, pulled hard on the wheel, and floored the accelerator. He made a U-turn on the narrow road and, pursued by bursts of gunfire, escaped with the wounded.

Private McClure was firing his carbine on full automatic just as fast as he could reload when Ranger expended the last of the machine gun ammunition and joined the remaining soldiers in the ditch. The survivors broke contact with the momentarily stunned NKPA and retreated in small groups back the way they had come. More than half of the forty men in the convoy had been killed or wounded, including the unarmed motor pool sergeant whose bullet-ridden body was discovered the next day. Without Ranger hammering away on the .50-caliber machine gun, few, if any, of the men would have survived.

Ranger was in the thick of the fighting during the grueling struggle for Sobuk-san and the desperate offensive that punched through the NKPA's iron ring at Waegwan. By November 1950, he was George Company's First Sergeant, an inspiration to all.

Ranger died on 16 November 1950 in a jeep that hit two antitank mines while driving slowly down a muddy road somewhere in North Korea. First Sergeant Albert Veenstra died on a day when the 5th RCT advanced four miles without firing a shot. Ironically, he was killed by an unreported American minefield, laid earlier in the month when the Eighth Army had withdrawn under the hammer blows of Chinese assaults.

Ranger's death was one of the few times the soldiers ever saw LTC John Throckmorton lose his composure. Prior to the combat team's deployment to Korea, Ranger had lost his stripes on a couple of occasions for minor infractions of military discipline. The Rock knew him well. On the day of his death, LTC Throckmorton praised the deceased NCO as the most fearless man he ever knew, adding that every man in the outfit felt the same way.[2] With tears in his eyes, the saddened regimental commander left the scene of the destroyed jeep and mangled hero to file an angry report damning the men who had left an unreported minefield in the path of his beloved soldiers.[3]

Ranger's battalion commander, LTC Albert Ward echoed his commander's sentiments, elaborating that First Sergeant Albert Veenstra "took patrols out every day and led the column when he was a corporal because that's the kind of soldier he was. Danger was his forte. He was idolized by his men. Any soldier would go anywhere when the sergeant led the patrol."[4]

Private First Class Robert T. Beste, Detroit, Michigan, summed up Ranger's death most eloquently: "It was a helluva way for the best soldier of us all to die."[5]

(source: Ray Warner)

CHAPTER TWENTY

THE HOME-BY-CHRISTMAS OFFENSIVE

A careful study of Eighth Army daily intelligence reports for the month of November 1950 reveals that, despite daily reference to the Chinese potential north of the Yalu River in Manchuria, there was a tapering off of concern about full Chinese intervention from about 10 November until 24 November, when Eighth Army resumed its offensive. In this connection it should be noted that the controlling Eighth Army viewpoint could scarcely avoid being influenced somewhat by that of Far East Command, which seems to have been that China would not intervene with major forces.
Lieutenant Colonel Roy E. Appleman, South to the Naktong, North to the Yalu

After Sonny was evacuated to Japan, the 5th RCT continued to fight, bleed and die in the rugged, frozen hills of North Korea. From 11-25 November, the combat team suffered nine battle and 109 non-battle casualties.[1] Ranger's death was recorded as a non-battle casualty. Firefights, sickness, accidents, and the cold took a terrible toll on the soldiers.

The one bright spot that rapidly turned sour was the snow. Contrary to popular belief, it does occasionally snow on the highest peaks of Hawaii. Yet few of the Islanders had ever seen snow before and, for a brief period of time, they were able to laugh, build snowmen, and throw snowballs at one another. The novelty wore off rather quickly, because the poorly clad soldiers were unprepared for the drastic dip in winter temperatures.

Following the entrance of the Chinese into the war, and the near destruction of the 8th Cavalry at Unsan, General Walker correctly concluded that he lacked the men, supplies, and equipment to mount a sustained offensive to the Yalu in the face of determined CCF resistance. His infantry divisions had suffered heavy losses and were on average thirty percent below their authorized strength.[2]

A few days following the 8th Cavalry's replay of the Little Big Horn, General MacArthur had preached that a calamity was at hand unless he was given immediate authorization to bomb the bridges spanning the Yalu. Now, his confidence restored by an inexplicable lull in the fighting, General MacArthur directed General Walker to advance to the Yalu without delay.

General Walker had a choice. He could either remain the Commanding General of the Eighth Army, or he could protest his orders and be relieved of his command. There is little evidence that General Walker disagreed vehemently with General MacArthur's assessment of Chinese intentions. We know that General Walker agreed with his G-2 Intelligence Officer's estimate that the Chinese had no more than a few divisions in North Korea.[3]

General Walker's previous training, experiences, and personality did not allow him to openly dispute General MacArthur's views, and he elected to remain at his post. He grew anxious, however, over the operational situation as the date for the planned offensive drew nearer. In private he instructed his commanders to exercise extreme caution in the forthcoming offensive and to break off the attack in the event of stiff Chinese resistance.[4]

President Truman and the JCS did not contest General MacArthur's optimistic perception of the strategic situation either. Washington shared General MacArthur's confidence largely because national intelligence organizations did not offer a substantially different strategic picture from the one presented in Tokyo. The Pentagon's optimism reached new heights of audacity when the JCS asked General MacArthur when the first infantry division fighting in Korea would be available for redeployment to Europe.[5] Sadly, the Truman Administration abrogated its responsibility to evaluate intelligence information that touched upon matters of the highest political im-

LTG Walker sits behind General MacArthur somewhere in North Korea. (source: NA)

portance. In essence, the Presidency authorized General MacArthur to determine American foreign policy by default.

Wishful thinking has been the bane of commanders since the dawn of organized warfare. An American intelligence debacle of this nature had not occurred since Pearl Harbor. The Chinese had in fact over 300,000 troops poised for offensive action in North Korea, superbly positioned to mount a counteroffensive once the Eighth Army played its first feeble hand.

As General MacArthur pondered matters of strategic importance, front line soldiers faced the daily, excruciating grind of small unit combat. On 17 November, SFC Horace Anderson led a reconnaissance patrol from Easy Company through the countryside to locate and report the presence of enemy forces operating in the vicinity of the 2nd Battalion. The soldiers were drawn from the 3rd Platoon, and SFC Anderson was their platoon sergeant.

The patrol moved out early that morning, weapons at the ready, trudging quietly through the rain and mud for several hours without making contact. A cold wind drove the rain at right angles into their faces as they walked under low gray clouds across a depressing landscape. Beads of cold water and splatters of mud adorned their clothing, weapons and equipment.

The patrol eventually encountered a lone civilian who informed SFC Anderson through a KATUSA interpreter that, at daybreak, he had seen ten armed Chinese moving in the opposite direction. Sergeant First Class Anderson reported this information over his radio and ordered the patrol to move out. The men walked warily across a wide rice paddy to a village populated by a small group of agitated and nervous civilians. The soldiers attributed the reactions of the villagers to their own foreign presence and kept on moving toward a low ridge on the far side of the yet another rice paddy.

When the patrol reached a predetermined point, the Chinese opened up with automatic weapons and small arms fire from camouflaged bunkers on the ridgeline. Bullets ripped into the mud around the soldiers, who immediately sought cover in the muck and returned fire. After a few minutes, SFC Anderson determined it was only a matter of time before the larger Chinese force overwhelmed his patrol. After ordering his men to withdraw to a paddy dike in their rear, SFC Anderson remained in place to direct an artillery fire mission over his radio. High explosive rounds arrived seconds later, bursting on target, and hurling shrapnel and clods of mud through the air.

Yet another CCF force struck the patrol's left flank as the soldiers withdrew. Sergeant Charles Krone, the Assistant Patrol Leader from Chicago, Illinois, was hit above his left lung. Two soldiers, Falk and Eagles, carried SGT Krone through a hail of small arms fire to a covered position behind the paddy dike where they applied first aid. Meanwhile, SFC Anderson quickly shifted the artillery fire to meet this new threat, and the impact of incoming 105-mm high explosive shells forced the Chinese threatening the patrol's flank to withdraw.

Once his men had reached the safety of the paddy dike, SFC Anderson shifted the artillery fire onto his own position. He ran through a drainage ditch seconds before the first rounds impacted in giant mushroom clouds of muddy debris. The patrol's mission accomplished, SFC Anderson led his men back to friendly lines. The 2nd Platoon intercepted the patrol on its return trip and helped to carry SGT Krone to a helicopter landing zone where he was subsequently evacuated. A doctor saved SGT Krone's life at a MASH unit in the rear. For his actions that day, SFC Anderson was awarded the Bronze Star for valor.[6]

On 23 November, the 5th RCT's soldiers enjoyed a traditional Thanksgiving Day turkey dinner with all the trimmings. It was a monumental logistical feat simply transporting the food to the front lines, much less thawing and cooking the frozen turkeys in the field. The mess cooks persevered and prepared a feast that they served to the grateful soldiers.

Private David Lomax, from Charlestown, Indiana, had recently joined Baker Company's 4th Platoon. He served with CPL Nathans, a tall, skinny soldier who was hungry all the time and could never get enough to eat. Baker Company was pulled off the line on Thanksgiving Day so the men could be served their meal. The soldiers were served by platoon: 1st, 2nd, 3rd, and 4th. A cheer was heard when the mess sergeant hollered, "All right men, line up for seconds!" Corporal Nathans quickly reached the head of the new line. His plate was already full of turkey, dressing, and mashed potatoes, so he started to eat as fast as he could to make room for more. Despairing of ever emptying his full plate in time, CPL Nathans grabbed the drumstick already on his plate and shoved it into his pocket. Half of the drumstick stuck out of his pocket as he happily served himself to seconds, piling his plate high. Every Thanksgiving since then, CPL Lomax has recalled the scene, "kind of funny… and kind of sad… [of] the tall, skinny soldier in Korea who for at least one day had all he could eat."[7]

First Lieutenant Randall Beirne wrote home on Thanksgiving Day from King Company's CP located next to three burnt-out T-34s still inhabited by their cremated crews. Nearby were the graves of three British soldiers. "Everything seems quiet and peaceful. We have a lot to be thankful for. At least we are alive and in good health. The weather has warmed up to about 40... The cooks stayed up all night getting Thanksgiving dinner ready. We actually have turkey (frozen) and we are going to set up a seated (in a way) meal. The Chinese better hadn't attack while we eat because they will have a hell of a time getting us away from our turkey. Besides turkey, we have cranberry jelly, minced pie, fruit cake, shrimp salad, candy, nuts, etc. So even on the front, a quiet front, we enjoy Thanksgiving."[8]

Quite a few men in K Company wore North Korean winter uniforms to dinner. Cold weather protective clothing had yet to reach the combat team in large quantities, so the men scrounged whatever they could wear to stay warm. When a cache of North Korean winter uniforms was liberated from a warehouse, the men donned the quilted overgarments. Lieutenant Beirne explained, "The American soldier is a very ingenious person. The world of the front line soldiers is quite a bit different from the world of the generals. Historians do a good job painting the blue arrows, describing the movement of generals and troops. The life of the front line soldier is another story in all the things they have to do to stay alive."[9]

A large quantity of mail arrived on Thanksgiving Day to the immense satisfaction of the homesick soldiers. As the men ate their turkey dinner, read letters, shared the contents of packages, and relaxed throughout this peaceful day, the 5th RCT's Operations Officer, MAJ Elmer G. Owens, was reading the 24th Infantry Division's mission statement for the offensive: "24th Division will attack West in zone from present position 24 Nov 50, and destroy enemy forces in zone. Seize line TAESAN-DONG, NAKCHONG-JONG, WON-NI [sic] prepare to continue the attack on order to South bank of the YALU RIVER."[10]

The 5th RCT had been on the receiving end of a dirty stick since the combat team was detached from the 25th Infantry Division the previous September. The problem quite simply was a shortage of men. Every unit serving in Korea was under strength, but there existed a marked disparity in manpower between the 24th Infantry Division's two organic regiments and the attached 5th Infantry. The Army's Table of Organization and Equipments called for each infantry regiment to have 153 officers, 26 warrant officers, and 3614 enlisted men. As of 9 November, the personnel figures were as follows:[11]

Veterans of the 5th RCT relax off the line. L to R: MSGT Alfred Alfonso, Wailuku, Maui; CPL Edward Kaulauli, Waikane, Oahu; PFC Felix Tormis, Kahuku, Oahu; CPL Wilder Chong, Honolulu; CPL William Silva, Wailuku, Maui; and CPL William Osorio, Palo Alto, California. (source: Chang)

UNIT	OFFICERS	WARRANT OFFICERS	ENLISTED MEN
19th INF	185	7	3,207
21st INF	185	5	3,288
5th INF	160	12	2,773

A manpower disparity also existed between the division's two 105-mm howitzer-equipped direct support artillery battalions and the attached 555th FAB.[12]

UNIT	OFFICERS	WARRANT OFFICERS	ENLISTED MEN
13th FAB	43	3	598
52nd FAB	47	2	615
555th FAB	45	3	546

The combat team would, therefore, participate in the "Home-by-Christmas Offensive" with an end strength considerably less than the Taro Leaf's organic units. That the 5th RCT subsequently accomplished so much, while supported so little, speaks highly of the officers and men assigned to LTC John Throckmorton's command. His soldiers sensed they belonged to a "Bastard Outfit," an elite combat team committed wherever the situation was most desperate, which in itself was a source of intense pride to the men. Nevertheless, one is forced to question the Taro Leaf's failure to bring the 5th Infantry up to the strength of at least the next weakest regiment in the division. Though LTC Throckmorton's command would be assigned the same missions as the 19th and 21st Infantry Regiments, it was going into action with approximately 500 fewer soldiers, a shortage equivalent to almost an infantry battalion.

Logistical problems abounded throughout the Eighth Army. Supplying the troops their traditional Thanksgiving dinner had stretched logistics to the breaking point. Airlift of vital cold weather clothing to the 2nd and 25th Infantry Divisions, for example, was suspended before Thanksgiving to ensure the frozen turkeys arrived on time. Moreover, the Eighth Army's maneuver battalions had barely a day's worth of ammunition and four day's supply of food on hand when their lead elements crossed the LD.[13]

General MacArthur flew to Korea to observe the Eighth Army's offensive commence against light enemy resistance on 24 November. Newspaper headlines in Honolulu triumphantly reported, "MacArthur Leads 'Final' Offensive Against Reds."[14] The following day, a feature article claimed, "Reds Talk Tough But It's Action by M'Arthur."[15] In an adjoining article, "an authoritative navy spokesman" questioned General MacArthur's public utterances that the troops would be home by Christmas. The anonymous official stated that sufficient ships did not exist to transport all the troops home even if the fighting ended on 1 December.[16] The Chinese promptly took care of this problem.

Contrary to General MacArthur's design, Eighth Army's offensive stalled almost immediately. The ambitious goal of reaching the Yalu took a cruel turn as the CCF mounted a savage counteroffensive. Comrade Peng Dehuai, Commander of the Chinese People's Volunteers, informed his subordinate commanders and staff on the eve of the counteroffensive that "our men face exceptional challenges. They have little artillery. No armor. No air support. They must perform heroically. But no more. They will never be called on to perform the impossible. Trust me. I give my word."[17]

At dusk on 25 November, Mao's peasant infantry departed their assembly areas and began a rapid approach march towards predetermined attack positions. Tens of thousands of lightly armed Chinese infantry exploded into action that bitterly cold night, attacking to the sound of blaring bugles, their paths lit by parachute flares, closing on American and ROK positions in a massive frontal attack, advancing at a dog trot under the stars.

The Eighth Army's soldiers had little time to react and, in many cases, no time to bring supporting artillery fires to bear before the battle was joined. Supported by deluges of mortar fire, CCF assault formations charged with ruthless determination. The fighting quickly degenerated into hundreds, perhaps thousands, of isolated firefights and close combat duels. Issues of victory or defeat and life or death were decided in the darkness by point-blank rifle fire, staccato bursts from submachine guns, the crump of grenade explosions, stabbing bayonets, slashing knives and even flailing fists. Within hours of the initial attack, the bulk of the ROK II Corps defending the Eighth Army's right flank had been overwhelmed, chewed-up, and decimated.[18]

American combat units incurred heavy losses that night, and over the course of the next couple of days, too. The 8213th Ranger Company, for example, attached to the 25th Infantry Division, was virtually destroyed on the night of 25-26 November, but the adjacent 27th Infantry "Wolfhounds" prevailed in the brutal close-combat struggle waged under the stars.[19] Easy and George Companies, 24th Infantry, fought toe-to-toe with the Chinese, while Charlie Company is reputed to have surrendered without a fight after blundering into a CCF assembly area.[20] The 2nd Infantry Division incurred heavy losses on the night of 25-26 November, but largely held its ground. The CCF 125th Division severely mauled the 7th Cavalry Regiment on the night of 29-30 November, but there was no replay of Unsan, largely because the troopers maintained unit integrity under heavy pressure.[21]

Although American combat units initially fared better than the ROK II Corps, the Chinese had successfully penetrated the Eighth Army's thin lines in several locations. By 28 November, the operational situation had deteriorated to the point where General MacArthur had concluded he was losing the battle.[22] No one was going home for Christmas.

Chinese commanders exploited their penetrations and quickly established roadblocks deep in the Eighth Army's rear. The 2nd Infantry Division incurred over 3,000 casualties in one ghastly day attempting to force a passage through a series of roadblocks during the hasty withdrawal from Kunuri.[23] One of its outfits, the 3rd Battalion, 9th Infantry was virtually wiped out, reduced to thirty-seven men after a couple of days of fierce close combat.[24] The FEAF intervened to halt the CCF advance, but due to a combination of poor flying weather, target acquisition difficulties inherent in mountainous terrain, and the virtual absence of a CCF logistical tail, air strikes failed to measurably slow the Chinese advance.

General MacArthur, perhaps seeking to preserve his military reputation for prosperity, began to call the Eighth Army's "Home-by-Christmas Offensive" a reconnaissance in force. He subsequently claimed that this reconnaissance had succeeded in its purpose, saving the Eighth Army and X Corps from disaster by prematurely forcing the Red Chinese to disclose their hands, thereby allowing General Walker's and General Almond's commands to evade the worst of the blow.[25] Reality intrudes at this point. The CCF caught a poorly deployed Eighth Army and savagely ground it to pieces at a time and place of its own choosing. The magnificent fighting withdrawal of the 1st Marine Division aside, X Corps fared little better.

General MacArthur has trivialized the damage inflicted on the Eighth Army during this period, claiming the 7,337 casualties it incurred, plus the 5,638 suffered by X Corps, were "about half the loss at Iwo Jima, less than one-fifth of that at Okinawa, and even less in comparison with the Battle of the Bulge."[26] His comparison does not stand up to scrutiny. Iwo Jima, Okinawa, and the Battle of the Bulge, American victories all, were fought and won over a longer period than the few days it took for the CCF to defeat the Eighth Army and X Corps. Within days of the Chinese counteroffensive, a battered, bloodied and defeated Eighth Army had commenced the longest retreat in the history of the United States Army.

CHAPTER TWENTY-ONE

REARGUARD

Rearguards are the safety of armies and often they carry victory with them.
Frederick the Great

On 24 November, the 24th Infantry Division crossed the LD and advanced on Eighth Army's extreme left flank toward the Yalu. Resistance increased during this brief phase of the "Home-by-Christmas Offensive." Chinese rifle, light machine gun, and mortar fires annoyed the progress of the 5th RCT throughout the long, frustrating day.

"We were crawling along behind one of the battalions in the afternoon," recalled PFC Arlen Russell who was driving a jeep carrying CAPT Vincent Marchesselli, the Artillery Liaison Officer attached to 3rd Battalion. "We came under very heavy small arms fire and it was almost like the enemy let the infantry pass before they engaged the column of vehicles. We all hit the ditches. The leaves of the bushes we had sticking out of our helmets for camouflage started disappearing with loud 'thwacks!' We knew something was up because we hadn't been hit that bad in a long time. The fire was concentrated and very heavy."[1]

The Chinese counteroffensive on 25 November did not strike the 24th Infantry Division in strength. As a result, the 5th RCT was spared the dismal fate of many other American infantry units during the next few days. On 26 November, the Eighth Army ordered the Taro Leaf to discontinue its advance until the deteriorating situation on other sectors of the front was clarified.[2] The combat team dug in on the division's eastern flank where it tied in with the battered ROK 1st Division, which had been under heavy assault from strong elements of the CCF 66th Army. Little opposition was encountered during the day.

At 0245 on 27 November, heavy machine gun fire forced one platoon from George Company to withdraw from its positions on a knoll located near Hill 222. The company counterattacked at 0745 and regained the lost ground two hours later after a sharp firefight with 50 enemy troops.[3] Later that day a patrol belonging to the 24th Infantry Division's Reconnaissance Company, temporarily attached to LTC Throckmorton's command, inflicted approximately 50-75 casualties on 500 enemy soldiers who were surprised while eating a meal in a village.[4] Yet another Reconnaissance Company patrol engaged a Chinese unit and killed twenty-five more enemy soldiers.[5]

At 2200, 27 November, the "Home-by-Christmas Offensive" officially ended when I Corps issued orders to subordinate commands to commence a withdrawal the following morning. Time did not allow for the 24th Infantry Division to type detailed written orders. It passed verbal instructions over the radio to subordinate units.

The combat team's withdrawal plan called for the 1st Battalion to disengage and head south at 0430, 28 November, to an assembly area north of Anju and the Chongchon River, followed by the 2nd Battalion at 0500. The 3rd Battalion was directed to cover the disengagement and link up with the combat team in the assembly area. Attached units consisted of D Company, 3rd Engineer Battalion; 1st Clearing Platoon; 1st Ambulance Platoon; and 1st

Bullets in their Christmas stockings. No one is going home. The 5th RCT makes contact with the CCF. (source: Chang)

153

Traffic Platoon, 24th Military Police Company. Once the 5th RCT reached its assembly area, it was going to be detached from the Taro Leaf to form a reserve for the I Corps.[6] The rest of 24th Infantry Division was going to be reassigned to IX Corps to help stabilize the deteriorating situation in the east.

As these orders were being disseminated, the 3rd Battalion occupied a perimeter defense on a low hill east of the main north-south MSR. The 2nd Battalion had dug in on another hill west of the MSR. A dense growth of pine trees covered the hills. The bitterly cold weather affected the entire combat team which still lacked adequate supplies of winter clothing. Thankfully, there had been little snowfall to date.

Love Company dug in on the right half of the 3rd Battalion's hill. King Company dug in on the left half of the hill in fighting positions facing due north and overlooking the road. One rifle platoon from Item Company, reinforced with a tank platoon, occupied a blocking position astride the road. King Company established its command post in a small building behind the blocking position. Lieutenant Colonel Benjamin Heckemeyer's CP was located farther to the rear along with the battalion trains and the 81-mm Mortar Platoon. The rest of Item Company was dug in farther to the east, providing flank security for the 24th Infantry Division.

Patrols had encountered small groups of Chinese troops in the vicinity of the 3rd Battalion earlier in the day. A flurry of artillery and air strikes worked over suspected CCF positions throughout the morning and afternoon as the soldiers laid trip flares, zeroed in their crew-served weapons, and waited for the fall of darkness. The 5th RCT had yet to experience the fury of the CCF counteroffensive that was crushing everything in its path farther to the east. This was about to change, for elements of the CCF 198th Division were stealthily moving into their attack positions to strike the 5th RCT.[7]

At approximately 0200 on 28 November, the shrill ring of a field telephone awakened CAPT Joseph Lukitsch, the CO of King Company, from a light sleep. Battalion informed K Company's commander that everyone was moving out at 0800. As usual, battalion failed to say where, and CAPT Lukitsch, who did not know about the impending withdrawal, gave his XO, 1st LT Randall Beirne, an exasperated look. Lieutenant Beirne shrugged his shoulders in agreement. Captain Lukitsch instructed the watch to awaken him at 0530. He would figure out what battalion wanted then. For the moment the weary company commander wanted to catch some sleep.[8]

At 0255, rifle shots punctuated the darkness, and the dull crump of grenade explosions echoed through the night.[9] Moments later, the roar of automatic weapons joined the din, and above it all could be heard the blaring, barbaric sound of Chinese bugle calls. Captain Lukitsch grabbed the phones to talk to his platoons while LT Beirne instinctively pulled his boots on. With no time to tie them, the XO ran out the door into the night with a carbine clutched tightly in hand.

The battle commenced near the crest of the hill above the King Company CP soon after the defenders first thought they heard movement farther down the slope. Corporal Arnett turned to CPL Bodie in his foxhole and asked, "Do you hear anything or is that the wind in the leaves?" A few seconds later, a KATUSA soldier in a hole nearby opened up with his rifle and received a hail of return fire from the base of the hill. Those soldiers not on watch struggled out of sleeping bags, grabbed their weapons, and prepared to fight.

Chinese machine gun teams commenced a hot and sustained fire, green and red tracers streaking directly over the heads of the assault elements of two CCF infantry battalions who were worming their way forward, on their bellies, up the slope. The first wave of Chinese soldiers hurled concussion grenades into the midst of King Company's fighting positions. Concussion grenades have little shrapnel effect, are easy to carry, and require little skill to employ, all of which made them the offensive weapon of choice for Chinese infantry in 1950. By 0300 concussion grenades were exploding throughout the battalion's defensive perimeter. In desperation, King Company's soldiers started to throw the concussion grenades back at the Chinese before they exploded. The sound of gunfire, grenade explosions, and bugles off to the right confirmed that Love Company was fighting for survival, too.

SFC Charles A. Falk, an 81-mm mortar FO, was requesting a call for fire when he was hit in the chest by gunfire. He refused to leave his position and continued to make increasingly more desperate appeals for fire support. For some inexplicable reason, Mike Company's 81-mm Mortar Platoon fired just two high explosive rounds in support of King Company's defenders that night. Perhaps Love Company had priority of fires, or maybe all radio and wire communications went down at the critical moment. In any event, SFC Falk continued to call for fire, yelling into his radio mike to make him heard above the roar of battle, until gunfire struck his head. He died shortly thereafter.

Lieutenant Beirne remained near the CP to assemble the headquarters personnel when CAPT Lukitsch ran up the hill with his company first sergeant and runners to direct the defense. The tanks on the roadblock fired a few rounds and pulled out leaving LT Beirne with the survivors from Item Company, and King Company's miscellaneous cooks, drivers, radio operators, and walking wounded.

Believing that the Chinese would soon overrun the CP, LT Beirne led his men up the hill to join the company. Corporal Arthur McClogan, from Pearl City, Oahu, fired a .50-caliber machine gun positioned near the CP to cover their movement.[10] During the ascent, LT Beirne encountered two wounded NCOs who mentioned the company's urgent need for litter bearers and ammunition. The XO no longer had a radio so he ran to Mike Company's 81-mm Mortar Platoon's position behind the hill to place a call to the battalion for assistance. After informing the battalion of the situation over Mike Company's radio, he grabbed the attention of two tank crews and a platoon of infantry and employed these units to establish a new roadblock covering the road. Just as the last tank was moving into position, the battalion directed him to establish a roadblock in the spot he had just chosen.

As King Company's defenders fought on top of the hill, one rifle squad from the 2nd Platoon withdrew without orders, and the CCF exploited the gap. The Chinese quickly expanded their penetration, splitting the 1st and 2nd Platoons from the 3rd Platoon, and assaulted the Weapons Platoon.

Weapons Platoon was overrun in a flurry of close quarters fighting. Sergeant Storms was firing at a group of Chinese hiding behind a grave mound when a grenade landed in his 60mm mortar pit. The explosion destroyed the mortar, but through a lucky zigzag on his part, SGT Storms survived the blast unhurt. Private Louis E. Armon defended a nearby hole with his carbine and .45-caliber pistol until a Chinese mortar round exploded and severed his foot. A group of friends grabbed Private Armon and hustled the wounded soldier down the hill.[11] The poor lad was in such excruciating agony that he begged his comrades to shoot him. They refused.

Lieutenant Fife emptied his carbine into a Chinese soldier trying to pull the pin from a grenade. Though badly wounded, the brave Chinese soldier kept trying to pull the pin until the lieutenant smashed his opponent's skull with a butt stoke that shattered the stock of his carbine.

Corporal Ferguson and Private More were shooting at Chinese soldiers to their front when a concussion grenade landed in their hole. Private More smothered the grenade explosion with his hand. He lost his hand but saved their lives, a fair trade for an infantryman in the Korean War.

Corporal Chickinanga was looking for targets when an unwelcome visitor jumped into his hole. He found himself face-to-face with a terrified Chinese soldier who screamed and leaped out of the hole and ran in another direction.

Corporal James D. Raines proved the tactical maxim that the machine gun is the backbone of a well-knit infantry defense. He waited until the Chinese were ten yards from his hole before he opened up with the Browning. The Chinese kept rushing into his fire, leaving a pile of torn and crumpled corpses lying within reach of the machine gun's muzzle. And still the enemy soldiers came on. A trip flare soared through the air, illuminating the battlefield, disclosing hundreds of Mao Tse Tung's peasant infantry crawling ant-like up the hill. Corporal Raines continued to fire, burning out the barrel of his machine gun. He changed barrels, recommenced firing, and expended six boxes of ammunition that night while killing an estimated fifty Chinese soldiers. Two of Mike Company's heavy machine gun teams fired off fourteen boxes of ammunition, killing scores more.

The blood price was high. Sergeant James R. Jackson was hit in the leg and walked down to the aid station. Master Sergeant Norman L. Bannister was hit in the head and died instantly. Private Hitchcock was shot through the chest with three tracers and died. Sergeant First Class Delmar P. Cole was hit in the arm and walked down the hill toward the aid station. He disappeared in the darkness and was never seen again. Sergeant Yoshikou was hit in the arm, earning his second Purple Heart of the war. Private Kenneth W. Clark was hit in the nose, his second wound of the war. Sergeant Troulius Adams was killed instantly by a concussion grenade. Both he and Clark had just rejoined the company after being wounded on Hill

King Company moves out. (source: Chang)

268. Private First Class Stanley J. Butts heard some Korean spoken, fired, and hit one of the KATUSA soldiers. Another soldier shot and wounded an Item Company soldier climbing up the hill in the darkness.[12]

Lieutenant Beirne was at the roadblock when he finally got through to CAPT Lukitsch on the radio. His CO said, "For God's sake get our vehicles and equipment out of the command post." The XO thought he was being sent on a mission to heaven when suddenly a jeep pulled up with two passengers coming from the direction of the command post. Lieutenant Beirne jumped in the jeep and sped back to the command post where much to his chagrin, he saw SGT William T. Akerley, Jr., the supply sergeant, and several other men calmly loading the company's vehicles, including their Russian truck.

The 1st Platoon withdrew to the CP after firing the last of their ammunition and helped to load the remaining equipment. Lieutenant Beirne never did understand why the Chinese failed to overrun the CP after their successful assault through Item Company's roadblock.

The estimated 150 casualties inflicted on the two Chinese assault battalions was the most likely explanation.[13] King Company's perimeter had been penetrated in three places, and neighboring Love Company's perimeter in two, but the enemy paid a steep price for his limited gains, and had expended much ammunition driving the Americans off the hill. Thus when the 3rd Battalion ordered King and Love Companies to disengage and withdraw to Item Company's positions located farther to the rear, the exhausted and bloodied Chinese did not pursue.

With the exception of one K Company rifle squad that abandoned its positions without orders, the 3rd Battalion's two forward rifle companies withdrew in good order, with their weapons and equipment, after expending all their ammunition, leapfrogging by platoons. King Company suffered twenty-nine casualties. Love Company's casualties are unknown.

Master Sergeant Hiram L. Ke, from Honolulu, died fighting with King Company that night. His body was not recovered. Corporal Nicholas Ke went AWOL from the 2nd Infantry Division when he heard that his brother was dead. Several days later he "joined" the 5th RCT to fight alongside the buddies of his departed brother and to exact his revenge.[14]

At dawn, CAPT Lukitsch requested permission to counterattack and retrieve the bodies of his dead. Permission was denied.[15] The Eighth Army's offensive had degenerated into a bloody rout farther east, and General Walker had directed a withdrawal to the vicinity of Pyongyang. The 3rd Battalion moved out at 0700 and headed for the combat team's assembly area north of Anju.

Later that day, the 24th Infantry Division detached the 5th RCT per previous instructions and commenced a motorized movement to reinforce IX Corps on the Eighth Army's shattered right flank. The I Corps directed the 5th RCT to remain on the left flank, covering the Eighth Army's withdrawal from blocking positions protecting the two bridges spanning the Chongchon River. The combat team performed this vital mission on 30 November, and held the crossing sites as the flotsam and jetsam of the Eighth Army's defeat limped across the river. Shivering in their foxholes, the soldiers huddled close together in a vain effort to ward off the bitter cold. At times, the wind chill factor brought temperatures down to twenty-two degrees below zero.

Earlier in the day, CAPT Hank Emerson witnessed two parachutes deploy from an American aircraft shot down by the Chinese near the river. He drove off in his jeep, accom-

SGT Mike Chalooga, Honolulu, examines a dead CCF soldier who was carrying an American short story magazine when he was killed. (sources: NA/Chang)

panied by a tank, to rescue the pilots. On the way he ran into the remnants of the 23rd Infantry, 2nd Infantry Division, retreating to the south. Colonel Paul F. Freeman, the CO of the 23rd Infantry, asked CAPT Emerson, "What outfit is this?" Upon hearing the company commander's reply, COL Freeman said, "Well God Bless A Company, 5th RCT!"[16] The 23rd Infantry had narrowly escaped annihilation a few hours before and was grateful to find an escape route securely held by the combat team.

After the 23rd Infantry crossed the river, I Corps ordered LTC Throckmorton at 1615 to begin blowing up the bridges. One and a half hours later, this had been done.[17] Shortly thereafter, the 5th RCT commenced its withdrawal in a snowstorm, serving as the Eighth Army's rearguard. General Walker congratulated the Rock over the phone on his battlefield promotion to colonel just before the combat team, mounted on trucks, moved out.[18]

When CAPT Emerson returned to A Company, COL Throckmorton directed him to hand over his trucks to expedite the withdrawal of the 23rd Infantry. Able Company was ordered to hold out in its present positions as long as practicable to give the combat team a head start. After receiving these instructions, CAPT Emerson reported that he had seen about thirty boxcars on a railroad siding while rescuing the aircrew. As a result of his report, it came to light that someone in I Corps had panicked and abandoned a trainload of ammunition. Captain Emerson was directed to destroy it. Once again he jumped into his jeep, and accompanied by his XO, 1st LT Austin R. Lord, they drove out to the railroad siding to blow up the train. Upon arrival, they opened the doors of each boxcar and readied a supply of thermite grenades. Then they both ran down the length of the train, hurling thermite grenades through the doors and onto the stacks of ammunition.

The boxcars smoldered and started to burn, but to the relief of the two officers, they were able to vacate the area before the first explosion. Indeed, for awhile the disgusted officers wondered if there ever would be an explosion. When CAPT Emerson returned to his company's blocking position, he had other things to worry about. A large column of Chinese soldiers could be seen moving toward A Company. It appeared that CAPT Emerson's outnumbered soldiers were going to be in for one hell of a fight. Suddenly, the long simmering boxcars exploded with a mighty roar. A massive mushroom cloud of smoke and debris spiraled into the air, and the Chinese dove for cover. No CCF commander was going to tangle with an opponent who possessed that kind of artillery support!

In the evening, CAPT Emerson mounted his company on the engine decks of five attached tanks and moved out in pursuit of the combat team. Several soldiers incurred frostbite riding exposed on the Shermans.[19]

The 5th RCT continued to serve as rearguard during the retirement to Pyongyang. Losses from 25 November to 2 December included 63 battle and 37 non-battle casualties.[20] On 2 December, the 5th RCT was awarded the Combat Infantry Streamer in honor of its superlative fighting performance.[21] Incredibly, as of this date, many of the combat team's soldiers fighting outside in the arctic winter had yet to be issued shoe-packs, parkas, and other winterized garments.[22]

The temptation existed in less disciplined units for frozen soldiers to rationalize their sordid predicament and hunker down inside their warm sleeping bags without posting security at night. Elements of the 1st Battalion witnessed the tragic results of this bad habit during the withdrawal.

One night, A Company drove into the 1st Battalion's assembly area after again serving as the regimental rearguard. The battalion was in reserve and warming fires were authorized. As CAPT Hank Emerson dismounted his jeep, the S-3 approached and told him to keep his men on the trucks. A company from another regiment had been overrun, and CAPT Emerson's outfit was assigned the mission of restoring that regiment's positions.

"You can imagine how that went over with the troops," explained CAPT Emerson. "It was dark as hell, and the men were cold and hungry."[23] The trucks roared off into the night, leaving the warming fires and hot chow far behind, on a journey of fifteen miles before the company reached its assembly area and dismounted on the frozen ground. As the men formed into squads and platoons, CAPT Emerson walked over to a hut where he supposed the regimental CP was located. He entered and found two senior officers drinking whiskey. A drunken battalion commander barely noticed CAPT Emerson's hulking presence in the hut, but the regimental commander promptly offered him a drink.

Captain Emerson wisely declined the proffered canteen cup of whiskey as he studied the regimental commander's situation map, which like so many at this stage of the Korean War had been drawn by Imperial Japanese Army surveyors and was of dubious accuracy at best. The shoddy, inaccurate map was of no value to the company commander who, lacking time to conduct a daylight reconnaissance, asked the regimental commander to at least show him what direction he had to travel. The colonel took the company commander outside, pointed into the darkness, and said, "Right about there."

Captain Emerson was worried that his company might accidentally stumble onto and assault a friendly unit dug in on the hill, but the regimental commander reassured him with the less than

Two Arson Easy machine gunners, Matthews (left) and Parish (right).
(source: Horace Anderson)

comforting statement that only one survivor had made it down the hill. Everyone else up there was either dead or Chinese. To make CAPT Emerson's task easier, the regimental commander assigned the sole survivor, a PFC, to help guide Able Company onto its objective.

Able Company deployed for combat and conducted its assault in accordance with the tactical manuals of the time. The company moved out in column until it hit predetermined platoon and squad release points. By the time A Company neared the crest, the soldiers were generally on line, advancing at a slow steady pace up the steep hill. Captain Emerson advanced with the center rifle platoon. "When I move, you move," he instructed his platoon leaders shortly before A Company crossed the LD. "When I stop, you stop. When I open fire, you open fire. We're going to quietly walk up the hill and get as close as we can."

As the company neared the enemy held crest, SFC Earl Davis gave the hand and arm signal for the company to halt. He whispered, "Listen to that, Sir." Captain Emerson replied, "What?" Davis motioned everyone to be quiet and listen, and sure enough, as the men stood silently on the hillside, they could hear the drunken voices of Chinese soldiers carousing around on the crest. Obviously, the Chinese had liberated a quantity of alcohol and were celebrating their victory. They clearly never expected the despised Americans to counterattack at night.

Captain Emerson motioned for his soldiers to advance, and so they did, eager to crash the party and teach the CCF a lesson or two about war. A startled Chinese soldier stood up as he saw the long line of soldiers loom suddenly out of the darkness. He never had a chance. Captain Emerson shot him down, and within seconds, the entire company was firing, their rifles cracking, BARs hammering, and Brownings stitching the hill. The drunken and terribly surprised Chinese never got off a round of return fire. Every one of them was killed.

Able Company assaulted over the crest, set up listening posts forward of the objective, and dispatched patrols off to either flank to make contact with adjacent companies. "About then it got light," recalled the company commander, "and it was the sickest thing I ever saw in my whole career. A whole rifle company. No foxholes dug. Nothing. Lying there in their sleeping bags. And they didn't have one sleeping bag for every two people. That way someone has to stay awake. Everyone was lying there, zipped up, including the company commander. There must have been a hundred men in the company, lying there dead. You can imagine what must have happened. The company had probably reached the crest near sun down. The men must have been tired, cold, and hungry. The company commander rationalized that no one would attack them there and decided to let the men have some sleep."

When the regimental commander met CAPT Emerson on the hill later that morning, he said, "That was the most professional night attack I ever saw. I'm going to put your company in for a citation. I'm going to get your whole company transferred to my regiment." Captain Emerson just stood there, thinking, "I don't want to have anything to do with your regiment."

After the regimental commander had departed, COL John Throckmorton walked up the hill. Captain Emerson reported to his CO who was obviously pleased with A Company's performance. The Rock's cheeks started to twitch in anger when the company commander informed him that the unit's regimental commander had been drinking with a drunken battalion commander the night before, and that one of this regiment's companies had been caught in their sleeping bags and annihilated. The Rock acknowledged the conclusion of the brief with a nod and said, "OK. I'm going to have a look around."

Captain Emerson thought, "Oh no!" The Rock was a strict disciplinarian who always kept his eyes open for one infraction or another. In this instance, a minor administrative failing would not escape the sharp eye of the RCT commander.

The 5th RCT, unlike other Army regiments in Korea, rarely suffered from trench foot largely because COL Throckmorton had directed his subordinate commanders to pay special attention to their men's feet. A standard operating procedure required each man to keep a change of socks tied to his belt and stuffed down into his trousers to keep dry. Whenever practical, small unit leaders made their soldiers take off their boots, remove their damp socks, rub down the skin, and place a pair of dry socks on their feet.

After checking two or three A Company soldiers, the Rock finally found one soldier, "a professional asshole," who only had one extra sock. Colonel Throckmorton looked angrily at CAPT Emerson, while off to the side the soldier's platoon sergeant appeared mad enough to take the miscreant out of sight and run him through with a bayonet. Captain Emerson was astute and mature enough to realize that this was simply the Rock's way of saying, "Good job last night. But you are still expected to maintain a damned disciplined outfit. Don't forget it."

After the Rock saluted and walked down the hill, it came to CAPT Emerson that he was working for a very special man. "That's when I realized the Rock had made something out of the 5th RCT that was visibly different from other regiments in Korea. I can't overemphasize the impact that one strong, strong, commander like the Rock had on the whole scene."

Morale is tenuous whenever an army is forced to retreat, yet LTC Clarence Stuart recalled, "The attitude of the men astounded me. They were proud of having done a good job and they had not been hurt much. Many of them thought the army would fight north of Seoul."[24] He thought morale in the Taro Leaf and Tropic Lightning, with the exception of the 24th Infantry, remained adequate. If directed, he felt the soldiers were prepared and willing to fight.

With the passage of time, a morale problem that began in the Eighth Army's rear echelons did spread to the combat units. When word of the 2nd Infantry Division's debacle at Kunu-ri reached the rear, morale in the service and support units plummeted. One manifestation of poor morale was the large amount of abandoned supplies and equipment left behind in the retreat. Chaplain Dick Oostenink watched in utter amazement as supply personnel torched immense stocks of parkas and other cold weather equipment while the 3rd Battalion's poorly clad infantry trudged slowly through the slush and snow in the frigid arctic cold.[25] On rare occasions the combat team benefited from the wastage that characterized the retreat. The 1st Battalion's S-4 Logistics Officer, for example, acquired fourteen abandoned trucks in perfect working order which the combat team quickly put to use.[26]

"We were not under enemy pressure," explained SGT Hibbert Manley, a platoon sergeant in Charlie Company. "For one thing, we were never kicked off of anything. We withdrew when we were ordered. We couldn't get over the waste we saw. At one point, we saw brand new tanks being destroyed because they didn't have the fuel to move them. But five miles down the road you'd see someone blowing up a fuel dump. The panic you may have heard about, it wasn't us, but the people behind us. We were madder than hell, and almost as mad as the Turks were. They just could not understand why we were pulling back."[27]

The morale problem infecting the Eighth Army was partially attributable to President Truman who had inadvertently belittled the Korean War as a mere Police Action or Conflict. Senior officers from General MacArthur on down had compounded the situation with bizarre promises that the men would be home for Thanksgiving, when they knew that for logistical reasons alone, such promises could not be kept. Incredibly, even after China's initial intervention, General MacArthur had continued to tell the men that they would be home by Christmas. It is easy to understand, therefore, why many soldiers felt betrayed and bitter. Morale was correspondingly low as the long retreat continued, and a sea of CCF infantry submerged the last hope for victory and an early resolution of the war.

It was bad enough that the ROKs broke and ran when pressured by the enemy, but even General Walker began to doubt the courage of the American soldier. For this reason, while the withdrawal to Pyongyang was in motion, General Walker began to contemplate abandoning the city and continuing the retirement south to the 38th Parallel. Fearing that the Eighth Army, if pressured, might panic and run, General Walker made one of the most controversial decisions of the Korean War. Believing that a protracted defense of Pyongyang was impractical and dangerous, General Walker ordered the Eighth Army to continue its withdrawal below the 38th Parallel to the Imjin River at a time when all contact with the enemy had been lost. In the words of one historian, "The essential to win such a battle — the will to fight, morale to contest the outcome, confidence of the professional leadership — were lacking in the officer corps, and in the rank-and-file as well. The rank-and-file might have responded had the leadership been up to it. But it was not. Eighth Army as a whole panicked and fled. It was a shameful performance."[28]

General Walker's decision to abandon Pyongyang exacerbated an already tense morale problem. Thousands of cold and hungry American soldiers were enraged to witness the destruction of supply dumps that could not be evacuated.[29]

Strangely, General MacArthur chose not to actively participate in General Walker's decision to withdraw at this crucial juncture of the fighting. Nevertheless, it is apparent from his cables to Washington that General MacArthur, however reluctantly, concurred. General MacArthur's star was descending in the hallowed halls of the White House and the Pentagon. For the first time in his long and illustrious career, General MacArthur's competence as a commander was being strongly criticized by his peers. General Matthew B. Ridgway, for example, believed that MacArthur's "insistence on retaining control from Tokyo, 700 miles from the battle areas, [was] unwarranted and unsound." He went on to state that this method of operations was largely responsible for the "heavy casualties and near disaster which followed."[30]

While these momentous decisions and colossal power plays were in motion, the 5th RCT continued to serve as rearguard. On 2 December, COL Throckmorton's command was reattached to the 24th Infantry Division. The 5th RCT immediately began a motorized movement to a blocking position at Yul-li.[31] Along the way, in the vicinity of Pyongyang, the regimental supply officer acquired enough Coca-Cola for every two men to share one bottle.[32] Unfortunately, Army regulations required the soldiers to purchase their cokes. How many men enjoyed a frozen bottle of Coke in the freezing North Korean winter remains a mystery.

During the withdrawal, COL Throckmorton implemented a standard operating procedure that had his battalions leapfrog through one another from one delay position to the next. The advance guard, usually a reinforced battalion, would drive until it reached a piece of key terrain, typically high ground, along the planned route of withdrawal. Here, the rifle companies would dismount their trucks and dig in to form a perimeter defense. Once the main body and the rearguard battalion had passed through their perimeter, the advance guard would assume the mission of rearguard and the process would be repeated.[33]

The 5th RCT occupied its blocking position at Yul-li from 4-7 December, at which time the retrograde continued.[34] About this time, LTC Albert Ward's 2nd Battalion began to acquire a reputation for burning down the North Korean villages it retreated through. An order emanating from the Eighth Army had directed scorched earth tactics to deny the CCF shelter from the elements as the Chinese continued their remorseless, if ponderous, advance. Easy Company acquired the nickname "Arson Easy" because of its enthusiasm in carrying out these destructive tasks.

When it became apparent that the war was not going to be over in a few days, LTC Clarence Stuart assigned 1st LT Frank Athanason the job of 555th FAB Communications Officer. Lieutenant Athanason said of the retreat, "It was cold as hell. We started moving south and morale was extremely low. Bumper-to-bumper traffic in the snow. The men were ill equipped for the weather and did not have proper winter clothing at the time. We didn't know what was going on. We'd get the word that we were going to stop and hold, and as soon as you'd stop, you'd be told to move again."[35]

Sergeant Samuel L. Lewis rejoined the artillery battalion's FDC section during the retreat after recovering from wounds incurred at Bloody Gulch. "The cold was terrible," he recalled. "One day during the retreat we received our first real eggs for breakfast in a long, long time. The grease would freeze as soon as the cook flipped the fried egg off the grill onto your plate. We were so hungry we ate them anyway."[36]

The 555th FAB learned how to fight in the winter through hard-earned experience. It took awhile to learn that in the zero-to-ten degree temperatures that prevailed in Korea, the first 105-mm howitzer rounds often impacted 1,000 to 1,500 yards closer than expected. A reserve officer, 1st LT Delbert A. Jurden, joined the battalion during the retreat. He understood the arcane art of artillery survey. As a result, the Triple Nickel increased its level of tactical sophistication and delivered increasingly more accurate fires.

The 555th FAB made its presence felt in support of the 5th RCT's infantry battalions throughout the withdrawal. At 2230, on 13 December, elements of K Company and the 3rd Battalion's supply trains were overrun in a surprise attack conducted by North Korean guerrillas wearing civilian clothes. King Company retreated under pressure into C Battery's perimeter where the howitzers fired over open sights throughout the night. The North Koreans attempted one final "banzai" attack the next morning, but it was repulsed with heavy enemy casualties.[37]

The North Koreans had captured a couple of K Company's mortars in their initial attack and quickly turned them against their former owners. Russian mortar ammunition had a single safety pin attached to each shell, while American mortar rounds had two, a detail the guerrillas overlooked. Lieutenant Randall Beirne explained, "The mortar rounds came in and nothing happened. They just went "bump" into the dirt." One round went through the fly of the mess tent, much to the annoyance of the mess chief.[38]

A leadership crisis brewing in the 3rd Battalion boiled over as a result of this firefight when LTC Benjamin Heckemeyer relieved CAPT Joseph Lukitsch of his command. Lieutenant Colonel

Heckemeyer justified the relief of the popular company commander after the guerrillas captured seven K Company infantrymen and one medic in the fighting. Captain Lukitsch's relief angered the company's officers and NCOs who were upset at the thought of losing their highly competent commander. Lieutenant Beirne approached LTC Heckemeyer and requested permission to speak to COL Throckmorton in order to explain to the regimental commander that the men did not want to lose CAPT Lukitsch. Lieutenant Colonel Heckemeyer, oddly enough, did not object, and LT Beirne led a delegation to the regimental CP to speak with the commanding officer.

When Colonel Throckmorton saw LT Beirne's small delegation, he asked, "What is this, Beirne, mutiny?"

A startled LT Beirne found himself at a rare loss for words. Not so 1st LT Arland H. Wagonhurst, West Point Class of 1945, who interjected, "Oh no, Sir! We just wanted to keep you informed."[39]

Colonel Throckmorton listened to the officers and made a quick decision to effect a compromise. To buttress the authority of his battalion commander, he upheld LTC Heckemeyer's relief of CAPT Lukitsch, who in turn was given another company to command in the regiment.

The bitterly cold night of 13 December found the 5th RCT retreating toward Uijongbu, one of its old stomping grounds from 1949. Second Lieutenant Edward P. Crockett was sitting with his head exposed to the freezing night air in the commander's hatch of his tank, attempting to recover his wits after being knocked nearly senseless by the unsecured barrel of the .50-caliber machine gun.

Lieutenant Crockett had won a coveted position in the Armor Branch upon his graduation from West Point with the Class of 1950. The Department of the Army had nearly nullified this achievement when it instituted a new and shortsighted personnel policy just before the Korean War that had regrettable consequences for many men. As a result of numerous complaints from second lieutenants who did not want to endure yet another year of instruction at a branch school following four years of instruction at West Point, the Department of the Army had decided in 1950 that all newly commissioned regular officers would spend their first three years of service with troop units. In theory the lieutenants would avoid the monotony of yet another year of instruction, while emerging from line service with a better appreciation for the relevancy of the subject matter taught at the branch schools. In hindsight this policy was implemented without giving due consideration to the possibility of having to wage a bloody war on a distant Asian battlefield. Regrettably, numerous second lieutenants went to war a couple of months after being commissioned in 1950 with little more than the theoretical knowledge they had gleaned from classroom instruction to sustain themselves in combat. One consequence was that the West Point Class of 1950 suffered particularly heavy losses in Korea.

Lieutenant Crockett was fortunate in that he had enjoyed a couple of pleasant months with the 2nd "Hell on Wheels" Armored Division at Camp Hood, Texas before he received orders to Korea as a replacement officer. His experience in armor was virtually nonexistent, however, because the 2nd Armored Division in 1950 was a basic training outfit that had no tanks. When LT Crockett reported to the 5th RCT in late November 1950, the Regimental Adjutant had crushed him with the news that Tank Company had its full compliment of officers. Therefore, the Adjutant recommended to COL Throckmorton that the armor officer be assigned to the infantry. The Rock had other ideas, and a grateful LT Crockett was assigned to the position of platoon leader in Tank Company, where he replaced LT Keith Whitham in the 2nd Platoon who in turn became the regimental aerial observer.[40] Tank Company, still commanded by CAPT Robert Kennedy, had been expanded to four tank platoons after recently absorbing the remnants of the 21st Infantry's Tank Company.[41]

Lieutenant Crockett's first task was to win the trust and confidence of his platoon sergeant. Master Sergeant Johnnie B. Walls, a Cherokee Indian, was a brave and experienced soldier who had served in the infantry before transferring in 1949 to the newly formed Tank Company at Schofield Barracks. Since the 5th RCT's arrival in Korea, MSGT Walls had proven his mastery of small unit armor tactics in many a desperate firefight from the Pusan Perimeter to Kunu-ri.

In the time-tested manner since Caesar's Legions conquered Gaul, the platoon sergeant's process of sizing up the new officer began immediately after LT Crockett joined the 2nd Tank Platoon. Lieutenant Crockett explained, "I asked my platoon sergeant to instruct me how to turn on the tank radio and manipulate the controls. Had there been any doubt in his mind regarding my raw inexperience, it vanished at that moment. Perhaps my unequivocal deference to his experience that first morning foretold his more gradually acquired respect for me."[42]

Lieutenant Crockett received a harsh initiation to warfare. A few nights after his arrival, the 5th RCT came under a furious Chinese assault and the order was given to withdraw. The 2nd Tank Platoon moved out in column, heading south without infantry escort. When one of the platoon's Easy Eights slid into a ditch, LT Crockett immediately backed up his Sherman to retrieve the immobilized tank. As the crews attached a towing cable, Chinese rifle fire from the left flank began to impact around the men. Lieutenant Crockett climbed out of his hatch and onto his tank's engine deck to unlimber the .50-caliber machine gun. He worked the bolt once, pressed the trigger, and nothing happened. In his haste, the platoon leader had forgotten that the bolt on a .50-caliber machine gun has to be worked twice to chamber a round. He worked the bolt a second time, pressed the trigger, and walked his red tracers into the Chinese muzzle flashes. Sergeant Walls calmly took cover next to the tank and watched with silent approval as his platoon leader fought a grim gunnery duel. He must have thought, "This one will do."

One exceptionally cold night, LT Crockett's platoon gave a lift to a group of Turkish soldiers. During the course of the journey, a Turkish soldier quietly froze to death while clinging to the turret of LT Crockett's tank.

The frozen days and nights blurred together as the combat team's withdrawal continued. Lieutenant Crockett did not have a sleeping bag, so he curled up as best he could in his blankets, wearing everything he owned, to catch a couple of hours of sorely needed rest. Master Sergeant Walls woke him at 0200, on 13 December, with the unwelcome news that the combat team was withdrawing forty-miles farther south to Uijongbu. Lieutenant Crockett climbed into his hatch as the Easy Eights roared into life and placed a helmet on his head. When LT Crockett ordered the driver, SGT Leonard Woods, to move out, the unsecured .50-caliber machine gun barrel slammed into the side of his head when the Sherman lurched forward. The lieutenant had not ensured it was locked down when he climbed aboard.

Lieutenant Crockett said, "I stood my position as tank commander and platoon leader in a semiconscious state of mind. Shortly after I regained full control of my faculties, we arrived at a fork in the road which was manned by a lone 24th Division MP who said, 'Lieutenant, where are you headed?' When I couldn't remember the name of the town where we were to assemble, I felt utterly stupid and certainly not in confident command of a combat armor unit. In an effort to disguise my embarrassment, I countered, 'Headed south, what's down that direction?' He called out the name of a totally unfamiliar town. 'And the other way,' I inquired? He answered — 'Uijongbu.' Bingo! "Wee johng boo," a familiar but difficult name indeed. We continued on in that direction."[43]

From its reserve position at Uijongbu, the 5th RCT dispatched its I&R Platoons on patrols to regain contact with the Chinese. Tanks accompanied most of the patrols. On the few occasions when the I&R Platoons made enemy contact, timely, accurate artillery fire from the 555th FAB often saved the day.[44]

Sergeant Bud Throne, from the 2nd Battalion's I&R Platoon, was walking beside a tank on one of these patrols when the Chinese initiated an ambush. A slug hit SGT Throne's left shoulder and knocked him to the ground. The tank's machine guns and main gun quickly silenced the enemy fire. Sergeant Throne was evacuated to the rear where the doctors patched him up so he could return to the 5th RCT. By this time he was one of a handful of survivors who had deployed with the battalion's original I&R Platoon to Korea. One of the others was CPL Jimmy Masuda from Ewa, Oahu.[45]

Although the 5th RCT had not been seriously mauled during the long retreat from North Korea, COL Throckmorton sought to redress the continuing disparity in personnel strengths between his outfit and units organic to the 24th Infantry Division. The personnel situation that existed on 12 December was as follows.[46]

SGT Bud Throne, Ada, Oklahoma, in North Korea wearing a fur hat he made for himself. (source: Bud Throne)

UNIT	OFFICERS	WARRANT OFFICERS	ENLISTED MEN
19th INF	168	7	3,045
21st INF	172	5	3,233
5th INF	161	13	2,770

Though the Triple Nickel now surpassed its sister battalions in total numbers of commissioned and warrant officers, it continued to lag far behind in enlisted strength.

UNIT	OFFICERS	WARRANT OFFICERS	ENLISTED MEN
13th FAB	39	2	576
52nd FAB	43	3	607
555th FAB	45	8	532

On 16 December, COL Throckmorton sent the 24th Infantry Division G-1 a request for 22 officers and 829 enlisted men to bring the 5th Infantry up to strength.[47] He exercised little administrative control over the 555th FAB, but the division artillery commander took the appropriate steps to bring the Triple Nickel up to strength, too. It was clearly going to be a longer war than anticipated just a few short weeks before, and 24th Infantry Division finally acted to replenish the combat team's decimated ranks with an infusion of replacements.

During a lull in the fighting, COL Throckmorton took steps to improve and sustain the morale of his soldiers. The Rock knew his soldiers took pride in service with the 5th RCT. Soldiers serving in Army infantry divisions, and a handful of independent outfits like the 187th Airborne RCT, wore a distinctive shoulder patch that identified their unit. Although the 5th RCT had been attached at varying times to the 1st Cavalry, 24th and 25th Infantry Divisions, the independent combat team did not yet have a distinctive patch of its own. A few veterans like CPL James Shaw wore the U.S. Army Pacific shoulder patch from their Schofield Barrack days just to have something distinctive to wear. Most soldiers wore the 24th Infantry Division's Taro Leaf on their shoulders, although technically, the 5th RCT was attached and not permanently assigned to this organization.

On 18 December, COL Throckmorton sought to redress this situation and requested a unit patch for his regiment from the Adjutant General of the Army. Included in the request was a proposed design: a scarlet pentagon with a white scroll underneath and the words "5th RCT" in infantry blue. After the inevitable bureaucratic modifications and delays, a patch depicting a scarlet pentagon enclosed within a white border was authorized for wear on 14 March 1952.[48]

The 5th RCT celebrated Christmas with church services and a sumptuous steak dinner. Lieutenant Ed Crockett's entire platoon huddled for warmth inside a single farmhouse that night. He said, "We cut a small tree and decorated it with unlikely ornaments: ration tins, can openers, shards of metal, and whatever else we could find." His bride Marcia had mailed him a fruitcake literally dripping with rum. Following their steak dinner, LT Crockett shared the present with his grateful men. His boys slept well that night.[49]

Colonel Throckmorton relayed his Christmas Greetings to all the 5th RCT: "As members of 'The Team' each of you may well be proud of your accomplishments during the past year. Your individual and collective efforts in training and in five months of combat have established the 5th Regimental Combat Team in the ranks of the Army's finest. During the coming year it will be our responsibility to maintain the 'Fighting Fifth's' reputation for efficiency, discipline and gallantry."[50]

CHAPTER TWENTY-TWO

RIDGWAY

If any war that our country ever engaged in could be called a forgotten war, this was it. The primary purpose of an army — to be ready to fight effectively at all times — seems to have been forgotten. Our armed forces had been economized almost into ineffectiveness and then had been asked to meet modern armor with obsolescent weapons and had been sent into subarctic temperatures in clothing fit for fall maneuvers at home. The people in the states, I knew, were often too preoccupied with the essential task of making a living to concern themselves with faraway battles, unless one in the immediate kin was involved. As for the men themselves, a good many had been reactivated after making a considerable sacrifice in a war that seemed hardly over, while the workings of the selective service had sent into action young men who often wound up in uniform simply because they were people of little influence at home. In view of all this, it is a miracle, and a credit to those who bred them, that our soldiers had fought so magnificently against such brutal odds and still retained their courage and the dogged willingness to go where their leaders sent them.
General Matthew Bunker Ridgway, The Korean War

General Walker was killed two days before Christmas in a tragic vehicle accident after visiting his son who had been awarded the Silver Star while serving in the 19th Infantry, 24th Infantry Division. General Matthew B. Ridgway was summoned from Washington to assume command of the Eighth Army. He would arrive in Korea in time to witness the CCF's next major offensive.

The 5th RCT's I&R Platoons continued their extensive patrolling effort through December while the rest of the combat team recuperated, absorbed replacements, trained, and maintained vehicles and equipment. On 27 December, COL Throckmorton received a map overlay from 24th Infantry Division for a tentative defense of the Seoul area, a strong indication that a further withdrawal was being planned. Verbal orders were issued to begin an immediate reconnaissance of the defensive positions.

On 29 December, the 72nd Engineers, Korean laborers, and one company from each battalion commenced construction of suitable defensive positions on the outskirts of Seoul. Two days later, the 5th RCT completed counterattack plans to back-stop the 21st and 19th Infantry Regiments' defensive positions on the MLR.[1] Clearly, the Eighth Army was anticipating a major CCF offensive.

In an attempt to boost flagging morale, the Eighth Army provided its guidance on Rest and Recuperation (R&R) in Japan on 28 December.[2] Each rest period was to consist of seven days, which would not be counted against accrued leave. The first six officers and thirty-four enlisted men from the 5th RCT departed on R&R two days later.

Losses in December had been light. No one was reported killed in action. Twelve WIAs, twelve MIAs, and 130 non-battle casualties were reported.[3] Moreover, everyone was pleasantly surprised when eight men, declared MIA after King Company's firefight with the guerrillas, returned on 23 December after an amazing nine-day trek through enemy territory. In contrast to the typical behavior of NKPA troops, the guerrillas released these men. All eight had to be evacuated for cold injuries, but at least they were alive.[4]

When General Ridgway arrived in Korea on 26 December, he was disappointed to find that the Eighth Army as a whole was a psychological wreck, always fighting with one wary eye over its shoulder, looking for a route of withdrawal.[5] Much of the Eighth Army's previous difficulties and defeats could be blamed on the easily panicked ROK Army. The bones of many of the best and bravest ROK soldiers lay in shallow graves from the Naktong to the Yalu, a grim reality that hampered the performance of the ROK Army for the rest of the war. There

Three of the men the North Korean guerrillas released. (source: Chang)

was plenty of dirty laundry to go around, however, and the performance of several American commanders and units had been equally poor.

General Ridgway was foremost a fighter and a leader. His arrival proved to be a decisive turning point in the Eighth Army's fortunes at this critical juncture of the Korean War. Like COL Throckmorton, General Ridgway possessed the uncanny knack of remembering the names of his soldiers, a gift that endeared him to enlisted men and officers alike. He also kept a large supply of gloves on hand, which he personally issued to soldiers in the field who had lost their own gloves in the confusion of a firefight.

He shook up the Eighth Army's command structure by quietly relieving numerous physically exhausted senior commanders who he replaced with fresh, innovative, and vigorous men. In Ridgway's words, "The leadership I found in many instances sadly lacking, and I said so out loud. The unwillingness of the army to forgo certain creature comforts, its timidity about getting off the scanty roads, its reluctance to move without radio and telephone contact, and its lack of imagination in dealing with a foe whom they soon outmatched in firepower and dominated in the air and on the surrounding seas—these were not the fault of the GI but of the policy makers at the top. I'm afraid my language in pointing out these faults was often impolite."[6]

General Ridgway brought a fresh tactical and operational perspective to Korea. In his opinion, Korea was excellent tank country, a view not previously shared by armor officers such as the deceased General Walker. Perhaps the difference in perspective was one of size and space. The armor officers who had led the victorious dash across Northwest Europe in World War II found the jagged mountains and narrow valleys of Korea to be inhibiting factors that prevented large scale, rapid advances by armored units. General Ridgway, a paratrooper, was not dreaming of wide envelopments and dashing armored drives to seize his opponent's vitals. Rather, he envisioned the battlefield from the infantry battalion and company commander's perspective — the gut wrenching, desperate advance through rough terrain into enemy automatic weapons and mortar fire that had characterized much of the fighting in Korea.

General Ridgway believed in offensive solutions, even to defensive problems. He viewed the tank's mission in Korea as that of a mobile, armored assault gun, one capable of shrugging off hits while battering down the enemy's defenses with direct fire at point-blank range in support of the infantry. General Ridgway ordered his subordinate commanders to use offensive tactics whenever possible on the tactical level with tank-infantry teams.[7] Regardless of the tactical situation, be it offensive or defensive, General Ridgway demanded that his commanders commit their tanks and infantry into battle as teams.

The previous performance of American and ROK artillery in Korea had disappointed General Ridgway. He believed that too many guns had been disgracefully lost during the long withdrawal from North Korea. One of his immediate concerns was to beef-up Eighth Army's artillery to counter the CCF's enormous influx of infantry. General Ridgway sensibly preferred to let the CCF expend lives while he expended high explosive shells. To provide his tank-infantry teams additional fire support, General Ridgway requested, and eventually received, a batch of long-range self-propelled artillery battalions that dramatically increased Eighth Army's hitting power.[8]

General Ridgway believed it prudent to trade space for his opponent's blood, believing lost terrain could be regained through counterattack once the foot-mobile Communist forces had overextended their weak logistical tail.[9] He desired above all else to pummel his opponent, to inflict horrendous losses on the CCF and NKPA, to make the Communists "scream uncle" and sue for peace. Implicit in General Ridgway's method of operations was his willingness to fight the war to a draw. Victory in the sense of overrunning North Korea, and the creation of a unified, democratic republic, was no longer General Ridgway's or President Truman's goal. That victory in the traditional sense remained General MacArthur's over-arching goal eventually led to his downfall, but that story need not concern us here.

General Ridgway was appalled by the living conditions of his soldiers and took immediate steps to increase supplies of tentage and cold weather clothing to shield the troops from the bitter cold. In an effort to improve the severe health problems plaguing the Eighth Army, he forbade units from establishing CPs and bivouacs inside homes and buildings. Unit commanders had previously enjoyed few alternatives to billeting their men and operating their CPs in the vermin-infested dwellings.[10]

"Up until the time General Ridgway came to Eighth Army, we had been living in Korean houses," explained CAPT Robert Lamb, the CO of Fox Company. "We did not have tentage. In January we started getting tents, we got winter clothing issued — it was late, we were already in the winter. That particular period was not one of the finer days of the American Army in that regard."[11]

The Commanding General's impact on the troops was electric. "General Ridgway restored our confidence in our ability to fight the Chinese," explained PFC Arlen Russell, now sixteen. "We finally had someone in command who was going to do something. We didn't realize at the time that all he'd done was tell us we could do it. His leadership turned us around."[12]

General Ridgway's arrival in Korea coincided with the onset of the "The Third Chinese Offensive."[13] On New Year's Eve the CCF crossed the 38th Parallel and invaded South Korea. The Chinese directed their main effort against the Eighth Army's left flank, where the I and IX Corps were dug in. Here the Eighth Army had established a corset defense, with American divisions laced between ROK ones. The CCF field commanders sought out divisional boundaries and hurled their main weight on the hapless ROK infantry, who promptly collapsed, leaving their American comrades holding the MLR, flanks exposed to Communist envelopment. As Chinese infantry pushed into the resultant gaps, many American combat units began to abandon their positions without orders, something even General Ridgway's presence proved incapable of stopping. After reviewing the situation, General Ridgway reluctantly issued orders to withdraw.[14]

The Chinese hit the 24th Infantry Division hard on the opening night of the offensive and achieved a penetration in the 19th Infantry's defensive sector. The 1st and 3rd Battalions, 5th RCT, advanced northwards, grimly determined to hold a blocking position long enough to cover the Taro Leaf's withdrawal.[15] Lieutenant Colonel Albert Ward's 2nd Battalion was placed under the command of the hard-pressed 27th British Commonwealth Brigade.

The Chinese, who had initiated their offensive in bad weather, were probably astounded when the sky suddenly cleared on 1 January and waves of FEAF fighter-bombers struck the exposed CCF infantry advancing in the open. Whenever the Chinese pressed too hard, COL Throckmorton could count on immediate CAS. The FEAF flew over 2,500 ground attack sorties on 1-5 January alone, bombing, strafing, and rocketing the exposed CCF infantry, and inflicting an estimated 8,000 casualties on the Communist forces.[16]

In a planning conference conducted prior to the Chinese offensive, General MacArthur had directed General Ridgway not to risk the destruction of the Eighth Army in a futile defense of Seoul.[17] This directive was in keeping with General Ridgway's willingness to trade space in order to inflict maximum punishment on the Chinese. General Ridgway, although dissatisfied with Eighth Army's performance, would have preferred to continue the battle, but the near total collapse of the ROK forces convinced him that Seoul could not be held, and the withdrawal continued south of the Han River.[18]

Throughout the withdrawal, COL Throckmorton made the force of his personality known, calmly issuing concise, logical orders to his commanders. In accordance with the combat team's standard operating procedures, the infantry battalions leapfrogged one another, falling back step-by-step under the protective range fan of the deadly accurate Triple Nickel gun crews. The cannoneers used white phosphorous shells to adjust their fire whenever the Chinese pressed too close and inflicted heavy losses on the enemy.[19] Under the cover provided by the Triple Nickel's volleys, the fatigued infantry marched south through the snow and slush, perhaps wondering if the strange war would ever end.

A blazing inferno greeted the soldiers as the combat team withdrew at night through Seoul. South Korean civilians, in their determination to leave nothing but ashes to greet the hated Chinese, fanned the flames of arson and created a sea of fire. With so many landmarks in ruins or flames, the 3rd Battalion's advance party became disoriented and lost contact with the main body during the withdrawal.[20] Late in the evening of 3 January, LTC Benjamin Heckemeyer approached Chaplain Dick Oostenink and asked him to lead the battalion through Seoul. Chaplain Oostenink agreed to this unusual request, because he had an intimate knowledge of Seoul's streets and alleys based on his prewar experiences in Korea. He placed his jeep at the head of the column and led it through the burning, rubble strewn streets of Seoul.[21]

Even in adversity, moments of levity accompanied the withdrawal. Lieutenant Randall Beirne said, "As we pulled back through Seoul, the soldiers cheered as they drove past the burning 31st Circle, because many had been robbed there before the war."[22]

Once across the Han, Chaplain Oostenink had his driver pull off the road so the command group could take

General Ridgway. (source: NA)

the lead and guide the battalion into its assembly area. Dawn was approaching as Chaplain Oostenink looked across the river to gaze at the hellish scene of a city in flames. As he gazed at the steeple of the Catholic Cathedral, silhouetted against the flames and sky, he thought, "They may destroy the city but the Cross of Christ always stands out above it."[23]

The 5th RCT observes a FEAF ground attack mission.
(source: NA)

Corporal Ronald Denton, in the Heavy Mortar Company, summed up the feelings of most of the men, "We were tired, dirty and angry. We didn't want to retreat. We'd rather have been attacking. But there were just too many Chinese and not enough soldiers."[24] Chinese pressure prevented the Eighth Army from holding the south bank of the Han, and the withdrawal continued to Changhowan-ni where the 5th RCT dug in for a protracted defense.

The I&R platoons and infantry companies conducted day and night reconnaissance patrols to regain contact with the enemy, maintain contact with adjacent units, and to question the thousands of refugees flooding the area.[25] Once again, an Eighth Army retreat had outpaced a Chinese advance, and from 5-17 January the 5th RCT made no contact with the enemy.

Since 28 November, the combat team had retreated 300 miles. The men were tired, hungry, filthy, and cold beyond our ability to imagine today as we sit comfortably in our homes. Soldiers serving in the 2nd Heavy Mortar Platoon were sitting around a small fire one bitterly cold night in a reserve position when PFC Oliver Holt departed his small circle of friends in a search to replenish the life-sustaining woodpile. When he entered a clearly marked minefield to gather small pieces of kindling in his arms, he stepped on an antipersonnel mine that exploded and ripped off one of his legs. The mangled soldier died shortly thereafter from loss of blood, shock, and the bone-numbing cold.[26]

The cumulative impact of sub-zero temperature, numbing weariness and ceaseless fear of the unknown drove some individuals to take extreme measures for self-preservation. Two soldiers in King Company, for example, shot themselves in the foot about this time, a serious breach of discipline that threatened to undermine unit morale.[27]

Major General John H. Church, the Commanding General of the 24th Infantry Division, thought poor morale pervaded his Taro Leaf soldiers. To counteract fears of imminent disaster, he took the unusual step of drafting a personal memorandum for his subordinate commanders that promised the division would not experience another Taejon.[28]

Colonel Throckmorton took immediate and aggressive steps to restore morale in the combat team, and under his sure hand, the soldiers responded. A strict training regime was the key. He instituted training and maintenance schedules for his units to follow when they were not actively patrolling. The Rock placed emphasis on antiaircraft and anti-paratrooper defensive tactics, due to the Eighth Army's fear that the Chinese Air Force was poised to enter the war in force.[29] He cracked down on disciplinary infractions and informed subordinate commanders that immediate improvement in convoy security and individual weapons handling was expected. The final terse line of one memorandum read, "Disciplinary action as necessary will be utilized to enforce infractions of these instructions."[30]

Colonel Throckmorton required each rifle squad to perform bayonet training designed to inculcate the infantry with a "determination to close with the enemy in hand to hand combat for the purpose of killing him."[31] If nothing else, the exercise succeeded in keeping the soldiers warm and limber.

One rare morning when the temperature rose above freezing, Tank Company's new CO, 1st LT George H. Gaylord, issued cans of white paint to his platoon leaders and instructed them to paint Hawaiian names onto the sides of their tanks.[32] The citizens of Hawaii had been very supportive of the 5th RCT and viewed the combat team as "Hawaii's Own." Wounded men recovering at Tripler Hospital on Oahu had experienced the true meaning of "Aloha Spirit" on pass out in the local communities. Colonel Throckmorton took this opportunity to show his appreciation while simultaneously boosting morale in his combat team. Though a handful of Sherman's already sported Hawaiian names such as *J. Aku Head Pupule*, the nickname of a Honolulu disk jockey, by the end of the day, the rest of Tank Company's Shermans sported Hawaiian names, too. *Mona Loa*, *Aloha*, *Leilani*, and *Hula Girl*, were just a few of the names that soon adorned the sides of Tank Company's Easy Eights.[33] Lieutenant Crockett's Sherman, *Hawaii Calls*, was the title of a popular song and musical group.

Shortly thereafter, LT Gaylord instructed his platoon leaders to paint a slogan that corresponded to the battalion they normally supported in smaller white letters next to each Sherman's Hawaiian name. The 2nd Tank Platoon's M4 A3E8's adopted the slogan "Ward's Boilers" because of LTC Ward's predilection to verbally state in his operations orders that "I want the tanks to go boiling down the valley."[34]

The New Year ushered in the Year of the Tiger. It was commonly believed that the Chinese would treat it as a bad omen to confront tigers in Korea. So roaring tiger faces with fierce eyes, black stripes, sharp fangs, and bloody claws were painted on the frontal armor of all but the 2nd Platoon's tanks. Lieutenant Ed Crockett preferred to rely on the traditional olive drab camouflage for protection rather than the outlandish caricatures of the noble Tiger. Thus, the 2nd Platoon missed out on some of the most bizarre art ever to adorn America's war machines.[35]

Sergeant James W. Hart, from Tulsa, Oklahoma, joined Fox Company in early January 1951. He had served with the 1st Cavalry Division in an 81-mm Mortar Platoon during the Philippines Campaign, and therefore enjoyed the benefit of previous combat experience. Discharged in 1946, he was working in Oklahoma's oil fields in October 1950 when President Truman recalled thousands of reservists to the colors. Thus SGT Hart joined Fox Company at a time when the 5th RCT had reached its lowest point in morale during the Korean War.[36]

Sergeant Hart was assigned to Fox Company's 60-mm Mortar Section as a squad leader. "I heard these guys start talking about 'bugging out.' This went on for two or three days. You know when you are new in an outfit you just keep your mouth shut and listen. I finally asked someone what 'bugging out' meant. They told me it meant to take off running when you were hit. I said, 'What do you mean take off?' And they said, 'Well, you just take off.' I said, 'We can't have this.' And they said, 'Well, that's what we do.' And so I went down to talk to the first sergeant and told him I'd like to have an NCO meeting. We did and I told them all how I felt; that we needed every man we had pointing their

A 4th Platoon Easy Eight celebrates the Year of the Tiger. L to R: CPL John T. Clark, SGT Frank G. Allen, SGT Theodore R. Liberty, CPL William J. Bohmback, and CPL James E. Kishbough. (sources: 25th ID Musem/Chang)

The 5th RCT covers the evacuation of noncombatants as they cross the frozen Han River on foot. (source: NA)

Donald Gottschall (right), Zephyr Hills, Florida, Heavy Mortar Company, tries to stay warm. An unidentified KATUSA stands on the left. The GI in the center is unidentified. (source: Donald Gottschall)

guns at the enemy and pulling the triggers. That way everybody got out. There must have been fifteen or twenty enlisted reserves, mostly sergeants, who joined Fox Company about the same time I did and they all felt the same way. I think that meeting added strength, or backbone, to the company. And I'm not trying to take anything away from the 5th because they were one hell of an outfit…. I felt strongly about this, and I felt it important enough, not just for my well being, but for the well being of the people involved there that we talk this over and decide what we needed to do. We went back and told the troops… if we had to withdraw, we'd do it in an orderly fashion. And anybody not doing so… well that wouldn't be considered too good. That's all it took."[37]

Offensive combat was a sure tonic to restore morale and, on 17 January, the 24th Infantry Division ordered the 5th RCT to conduct platoon-sized patrols every other day to Ichon, alternating with the 27th Commonwealth Brigade. On 21 January, G Company, reinforced with tanks, recoilless rifles, mortars and two squads from the 2nd Battalion I&R Platoon departed on a patrol. After reaching Ichon, a platoon-sized force advanced to the south bank of the Han, captured two Chinese soldiers, and at this time was farther north than any other UN unit in Korea. Another platoon-sized patrol from G Company participated in a fierce firefight until it was forced to withdraw with seven WIA after expending all its ammunition.[38]

When LTC Albert Ward flew to Japan for a well deserved spell of R&R, COL Throckmorton decided it was time to give MAJ Claude Baker a taste of battalion command. Regrettably, the 2nd Battalion's zeal in burning villages to the ground had not abated once the outfit retreated into South Korea. After MAJ Baker caught a couple of his units burning villages, he ordered the company commanders and battalion staff to knock it off. Henceforth, arson was no longer tolerated in the 2nd Battalion. This policy remained in effect when LTC Ward resumed command of the battalion seven days later.[39]

Replacements began to arrive in increasing numbers, with 503 replacements and hospital returnees joining the 5th RCT on 21 January alone. Colonel Throckmorton directed that all

Crew of the Easy Eight J. Aku Head Pupule *takes a break. L to R: unknown; Platoon Sergeant Herman Wedding, Hampton, VA; Driver Bill Kapaku, Waianae, Oahu; Gunner SGT Douglas Lay of 1st LT "D.J.'s" 3rd Platoon. (sources: Bill Kapaku/Chang)*

5th RCT tankers. L to R: LT Ed Crockett, Oakland, CA; SFC William Puaoi, Hoolehua, Molokai; CPL Robert Rucinski, Minneapolis, MN; LT George Gaylord, Wausau, WI; and CPL William Anderson, Louisville, KY. (source: Chang)

replacements would receive seven days of refresher training to acclimatize the soldiers and give them a psychological boost before they were assigned to their units.[40] Thus the replacements gained self-confidence and the belief that they belonged to an elite combat team that cared for their individual welfare. During this period, several veteran platoon leaders and NCOs rotated to the rear for two-week intervals to train the replacements.[41]

On 22 January, the 2nd Battalion, with Tank Company, and the entire 555th FAB attached, conducted an aggressive reconnaissance in force with the 7th Cavalry Regiment north of the MLR.[42] Much to everyone's surprise, they did not make contact with the enemy.

Thus emboldened, on 29 January, the 24th Infantry Division ordered the 5th RCT to move to Ichon and prepare to attack northward toward a series of ridgelines on the far side of a wide valley. While truck convoys rolled toward the combat team's assembly area, COL Throckmorton made a personal reconnaissance of the snow-covered terrain from an L-5 aircraft. After seeing the lay of the ground, COL Throckmorton ordered the 1st Battalion to seize Objective Baker, Hill 475 and Hill 406. The 2nd Battalion, which had rejoined the 5th RCT in its assembly area, was ordered to seize Objective Able, Hill 256.[43] The 3rd Battalion remained in reserve.

While the soldiers moved into their attack positions in the pre-dawn darkness, each American and KATUSA enlisted man received a gratuitous PX ration of four candy bars.[44] The 2nd Battalion crossed the LD at 0730. An hour later, the 1st Battalion commenced its attack. The combat team moved out through a heavy morning fog, the soldiers advancing warily through the snow as sporadic enemy bullets whispered through the bitterly cold air. Although fog concealed the soldiers moving across the open ground, as the assault battalions closed on their objectives, it began to interfere with the adjustment of artillery fire and close air support. By 1330, the fog had lifted, and enemy resistance had increased dramatically. A coordinated infantry assault, supported by artillery and FEAF air strikes, proved necessary to eject the tenacious CCF defenders from their positions.

The 1st Battalion fought its way onto Objective Baker through fierce Chinese resistance. Corporal Wilfred Parks, from Honolulu, led a rifle squad in Baker Company. Intense Chinese fire pinned this rifle squad to the ground, all except CPL Parks who took little notice of the enemy fire and rushed forward hurling hand grenades into the enemy trenches. His soldiers dutifully followed their intrepid leader and assaulted through the Chinese position.[45]

By 1630, the 1st Battalion had cleared its objective, "and many enemy were killed during the ensuing mop-up." A fierce Chinese counterattack ejected C Company from its positions in furious close quarters fighting. The official report states, "The company reformed and by constant assaults on the position was able to retake the lost ground." Objective Baker was declared secure at 2110.[46]

The 2nd Battalion had likewise encountered only light resistance early in its assault, but when the fog cleared around 1000, the Chinese lashed out with intense and deadly accurate mortar and automatic weapons fire. George Company led the assault that morning and took considerable losses securing its objective on the lower part of a long ridgeline dominated by Hill 256, which remained in Chinese hands.

It was nearing the moment when E Company was going to have to conduct a passage of lines through G Company and continue the attack to seize Hill 256. Captain William Conger, the CO of E Company, went forward with his 3rd Platoon Leader, 1st LT Carl Dodd, to confer with CAPT William L. Cooper, the CO of G Company, before the passage of lines took place. The three officers were standing together on a spur discussing the tactical situation when a mortar round exploded nearby, the concussion knocking all three to the ground. Shrapnel had seriously wounded both CAPT Conger and CAPT Cooper and they were evacuated down the hill.[47] Lieutenant Dodd returned to Easy Company and briefed the men on the forthcoming attack.

First Lieutenant Lucian R. Rawls took over Easy Company, but since he was not present when CAPT Conger devised the offensive scheme of maneuver, LT Dodd briefed the plan. Easy Company's mission was to secure three knolls on the ridgeline, identified by height as the lower position, the center position, and finally, the summit of Hill 256. The scheme of maneuver tasked the 3rd Platoon with an assault directly up a saddle to break into the center position. At this point, one of the other platoons would pass through the 3rd Platoon and continue the attack on Hill 256 while yet another platoon attacked downhill and took the lower position.[48] Lieutenant Rawls briefed the fire support plan, which included a flight of P-51s that was going to drop napalm on the center position while the company assaulted up the ridge. The company's organic and attached machine guns would support the attack on all three objectives from a base of fire with long range gunnery.

First Lieutenant Carl H. Dodd, a former NCO who had earned a couple of Silver Stars and a battlefield commission earlier in the Korean War, was the sole officer leading a rifle platoon in Easy Company on 30 January. Born with a twisted foot that caused him immense pain when he walked long distances carrying heavy loads, he had successfully concealed this fact when he enlisted in the Army in 1943. Quite naturally, he ended up in the infantry. World War II was over when Private Dodd shipped out to partake in the occupation of Korea. When his enlistment expired, he returned to his home in Harlan County, Kentucky, but civilian life did not appeal to Carl Dodd. He reenlisted and took his bride, Libbie, to Schofield Barracks.

Sergeant First Class Dodd had been 1st LT Gordon Strong's platoon sergeant when the latter was KIA near Chindong-ni. His courage, tactical skill, and sheer audacity had earned him a battlefield commission in late October 1950 when his unit was operating deep inside North Korea. He was now the 3rd Platoon Leader in E Company, and SFC Horace Anderson was his platoon sergeant.

Before the 3rd Platoon moved out, a flight of P-51s dropped napalm in the vicinity of the center position. The fiery explosions killed few Chinese. Only direct hits had any effect on the occupants of the skillfully constructed trenches and bunkers. Yet the napalm did keep the enemy's head down as Easy Company advanced with fixed bayonets up the slope.[49]

MSGT Horace Anderson (left), Adrian, Georgia, on a route march at Fort Benning, July 1951, after he rotated from Korea. (source: Horace Anderson)

Sergeant First Class Anderson accompanied one of the 3rd Platoon's rifle squads when the assault commenced.[50] He had instructed his men to keep moving no matter what happened, so they could bust into the Chinese trench as a unit. On his way up the ridge, he encountered a camouflaged Chinese fighting position. He hurled one of the eight hand grenades he carried on his person into the hole. After the explosion, he scrambled past the smoking hole and pumped several M-1 rounds into a pile of bloody rags lying in a mangled heap at the bottom.

When SFC Anderson reached a concealed position overlooking the center position, he noticed that the Chinese were stacked back-to-back, two in a row, in a trench with one group shooting and throwing grenades while the other scanned the skies for the dreaded FEAF fighter-bombers. Glancing around, SFC Anderson was shocked to discover that, except for the Chinese, he was alone. Looking down the hill, he saw that his rifle squad was pinned down on the lower slope by automatic weapons fire.

Fox Company advancing past dead CCF soldier on Hill 256. L to R: SGT Oliver Waiau, Hilo, Hawaii carries a captured CCF machine gun; SFC Robert Muramoto, Honolulu; PFC Arlo Perdue, Griswold, IA; and PFC James Sunser, Patlon, PA. (sources: NA/Chang)

At this juncture, SFC Anderson made a mistake that nearly cost him his life. He cupped his hands together and shouted down to his men, "You people get the hell up here!" As he returned his attention to the Chinese trench, he saw much to his dismay a sky full of hand grenades arching through the air heading his way. That the Chinese used less powerful concussion grenades, rather than the American high explosive ones stuffed full of shrapnel, saved his life a few seconds later when a multitude of grenade explosions lifted him off the ground. Though hit by fragments in the left shoulder blade, he could still move. The explosions had shattered his rifle, so he started pitching his seven remaining grenades into the trench at different angles to ensure he covered the entire enemy position. The platoon sergeant fought a lively grenade duel with the Chinese who replied with ten grenades for every one he threw. One explosion paralyzed his body, all but his right arm, which he used to toss his last grenade at the enemy. Then he lay back in the snow wondering who would reach him first, the American rifle squad or the Chinese.

When SFC Anderson heard the crackle of small arms fire down below, he knew the rifle squad had commenced its assault on the trench. He could not lift his head due to his wounds and, therefore, did not see the Chinese shoot Corporal Pete Peterson through the stomach while he stood upright firing his BAR from the hip into the Chinese defenders. Nor did he see the KATUSA, known only as "Jim", who grabbed the BAR and stood in full view on the lip of the trench as he raked the screaming Chinese soldiers with magazine after magazine of automatic rifle fire. After the firing died down, SFC Anderson saw a pair of combat boots staring him in the face, and one of his boys told him, "Don't worry, you'll be alright."

The company was in the attack and could not stop for anyone. An Army Signal Corps cameraman, MSGT Albert "Al" Chang who was recording the battle on film for prosperity, found SFC Anderson lying in the snow. The cameraman said that he would stay with SFC Anderson until a medic arrived. The wounded platoon sergeant suggested another idea. The Chinese habit of mounting counterattacks made it imprudent to be found lying next to a bunch of their dead friends if they returned. So MSGT Chang helped SFC Anderson walk down the ridge to a collection point where he was loaded into an ambulance and evacuated to an aid station.[51]

Fox Company participated in the attack on Hill 256. "Our battalion objective was a rather large hill," said CAPT Robert Lamb, "with E Company attacking on the left and F Company on the right. The hill was heavily defended with little cover except for some natural folds in the ground."[52] First Lieutenant Arthur E. Mahoney's hard fighting 1st Platoon, G Company, was fighting on Easy Company's left flank.

Meanwhile, Easy Company, spearheaded by LT Dodd's platoon, pressed home the assault through heavy Chinese defensive fire. "We had hardly moved out," SGT James, a rifle squad leader in the 3rd Platoon, E Company, recalled, "before the gooks started throwing grenades and firing automatic weapons from positions right in front of us that we didn't know were there. When the fire got too heavy I hollered at my squad to take cover. The lieutenant heard me. 'Take cover, hell!' he yells. 'Use marching fire and follow me!' He kept on going up. Some of the fellows got hit and I hung back to see if I could help them. But LT Dodd looks back and yells, 'Come on! Follow me!' So we do. Right up that hill."[53]

Lieutenant Carl Dodd rushed up the slope carrying his .45-caliber pistol and seven grenades. When he used up his own grenades, he gathered more from the dead and wounded and threw those too. One particularly troublesome Chinese machine gun kept his soldiers pinned down, inflicting losses on his men. Lieutenant Dodd charged the gun, firing his pistol to keep the Chinese heads down. When he reached the bunker's aperture, he hurled a grenade inside and killed the crew. At times three, four, and even five CCF machine guns were firing at the courageous officer. Lieutenant Dodd kept advancing, knocking out a gun here, and shooting a Chinese soldier there, as he continued up the ridge toward the summit of Hill 256. Whenever his soldiers bogged down, he would continue to attack alone, setting the example as he closed on the Chinese with a remorseless will to prevail. His soldiers followed, and many fell killed or wounded, as LT Dodd led the way, clawing and kicking his way to the summit. They almost made it, but not quite, and at 2110, COL Throckmorton ordered the 2nd Battalion to dig in for the night.

The 2nd Battalion's tactical aggressiveness and initiative stunned observers from corps and army who witnessed the bitter, close-range infantry fighting that raged throughout the hotly contested struggle for control of Hill 256. The combat team incurred 64 casualties during the day's fighting.[54] Lieutenant Carl H. Dodd, and his 3rd Platoon, E Company, and LT Mahoney, and his 1st Platoon, G Company, had conducted a series of audacious bayonet charges that disproved once and for all the myth of Chinese invincibility in infantry close combat. The two hard-fighting rifle platoons received well justified praise from their corps commander on down for their aggressive leadership which succeeded in inflicting heavy losses on the Chinese for relatively light losses in return.[55]

General Ridgway was present the following morning when the 2nd Battalion rapidly cleared the remainder of Objective Able. As General Ridgway climbed the hills beside LTC Albert Ward, he expressed his admiration for the 5th RCT's tactical performance. Moreover, he sent a telex to all American and South Korean corps and division commanders, "The U.S. Fifth Infantry Regiment, COL Throckmorton commanding, attacked in daylight across a mile wide open plain and took a series of ridges up to 150 feet above the valley which completely dominated the ground this regiment had to cross.

"Chinese Communist forces had organized and defended these ridges tenaciously with individual foxholes and underground shelters, one of which with a connecting galley was large enough for a crew of the 120-mm mortar in which this weapon was emplaced.

"In late afternoon I personally visited the 2nd Battalion, LTC Ward commanding, and went over the ground taken by E and F Companies. This operation achieved the true measure of tactical success — key terrain, a vital mountain pass — seized with heavy losses inflicted and only light losses sustained.

"The reason was due to proper appreciation and use of terrain and high leadership whereby high class infantry with supporting air and artillery worked its way along the ridges until all dominating ground was taken. This operation furnishes a fine example of how it ought to be done."[56]

Before the Commanding General could send his telex, Hill 256 had to be won. Lieutenant Carl Dodd's foot had hurt throughout the long night, which in a strange way proved a godsend as it helped to keep him awake positioning his men, comforting the wounded, and keeping his platoon's guard up to repel any Chinese counterattacks. He led his men up the slope at dawn, through intense Chinese defensive fire, and took the crest of Hill 256. It was a costly assault, and several men were killed and wounded in the short time it took to overrun the last enemy resistance on Hill 256. Easy Company was king of the mountain, however, much to the dismay of the Chinese who mounted several furious and futile counterattacks to regain possession of the hill.

The 5th RCT committed its reserve that morning, and the 3rd Battalion passed through its sister battalions, seizing yet another objective, this time without meeting resistance. Over 150 enemy dead were counted on the 1st and 2nd Battalions' objectives.[57] President Truman subsequently awarded the Medal of Honor to 1st LT Dodd in a ceremony held in the White House.

Elements of 2nd Battalion in action, Hill 256.
(sources: NA/Chang)

The month of January had witnessed yet another fine tactical performance by the 5th RCT. It was fitting that the Department of the Army recognized the regiment's superb combat record when the 5th RCT was awarded the Combat Infantry Streamer on 23 January 1951.[58] The combat team incurred 25 men KIA, 65 WIA, 3 MIA and 178 non-battle casualties in January 1951.[59] The successful outcome of the recent offensive operations, combined with the recognition General Ridgway bestowed on the men, led to an upsurge in morale.

During the first week of February the 5th RCT fought the CCF in the vicinity of Subuk, where the defenders opposed the combat team's advance from bunkers tunneled into both the forward and reverse slopes of steep ridgelines. In-

Easy Company soldiers rest in a reserve position. L to R: Hulse, Horace Anderson, Paris, and "Chief." (source: Horace Anderson)

terlocking machine gun fire and concentrated mortar barrages took a steady toll on the combat team as it fought its way into the teeth of the enemy defenses. Grueling close-quarters combat was the norm, with most engagements fought in the mountains, often above the clouds, at point-blank range.

Love Company's mission on 5 February was to attack and seize Hill 514. Sergeant First Class Samuel L. Kealoha, Territory of Hawaii, one of Sonny's former drill sergeants, commanded a 75-mm Recoilless Rifle Section from Mike Company that was following in trace of the infantry. During Love Company's advance, the infantry came under concentrated bursts of accurate machine gun fire. Wounded soldiers fell screaming in pain, their torn bodies writhing on the frozen ground. With Love Company pinned down and taking losses, the cry went out to bring up the recoilless rifles.

Sergeant First Class Kealoha led his section forward through the intense enemy fire and designated a position for the gun crew to set up the cumbersome weapon. While his men placed the mount on the tripod, and slapped the barrel and gun sight into place, SFC Kealoha continued to crawl forward, alone, through bursts of machine gun fire. He reached an exposed location where he could point out the first target, a cleverly camouflaged bunker that dominated a killing zone with the muzzle of its automatic weapon. The efficient 75-mm recoilless rifle crew responded to SFC Kealoha's hand-and-arm signal with a high explosive round they slammed through the bunker's aperture. An infantry platoon rushed the ruins of the smashed bunker and shot the surviving Chinese defenders.

Love Company resumed the advance until yet another invisible enemy machine gun opened up on the exposed infantry. Undaunted by the enemy's fire, SFC Kealoha advanced through the rugged, undulating terrain to pinpoint the location of the Chinese machine gun. With complete disregard for his own safety, he closed to within a few yards of the nearly invisible bunker before the Chinese gun crew inside opened up on him. A seriously wounded SFC Kealoha returned to his section and directed its fire at the enemy bunker, which was quickly knocked out by a high explosive shell. Love Company overran the Chinese position, killing the gun crew. Sergeant First Class Kealoha survived the ordeal and was awarded the Silver Star for gallantry.[60]

The 5th RCT gained ground slowly. The men attacked in the day and dug in at night. The exemplary support of FEAF aircraft reduced friendly casualties from CCF rearguards to a minimum. The advance would resume in the predawn darkness as the infantry moved out carrying their world upon their backs: individual and crew-served weapons, sleeping bag, grenades, rifle, ammunition, trip flares, extra socks, water, and rations. General Ridgway had demanded that his commanders get off the roads and into the hills, and this was done. The Chiggy-bearers, who physically carried much of the heavy ammunition crates, water cans, and ration boxes normally carried on vehicles, made fighting in the mountains possible.

"I quickly found out how ill-equipped I was for the fighting in Korea because it was murderous going up those hills," recalled SGT James Hart. "It was physically, mentally, and actually murderous. The first time, after I'd gone about thirty minutes, I was just completely out of breath, exhausted, and it was now my turn to carry the baseplate."[61]

1st LT Carl Dodd is awarded the Medal of Honor by President Truman.
(source: NA)

The unceasing strain of continuous close combat took a steady toll in battle casualties, sickness, and sheer physical and mental exhaustion. Although the combat team inflicted punishing losses on the Chinese, it witnessed a corresponding decline in fighting power. After one particularly tough objective proved impossible to crack, the 5th RCT reverted to 24th Infantry Division's reserve for a well-deserved rest.[62]

The latest batch of infantry replacements to reach Korea contributed to the problems combat units encountered on the front lines. Generally speaking, the replacements consisted of two broad categories — those who were trained infantrymen and those who were not. Reservists and National Guardsmen recalled to active duty were by and large well-trained soldiers. Many of these men had previous combat experience dating from World War II. Too many replacements, however, reported to their combat units after having received rudimentary training, little of which was combat related. The situation appalled the 24th Infantry Division, which noted, "Replacements received by this command received a minimum 3 days training in a Replacement Company before being assigned to their unit. This has been necessary because of the fact that men are being received that have fired only 9 rounds from their weapons and have no knowledge how to disassemble their weapons."[63]

Since the combat team's last thorough training period during the previous October, corporate knowledge in the employment of crew-served weapons had witnessed a decline in expertise in the line companies. This was particularly true in the 60-mm Mortar Sections, probably because the Heavy Mortar Company and 81-mm Mortar Platoons drew the bulk of the trained mortar men who arrived as replacements.

"I'm very proud to have been in Fox Company, and very proud to have been in the 5th RCT, and extremely proud to have served under CAPT Lamb," explained SGT James Hart. "The fact of the matter was those guys weren't well trained in mortars. When I went into the 1st Cavalry Division [in World War II] they gave me a charge card. One came with each box of ammunition, and they told me to memorize it. My God, there had to be 500 squares on it. I had to know at 3,200 yards what the degree was, what the charge was, and all that, and I had to know it. And those guys could put rounds in your hip pocket. The first thing I asked my guys in Korea was 'have you guys sighted your mortars in from a defilade position,' and they said, 'What do you mean?' So I told them that if we get attacked, we had to be able to fire from a covered position. And they said, 'No, we've never done that.' Well I told them that you're going to get ready to do it…. It wasn't that the men weren't capable or willing, they just hadn't had anybody who really knew. They had done a tremendous job, a much better job than any other outfit over there…. I don't know what I'd have done if I'd wound up in my old 5th Cavalry, because those guys apparently didn't know anything."[64]

While the combat team rested in its reserve positions, COL Throckmorton emphasized discipline. He insisted on constant adherence to orders and strict discipline in the ranks. He directed unit commanders to ensure that their soldiers wore their helmets at all times. He ordered canvas tops and side curtains removed from vehicles to prevent officers and NCOs from remaining dry while the infantry floundered through the mud, slush, and rain. Additional orders and warnings were published with COL Throckmorton's signature relating to every aspect of a soldier's life from the care of his personal weapon, to saluting, and the prevention of typhus and cold-weather injuries.[65]

One hundred and fifty-two replacements and sixty-eight hospital returnees joined the 5th RCT on 19 February.[66] Two weeks before an unusual incident had occurred when Private C.D. Dooley arrived at the 5th RCT reception center and reported for duty. Upon a review of Private Dooley's records, it was determined that the poor soul had yet to attend to Basic Training. Since the soldier's enlistment in October 1950, Private Dooley had spent all his time either processing or in transfer to new locations. The hapless soldier was sent to a rear area where someone could at least teach him how to field strip, clean and fire his M-1 rifle.[67]

The 5th Cavalry, 1st Cavalry Division, made a determined bid at this juncture to lasso hospital returnees from the 5th RCT into their outfit. Poor relations had existed between the 5th RCT and the 1st Cavalry Division ever since an issue of *Stars and Stripes* had erroneously announced that the 5th Cavalry Regiment had captured Waegwan. Moreover, it was widely suspected within the ranks of the

5th RCT that the 1st Cavalry Division had padded its own casualty figures during that battle with the names of men who had actually fallen fighting as members of the combat team.[68]

Sergeant First Class Horace Anderson and Sergeant Charles Krone were standing in line at the I Corps Replacement Center after recovering from their respective wounds, when a second lieutenant from the 5th Cavalry attempted to use his rank to force the two veterans to report to his unit. Sergeant First Class Anderson faced the officer down, and replied, "No Sir! We're either going to the 5th RCT or the stockade." The lieutenant retreated in the face of this blunt refusal. Later, when SFC Anderson related the incident to COL Throckmorton, the Rock chuckled and said, "I'll look into it. And you don't have to worry about going to the stockade."[69]

One of the hospital returnees who returned to the 5th RCT in February was the soldier from Lanikai, SGT Ernest M. Calhau, known to friends and family alike as "Sonny."

Baker Company advancing, 5 February 1951. (sources: NA/Chang)

CHAPTER TWENTY-THREE

KILLER AND RIPPER

...so the Army developed men who learned to fight in Asia. Soldiers learned to travel light, but with full canteen and bandoleer, and to climb the endless hills. They learned to hold fast when the enemy flowed at them, because it was the safest thing to do. They learned to displace in good order when they had to. They learned to listen and obey. They learned all the things Americans have always learned from Appomattox to Berlin. Above all, they learned to kill. On the frontier there is rarely gallantry or glamour to wars, whether they are against red Indians or Red Chinese. There is only killing.
T.R. Fehrenbach, This Kind of War

Under General Ridgway's inspired leadership, the Eighth Army made a rapid moral recovery. Buoyed by the success of its reconnaissance in force operations in January, the Eighth Army planned a series of limited objective attacks designed to inflict the largest number of enemy casualties for the minimum expenditure in blood.

Communist field commanders were not content to remain passive spectators in the unfolding drama and had ambitious operational plans of their own. In the middle of February the CCF commenced a massive offensive against the central sector of the Eighth Army's defensive line. For the first time the valor of Mao's peasant infantry proved unequal to the task, and the CCF offensive collapsed under a hurricane of high explosive shells. Over 5,000 Chinese soldiers were killed on 14 February alone. Probably three times that number fell wounded.[1] China's failure to win a decisive victory in the central sector encouraged General Ridgway to commence an offensive in the west.

On 16 February, I Corps attacked with four infantry regiments from the 24th and 25th Infantry Divisions. Their mission was to cut enemy supply lines and destroy all enemy forces in their zones of action. Artillery support was massive, accurate, and incredibly destructive. The 5th RCT was temporarily attached to the 25th Infantry Division for the duration of this offensive. When COL Throckmorton's assault battalions reached the Han River on 18 February, his soldiers counted 400-500 dead enemy soldiers lying in demolished bunkers and foxholes.[2]

About this time, CAPT William Perry, the S-3 of the 2nd Battalion, received a radio message from a rifle company commander who requested permission to bivouac in a village on the south bank of the Han. General Ridgway disapproved of the practice of bivouacking in villages due to the menace posed by disease. Yet, it was a bitterly cold day, and when the sun finally dipped behind the mountains, this company commander wanted to have his men billeted inside the huts where they could take turns sleeping on top of the warm ceramic stoves that adorned all Korean homes.

Captain Perry responded by asking, "Are all the Chinese gone?"

The company commander replied, "They're all on the other side of the river."

"Are you sure of that?" queried Captain Perry. "Because otherwise you're going to have to discuss that with the Chinese."

"Well," replied the freezing company commander, "they're either going to have to get out or move over. I'm going in there." The Chinese moved out.[3]

As the overextended CCF withdrew in the face of the Eighth Army's effective combination of firepower and maneuver, General Ridgway stunned his commanders and staff by ordering a full-scale offensive on the central sector. The combat team's mission during Operation KILLER was to screen south of the Han River while conducting aggressive patrols to the north bank in order to maintain steady pressure on the Chinese.

Operation KILLER commenced on 21 February, its primary purpose being to inflict maximum casualties on the CCF through a massive application of firepower. The offensive

A soldier from the 5th RCT fires a BAR during Operation KILLER, February 1951. (source: 25th ID Museum)

floundered in a sea of mud, however, and enemy casualties were light.[4] On a positive note, KILLER provided a moral boost to the troops who enjoyed being on the offensive.

When a senior State Department official attacked General Ridgway's use of KILLER as the code-name, the gutsy Eighth Army commander replied it was about time someone reminded the American people what the war was all about.[5] General Ridgway was sensitive to the powers of the press, however, and he issued a politically neutral code-name for his next offensive, Operation RIPPER, scheduled for early March.

While the fighting raged in Korea, on Oahu, Mrs. Connie Torres was praised in the Honolulu newspapers as "Mom of the 5th RCT." Mrs. Torres and her husband, A. T. "Tony" Torres, a lieutenant in the Honolulu Fire Department, had made their restaurant in Wahiawa, the "Chili Bowl", a home-

Tank Company, with infantry riding on the engine decks, advances on the Han River. (sources: NA/Chang)

away-from-home for the Mainlanders serving in the 5th RCT before the war. When the combat team sailed to Korea, several soldiers had left their cars in her care. She kept the cars clean and in running condition during their absence. Mrs. Torres received at least seventy-five letters a week from "her boys" in Korea, and she answered every one, usually writing ten or more return letters each day. She was often found at Tripler Hospital, visiting wounded soldiers and inviting them to her home when they were allowed out on pass. To many 5th RCT soldiers, she was "Mom."[6]

The 5th RCT's mission during Operation KILLER was confined to running patrols across the Han to keep the enemy off balance.[7] Lieutenant Randall Beirne observed a small patrol slip across the Han one evening, the men disappearing into the mist. No one from this patrol returned, leaving the saddened officer to ponder the terror and misfortune they must have endured when finally discovered and run to ground by the Chinese.[8]

Sergeant Bud Throne had rejoined the 2nd Battalion's I&R Platoon while Operation KILLER was in progress. His platoon conducted several reconnaissance missions at night across the Han. "We crossed the Han in a small boat, paddling as hard as we could through the swift current," he explained. "One of the guys from Hawaii, who used to always sing Nat Cole's 'Mona Lisa,' said the heck with this and got out of the boat in mid-stream. We didn't know the water was only hip deep. So we all got out of the boat, too, and simply walked across the Han. This was one of the few times I can recall laughing in a combat situation."[9]

General Ridgway's insistence on confronting Chinese manpower with firepower won many converts in the 5th RCT. Lieutenant Ed Crockett's 2nd Tank Platoon, for example, overwatched the Han River from firing positions on the south bank during Operation KILLER. Across the river, a deeply entrenched CCF detachment occupied Hill 192, a piece of key terrain that dominated the area. One day an FO from the 555th FAB joined LT Crockett's platoon to observe a "Time on Target" fire mission on Hill 192 that was going to be fired by every tube of divisional and corps artillery. At the appointed second, a multitude of 8-inch, 155-mm, and 105-mm howitzer shells impacted simultaneously on Hill 192 with a tremendous roar, hurling boulders, dirt, and lumber high into the air. After the smoke cleared, LT Crockett observed through his binoculars that the impact of hundreds of high-explosive shells had nearly removed the top of the hill.[10]

As KILLER drew to a close, it became apparent that the Eighth Army's successful application of firepower and maneuver had destroyed the mystique of the invincible Chinese hordes. Eighth Army's success did not occur without casualties. In February the combat team had suffered 9 men KIA, 59 WIA, 4 MIA, and 264 non-battle casualties.[11]

The first week of March found the 5th RCT occupying defensive positions south of the Han. Colonel Throckmorton dispatched combat patrols across the river every day to make contact with the enemy.

Meanwhile, Sonny settled down in Fox Company and got on with the business of soldiering. He was blessed with a superb company commander in CAPT Robert Lamb. Sergeant First Class James Hart, a 60-mm mortar squad leader, explained, "What I always admired about CAPT Lamb was his combat demeanor. He was the calmest man in combat that I ever served with. He also didn't charge the hill with a Forty-five. He took care of what he was supposed to take care of directing the platoons and calling in the supporting arms. He was the best I ever saw."[12]

Operation RIPPER commenced on 5 March, its purpose being to "seize or destroy enemy personnel or equipment."[13] In keeping with General Ridgway's demands that the artillery pave the way for his infantry, RIPPER opened with the mightiest artillery barrage of the war to date. In 25th Infantry Division's sector alone, 148 guns fired 5,000 rounds on the CCF positions north of the Han that day.[14] The Eighth Army exploited its artillery fires with a determined assault conducted on a fifty-mile front by six corps and eleven divisions.

The 5th RCT forced a crossing over the Han on 5 March, during the opening hours of Operation RIPPER. A Chinese counterattack was repulsed that night.[15]

About this time, SGT Kenny Freedman was blown several feet into the air by an exploding mortar shell. While lying in the dirt, he checked himself for visible wounds, found none, stood up, and promptly passed out. He awoke on a stretcher slung on the outside of an airborne helicopter that was flying him to a MASH unit. After X-rays were taken, it was determined that the tough young soldier had several fractured vertebrae. He was evacuated to Osaka, Japan, where he enjoyed a short convalescence before rejoining his unit in April.[16]

The 5th RCT, assigned a supporting role in RIPPER, was heavily engaged on 6 March near Yangpyong. A CCF machine gun took Love Company under intense and accurate fire, temporarily pinning the men to the ground. Sergeant Clarence Y. Choy, from Honolulu, crawled to within grenade range of the enemy automatic weapon before taking it out with a well-thrown hand grenade.[17]

Enemy resistance rapidly diminished, and by 10 March the Eighth Army had succeeded in outflanking Seoul. Five days later, an intrepid group of soldiers from the ROK 1st Division crossed the Han without authorization from General Ridgway and raised the South Korean flag over the ruins of their beloved capitol.[18]

Sonny used U.S. Army Special Services stationery to write to his parents on 6 March. "Things here, where we are dug in, are pretty quiet. It snowed a little a few times, but the sun has been shining all day. Our foxhole has a roof over it, so it's pretty warm. Otherwise things here are pretty good. So far, since I've been in Korea, I haven't received any letters yet. I will write every three days. Mom, I wonder if you could send me some [dried] squid. All the Island boys are getting some, and it sure is good to chew on…. How is [sic] Buddy and Manley making out in school? Say hello to Granny and give her my love. Mom, I love and miss you folks very much. I hope I can come home one of these days. I'm still waiting for the pictures. I hope Dad is [doing well] in business. So until I hear from you, all my love. Sonny."

During the period 9-16 March, while the 5th RCT rested in reserve, LT Randall Beirne was reassigned from his XO duties to be the platoon leader of his old outfit, the 2nd Platoon, King Company. Master Sergeant Kermit Jackson, the "twenty-eight-day soldier" of Hill 268 fame was his platoon sergeant. Sergeant First Class James Jackson was his platoon guide. Together, the three men were the only remaining members of the original 2nd Platoon that had deployed to Korea the previous July.[19] Meanwhile, the battle weary combat team passed the time absorbing replacements, cleaning weapons, and preparing for the ordeals ahead.[20]

Private First Class Arlen Russell was going home. His terrified mother, convinced that she would be in trouble with the authorities for conspiring to help her son's fraudulent enlistment, was afraid to inform anyone that her underage son was fighting in Korea. Not so his feisty grandmother, who turned him in. The sixteen-year-old combat veteran returned home to a nation that hardly knew her sons were fighting a war.[21]

Major Bert Nishimura, an Eighth Army Public Relations Officer and veteran of the famous 442nd RCT, did his best to inform the public about the war. The Honolulu newspapers routinely published his articles about the exploits of the 5th RCT.

Yet it was MSGT Albert Chang, from Laie, Oahu, a

A Tank Company 76-mm gun hitting targets across the Han. The vane sight of the .50-caliber antiaircraft weapon is visible. (source: Ed Crockett)

Three Hawaiian soldiers in the snow. L to R: SGT Elmino Colon, Honolulu; MSGT David Broad, Laie, Oahu; and CPL Arsanio Vendiola, Waipahu, Oahu. (source: Chang)

combat photographer serving with the 5th RCT, who brought the Korean War to life for the American public. Hundreds of his superb photographs were published in Honolulu and Mainland newspapers and magazines during the first year of the war. Master Sergeant Chang received a Pulitzer Prize nomination for his combat photography in Korea.

Sonny wrote his last letter home on 13 March from the regimental reserve position. "Dearest Mom and Dad, I hope this letter finds you in the best of health. I'm fine. We are across the Han River now. We are in reserve for a week. It's still cold here at night, but kind of warm during the day. We are camped on the shore of a little river. That's why it's kind of cold. I'm squad leader again. Same old job. Everything is about the same here. We have lots of new men. All of them are a bunch of swell guys. The other day, I got a letter from Johnnie Blyth. He is back in Korea, too. That is the only letter I received since I've been here. I should be getting mail soon from you folks. My first letter must have got there already. I sure like to get mail when I'm here. That's about the only good morale builder. Without mail, you're lost. Well Mom, how are things at home? Fine I hope. Must be nice weather there now. I could sure use some of that sunshine now. Don't forget to have Buddy and Manley write. I like to hear from them. I won't write to everybody till I get a letter from them. There is not too much time to write. This is my third letter to you. I still miss you folks very much. Sure wish I was home. Give my love to Granny and the rest of the family. I'll say bye for now, Mom and Dad, and God Bless you. Love Sonny. P.S. I'll try and write every three days."

Two Able Company soldiers take a break on the Han River front. L to R: SFC Alvin Kalawe, Kapoho, Hawaii, and SFC Harold Moniz, Hilo, Hawaii. Note the dead CCF soldier in the background. (source: Chang)

Two 5th RCT infantry warily approach a dead CCF soldier. (source: Chang)

2nd Platoon, Fox Company in reserve. LT Montague is standing in the center without his hat on. PFC Charles Myers is kneeling, far right. (source: Charles Myers)

CHAPTER TWENTY-FOUR

Good Friday

Mama, Mama,
you're so tired I know
watching over me
night and day.
Soon you'll rest
for I must go away.
I must die I heard them say.
All those tears
roll down your cheeks.
Mama, Mama,
do not weep
because it is such a pretty place.
Kiss me now, I fall asleep.[1]

After a brief rest in divisional reserve, the 1st Battalion commenced an attack on 18 March, Palm Sunday, against light Chinese resistance.[2] The entire 5th RCT jumped off into the attack the next morning as the soldiers pursued the Chinese through the rugged hills. Enemy fire wounded five men during the day's advance.

King Company fought a stiff engagement on 19 March as it struggled to seize a Chinese hilltop defensive position. Lieutenant Randall Beirne was startled to see one sergeant calmly walking up the hill with his hands in his pockets as Chinese bullets impacted around him. "He has already been seriously hit once," the platoon leader wrote home, "but doesn't seem the slightest bit afraid. He hopes for a leg or arm wound to get to Japan. If he gets killed, he figures he won't have to worry about Korea anymore."[3]

Fighter-bomber strikes and artillery fire hammered the Chinese defenders as the infantry wormed their way closer to the objective. Overhead machine gun fire supported the infantry's final assault up the jagged mountain peak. Lieutenant Beirne watched a squad from another platoon yelling as they overran a portion of the objective with fixed bayonets. One Chinese soldier rose out of his hole to draw a bead on the large, muscular, Samoan NCO leading the charge, but SFC Amatuani Faamaile side-stepped just in time and butt-stroked the enemy soldier with his carbine, breaking the stock in the act of crushing his opponent's skull. The surviving Chinese soldiers broke rather than tangle with the likes of SFC Faamaile. Twenty-five CCF corpses littered the crest. Several Chinese were shot to death when the enemy withdrew down the reverse slope.[4]

No one in K Company was hit. Lieutenant Beirne attributed this to the Eighth Army's recent emphasis on bayonet fighting, which he believed gave the American soldiers a psychological advantage over the already outgunned Chinese.

The 5th RCT dug in for the night and was occupying defensive positions on the morning of 20 March. Two soldiers were WIA that morning, one from Sonny's company. The 35th Infantry Regiment, along with elements of the Turkish Brigade, began to conduct a relief in place with the 5th RCT at noon. By 1630 the entire combat team had withdrawn a short distance to rest and reorganize for the night in the vicinity of Ochon.[5]

After a fitful night's rest in their frozen foxholes, the weary soldiers were roused and mustered in the early morning darkness. The LD was the MLR, occupied that morning by the 35th Infantry and the Turkish Brigade. The 5th RCT conducted a passage of lines at 0600 through the 35th Infantry and commenced the assault with all three infantry battalions in the attack. According to the 5th RCT's Unit Report, "All objectives were secured for the day and resistance was negligible."[6] No casualties were reported.

As Sonny and his comrades kept a wary eye on their perimeter that night, Ernest was writing a letter that his son would not live to read. "Dear Sonny, I came home early from work so decided to write you this letter. Hope you are OK. We are all fine. The weather here is lousy again. Talk about rain. It has been raining all day. There are some crazy fishermen on the beach trying to fish. Mahollich is one of them. I think the fish are coming back. Mahollich caught a Papio and an Oio yesterday at 5 P.M. The day before a Mr. Nelson caught an 11 pound Olua. This is getting me jealous so I bought a new reel today and will try casting again. I could not get any squid at the market. We'll ask Buddy and Manley to go out and find one for me tomorrow. Buddy went to Hickam Field today to try and join the National Guard Air Reserve. He has to go to Fort Ruger Monday night for a physical. If he passes that, then he has to take the written tests, and if he passes, he is then in the Air Reserve. He wants to take aviation mechanics. I hope he makes it. Yesterday the Buick Company called me to take up a green Buick Super. Nice car, but I don't like green. I phoned Mama and she told me not to take it. I should have taken it anyway as it had white walls, radio, plenty of chrome, and it was good looking. Besides the new cars coming in a couple of months won't have much chrome and will cost more because of the increase in taxes. I don't know why I let Mom talk me out of it, just because I want an Imperial Blue Job. Oh well! That is that. I see by the papers, that you fellows are just about at the border of the 38th Parallel. MacArthur has authority to cross, but is waiting for the UN to decide first. The UN should send about 200,000 more men there and let you fellows come home for a rest. Headlines say U.S. Armed Forces now double what it was before the Korea outbreak. That is good news, but I hope it means replacements for you fellows in Korea. I hope you fellows do not have to cross the border until they send another 100,000 men there so our forces can be real strong. Not much going on in Kailua. I went to confession today and will go to communion Easter Sunday for the men in Korea and for you. We pray hard for you. The Calhau families are pulling for you so keep your chin up. Keep a cool and level head and don't take wild chances and you will come home safely. I suppose the weather there is terrible. Must be the rainy season now. God Bless you and keep you safe. Dad."

LT Randall Beirne calmly observes CCF mortar rounds exploding nearby. (source: Chang)

Theresa enclosed another letter to her son in the same envelope. "My Dear Son, Daddy wrote tonight, also Buddy and Manley. So I thought I'd put a few lines in too. Tomorrow I'm going to visit 4 Catholic Churches. I'm going with a group of women from our church. We will stay on the Windward side. This is a pilgrimage. A special blessing is attached to it from the Pope. I will offer mine up for your safe return, which we hope is real soon. Take care of yourself. Pray to the Lord to give you strength and courage to do your part well. We at home will pray for you. Chin up. Write home to us often so we know you are OK. So far we [have] got one letter since you are back [in Korea]. I know you are doing your best all around. Just keep on the alert. Sleep and rest when you know it is safe to do so, when you have a lull period, as they call it. I know it's tough going. But what can we do? Those war mongrels want war. Hope you're OK.

The 2nd Battalion advances on a Hill of Sacrifice, 22 March 1951. (source: NA/Chang)

Where are you? Seems those Chinese keep hitting the Central front. Isn't that where you are? By the time you get this, it should be decided if they are going over the 38th Parallel…. Stop and get it over and done with I say. Well dear son, I better get to bed. Not before I say my Rosary and some special prayers I say every day. May God Bless you and protect you always. Good Luck & always Love. Mom."

On 22 March, the 5th RCT crossed the LD at 0800. After securing its objectives, tank-infantry patrols maintained contact with adjacent units on each flank. One soldier from Able Company was wounded.[7] Master Sergeant Robert P. Noneman, Easy Company, who had boldly stood in full view of the enemy hurling hand grenades when the NKPA had overrun 1st LT Gordon Strong's platoon on 7 August 1950, so long ago, perished during the day.[8] As usual, he was out front doing his job when a sniper shot him. He died on a day when staff officers at higher headquarters reported negligible resistance. The Chinese appeared to be withdrawing, but appearances can be deceptive.

The 5th RCT was occupying defensive positions on the morning of Good Friday, 23 March 1951. The first inclination that this was not going to be an easy day occurred at 0437 when a CCF combat patrol struck Item Company's perimeter. Intense mortar fire and at least four light machine guns supported the enemy assault. The attack was repulsed with the aid of friendly mortar and artillery fires. Shrapnel wounded one Item Company soldier. At 0500, Easy Company reported it was taking mortar fire. George Company was hit by small arms fire five minutes later. By dawn, with both the 2nd and 3rd Battalions, 5th RCT, under fire, it was becoming evident that this was going to be a rough day.[9] The CCF's message was easy to decipher. They planned to contest any further advance.

At 0810 and 0815 respectively, George and Fox Companies crossed the LD in the attack. The soldiers advanced with weapons at the ready, bayonets fixed, under a bleak, forbidding, overcast sky, their uniforms and canvass field equipment drenched by fine droplets of cold rain that drizzled intermittently throughout the windy, dreary day. By 0820, the 3rd Battalion was advancing, too. The 1st Battalion remained in reserve.

The 5th RCT's mission on 23 March was to secure a series of hills, destroying all enemy forces in its zone of action. Two of Tank Company's Easy Eights struck mines at 0845, putting them out of action. Regimental Objective 34 was secured at 0916 without opposition. Regimental Objective 32 was secured five minutes later. At 0924, 2nd Battalion reported that an enemy platoon was occupying Hill 637. Regimental Objective 30 was secured at 1130.[10]

The morning was going reasonably well for 1st LT Thomas P. Bartow, the 1st Platoon leader, Fox Company, who had taken over Sonny's platoon the day before. A graduate from the University of Hawaii, LT Bartow had received his commission through the ROTC program in June 1950. He was awaiting assignment to Quartermasters school when the combat team was alerted for movement to Korea. Second Lieutenants Bartow and Vance B. McWhorter, another recent University of Hawaii graduate, had volunteered to accompany the combat team to Korea. The two officers were assigned to Tank Company.

Lieutenants Bartow and McWhorter shared a few things in common. That both officers hailed from Honolulu was of little importance. Of supreme relevance was the sad truth that neither officer had attended a branch school, just another example of the desperate manpower situation the Army faced in the summer of 1950. Thus the two officers went to war with little more than the most basic theoretical tactical knowledge gleaned from dusty ROTC manuals to sustain them in combat.[11]

Lieutenant McWhorter was dead. He had taken over a tank platoon in the Pusan Perimeter when his predecessor was wounded. On 9 November 1950, an Easy Eight from his platoon lost a track when it rolled over an antitank mine. When LT McWhorter dismounted his tank to supervise the retrieval of the damaged Easy Eight, he had no idea his luck had just run out.

The North Koreans were devious, cunning fighters, and they loved mines. They also knew it was standard operating procedure for a tank that had been disabled by a mine to be towed out of the way by another that carried, like all Army tanks, a steel towing cable for this purpose. Thus the NKPA initiated the cunning practice of laying an inverted V-shaped pattern of three antitank mines on likely armor avenues of approach. The antitank mine at the tip of the inverted "V" was buried at the normal depth, while two additional antitank mines were buried at an angle and to the rear of the first, but too deep to explode under normal pressure if driven over by a tank or vehicle.

Lieutenant McWhorter never suspected that there were two more mines behind the damaged tank. His crew quickly rigged the towing cable and remounted their Sherman as the young officer stood off to the side giving hand and arm signals to his driver who put their tank into reverse. Lieutenant McWhorter's Easy Eight pulled taut the slack on the towing cable and commenced dragging the damaged tank slowly across the ground, an action that generated the necessary ground pressure to detonate the two deeply buried mines. The force of the explosions hurled

L to R: LT Vance McWhorter, Honolulu, KIA 9 November 1950; SGT Bill Kapaku, Waianae, Oahu; followed by four unknowns. SFC Hap Easter is standing. (sources: Bill Kapaku/Chang)

chunks of the steel tank track through the air. Lieutenant McWhorter died instantly. Second Lieutenant Frank D. Bullano, who had received a battlefield commission at Waegwan and two Silver Stars in Korea, was severely wounded.[12]

Second Lieutenant Bartow was a nervous individual, and there is reason to believe that CAPT Robert Kennedy did not have enough confidence in him to make him a platoon leader in Tank Company. With that option closed, LT Bartow became the combat team's aerial observer when he arrived in Korea. He flew as an observer in an L-5 aircraft along the front lines to gather reconnaissance information of value to the combat team. It was a dangerous job, but one that did not require the officer to demonstrate leadership ability. Heavy casualties in the company grade officer ranks ensured that LT Bartow was eventually transferred to the infantry. A recently promoted 1st LT Bartow joined Fox Company on 22 March. The next day, Good Friday, found LT Bartow leading his rifle platoon into combat for the first time.

"He was a nice guy," said SGT James Hart. "I recall that he had just been assigned to us. We were walking down the road to approach the hill. Lieutenant Bartow and I were walking together, or I guess I was ahead of him a little bit. He said something to me, so I dropped back a bit and we started talking. 'Sergeant, I'm really new here,' he said, 'and I'm really a Quartermaster officer. I know nothing about the infantry and combat. What should I do?'"

SFC Amatuani Faamaile, Somoa, was awarded the Silver Star and Purple Heart fighting in King Company. (source: Chang)

Sergeant Hart calmed the inexperienced officer with sage words of advice. "You have a good platoon sergeant," replied SGT Hart. "Tell him what's troubling you, and let him lead you and tell you what to do."[13]

As the day wore on, the point rifle squads in the 3rd Battalion made contact with Chinese infantry. King Company encountered heavy enemy defensive fire as it closed on Regimental Objective 35. Sergeant First Class Amatuani Faamaile threw a grenade into a Chinese machine gun position. Following the blast, the large, powerful infantryman leaped into the midst of three Chinese soldiers, swinging his carbine like a club, killing two, and taking the lone, utterly terrified survivor prisoner. Once again, SFC Faamaile had to find a replacement for his broken carbine. The shattered stock lay at his feet next to the bodies of the two dead Chinese soldiers.[14]

King Company declared the objective secured at 1215. One hour and ten minutes later, a Chinese counterattack swarmed up the rocky slope in company strength, firing burp guns and hurling grenades, as they scrambled up the hill to close with the Americans. The 3rd Battalion committed Love Company to support King Company's defensive effort, but the CCF counterattack was repulsed before the reinforcements arrived on the scene. Fifty-six enemy bodies littered the hill.[15]

A few miles west of the King Company, Sonny led the 1st Squad, 1st Platoon, Fox Company, up the muddy hillside of Regimental Objective 42, which his outfit secured at 1435. The 2nd Battalion continued to advance, securing Regimental Objective 38 at 1630. Fox Company's fatigued soldiers had hiked all day while carrying their heavy combat loads, but light resistance with no losses incurred made their burdens easier to bear. The 2nd Battalion ordered CAPT Robert Lamb to continue the advance and seize Regimental Objective 43, Hill 814, where Fox Company would dig in for the night.[16]

As Fox Company struggled up the steep, slippery slope of Hill 814, the soldiers came under a smattering of enemy small arms fire from the crest. Captain Lamb directed his 2nd and 3rd Platoons to place fire on the enemy positions while LT Bartow's 1st Platoon maneuvered to seize the objective.

Lieutenant Bartow's 1st Platoon advanced into the enemy small arms fire. Sonny was up front, walking point, as he led the young soldiers he always referred to as "the boys" in his letters home up the rugged hill. As a squad leader, Sonny did not have to walk point, but it was his nature to advance to the scene of greatest danger, and today was no exception.

Approximately twenty yards beneath the crest of Hill 814, known as Tokkum-san to the South Koreans, a determined disciple of Chairman Mao Tse-tung manned a captured .50-caliber machine gun. The lay of Hill 814 facilitated the enemy defense. The only avenue of approach funneled the attackers into an inverted V-shaped killing zone, no more than twenty-five yards wide, just below the jagged crest. This killing zone was dominated by the .50-caliber machine gun located inside a superbly camouflaged bunker. Chinese riflemen and burp gunners provided the bunker flank protection from foxholes and trenches.[17]

The Chinese had suffered onerous casualties over the past few weeks, and the poorly supplied soldiers of the revolution were tired, hungry, low on ammunition and desperately afraid of American firepower. What thoughts raced through the mind of the Chinese soldier as he sighted the .50-caliber machine gun in on the American platoon advancing up the steep, rocky slope of Tokkum-san will

CAPT Lester, CO of George Company, 23 March 1951. Hill 814 where Sonny died is probably one of the hills behind him. (sources: NA/Chang)

This photo of Lona sitting on Sonny's car was en route to him when he fell KIA on 23 March 1951. Her sister, Dawn, stands in the background. (source: Calhau family)

never be discerned. Perhaps he desired an opportunity to strike a blow for Communism. Conceivably he wanted to exact revenge for fallen comrades. More likely, he was too numb from fatigue, hunger, and fear to care.

Sergeant Calhau's thoughts are also unknown. It was a steep hill, and the young soldier was probably exhausted from the long day's advance. He knew the enemy was waiting for him on top of Hill 814. Possibly Sonny harbored hopes that the Chinese would abandon the crest and continue their withdrawal. Maybe the soldier from Lanikai was thinking of family and home.

As Sonny advanced up the Hill of Sacrifice, the Chinese soldier fed a belt of ammunition into the weapon, pulled back the charging handle once, then twice, sighted down the barrel, and awaited the order to open fire. When Sonny's squad reached a predetermined point, an order was barked in Chinese, and the machine gunner pressed the trigger.

The 5th RCT's Unit Report reads, "At 1745 as White [2nd Battalion] advanced to objective 43 it began receiving small arms fire. One platoon prepared to assault the position when it received a heavy volume of fire from a large enemy force occupying the objective. Platoon withdrew."[18]

Several bullets struck Sonny in the chest and stomach from the initial burst of automatic weapons fire. As he lay mortally wounded in the mud on the rocky slope of Hill 814, his buddies in the 1st Platoon, Fox Company, were being hit hard, and men were going down. The platoon was unable to bring supporting artillery to bear, probably because they were too close to the Chinese positions. During the terrifying confusion, Sonny died in the midst of the firefight, his body exposed to automatic weapons fire and bursting grenades.

Lieutenant Bartow sensibly gave the order to fall back. In the chaos of the withdrawal, Sonny's lifeless body was left on the hillside, as his body was lying within the killing zone of the Chinese automatic weapon. One other soldier was KIA in the vicinity of Sonny, Private David L. Pugh from Randolph County, North Carolina.[19] As the men stumbled down the hill, dragging seven wounded soldiers with them, they reached the relative safety of the rest of the company. When the company had withdrawn a safe distance, the Heavy Mortar Company hammered the Chinese with high-explosive rounds.[20]

Tragedy compounded tragedy on Good Friday. A couple of tanks fired in support of Fox Company as the men staggered down the hill and took temporary refuge behind a finger. A flat trajectory main gun round impacted on top of this finger and showered the men with shrapnel which severely wounded several soldiers, including LT Bartow.[21]

Total reported casualties within the 5th RCT on Good Friday were two KIA, and twelve WIA, though one survivor believes that Fox Company's casualties alone were much higher.[22]

It is extremely doubtful if the Chinese soldier who killed Sonny managed in turn to survive the war.[23]

CHAPTER TWENTY-FIVE

EASTER SUNDAY

And if ye go to war in your land against the enemy that oppresseth you, then ye shall blow an alarm with the trumpets; and ye shall be remembered before the Lord your God, and ye shall be saved from your enemies.
Numbers 10:9, Holy Bible (KJV)

Strong elements of the CCF 226th Regiment, 76th Division, 26th Army, barred the combat team's advance.[1] The CCF 26th Army was rated a crack unit by the Chinese themselves, for it had repeatedly demonstrated superior fighting ability and high morale on the battlefield. The tenacious and skillful Chinese defense of Hill 814 illustrated the 226th Regiment's iron discipline under heavy fire.[2]

Sporadic Chinese artillery and mortar fires slammed into the 5th RCT's defensive positions throughout the night, adding to the fear and misery experienced by the soldiers. With bugles blaring, a sudden counterattack materialized out of the darkness, the Chinese advancing at a rush, firing burp guns and hurling grenades. A platoon from King Company was knocked out of its positions an hour after midnight. The platoon rallied, counterattacked up the slope, and regained its positions after a brisk firefight at 0430. The ferocious Samoan rifle squad leader, SFC Amatuani Faamaile, fell wounded on the battlefield.[3]

At dawn, the 5th RCT's bone-weary soldiers resumed the attack. Air strikes and artillery fire blasted a path for the infantry. Fox Company assaulted Hill 814 through intense automatic weapons fire and an inferno of exploding mortar shells. One platoon clawed its way to the crest only to be hurled back down the slope by a resolute Chinese counterattack.

The 5th RCT's losses mounted throughout the long, dreary, overcast day. One soldier, PFC Robert L. Geise, was KIA in Fox Company. Forty-nine of the combat team's soldiers fell.[4] A seriously wounded soldier was evacuated by helicopter after suffering a gunshot wound to the head.[5] His subsequent fate remains a mystery.

At 1500, the 2nd Battalion ordered Fox Company to withdraw to Objective 42 where the exhausted soldiers hunkered down for another miserable night. Captain Robert Lamb, a brave

CAPT Robert Lamb, CO of Fox Company, was a brave and beloved commander. (source: Robert Lamb)

soldier and beloved leader, was the last man off the hill. Sonny's lifeless body remained on the blasted, burned, and battered hillside where he had fallen the day before.[6]

"That was the worst beating we took in all the time I was with Fox Company, including the time I was captured," recalled SGT James Hart. "When we went up that hill [on 23 March] it was the first time we had a full complement of forward observers for approximately 220 men. We came off that hill with about fifty or sixty men. Over fifty of our men had battle fatigue, men who were exhausted and just stumbling and wandering around. I can't get over the futility of going up that hill. It was almost as if they could have held us off with rocks if they had wanted to."[7]

The situation was deemed ripe for a Chinese counterattack. To counter this threat, the 24th Infantry Division transferred a battalion from the 21st Infantry to an assembly area behind the 5th RCT where it could, if necessary, restore the MLR through counterattack or block an enemy penetration. Sporadic fighting continued throughout the interminable, tension-filled hours of the night, but the dreaded CCF counterattack never materialized.[8]

A Chinese rearguard withdrew from Hill 814 before dawn on Easter Sunday. Sonny was retrieved the same day. After his body was identified, it was sent to graves registration in the rear. The soldier from Lanikai was finally going home.

A wounded 5th RCT soldier is evacuated by helicopter, March 1951. (sources: NA/Chang)

5th RCT soldiers take communion on Easter Sunday. (source: 25th ID Museum)

CHAPTER TWENTY-SIX

Hurry Up And Die

Aptitude for war is aptitude for movement.
Napoleon

Corporal James Shaw returned to Korea shortly after Sonny and was promptly promoted to sergeant. King Company kept the FO gainfully employed during the combat team's grueling advance. It was not until after Easter that he had an opportunity to visit his friend.

"I went over to Fox Company when both our outfits were off the lines," SGT Shaw explained. "I asked someone where Sonny was and he didn't want to talk. I eventually found his squad. About five or six guys were left, mostly guys from Hawaii. They were pretty quiet at first and didn't answer my questions. When I told them I was a good friend of Sonny's, they invited me into their tent and told me that Sonny had been killed walking point up a hill. Now Sonny was a squad leader and he didn't have to walk point. I was angry and asked these guys why Sonny was walking point, and one of them replied, 'Because that's the way he was. He wanted to and just did it.' Now Sonny could have picked someone else to walk point that day, and that person would probably have died in his stead. But not Sonny. Oh no, not Sonny. That's the kind of soldier he was. My greatest regret is that I never had a chance to see him again. It made me sick to even think that he'd died. It hurt bad. It still does. I look at our picture every day."[1]

As Sonny began his slow journey home, the 5th RCT fought its way northward, taking one contested hill after another as the physically drained, foot-sore infantry pushed their opponent across the 38th Parallel. Chinese rearguards suffered heavy losses, primarily from air strikes and artillery fire, as they endeavored to screen the arrival of fresh CCF armies gathering in North Korean assembly areas in preparation for a renewed offensive. The 5th RCT captured two artillery pieces during the advance, but only a handful of Chinese soldiers willingly surrendered. On a happier note, the combat team liberated twenty-one ROK soldiers on 29 March from their Chinese captors.[2]

On the evening of 28 March, Baker Company was advancing up Hill 581 near Pochon when it encountered a strong Chinese defensive position. Three soldiers were WIA in the ensuing firefight, and the company withdrew leaving the crest in Chinese hands. The struggle resumed the following morning, 29 March, as Baker Company clawed its way to within 100 yards of the crest. The assault bogged down when mortar shells exploded amongst the men, and intense automatic weapons and small arms fire raked the soldiers caught in the open on the naked slope of the disputed hill.

Baker Company lost PFC John F. Summers KIA and five others WIA. Second Lieutenant Kense Suga, a former MSGT who had just earned a battlefield commission, was wounded leading the 2nd Platoon up the hotly contested hill. Two men from Able Company, and three from Charlie Company, fell wounded nearby.

Sergeant First Class Robert H. Middleton, having recovered from wounds incurred on Sobuk-san, led the 1st Platoon, Baker Company, into the firestorm until they reached a position within twenty-five yards of the crest. Here, intense enemy fire pinned the soldiers down. Suddenly, with complete disregard for his own safety,

COL Throckmorton (left) discusses the tactical situation with LTC Elmer Owens, CO 3rd Battalion (center) while CPL Lorrin Thurston, the Rock's driver, looks on. CPL Thurston's father was the editor of the Honolulu Advertiser. *(source: Chang)*

MSGT Johnnie Walls, St. Louis, MO, gives a candy bar to a child sitting on Leilani. (sources: 25th ID Museum/Chang)

SFC Middleton stood up and started hurling hand grenades at the automatic weapons positions. He eliminated two machine guns in this fashion, but the Chinese fought back hard, and soon their own grenades were landing at his feet. The force of the explosions knocked SFC Middleton to the ground and temporarily stunned the courageous soldier. He quickly recovered and led his men in a bayonet charge that routed the CCF defenders from the crest of Hill 581. For this action, SFC Middleton was awarded the Silver Star.[3]

Tank Company often supported the infantry's movement along the ridgelines from firing positions on the valley floor. One day the 2nd Tank Platoon was overwatching the advance of a battalion when COL Throckmorton and his operations officer rode by in a jeep on a personal reconnaissance. Shortly after the jeep passed LT Ed Crockett's tank, it rounded a bend in the road and drove into a column of Chinese soldiers marching in the opposite direction with their weapons slung nonchalantly over their shoulders. Colonel Throckmorton's driver quickly made a U-turn and floored the accelerator before the startled Chinese had time to fire. The Chinese infantry ran around the bend in pursuit, only to run into the 2nd Tank Platoon. A concentrated barrage of point-blank high explosive shells and machine gun fire killed the hapless Chinese.[4]

To counter boredom the tank crews often indulged in long range sniping with their 76-mm guns. Admittedly, this was an expensive endeavor, for each high explosive shell cost the taxpayers $50. Nevertheless, the tankers were taxpayers, too. As far as they were concerned, civilians who disapproved of the expenditure were welcome to join them in Korea.

The challenge was to see who could attain a first round hit on an enemy soldier at the greatest possible range. Lieutenant Crockett's gunner, SFC William J. Puaoi, from Molokai, was recognized as one of the best gunners in Tank Company. He and LT Crockett continually challenged one another to see who was the better shot. One day, a CCF soldier was observed on a hillside beyond the maximum effective range of the 76-mm gun. It was LT Crockett's turn to shoot, and he obliterated the unlucky individual with his first round. The "Platoon Best" stood for several months, at which time it was LT Crockett who broke it again.

Master Sergeant Johnnie Walls' approval rating for LT Crockett soared as the days and weeks went by. Lieutenant Crockett in turn was so enamored with his platoon sergeant's leadership and tactical skills that he recommended him for a battlefield commission. Master Sergeant Walls remained the platoon sergeant of the 2nd Platoon while the paperwork for his well-deserved commission was in motion.[5] In anticipation of MSGT Walls' pending commission, MSGT Morris B. Helm, a seasoned tanker, but new to Korea, joined LT Crockett's platoon as a platoon sergeant in waiting.

The 5th RCT reached the 38th Parallel on 31 March after establishing its CP at Pisi-gol the day before. Pisi-gol would figure prominently in the saga of the 5th RCT later in April, but for the present, it was of little significance.[6] Colonel Throckmorton ordered the 3rd Battalion to send a tank-infantry patrol across the border on the last day of March. This patrol encountered strong enemy forces and withdrew after killing approximately thirty CCF soldiers.[7] Lieutenant Crockett's 2nd Tank Platoon spearheaded the drive, shooting up a CCF rearguard that attempted to bar their path. The following day, LT Crockett led another patrol that erected a red pentagon sign post with the words "38th Parallel Courtesy of the 5th RCT," scrawled in toothpaste to mark the spot.[8]

The night before the combat team crossed the 38th Parallel, CAPT Kenneth L. Sutherland, the CO of M Company, was blessed with a letter from the oldest of his two little girls. He proudly read his daughter's letter to 1st LT Harold Thralls, the Machine Gun platoon leader, who had just returned from a two month stay in Japan recovering from a leg wound. The two officers conversed softly into the night, exchanging news from home and discussing combat operations at the front. Lieutenant Thralls was content to serve under his personable commanding officer, a soldier who was truly beloved by his officers and men.

The next day, 31 March, found LT Thralls limping from one machine gun section to the next as Mike Company supported the 3rd Battalion's attack across the 38th Parallel. The platoon leader had visited two of his three machine gun sections, and was on his way to visit the third, when a rifle company recovered the bodies of two GIs during the advance. Their captors had bound these unfortunate men with barbed wire and shot them, execution-style, in the back of the head at point-blank range. The Battalion Commander, LTC Elmer G. Owens, arrived on the scene to discuss the murdered GIs with LT Thralls. Shortly thereafter, CAPT Sutherland drove up in his jeep and joined them.[9]

Captain Sutherland noticed LT Thralls' limp and directed him to use his jeep and return to the company CP for a rest. Lieutenant Colonel Owens concurred and invited CAPT Sutherland to accompany his visit to a rifle company where the latter could check on LT Thralls' third machine gun section.

Lieutenant Colonel Owens and CAPT Sutherland drove approximately a half-mile down a road where their jeep encountered a tank approaching from the opposite direction. The driver halted the jeep at the entrance to a narrow cut in the road for a few seconds to let the battalion commander dismount. Meanwhile, the tank pulled over to the side of the road to let the jeep through. Captain Sutherland remained in the jeep, and as it passed the tank, the right front wheel struck a mine that exploded and mortally wounded the company commander.[10] He lived for about one hour while awaiting a helicopter medical evacuation. Regrettably, the helicoptor pilot refused to evacuate the wounded company commander because the landing zone lay under enemy observation.[11] Captain Sutherland was one of nineteen men reported KIA by the 5th Infantry for the month of March.[12] An additional 137 WIA, and 145 non-battle casualties, rounded out the 5th Infantry's losses.

The combat team advanced deeper into the mountains, pressing stubborn Chinese rearguards ever northward. On 2 April, 1st LT Randall Beirne described his experiences in a letter home. "Each hill the infantryman sweats out. They point out a hill and say that's our objective. It's probably a 3,000-foot peak with sheer rock cliffs on several faces. The 'wheels' say some enemy is on it, but that artillery and air will work it over before we go up. The CO says your platoon will lead off… you move out. The mountain looms over you and seems to almost grin. In your mind you are thinking, 'If they have a machine gun there on that knob, and on that knob, they will get me in a crossfire. I'll use the best covered route.' You work up slowly, one squad at a time, always taking covered routes, and always staring at that knob that might have a machine gun. There's an open area. You move across. No enemy fire comes from the hill. You think, 'Is he holding back and waiting for you to get closer?' The mountain begins to go straight up. The men crawl from behind one huge boulder to the next. They always watch that knob. Sweat pours off everyone. The wools we wear to keep us warm at night definitely hold us back now. The machine gun and ammo are heavy. The rations are heavy. The hill is steep, it's like walking up large steps. Everyone is waiting for that first burst of enemy fire. Every inch of the hill is being scanned. The machine gun fires at random to try to draw fire and see if anyone is up there. Everyone is flushed and panting. Each step is an effort. Then over the radio comes that familiar question: 'What are the coordinates of your location?' And 'Hurry up.' It's always hurry up. It's always the 'brass' sitting in their jeeps looking at you through glasses that say 'Hurry up.' To them the hill is like a piece of paper. They see only the map and the red pencil marks…. If that hill is taken they see for themselves a new silver leaf or an oak leaf cluster to their Silver Star…. The lead squad or platoon keeps working its way up the hill. The men relax a little because they feel if any enemy were on the hill, they would have fired at them by now. Perhaps a single enemy does fire. They keep moving up and finally the enemy may quit and run. The top is reached. The men are nearly exhausted. A little flushing out is done…. Finally the rest of the company arrives. The men sit and eat a ration. Some just sit and stare into space. Then the order comes, 'Move on to the next hill.'"[13]

First Lieutenant McKinley G. Buckner, a former assistant hangman at the Nuremberg War Crimes Trials, earned a battlefield commission early in the Korean War. He was KIA on 4 April by friendly fire.[14] Easy and George Companies were

SFC William Puaoi, Hoolehua, Molokai, was one of Tank Company's best gunners. (sources: NA/Chang)

189

attacking along a narrow ridgeline when they encountered a Chinese bunker located on the far side of a long saddle. The soldiers had fought their way through mortar and automatic weapons fire to reach this point, but a further advance across the open, fire-swept ground was impossible. Several attempts to rush the bunker had already failed under withering automatic weapons fire. The bunker's weapons commanded every possible approach. Envelopment was out of the question. Moreover, the narrow spine of the ridgeline was not amenable to the employment of recoilless rifles and other crew-served weapons.

First Lieutenant Lucian R. Rawls, Columbia, South Carolina, commanded Easy Company with consummate tactical skill throughout the engagement. Yet as the sun set behind the mountains, the bunker continued to dominate the battlefield, mocking the men lying exposed under the muzzles of its machine guns. Decisive action was called for. The company commander discussed the tactical situation with his FO, LT Buckner, from B Battery, 555th FAB, who also hailed from South Carolina. Lieutenants Rawls and Buckner agreed that shifting a previously planned target onto the bunker would be the best way to deal with the Chinese. Lieutenant Rawls was very concerned that the artillery fire would be too close to allow the lead platoon to remain safely in its present position. Lieutenant Buckner agreed and suggested it was best for him to remain in the most forward area to direct the fire while the platoon withdrew a safe distance. Lieutenant Rawls said fine, but he would keep LT Buckner company. When LT Buckner's radio operator, CPL Dan M. Gonzales, from Las Vegas, New Mexico, requested permission to remain behind, the FO hesitated to reply out of concern for his safety. He finally said, "OK."

LT Crockett's 2nd Tank Platoon confers with ROK civilians on 31 March 1951. (source: Chang)

The three soldiers crowded into a foxhole for cover. Lieutenant Buckner requested a fire mission, which CPL Gonzales transmitted over the radio. The 11th FAB, armed with 155-mm howitzers, fired the mission. Within seconds, the first shells came screaming in, bursting on and around the Chinese bunker, and throwing debris and shrapnel through the air. Lieutenant Buckner appeared satisfied with the results when, suddenly, he sensed a short round coming and yelled for everyone to get down. The round plowed through a group of nearby tree tops and exploded within a few feet of their position. The force of the explosion threw LT Rawls out of the hole and knocked him senseless. Otherwise, he was not seriously hurt. Lieutenant Buckner and CPL Gonzales were pinned to the

5th RCT soldiers attempt to save the life of CAPT Kenneth L. Sutherland, CO of Mike Company. The force of the mine explosion flipped the Jeep completely around. (sources: NA/Chang)

ground by rocks and debris. Corporal Gonzales grabbed the handset and started yelling "Cease Fire! Cease Fire!" It took a moment to realize his damaged radio would never work again.

Lieutenant Fred T. O'Keefe, from George Company, quickly arrived with a group of medics who did everything possible to save LT Buckner's life, but the valiant FO bled to death from a severed artery as he was being carried down the hill.[15] One of his many friends, 1st LT Roy T. Nakashima, from B Battery, took over as Easy Company's FO the next day.

Lieutenant Earl Law was LT Buckner's best friend. They had served as NCOs together at Schofield Barracks, where they had enjoyed one another's company on many a payday weekend in Honolulu's watering holes. When LT Law heard that his friend was wounded, he thought his buddy was recovering in the rear.

Major Perry Graves, the S-3 of the 555th FAB, visited C Battery with LTC Clarence Stuart for lunch the next day. He asked LT Law, "Have you heard about Buckner?"

Lieutenant Law replied, "Yeah, that gold bricking S.O.B!" Major Graves told the shocked lieutenant, "No, no! He's dead."

Lieutenant Law stood speechless for a moment and then stalked out of the tent. He stood alone in a nearby rice paddy, crying for his departed friend.[16]

A rifle squad moves out, carrying their world on their backs as they prepare to ascend another nameless hill. (source: Chang)

A 555th FAB FO team in Korea. (source: Chang)

The 3rd Battalion was fighting to the west of the 2nd Battalion when LT Buckner died. The Chinese allowed the lead platoon from Love Company to advance into the middle of an icy stream before they opened fire. Tracers whipped through the platoon, killing and wounding several men with the first bursts of deadly accurate automatic weapons fire. One group attempted to retrace their steps while green and red tracers slapped at their heels. The rest of the platoon charged with fixed bayonets, but the soldiers ran into an anti-personnel minefield raked by machine gun fire.

King Company inched its way up the steep slope through the "crump, crump, crump" of enemy mortar fire. The Chinese were using captured American 4.2-inch and 81-mm mortars that day, much to the discomfort of the soldiers. The 3rd Platoon was pinned down with nowhere to go but forward, so it stood up and assaulted through one Chinese position, losing half its men, but taking the objective with grenades, rifles, and bayonets.

When Lieutenant Randall Beirne's 2nd Platoon moved up to assist the 3rd Platoon, the soldiers came under heavy small arms and automatic weapons fire from the reverse slope when they reached the crest. All the while, mortar rounds impacted among the men, hurling white-hot shrapnel through the air. Cries for medics echoed along the line as the fire intensified, and more men went down, killed or wounded.

Lieutenant Beirne said, "Suddenly grenades began landing in our line and someone yelled, 'They are counterattacking!' and then he started back down the hill. Almost the whole line started to turn and run…. My first instinct… on seeing all those men turning back was to do the same but fortunately pride and discipline put these words into my mind: 'What the hell are you doing?' At the same time SGT William T. Akerley, Jr., the Supply Sergeant, and a group of other sergeants, ran back at the enemy while yelling, cursing and calling the men cowards. The individual soldier suddenly became ashamed and then mad. The whole line turned and went charging back up that hill…. It looked like Pickett's Charge. The enemy counterattack was completely routed."[17]

Lieutenant Beirne gave full credit to his NCOs for the charge. Most of his soldiers were recent draftees, good men who nevertheless had yet to acquire a strong sense of unit pride. They would learn through experience that it was almost always safer to hold one's ground. Units that broke and ran were usually chewed to pieces during the merciless enemy pursuit. Tactical skill, and pride in self and unit would come, but first a handful of brave veterans had to teach their young soldiers the brutal trade of war. The price was steep. All too many veterans paid the butcher's bill.

Sergeant First Class James R. Jackson, one the men who had helped turn the tide on Hill 268 so long ago, grabbed a light machine gun in this firefight. Shooting from the hip, he advanced uphill until a Chinese mortar round exploded at his feet, knocking him to the ground.

Corporal John Sonley, a soldier serving in Mike Company, was one of several men who held SFC Jackson down as the medics gave him a dose of morphine. He recalled, "Jackson was trying to sit up and look at his feet. He mustered some superhuman strength, threw off the men holding his arms and sat up. As he looked at where his feet had been, he said, 'Oh my God,' and died."[18] Sergeant First Class James Jackson, an Indiana farm boy with three years' service under his belt, was a nineteen-year-old noncommissioned officer of the Forgotten War.

Among the dead was a seventeen-year-old veteran machine gunner who was about to be sent home for being underage. All told, the "Chiggy-bearers" carried four basic loads of ammunition up the hill and thirty litter cases back down.[19]

First Lieutenant Smith,[20] West Point Class of 1949, was a rifle platoon leader in Able Company. After months of continuous combat in Korea, LT Smith began to experience great difficulty concealing his personal fear. Captain Hank Emerson, the CO of Able Company, was worried about the bad effect LT Smith was beginning to have on the men. One morning, CAPT Emerson returned to his company CP after receiving orders for the day's advance. Lieutenant Smith approached him with a mournful expression on his face and asked, "What is the mission? Is it going to be bad?"[21]

Captain Emerson exploded, "Hell no, LT Smith! The Goddamn war is over and we're all going on R&R to fucking Japan! What in the hell do you expect?"

CPL John Sonley, Mike Company, from Chandler, AZ, was one of several men who tried to save SFC James Jackson's life. (source: John Sonley)

Lieutenant Smith recoiled under his company commander's wrath and returned to his rifle platoon where he stood off to the side of his men fidgeting in fear. Captain Emerson immediately felt badly about how he had treated his platoon leader and resolved to have the combat-fatigued officer transferred out of a line company.

"Hell," explained CAPT Emerson, "LT Smith was probably braver than all of us. He always did his job in combat, leading his men forward into the enemy fire. It wasn't his fault that he couldn't control his fear anymore. But the Rock had always told us that we couldn't afford to let the men see us afraid, and he was right. The men were starting to make fun of LT Smith because he couldn't control himself anymore. Some of the more sarcastic NCOs asked me that day if he was 'my West Point friend' as they nodded toward LT Smith who was obviously trembling in fear."

Lieutenant Smith did his part in the day's fighting as he led his men into the Chinese defensive fire. A few days later, CAPT Emerson discretely requested that LTC Thomas Roelofs transfer LT Smith, and this was done. Lieutenant Smith was obviously relieved to join the Heavy Mortar Company, a comparably safe job, one step removed from the immediate hazards of the infantry firing line. He died on 3 April 1951 after his jeep hit a mine.[22]

Rumors of a rotation policy ran rampant through the combat team. In case this rumor proved accurate, 1st LT Lucian Rawls, the CO of Easy Company, instructed his first sergeant, MSGT Horace Anderson, to draw up a roster of the men who had deployed from Schofield Barracks in July 1950. Lieutenant Rawls wanted the men with the longest time on the lines to rotate first if the rumored policy was implemented. Of the 145 officers and men who had deployed from Schofield Barracks with Easy Company, just fifty-nine remained, and every one of these soldiers had been wounded, several as many as four times.[23]

Colonel Throckmorton's days in Korea were numbered. After General Ridgway received a request for a combat experienced officer to serve as the senior aide for the Chief of Staff of the Army, General J. Lawton Collins, he offered one of his best regimental commanders, COL Throckmorton, the job. The Rock was loath to leave his beloved soldiers, but the courageous regimental commander knew that when the rotation policy took effect, he would be replaced. The Army's

COL Throckmorton confers with MG Blackshear Bryan, CG 24th ID. (source: Chang)

foremost airborne soldier, General Ridgway, handpicked LTC Arthur H. Wilson, from Brownsville, Texas, to command the 5th RCT.[24]

Lieutenant Colonel "Harry" Wilson was an experienced airborne infantry officer who had learned his trade in the Pacific Theater of Operations in World War II while serving as a battalion commander, and later regimental executive officer, in the 187th Glider Infantry, 11th Airborne Division.[25] His bravery under fire during the grueling struggle to recapture the Philippines was unquestioned, for one does not earn the Silver Star, two Bronze Stars, and the Purple Heart leading from the rear. He had a deep appreciation for airborne tactics which usually called for paratroopers to jump into a drop zone located deep in enemy territory where they defended a perimeter at all costs until relieved by an overland advance. His combat experience in Korea, however, was limited to two daring, if brief, combat jumps in command of the 1st Battalion, 187th Airborne. Neither combat jump had encountered heavy enemy opposition.

Anyone who took over from the Rock was bound to have a hard act to follow. Oddly enough, LTC Wilson's first hurdle was that he had graduated from the United States Military Academy, the cradle of Army leadership, with the Class of 1937. He was in fact the first man from his class to command a regiment in Korea, and this at a time when most of his classmates were battalion commanders at best. True, COL Throckmorton, a West Pointer to the bone, had also assumed command of the combat team as a lieutenant colonel, but the soldiers Harry Wilson would have to lead in combat did not automatically view him in the same league as the Rock.[26] Many officers perceived LTC Wilson to be a "ring knocker," one who used the combination of his West Point and Airborne connections to secure a prized position. This perception became the source of considerable, if subdued, grumbling on the part of some of the combat team's officers. Most of these officers believed their own combat proven LTC Albert Ward should have replaced the Rock. This attitude was by no means universal, and remained muted out of respect for the chain of command, yet it was prevalent in sufficient force to give cause for worry if the new commander did not quickly measure up to the expectations of key subordinates.

It is important to understand that LTC Wilson's previous airborne experience held little weight in the eyes of the 5th RCT's officers and NCOs. The Army's infantry branch had split along three distinct lines during World War II. Of the three, mechanized infantry played no prominent role in Korea. Of the remaining two, the straight-leg infantry considered themselves a superior breed, largely because the flashy, headline-grabbing, airborne infantry had garnered little in the way of practical combat results in Korea to justify their elite status. Sustained straight-leg infantry combat conducted on a regimental scale in mountainous terrain was a great deal different from LTC Wilson's previous combat experience.

Lieutenant Colonel Benjamin Heckemeyer departed on emergency leave, never to return to Korea, when COL Throckmorton rotated home. Few of the soldiers serving in the 3rd Battalion regretted his departure, largely because many of the men felt he took care of himself and his staff at the expense of the line companies. In October 1950, for example, during a battalion awards formation conducted near Seoul, the soldiers standing in the ranks, veterans of Waegwan and Kumchon, had started to boo and hiss when they noticed most of the awards recipients were none other than LTC Heckemeyer and members of the staff. It took a great deal of effort on the part of their company commanders and platoon leaders to silence the combat infantrymen.[27] Following LTC Heckemeyer's departure, LTC Albert Ward fleeted up to become the combat team's executive officer.

Lieutenant Colonel Thomas Roelofs reportedly departed Korea under a cloud. The battalion commander had submitted an awards recommendation for himself that he did not deserve, and the Rock had challenged him on it. Colonel Throckmorton was extremely loyal when it came to covering for the shortcomings of his battalion commanders, but LTC Roelofs' transgression was not allowed to stand, and the battalion commander was quietly relieved of his command. The relief was without prejudice, for LTC Roelofs was promoted to colonel shortly thereafter, the rank he and LTC Heckemeyer retired at long after the war.[28]

The capable MAJ Claude Baker took command of 1st Battalion from LTC Roelofs. "I liked him," said SFC Hibbert Manley who served in Charlie Company. "He was more personable than LTC Roelofs. Before we went on patrols, we'd receive a briefing at battalion. Major Baker really made you feel like he cared. Roelofs might have cared, but you'd never know it from the way he acted."[29]

Major Rufus Pope, a recent replacement, took command of the 2nd Battalion.[30] Major James P. Alcorn, the former regimental Adjutant, assumed command of the 3rd Battalion from LTC Elmer Owens who rotated home. Finally, MAJ Frederick A. Wells fleeted up from his position as S-3 of the 1st Battalion to assume the responsibilities of regimental operations officer.[31]

Lieutenant Colonel Wilson's newness to regimental command, combined with the fact that three of his four battalion commanders and several key staff officers, were new to their posts, would have been surmountable if the front had remained stable. Unfortunately, the Communists had plans of their own, and LTC Wilson's learning curve during the forthcoming Chinese Spring Offensive was destined to be as brief as it was steep.

Meanwhile, as the Chinese continued to withdraw their forward screen, while amassing an assault force that dwarfed anything the Eighth Army had faced before, events on the American political scene took an unanticipated turn that suddenly converged on the CP of the 5th RCT.

The Honorable Mr. Frank Pace, Secretary of the Army, toured the front lines in Korea on 11 April to observe Operation DAUNTLESS, yet another Eighth Army offensive designed to inflict maximum punishment on the Chinese. The 5th RCT was in reserve while COL Throckmorton conducted a turnover with LTC Wilson. Earlier in the day the Eighth Army's Chief of Staff had called COL Throckmorton trying to contact the Secretary of the Army. Colonel Throckmorton informed Mr. Pace of the call at 1500 when the latter arrived with General Ridgway at the command post. When Mr. Pace placed a call to the Chief of Staff, he was informed that President Truman had just relieved General MacArthur and that General Ridgway had already been chosen to succeed him in Tokyo. Thus, General Ridgway received the stunning news of General MacArthur's relief, and of his own appointment to succeed him, from the Secretary of the Army at the combat team's command post.[32]

General MacArthur's relief was mourned by some. Others were pleased to have General Ridgway in command. Private First Class Donald Gottschall said, "When MacArthur was there we got, if you'll pardon the

LTC Stuart, CO 555th FAB, is awarded the Legion of Merit by MG Blackshear Bryan. LTC Stuart was the only one of the 5th RCT's four battalion commanders to remain at his post when LTC Harry Wilson assumed command of the combat team. (source: NA)

expression, 'shit and shoved at.' When General Ridgway took over we received food, clothing, and decent stuff."[33]

The Army's long awaited rotation policy went into effect shortly before COL Throckmorton's departure.[34] The first group of 190 5th RCT soldiers departed Korea on 10 April. Included in this number were several veteran officers and NCOs, to include CAPT Hank Emerson, LT Keith Whitham and MSGT Horace Anderson. More followed. The rotation policy was a definite morale boost for, in the past, the soldiers had little to look forward to other than endless hours of horrifying combat until they too became casualties, bloody statistics in a seemingly endless war. On the downside this policy led to a the steady drain of combat experienced leaders, and a corresponding increase of inexperienced replacements, just when it appeared the CCF was on the verge of mounting yet another massive offensive. The loss of so many experienced soldiers would be felt in the coming battles.

Of the 532 replacements who reported for duty between 4-13 April 1951, most were lads eighteen or nineteen years of age, old enough to fight, kill, bleed and die, yet too young to legally drink a cold beer in most of the Forty-eight States or Territories.[35] Youthful and well fed, their outward appearance would change in short order, muscles hardened through arduous marches bearing heavy loads; faces and hands weather-beaten, chapped and mauled; feet blistered,

CAPT Norman Cooper of Chattanooga, TN, with his wife Inez and son Gregory, after he rotated home from Korea in August 1951. (source: Norman Cooper)

callused and bruised; their eyes silent witness to innumerable tragic nightmares far beyond the comprehension and experience of America's civilians who lived in comparative luxury, far removed from the blood price of this distant Asian war. Henceforth, the war would be waged primarily by citizen-soldiers, otherwise known as draftees. The days when the Army was manned exclusively by long-service volunteers would not return until 1973.

CHAPTER TWENTY-SEVEN

SPRING OVERTURE

At approximately 2105 hours, I Company of the 19th Infantry was attacked by an unestimated number of enemy using grenades. By 2200 the enemy had broken into F Company and was occupying some of its positions and firing into I Company's positions. By 2400, K Company was out of communications with its battalion and, while there were portions of the company known to be in the forward positions, it was believed they were very low on ammunition. The 3d Battalion Commander stated that more Chinese made this attack than he had ever seen before — this from an officer who had been with the division since it landed in Korea in July, 1950. In the area of the 5th Infantry, the same thing was happening.
24th Infantry Division Command Report, 22 April 1951

Sonny's comrades in the 5th RCT still had their toughest week ahead of them. Enemy resistance solidified on 22 April as the Eighth Army's offensive ground to a halt in the face of dogged resistance. Chinese rearguard actions in February, March, and early April had skillfully covered the assembly of 337,000 CCF soldiers poised to regain the initiative through offensive combat. Radio Pyongyang confidently boasted that the combined weight of the reinforced CCF and the rejuvenated NKPA would overrun the Eighth Army, capture Seoul, and win the war.[1]

The combat team hastily dug in near nightfall on a 6,000-meter front in the vicinity of Unjimal. The MLR ran from east to west and straddled a narrow valley between two rugged ridgelines on which rested the combat team's flanks. The MSR ran generally north to south through the valley. Though the 1st and 2nd Battalions defended the MLR with all six rifle companies abreast, the broken nature of the terrain made it nearly impossible for the companies to physically tie in. One platoon of Sherman tanks, and one of 4.2-inch mortars, was attached to each of the forward battalions. The 3rd Battalion, with the rest of Tank Company and a platoon of 4.2-inch mortars attached, was in reserve on the valley floor 1,200 yards south of the MLR. The 555th FAB had hastily registered its defensive fires.[2]

The terrain was unfavorable for a protracted defense. The razor back ridgelines dominating each flank were covered with dense vegetation that considerably reduced the visibility of the defending riflemen. Fields of fire were often blocked by jumbled masses of huge boulders. "We went into this position very late in the day," explained CAPT Robert J. Lamb, the CO of Fox Company. "We had very little time to dig in before we were hit."[3]

The combat team's left flank rested on the crest of Hill 795 where E Company, 2nd Battalion, tied in with K Company, 19th Infantry. The 24th Infantry Division viewed retention of Hill 795 as critical, for it was located on a north-south ridgeline that led south through the entire divisional sector. The Chinese were notorious for using the crests of ridgelines as their axis of advance, and division G-2 therefore believed Hill 795 would be the enemy's most likely initial objective.[4] From the crest of Hill 795, the 2nd Battalion's sector on the MLR ran downhill due east. Easy Company was on the left, Fox in the center, and George on the right where the latter tied in with the 1st Battalion on the valley floor.

4.2-inch mortar digging in. L to R: PFC Donald Gottschall and PFC Salvatore Brocato. (source: Donald Gottschall)

The 1st Battalion's sector on the MLR climbed from the valley floor to the crest of a 1,000-meter high ridgeline on the combat team's right flank. Here, Able Company was unable to physically tie in with the ROK 6th Division due to the lateness of the hour, a shortage of men, and the broken nature of the extremely rough terrain. This was a particularly dangerous development in that Able Company's boundary with the ROK 6th Division doubled as the boundary of I and IX Corps, Eighth Army.[5] And the CCF exploited boundaries.

The ROK 6th Division suffered from a justifiably poor reputation for its repeated failures to hold ground when assaulted by the Chinese.[6] South Korean soldiers feared their Chinese opponents with a pathological dread that transcended Western understanding, a fact which nonetheless remained a source of grave concern whenever American commanders found themselves located on an ROK Army unit's flanks.

Able Company gained and maintained visual contact with the ROKs in the remaining hour of day light, and covered the resultant gap as best they could with fire. Yet given the CCF's demonstrated predilection to seek out and strike unit boundaries, and the coordination difficulties inherent in all cross boundary operations, the tactical deployment of the unreliable ROK 6th Division was bound to have serious consequences for the 5th RCT if the ROKs collapsed under enemy pressure.

The 3rd Battalion's position would in theory enable it to counterattack in support of the infantry battalions defending the MLR. In practice, however, a night ascent from the valley floor to the top of either ridgeline would require several hours of hard climbing, so a decision to commit the reserve would have to be made early if it was going to be made at all. One rifle platoon from I Company was detached and dug in on an isolated hilltop 2,000 yards south of the 1st Battalion to cover the right flank in case the ROKs broke and ran. A rifle platoon from Love Company occupied Hill 752, approximately 1,000 yards behind Easy Company's positions on Hill 795 to block any penetration there.[7] The rest of 3rd Battalion remained on the valley floor.

Chinese 150-mm artillery and 120-mm mortar fires began to impact on the 1st Battalion at 1835, and twenty minutes later, the first rounds came crashing down on the 3rd Battalion, too. Immediately after these salvos impacted, artillery hammered the 2nd Battalion along its entire frontage. Sergeant Turner, an S-3 Clerk in the 5th RCT CP, phoned all battalions at 1900, "Enemy movements and PW report indicate tonight is critical. Be especially alert. Occupy best defensive positions immediately available; adjust defensive fires of artillery and mortars and take other measures to meet an attack in force tonight."[8]

Major Claude Baker was experiencing problems with his XO long before the first Chinese rounds impacted on the 1st Battalion. This particular officer, LTC Heckemeyer's former XO in the 3rd Battalion, had unfortunately mastered many bad habits in Korea. The 1st Battalion's soldiers had participated in sporadic, yet occasionally intense, fighting to their immediate front all day, during which CAPT Fred F. Hipley, the CO of Charlie Company, had been wounded in the heel and evacuated. Major Baker and his S-3, CAPT George C. Viney, toured the lines before sunset in order to confer with the company commanders, particularly with 1st LT Charles E. Brannon, a recent replacement and World War II combat veteran, who had taken command of Charlie Company.

During MAJ Baker's absence, enemy mortar fire impacted in the vicinity of his battalion's CP. The XO panicked and ordered the CP to withdraw. When MAJ Baker walked back down the hill, soldiers from the 81-mm Mortar Platoon informed their battalion commander that the XO had withdrawn the CP without informing anyone where he was going. After MAJ Baker finally found his CP, he discovered to his dismay that it was located even farther south than regiment's! He relieved his XO on the spot.[9]

At 1920, the regimental liaison aircraft spotted Chinese infantry moving south along the ridgeline leading toward Hill 795. Ten minutes later, the 2nd Battalion's combat outpost, a platoon-sized element, commenced a withdrawal under heavy enemy pressure to the MLR. The Taro Leaf G-3 informed LTC Wilson at 1950 that the 3rd, 25th, and elements of the 24th Infantry divisions were under heavy attack all along the front. Lieutenant Colonel Wilson reported to the Taro Leaf G-3 at 2010 that the 5th RCT was experiencing heavy enemy artillery fire, and that he expected a major enemy assault to hit his lines soon. In anticipation of the CCF assault, he alerted the 3rd Battalion for immediate employment in support of either the 1st or 2nd Battalions.

The CCF commenced the Chinese Spring Offensive across a forty-mile front with nine armies that slammed into the UN ranks in what was subsequently determined to be the single largest Communist offensive of the entire Korean War. The Chinese troops, who had recently been re-equipped with large quantities of new Russian small arms, automatic weapons, and mortars, advanced down the ridgelines wearing their new green cotton uniforms, confident of victory.

The 20th Army, CCF Third Field Army, had the mission of destroying the 24th Infantry Division. Its three infantry divisions, the 58th, 59th, and 60th, averaged 6,000 to 7,000 men each. Most of the 20th Army's soldiers were peasants from the province of Shantung, China, who had fought the X Corps in the Chosin Reservoir Campaign the previous winter. Though the 20th Army had incurred heavy losses in bitter combat against the 1st Marine Division and Army units in North Korea, it had seen little action since then and was considered well rested.

The Taro Leaf's artillery hammered away through the late afternoon and evening at CCF troop concentrations reported moving southward. A Chinese artillery battery, for example, was pounded into submission by the 13th FAB

Tanks and infantry on the valley floor. (source: Chang)

at 1845. The 555th FAB's S-2, 1st LT Delbert A. Jurden, reported 200 casualties inflicted on a Chinese column caught in the open by the battalion's 105-mm howitzers five minutes later. When an aerial observer reported the location of six mules believed to be hauling pack howitzers at 1935, an artillery concentration was fired that killed the mules and destroyed the howitzers. In truth, however, the sheer multitude of targets overwhelmed the best efforts of the firing batteries, and masses of CCF infantry continued their relentless approach march in column formations down the ridgelines with apparent disregard for casualties.[10]

With the onset of darkness, the 20th Army hurled its assault regiments against the Taro Leaf defenders who endeavored to defend the MLR. Mao's tough peasant soldiers pressed home their assault with ruthless determination and admirable valor, accepting horrendous losses as they advanced into withering defensive fire.

On the combat team's left flank, the 19th Infantry was hit hard in the opening engagements. The tactical situation in the 5th RCT's sector remained stable, however, largely because the CCF restricted their initial activities here to infantry probes. This was about to change, for the CCF 59th Division had two regiments massing for an assault that would not be long delayed. Enemy mortar and recoilless rifle fire slammed into Able Company, inflicting many casualties, as Chinese reconnaissance patrols probed the combat team's right flank.[11]

Major Frederick Wells reported to LTC Henry H. Mauz, G-3, 24th Infantry Division, at 2100 that the MLR, though under heavy small arms fire, had yet to be struck by the Chinese.[12] Lieutenant Colonel Wilson's veteran soldiers nevertheless hunkered down in their fighting positions to await the shrill bugle calls they knew from experience heralded every major CCF assault. Twenty minutes later, the 2nd Battalion heard the barbaric musical notes, and, within seconds, the battle was joined.

Hundreds of Chinese soldiers advanced rapidly through the underbrush, and guided by the light of a full moon, struck the boundary between Easy and Fox Companies.[13] Grenades exploded, burp guns fired, rifles cracked, and men fell killed and wounded on the disputed ground. Another CCF assault troop hit the boundary shared by Fox and George Companies and achieved a shallow penetration. Captain Lamb's Fox Company restored the MLR through counterattack fifteen minutes later.[14]

A more ominous development occurred in the 19th Infantry's sector where its K Company was overrun. From their newly won positions on the western side of Hill 795, the Chinese poured fire down into L Company, 19th Infantry. The fighting spread rapidly downhill as the Chinese extended the close quarters combat duel into the 2nd Battalion, 19th Infantry's positions. Lieutenant Colonel Mauz directed the CO of the 19th Infantry at 2200 to "try and hold onto ground. 5th Infantry E and F Companies still holding their positions."[15]

Easy Company, 2nd Battalion, 5th Infantry was terribly exposed when physical contact with the 19th Infantry was lost. The men could hear the sounds of an intense firefight coming from that direction, but they could see no targets in the densely wooded, broken terrain, and thus held their fire. The Chinese probed Easy Company's lines at 2350 with infiltration detachments that attempted to draw return fire by spraying the area with burp guns and hurling grenades, but MAJ Wells promptly informed LTC Mauz that there was "nothing to worry about yet."[16]

The 2nd Platoon occupied defensive positions on the combat team's extreme left flank, on higher ground overlooking the rest of Easy Company. Most of the soldiers were experienced fighters, not a "bush shooter" in the lot, so if the M-1s started to crack, the men knew it was for real. A machine gun was sighted to fire across the platoon's defensive front, with a direction of fire to the northwest into the 19th Infantry's defensive sector. The machine gun's sector of fire had been coordinated with K Company, 19th Infantry, which had emplaced one of its machine guns to fire across its front into Easy Company's sector, but that gun was no longer firing. A BAR man was dug in next to the 2nd Platoon's machine gun, to cover this field of fire if the Browning was knocked out, jammed, or had to change barrels. The best grenade throwers were given a box of grenades each, and told to cover the dead space in front of the platoon's automatic weapons.

The platoon sergeant, SFC E. C. Lundquist,

A 105-mm battery replies. (source: Arlen Russell)

shared a foxhole with the platoon leader, 2nd LT Henry Lang, and the FO, 1st LT Roy T. Nakashima, from B Battery, 555th FAB. Of the three men, SFC Lundquist did not have to be there that night. He had passed up a rare opportunity to enjoy a well-deserved R&R in Japan when it appeared the Chinese were planning to attack. No one was going to accuse SFC Lundquist of "flaking-off."[17]

First Lieutenant Roy T. Nakashima, an ROTC graduate from the University of Hawaii, was probably the most experienced FO still on his feet from the original group of Triple Nickel artillerymen to deploy to Korea. He joined the 555th FAB just before the combat team deployed from Schofield Barracks. "He always had a smile on his face, a real positive officer," recalled another FO, 1st LT Earl Law.[18] "He was a well liked man," said PFC Albert F.

Chinese mortar and artillery fire impacting near the 2nd Tank Platoon. Troops on right take cover under a 1/4-ton truck. (source: Ed Crockett)

Semasko, a cannoneer in B Battery, 555th FAB. "Everyone in the 5th RCT knew that man. I never heard anything but good about him. He was one heck of a guy."[19]

One error the Triple Nickel repeated time and again was its propensity to leave its FOs on this hazardous duty too long. Few FOs, or their radio operators, survived combat tours in Korea without being wounded. Many were killed. Of the original nine FOs who deployed to Korea with the 555th FAB, on the night of 22 April only two were left.[20]

Lieutenant Nakashima had called in too many fire missions to count since that day on Fox Hill near Chindong-ni when an artillery liaison aircraft had dropped a crate of ammunition on top of his radio. He should have been replaced much earlier and given a break in Headquarters Battery or on B Battery's gun line. Not one to complain, LT Nakashima continued to climb into the mountains with the infantry, an SCR-300 strapped to his back, binoculars around his throat, a map case over his shoulder, and .45-caliber pistol holstered on his hip. He carried an 8-mm movie camera in his pack, loaned to him by Warrant Officer Sal Bosco, so he could take some movies of the fighting. Before LT McKinley Buckner's death, Warrant Officer Bosco, LT Law, and LT Nakashima had often shared a bottle of Canadian Club with LT Buckner on rare occasions when off the line. Now LT Buckner was dead, and LT Nakashima had taken his friend's place in the mountains with Easy Company.[21] Replacement officers were available to take LT Nakashima's FO job, yet when no one volunteered to assume this hazardous duty, he never complained, knowing that others declined to share the risks.

Lieutenant Nakashima was crouched in the foxhole, showing SFC Lundquist a technique of using the binoculars in low ambient light conditions, when a handful of survivors from K Company, 19th Infantry, came running through the 2nd Platoon's positions. These soldiers shouted that the Chinese were behind them and that their company had been overrun. When SFC Lundquist relayed this information to the company CP over the landline, it was confirmed. Moreover, he was informed that the Chinese had enveloped the rear of the company. The 60-mm Mortar section was already engaged in a hand-to-hand struggle for control of its gun pits. At 0020 MAJ Wells reported to LTC Mauz that Easy Company was being struck from the rear.[22] Five minutes later, the Chinese slammed into Easy Company from three sides.

Easy Company was hit hard by the advance guard of a CCF regiment. The company stood its ground, killing scores of Chinese with their rifles, BARs and machine guns. In spite of appalling casualties, the Chinese pressed home their assault, advancing through a hellish inferno of grazing fire, acrid smoke, and thunderous explosions. And through it all, men from Jinan and Weifang grappled with soldiers from Kona and Pittsburgh, killing one another at close range as parachute flares whistled eerily overhead.

After an hour of steady fighting, the MLR began to buckle under the enemy's remorseless pressure. Easy Company's tactical situation was perilous, for at 0130, the CO of the 3rd Battalion, 19th Infantry reported to G-3, 24th Infantry Division, that: "a large number of enemy pouring through gap on Hill 795 in column of twos."[23]

Lieutenant Nakashima was calling for fires and passing the locations of other units, that for whatever reason could not contact higher headquarters over the radio net, when his last radio transmission was heard at 0145.[24] Sergeant First Class Lundquist was speaking on the field phone to Easy Company's CP when a shell exploded immediately in front of his foxhole. Lieutenant Nakashima bore the brunt of the blast, and in doing so, saved SFC Lundquist's and Lt Lang's lives. The platoon leader was knocked senseless to the bottom of the hole. Lieutenant Nakashima was thrown lifeless against the side of the foxhole, his radio and the phone link to company blown apart.

Sergeant First Class Lundquist recovered his senses as he dug himself out of a pile of debris. To his horror, he discovered that his uniform was saturated with LT Nakashima's blood. Rifle fire was crackling up and down the platoon's defensive line when he attempted to locate the field phone in the darkness. The landline no longer existed, so he ran to the company CP to report his platoon's situation. The company commander told him to return to his unit, set-up an all round defense, and cover the withdrawal of the main body down the hill. Lieutenant Colonel Wilson had ordered the 2nd Battalion to withdraw from the MLR when it became apparent that the CCF had enveloped the combat team's left flank in great strength.[25] It would take time to conduct an organized, fighting withdrawal in the darkness, and Easy Company's 2nd Platoon was ordered to buy that time. When the 2nd Platoon ran out of machine gun ammunition, it was to withdraw in small groups through the Chinese and link up with the company. The platoon sergeant ran back to his foxhole and passed the CO's orders on to LT Lang, who had recovered from the blast.

Shortly thereafter, the 2nd Platoon was hit extremely hard — front, flanks and rear. Rifles cracked, machine guns roared, and BARs hammered out bursts of fire, as the Chinese closed to within grenade range of the platoon's foxholes. Burp gunners dueled with riflemen at point-blank range, as the crump of grenade explosions resounded through the night. When ammunition for the automatic weapons was expended, LT Lang and SFC Lundquist started to order small groups of men to breakout.

Private Hugh N. Sommer, Jr., served in the last 2nd Platoon rifle squad to disengage. While attempting to reach a rally point, Private Sommer walked point for his squad. He mistook an enemy soldier silhouetted to his front for an American. Private Sommer called out that he was bringing his squad through and received an affirmative reply in English. As Private Sommer's squad approached, the Chinese soldier hurled several grenades in rapid succession. Private Sommer retrieved a couple of these grenades and hurled them away from his comrades before they exploded. He was in the process of throwing yet another grenade when it exploded in his hands and killed the valiant soldier. The survivors, who finally killed the CCF grenadier, later reported Private Sommer's heroism to their superiors. The fallen soldier was awarded the Distinguished Service Cross, posthumously.[26]

Sergeant First Class Lundquist lost contact with LT Lang in the darkness as they were making one last tour of the lines to determine if everyone had left. Numerous bodies, mostly Chinese, lay sprawled on the ground as SFC Lundquist moved through his platoon's perimeter. Once assured that he was the only one remaining in the position, SFC Lundquist attempted to evade capture going down the hill. He almost made it. A CCF patrol captured him and he spent the next twenty-nine months in the living hell of a Chinese Prisoner of War camp.[27] The Chinese intercepted and captured LT Lang, too.[28]

Fox Company gave a good account of itself throughout the bitterly contested night as the Chinese pressed hard against its lines. When CAPT Lamb received the order to withdraw, he had reason to believe the CCF already occupied part of the valley below. Furthermore, CAPT Lamb knew that his field first sergeant was en route to his position with a team of bearers who carried a resupply of ammunition, but he had no means to warn them that the company was pulling out.[29]

Sergeant First Class James W. Hart, recently promoted and elevated to the position of Fox Company's field first sergeant, was sitting in the 2nd Battalion CP earlier that afternoon when he heard that the Chinese would prob-

L to R: SGT Oliver Waiau, Hilo, Hawaii; SFC David Kauanui, Nanakuli, Hawaii; and PFC Miles Adair, Leon, Iowa, set up a machine gun. (source: Chang)

Four Easy Company soldiers on an M-46 Patton. L to R: SGT Leatherman, French, Anderson, and SFC E.C. Lundquist sitting on the gun tube. (source: Horace Anderson)

ably commence a major offensive that night. He knew his company would require a resupply of ammunition, so he loaded up a jeep and trailer and drove off to the front in the late afternoon, accompanied with a group of Chiggy bearers and soldiers. When they finally reached the MLR around 1900, SFC Hart led the small, intrepid group of soldiers and civilian laborers up the ridgeline, carrying the ammunition. Regrettably, the men found themselves in front of George Company, which promptly took them under fire. So did the Chinese. Caught in a crossfire, the detachment split-up. One group with most of the Chiggy bearers managed to make its way to friendly lines, while a smaller group, led by SFC Hart, withdrew down a finger with the Chinese in pursuit.[30]

5th RCT infantrymen. (sources: NA/Chang)

Six soldiers accompanied SFC Hart down the finger, including SGT Oliver Waiau, PFC Gadlin, PFC Gerald M. Flowers, and PFC Jesse Bingham. A couple of Chiggy bearers followed. As the Chinese closed in, SFC Hart chose a defensible piece of ground to make a stand. A platoon of Chinese infantry, equipped with burp guns, attempted to overrun the detachment in one decisive rush, but was repulsed with heavy losses. A second attempt to overrun the detachment failed with even heavier Chinese losses. PFC Gadlin, a recent replacement from Liberal, Kansas, went through two bandoleers of ammunition, 128 rounds, in the two Chinese assaults. The expert shot killed numerous Chinese with accurate, point-blank rifle fire under the light of a full moon.[31]

Sergeant First Class Hart used an SCR-300 radio to keep abreast of the battle's progress. Just as SFC Hart heard an FO say over the radio that he had lost an adjusting round, the shell exploded nearby, killing a large number of Chinese who were attempting to rush the small hornet's nest for the third time. Not one to waste an opportunity, SFC Hart butted into the radio traffic. He said, "'I got it, and I'd sure like a bunch more.' And so they had a battery fire for us that wiped out all the Chinese."[32]

The Chinese reorganized their shattered assault unit while SFC Hart attempted to contact help without success over the radio. At about 0200 SFC Hart told his men they would have to fight their way through to the MLR. The soldiers came under intense fire as soon as they moved out. In short order most of the unarmed Chiggy bearers were killed. Sergeant First Class Hart led the survivors higher into the mountains with the Chinese close behind. Dawn found the men caught far behind enemy lines.

Meanwhile, across the valley, the ROK 6th Division lived up to its poor reputation. It quickly collapsed without offering effective resistance, a disgrace that left the 5th RCT's right flank wide-open to assault. The wholesale flight of the ROKs was first reported at 0250 when the 5th Infantry's I&R Platoon collared forty stragglers from the ROK 19th Infantry on the valley floor. How these men managed to run so far, so fast, over the incredibly rough terrain into the combat team's sector boggles the imagination.[33]

Able Company had deployed its three rifle platoons in an inverted "T" across the top of a razor-sharp ridgeline on the combat team's right flank. Chinese mortar fire commenced pounding A Company at 2147, as machine gun tracers streaked overhead. Sergeant Kenny Freedman, the 81-mm FO, attempted to suppress the enemy automatic weapons fire, but the roar of incoming American mortar and artillery explosions brought no discernable relief.[34]

Shortly after midnight, the company commander, CAPT Horace W. West, from Nazareth, Pennsylvania, reported to battalion that he thought he could hold his ground in spite of heavy casualties. A platoon from the adjacent Charlie Company reinforced Able Company at 0200. About this time, 1st LT Charles E. Bannon led elements of Charlies Company in a bold counterattack that destroyed an enemy penetration. For this action he was awarded a Distinguished Service Cross. An hour later, two Chinese companies slammed into Able Company's forward most rifle platoon, which was virtually destroyed in furious close combat. A handful of survivors escaped death or capture. Two 75-mm recoilless rifle crews were also overrun about this time, the crews killed or captured. Cries went out for 4.2-inch mortar support, but the 1st Battalion's attached heavy mortar platoon had come under attack from a Chinese patrol farther down in the valley and no fires were forthcoming from this unit.[35]

Captain West gathered the few survivors he could find in the darkness and prepared to lead them off the ridge. His radio operator's SCR-300 was smashed by a shell fragment, which had left the shaken lad otherwise unscratched. Captain West's command group evaded the Chinese who swarmed around them in the darkness. On the valley floor they found more survivors from Able and Charlie Companies. Captain West led these men through groups of roving Chinese infantry, and after a har-

Awaiting the order to move out. (source: Chang)

rowing trek that included an occasional strafing run by overzealous FEAF pilots, the battered remnants of Able Company finally reached friendly lines. One of those wounded in the strafing was PFC James Baumgarner, a rifleman serving in Able Company, who survived the war to earn accolades in the hearts of the American people as James Garner, a most talented Hollywood movie star.[36]

Following the collapse of the ROK 6th Division on the combat team's right flank, and the breakthrough along the boundary shared with the 19th Infantry on the left, the 5th RCT was in danger of being caught in a double envelopment. The CCF thrusts along both ridgelines had obviously been undertaken to avoid the armor concentrated on the valley floor. By midnight, it was clear to LTC Wilson that the danger of a major enemy assault through the valley had passed. The 3rd Battalion's rifle companies were urgently required to shore up the combat team's crumbling flanks, and a decision was therefore made to commit the regimental reserve.

Love Company, CAPT Barnados commanding, formed into a column at the base of the western ridgeline, strong backs cruelly bent under an oppressive load of weapons, ammunition, water, rations and equipment. Officers and NCOs issued crisp orders to the gathered men, the steamy fog from their collective breaths lingering briefly in the frigid April night's air. At 0110 the long column of soldiers moved out in single file to join the rifle platoon already on Hill 752. The column snaked its way up the mountain, climbing slowly in the darkness to the heights above, where the men would be called upon to fight and kill, and if need be, to die. The climb was long and hard, a steep, exhausting and torturous path on which men occasionally slipped and fell, with a clatter and crash of weapons and equipment, silently cursing the endless war and their role in it.

The soldiers understood the gravity of the situation, for they knew that the combat team's left flank was exposed. The Chinese were good, that they granted. Yet the soldiers believed in themselves and their leaders, and they knew the combat team was a match for the Communists. And so they climbed the mountain in the darkness, weapons ready, bayonets fixed, carrying a full issue of grenades. Extra bandoleers of ammunition swayed across their chests, draped over the shoulders of teenage youths, lads aged and wizened far beyond their years, who climbed steadily into the unknown, sweating from physical exertion in the cold.

At the suggestion of LTC Mauz, LTC Wilson committed King Company shortly after Love Company moved out, its mission to occupy a blocking position on the western ridgeline, south of Love Company, to prevent the CCF from enveloping the combat team from the west and overrunning the rear area. At 0240 Item Company, minus the one platoon already positioned on the eastern flank, was ordered to establish a blocking position south of Able Company in order to prevent the CCF from enveloping and destroying that outfit. By 0300, all of the 3rd Battalion was in motion, climbing steadily into the mountains to fight the Chinese.

Daybreak found a bruised and battered combat team defending its ground, the defiant rifle companies holding onto part of the original MLR after killing a large number of Chinese. Contact with Easy Company had been restored, but that unit had lost a platoon's worth of soldiers in the swirling close combat struggle that had raged throughout the night. The CCF engaged Love Company in a fierce firefight as the soldiers climbed the steep ridge under heavy fire. King Company reached the top of the ridgeline unopposed and, by 0600, it had advanced northward along the crest and was heavily engaged with the Chinese. Through the skillful employment of air strikes and artillery fire, these two companies blocked the CCF from advancing south along the ridge and down into the valley floor. The situation on the right flank, where Able Company had been badly mauled, was dangerous, but Item Company's steady presence had prevented it from reaching critical mass.

Stiff fighting continued on both ridgelines until 0915, when the 24th Infantry Division ordered the 5th RCT to withdraw through the 21st Infantry, division reserve, and occupy an assembly area in the rear. King Company covered the combat team's withdrawal from a commanding height on the western ridgeline, holding the Chinese at bay with supporting arms.

Lieutenant Randall Beirne recalled, "This was one of the few times in the war when we could see the Chinese attacking in daylight. I even took pictures of the engagement, but of the 31 rolls of film I took in the war, this was the only one lost."[37]

Sergeant James Shaw was on the SCR-300 radio calling in fires in support of King Company.

"We were scared to death," he said. "But we fired off so much artillery that you couldn't believe it that day. And when they finally told us we could withdraw, we got out of there fast."[38]

In the vicinity of Hill 1046, elements from Able, Item, and Charlie Companies fought a desperate, confusing, close range firefight with a large CCF combat patrol during a critical phase of the disengagement. Casualties were heavy on both sides. Private First Class Darrel D. Council, a machine gunner in Dog Company, remained at his machine gun to cover the withdrawal. He steadfastly manned his weapon alone, pouring fire into the attacking masses of Chinese until his position was overrun. He was subsequently awarded the Distinguished Service Cross.[39] One platoon from Item Company, led by 1st LT William P. Keenan, became separated during this engagement and, through an error in navigation, drifted off onto a ridgeline occupied in force by the Chinese.

Lieutenant Keenan had joined Item Company the previous January. On the morning of 31 January, after the 2nd Battalion had crossed the LD to seize Hill 256, LT Keenan had heard a strange wailing sound through the thick morning fog. After a moment's hesitation, LT Keenan asked Item's artillery FO, 1st LT Earl Law, "Do you hear those roosters crowing?" Lieutenant Law replied, "Roosters Hell, those are Chinese bugles!"[40]

During several months of continuous combat operations, LT Keenan had developed a reputation as a capable and courageous platoon leader. On the morning of 23 April, the roosters were crowing in spades. Bugle calls announced the Chinese were gaining on the soldiers as bursts of automatic weapons fire snapped at their heels. In the midst of a short, bitter, engagement, LT Keenan was hit by burp gun fire. Sergeant Grey, the platoon sergeant, detailed a couple of soldiers to carry the lieutenant as the platoon attempted to break contact. Several men were killed or wounded in the running gun battle as the Chinese closed on the outnumbered platoon, with bugles blaring, like a pack of hounds. Sergeant Grey transmitted a frantic radio message asking for assistance.[41] The 5th RCT CP heard the radio transmission and organized a task force to rescue the embattled platoon.

Sergeant James Shaw overheard the unfolding drama on the tactical radio net. The FO recalled, "We heard the aerial observer say, 'Oh my God! I don't think they are going to get down that mountain soon enough. The Chinamen are coming around and are going to flank 'em and get 'em.' And sure enough the Chinese did. The platoon from Item couldn't get down fast enough. I don't know how many of those guys ever got out of that mess. It was terrible. We could hear them on the radio, but we couldn't do anything for them because they were too far away. The aerial observer called in some artillery fire but I don't know if it ever did any good."[42]

Lieutenant Colonel Wilson scraped together a miniature task force consisting of a platoon of tanks and infantry, and A Battery, 555th FAB, to rescue LT Keenan's platoon. First Lieutenant Frank Athanason, newly elevated to command A Battery, participated in this action. Lieutenant Colonel Clarence Stuart led the task force. Major Frederick A. Wells, the newly appointed regimental S-3, and MAJ Perry Graves, the S-3 of the 555th FAB, accompanied A Battery.

The top-heavy task force traveled three miles heading due north until it reached an area that had a very narrow cut in the road.[43] At the northern end of the cut, a fast flowing stream bisected the road. A shallow ford led to a confined valley on the far side. Against LT Athanason's wishes, LTC Stuart directed A Battery to ford the river and establish firing positions in the valley.

The beautiful sunny day afforded excellent visibility for 800-900 yards across the clearing to the north where a tree-covered ridgeline blocked the view. At its widest point the valley was 800 yards across. Able Battery went into position, with its six 105-mm howitzers on line, facing north. A prime mover was positioned immediately behind each howitzer, ready to hook up and move out on order. One M16 "Quad 50" was positioned on each flank, the wicked-looking machine gun barrels parallel to the ground, ready to open fire instantly.

A 57-mm Recoilless Team in action. (source: NA)

James Hart immediately following his release from captivity. (source: James Hart)

Lieutenant Colonel Stuart led the rest of the Task Force in his jeep and was soon lost to view in the tree line to the direct front of the guns. Every so often the plan called for LTC Stuart to radio LT Athanason and let him know he was OK. After hearing a few reassuring messages, the battery lost radio contact with LTC Stuart. When LT Athanason requested permission from MAJ Graves to retrograde his non-essential vehicles, the request was denied. Soon enough, a tank was seen barreling down the road, returning the way it had come. The battery commander tried to stop the tank, but it raced past, headed for the rear. A jeep roared down the road in trace of the tank and stopped briefly at the battery position. Out jumped MAJ Wells, who told LT Athanason, "You better get the hell out of here now! They were ambushed up there and your battalion commander is dead!"[44]

Major Wells sped off in his jeep, leaving A Battery shaking their heads and trying to make sense of a dangerous situation. Lieutenant Athanason informed MAJ Graves that he was sending his first sergeant with all the battery's non-essential vehicles to the rear, and this was done. As the last of these vehicles crossed the river, A Battery started taking small arms fire from the north. Shortly thereafter, literally hundreds of densely packed CCF infantry emerged from the tree line, advancing across the open field. Lieutenant Athanason directed his "Quad 50s" to open up, and within seconds the heavy machine guns were hammering away, cutting the Chinese down. All six howitzers joined in seconds later, slamming high explosive shells down range that ricocheted off the ground and exploded over the heads of the Chinese with fearful execution.

Lieutenant Athanason surveyed the carnage through his binoculars and noticed in the midst of this hellish scene an American soldier carrying a helmet under his arm who was running as fast as he could just a few hundred paces ahead of the Chinese. Closer examination revealed that this intrepid soldier was none other than LTC Stuart, who appeared very much alive, and running as fast as his forty-year-old legs could carry him. The battery commander ran from gun-to-gun to ensure they did not target the battalion commander in the heat of the action. As LTC Stuart closed on A Battery, LT Athanason started displacing his guns, one at a time, getting them out of the clearing and across the river, heading south to rejoin the rest of the combat team.

Unfortunately, when it came time to hook up the last howitzer to its prime mover, someone tried to close the trails without pulling the trail pin and jammed the trails in place. Seeing as how it would be impossible to fix the problem before the Chinese overran the position, LT Athanason directed the gun crew to remove the breech block, abandon the gun, and leave. He remained behind with his jeep and one "Quad 50" until LTC Stuart reached him. Chinese small arms fire was chewing up dirt around the two vehicles when an out-of-breath LTC Stuart reached the battery commander's jeep. By this time, the Chinese were so close to the "Quad 50" that it could no longer depress its barrels far enough to hit them. Nevertheless, A Battery managed to get out of this mess having lost one gun and one soldier wounded in action.

After LT Athanason's jeep caught up with the rest of his battery about a mile down the road, LTC Stuart directed him to stop and assemble the men. Expecting to hear words of praise from their commander, the battery personnel were startled to hear LTC Stuart say, "I want to apologize for running from the enemy. I think if we had stayed there we could have held them."[45] No one believed him and saying it did nothing to improve morale.

Lieutenant Colonel Wilson remained forward of the reconstituted MLR with his command group and seven tanks trying to rescue LT Keenan's platoon. The 1st and 2nd Battalions had already reached their assembly area far to the rear, and the 3rd Battalion was closing, when the Commanding General of 24th Infantry Division, Major General Blackshear M. Bryan, gave LTC Wilson a direct order at 1815 to return to friendly lines.[46] At 1955, LT Cochrane notified G-3, 24th Infantry Division, from the 5th RCT CP that LT Keenan's platoon was going to try to infiltrate down the valley that night along the MSR to safety. An airdrop of food and ammunition for the platoon was requested.

Lieutenant Keenan was hurt, having lost much blood from multiple bullet wounds, and he was slowing down his men. As night fell, LT Keenan ordered SGT Grey to leave him and lead the handful of survivors to safety. It was their only chance, LT Keenan implored, but SGT Grey refused to abandon his platoon leader. Lieutenant Keenan threatened SGT Grey with a courts martial if he refused a direct order. Finally, after a brief and heated exchange, SGT Grey shook hands with his lieutenant and, with tears in his eyes, he led the remnants of their platoon back to friendly lines.[47]

Lieutenant Keenan miraculously survived his wounds. The Chinese captured him four days later, and he suffered through twenty-nine months of harsh imprisonment before his release from captivity at the end of the war.[48]

While the drama of LT Keenan's platoon was reaching its climax, cut off soldiers from other elements of the combat team were attempting to reach the MLR. Sergeant First Class James Hart had spent a nerve wracking day hiding in the bushes with two other soldiers in the middle of a large Chinese bivouac. At dusk on 23 April, SFC Hart's men field stripped their weapons and buried the pieces so the Chinese could not use them if the soldiers were captured. After discarding their distinctive helmets, the detachment headed south, stepping over sleeping Chinese lying in the field.

"We hadn't gone very far when we ran into a guard on one of the trails," recalled SFC Hart. "His eyes got big, and I'm sure mine did too. I didn't know if I should jump him or just walk past him. I decided to walk past him, and, sure enough, all three of us got past."[49]

When the sentry shouted a belated alarm, the three soldiers ran into the valley to evade pursuit. A CCF patrol followed them to the MSR where the men split up to evade capture. Sergeant First Class Hart almost jumped into a foxhole occupied by a CCF infantryman.

James Hart being awarded the Silver Star, February 1954. (source: James Hart)

He took cover in an adjacent foxhole instead. When he looked over the rim, he saw the Chinese soldier in the first hole smiling at him. Not wanting to press his luck, SFC Hart left his foxhole a few moments later and boldly joined the end of a Chinese column marching southward along the road.

During the march, the other two American soldiers joined SFC Hart in the column. After marching a couple of miles down the road, the CCF column took a short break. The three men separated in the darkness. Shortly thereafter, SFC Hart was captured. After twenty-nine nightmarish months in Chinese captivity, SFC Hart returned to friendly lines. When he reached the United States, the modest soldier discovered that CAPT Robert Lamb had recommended him for the Silver Star.

"My greatest regret was in the capture of my First Sergeant," explained CAPT Lamb. "I knew during our service together that he was one of the absolutely first class soldiers one could know. My conversations and correspondence with him since then have confirmed that judgment."[50]

CHAPTER TWENTY-EIGHT

Death Valley

Those who wage war in the mountains should never pass through defiles without first making themselves masters of the heights.
Maurice de Saxe, Mes Reveries, Vol. XXII

As the 5th Infantry awaited orders near Ukkalgye in division reserve, LTC Wilson knew it was only a matter of time before the combat team assumed a rearguard mission to cover the withdrawal of the Taro Leaf from the deteriorating operational situation on the MLR. With this grim thought in mind, the 1st and 2nd Battalions dispatched patrols to the north on 24 April to reconnoiter possible blocking positions. The 3rd Battalion dug in on high ground to the east of Ukkalgye, to protect the eastern flank of the MSR from Chinese units moving south through the shattered ROK 6th Division's sector.

All through 24 April, the Triple Nickel hammered the CCF in support of the hard-pressed 19th and 21st infantry regiments holding the MLR. As Chinese pressure intensified on the Taro Leaf's defenders, strong CCF detachments marched unopposed on their right flank through the void left by the disintegration of the ROK 6th Division.

Shortly before midnight, on 24 April, the Eighth Army concluded that it was no longer capable of expelling the CCF penetrations through local counterattack. With the collapse of the ROK 6th Division, there existed a 13,000-meter gap between the right flank of the 24th Infantry Division and the left flank of the nearest friendly unit, the 1st Marine Division. The left flank of the Taro Leaf was threatened, too, where the Chinese had achieved a penetration on the boundary shared with the 25th Infantry Division. With its reserves exhausted, the Eighth Army, now commanded by General James A. Van Fleet, reluctantly ordered a withdrawal to Line Lincoln, a few miles north of Seoul.

The Taro Leaf's withdrawal plan called for the 19th and 21st infantry regiments to pass through the 5th RCT's lines, at which time LTC Wilson's command would assumed the mission of divisional rearguard. Of the combat team's three maneuver battalions, the 3rd Battalion continued to occupy a hilltop blocking position on the 5th RCT's eastern flank. The 2nd Battalion, with Tank Company and D Company, 6th Tank Battalion attached, moved north a short distance to block a Chinese advance down the valley floor.[1] When the 1st Battalion moved out at 0300 to occupy its blocking position, a hilltop behind the 19th Infantry on the western side of the MSR, strong CCF combat patrols were known to be roving behind the MLR.

During the 1st Battalion's ascent of the steep Gold Mine Trail, a strong force of Chinese infantry ambushed the point elements of Able and Charlie Companies near daybreak in a kill zone 600 yards short of their objective. Both sides suffered heavy casualties in the ensuing engagement, which prevented 1st Battalion from reaching its blocking position. However, Major Claude Baker's hard-fighting infantry repulsed repeated Chinese attempts to descend to the valley floor which, if successful, would have cut the MSR behind the 19th Infantry.

Triple Nickel gun crews fired volley after volley in support of the 1st Battalion's infantry and, by late morning, ammunition for the 105-mm howitzers was low. The regimental Tactical Air Controller, 2nd LT Walter Fay, USAF, who had arrived in Korea three days earlier, directed air strikes on CCF units moving through the hills. Without near continuous artillery support, and periodic CAS, the CCF would have overrun the 1st Battalion.[2]

The 19th and 21st infantry regiments disengaged from the MLR under heavy pressure. Both units completed a passage of lines through the 5th RCT at approximately 1100 and withdrew to the new MLR. Once the new MLR was occupied, the 24th Infantry Division intended for the 5th RCT to withdraw through it in daylight and take up position in divisional reserve.

Lieutenant Colonel Wilson ordered the 2nd Battalion, reinforced with both tank companies, to serve as rearguard. The 3rd Battalion would serve as advance guard when it displaced on order for an assembly area located behind the new MLR. The 1st Battalion and the 555th FAB would follow the 3rd Battalion, the infantry riding out on the artillery prime movers. Once the artillery was on the road and heading south to the assembly area, the rearguard would move out and follow.

This simple plan fell apart before it could be implemented. First, the combat team violated its own standard operating procedures when it failed to designate intermediate objectives for the advance guard to occupy on key terrain features overlooking the route of withdrawal. Second, and of critical importance, the 8th Ranger Company (Airborne), attached to the 21st Infantry, was unable to disengage from the MLR as planned. Strong elements of the CCF 60th Division barred the withdrawal of the 8th Rangers, now encircled and engaged in heavy fighting. The Taro Leaf handed off a problem when it attached the 8th Rangers to the 5th RCT and instructed LTC Wilson to extradite them from their predicament.

The 8th Ranger Company was an old idea fighting a new war. The Rangers, who had performed with distinction in World War II, were discarded at the close of hostilities. When the NKPA invaded South Korea, the need for high-quality infantry trained to execute special missions was belatedly recognized and the Rangers were quickly resurrected. By April 1951, a company of Rangers had been attached to each of the Army's infantry divisions fighting in Korea. Their mission, to conduct raids and other missions of operational importance to senior commanders, was quickly forgotten by manpower-starved divisional commanders in the maelstrom of Korea.[3]

The 8th Ranger Company had recently joined the 24th Infantry Division after receiving intensive training in the States. Initially, the Taro Leaf employed the 8th Rangers in a series of long range patrols behind enemy lines, and it was in the course of one of these patrols that the jaunty Rangers first made their mark. On the night of 15 April, a patrol from its 3rd Ranger Platoon had seriously mauled a larger CCF unit, killing an estimated seventy Chinese, "fifty of which were counted dead." The Rangers lost two KIA and three WIA in this fierce action.[4]

Following the collapse of the ROK 6th Division, the 24th Infantry Division committed the 8th Rangers to screen the Taro Leaf's right flank from atop Hill 1010. The 8th Rangers reported CCF troop movements and brought observed artillery fire missions to bear on the enemy. By the evening of 24 April, the CCF had encircled the Rangers and the men knew they would have to fight their way out to reach the safety of friendly lines. At 0425 the following morning, the G-3, 24th Infantry Division, directed the S-3, 21st Infantry, to "Move Rangers at first light back to the vicinity of 2nd Battalion, 21st Infantry and then down the ridge to join 3rd Battalion, 5th Infantry. Attached to 5th Infantry on arrival."[5] The Rangers would have to move fast because the entire 21st Infantry was under orders to withdraw later that morning through the 5th RCT to form a new defensive line.

Daybreak, 0541, found the Rangers moving out under fire, heading southwest down a steep and narrow ridgeline. In places the men had to move and fight in single file. The fighting reached an epic level of ferocity as the Rangers struggled to overrun Hill 628, a heavily defended piece of key terrain that barred their path. Captain James A. Herbert, the company commander, was badly wounded in the neck and shoulders. He continued to direct the combat actions of his Rangers even as he stanched the flow of blood by sticking his fingers deep inside the holes in his flesh. Shortly before 0900, the Rangers overran the crest in furious close combat. The bodies of dead and wounded Rangers lay sprawled on the disputed ground, among an even larger number of dead Chinese. Almost immediately, the Rangers repulsed the first of a series of resolute CCF counterattacks. No quarter was asked or given.[6]

Meanwhile, at 0650, the Taro Leaf attached the 8th Rangers to the 5th RCT even though the Rangers had yet to reach the 2nd Battalion, 21st Infantry, much less LTC Wilson's own 3rd Battalion.[7] Regrettably, LTC Wilson was not in direct radio communications with the Rangers, and his CP had to rely on the 2nd Battalion, 21st Infantry to relay messages.

Tragically, the 3rd Battalion, 5th RCT was in radio communications with "Old Rose," the call sign for the 8th Ranger Company. The signalers had never heard of "Old Rose" and discontinued the connection. They probably believed that Old Rose's requests for assistance were a Communist ruse designed to sucker the Americans into a trap. That no one checked the Signal Operating Instructions to confirm the identity of Old Rose compounded the tragedy.

Major Frederick Wells, the combat team's S-3, sent the 2nd Battalion, 21st Infantry the following message at 0910: "Send message to Ranger Company. Get out best way possible."[8] He clearly did not believe the 5th Infantry was in a position to extradite the Rangers. Nevertheless, the 5th RCT had to try, and he issued the appropriate orders to the 3rd Battalion.

The 3rd Battalion was coming under increasingly heavy enemy pressure when it was informed of the 8th Ranger's plight. Two platoons from Love Company crossed the LD at 0935 in an attempt to reach the Rangers. Intense CCF small arms fire stalled the attack, however, and the platoons were recalled.[9] Meanwhile, the Rangers remained locked in combat on Hill 628, 2,500 impossible yards from friendly lines.[10]

The 5th RCT Command Report for April 1951 states that LTC Wilson dispatched elements of B Company, 6th Tank Battalion at 0600 to link-up with the Rangers.[11] The unit and time are probably both in error. As previously discussed, D Company, and not B Company, 6th Tank Battalion, was the outfit attached to the 5th RCT on 25 April.[12] Due to incessant combat operations and a high personnel turnover, the command report for April 1951 was actually written in late June.[13] By then, several key personnel who participated in this engagement had either transferred or rotated home. Others had been evacuated for wounds. The regimental S-3, as we shall see, had been killed in action. It is doubtful that LTC Wilson dispatched D Company before the Taro Leaf attached the Rangers to his command. One suspects that D Company received its orders to rescue the Rangers when it became apparent that Love Company's attack was not going to succeed. In any event, sometime that morning a platoon of the large, garishly painted Patton tanks, with bizarre tiger faces and claws decorating their frontal armor, rumbled off to the north to rescue the Rangers.

Oddly enough, the first tanks to reach the Rangers were from the 3rd Platoon, C Company, 6th Tank Battalion, which had been supporting the 21st Infantry until approximately 1100 when the latter withdrew from the MLR. The tankers probably knew of the 8th Ranger Company's plight from a group of five wounded Rangers who had fought their way down the slope of Hill 628 to the 21st Infantry.[14] Yet it was not until 1105 that the tanks established radio contact with the Rangers.

At 1155, the 5th RCT Command Report claims that B Company's (actually D Company's) Patton tanks succeeded in reaching sixty-five mostly wounded Rangers, who had broken out of the encirclement. No mention is made of the 3rd Platoon, C Company, 6th Tank Battalion's participation. Two Rangers informed the tankers that they had hidden a wounded officer they could not physically move earlier in the day. In response, a small task force moved out to recover the missing Ranger officer. This action, however noble, took precious time.[15]

Lieutenant Colonel Wilson's near total tactical fixation on the various rescue attempts to free the entrapped Rangers is understandable in that he deeply cared for his soldiers. Moreover, he had been ordered to execute this unanticipated mission by the 24th Infantry Division. Yet when the 3rd Battalion withdrew from its blocking position in accordance with LTC Wilson's orders at 1210, the 5th RCT was left in a dangerously exposed position. Following the 3rd Battalion's disengagement, there remained no friendly unit in position to screen the combat team's elongated and wide-open eastern flank.

The 3rd Battalion rode out on trucks, heading south along the MSR, with most of Headquarters

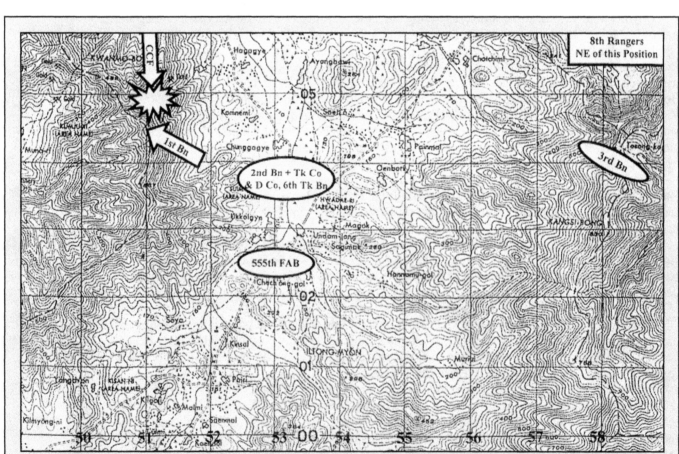

DEATH VALLEY, 0001-0700, 25 APRIL 1951. *The 19th and 21st Infantry Regiments are fighting several kilometers to the north of the 5th RCT, which is in division reserve. Elements of the 555th FAB may have been north of the position depicted on this map, supporting the Taro Leaf's hard-pressed infantry on the MLR. The lead elements of the 1st Battalion are ambushed at daybreak as they ascend the Gold Mine Trail. The 8th Ranger Company (Airborne) has commenced its breakout, but it is still a few thousand meters northeast of the 3rd Battalion's blocking position. The CCF is marching south on the 3rd Battalion's right flank through the void left when the ROK 6th Division collapsed on 22-23 April.*

and Headquarters Company, 5th Infantry, following in trace. The latter included a large portion of the combat team's tactical CP. At 1410, the column reached the combat team's assembly area in the vicinity of Sopa after passing through the new MLR. No effective enemy resistance was encountered during the withdrawal. When the truck-mounted soldiers witnessed a handful of mortar shells impact near the road as the convoy approached a narrow pass in the vicinity of Pisi-gol, they casually assumed the 19th Infantry was registering its mortars. Actually elements of the CCF 60th Division had fired the mortars from the high ground that dominated both sides of the pass. As the last of the trucks cleared the pass, CCF infantry were feverishly digging in and sighting heavy weapons to oppose the passage of the next convoy to use that road.[16]

Lieutenant Colonel Wilson failed to recognize that elements of the CCF 60th Division had enveloped his right flank. Strangely, the combat team's intelligence officer later claimed, "There was no evidence which would point to this maneuver."[17] The evidence was apparent, yet the 5th RCT's senior leadership did not see what their troops saw so clearly as the long morning turned into afternoon.

First Lieutenant Ed Crockett's 2nd Tank Platoon occupied a blocking position that day with the 2nd Battalion on the valley floor. He said, "By mid-day we could observe the enemy moving past us along the high ridgeline running parallel to the withdrawal route. Small groups of Korean refugees had been passing through our position all morning. They were going south, moving ahead of the advancing Chinese. About 1400 I was surprised to see one group heading the opposite direction — north. I recognized some of the people as those who had passed our position headed south about an hour earlier. It was at that point that I realized the Chinese were to our rear, blocking passage."[18]

Fox Company occupied a blocking position in the valley on the western side of the blocking position. "We had a clear view of the road and the hills northeast and east of the MSR," recalled CAPT Robert Lamb. "During the morning and into the early afternoon we could see Chinese in considerable numbers on those hills. Moreover we had been informed that there was a major Chinese penetration of the division on the right of the 5th RCT."[19]

When two KATUSA interpreters in A Battery heard oriental voices coming over the short-range PRC-526 "Walkie Talkie" radio 1st LT Frank Athanason carried in his jeep, one said, "Not Korean, that's Chinese." The Chinese, obviously using captured American equipment, could not be far away.[20] Why the combat team's senior leadership failed to recognize the potential for disaster remains a mystery.

Meanwhile, the 1st Battalion broke contact on the Gold Mine Trail late that morning under the covering fire of the Triple Nickel's fires and air strikes flown by twin-engine B-26s. The soldiers trudged down the trail, carrying their dead and wounded, to the MSR where they mounted the 555th FAB's trucks.

The day before, the Commander of 24th Infantry Division Artillery had directed all infantry regiments to comply with the following message: "In the event that a withdrawal is ordered, vehicle columns will be so organized that foot troops and supporting weapons will be readily available to reduce road or fire blocks. Infantry type action will be initiated with minimum delay."[21]

The 5th RCT's response to this message was to have its 1st Battalion provide security for the artillery during the withdrawal. One rifle company was assigned to protect each firing battery, with the infantry mounted on the Triple Nickel's trucks. This solution looked good on paper and solved the logistical nightmare of providing enough transportation to motorize the infantry. Yet the 5th RCT was conducting a rearguard mission, not an administrative movement. Squad and platoon integrity was quickly lost when the infantry was crammed into whatever trucks had extra room to carry a complement of riflemen. There was also the question of who was guarding whom. The 1st Battalion's rifle companies may have averaged fifty to seventy-five men apiece by this time, having suffered murderous losses in the past few days of intensive combat. How much aid they could realistically provide the artillery remained conjectural at best. The combat team's command group gave this problem little thought as it focused on the rescue of the embattled Rangers. It was probably surmised that if serious fighting had to take place, the regimental rearguard, 2nd Battalion reinforced by Tank Company and D Company, 6th Tank Battalion, would take care of it.

Lieutenant Colonel Wilson planned on traveling with the regimental rearguard. There is no doubt that he anticipated the greatest danger to materialize from the north. Oddly enough, he sent MAJ Frederick Wells, his operations officer, to supervise the march order and assembly of troops and vehicles near Pisi-gol, a considerable distance south of the 2nd Battalion's blocking position. In view of the critical tactical situation, this decision is difficult to fathom today. Major Wells' responsibilities would not normally have entailed such a task, one better suited to the Regimental S-4 or the motor transport officer.

Once the bulk of Headquarters and Headquarters Company, 5th Infantry had withdrawn with the

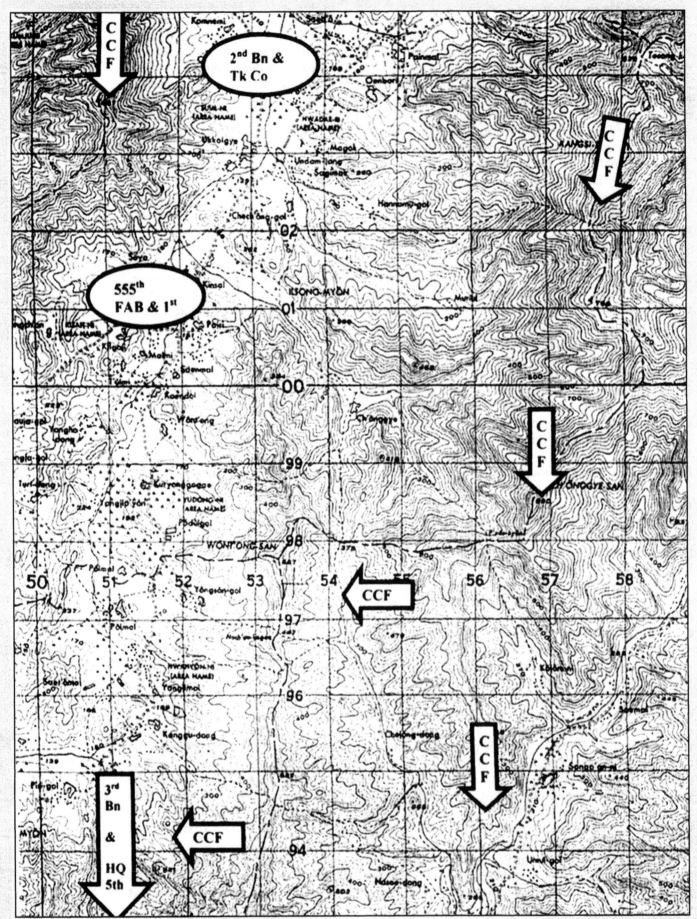

DEATH VALLEY, 1400-1700, 25 APRIL 1951. *The 3rd Battalion withdraws on order and clears the pass at Pisi-gol at 1410 just as the CCF commences to dig in and register mortars. Meanwhile, the 1st Battalion breaks contact on the Gold Mine Trail and links up with the 555th FAB to commence a motorized movement to the new MLR. D Company, 6th Tank Battalion returns to the 2nd Battalion's blocking position at 1700 with the remnants of the 8th Ranger Company.*

3rd Battalion to Sopa, little of the combat team's command and control apparatus remained with LTC Wilson. That LTC Wilson's communications difficulties would be magnified if the withdrawal did not go according to plan is an understatement.

Exactly when the last of D Company's Patton tanks roared back into the 5th RCT's lines following the final pick-up of Ranger stragglers is open to dispute. One historian has quoted the S-3 Journal, 6th Tank Battalion, which includes an entry at 1200 that the 3rd Platoon, C Company was on its way back to friendly lines with 107 men, including 25 wounded.[22] The 5th RCT's Command Report for April 1950 hints that the Ranger pick-up was actually a continuing action, in that elements of the Rangers were retrieved by 1200, while the final pick-up was not completed until approximately 1700. In determining the moment when the last Patton re-entered friendly lines, the recollections of the S-3 of the 2nd Battalion have proven most helpful.

Captain William O. Perry had served as an 81-mm Mortar Platoon Leader in Dog Company and as the S-3A for the 2nd Battalion since he initially joined the 5th RCT in late September 1950. On 25 April, he was serving as the S-3 for the 2nd Battalion.

"We received a radio message early that morning," CAPT Perry recalled. "Maybe from division, but frankly, I think from corps. This was unusual because we'd never had a message come in that had not gone through regimental channels. We were told to stay in position because the Ranger company was out there still. By that time, our people were already beginning to move out on the available transportation. I talked to Jim Herbert [CO 8th Rangers] recently about this, and he said something that I didn't remember... that I'd sent forward a tank platoon... from Dog Company of the 6th Tank Battalion. Anyway, we sent them forward. I was concerned because we were behind schedule. We had reports that the enemy was moving south of us on our right flank, and there was only one road back that I knew about. We wanted to get the Rangers back as soon as we could so we could get out of there.... The tanks brought the wounded back, and Jim Herbert from my West Point class was one of the wounded... badly wounded, he passed out on the back of the tank if I remember right. When the Rangers got through, we began to pull out. I believe George Company was the last unit out. They rode out on the tanks. I rode out in a jeep with MAJ Pope.... As I recall, it was still daylight, maybe around 1630 or so when we finally moved out."[23]

Meanwhile, the Chinese had completed their blocking positions astride the MSR near Pisi-gol. The 5th RCT, delayed in commencing its withdrawal until approximately 1700, was destined to pay a terrible price for the lost time. In the words of Command Report, "This last delay was costly."[24]

Able Battery was in the vicinity of Malmi when it loaded the remnants of one of the 1st Battalion's rifle companies (probably Baker Company), no more than fifty men, onto 1st LT Frank Athanason's trucks and drove south to link up with Headquarters Battery. Able Battery pulled off the MSR onto a dead-end road that ran a short distance due west where Headquarters Battery was located, probably in the vicinity of Polmal.[25] Baker and Charlie batteries, with an infantry company apiece, were positioned to A Battery's immediate north. Even though the 1st Battalion was mounted on the artillery's trucks and ready to roll, LTC Clarence Stuart directed his battery commanders to dismount the infantry and feed them a hot meal. Here too, a lack of urgency was apparent. The famished and exhausted infantry, fresh from a casualty intensive engagement on the Gold Mine Trail, enjoyed what for many soldiers was a Last Supper prepared by the Triple Nickel's field kitchens. Meanwhile, the Chinese continued to interpose more men and crew-served weapons on the ridgelines overlooking Pisi-gol.

Lieutenant Athanason placed his howitzers in position, the barrels laid in on an azimuth facing due north, while the wretched remnants of the rifle company that accompanied his battery ate their meal. He watched the infantrymen wolf down their food as an advance party from Headquarters Battery sped by heading south for the rear. Baker Battery followed a few minutes later, the artillery prime movers packed with gunners, infantrymen, supplies and equipment. A few minutes later, the battery commander heard B Battery's frantic appeal for help over the radio. They had been ambushed and were under fire.

Strong elements of at least two CCF infantry battalions were perched to pounce from both sides of the defile overlooking the pass at Pisi-gol when B Battery drove into the killing zone.[26] Additional CCF battalions were moving into position onto the eastern heights, north of Pisi-gol and overlooking the MSR, when the overloaded trucks carrying the unsuspecting soldiers of B Battery and their infantry escort (probably Charlie Company) drove south under the muzzles of their guns. Intrepid CCF squads and platoons had in several cases already entered the valley floor, and now occupied firing positions astride both sides of the MSR. One CCF unit of indeterminate size was stealthily entering a village immediately north of Pisi-gol (probably Kanggu-dong) when the trucks roared past. The Chinese in the village held their fire to allow the column of vehicles and guns to enter the pass. Here, the two battalions on the high ground overlooking the MSR would initiate the ambush to disable vehicles on the road, thus blocking the defile.

For B Battery, and its infantry escort, the day's combat actions had up to this point appeared almost like old times. The Eighth Army was in full retreat, and the 5th RCT had been called upon once again to cover 24th Infantry Division's withdrawal. After a bloody firefight on the Gold Mine Trail, the men in Charlie Company knew they were heading for a short respite in divisional reserve. For many men, thoughts of reading a letter from home, or curling up in a sleeping bag for a well-deserved rest, were dreams the merciless god of war shattered forever.

Major Claude Baker rode in his jeep at the head B Battery's column of trucks and guns. As the battalion commander neared the summit of the mountain pass southeast of Pisi-gol, he noticed a large number of oriental soldiers occupying positions on both sides of the narrow defile. His S-3, Captain George Viney, had just shouted that he thought these were enemy troops, when the Chinese opened fire. A burst of automatic weapons fire hit a 3/4 ton truck following immediately behind MAJ Baker's jeep, killing the driver, which caused the truck to jack-knife and block the road. Major Baker's jeep was the last 5th RCT vehicle to clear the pass that day. Few American soldiers made it out on foot that way either.[27]

Two CCF battalions opened fire at 1730 with intense automatic weapons fire that swept the motorized column. Mortar explosions added to the slaughter. A few of B Battery's trucks skewed out of control, turned over, caught fire and exploded. The remaining trucks halted as orders were passed from one end of the convoy to the other for the infantry to dismount, form up, and assault the Chinese. While the infantry attempted to form up into squads and platoons, a few cannoneers tried to unlimber the 105-mm howitzers to return fire over open sights, but they never stood a chance and died next to their guns. Most of the survivors leaped for cover in the drainage ditches on both sides of the road.

Heavy and accurate Chinese fire knocked the infantry over like bowling pins as they attempted to deploy for combat. The infantry company, crammed like sardines in the back of whatever artillery prime mover had room to carry a few extra men, with no regard for squad and platoon integrity, was unable to deploy and fight as a coordinated unit. Here and there, small groups of grimly determined soldiers fought their way up the ridgeline to assault the Chinese, but their courageous, uncoordinated actions lacked momentum, enjoyed no fire support, and failed to dislodge the entrenched Chinese. Losses were severe.

"The Chinese were on the ridges on either side of us when they closed the door," said SGT Hibbert Manley, a platoon sergeant in Charlie Company. "We started dismounting the vehicles to find out what was going on. And here they come from both sides. It was mass confusion. We gathered together in small groups and fought shoulder-to-shoulder to hold the Chinese off."[28]

The FDC Section, Headquarters Battery, moved out on the MSR a few minutes after B Battery. Sergeant Samuel L. Lewis was riding in a jeep when the FDC Section suddenly ran into the rear of B Battery's column of burning vehicles. "I jumped out of my jeep and ran about ten feet before I noticed three Chinese soldiers a few yards away who opened up on me," recalled SGT Lewis. "I pulled out my .45, fired off a magazine, and managed to miss every time. So I dropped my useless pistol and ran back the way I had come where I joined a few other soldiers behind some cover. I also found a carbine. From that day on, I never relied on a .45 again."[29]

Major Frederick Wells was directing traffic near Pisi-gol when the Chinese sprang the ambush. The operations officer jumped into his jeep and sped to B Battery's location. While his jeep covered the short distance, enemy automatic weapons and rifle fire rapidly spread northwards like a prairie fire up the length of the MSR. Scenting blood, more CCF formations had entered the fray.

Major Wells found B Battery hopelessly stalled on the road. Most of the key unit leaders lay dead or wounded. After reporting the situation over the radio, he attempted to jump-start the convoy, not realizing the pass was blocked. Lieutenant Colonel Wilson immediately dispatched a tank platoon to B Battery's assistance, while the 2nd Battalion, the remainder of the regimental Tank Company, and D Company, 6th Tank Battalion, prepared to move out.

First Lieutenant Ed Crockett's 2nd Tank Platoon was deployed that afternoon approximately 800 yards east of the MSR near Kinsal. All five of the platoon's tanks were operational. A group of infantry was relaxing on the engine decks of the tank platoon, ready to move out, when a senior officer ran up to the platoon leader. The officer directed the infantry to dismount and gave LT Crockett verbal orders to head south with a section of his tanks as quickly as possible to eliminate "some small arms fire striking the Triple Nickel."[30]

The 2nd Tank Platoon's heavy section moved out with three Easy Eights. Master Sergeant Johnnie Walls, who had yet to receive his battlefield commission, remained behind in command of *Leilani* and another Easy Eight. Lieutenant Crockett led the heavy section's advance in *Hawaii Calls*, followed by MSGT Morris Helm's crew in *Aloha*, and SFC Herb Glesener's crew in *Mona Loa*.

The intrepid tank crews soon encountered a CCF squad crawling along a ditch on the eastern side of the road a couple of hundred yards south of Podulgol, and an easy 3,000 yards north of where B Battery was under fire. To LT Crockett's amazement, the Chinese kept crawling slowly along the ditch in plain view, with some of the men occasionally glancing apprehensively over their shoulders at the tanks. After observing this surreal scene for a few seconds, the three tanks opened fire and obliterated the enemy squad.

Immediately thereafter, a lone Chinese soldier rose up from a ditch on the opposite side of the road and charged *Hawaii Calls* with a wooden club in hand. The brave and very determined enemy soldier was clearly aiming to brain the young platoon leader, who stood with his head and shoulders exposed in the commander's hatch. Lieutenant Crockett could have reached for the M-1 rifle hanging within easy reach on the top rear of the turret, or he could have grabbed the carbine mounted at knee level inside the turret. Instead, he made the mistake of reaching for his personal side arm, a .45-caliber automatic pistol suspended under his left arm from a shoulder holster.

Lieutenant Crockett explained, "The problem at the moment was that the pistol happened to be under my field jacket which I had slipped on hastily as we departed the blocking position up the valley. It was frightening to realize how the slightest lapse in vigilance can defeat one in combat. As it turned out, I struggled with the jacket buttons and extracted my pistol only at the moment he reached the front of the turret, three feet away from my face. As he raised his club to pound me on my head, the muzzle of my .45-caliber pistol arrived twelve inches from his forehead. I pulled the trigger and despaired at the sound of the 'click' as the pistol failed to fire. To my astonishment, the Chinaman turned and scurried down the front slope of the tank. As quickly as possible, I retracted the slide of my weapon to chamber another round. With my sights in the middle of his back as he leapt off the tank, I squeezed the trigger. He appeared to leap forward and fell on his face. He did not arise."

Lieutenant Crockett's tanks moved out again, down the road toward B Battery where even now MAJ Wells was running along the column of stalled and burning vehicles ordering the men to seek

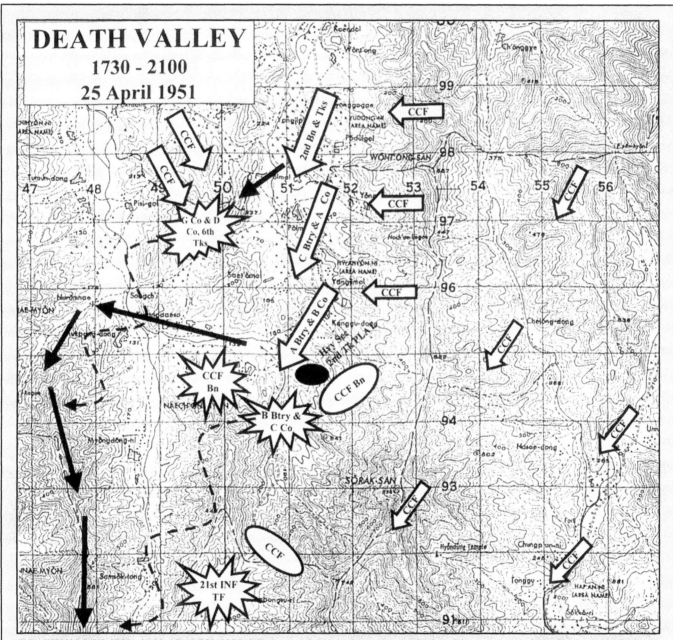

DEATH VALLEY, 1730 - 2100, 25 APRIL 1951. B Battery and C Company are ambushed at 1730. Attempts to force the pass fail with heavy U.S. losses. A Task Force from the 21st Infantry is ambushed when it attempts to breakthrough from the south. The 5th RCT errs when it directs A and C Batteries to drive into the CCF killing zone. The Heavy Section of the 2nd Tank Platoon holds the CCF at bay. Triple Nickel artillery fire blasts the CCF off the western hills, while the 2nd Battalion and the two tank companies enter the fray. The combat team breaks out using a road the 72nd Engineers had previously constructed on a ridgeline to the west (black arrows). Units pinned down in the killing zone breakout in small groups (dotted lines). G Company and D Company, 6th Tank Batalion, suffer heavy losses while serving as the regimental rearguard.

cover and return fire. Shortly thereafter, the brave operations officer fell mortally wounded, hit by a deadly combination of bullets and mortar shrapnel.[31] As if on signal, a CCF assault struck the head of the stalled column from the east, blowing bugles, throwing concussion grenades, and shooting burp guns from the hip. Caught between the enemy and burning trucks, the soldiers here never had a fighting chance. A pitiful handful of survivors were taken prisoner.

Lieutenant Frank Athanason could clearly see from A Battery's position the Chinese on the ridgelines who were shooting down at B Battery. The range from A Battery to the nearest enemy held ridgeline was 1,800 yards at most, so he ordered his gun crews to turn their howitzers around and commence direct fire at the Chinese. Charlie Battery was still in position farther north and the weight of their combined fires could have taken a tremendous toll on the enemy, "but everybody was excited and wanted to move."[32] Shortly after A Battery fired a couple of direct fire volleys, LTC Clarence Stuart, who may have been under the impression that MAJ Wells had cleared up the situation at the pass, directed LT Athanason over the radio to limber up his guns and move south. Lieutenant Athanason flagged down a tank heading south and instructed the commander standing in the turret to lead his battery down the road.

As the column of A Battery trucks rolled through a village (probably Kanggu-dong) still north of where B Battery and C Company were being cut to pieces, the soldiers came under heavy small arms fire from the houses. Lieutenant Athanason dismounted his jeep, and ran abreast of the Sherman, where he stood pointing out targets for the tank commander. Everytime the Easy Eight's main gun roared, the muzzle blast knocked the battery commander to the ground. At first he thought concussion grenades were knocking him down, until he realized otherwise. Meanwhile, the battery first sergeant, a magnificent soldier, both professional and brave, charged into an enemy occupied building, firing his carbine from the hip. He was not seen again.

The first sergeant's sacrifice, combined with point-blank tank main gun and machine gun fire, beat down the Chinese opposition, and the column soon found itself moving south again on the MSR. A short distance down the road, A Battery encountered the end of B Battery stalled on the road. Survivors crowded the roadside ditches, firing their weapons at the Chinese dug in on the ridgeline. Lieutenant Athanason halted his column and ordered his cannoneers to uncouple their howitzers and commence fire.

As the cannoneers unlimbered their 105s, automatic weapons fire raked the battery and men fell dead or wounded around their comrades. The range was down to 200 yards as veteran gun commanders ignored the carnage and laid their howitzers on the muzzle flashes winking at the soldiers from the ridgelines to the east and west of the road. Noncommissioned officers shouted fire commands above the din, as the cannoneers loaded high explosive shells, and gunners manipulated the traverse and elevation wheels to bring the howitzers to bear. The gun crews slammed round after round of high explosive ammunition down range and succeeded in blasting their Chinese tormentors off the face of the western ridgeline, but murderous enemy fire from the east continued unabated.

The battery had expended much of its basic load of artillery ammunition earlier in the day supporting the 1st Battalion's engagement on the Gold Mine Trail, so there was very little remaining at this point. After the battery expended its last high explosive rounds, the gun crews fired their white phosphorous shells. Finally, just the smoke rounds were left. And then, these too were gone.

When LT Athanason had initially assumed command of A Battery, one of his first orders was for every man in his battery to always keep his personal weapon within easy reach. Moreover, he ensured that his battery traveled with a full allowance of readily accessible infantry ammunition: boxes of rifle, carbine, and machine gun ammunition, and cases of hand grenades. Armed with their individual weapons, and six bandoleers of ammunition apiece, in addition to their hand grenades, Able Battery was prepared to fight as infantry that desperate evening as the sun set and the battle raged.

From his position in a corpse-strewn, muddy ditch, LT Athanason surveyed the carnage and concluded that his howitzers would not prevail that afternoon. Death or capture awaited those who remained in the Chinese kill zone. Lieutenant Athanason decided he had nothing to lose when he gathered what men he could into a ragged skirmish line and led them up the ridge in a daring bid to regain the initiative through counterattack.

About the time LT Athanason jumped off in his counterattack, LT Ed Crockett's section of tanks arrived and found the road blocked with burning vehicles near the mouth of the pass. Gunners huddled behind the shields of their howitzers as they engaged the enemy with direct fire. Soldiers lay in ditches on both sides of the road, some dead, others wounded, the rest returning fire. The three Easy Eights left the congested road to bypass the wrecks and advanced as far as they could toward the mouth of the pass.

Hawaii Calls halted in front of a large rock formation about forty yards to the left front of the tank. *Aloha* and *Mona Loa* overwatched *Hawaii Calls* from firing positions a little farther back. One

Chinese squad at a time would form up behind the rocks before it charged across the open ground toward *Hawaii Calls*. Lieutenant Crockett's crew shattered every CCF assault with the concentrated, deadly fire of the tank's main gun and the bow and co-axial-mounted .30-caliber machine guns. A blizzard of enemy automatic weapons fire, however, prevented employment of the tank's .50-caliber machine gun. As the Chinese charged, squad after squad, armed with satchel charges and grenades, advancing at the double time across their dead and dying comrades, other component parts of the 5th RCT were in motion.

Earlier that afternoon, C Battery had received orders to limber up their 105-mm howitzers and head south on the MSR. "We could see the Chinese on the ridgelines on both sides of the road marching south to get behind us," recalled the Battery XO, 1st LT Earl Law. After C Battery had driven a short distance, they heard B Battery's frantic radio appeal for fire support, stating they were pinned down by heavy enemy fire. First Lieutenant Cecil J. Burton, the CO of C Battery, and a former Marine staff sergeant in World War II, pulled the battery off the road. He laid three guns on an azimuth due south. These 105s commenced pumping high explosive rounds downrange in support of B Battery's call for fires. Lieutenant Law laid the remaining three guns for direct fire to cover both sides of the road. Lieutenant Burton admonished his XO to hold his fire until he saw the "whites of their eyes."[33]

Everyone not manning the howitzers joined the perimeter defended by their infantry escort, the pitiful remnants of CAPT Horace West's Able Company. Moments later, CCF automatic weapons fire began to rake the battery and mortar rounds exploded in the rice paddies on both sides of the road. With bullets kicking up dust around his feet, CAPT West cussed, swore, and walked the line kicking people in the butt to make them return fire. "Start shooting boys!" he roared as tracers streaked by on all sides.

In the midst of this firefight, C Battery suddenly received word to limber up the guns and head south as fast as they could. "So we got on the road," said LT Law. "And, oh man, we were making it south when suddenly we came around this corner and there was this Quad 50 sitting right in the middle of the road. It was shaking as all four barrels fired, but I couldn't hear it for all the other noise going on. But I knew it was firing. We got slaughtered that day, but we piled up some Chinese."

Charlie Battery had reached the end of A Battery and could go no further. The cannoneers dismounted and laid their 105s for direct fire as Able Company deployed for combat. Captain West stood upright amidst the carnage directing the fire of his soldiers. Though hit several times, the company commander remained on his feet exhorting his men until yet another burst of automatic weapons fire finally knocked him senseless to the ground. A handful of soldiers carried their badly wounded commander to the tank commanded by 1st LT Gordon W. Campbell, the 4th Tank Platoon Leader, and lifted him to the engine deck under the cover of the Sherman's suppressive fire. Captain West rode out on LT Campbell's tank, survived his wounds and, during a lengthy recovery period at various Army hospitals, was awarded the Distinguished Service Cross for valor.

Lieutenant Earl Law ran toward the head of the column with 1st LT Joe Burton to ascertain the cause for the halt. When Chinese soldiers lying in a rice paddy took the two officers under fire, they both hit the dirt and returned fire with their ludicrously inadequate .45-caliber pistols. After a bullet tore through LT Law's kneecap, LT Burton carried his XO a considerable distance back towards the battery under heavy fire. Lieutenant Law finally asked LT Burton to return to the battery without him, because he was clearly slowing the battery commander down. Lieutenant Burton said farewell to his friend and took off running down the column of burning vehicles. As LT Law watched him go, he calmly reloaded his pistol and awaited his fate.[34]

Meanwhile, MAJ Claude Baker had formed a mental picture of the desperate situation on the northern side of the pass based on radio reports he was monitoring over the 5th RCT's command net. He immediately contacted the 5th RCT CP, which had traveled with the regimental trains in trace of the 3rd Battalion, and was thus clear of the ambush. Lieutenant Colonel Ward, who in his capacity as the regimental XO had accompanied the combat team's CP to Sopa earlier in the day, received MAJ Baker's SOS and appraised the G-3, 24th Infantry Division of the situation at 1745.[35] The 21st Infantry was directed to dispatch a company of tanks, reinforced with an infantry company, to break through from the south to the embattled combat team. During its approach march, the Chinese ambushed this task force, knocking out two M-46 Patton tanks and inflicting heavy losses on the infantry. The survivors retreated. Clearly, the 5th RCT was on its own.[36]

Regrettably, the 5th RCT CP inadvertently passed misleading information to G-3, 24th Infantry Division when it reported that, based on the accounts of a few soldiers who had broken out of the trap, the CCF road block appeared to be "at least one company."[37] In reality, the CCF had commenced the ambush with a force of two battalions. Even now, additional CCF units were joining the battle, determined to be in on the kill. The combat team was fighting hard, however, and the CCF would pay a steep price.

A Sherman tank crew's panorama of the battlefield was restricted due to the nature of the armored beasts. The driver and bow gunner could see only to their immediate front through narrow slits in their armored hatch covers. The gunner was restricted to viewing the carnage through his telescopic gun sight. It was imperative therefore for a tank commander to fight unbuttoned, with head exposed, to direct the fight. Lieutenant Ed Crockett was doing just that, calmly speaking to *Aloha* and *Mona Loa* over the radio and to his crew over the intercom, as he directed his heavy section's combat actions. The crew, though aware of the gravity of the situation, remained calm and deliberate in their duties, occasionally joking and bantering to relieve the tension filled air. The bottle of bourbon helped.

Though neither Mrs. D. Leigh Colvin nor her staunch comrades in the WCTU would have approved. LT Crockett had returned from R&R in Japan just a few days before with a fifth of bourbon in hand to celebrate the birth of his newborn daughter with his crew. As the firing picked up in intensity, and the reality of imminent death appeared evident to all, LT Crockett must have thought, "What the hell," and presented the bottle to his grateful crew. Each tanker took a swig, and perhaps two, before passing it to the next man. In short order the bottle was consumed.

Lieutenant Crockett was searching a ridgeline to locate a machine gun that was engaging his tank when a terrific explosion resounded with a distinctive "whoomp" between *Hawaii Calls* and *Mona Loa*, SFC Glesener's tank. Lieutenant Crockett's crew asked in unison, "What in the ⸺ was that!" Lieutenant Crockett calmly reassured his men that a 120-mm mortar explosion probably caused the sound they heard. In truth he had clearly seen the 3.5-inch high explosive antitank (HEAT) rocket whiz by within two feet of his head before it exploded behind *Hawaii Calls*. Obviously the Chinese had captured a 3.5-inch rocket launcher. He would soon find out if they knew how to use it. Regrettably, neither LT Crockett, MSGT Helm, nor SFC Glesener had seen the distinctive back-blast of the rocket launcher, otherwise they would have pulverized the position with a volley of fire.

In the distance a Chinese loader pulled the safety pin from another HEAT rocket, pushed it into the rear of the tube, lifted the arming handle, and informed the gunner with a pat on his back that the weapon was ready to fire. The gunner, who balanced the bazooka on his shoulder as he squinted carefully through the sight, lined up the nearest Easy Eight and squeezed the trigger. An electrical charge ignited the rocket engine, propelling the large black HEAT rocket out of the tube at several hundred feet per second. The rocket arched through the air and impacted on the frontal armor of *Hawaii Calls* where the point initiating, base detonating, fuse exploded the shaped charge warhead in a blow torch pattern of directed energy that blasted a hole half an inch in diameter and five inches deep through the armor plate.

Lieutenant Crockett was stooped over, head and shoulders under armor, conferring with Sergeant Bill Gunzleman, his gunner, when the rocket exploded. He therefore escaped the flash of flame that engulfed the exterior of the turret. The HEAT rocket exploded against the thickest part of the tank's frontal armor, where it began to fold back under the tank. The huge final drives of the Sherman's propulsion system are housed inside the hull at that point. Had the rocket struck higher on the hull, or on the turret, few, if any, of the crew would have survived the sympathetic detonation of stored fuel and ammunition. Luckily for LT Crockett's crew, the shaped charge warhead that so easily penetrated the hull's armor plate, expended itself in the gears. Corporal Masterson, the loader, suffered shrapnel wounds on his hands and face from spalling. The driver, Sergeant Woods, suffered minor burns when the rubber grommet on his hatch cover melted and fell around his shoulders.

Quite naturally, LT Crockett's first thought after the explosion was that he was never going to hold his newborn daughter or see his wife again. Though the Sherman's engine stalled immediately after the explosion, the entire crew was pleasantly surprised that the tank did not explode or catch fire. The shaken crew returned to their armament a few seconds later and recommenced the fight.

Meanwhile, SFC Glesener's crew in *Mona Loa* had observed the back-blast of the Chinese bazooka team this time. His gunner killed the bazooka team with a high explosive round.

Farther to the north, the 2nd Battalion moved out, a long motorized column snaking down the MSR, coming to the aid of the 1st Battalion and the Triple Nickel. "We didn't have much time to issue an order," said CAPT Robert Lamb, the CO of Fox Company. "We knew there was a road block, and we had an idea where it was. We were to fight our way through it and open the road."[38]

Captain Lamb led two rifle platoons mounted on a platoon of Easy Eights

SGT Leonard A. Woods, Crown Point, NY, driver of Hawaii Calls, *was wounded in the ambush. (source: Ed Crockett)*

down the MSR. Well short of the objective, "We came to disabled vehicles on and near the road and we came under intense small arms fire from relatively close range," recalled the company commander. Captain Lamb was hit in the arm almost immediately, and the force of the blow knocked him off the engine deck to the ground.

"Our casualties were heavy," said Captain Lamb, "but the tanks and infantry along the road were returning fire and continued to do so during the afternoon. From my perspective, the action was being controlled by small groups. I no longer had control of the tanks or the men who were on them and I was not in contact with battalion. I have never known what command and control existed along the column of men and vehicles, including considerable artillery.

"We stayed there all afternoon," continued Captain Lamb. "Later … we learned that COL Stuart, the commander of the Triple Nickel, remembered that there was an unimproved road that led west from the MSR which he had used earlier. That's the way we got out. We got as a many men and vehicles through that route as we could. My last recollection of that valley, as the sun went down, was the vision of our Air Force bombing and destroying the tanks, artillery and vehicles which had been left north of the pass."[39]

George Company was assigned the mission of battalion rearguard with at least six Pattons from D Com-

PFC Estes Philpott (standing right) and his G Company 60-mm mortar squad rendered supporting fire as best they could during the struggle. (source: Estes Philpott)

pany providing both transportation and fire support. When George Company's mortars withdrew on order, the battalion command group followed in trace. The rifle platoons, mounted on D Company's Pattons, brought up the rear of the column.

Private First Class Estes Philpott, from Decatur, Arkansas, served in G Company's 60-mm Mortar Section. All day the men had seen hundreds of Chinese march past on the ridgelines to the east and west of the valley. Late that afternoon, his mortar section drove south along the MSR in trucks while the rifle platoons remained at the blocking position with the tanks from D Company, 6th Tank Battalion. The trucks stopped near the crest of a small hill, and the men dismounted to see why. In the distance the soldiers could clearly see the artillery being shot to pieces in the valley. Captain William Perry, the battalion S-3, drove up in a jeep and gave the men their orders. As the 60-mm mortars lobbed shells in the direction of the Chinese, another soldier opened up with a .50-caliber machine gun mounted on a tank turret, raking a column of Chinese soldiers seen moving on the hills. About this time, a column of Pattons drove past their position and took a trail that led to the west where they disappeared.[40]

The mortars were nearly out of ammunition when a soldier brought back a truckload of 60-mm rounds he had found scavenging in the decimated column ahead. The men formed a bucket brigade, opening the crates, passing the rounds, tearing off increments, and handing them to the aid-gunners who stuffed the shells down the smoking gun tubes. The 60-mm shell bursts killed scores of Chinese, yet the CCF shrugged off its losses while concentrating its fires on the hapless artillery batteries trapped in the valley below.

On order, George Company's rifle platoons climbed onto the engine decks of the six tanks belonging to D Company, 6th Tank Battalion. Though the Patton tanks were relatively invulnerable to Chinese mortar and automatic weapons fire, the infantry was not. "We were riding on tanks," said CPL Bill Welch, the platoon sergeant of the 2nd Platoon, George Company. "All of a sudden we received this terrific mortar fire from the hills to our east. I was standing on a tank as we were moving. All Hell was breaking loose. We dismounted and started returning fire."[41]

Sergeant First Class Clarence Young, from Honolulu, had deployed with the 5th RCT from Schofield Barracks. He was supposed to rotate in a few days. Corporal Welch watched him climb into the turret of an anti-aircraft half-track to return fire. This half-track took three direct hits from mortar rounds in rapid succession. "That's the last of Clarence," thought CPL Welch.[42] Thankfully, such was not the case. The Chinese took the stunned SFC Young prisoner when they overran the column later that evening.

Major Rufus Pope, the new CO of the 2nd Battalion, and his S-3, CAPT William Perry, tried to organize order out of chaos. They were in radio contact with some of their company command groups, but the span of control of the company commanders no longer extended further than the soldiers they could see to their immediate right and left.

"We were taking an incredible volume of small arms fire," said CAPT Perry. "Some mortar rounds were coming in, but they weren't bothering us too much. Major Pope and I ran over to a couple of the Pattons, and tried to direct their return fire over the tank-infantry phones, but I doubt if this fire had much effect."[43]

Lieutenant Colonel Wilson's role in the unfolding debacle remains conjectural at best. His operations officer was dead, and the bulk of the combat team's command and control apparatus was located in the combat team's assembly area with LTC Ward. The 3rd Battalion was also in the assembly area and of no immediate use to the main body getting chewed to pieces in the vicinity of Pisigol. Major Claude Baker, the CO of the 1st Battalion, was cut off from his command, and the remnants of his scattered rifle companies were pinned down along the length of the column of burning vehicles, disorganized, and unable to fight in a coordinated fashion. The Triple Nickel, though fighting hard, was nearing the point when the batteries would exhaust their ammunition and succumb to the weight of sheer numbers. Finally, LT Walter Fay, the Tactical Air Controller, was wounded, which left no one to request and direct air strikes.

Lieutenant Ed Crockett believes he saw LTC Wilson and LTC Stuart crouched beside *Hawaii Calls* early on in the ambush.[44] If so, the two officers had survived heavy enemy fire to reach the head of the column only to find it irretrievably blocked by the mangled remnants of B Battery's trucks and howitzers.

LT Ed Crockett was recommended for the Distinguished Service Cross which was downgraded to the Silver Star by Corps Headquarters. (source: Ed Crockett)

Lieutenant Colonel Wilson's mounting frustration and rising anxiety for the safety of his command may have interfered with his capacity to command at this juncture of the fighting. After Baker Company finally formed up as an organized unit, its CO found LTC Wilson on the battlefield and asked him where he wanted to commit the company. Lieutenant Colonel Wilson's reply, "I don't know where to put them," reportedly shocked the company commander.[45]

Lieutenant Colonel Clarence Stuart deserves praise for saving the lives of those soldiers who escaped the engagement the survivors subsequently called "Death Valley." During the previous March the 72nd Engineers had improved a narrow mountain trail west of Pisi-gol that ran parallel to the MSR. While the fighting raged, LTC Stuart recalled the existence of this road, which trucks and tanks could traverse. As this route had yet to be added to any maps, it was probably unknown to the Chinese, and hopefully unguarded. Lieutenant Colonel Stuart conducted a route reconnaissance and found the improved trail to be free of Chinese troops. He relayed this information to LTC Wilson, who in turn contacted MAJ Claude Baker on the radio to confirm if the route was still open on the far side of the ridge. When MAJ Baker replied that, as far as he could tell, the Chinese had not sealed it off, LTC Wilson ordered the combat team to break contact along this route to the MLR.[46]

All of this took time. And still the fighting raged near the mouth of the pass. Chinese automatic weapons fire ricocheted off *Hawaii Calls'* armor, and mortar shrapnel cleaved the radio antennae in half. *Aloha* and *Mona Loa* fought their respective battles while bullets and shrapnel pinged off their scarred armored sides. The heavy tank section was running out of ammunition when LT Ed Crockett removed his rank insignia and class ring and rolled them up in a handkerchief that he placed in a pocket. He intended to throw the handkerchief over the side when the end came.

The sun was setting when MSGT Helm relayed a radio mes-

"Death Valley" looking south to the ambush defile; taken on 25 April 1965. (source: John R. Burke)

sage to LT Crockett that directed the combat team to withdraw to the west. An anxious crew awaited *Hawaii Calls'* response when SGT Woods attempted to restart the engine. They felt like cheering when the rugged Easy Eight's engine turned over, did not catch fire, and the transmission slipped easily into reverse gear.

Lieutenant Crockett's initial euphoria quickly evaporated. He stared transfixed from his open turret hatch at the sight of eight wounded soldiers lying in the bed of a field ambulance, their mutual gazes locked for eternity across the fire-swept ground, mournful eyes pleading for assistance he was unable to provide. The ambulance driver had disappeared, perhaps killed or wounded, that we will never know. There was nothing LT Crockett could do to help these men, for the Chinese, having noted the withdrawal, were swarming off the hills in pursuit. The tanks were drawing intense small arms fire, and any attempt made to dismount would have been suicidal. Lieutenant Crockett's only consolation was that the Chinese, unlike the North Koreans, usually took prisoners. The enemy appeared to be respecting the Red Cross insignia painted on the sides of the ambulance, the only undamaged vehicle in a long column of burning trucks. Regrettably, LT Crockett's conscience was not appeased, and recurring nightmares have troubled his sleep evermore.

Hawaii Calls traversed 500 yards of ground before its engine overheated and stopped. Lieutenant Crockett notified *Aloha* and *Mona Loa* that his crew was going to bail out and hitch a ride. For some reason, unknown even to LT Crockett, he found himself standing on the engine deck, attempting to untie his personal gear from the turret of *Hawaii Calls*, when a string of bullets ripped into his bed roll just above his fingers. He quickly regained his senses, abandoned his gear, and ran as fast as he could to *Mona Loa*. Once aboard, *Mona Loa*'s gunner pumped an armor piercing round into *Hawaii Calls*, a fitting coup de grace for an armored vehicle.[47]

Meanwhile, LT Frank Athanason's mixed force of cannoneers and infantry had overrun a couple of Chinese machine gun and mortar positions in their counterattack up the ridgeline. When he had the opportunity to look over his shoulder down the hill, it became apparent that the situation had changed in the valley below. Able Battery's vehicles could no longer be seen, having apparently turned around to escape the trap by another route. Moreover, the Chinese had moved down the opposite ridge to encircle the men trapped below, so LT Athanason, now wounded, led his men back down the slope where they regrouped in a ditch.[48]

As LT Athanason dressed his wound, he noticed MAJ Wells lying motionless nearby. He watched his helmetless driver, a private, and an occasional troublemaker, place the deceased officer's helmet with the gold oak leaf insignia on his head. A few moments later, a rifle platoon leader ran up asking, "Major! Major! What are we going to do?" The private pointed at his battery commander and replied, "Talk to this guy next to me. He won't even make me a PFC, and you're calling me a major!"[49]

Lieutenant Athanason gathered about 20 men and led them southwest across a rice paddy. As 1st LT Delbert A. Jurden, the S-2 for the 555th FAB, ran across the paddy, a Chinese soldier rose out of a spider hole and shot him in the back. Lieutenant Athanason took out the spider hole with a grenade before he rushed to the side of the wounded officer. Unable to walk, the men carried LT Jurden to a clearly marked ambulance full of wounded soldiers that was stalled behind them on the road.[50] The Chinese appeared to be respecting the Red Cross insignia painted on each side, for although vehicles to its fore and aft had been hit by enemy fire, the ambulance remained unscathed. They left LT Jurden in the ambulance with the other wounded men in the hope that the CCF would take care of them.[51]

Lieutenant Athanason's group ran over a low hill to the west, dodging their Chinese pursuers, who were blowing whistles and, luckily, shooting high. A flight of Navy F4U Corsairs saved them. The Chinese hit the dirt as the aircraft made three runs without expending any am-

Hawaii Calls, *where she came to rest in Death Valley. The 3.5" rocket penetration is visible on the front slope (lower left). An inspector examines the hulk after the valley was recaptured. (source: Ed Crockett)*

munition. The planes may have been out of ammunition, but their dogged persistence managed to bluff the Chinese pursuers into keeping their heads down.

Meanwhile, other desperate men began to break out of the trap in small groups. Sergeant Samuel Lewis struck out across a rice paddy, heading west, accompanied by a couple of soldiers from Headquarters Battery. One soldier from West Virginia, identity unknown, was shot in the head and killed. A few other men were hit, but once the group crossed a low rise to the west, they received no more fire and escaped to safety.[52]

Lieutenant Earl Law decided to strike out on his own. He grimaced in pain as he hobbled across a rice paddy on his wounded knee, with bullets impacting uncomfortably close by. "I'd lost a lot of blood and decided to stop to catch my breath behind a rice paddy dike," he recalled.

While LT Law rested, a cannoneer from A Battery, A. J. Jenkins, approached and said, "Take me with you lieutenant. I'm hit in the gut."

Lieutenant Law relied, "Well let me tell you buddy, I'm hit, too, in the leg. The only way we're going to get out of here is on our own power, and you were doing pretty damn good."

Lieutenant Law informed Jenkins that they would go out together, and the relieved soldier followed the officer when he moved out a few minutes later. Lieutenant Law walked as fast as his damaged knee would carry him up a ridge. A sergeant, who happened to be one of LT Law's friends, emerged from behind some bushes and half carried the officer to cover. Together with Jenkins, the three men reached the MLR.[53]

Charlie Company broke out in small groups. Sergeant Hibbert Manley's group infiltrated at night through a sleeping Chinese company before they finally reached friendly lines. Another group, led by the legendary SGT Joseph Tupa, arrived at the MLR after midnight. The fearless SGT Tupa, who had already earned three Silver Stars, a Bronze Star, and four Purple Hearts in eight months of continuous combat, went out alone to guide in stragglers. Somewhere in the darkness a CCF combat patrol took him prisoner. The Communists spent the next twenty-nine months trying to break the spirit of this magnificent soldier. Sergeant Tupa refused to bend to their will and attempted to escape on several occasions. His heroics so impressed Major General William F. Dean, the highest ranking American officer captured in the Korean War, that he asked SGT Tupa to accompany him to Japan in his plane upon their release from captivity in 1953.[54]

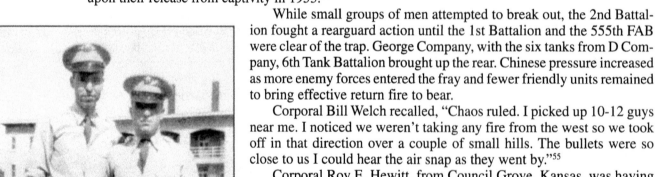

While small groups of men attempted to break out, the 2nd Battalion fought a rearguard action until the 1st Battalion and the 555th FAB were clear of the trap. George Company, with the six tanks from D Company, 6th Tank Battalion brought up the rear. Chinese pressure increased as more enemy forces entered the fray and fewer friendly units remained to bring effective return fire to bear.

Corporal Bill Welch recalled, "Chaos ruled. I picked up 10-12 guys near me. I noticed we weren't taking any fire from the west so we took off in that direction over a couple of small hills. The bullets were so close to us I could hear the air snap as they went by."[55]

Corporal Roy E. Hewitt, from Council Grove, Kansas, was having a tough war. He had already spent three months recovering in Japan from wounds incurred at Waegwan. On 19 February, shortly after he rejoined the company, he was wounded again. When CPL Hewitt returned to George Company after recovering from his second wound, his rotation date was only days away.

Corporal Hewitt's squad had hitched a ride on a Patton tank during the breakout. This tank exploded when the Chinese hit it with a bazooka rocket. Corporal Hewitt tumbled to the ground bleeding from his third wound of the war. A few days later, he and several other soldiers were captured. Corporal Hewitt's rotation date was delayed for twenty-nine months.[56]

The Chinese bazooka team knocked out the Patton CPL Hewitt's squad was riding on as it entered a cut in the road. When the remaining five tanks attempted to bypass the burning Patton, they were hit by bazooka rockets and set on fire. Automatic weapons fire cut down the tankers who tried to escape from their flaming coffins. There were few survivors from this tank platoon.[57]

One soldier from George Company, John King, from Cochrane, Georgia, recalls the slaughter: "They hit the number one tank stopping it, then hit the rest," he recalled.[58] "All were knocked out. I can tell you

John King (right) was wounded and captured in Death Valley. He was not released until the prisoner exchange in 1953. Louis Frezzo (left) was killed earlier on Sobuksan. (source: Ray Warner)

those tanker crews put up a fight. Most of them were KIA, MIA or taken prisoner.... As I came off the tank I was standing on, a mortar round came in. I got hit in my back, in my hip.... My whole left side was paralyzed... so I started crawling right besides the tanks. By now it was dark. I could see the tanks on fire as I crawled past them. I could see the tank crews as they were killed by the Chinese, coming out of their tanks bent over the hatches. I can still see those tankers today."

King took shelter in a foxhole. After the fighting died down, a squad of heavily armed Chinese walked up and pointed their weapons at him. King thought the CCF did not take wounded prisoners. Much to his surprise, a Chinese soldier carried him to a prisoner collection point. He was released from captivity at the end of the war.

After PFC Estes Philpott's mortar section had fired the last of its 60-mm rounds, an order was given to move out. He recalled, "We climbed aboard the tanks and decided to try and bust through. There wasn't room for everyone on the tank I was on... Fred Broghammer... stood on the top of one of the mufflers on this Patton tank. And you know how hot they get. Some of the tanks were knocked out. The one I was on tried to go around them and through the cut, but could not make it. It turned around and headed back north. At this time the tank was hit.... I landed in soft dirt with both eardrums ruptured from the blast.... We got up and ran between the rocks and the tank, through a pass, down into a field where the tracers were coming from every direction." After a harrowing adventure, PFC Philpott reached the MLR with a small group of lucky comrades.[59]

At 1900 the 5th RCT reported it was clear of the ambush, and two hours later the last organized units cleared friendly lines. Individual soldiers and small groups of men trickled in through the night and over the course of the next few days.[60] Lieutenant Athanason, for example, led his group south through the darkness, avoiding low ground because the Chinese usually left the ridgelines at night in search of food. American artillery fire occasionally crashed around the group of men who pressed on until they linked up around 0400 with an armor platoon from the 6th Tank Battalion on the MLR. The tank platoon leader asked LT Athanason to place his men around the tanks because he did not have infantry support. When LT Athanason informed the tank commander that several of his men were wounded, the platoon leader feigned ignorance of the aid station's location and advised him to remain near the tanks until daybreak. So the worn and injured men provided the tanks infantry protection. When the first rays of sunshine graced the sky, LT Athanason discovered that the aid station was located just a few hundred yards away, something the frightened tank platoon leader had known all along.

The 5th Infantry's command report for April 1951 claims the combat team's morale remained high even after the ambush.[61] Perhaps this was true, but the combat team had suffered appalling casualties. Personnel losses will never be exactly known. According to Brigadier General George Barth, originally 800 men were reported missing, but as stragglers reached the MLR, this number was considerably reduced.[62] The 1st Battalion alone incurred approximately thirty-percent casualties. First LT Charles E. Brannon, who earned his second Distinguished Service Cross in two days, prevented even heavier losses from occuring through the force of his leadership by keeping the rennents of scattered units in a desperate breakout that suceeded in reaching the MLR.[63]

The Taro Leaf reported a total of 1,706 battle casualties in April, nearly 600 more than the 25th Infantry Division and over twice as many as the 3rd Infantry Division.[64] As far as casualties in the 5th RCT goes, one report states the 5th Infantry incurred 559 battle casualties in April: 20 KIA, 289 WIA, and 243 MIA, the near equivalent of one of its three infantry battalions.[65] In addition, 1 officer and 186 enlisted men were listed as non-battle casualties: 125 the result of disease, 61 due to injuries. A Triple Nickel personnel report submitted to 24th Infantry Division Artillery for the period of 1800 15 April to 1800 30 April lists 3 enlisted men KIA; 6 officers, 1 warrant officer and 43 enlisted men WIA; and 4 officers and 45 men MIA.[66] A handful of men who were initially reported MIA did trickle in over time. Of the men who were captured, a significant number died in captivity from wounds, maltreatment, and starvation.

The 7 officer and 366 enlisted replacements received in April did not cover the 5th RCT's losses, but, oddly enough, the combat team's enlisted strength was greater at the end of the month than it had been at the beginning. This was accounted for by the return of 312 veteran enlisted men and three officers from various hospitals.

The 5th RCT inflicted severe casualties on the Chinese in April 1951. Precise body counts are difficult to arrive at if only because it was quite a challenge to count bodies, at range, when "they are in piles and you are under intense incoming fire."[67] The infantry physically counted the bodies of 363 dead Chinese soldiers in April and believed they had wounded 212 more. *Hawaii Calls* was credited with killing 150 CCF soldiers at Pisi-gol, and *Aloha* 100 more. Triple Nickel gun crews probably killed hundreds, and wounded thousands, of enemy soldiers in a hurricane of high explosive shells.[68] Certainly, the Chinese lost heavily on the night of 22-23 April and in the ambush on 25 April, but no

Two G Company survivors of the ambush. Robert White (left) was wounded and captured. A CCF surgeon amputated his leg before his release in the 1953 prisoner exchange. Raymond J. Warner (right) survived wounds from a November 1950 action and escaped Death Valley with a small group of stragglers. (source: Ray Warner)

one had time to count the enemy corpses or to shed tears for the fallen People's Volunteers. Not even Chairman Mao.

The 24th Infantry Division reported the loss of twelve 105-mm howitzers to enemy action on 25 April.[69] Six of the lost howitzers belonged to B Battery. Able Battery had lost one howitzer on 23 April and two more at Pisi-gol.[70] Charlie Battery managed to extradite four of its six howitzers from the trap. The mystery of who owned the one unaccounted for howitzer remains. It may have belonged to a field artillery battalion other than the Triple Nickel, or perhaps it was a badly damaged weapon that had to be replaced following the ambush.[71]

Particularly heavy tank and vehicle losses characterized the engagement. Tank Company lost three Easy Eights in the fighting. Of these, LT Ed Crockett's crew abandoned *Hawaii Calls* as previously related. Master Sergeant Johnnie Walls' crew bailed out of *Leilani* after its engine blew a rod at the worst possible moment while under heavy enemy fire. First Lieutenant Gordon W. Campbell prudently abandoned one of his 4th Platoon Easy Eights that was being towed due to a mechanical malfunction. The 6th Tank Battalion lost nine Pattons. We know that six Pattons supporting G Company were knocked out. Two more were lost when the 21st Infantry attempted to break through to the trapped 5th RCT. The fate of the ninth Patton is unknown. Eighty-five 5th RCT vehicles, including thirty-two 2 1/2 ton trucks, were destroyed.

The reported loss of just 23 M-1s, 12 carbines, and 15 BARs is difficult to reconcile with the large number of dead and missing who remained lying on the battlefield. One suspects this number reflects those soldiers present for duty who had lost their weapons in the ambush. If so, this indicates that most of the men retained their personal weapons, and thus their discipline and self-respect. As far as crew-served weapons go, four M1917A1 .30-caliber heavy machine guns, fourteen M1919A6 Brownings, three 81-mm and five 60-mm mortars, in addition to one 57-mm recoilless rifle, were also lost, probably abandoned by reasonable men who attempted to breakout of the trap on foot.[72]

It would sound trite to say the 5th RCT was unlucky on 25 April. Moreover, it would not be entirely true. Combat units to a large extent make their own luck and, on 25 April 1951, a chain of events and serious tactical errors culminated in the tragic engagement that ensued. Although LTC Wilson was new to the command, and did not yet know his officers or men, most of the errors fall squarely on his shoulders. When the 24th Infantry Division directed LTC Wilson to rescue the Rangers, it appears that he lost touch with the battlefield while focusing his eyes and energy on what was essentially a battalion commander's task. Since the combat team had rescued most of the Rangers by 1200, the five-hour delay between that moment and B Battery's first frantic appeal for help remains nearly incomprehensible. War has a cold logic all its own. The fate of a couple of Rangers, no matter how harsh it may sound in the peace and quite of one's home, was not worth the risk thrust upon the entire combat team — a significant force of arms the Taro Leaf was counting on to help reestablish the MLR.

Chinese infantry were clearly moving southward in large numbers on the ridgelines to the combat team's east and west as the long day wore on. The leadership's lackadaisical response to this threat remains difficult to fathom. Lieutenant Colonel Wilson made no provision to protect the combat team's flanks or rear when he ordered the 3rd Battalion to commence its withdrawal. In spite of all the hard-learned lessons accumulated over the past months of combat against the Chinese, LTC Wilson failed to understand the significance of the pass at Pisi-gol. The 5th RCT would have been better served if the 3rd Battalion had secured this key terrain and held it until the rest of the combat team passed through later in the day. Such leapfrog tactics had been used with great success under COL Throckmorton's sure hand in previous rearguard actions.

"We violated our own standard operating procedures," explained CAPT William Perry. "It was standard procedure to position a battalion, or at least a company, on the next defensible hilltop position. We didn't do that this time. As a result we lost control of the people. As soon as you put your soldiers on trucks you lose control of your people anyway. But we could have kept control of some of the units. Of course, what happened, was that all the companies got hit, like Lamb's, when they were still mounted on vehicles. It's a little hard to get people off of vehicles and form them up to fight because you don't know where all your people are. Of course, I'm glad we stayed for the Rangers, but it was an expensive thing in people and equipment."[73]

The combat team had, moreover, commenced its withdrawal in small motorized columns that resembled an administrative retrograde rather than a withdrawal under pressure. Lieutenant Colonel Wilson appears to have focused only on the threat from the north. The possibility that the combat team would have to fight in every direction seems to have escaped him. A sense of urgency does not enter the picture until after B Battery drove into the ambush. It is difficult to escape the conclusion that the senior leadership misjudged the situation at this point and contributed to the disaster. Able and Charlie batteries were firing at clearly visible targets on the ridgelines overlooking Pisi-gol when they were essentially directed to limber up and drive into the Chinese killing zone. That the gun crews fought like tigers, firing over open sights, and still managed to extradite many of their howitzers and much of their equipment, speaks volumes for the heroism of the soldiers and the small unit leadership displayed by officers and NCOs. Nevertheless, this disaster was not a foregone conclusion. If the two batteries had continued shooting as LTC Wilson brought the 2nd Battalion southward with the tank companies, the result would probably have been dramatically different. The 5th RCT might still have had to use the escape route to the west, but the combat team would have come out fighting in cohesive platoons, companies, and batteries — and more men and equipment would have been saved.

Lieutenant Colonel Wilson was a brave man who was elevated to a position of immense responsibility with little time to learn the part. Moreover, he did not enjoy the confidence of several key officers who were annoyed that a man they considered an unqualified outsider was to command them in battle. General Ridgway apparently had cause to rue his decision to "hand-pick" LTC Wilson for the job. For though LTC Wilson was promoted to colonel shortly after the ambush, he was never promoted again.

COL Arthur H. Wilson bids farewell to officers of the command, upon being replaced by COL Alexander D. Surles, 20 August 1951. (source: NA)

CHAPTER TWENTY-NINE

THE COLOR OF BLOOD

Blood is the price of victory.
Clausewitz, On War

First Lieutenant Earl Law lay on a cot nursing his wounded knee in a crowded hospital tent full of badly wounded enlisted men. Their bloodstained bandages marked the soldiers as members of an exclusive club, one few men sought to join. As the lieutenant conversed with a young rifleman who had lost a kidney in the ambush, a doctor entered the tent with a female nurse. The doctor, who wore the rank insignia of a colonel, took one glance at LT Law and said, "Lieutenant, you're in the wrong tent. The officer's tent is up the hill."

Lieutenant Law replied, "Well colonel, I got hit with these guys, and I don't think I'll be contaminated too much. I guess I'll stay right here." The colonel stiffly informed LT Law that he could do whatever he pleased and started fiddling with the wounded officer's leg.

The knee was badly swollen, stiff, and would not bend. When it appeared the colonel was going to bend it anyway, the lieutenant asked him to desist. The colonel angrily replied, "I know what I'm doing." The doctor placed one hand on LT Law's ankle, and another on his thigh, and bent the tortured officer's damaged leg.

Sweat popped out of LT Law's forehead, and in agony, he yelled at the colonel, "Let go of my leg you son of a bitch!" The colonel dropped the leg and shouted back, "If that's how you feel, I'll send you back to the front!"

"Get my britches!" LT Law roared at the doctor as the stuffy colonel stormed out of the tent. The nurse, clearly shocked at the exchange, admonished the wounded officer, "You shouldn't talk to a colonel like that."

"I'll knock the colonel on his butt, lady," replied the former master sergeant. Lieutenant Law left the hospital on crutches and returned to duty with the Triple Nickel. Two weeks later LTC Stuart directed that LT Law return to the States. The battalion commander was afraid that if C Battery got into another firefight, someone would probably get killed trying to rescue the injured officer.[1]

The 5th RCT captured just six Chinese PWs in April, a testimony to the morale and discipline of the CCF soldiers fighting in Korea.[2] Few Chinese soldiers had been captured up to this stage of the war, largely due to the enemy's firm belief in the justice of their cause and unflinching confidence in their leaders. Though poorly supplied and inadequately armed, the Chinese soldier had proven brave and determined in the attack, and both resolute and tenacious in the defense.

The moral facade of the Chinese soldier cracked toward the end of April, a direct result of the unrealistic demands Mao had placed on his men. Blind faith collapsed in the face of overwhelming American firepower and inadequate food supplies. Approximately 70,000 Chinese soldiers had fallen killed or wounded in the Spring Offensive alone, a horrifying loss of trained soldiers and commanders that even the manpower rich CCF could ill afford to lose.[3] A significant percentage of these casualties were borne by the cadre, to the detriment of the overall effectiveness of the CCF. Thousands of CCF soldiers perished from exhaustion, starvation and disease.

Recent drafts of untrained conscripts could not hope to equal the tactical skill and morale of the original "Iron" troops who had spearheaded the CCF intervention forces in Korea. Severe losses in the cadre had reduced the overall effectiveness of the surviving veterans. Party slogans could not overcome the obvious disparity in weapons and supplies the Chinese faced in daily firefights with American soldiers and Marines. A CCF squad leader wrote in captivity, "'Human wave' tactics are supposed to overwhelm the enemy's firepower with predominance of manpower and thus win the

By 1952 integration was a fact of Army life. B Battery soldiers at rest. (source: 5th RCT Association)

victory. From my experience in the present war, I found this tactic had no sense and no value. It also cannot be approved from a humanitarian point of view. In actual combat it was nothing but a mass loss of lives and defeat."[4]

Mao did not concur and directed his commanders to mount yet another major offensive. Communist cadres promised their troops that military support would be forthcoming from the Soviet Union. Until it materialized, the lightly armed CCF infantry would bear the brunt of the fighting, and suffer appalling losses, in the face of absolute American fire superiority.[5]

As Mao's armies prepared for another human wave assault on the Eighth Army's lines, the 5th RCT licked its wounds. Lieutenant Colonel Clarence Stuart wisely refused to let his batteries go south to be refitted. "We'll stay here and have the equipment come to us," he informed his battery commanders.[6] "That was a wise decision, for if we'd gone to a rear area to recoup, I think our morale would have plummeted," said SGT Samuel Lewis.[7]

C Battery, 555th FAB, falls in for an inspection in Korea, summer 1951. CPL James Shaw, Ogden, Utah, front rank, right file. The Red Leg at the end of the first rank is an African-American cannoneer. (source: James Shaw)

First Lieutenant Gordon W. Campbell, the senior armored platoon leader, assumed command of Tank Company after LTC Wilson selected CAPT George Gaylord to be his regimental S-3. One of LT Campbell's first acts was to send LT Ed Crockett to Taegu to expedite the return of a couple of repaired tanks to the front. While in Taegu, LT Crockett and his crew parked one of the repaired tanks in front of a field hospital before going inside to visit the company's soldiers who were recovering from sickness or wounds. After a cheerful visit with their friends, the tank crew walked outside the hospital in time to witness a group of Military Police scratching their heads over how to write a ticket for an Easy Eight. Lieutenant Crockett's crew solved their problem by driving the tank to the train station where it was loaded onto a flat car.[8]

Upon LT Crockett's return, he was directed to report to the Quartermaster who demanded that he reimburse the government for a .45-caliber pistol lost when he bailed out of *Hawaii Calls*. Lieutenant Crockett stormed out of the flustered officer's tent after refusing to pay the bill. Thankfully, no one ever asked him to reimburse Uncle Sam for *Hawaii Calls*.[9]

Reason triumphed over racial prejudice throughout the Army as the first casualty intensive year of the Korean War ended. Skin tone lapsed into insignificance as the firestorm consumed lives at a prodigious rate. Racially segregated units slowly disappeared from the Army's order of battle. Only one color mattered in the Army anymore, and all soldiers shared it — the color of blood.

First Lieutenant Clarence H. Jackson had paved the way, fighting with Easy Company from Chindong-ni to Kusong. Lieutenant Jackson was a brave and respected leader who took care of his men. Colonel Throckmorton had the honor of presenting LT Jackson the Silver Star on 11 March 1951 for gallantry in action.[10] Lieutenant Jackson was the first step, an experiment in fact, that would reach its logical conclusion the day General Colin Powell assumed the mantle of Chairman of the Joint Chiefs of Staff. Now LT Jackson was gone, having rotated to the States with the first group of veterans to leave Korea.

Lieutenant Brooker T. Morris, from Houston, Texas, was the second Black officer to join the combat team. He served as a rifle platoon leader and never lost a man in combat. Although several of his soldiers were wounded, he was justly proud that he always recovered his casualties from the battlefield. Much later, on another battlefield, he became the first African American to teach Caucasian students in Houston's newly integrated school districts.[11]

The manpower starved 5th RCT absorbed its first Black enlisted replacements in the winter of 1951. More Black soldiers followed, slowly making their presence known in the combat team. Ten days before the Chinese Spring Offensive, of the 123 Black soldiers serving in the entire 24th Infantry Division, 38 were serving in the 5th Infantry, and 5 in the 555th FAB.[12]

Private First Class Augustus "Gus" Campbell was the first Black soldier to join Tank Company. He was assigned to LT Ed Crockett's crew as a loader in *Kathy's Kiddy Kar*, an Easy Eight named in honor of the platoon leader's infant daughter. If PFC Campbell was apprehensive about being the lone Black soldier in the 25-man tank platoon, he kept it to himself. Not surprisingly, in view of the platoon's already diverse racial mixture, PFC Campbell was quickly accepted.

Private First Class Campbell did not have long to wait for his baptism of fire. A few days after he arrived, *Kathy's Kiddy Kar*'s armor was literally pinging from hits by small arms fire as the tank platoon advanced into the midst of a Chinese defensive zone. Lieutenant Crockett issued the gunner a fire command, who in turn lined an enemy machine gun in his sights. Private First Class Campbell properly slammed home a forty-pound high explosive shell into the gun chamber tripping the breach block cover into the firing position. The next thing the crew heard was the dreaded sound of a separated round as the warhead departed the shell casing and slid a few feet down the gun barrel. With the main gun rendered impotent, PFC Campbell quickly opened the breach and removed the shell casing without dropping any of the explosive powder on the turret floor. Once he finished the first of his immediate action duties, the more hazardous task remained. Lieutenant Crockett turned to his loader and said, "You know what you have to do."

Rather than waste time responding in the affirmative, the gutsy young loader opened his hatch, pulled himself out of the tank, leaped onto the ground, and sprang into action. As bullets impacted on the ground around his feet, and ricocheted off the Sherman's armor plate, PFC Campbell removed two five-foot sections of wooden ramrod from the side of the tank, and quickly attached them together. Standing upright in full view of the enemy, he gently pushed the ramrod down the barrel until the warhead fell into the gunner's waiting hands inside the turret. A twenty-second eternity later, PFC Campbell scrambled unscathed through his hatch and resumed his loader functions.

Lieutenant Crockett said in admiration, "Wow Campbell, that was fast work."

The loader nodded and replied, "Sir, I even took time to relieve myself out there." The tension broken, the crew laughed together over the intercom and returned to the deadly business of war.[13]

A newly promoted CAPT Frank Athanason received a message a few weeks after the ambush to report to LTC Stuart and pick-up a replacement. Normal operating procedure did not call for battery commanders to personally pick-up replacements, so the mystified CO of A Battery hurried over in his jeep to find out what was going on.

Lieutenant Colonel Stuart called CAPT Athanason into his tent and told him to grab a seat. Black soldiers had first joined the Triple Nickel the previous winter, but they had all been assigned to either Headquarters or Service batteries. This was about to change. Private Jim Brown had just reported for duty and LTC Stuart was assigning him to A Battery. Since CAPT Athanason was from the South, LTC Stuart believed that if Private Brown succeeded in A Battery, and the battalion commander wanted him to succeed, it would be taken as a good sign for the other batteries to emulate.

Private Jim Brown, an eighteen-year-old cook by military occupational specialty, was standing outside the tent waiting to meet his battery commander. Able Battery was short of cooks, so CAPT Athanason meant it when he told the young soldier that he was glad to have him in his unit. They returned together to the battery where Private Brown was dropped off into the capable hands of the first sergeant, who in turn took the soldier over to the tent where the cooks were billeted.

Half an hour later, the first sergeant entered CAPT Athanason's tent with Private Brown at his side, and reported that the cook wanted to speak to the battery commander about a matter of utmost importance. A thoroughly mystified CAPT Athanason asked Private Brown, "What is the problem?"

Private Brown looked him square in the eye and responded, "Sir, I don't want to cook. I want the most dangerous job in the battery so I can prove myself to the men." Captain Athanason mulled the soldier's heartfelt request over for a brief moment, and agreed to make it so. He assigned Private Brown to the FO Team in support of A Company and, for the next couple of weeks, the soldier carried the SCR-300 radio on his back into the mountains to do battle against the Chinese. After a particularly grueling firefight, Able Company limped off the line to enjoy a short breather in reserve. Private Brown marched down with the infantry, head held high, looking just as filthy, bleary-eyed, exhausted, and foot-sore as the rest of the soldiers. As Private Brown approached CAPT Athanason, the FO radio operator smiled and said, "Sir, I'm ready to start cooking again." Private Brown returned to the mess tent a proven cannoneer who had paid his dues in Hell.[14]

As time went on, more Black soldiers joined the combat team. Performance counted, not skin tone, in the eyes of the soldiers. Men who performed well were accepted. Those who let their comrades down, regardless of race, were not. Master Sergeant William T. Welch, the platoon sergeant of the 2nd Platoon, George Company explained, "I had three Black soldiers in my platoon. Priestly was a BAR man. In fact I had two Black BAR men in my platoon. One I would have shot if I'd got a chance to. He would point the BAR at our own guys and threaten them all the time. Another guy, I would have given my life for. I think his name was Earl Renfrew. He ended up as assistant squad leader. And then we had a medic by the name of 'Doc' who treated our wounds when we were hit."[15]

On 4 May, the 5th RCT received orders to establish a regimental-sized outpost line of resistance (OPLR) in the vicinity of Masogu-ri, a rubble-strewn village approximately 5,000 yards forward of the 24th Infantry Division's sector of the MLR. The Eighth Army had recently added depth to the defense when it initiated the practice of using a regiment from each of division to defend an OPLR.

The mission of the 5th RCT on 4 May was to "Seek out the enemy, attempt to determine his plan and to deceive him as to the location of the Division Main Line of Resistance."[16] The combat team occupied the OPLR the following day with each infantry battalion deployed in a hilltop perimeter defense astride the Pukhan Valley in anticipation of a CCF offensive down the valley with the enemy's objective being the capture of Seoul.

Lieutenant General James A. Van Fleet, the commanding general of the Eighth Army, wanted to turn the Pukhan Valley into a death zone for the CCF. He directed his commanders to build bunkers for their troops and weapons, lay swaths of barbed wire, and liberally sprinkle the ground with mines. Convinced that the CCF would direct their main effort on this sector of the front, General Van Fleet planned his defensive measures accordingly. That the Chinese might have other operational plans in mind was not given serious consideration.[17]

Aggressive infantry patrolling commenced along the length of the combat team's 10,000-meter frontage which resulted in the capture of one CCF PW. No further contact was made with the enemy until nightfall, on 5 May, when a Fox Company patrol exchanged gunfire and grenades with a fifteen-man CCF patrol. On the morning of 6 May, seven infantry patrols moved out. Two CCF stragglers were killed in brief firefights and one PW taken.[18]

Tank-infantry patrols operated forward of the OPLR over the course of the next several days. Some of these patrols penetrated to a distance of 10,000 yards forward of the outpost line. The virtual absence of enemy contact indicated the CCF had withdrawn its forces to regroup in preparation for another offensive. On 10 May, a patrol from the 1st Battalion engaged approximately thirty CCF soldiers who fled northward into the hills after a brief exchange of tank and artillery fire.[19]

The Chinese resumed aggressive offensive patrolling on the night of 12-13 May. Easy Company's perimeter was hit by a CCF combat patrol that threw hand grenades into the American positions. An ambush patrol from the 2nd Battalion shot-up this Chinese patrol, as it withdrew to the north, killing four CCF soldiers and wounding six more.[20]

Item and King Companies were dispatched the next morning, reinforced with tanks and artillery, to attack an enemy concentration reported in the vicinity of Hyon-ni. This task force encountered a stubborn, dug in, opponent who fought back with automatic weapons, 76-mm field guns, and mortars. Air strikes and artillery fire inflicted losses on the CCF, but the task force withdrew on order at 1530 to the OPLR without eliminating the enemy defenders.[21]

On 14 May, an angry General Van Fleet toured the 24th Infantry Division's sector. He chewed out the corps and divisional commander for not making the defensive positions as strong as he had repeatedly demanded.[22] Later that night, a 1st Battalion patrol called in artillery fire on a group of 150 CCF soldiers, killing fifty-five of the enemy. A prisoner taken on 15 May stated that the CCF 191st Division, 64th CCF Army, was massing for an offensive against the combat team. The lull before the storm was over, for Mao's infantry had recovered from their bloody wounds and the CCF was poised to mount another offensive.

The American soldiers were exhausted from the long, intense period of patrolling. In the rugged terrain, even a 4,000 meter foot patrol could take up to an entire day of non-stop marching. Nevertheless, the benefits derived from the patrolling "outweighed the disadvantages particularly since heavy fighting of the 22nd and the 23rd of April and the ambush fight of 25 April might well have reacted to weaken the Regiment's offensive spirit if the Regiment had not been so actively employed."[23] More importantly, aggressive small unit actions in the face of comparatively light resistance had blooded the replacements who now enjoyed confidence in themselves and their units.

The daylight hours of 16 May passed quietly enough. Each battalion pulled back a few hundred yards to higher ground in an effort to deceive

B Battery, 555th FAB, 1952. (source: 5th RCT Association)

the Chinese. Listening posts and ambush patrols departed friendly lines at dusk to report and, if possible, to disrupt the enemy's advance. Artillery interdiction fires rained down on likely enemy avenues of approach throughout the night. Tank Company consolidated its platoons between the 1st and 2nd Battalions while Able Company, 6th Tank Battalion, occupied firing positions on the combat team's right flank.

The anticipated enemy offensive commenced with CCF platoon-strength combat patrols probing all three battalions in the early hours of the night. At 0015 on 17 May, CAPT George Gaylord informed COL Mauz, division G-3, that Love and Item Companies were under small arms fire.[24] Fifteen minutes later, he informed division that King Company had incurred four WIAs from 81-mm mortar fire. Tank Company's four platoons were heavily engaged from the start, killing scores of Chinese with high-explosive rounds and concentrated machine gun fire. Love Company repulsed an assault by two CCF platoons with heavy defensive fire.

By 0130, the CCF attack had spread to the 1st Battalion's sector. The 2nd Battalion was hit too, particularly Fox Company, but the enemy's main effort appeared to be developing in the 3rd Battalion's sector where the pressure continued to mount. At 0145 Item Company came under heavy fire from approximately eighty CCF soldiers operating to its rear. Captain Gaylord passed this discomforting information up to division. Five minutes later, a bizarre incident occurred when George Company reported, "Estimated enemy battalion coming down the road from west on horses. Engaging with fire now."[25]

Able Company was clobbered at 0150, with COL Wilson on the line to COL Mauz reporting that one of its three rifle platoons was overrun. The remnants of Able Company were locked in a desperate close combat struggle in their defensive positions. Colonel Wilson reported that the enemy had forced a penetration between George and Easy Companies. By 0220, COL Mauz estimated that a CCF regiment had engaged the 5th RCT.

Five minutes later, COL Wilson lost contact with George Company. With the nightmare of Death Valley ever present in COL Wilson's mind, he ordered all non-essential vehicles to withdraw to the MLR at this time. The combat team regained contact with George Company at 0305 while the hard-

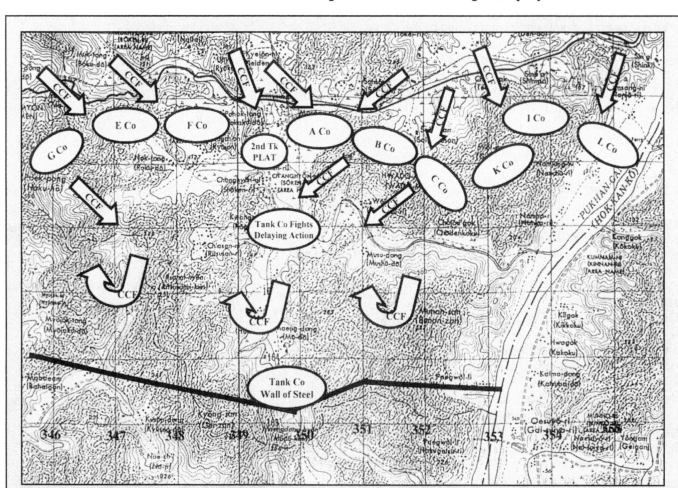

MASOGU-RI, 0001 - 0700, 17 MAY 1951. The CCF offensive penetrates the 5th RCT's defensive line. Hit hard, the companies withdraw under heavy pressure, to the dark line on the map. Tank Company fights a classic delaying action. At dawn, the "Wall of Steel" breaks up the final CCF assault. The Chinese withdraw, having sustained heavy losses.

pressed infantry withdrew under intense pressure to a tighter battalion defensive perimeter.[26]

First LT Charles E. Brannon was shot int he head in Charlie Company's sector while manning a machine gun. He died of wounds in Tokyo. During the 45 days he served in Korea, he earned two Distinguished Service Crosses, two Purple Hearts and a Silver Star. Meanwhile, LT Ed Crockett's tank platoon covered the 2nd Battalion's withdrawal, until it too was facing encirclement. Lieutenant Crockett gave the order to withdraw, and the platoon's Easy Eights lumbered 300 yards to the rear, their respective armaments lashing out at the advancing CCF squads and platoons. Master Sergeant Johnnie Walls' 3rd Tank Platoon overwatched the movement.[27] After the neighboring 1st Battalion withdrew a short distance, the 3rd Tank Platoon withdrew through the hard-fighting 1st and 2nd Tank Platoons. Tank Company fought a textbook delaying action, to the probable dismay of the decimated CCF assault battalions that had to pay the price.[28]

As pressure built on the OPLR, CAPT George Gaylord requested to continue the withdrawal started when George Company was pulled in. Colonel Mauz thought this over for a moment and replied, "Hold present position for time being."[29]

CPL Estes Philpott, Decatur, AR (center) with two friends: (left) Thomas Andrewjewski was KIA 1 November 1951 and (right) Donald P. Bellis was KIA on 20 October 1951. (source: Estes Philpott)

Clearly, the Taro Leaf G-3 was against a night withdrawal in mountainous territory.

Colonel Wilson disagreed and requested at 0345 to withdraw the combat team to the MLR. The Commanding General 24th Infantry Division, Major General Blackshear M. Bryan, fired COL Wilson's request up to IX Corps G-3, Colonel Kunzig, who replied twenty minutes later, "Hold until daylight and further instructions will be issued."[30]

An unidentified 5th RCT radio operator informed the Taro Leaf G-3 section at 0410 that "1st Battalion is being outflanked and 2nd Battalion has been ordered to withdraw to phase line one. Believe we will be unable to hold line due to increasing pressure."[31] Chinese 81-mm mortar and artillery fire crashed down on the 2nd Battalion, inflicting losses and adding to the confusion as it attempted to reorganize in the darkness. Meanwhile, the 2nd Tank Platoon shifted its front to face the growing enemy threat from the northwest.[32]

Colonel Mauz responded at 0425, "Ordered to hold present positions, further orders at daylight." The combat team's leadership noted their disagreement ten minutes later. "1st Battalion hit by estimated enemy battalion. 2nd Battalion hit by estimated enemy battalion. 3rd Battalion hit by estimated enemy battalion plus. If hit again in same strength will be unable to hold, do not have stabilized line."[33] At this time, all four of Tank Company's platoons were heavily engaged, maneuvering as necessary to face the rapidly developing threat.[34]

General Bryan relayed the 5th RCT's estimate of the situation to IX Corps. Major General William M. Hoge, the corps commander, reiterated that it was Army doctrine to avoid night withdrawals. General Hoge was concerned that a night withdrawal might turn into a disaster. He directed that "5th Infantry move into perimeters and hold those positions until daylight."[35]

Tank Company recorded that the stiffest fighting occurred at 0530. "Enemy machine guns lined the ridges and their fire was of such magnitude that neither its accuracy nor violence has ever been paralleled in any of the intense fighting that this unit, and possibly any unit has undergone in the present conflict," wrote CAPT Gordon Campbell after the engagement. "The night was starkly illuminated by flashes from weapons of all calibers and the darkness was veiled by the mass of tracers arcing through the night."[36]

General Hoge was vindicated when the crisis peaked at dawn. The powerful CCF assault down the Pukhan Valley led many in the 5th RCT to believe theirs was the biggest fight in Korea that night. They were wrong. For even as the Chinese infantry hurled themselves into their assault against the 5th RCT, farther to the east the CCF unleashed its main effort in a massive offensive that struck X Corps in the trackless mountains on the No Name Line. Once again the ROKs broke, but X Corps held on and inflicted murderous losses on the Chinese. Tenth Corps' artillery blasted entire CCF battalions and regiments into oblivion, firing 17,000 rounds on 16 May, 38,000 rounds on 17 May, and an amazing 50,000 rounds on 19 May alone.[37]

Meanwhile, the 5th RCT fought on the OPLR. During the night of 17-18 May, the CCF struck the 1st and 3rd Battalions on Hill 537. One company from the 1st Battalion was dislodged at 0415 after heavy fighting. A counterattack recaptured Hill 537 later in the morning.[38] Able Company, 6th Tank Battalion, supported the assault with their heavy 90-mm cannons. A CCF battalion overran Hill 537 in seesaw fighting early on the morning of 19 May. The position was restored by counterattack at 1000.

In a calculated attempt to take the pressure off X Corps, the Eighth Army jumped off in a counter-offensive code-named DETONATE on 20 May.[39] The 5th RCT advanced in a driving rain, the men carrying their heavy combat loads up and down the steep ridgelines, engaging the CCF at every opportunity. Heavy fighting characterized the advance, particularly in the vicinity of Hills 373 and 388 where the 5th RCT fought a deeply entrenched, well-armed opponent. Hill 388 fell on 20 May, but the CCF defenders on Hill 373 doggedly contested the advance until they were finally overrun in bitter fighting the following day. The combat team estimated it had inflicted 176 KIA and 175 WIA on the CCF in the previous few days of fighting.[40]

The 5th RCT advanced on 22 May through resistance that ranged from light to heavy. Fox Company overran Hill 192 in a stiff engagement, capturing nineteen CCF soldiers and killing thirty-three more.[41] In contrast the 1st Battalion was mildly surprised to witness the Chinese abandon their positions on Hill 254 without a fight.

Morale soared as the combat team pursued the fleeing CCF. For the first time since Mao's entry into the Korean War, large numbers of Chinese soldiers voluntarily laid down their arms. A sense of despair gripped the starving, ill-equipped CCF soldiers, who had incurred murderous losses for no discernable gain in the recent fighting. Political officers no longer held sway over men who had watched their units decimated in fruitless attacks in the face of overwhelming American fire superiority. Losses in the cadre had reached catastrophic levels. Incessant hunger had sapped the will of the survivors.

On the night of 26-27 May, George Company dispatched an ambush patrol led by MSGT Massingill. A Chinese column blundered into George Company's ambush and lost twenty KIA in the killing zone.[42] Private First Class Roberto L. Casillas, from the Bronx, New York, was mortally wounded by return fire. Master Sergeant Bill Welch carried the wounded soldier for a half-mile to the aid station, but PFC Casillas died in his arms before he covered the distance.[43]

The Chinese soldiers had been moving toward an attack position when they walked into George Company's ambush. Additional CCF units had already reached this attack position and were preparing to strike Hill 192 in a desperate bid to regain the tactical initiative. George Company, alerted by the ambush, was ready for action when the CCF struck at 0400. A simultaneous assault hit the 21st Infantry's CP, located on the road immediately behind George Company. In heavy fighting the Chinese overran a portion of the disputed hill.[44]

MSGT William Welch, Mahtomedi, MN (sitting foreground) carried the mortally wounded PFC Roberto Casillas, Bronx, New York, to the aid station. (source: Mrs. William Welch)

The first reinforcement to reach George Company was LT Ed Crockett's 2nd Tank Platoon. Captain Gordon Campbell had selected LT Crockett's platoon to lead the counterattack because they were familiar with the terrain, having just completed a stint on the portion of the front lines under attack.[45]

Oddly enough, it was judged too dangerous to commit the 2nd Battalion's rifle companies in a counterattack until dawn. It was feared that the infantry might be ambushed and shot up in the darkness. The known shortage of CCF antitank weapons contributed to this curious reversal of tactical roles that witnessed the armor's dispatch ahead of the infantry. Although LT Crockett's bow

CAPT Chauffer, CO George Company, lines up the day's haul in CCF PWs. (source: Ed Crockett)

gunner suffered a severe head wound, no tanks were lost during the engagement. Heavy casualties were inflicted on the Chinese.

At dawn, Fox Company, Sonny's old outfit, gained a measure of revenge for Death Valley when it spearheaded a 2nd Battalion counterattack to rescue the soldiers still holding out on Hill 192. The CO of Fox Company at this time was 1st LT John R. Henderson, of Waynesburg, Pennsylvania, who sported a handlebar mustache and packed two pearl-handled six-guns on his hips. A gambler by nature and with the cards, his soldiers followed their courageous company commander wherever he led.

During their ascent up a trail, Fox Company came across two armed Chinese soldiers who quickly laid down their weapons and surrendered to LT Henderson. Just a few days before, any CCF soldier worth his salt would have sprayed the Americans with burp gun fire, for until

A 5th RCT soldier marches CCF PWs down a hill as other 5th Infantry soldiers ascend it. (source: Chang)

then voluntary surrenders on the part of Chinese soldiers had been a rare event. The pleasantly surprised company commander whipped out a pack of cigarettes and gave each of the Chinese soldiers a light. As soon as the two prisoners had taken their first tentative puffs and smiled in gratitude, hundreds of heavily armed CCF soldiers emerged from behind the rocks above and laid down their weapons in surrender. Fox Company was mightily surprised and quickly ran out of smokes. If the Chinese had chosen to resist, many men would have died on that nameless hill, but LT Henderson's compassion for his defeated opponents had clearly won the day.[46]

When Fox Company reached the 21st Infantry's CP, they found that unit's medics shooting it out in the trenches with their .45s, in a desperate close combat struggle to hold off the Chinese. Suddenly, and much to everyone's amazement, the Chinese will to resist abruptly collapsed at 1430 when 1,141 soldiers laid down their arms and marched into captivity, the single largest haul of Chinese PWs to date. Over 250 Chinese surrendered to the 2nd Tank Platoon alone.[47] The Chinese still possessed a plentiful supply of ammunition when they surrendered.[48]

"It's like a holiday," remarked PFC Raymond Aokiona, from Honolulu, to a reporter as he led his fourth group of PWs to the rear that day. Sergeant First Class Y.S. Lee, from Honolulu, shouted cadence and marching commands in English to the Chinese. "The rhythm is the same," SFC Lee explained to the reporter. "It worked on the North Koreans last Fall."[49]

General Ridgway's operational philosophy of employing massive firepower, combined with aggressive maneuver, to combat Chinese manpower appeared to be working. Cracks in CCF morale grew into a torrent of PWs the longer the counteroffensive continued, much to the dismay of the Communist leadership. It was probably no accident that the Communists initiated peace feelers with the United Nations shortly after the 5th RCT's victory on Hill 192.

The 5th RCT went on to participate with honor and distinction in every campaign over the next two bitter years of the Korean War. On the blood-drenched Hills of Sacrifice, the 5th RCT served with intense pride and selfless valor. When the 24th Infantry Division was withdrawn to Japan in late 1951, the 5th RCT remained in Korea as an independent combat team. During the next two years, the 5th RCT served at various times as a corps level reserve and under the operational control of the 3rd, 25th, 40th and 45th Infantry Divisions. With the sole exception of a brief spell guarding PWs on Koje-do Island, the 5th RCT was always on the firing line.

In many respects the fighting increased in ferocity. Mao exploited the peace negotiations as an umbrella to increase the CCF's firepower, which in turn played a significant role in restoring the shattered morale of his soldiers. The Soviet Union, for a price Mao later had cause to regret, began to provide the CCF with modern heavy weapons and logistical support.

Men died every day in a war America no longer planned to win. Major William Perry, recently promoted and now serving as the CO of the 2nd Battalion, recalls one of the thousands of forgotten soldiers who fell in Korea. "I received a replacement officer, a reserve second lieutenant, who had served as an enlisted man fighting in Europe during World War II. He had three kids. I know that because we talked about his family on the day he joined my battalion and, you see, I had three kids, too. We were comparing notes, talking, and he was probably two years older than me. He was a replacement, a reserve lieutenant who had been called to active duty. I informed him that I was sorry, because I was going to have to send him to his unit that night. He was going to have to go up the hill with the chow. Normally, I would have preferred to keep him at battalion for a couple of days until he got his feet on the ground. But the unit I was sending him to join was short of officers, and he was needed on that hill. He said, 'It's all right, Sir. I know what it's like. It will take me a few days to get back in the middle of things, but I knew what I was doing when I signed up for the inactive reserves. I knew that if something came along, then I might have to get involved. And I knew that, being an infantry platoon leader, when Korea broke out, I'd probably have to go. I know it's tough, that casualties have been heavy, and it's going to be chancy. That said, I'm proud to serve.' He went up that night with the chow. The next morning, his soldiers carried his body down the hill wrapped in a poncho."[50]

The 5th RCT fought on. Able Company was the only company or battery-sized unit in the 5th RCT to earn a Distinguished Unit Citation. It did so while participating in the dogged defense of Outpost Harry on 12-13 June 1953. This most sanguinary engagement witnessed 456,995 incoming CCF artillery and mortar rounds impact on the Outpost Harry garrison during the second week of June alone.[51] The CCF hurled elements of three divisions into the struggle, losing battalion after battalion in human wave assaults to intense American defensive fire. Penetrations of the MLR were expelled in vicious close combat. True to form, the 555th FAB made its presence known, firing 50,000 rounds in five nights of continuous combat.[52]

On yet another summer day in July 1953, the Chinese unleashed 13 divisions to teach the ROKs a final lesson. The CCF juggernaut overran two regiments of the elite ROK Capitol Division, but then ran into the depressed barrels of the Triple Nickel. The 555th FAB fired some 15,000 rounds alone that day, many over open sights. A human tidal wave swamped B and C batteries in bitter, close combat that witnessed appalling casualties on each side. Elements of Service and Headquarters batteries went under too. Able Battery, commanded by 1st LT Ted Griesinger, successfully disengaged five of their howitzers as waves of Chinese infantry rushed the guns. Casualties in the Triple Nickel ranged on the order of 275 men. Approximately 75 soldiers were KIA. The unfortunate men who marched into CCF captivity that day were exchanged a few weeks later when the Armistice went into effect. Meanwhile, men continued to die.[53]

Sergeant First Class Harold R. Cross, from western Michigan, had served in the Army Occupation Forces in Germany before mustering out of the service in November 1952 and returning home with Ilse, his German war bride. He reenlisted in the Army and joined King Company, 3rd Battalion, 5th RCT in March 1953. At 2030, on 27 July 1953, SFC Cross was sitting with five of his comrades and friends inside a heavily sand-bagged bunker one mile west of Christmas Hill and 500 yards south of the dominating heights of Hill 931, an imposing Chinese fortress. The soldiers were calmly awaiting the long hoped for Armistice to go into effect at 2200 along the length of the embattled front when the first of thousands of Chinese mortar and artillery shells burst in the vicinity of their position.

Explosions rocked the bunker as SFC Cross moved through the dust-filled air to the entrance where he sat down by the field phone to relay reports of incoming rounds to King Company's CP. A heavy caliber mortar or artillery shell made a direct hit on the bunker ten minutes later, the force of the explosion snapping in half the sixteen-inch log that served as the support beam for the doorway. The bunker promptly collapsed, pinning the six men inside under the fallen debris. Their shouts for help could not be heard above the roar of exploding shells.

Nearby, PFC Maxwell Feiner cringed inside his bunker as the howling, shrieking rain of high explosives pounded the tortured ground. He had escaped from Nazi Germany as a youth with his younger brother. Raised by foster parents in Boston, Massachusetts, he had learned at an early age that freedom is not free; Maxwell Feiner's beloved father had perished in the infamous Dachau Concentration Camp. His attempts to enlist in the Army, and later the Navy, at the outbreak of the Korean War had been rebuffed due to his alien status. Oddly enough, the Army drafted him on 13 August 1952, and Private Feiner found himself serving as a combat medic in Love Company.

After surviving the ferocious battles for the Punchbowl and Outpost Harry, PFC Feiner found himself inside the dubious shelter of a bunker as 8,800 CCF high explosive rounds impacted on Christmas Hill less than two hours before the Armistice was due to go into effect. The regimental Chaplain, Father Bull, advised the medics to remain under cover as the hurricane of explosive shells rained down on the hapless soldiers.

Following the barrage, the medics emerged from their bunker and went to work. When a group of soldiers, including PFC Feiner, reached the smoking ruins of one collapsed bunker, they heard the muffled voices of entrapped men. A rescue team pulled six men from the rubble of shattered support beams and perforated sandbags, including a mortally wounded SFC Cross who never

MAJ William Perry, Denver, CO, the CO of 2nd Battalion, is awarded the Silver Star by COL Alexander Surles, CO 5th RCT, on 20 September 1951. (source: NA)

whimpered or complained during or after the rescue attempt. Private First Class Feiner helped carry SFC Cross to an evacuation point where an ambulance whisked the wounded man away to an aid station. Sergeant First Class Cross died at 0200, four hours after the Armistice finally took effect. He was the final American to die in the war.[54]

Or was he? Strong evidence exists that the Communists failed to exchange all their prisoners of war when the so-called prisoner exchange occurred after the Armistice went into effect.[55]

In the winter of 1951, PFC Gene Bleuer's combat patrol from Baker Company was ambushed north of the Han River. After exhausting their ammunition, the squad was overwhelmed by a superior Chinese force. During the tortuous march to Pyongyang, their guards beat to death some of the prisoners. Upon arrival at a PW compound, most of the 5th RCT captives were split up and sent to different camps.[56]

Private First Class Bleuer's interrogator, a Chinese officer, claimed to have graduated from Stanford University. During his incarceration, PFC Bleuer occasionally witnessed Soviet officers visiting the compound. Rumors abounded that the Soviets escorted American prisoners on one-way trips to the Soviet Union.

Escape attempts brought swift and brutal retaliation. When an attempt was thwarted or escapees recaptured, the guards routinely lined up the PWs along the barbed wire to face a firing squad. Sometimes the Communist weapons were loaded; sometimes they were not. "Between 25-30 Americans were executed in my compound alone," PFC Bleuer states. On one occasion, a tunnel under the wire granted freedom to about a dozen

SFC Harold Cross, K Company, was the last American killed in the Korean War. (source: Ray Warner)

GIs. The CCF claimed to have recaptured all of these men. However, none of these GIs was ever returned to PFC Bleuer's compound; all were probably executed or perished as slave laborers.

When the reality of the prisoner exchange reached the Pyongyang compounds, the Communists chose very carefully who would be released and who would remain. Gene Bleuer was released, but he is convinced that many men remained behind in Communist captivity, including soldiers he once served with in the 5th RCT. These unfortunate men disappeared into the Communist Gulag.

The 5th RCT no longer exists other than in the hearts and memories of the men who fought the Korean War. Yet if just two Army infantry regiments deserve the title elite for their actions in Korea, one is the 27th "Wolfhounds" and the other is the 5th RCT. The former was the premier regiment of the Tropic Lightning Division, soldiers who earned their justifiably fierce reputation with the tips of fixed bayonets, their heroism embellished in every paper across the land. Colonel Throckmorton, on the other hand, disliked the press, and except for reporters from the Honolulu papers, he rarely gave interviews. One result is that the combat team's superlative combat performance in Korea is not well known outside the dwindling circle of men who themselves fought in the Korean War.

If one measure of the quality of a combat organization is the number of general officers produced, then the 5th RCT clearly earned its keep.[57] In addition to General John L. Throckmorton, the following officers who served in the 5th RCT are known to have achieved general officer rank: Lieutenant General A. D. Surles, CO 5th RCT, 1951-52; Lieutenant General Henry E. Emerson, C, HHC 1st Battalion, CO A Company, 1949-51; Lieutenant General James M. Lee, M, K, & CO L Company, 1950-52; Lieutenant General Harvey H. Fisher, CO 5th RCT, 1953; Lieutenant General Herbert R. Temple, CO A Company, 1951-52; Major General James A. Johnson, Platoon Leader 72nd Engineers and CO B Company, 1949-1951; Major General Robert L. Shirkey, CO B Company, 1951-52; Major General Gordon J. Duquemin, A & HHC Companies, 1st BN, 1949-51; Major General Ben Sternberg, CO 5th RCT, 1953-54; Brigadier General Irwin Cockett, Jr., D Company 81-mm Mortar Platoon, 1950-51; Brigadier General John H. Daly, CO 555th FAB, 1949-50; Brigadier General Lester L. Wheeler, CO 5th RCT, 1953; Brigadier General Robert J. Koch, Battery Commander, 555th FAB; Brigadier General Frederick A. Smith, Jr., 1953-54.

Less reliable measures of a unit's combat worth are the awards its soldiers receive for valor. Colonel Throckmorton, for all his leadership skills as a commander, was "chintzy" when it came to approving awards.[58] Men often earned Bronze or Silver Stars in other outfits for actions that would have warranted a pat on the back or a handshake in the 5th RCT. Regrettably, company commanders, who often wrote their award recommendations by flashlight while sitting in a foxhole at night under a poncho in the rain, received little administrative help from their respective battalion headquarters. Awards recommendations were often downgraded at battalion, regiment, or division — posthumous ones, too.

1st LT Peter Foss, the CO of K Company, poses for a snapshot during a lull in the fighting of the Punchbowl, 1952. Note his armored vest. (source: Peter Foss)

Another unreliable gauge of combat effectiveness is to examine the number of unit awards an outfit receives in wartime. To begin with, the Distinguished Unit Citation was the highest award a combat unit could earn in the Korean War. In contrast to the Vietnam War, where Army brigades, Marine regiments, and even entire divisions, were awarded the Presidential Unit Citation, and often more than once, the Korean War era Distinguished Unit Citation was rarely presented to units larger than battalions. The 3rd Battalion, 5th Infantry, and attached units, were presented the Distinguished Unit Citation for actions during the Task Force Kean offensive. Oddly enough, neither of the combat team's remaining battalions, including the 555th FAB, ever received this prestigious award, even though they were much more heavily engaged in the Task Force Kean offensive than LTC Heckemeyer's battalion. Able Company, and attached units, received the Distinguished Unit Citation for their role in the defense of Outpost Harry, but no other companies or batteries were ever so honored. One reason was that "Bastard Outfits," like the 5th RCT, were shuttled from division to division as the situation demanded. Regrettably, overworked divisional staffs rarely took the time to write a citation for a non-divisional unit.[59]

It should come as no surprise to hear that the 5th RCT made mistakes in combat. Men were killed, wounded, and missing because of those mistakes. Human error, rather than hard luck, causes military disasters great and small. Yet the 5th RCT consistently demonstrated an ability to rebound in the face of adversity. The individual soldier's pride was the key. This pride was based on a tradition of excellence, confidence in comrades and arms, and trust in the chain of command. Colonel Throckmorton's leadership set the tone during the first year of the war, but the company grade officers and NCOs maintained and reinforced this strong sense of self-confidence and unit pride through the force of their individual personalities and courage under fire. Of equal importance is that COL Throckmorton's successors maintained the high standards he originally set for the command. In short, the commanding officers of the 5th RCT treated their subordinates like men, and the soldiers acted accordingly.

According to Lieutenant General Hank Emerson, "What made us different was having Throckmorton in command. A secondary factor was having people like SGT Adrian J. K. Sylva who put a little backbone into the unit that might otherwise not have been there. We were very fortunate to have those Hawaiian guys. Another one was Santiago Bunda, a brave man and a superb athlete who thankfully survived the war."[60]

Colonel Randall Beirne agrees, and would only add MSGT Kermit Jackson, SFC James R. Jackson, SGT William T. Akerley, Jr., and all the World War II combat veterans who did everything that was asked of them, and more, in Korea.[61]

When one of the combat team's former battalion commanders was asked why he considered the 5th RCT to be the "outstanding" unit of his career, he explained, "Colonel Throckmorton was a very, very dynamic leader of men. He was a quiet, thoughtful, yet forceful man who inspired confidence in his soldiers. He quickly replaced a bunch of officers who did not measure up to his standards. The unit had been together for some time, and by and large, the backbone of the Fifth were the large number of soldiers from Hawaii. They were a bunch of doggoned good soldiers. They were hot, and they were Island boys. They liked soldiering, and by that, I mean they liked to fight. I don't think they were worth a hoot in garrison! They were

CAPT Thomas E. Waldie, beloved chaplain, was presented the Silver Star by the RCT CO, COL A. D. Surles. Father Waldie was always at the site of greatest need, ministering to the men of the regiment. (source: NA)

the kind of men you wanted around when the chips were down. When I was a battalion commander, my driver was a short Hawaiian guy who stood maybe five-foot-three. He could barely see over the hood of our jeep, and as a consequence, we were always hitting bumps that threw me around. But I never replaced that man. He was just too good of a soldier. We had a great deal of camaraderie. On the rare occasions when we were off the line, we had battalion formations where we played Taps and Echo Taps for the guys who were gone. We also welcomed the replacements to the unit. This made a big impression on the people. We were tough on personal appearance, cleanliness and ensuring our people were awake when they were supposed to be awake. We took care of our people's feet, made them change socks, and as a result had very few frostbite cases, where in other units frostbite was a big problem. It was a little thing, but it was people, and saying to the men, 'Hey, we think you're important.' And finally, when off the line, we trained hard. Once we lost two guys in a live-fire exercise, but as callous as this may sound, learning from our mistakes in training was better than losing a platoon in combat."[62]

SGT Kenny Freedman (left), Kahuku, Oahu, was an 81-mm Mortar FO. SGT Hibbert Manley (right), Honolulu, took a sniper's bullet through his helmet a few days after this photo was taken. He survived his first tour in Korea and later went back "for seconds." (source: Hibbert Manley)

To gauge the combat effectiveness of a unit, it is necessary to examine the morale and motivations of the soldiers rather than conduct a simple bean count of the number of awards the unit earned in combat. As 1st SGT Kenny Freedman eloquently explained, "A lot of units get beat up and they are down — way down — for a long time in combat. Some of the units in Korea didn't have any morale. You'd ask someone what outfit they were with, and they'd hold their heads down and mumble some reply, 'I'm with the stinking uppity-ump.' Now if they asked us the question, we'd reply, 'I'm in the 5th RCT!' No one dared to talk about the 5th RCT. We could talk about the 5th RCT, but no one else."[63]

First Sergeant Hibbert Manley sums up the attitude prevalent in the 5th RCT throughout the Korean War: "We fought a hell of a battle in Korea. And to all of us, we thought we did what we were trained for — ain't no big thing — and many of us went back for seconds. I wish I could tell you of all the brave men who were in my platoon, and the ones I held while their lives left them. I know you know of Kenny Freedman, the best FO I ever had and a hell of an 81-mm mortar man."[64] When Kenny Freedman passed away, Hibbert Manley, and a close group of family and friends, scattered the valiant soldier's ashes in Oahu's surrounding waters.[65]

The 5th RCT is reputed to have lost 867 men KIA, 3,188 WIA, 16 MIA, and 151 men captured during the Korean War.[66] Actual losses were much heavier, for this total does not appear to include the bulk of the soldiers who fell during the Task Force Kean offensive. Nor does it include all the casualties incurred during the desperate defense of Sobuk-san, the epic breakout at Waegwan, and the sanguinary engagement at Kumchon. Recent research has that 950 men were KIA, MIA, perished in captivity, or DOW. When combined with the 84 suspected dead, even these numbers are probably lower than the actual loss of life. No comprehensive records exist of the KATUSA boys who died alongside their American comrades in the 5th RCT. The Triple Nickel's extensive losses at Bloody Gulch and Death Valley are not included in their entirety either. Sonny died in good company, alongside "his boys," honorable men who performed their duty in a horrifying inferno of fire and steel.

EPILOGUE

RETURN TO LANIKAI

The military forces of this country suffered 142,277 casualties in the Korean War. The invasion of South Korea by the Communists of the North came swiftly and without warning slightly more than three years ago. It was necessary for this country to act promptly, and it did. Among the troops immediately available were those from Hawaii. The rate of casualties among troops from Hawaii was especially high. Final figures show that on a per capita basis our people suffered one casualty for each 302 civilians residing in the Territory, whereas on a national basis, the loss was one casualty for each 1,125 Americans. The service of our boys was not only marked by heavy losses but by especial bravery. By the time a total of 53 Congressional Medal of Honor had been awarded, 2 of the 53 had gone to sons of Hawaii. The first was Herbert K. Pililaau of Waianae and the second was Leroy Mendonca of Honolulu.
Joseph R. Farrington, Delegate to Congress, Territory of Hawaii, July 1953[1]

Ernest and Theresa suspected something was wrong when Sonny's once prolific letters stopped being delivered to their home in Lanikai. On 13 April, an Army officer assigned to Fort Shafter handed Sonny's father the long dreaded telegram in his real estate office on Alakea Street in downtown Honolulu.[2] After recovering from his shock, Ernest politely thanked the officer for his time. He immediately phoned the principal at Roosevelt High School to inform him that he was going to drive over and pick up Sonny's brothers from school.

After the longest and loneliest drive in Ernest's life, he arrived at the school and showed Buddy and Manley the telegram.[3] After everyone stopped crying, Ernest drove the boys home over the Pali to confront Theresa with the news. She knew something was wrong as soon as they arrived and hysterically burst into tears. Until the day she died, the grief stricken mother never stopped yearning for her departed son.[4]

In the bureaucratic halls of the immense military machine waging a war in Korea, a number of serious paper work errors were committed which contributed to the family's grief. What faith the family retained in the Army following Sonny's death was soon shattered. Although the Army had correctly informed Ernest and Theresa that their son had died on Hill 814 on 23 March 1951, when the letters family and friends had written to Sonny started to return, they were all marked: "Return to Writer — Deceased: 19 March 51." The most terrible thing about the family's ordeal had little to do with the contradiction in dates. Rather, it was the stunning realization that not one of the letters they had written Sonny since his departure from the 35th Station Hospital in Kyoto, Japan, had reached him in Korea.[5] Sonny's refrain from the last letter he ever wrote returned to haunt Theresa and Ernest for the rest of their lives: "Without mail, you're lost."

Theresa started to blame Ernest for Sonny's death.[6] After all, she reasoned in her grief, Ernest was the one who had encouraged Sonny to join the Army in the first place. Ernest in turn took his grief out on the Army's shocking inability to deliver the mail on time. In his opinion there was absolutely no reason other than sheer incompetence that the Army could not deliver a letter within five weeks of it being sent. The thought of his beloved son dying on a lonely hill without a single letter from home to sustain him was too much for Ernest, who mounted a letter writing campaign to the newspapers and local politicians in a determined attempt to rectify this ridiculous situation.

Sonny returns home to repose eternally in the Punchbowl. (source: Calhau family)

236

On 3 July, the *Honolulu Star-Bulletin* published an article entitled, "Amazing Mail Delays," based in part on Ernest's research.[7] The results of an investigation by the Adjutant General, Department of the Army, failed to placate the angry father. At Ernest's request, Hawaii's delegate to Congress, the Honorable Joseph R. Farrington, discussed the issue on the floor of the House of Representatives.[8]

The Department of the Army, Army Effects Bureau, mistakenly shipped the personal effects of an officer who had been killed in action in Korea to Sonny's parents. Ernest returned the effects of the deceased officer, but Sonny's effects were never recovered.[9]

As letters of condolences poured into the Calhau home, a resolution was adopted by the Mayor and the Board of Supervisors of the City and County of Honolulu, Territory of Hawaii, paying honor and tribute to SGT Ernest M. Calhau.[10] The Secretary of the Army, Frank Pace, Jr., sent the Calhau family his condolences in a formal letter that also announced the posthumous award of Sonny's Purple Heart.[11] General Matthew B. Ridgway, true to form for this magnificent officer, sent Ernest a personal letter expressing sympathy for his son's death.[12]

Taps being played at Sonny's funeral. (source: Calhau family)

24 April 1951
Dear Mr. Calhau:
The untimely death of your son, Ernest, has been a tragic loss. While no one can fully share the sorrow which the death of your loved one brings, he will be sorely missed by his comrades, too.

We earnestly hope that you may find some comfort in the knowledge of the understanding sympathy of those who knew him and shared service with him in this Command. There should also be some measure of consolation in knowing that he met his death pridefully and manfully in the service of his Country.

I have faith that his devotion to duty, in defense of all that we and the free peoples of the world hold most dear, has helped us on the long, hard road by which alone we may expect some day to reach a just, an honorable, and an enduring peace.

May God grant we continue to follow that road whatever be the sacrifices entailed.
With sincere sympathy, I am,
Respectfully,
M. B. Ridgway
Lieutenant General, U.S. Army.

Theresa and Dorothy Kenawell continued their lively correspondence for several years after Sonny's death. In the era before stress management and grief therapy, written correspondence was one of the few emotional outlets available to people. When Dorothy heard about Sonny's death, she immediately responded in her charming way with a lovely card entitled:

The Home Beyond
'I go to prepare a place for you.'
    John 14:2
We are so sad when those we love
Are called to live in that HOME ABOVE,
But why should we grieve
when they say good-by
And go to dwell in a 'cloudless sky,'
For they have but gone to prepare the way
And we'll join them again some happy day.
The Kenawell family

Sonny's grieving mother receives the traditional fallen warrior's flag. (source: Calhau family)

Mrs. Calhau, once again, pays loving respect to her lost son, as mothers have done throughout the course of warfare. (source: Calhau family)

Dorothy wrote Theresa on 21 July 1951 that her revered son, Johnnie Kenawell, was finally coming home too.[13]

"Dear Theresa,

Just a few words to tell you that they have brought Johnnie home for burial. As yet we have not received his body, but it will be here for services next Saturday. I will answer your letter as soon as we get settled over the services. Right now I am mixed-up. I hardly know what I am doing. I am still trusting in the Lord to give us all strength. I have found Isaiah 41:13 helps a lot; "For I the Lord thy God will hold thy right hand, saying unto thee, Fear not: I will help thee." How wonderful it is to put all our faith and trust in God for I have found that He has taken so much of my burdens away. Love and prayers, Dorothy."

Sonny returned home to his beloved Hawaii later that year. A Mass was held at Our Lady of Peace Cathedral at 9:30 A.M. on 9 November 1951. The internment service was conducted one hour later at the National Memorial Cemetery of the Pacific where Sonny was buried with full military honors.[14] Soldiers from the U.S. Army Pacific ceremonial unit served as honor guards and pall bearers, a duty Sonny had performed little more than a year before. Family and friends were present in large numbers, for Sonny's special ray of sunshine had warmed many lives in the years of his youth.

As the solemn ceremony commenced, a gathering of Sonny's comrades from the 5th RCT silently observed the proceedings. The combat-hardened soldiers, some of whom were still recovering from wounds, felt a special bond with the soldier from Lanikai, one that can only be forged in the fiery crucible of war. These unappreciated warriors would march in no victory parades. Standing tall and proud that day, they asked and received nothing from their country other than an opportunity to honor one of their fallen comrades and friends. Those present included Captain Stanley Howarth, F Company; Captain Kenneth Hino, F Company; MSGT David Broad, G Company; MSGT James Okita, F Company; SFC David Kauanui, F Company; SFC Mamoru Ekimura, F Company; SFC Douglas McQullian, E Company; SFC Kaae, I Company; SGT James Kawamura, E Company; SGT Richard Saki, F Company; SGT Komura, F Company; SGT Ward, F Company; SGT John Phillips, F Company; SGT Fuji, Medical Company; CPL Todd, F Company; CPL Richard Nogami, F Company; CPL Tamao T. Sugata, F Company; CPL Charles Oh, E Company; CPL Shigeo Toyama, Medical Company; CPL Fredricko Acoba, H Company; CPL Alfred Bode, I Company; CPL Joseph Gonzales, G Company; CPL Frank Cordero, G Company; CPL Horace Nakamura; CPL Robert K. Young; PFC Richard Matsuda, F Company; PFC Salvador Emellio, F Company; PFC Aquino, F Company; PFC William Millan, F Company; PFC Albert Oshiro, F Company; and PFC Florencio Mangosing, Medical Company.

The civilians in the crowd flinched as the rifle volleys rang out. As the bugler played taps, a master sergeant presented Theresa with Sonny's burial flag. Theresa, wearing the white dress of a Gold Star mother, was magnificent that day, gracefully accepting the flag in honor of her fallen son. Granny stood by Theresa's side, her anguished soul reaching out beyond eternity for her grandson.

The Korean War ended with an armistice rather than victory. The soldier from Lanikai was one of 33,629 Americans killed in action during the Korean War. A depressing 20,617 more men perished from non-battle causes. An appalling 103,284 men were wounded, many so severely that they can never leave the confines of a Veterans Hospital for the rest of their lives. Tragically, over 8,000 men remain missing in action, their mourning families forever wondering "How, where, and why?"[16]

Those men and women who served in the Korean War returned home and quietly melted back into a society that wanted to hear no more of war. No brass bands or parades honored their valorous deeds. A visit to any public library will quickly reveal a tragic truth. Although thousands of historical works exist on World War II, and hundreds on the Vietnam War, you will find the shelves conspicuously bare on Korea, America's Forgotten War.

Sonny's tale has been told. Born two weeks before Christmas, he perished on Good Friday. The fallen squad leader lay for three days on the fire-swept slope of Hill 814, a miniature hell, until his faithful comrades recovered him on Easter Sunday. He lies in state today, flanked on all sides by his comrades in the 5th RCT.

Visitors to Oahu are cautioned not to waste time in a futile search for Sonny's home in his beloved Lanikai. The house is gone, a victim of age and the relentless advance of the sea. The ill-advised construction of seawalls played a role in the home's demise, and that of the once sandy beach, where Sonny's family and friends used to relax in their leisure hours fishing, and engaged in congenial conversations through the tropical Lanikai nights. The ocean has swept the sparkling white sand out to sea, leaving a naked coral ledge in its wake. The fish rarely bite anymore, for they are few and far between now, victims of foreign commercial fishing fleets, snagged on long-lines and drowned in huge nets.

The Aloha Spirit still exists on Oahu, but you have to be patient and search for it, something tourists rarely have the time or inclination to do. There is one place where you can readily find it, however — at the Punchbowl, where you can visit Sonny and his comrades who fought the good fight in some of our Nation's bloodiest wars. And while you stand there, on the rim of the crater in the shade of the trees, listen closely, if you care, for you will hear in the breeze many other tales at Puuowaina, the Hill of Sacrifice.

MSGT Alfred Los Banos, Honolulu, survived one of the nation's most gruesome wars to become Ambassador of the Forgotten War. He was the only former enlisted man ever appointed to the American Battle Monuments Commission. He departed this world for a better place in 1999. (source: Fred Los Banos)

ACKNOWLEDGMENTS

Upon returning to Marine Corps Air Station, Kaneohe Bay, Hawaii, after service with the 2nd Battalion, 3rd Marines, "Task Force Taro," during Operation Desert Storm, my outfit experienced the true meaning of the Aloha Spirit. Our Marines marched smartly in an unforgettable victory parade through downtown Honolulu past thousands of cheering civilians. Near the end of the parade route, one elderly Hawaiian gentleman stood off to the side, waving a placard that read, "Thanks Marines for kicking Saddam's Ass." That man wore a Veteran of Foreign Wars cap, and on this cap there was a small red pentagon insignia with a white border, the shoulder patch of the U.S. Army's 5th Regimental Combat Team.

My wife's Uncle Sonny had been killed in action during the Korean War while serving in the 5th RCT. My father-in-Law, Manley, was always reticent about discussing his oldest brother, and I had learned not to press this subject long before. After the parade Darlene drove me to her parents' house where we spent the night. Later that evening, I mentioned to Manley that, while I had enjoyed the day's festivities, my conscience was bothered. I knew the veterans of the Korean and Vietnam Wars had never received such wonderful treatment when, in reality, their respective achievements and combined sacrifices had dwarfed those of ours in the desert just a few short weeks before. Our conversation shifted to the subject of Sonny, and for once the atmosphere was just right. The next morning, Manley gave me a box full of the letters Sonny had mailed home from Korea before a burst of machine gun fire ended his life.

Reading Sonny's letters was an emotional experience. Sonny, the troublemaker and high school drop out, had grown up quickly in Korea. He had tried hard to reassure his worried parents and rarely wrote about combat. Rather, Sonny's mud-splattered stationery speaks of his joys and sorrows, and love for family, comrades, and friends. I found myself desperately hoping to find another of Sonny's letters to read in the dwindling pile of dusty envelopes, knowing full well that time was running out. No more letters would be forthcoming after 23 March 1951.

The Marines transferred us a few weeks after my return from the desert. Sonny stayed close by, his words never far from my mind. While living in Norfolk, Virginia, I began to write a book on Sonny's experiences in the Korean War. Naturally, I read everything I could find, but there is a reason why Korea has been called The Forgotten War. There was precious little to read, and of the books that are in print, most dwell on either the big picture or the Marines.

Dallace Meehan, a professor with American Military University, gave me the courage to persevere. With his moral support and guidance, we went to the National Archives to conduct research for a manuscript on Sonny's experiences in the 5th RCT. Darlene made it possible. While I read after action reports, she copied and filed the immense stacks of material.

We took the opportunity during a short vacation to scour the Honolulu Archives and the Public Library for more information on the 5th RCT. During our brief stay on Oahu, the manuscript began a subtle metamorphosis. Sonny's tragedy aside, I concluded the manuscript's focus should properly be on the 5th RCT, an outfit that proved itself on the battlefield when other units often failed the test.

Shortly after our vacation, Manley discovered the existence of the 5th RCT Association. I contacted Arlen Russell, the association's editor, who put me in touch with the combat team's veterans. Colonel Randall Beirne, for one, invited me to spend the night in his home. In addition to giving me a stack of his maps and personal letters from the war, Randall showed me a color film he made in Korea while fighting as a platoon leader in King Company. Through his movie camera's lens, I saw the ships slip anchor in Honolulu, the rolling blue breakers at sea, Hap Easter's burning Easy Eight tank at Chindong-ni, and the men of King Company marching down tree-lined, dusty roads, many never to return home again.

Lieutenant General Hank Emerson, "The Gunfighter," brought General John L. Throckmorton, "The Rock," to life for me. The Rock deserves most of the credit for transforming the 5th RCT into a crack outfit. It is only fitting that one of his closest friends has helped to explain this man's tremendous impact on the combat team when it was stand or die on Sobuk-san. A modest man, General Emerson gave full credit for his own personal success as the Commanding Officer of Able Company to the valor and skill of his soldiers.

Lieutenant General Alpha Bowser, USMC, volunteered to write a foreword for the manuscript. Those soldiers who served their 105-mm howitzers in the Triple Nickel will be pleased to note that he is a cannoneer. He led artillery battalions on the battlefields of Guam and Iwo Jima, and while the 5th RCT was stationed at Schofield Barracks, he served at FMF PAC on Oahu. He transferred to the 1st Marine Division in time to become its G-3 Operations Officer at the outbreak of the Korean War, and served most competently in this capacity through the Inchon Landing, the capture of Seoul, the Chosin Reservoir Campaign, and the Chinese Spring Offensive.

Major General James Johnson told me of the exploits of the 72nd Engineers and Baker Company. In addition to his interview with me, he gave me a copy of his oral interview with Dr. Charles Hendricks, Office of History, U.S. Army Corps of Engineers.

Lieutenant Colonel Keith Whitham filled me in on the combat team's activities in Korea before the war, the peacetime routine at Schofield Barracks, and on Tank Company's wartime exploits. His insight brought this manuscript to life.

Colonel Ed Crockett's invaluable assistance requires elaboration. In addition to giving me a copy of his unpublished memoirs of his Korean War experiences, he personally went to the National Archives with and without me to assist in the research. He contacted friends who scrubbed their memories to provide the most thorough accounting of Tank Company's combat actions at Death Valley and Masogu-ri. Moreover, he was the manuscript's unofficial editor, a man devoted to truth and accuracy, and one who labored long hours through numerous drafts to make sense of my often confusing prose.

It is difficult to list everyone else who helped, because so many people helped in so many different ways. Please forgive me if I have overlooked someone. It is appropriate to mention Horace Anderson; Frank Athanason; Claude Baker; Sal Bosco; Frank Brooks; Norman Cooper; Ronald Denton; David Eckert; Jim Evans; George "Kenny" Freedman; Dan Gonzales; Joseph Gonzales; Donald Gottschall; Perry Graves; James Hart; Herbert Ikeda; William Kapaku; Alton Kenawell; Robert Lamb; Earl Law; Richard Lewis; Samuel Lewis; Alfred Los Banos; Hibbert Manley; Albert McAdoo; Gene McClure; Robert Middleton; Dawn Mladinich; Dick Oostenink, Jr.; Gerald Pack; William Perry, Jr.; Jerome Prather, Jr.; Robert C. Sebilliani; Albert Semasko; James Shaw; Charles Shepherd; John Sonley; William Straney; Thomas Throckmorton; Albert Throne; Frank Valvo; Raymond Warner; and William Welch.

The staffs at the National Archives, Center for Military History, Institute of Heraldry, and the Tropic Lightning Museum are commended for their hospitality and willingness to assist an unknown author complete his quest.

In addition to Roselie and Manley, I thank my parents, Jim and Marcianne, and LTCOL Stephen Giusto, USMC, and MAJ William Ridenour, II, USMC, for their support and encouragement. In conclusion I wish to express my special thanks to Darlene for her unqualified support. Her Uncle Sonny would have been extremely proud of her. To everyone else, I extend a hearty Aloha, Mahalo, and Semper Fi.

As a final note, memories fade, and official reports are sometimes incorrectly written or interpreted. As it is the historian's job to keep the facts straight, I bear full responsibility for any errors contained in the text.

Many photographs of the most accomplished combat photographer of the Korean War, MSGT Albert Chang, appear in this volume. Some were found at the National Archives in College Park, Maryland; others derive from individual contributions; still others were provided by the 5th RCT Association (many, courtesy of COL Elmer G. Owens, USA Ret.), loaned to the author for use in this book. (source: NA)

ENDNOTES

PROLOGUE

[1] Elspeth P. Sterling and Catherine C. Summers, *Sites of Oahu* (Honolulu: Bishop Museum Press, 1978), pp. 291-292; and Doug Carlson, *Punchbowl: The National Memorial Cemetery of the Pacific* (Aiea: Island Heritage Publishing, 1992), pp. 12-14. McKinley High School sits on the former site of the Kewalo fish pond, also known as Kawailumalumai, or drowning pond.

[2] *The American Battle Monuments Commission World War II Commemorative Program* (Washington, D.C.: American Battle Monuments Commission), p. 34. The Manila American Cemetery and Memorial, Fort Bonifacio, Manila, Philippine Islands, hosts the remains of 17,206 Americans who perished in the Southwest Pacific and 36,281 MIA. Military personnel KIA in the European Theater of Operations are also buried at the Punchbowl in large numbers.

CHAPTER ONE

[1] Author interview with Mr. Manuel G. Calhau.

CHAPTER TWO

[1] Author interview with Mr. Joseph Gonzales, Sr.

[2] Author interview with Commissioner Alfred S. Los Banos

[3] Author interview with Mr. Manuel G. Calhau.

[4] Author interview with Mr. Alton Kenawell, Johnnie's youngest brother.

CHAPTER THREE

[1] MAJ Mark M. Boatner, III, *Army Lore and Customs of the Service: Regular Regiments of the Korean Conflict* (Tokyo: Pacific Stars and Stripes, 1954), pp. 146-150.

[2] General J. Lawton Joe Collins, *Lightning Joe: An Autobiography* (Baton Rouge: Louisiana University Press, 1979), p. 29.

[3] *Veterans of Foreign Wars Memorial Edition Pictorial History of the Korean War: MacArthur Reports* (Veterans' Historical Book Service, Inc., 1951), p. 3.

[4] Clay Blair, *The Forgotten War: America in Korea 1950-1953* (New York: Time Books, 1987), pp. 44-45.

[5] Goncharov, Sergei N., John W. Lewis, and Xue Litai, *Uncertain Partners: Stalin, Mao, and the Korean War* (Stanford: Stanford University Press, 1993), pp. 140-141 and 146-150.

[6] James F. Schnabel, *U.S. Army in the Korean War: Policy and Direction: The First Year* (Washington, D.C.: Office of the Chief of Military History, Department of the Army, 1971), pp. 45-46.

[7] *Ibid.*, pp. 46-47.

[8] Blair, *The Forgotten War*, pp. 42-43.

[9] Author interview with LGEN Henry E. Emerson, USA Ret.

[10] *Ibid.*

[11] Author interview with Mr. Horace Anderson.

[12] *Ibid.*

[13] *Ibid.,* SFC Burton was KIA on 30 January 1951 while serving in Easy Company, 5th RCT.

[14] Author interview with Mr. Frank Valvo.

[15] MAJ Robert K. Sawyer, *Military Advisors in Korea: KMAG in Peace and War* (Washington, D.C.: Office of the Chief of Military History, Department of the Army, 1962), p. 36-37; and 5th RCT Unit History dated 9 January 1951. The 5th RCT Unit History mistakenly states that the 32nd Infantry was "redesignated" as the 5th Infantry. If true, then the 5th Infantry would have acquired the lineage and traditions of the 32nd Infantry. That did not happen. Rather, the 5th Infantry was reactivated using personnel and equipment transferred for this purpose. The 32nd Infantry was subsequently transferred minus equipment and personnel to Japan where it was rebuilt.

[16] Author interviews with MGEN James A. Johnson, USA Ret., and LGEN Henry E. Emerson, USA Ret.

[17] Author interview with MAJ Frank B. Brooks, Jr., USA Ret.

[18] 5th RCT Unit History, 9 January 1950.

[19] One-third of the 37-mm cannons mounted on the M-8 armored cars were inoperable due to a shortage of spare parts. Author interview with LTC Keith W. Whitham, USA Ret.

[20] Author interview with Mr. Ronald Denton.

[21] Author interview with COL Dick J. Oostenink, Jr., USA, Chaplain Corps, Ret.

[22] Author interview with LTC Keith W. Whitham, USA Ret.

[23] Author interview with MAJ Frank B. Brooks, Jr., USA Ret.; and 5th RCT Unit History, 9 January 1950. The pilot's name was Captain French.

[24] 5th RCT Unit History, 9 January 1950.

[25] *Ibid.*

[26] *Ibid*

[27] The 32nd Infantry was billeted here. There was also a 31st Street Circle, where the 31st Infantry was billeted at one time.

28 Author interview with MGEN James A. Johnson, USA Ret.
29 Sawyer, *Military Advisors in Korea*, p. 43-44; and author interview with MAJ Frank B. Brooks, Jr., USA Ret. Originally, KMAG standards required captains with a year remaining on their overseas tours to serve as advisors. Revised standards allowed 1st lieutenants with six-months or more remaining on their overseas tours to serve. In desperation 1st lieutenants with less than six-months remaining on their overseas tours were accepted.
30 Author interview with MGEN James A. Johnson, USA Ret.
31 Author interview with LGEN Henry E. Emerson, USA Ret.
32 "U.S. Koreans Beat Attack," *The Honolulu Advertiser*, 5 May 1949.
33 "Undeclared War Along Korea Frontier Reported," *The Honolulu Advertiser*, 10 May 1949.
34 Author interview with Mr. Frank Valvo.

CHAPTER FOUR

1 "First of New Army Troops Arrive Here," *The Honolulu Advertiser*, 10 June 1949.
2 Gene E. McClure, "An Autobiography" (University of Texas, unpublished manuscript), p. 10.
3 Author interview with Mr. David Eckert.
4 The men often wore brightly polished helmet liners at Schofield Barracks.
5 Johnson's determination to gut the USMC is discussed in Lieutenant General Victor H. Krulak, *First to Fight: An Inside View of the U.S. Marine Corps* (Annapolis: Naval Institute Press, 1984).
6 "'Bocquet' Reveals How He Captured T.H.," *The Honolulu Advertiser*, 5 October 1949.
7 Author interview with LGEN Henry E. Emerson, USA Ret.
8 "50-Minute War is Staged at Schofield," *The Honolulu Advertiser*, 11 October 1949.
9 "US Invaders win MIKI Climax Verdict," *The Honolulu Advertiser*, 26 October 1949.
10 "First Wave Expected About 9 A.M.," *The Honolulu Advertiser*, 26 October 1949.
11 "New Uniform Worn by MIKI Personnel," *The Honolulu Advertiser*, 1 November 1949.
12 General Aurand's comments probably raised a few quizzical eyebrows in the Marine Corps and the Navy, especially since the Chairman of the JCS, General Omar N. Bradley, USA, had derided the value of amphibious warfare in a speech before the House Armed Services Committee on 19 October 1949 while MIKI was in progress. See COL Robert Debs Heinl, Jr., *Victory at High Tide: The Inchon-Seoul Campaign* (New York: J.B. Lippincott Company, 1968), pp. 3 and 6-7.
13 "Oahu Troops Slated for Airborne Training," *The Honolulu Advertiser*, 3 November 1949.
14 The 5th RCT Unit History, 9 January 1950.
15 *Ibid*; and "Korean Army to Honor U.S. Unit Today," *The Honolulu Advertiser*, 10 November 1949. Yeungsup Kim, the Consul General, was in Korea, and thus unavailable to make the presentation.
16 Author interview with MSGT Arlen Russell, USAF Ret. The Army required the written consent of his mother because he was "seventeen" years old.
17 *Ibid.*
18 Author interview with MAJ Earl J. Law, USA Ret.
19 1st SGT George Freedman, "Remember When", 5th RCT Newsletter, (hereafter known as the 5th RCT NL), October 1993.
20 *Ibid.*, November 1993.
21 A crew-served weapon is one manned by two or more men.
22 1st SGT George Freedman, "Remember When?," 5th RCT NL, November 1993.
23 *Ibid.*
24 Author interview with Mr. Ronald Denton.
25 Author interview with MGEN James A. Johnson, USA Ret.
26 Author interview with Mr. Robert H. Middleton.
27 Author interview with Dr. D. Randall Beirne, COL, USAR Ret.
28 Author interview with 1st SGT George Freedman, USA Ret.
29 Air Force personnel were paid on the same day. The Navy and Marine Corps paid their personnel on the first day of each month.
30 Author interview with Mr. David Eckert.
31 Author interview with MSGT Arlen Russell, USAF Ret.
32 Author interview with Mr. Robert H. Middleton.
33 Author interview with 1st SGT George Freedman, USA Ret.
34 Lieutenants Emerson, Strong, and Krause had graduated from West Point with the Class of 1947.
35 Author interview with LTC Keith W. Whitham, USA Ret.
36 Author interview with Dr. D. Randall Beirne, COL, USAR Ret.
37 Author interview with LTC Keith W. Whitham, USA Ret.
38 Author interview with Dr. D. Randall Beirne, COL, USAR Ret.
39 *Ibid.*
40 *Ibid.*
41 *Ibid.*
42 Roy E. Appleman, *South to the Naktong, North to the Yalu* (Washington, D.C.: Office of the Chief of Military History, Department of the Army, 1961), p. 21, p. 35. Of the 98,000 men serving in the ROK Army on 25 June 1950, 44,000 had been reported killed, missing or captured by 31 July 1950.

43 Author interview with MSGT Arlen Russell, USAF Ret.

44 1st SGT George Freedman, "Remember When?," *5th RCT NL*, December 1993.

45 Author interview with MAJ Earl J. Law, USA Ret.

46 Brigadier General G. B. Barth, *Tropic Lightning and Taro Leaf in Korea July '50 - May '51* (Athens, Greece: Chief of Public Information Division, Department of the Army, 1955), pp. 90-91. Moreover, General Matthew B. Ridgway, *The Korean War* (New York: Doubleday and Company, Inc., 1967), pp. 34-35, states that the Eighth Army's four combat divisions were short an average of 6,400 men each. For budgetary reasons, every division had deactivated all of its antitank gun units, one-third of its infantry battalions and artillery batteries, and all regimental tank companies. Only the 1st Cavalry Division had a medium tank battalion.

47 General Douglas MacArthur, *Reminiscences* (New York: McGraw-Hill Book Company, 1964), p. 335.

48 Appleman, *South to the Naktong*, pp. 60-76.

49 Schnabel, *Policy and Direction*, pp. 91-92.

50 "Sound and Fury of Battle at Schofield," *The Honolulu Advertiser*, 13 July 1950; and "Army's Firepower Given Tryout in Exercises at Schofield," *The Honolulu Advertiser*, 16 July 1950. The demonstration was repeated for a couple of days. General Aurand was present at the first demonstration on 13 July. The alert order arrived following the last demonstration on 15 July. The new 3.5-inch rocket launcher had yet to be delivered to the 5th Infantry's antitank gunners. The troops were still equipped with the 2.36 rocket launcher that had already demonstrated its inability to defeat North Korean T-34 tanks.

51 Author interview with MSGT Arlen Russell, USAF Ret.

52 Author interview with Mr. Alton Kenawell.

53 Author interview with Mr. Manuel G. Calhau.

CHAPTER FIVE

1   "Reds Near Taejon," *The Honolulu Advertiser*, 16 July 1950.

2   Author interview with 1st SGT George Freedman, USA Ret.

3   Author interview with Dr. D. Randall Beirne, COL, USAR Ret.

4   Author correspondence with Mr. Herbert H. Ikeda. Carl F. Knobloch died on 11 August 1950, eleven days after the combat team arrived in Korea. Vernon Jernigan fell on 27 August 1950, while leading a platoon from K Company on a patrol. Vance B. McWhorter died on 9 November 1950 when his tank hit a mine. Thomas P. Bartow was wounded on 23 March 1951 while leading Sonny's 1st Platoon, F Company, up Hill 814. Roy T. Nakashima, an artillery Forward Observer in B Battery, and Leonard K. Warner, a platoon leader in H Company, perished on 23 April 1951.

5   Author interview with COL Dick J. Oostenink, Jr., USA, Chaplain Corps, Ret.

6   1st SGT George Freedman, "Remember When?," *5th RCT NL*, January 1994; and Gene E. McClure, p. 14.

7   Author interview with LGEN Henry E. Emerson, USA Ret.

8   Schnabel, *The U.S. Army in the Korean War: Policy and Direction*, p. 92, states the 5th RCT departed on 25 July. Other veterans maintain the ships sailed on 22 July. Actually, not all the ships sailed on the same date. While the *Mann*, the *Gaffey*, and the *Merrill* may have sailed in convoy, the *Ventura* steamed independently and did not reach Pusan until 8 August.

9   "5th Dependents Can Stay; 600 Seek Transport," *The Honolulu Advertiser*, 3 August 1950.

10 Author interview with MAJ Thomas B. Throckmorton, USA Ret.

11 Author interview with Mr. Sal Bosco.

12 *5th RCT NL*, 3 January 1992.

13 Author interview with MAJ Frank Brooks, Jr., USA Ret.

14 Author interview with MSGT Arlen Russell, USAF Ret.

15 McClure, *Op. Cit.*, p. 15.

16 Author interview with LGEN Henry E. Emerson, USA Ret.

17 Author interview with Dr. D. Randall Beirne, COL, USAR Ret.

18 Author interview with COL Dick J. Oostenink, Jr., USA, Chaplain Corps, Ret.

19 Collins, *Lightning Joe*, pp. 132-133. Following 7 December 1941, many senior Naval and Army officers doubted the loyalty of the Japanese-Americans serving in the Hawaiian Army National Guard's 298th and 299th Infantry Regiments. General Delos Emmons, Commanding General of the Hawaiian Department, did not concur, and with the support of the Honorable Mr. John J. McCoy, Assistant Secretary of War, the 100th Battalion (Separate), and later the 442nd Infantry, were formed from Japanese-American volunteers. Both outfits repaid their fellow countrymen's distrust with an epic saga of heroism and bloodshed. The 442nd Infantry was the most highly decorated Army regiment in World War II.

20 Melvin M. Johnson and Charles T. Haven, *Automatic Weapons of the World* (New York: William Morrow and Company, 1945), pp. 116-117. The BAR M1918A2 fired a .30-caliber (.30-'06) bullet from a twenty-round box magazine. It weighed 19 pounds and could be fired at either a high or low cyclic rate of fire. The lack of a changeable barrel was the BAR's weakness.

21 *Ibid.*, pp. 179-180. The M-1 semi-automatic rifle fired the same .30-caliber round as the BAR. It weighed 9.7 pounds empty and without a sling.

22 MAJ John A. English, *On Infantry* (New York: Praeger, 1984), pp. 164-168 and 174-175; and *The Senior R.O.T.C. Manual* (Washington, D.C.: Department of the Army, July 1950), pp. 267-268.

23 Melvin M. Johnson and Charles T. Haven, *Automatic Weapons of the World*, p. 117; and Will Eisner, *America's*

Combat Weapons (New York: Sterling Publishing Co., Inc., 1960), p. 17. Both machine guns were air-cooled, recoil operated, tripod mounted, and fired linked belts of .30-caliber ammunition. The M1919A6 differed from the M1919A4 in that it had a bipod, pistol grip, and wooden shoulder stock affixed. The M1919A4 weighed 31 pounds with its tripod. The A6 variant weighed one pound, eight ounces more. The barrel was changeable.

[24] Captain Martin J. Sexton, "Machine Guns in the Attack," *The Marine Corps Gazette*, October 1948.

[25] Army infantry officers acknowledged the superiority of the fire team organization early in the Korean War. See Captain Henry G. Morgan, "Stronger Fighting Teams in the Rifle Platoon," *United States Army Combat Forces Journal*, April 1952. Army squad leaders often reacted to the lack of automatic weapons firepower by employing a second, bootleg BAR. The Army officially adopted this organization in 1952, but, by then, much damage had been done. A second machine gun was added to the 4th Squad of each rifle platoon at this time, too. It should be pointed out that the 5th Marines arrived in Korea seriously under strength. Each of the regiment's three infantry battalions had two rifle companies, rather than the three called for under the T/O, and one weapons company. The rifle companies did not receive their third rifle platoons until shortly before the 1st Provisional Marine Brigade embarked on its ships for movement to Korea. The third rifle company was added to each battalion when the 5th Marines departed the Pusan Perimeter to participate in the Inchon landing. See Lynn Montross and Captain Nicholas A. Canzona, USMC, *U.S. Marine Operations in Korea.* Vol. 1. (Washington, D.C.: Historical Branch, G-3 Headquarters, U.S. Marine Corps, 1954), pp. 49-50, and 57; and Krulak, p. 135. The 1st Battalion, 11th Marines, however, deployed 20% over its T/O strength and was able to use these extra men for security duties. See, LTCOL Ransom M. Wood, "Artillery Support for the Brigade in Korea," *The Marine Corps Gazette*, June 1951.

[26] For a prewar view of Marine CAS doctrine, see, Brigadier General Vernon E. Megee, "Control of Supporting Aircraft," *The Marine Corps Gazette*, January 1948. For a Korean War view read Major General Vernon E. Megee, "The Tactical Air Support of Ground Forces," *The Marine Corps Gazette*, December 1955; and Ernest H. Giusti, "Marine Air Over the Pusan Perimeter," *The Marine Corps Gazette*, May 1952. Richard P. Hallion, *The Naval Air War Over Korea* (Baltimore: The Nautical and Aviation Publishing Company of America, 1986), pp. 41-50, explores the strengths, weaknesses, and differences between Air Force and Naval aviation aircraft, tactics, weapons and CAS doctrine.

[27] MAJ Michael P. Dolan, "What's Right and Wrong with Close Air Support," *United States Army Combat Forces Journal*, July 1951. Robert Frank Futrell, *The United States Air Force in Korea, 1950-1953* (Washington, D.C.: Office of Air Force History,1983), p. 463, states the USAF increased the length of a TACP tour to sixty days after February 1951.

[28] Author correspondence with 1st SGT Hibbert Manley, USA Ret.

[29] Futrell, *The United States Air Force in Korea*, pp. 106-109, 462-463.

[30] *Ibid.*, pp. 123, 704-708.

[31] Barth, *Tropic Lightning and Taro Leaf*, p. 2.

[32] *The Senior R.O.T.C. Manual*, p. 283.

[33] *Ibid.*

[34] *Ibid.*

[35] *R.O.T.C. Manual. Infantry.* Vol. III. (Harrisburg: The Military Service Publishing Company, 1949), pp. 200-223. The minimum range was 565 yards.

[36] Author interview with Mr. Donald L. Gottschall.

[37] *Ibid.* This support relationship lasted for at least the first nine months of the war.

[38] Later in the Korean War, an M-26 Tank Platoon was added to each Marine infantry regiment's organic antitank company. Not every Army regiment was assigned a Tank Company.

[39] Author interview with LTC Keith W. Whitham, USA Ret. Several sources state that the 5th RCT deployed to Korea with fourteen M-26 Pershing Tanks. This is incorrect. The 1st Provisional Marine Brigade deployed with the M-26, but the 5th RCT deployed with Shermans.

[40] Author correspondence with Mr. Charles Shepherd.

[41] Author interview with COL Albert R. Throne, USA Ret.

[42] *The Senior R.O.T.C. Manual*, p. 278; and author interview with LTC Norman W. Cooper, USA Ret.

[43] *R.O.T.C. Manual. Infantry*, pp. 147-178 and 255-296. The smooth bore, man-portable M19 60-mm mortar weighed 49 pounds and fired a 3-pound high explosive round to 1,900 yards. A white phosphorous round, weighing approximately 4 pounds, had a maximum range of 1,700 yards. The manportable M18 57-mm Recoilless Rifle weighed 44 pounds. It fired high explosive, canister, high explosive antitank, and smoke munitions to an effective range of approximately 500 yards.

[44] *Ibid.*, pp. 362-365.

[45] *Ibid.*, pp. 359-362. CWO-4 William J. Straney, USAR Ret., in correspondence with the author dated 18 December 1994, believes Fox Company deployed with just one SCR-300 and five PRC-526s, which means the combat team deployed with fewer than the authorized complement of radios. The opinions concerning the reliability of this equipment are the author's.

[46] *R.O.T.C. Manual. Infantry*, pp. 33-35 and 46-48. The M1917A1 water-cooled machine gun fired the same .30-caliber round as the M1919A4 or A6. The weapon weighed 41 pounds with water. Its chief advantage over either the A4 or A6 was its capability to conduct longer periods of sustained automatic fire.

[47] That Mike Company formed a third machine gun section for its heavy machine gun platoon is confirmed in the 5th RCT NL, March 1992.

48 *R.O.T.C. Manual. Infantry*, pp. 35-36 and 297-310. The M20 75-mm Recoilless Rifle fired a 4-pound high explosive, high explosive anti-tank, and smoke round to a maximum range of 6,960 - 7,300 yards depending on the type of ammunition. The high explosive round could be armed with either point detonating, instantaneous and delay action fuses. Its effective range was approximately 1,000 yards.

49 McClure, *Op. Cit.*, p. 138.

50 *R.O.T.C. Manual. Infantry*, pp. 35, 179-199; and author interview with 1st SGT George Freedman, USA Ret. The Marines initially equipped their battalions with six 81-mm mortars. After Inchon, the 1st Battalion, 1st Marines integrated two additional 81s to form an eight-tube platoon that remains the official T/O for Marine infantry battalions to date. See, 2nd LT Eugene J. Paradis, "Reorganized 81-mm Mortar Platoon," *The Marine Corps Gazette*, March 1951.

51 Author interview with MGEN James A. Johnson, USA Ret. The other two platoon leaders were 1st LT Kenneth M. Hatch and 1st LT Albert A. Van Petten, both of the Class of 1947.

52 John Toland, *In Mortal Combat: Korea 1950-1953* (New York: William Morrow and Company, Inc., 1991) p. 142, is an example.

53 Author interview with COL Frank A. Athanason, USA Ret.

54 Author interview with Dr. D. Randall Beirne, COL, USAR Ret. Second Lieutenants Beirne and Jackson were classmates at Fort Benning in 1949.

55 Clay Blair, *The Forgotten War*, p. 193.

56 Charles R. Cawthon, *Other Clay: A Remembrance of the World War II Infantry* (Niwot: University Press of Colorado, 1990), p. 79.

57 Joseph Balkoski, *Beyond the Beachhead: The 29th Infantry Division in Normandy* (Harrisburg: Stackpole Books, 1989), pp. 244-245, 248-250, 255, 258, 260, 265 and 267.

58 Blair, *The Forgotten War*, p. 193.

59 Collins, *Lightning Joe*, pp. 172-173.

60 The provisional battalion was disbanded when the 5th RCT deployed to Korea.

61 Author interview with MAJ Thomas B. Throckmorton, USA Ret.

62 Blair, *The Forgotten War*, pp. 197-198.

63 Author interview with Dr. D. Randall Beirne, COL, USAR Ret., and MAJ Thomas B. Throckmorton, USA Ret. Lieutenant Colonel Throckmorton's reduction in rank after World War II was not unusual.

64 For details on LTC Daly, see: "Hawaii GI is Killed, Three Hurt," *The Honolulu Advertiser*, 17 August 1950.

65 Author interview with MAJ Earl J. Law, USA Ret.

66 Author interview with Mr. Sal Bosco.

67 Author interview with Judge Samuel L. Lewis.

CHAPTER SIX

1 Blair, *The Forgotten War*, p. 172.

2 Appleman, *South to the Naktong*, p. 210.

3 *Ibid*, p. 212.

4 Blair, *The Forgotten War*, p. 179.

5 Montross and Canzona, *U.S. Marine Operations in Korea*. Vol. 1, pp. 96-98.

6 *Ibid.*, pp. 26-30.

7 *25th Infantry Division War Diary* (25th ID WD) entry, 6 August 1950.

8 1st Cavalry Division (CD) WD entry, 2 September 1950.

CHAPTER SEVEN

1 Captain Allan A. David and Sergeant Norwin E. Austin, *Battleground Korea: The Story of the 25th Infantry Division* (25th Infantry Division History Council, 1951). The pages of this book are not numbered.

2 Blair, *The Forgotten War*, p. 193; and MAJ Daniel P. Bolger, "Zero Defects: Command Climate in First US Army 1944-1945," *Military Review*, May 1991, pp. 61-73, who compares the command climate between the First and Third Armies in WWII. General Kean, as the Chief of Staff of the First Army in Normandy, would probably have been aware of all firings.

3 "Buddy System Found Effective in Protecting 5th RCT Orientals," *The Honolulu Advertiser*, 9 September 1950. Corporal Miguel Taoy stated in this article, that "This is not like the last war. You can't tell who you're fighting half the time. I feel a lot better with the buddy system working the way it is and so do a lot of other guys."

4 Author interview with Mr. Johnnie B. Walls.

5 McClure, *Op. Cit.*, p. 31.

6 Author interview with MSGT Arlen Russell, USAF Ret.

7 Author interview with Mr. Horace Anderson.

8 5th RCT NL, 5 December 1991; and author interview with CWO-4 William J. Straney, USAR Ret.

9 Author interview with MAJ Frank B. Brooks, USA Ret.

10 Appleman, *South to the Naktong*, p. 271. Military maps mark the summit of a hill with a number corresponding to its height in meters. In this case the hill was 342 meters in height. "San" means hill in Korean.

11 Author interview with MAJ Frank B. Brooks, USA Ret.; and CWO-4 William J. Straney, USAR Ret.; Appleman, *South to the Naktong*, p. 271, states that a platoon for G Company was driven from the crest by the NKPA that morning.

12 Author interview with CWO-4 William J. Straney, USAR Ret.

13 Oral Interview with MGEN James A. Johnson, USA, Ret., conducted by Dr. Charles Hendricks, Office of History, U.S. Army Corps of Engineers, on 25 February, 4, 11, 25, and 31 March, and 7, 20, 21 April 1993.

14 5th RCT NL, July 1991; and author interview with MGEN James A. Johnson, USA Ret.

15 Oral Interview with MGEN James A. Johnson, USA, Ret., conducted by Dr. Charles Hendricks.

16 One of Sonny's subsequent letters home indicate that Yaban-san was rechristened in honor of his unit after the successful night attack. An author interview with MAJ Frank B. Brooks, USA Ret., confirms this information.

17 Author interview with Mr. David Eckert.

18 From a photo-caption in the 3 April 1951 edition of *The Honolulu Advertiser*.

19 5th RCT NL, July 1993. Mr. Frank Valvo believes that CPL Fain was KIA on 3 August, but subsequent research has determined that he fell (or DOW) on 6 August.

20 Montross and Canzona, *U.S. Marine Operations in Korea*. Vol. 1, pp. 99-100.

21 25th ID WD, 6 August 1950.

22 *Ibid.* The term MLR describes the location of a strong, fixed position. The LD is an imaginary line drawn on a map, preferably located on a readily identifiable terrain feature such as a road or stream. When a unit advances across this line, it is said to be in the attack.

23 The parlance "5th Marines" denotes a Marine infantry regiment. In this case, it was the 5th Marine Regiment, commanded by LTCOL Raymond L. Murray, a veteran battalion and regimental commander who had participated in combat operations against the Japanese on Guadalcanal, Tarawa and Saipan, earning the Navy Cross, two Silver Stars, and a Purple Heart. The 5th Marines was reinforced with Company A, 1st Tank Battalion (M-26 Pershing Tanks armed with 90-mm guns); Company A, 1st Combat Engineer Battalion; 1st Battalion, 11th Marines (an artillery outfit); and various service units. (Note that Marine units, unlike Army units, place the letter designation after the word "company.") Together, the 5th Marines and Marine Air Group 33 formed the 1st Provisional Marine Brigade. Montross and Canzona, *U.S. Marine Operations in Korea*. Vol. 1, pp. 49-53.

24 Lieutenant Colonel Ransom M. Wood, "Artillery Support for the Brigade in Korea," *The Marine Corps Gazette*, June 1951.

25 Montross and Canzona, *U.S. Marine Operations in Korea*. Vol. 1, p. 106, state that the weapons fire was determined to have come from one of the 2nd Battalion, 5th Infantry's units located on an adjacent hill, the soldiers apparently being unaware that a Marine platoon was moving through their area. An Army guide who accompanied the Marine platoon believes the source of the fire was an NKPA machine gun. He further states that he warned the Marines of the presence of this weapon, but that they disregarded his warnings and paid the consequences for their error. See 5th RCT NL, 1 September 1991. For yet a third opinion, see Lynn Montross,"The Pusan Perimeter: Fight For a Foothold," *The Marine Corps Gazette*, June 1951, which attributes the Marine casualties to NKPA artillery fire.

26 Author interview with CWO-4 William J. Straney, USAR Ret.

27 Author interview with Mr. David Eckert.

28 Author interview with CWO-4 William J. Straney, USAR Ret.

29 Author interview with MAJ Frank B. Brooks, USA Ret.; and CWO-4 William J. Straney, USAR Ret. Corporal Starkey was awarded the Distinguished Service Cross and is buried at Arlington Cemetery.

30 Author interview with MAJ Frank B. Brooks, USA Ret.

31 Montross and Canzona, *U.S. Marine Operations in Korea*. Vol. 1, pp. 108-110; 25th ID WD, 7 August 1950. 25th Infantry Division was under the mistaken impression that the drop was successful; and Author interview with Mr. David Eckert.

32 Author interview with Mr. Frank Valvo.

33 *Ibid.*; and "Kauai Gunner Bags 41 North Koreans," *The Honolulu Advertiser*, 7 November 1950.

34 Author interview with LTC Keith W. Whitham, USA Ret.; and 5th RCT NL, July 1993, and December 1990.

35 Author interview with MAJ Earl J. Law, USA Ret.

36 Appleman, *South to the Naktong*, p. 272.

37 1st SGT George Freedman, "Remember When?", 5th RCT NL March 1995. Other accounts state that the tank hit a mine.

38 The Marines would have cause to rue the poor quality of the maps a few days later, when one of their battalions made a nearly identical error. Montross and Canzona, *U.S. Marine Operations in Korea*. Vol. 1, pp. 127-129.

39 "5th RCT Hits a Snag," *The Honolulu Advertiser*, 7 August 1950.

40 Author interview with COL Claude W. Baker, USA Ret.

41 The MSR was a route assigned to a unit for logistical purposes.

42 Appleman, *South to the Naktong*, pp. 273-274.

43 Lieutenant Colonel Ransom M. Wood, "Artillery Support for the Brigade in Korea," *The Marine Corps Gazette*, June 1951.

44 Senior Army officers had yet to forgive the Marine Corps for relieving one of their divisional commanders on Saipan in June 1944. Moreover, the bitter and protracted postwar roles and mission debates had left deep scars that had yet to heal. Thus, General Kean took a courageous stand within his own Army when he placed General Craig in tactical command of the Army units.

45 25th ID WD, 7 August 1950.

46 Author interview with Mr. David Eckert.

47 Appleman, *South to the Naktong*, pp. 272-273.

48 Author interview with MAJ Frank B. Brooks, USA Ret.

49 *Ibid.*

50 Author interview with Mr. Gerald Pack.

51 Author interview with Mr. David Eckert. He remained in the hospital until November 1950, his recovery complicated by the onset of malaria contracted on Fox Hill.

52 Author interview with MAJ Frank B. Brooks, USA Ret. Lieutenant Brooks rejoined F Company the next day. He was badly wounded a few days later and did not return to the 5th RCT until the middle of September 1950.

53 Author interview with Mr. Horace Anderson; and 5th RCT NL, 29 October 1991.

54 Author interview with SFC Richard F. Lewis, USA Ret.

55 Author interviews with LTC Keith W. Whitham, USA Ret., and SFC Richard F. Lewis, USA Ret.

56 Author interview with SFC Richard F. Lewis, USA Ret.

57 Barth, *Tropic Lightning and Taro Leaf*, P. 17.

58 25th ID WD, 8 August 1950.

59 Appleman, *South to the Naktong*, p. 274.

60 *Ibid.*

61 25th ID WD entry, 8 August 1950.

62 "Enemy Retreats Toward Chinju Base; Hawaii 5th in 2nd Big Night Attack," *The Honolulu Advertiser*, 10 August 1950. LTC Throckmorton rarely spoke to newspaper correspondents. He made an exception to correspondents from Honolulu because he wanted the people of Hawaii to read about the exploits of their friends, family, and loved ones. That CPL Lorrin Thurston, his driver, was the son of the editor of *The Honolulu Advertiser*, probably accounted for his willingness, too.

CHAPTER EIGHT

1 Montross and Canzona, *U.S. Marine Operations in Korea.* Vol. 1, pp. 139-142.

2 "5th Dons Masks to Push Ahead in Dust," *The Honolulu Advertiser*, 9 August 1950.

3 25th ID, Assistant Chief of Staff, G-2, letter to Division Historian, 9 August 1950.

4 25th ID WD entry, 9 August 1950.

5 Author interview with LTC Keith W. Whitham, USA Ret.

6 Lieutenant Whitham earned the Silver Star for this action.

7 Author interview with Mr. Robert H. Middleton.

8 Author interview with COL Claude W. Baker, USA Ret.; MGEN James A. Johnson, USA Ret.; and LGEN Henry E. Emerson, USA Ret.

9 Author interview with Mr. Robert H. Middleton.

10 The 90th FAB had just two four-gun batteries. One was with the 5th RCT, the other with the 35th Infantry. Later in the war, it received its third firing battery, and each battery was increased in size to six howitzers.

11 Author interview with Dr. D. Randall Beirne, COL, USAR Ret.

12 Author interview with LTC Keith W. Whitham, USA Ret.

13 Appleman, *South to the Naktong*, pp. 277-278. The 25th ID WD has little to say concerning this action.

14 Author interview with COL Claude W. Baker, USA Ret. Appleman, *South to the Naktong*, p. 277, states that LTC Daly assumed temporary command of 1st Battalion. COL Baker disagrees. He recalls that he commanded the battalion until LTC Roelofs assumed command the next day.

15 He recovered and rejoined the combat team. Author interview with LTC Keith W. Whitham, USA Ret.

16 Author interview with LTC Norman W. Cooper, USA Ret.

17 Author interview with Mr. Horace Anderson. A gunner usually fired the 57-mm from his shoulder, so the loss of the tripod was not important.

18 Author interview with LTC Keith W. Whitham, USA Ret.

19 *Ibid.*

20 Author interview with 1st SGT George Freedman, USA, Ret.

21 Barth, *Tropic Lightning and Taro Leaf*, pp. 18-19. "Red Legs" is another term used to describe artillerymen.

22 Author interview with COL Claude W. Baker, USA Ret.

23 Author interview with COL Dick J. Oostenink, Jr., USA, Chaplain Corps, Ret.

24 Appleman, *South to the Naktong*, p. 279.

25 Baker Battery was no longer combined with C Battery. Author interview with Mr. Albert F. Semasko.

26 Author interview with LTC Norman W. Cooper, USA Ret.

27 McClure, *Op. Cit.*, pp. 56-57.

28 Author interview with MSGT Arlen Russell, USAF Ret.

29 Author interview with SFC Richard F. Lewis, USA Ret.

30 Author interview with COL Claude W. Baker, USA Ret. Note that COL Baker's recollection of events is at variance with LTC Roelofs' as recorded in Appleman, *South to the Naktong*, pp. 280-284. Baker disputes Roelofs' claim that he awakened the battalion commander at 0100 with the news that C Company was being overrun. Baker states this was impossible because no one knew where LTC Roelofs had gone to sleep.

31 Author interview with COL Claude W. Baker, USA Ret.

32 Author interview with LTC Keith W. Whitham, USA Ret.

[33] Author interview with Mr. Albert F. Semasko.

[34] *Ibid.*

[35] Oral Interview with MGEN James A. Johnson, USA, Ret., conducted by Dr. Charles Hendricks.

[36] Author interview with Judge Samuel L. Lewis.

[37] Author interview with Mr. Albert F. Semasko.

[38] Apparently, no high explosive antitank rounds were available to the gun crews.

[39] The origin of this Heavy Machine Gun Platoon has been disputed. Some eyewitnesses claim it belonged to D Company, while others insist it was from H Company. The author believes it was D Company's platoon because LTC Throckmorton would probably not have left his battalion's platoon behind.

[40] Author interview with COL Claude W. Baker, USA Ret.

[41] Author interview with SFC Richard F. Lewis, USA Ret.

[42] Appleman, *South to the Naktong*, p. 284.

[43] 5th RCT NL, 5 December 1991.

[44] Author interview with LTC Keith W. Whitham, USA Ret.

[45] Author interview with WO Sal Bosco, USA Ret.

[46] Author interview with Judge Samuel L. Lewis.

[47] Barth, *Tropic Lightning and Taro Leaf*, pp. 18-19.

[48] Author interview with SFC Richard F. Lewis, USA Ret. Presumably, they moved out ahead of COL Ordway and the regimental trains.

[49] Author interview with MSGT Arlen Russell, USAF Ret.

[50] 25th ID WD entry, 12 August 1950.

[51] Barth, *Tropic Lightning and Taro Leaf*, p. 19, stated eight howitzers were lost, however, this total includes the two knocked out on 8 August 1950. The S-4 Maintenance Staff Journal, HQ 24th Infantry Division Artillery, includes an entry on 21 April 1951 that lists all the 24th ID's 155-mm and 105-mm losses to date. Though the 555th FAB did not join the 24th ID until September 1950, its loss of six 155-mm howitzers in August 1950 is included in the report. Major Earl Law, in an interview with the author, stated that survivors informed him the gun crews deliberately blew up their howitzers with their last shells just before the batteries were overrun.

[52] 25th ID WD entry, 13 August 1950.

[53] Appleman, *South to the Naktong*, p. 284. Strangely enough, the 90th FAB received a Distinguished Unit Citation for this action while the heroics of the 555th FAB went unrewarded.

[54] *Ibid.*

[55] Author interview with Dr. D. Randall Beirne, COL, USAR Ret. The "great military expert" referred to was S.L.A. Marshall who wrote *Men Against Fire* (New York: William Morrow, 1941), a book that claimed just one in four or five riflemen fired his weapon in combat.

[56] Author correspondence with Commissioner Alfred S. Los Banos.

[57] Author interview with Dr. D. Randall Beirne, COL, USAR Ret.

[58] Author interview with Mr. Albert F. Semasko.

[59] Appleman, *South to the Naktong*, p. 285.

[60] Oral Interview with MGEN James A. Johnson, USA, Ret., conducted by Dr. Charles Hendricks.

[61] 25th ID WD entry, 16 August 1950.

CHAPTER NINE

[1] Author interview with Mr. Donald L. Gottschall.

[2] Author interview with LGEN Henry E. Emerson, USA Ret.

[3] Author interview with Dr. D. Randall Beirne, COL, USAR Ret.

[4] Author interview with LTC Keith W. Whitham, USA Ret.

[5] Author interview with LTC Norman W. Cooper, USA Ret.

[6] Author interview with CWO-4 William J. Straney, USAR Ret.

[7] Author interview with Mr. Donald L. Gottschall.

[8] Author interview with Mr. Horace Anderson.

[9] 25th ID WD entry, 14 August 1950.

[10] Lieutenant Colonel Daly was subsequently awarded two Purple Hearts and the Distinguished Service Cross for his actions at Pongam-ni. He should have received a third Purple Heart, but being too modest to ask, he never received it. He retired disabled as a brigadier general in 1964. Author interview with SFC Richard F. Lewis, USA Ret.

[11] Author interview with COL Frank A. Athanason, USA Ret.

[12] Author interview with MAJ Earl J. Law, USA Ret.

[13] Barth, *Tropic Lightning and Taro Leaf*, p. 23. Not all of the 555th FAB's officer casualties fell killed or wounded. The battalion XO, S-2, and the Headquarters Battery commander were relieved of their duties for combat fatigue. Author interview with SFC Richard F. Lewis, USA Ret.

[14] Author interview with COL Frank A. Athanason, USA Ret.

[15] The lack of knowledge and skill relating to artillery tactics and techniques was endemic for the same reasons, losses and lack of experience, to virtually all the FABs in Korea.

[16] Author interview with SFC Richard F. Lewis, USA Ret.

[17] Mesko, *Armor in Korea*, pp. 9-10.

[18] 25th ID WD entry, 18 August 1950.

[19] Author interview with SFC Richard F. Lewis, USA Ret.

[20] "Tropic Lightning" is another name for the 25th ID.

[21] Author interview with Dr. D. Randall Beirne, COL, USAR Ret.

[22] 25th ID WD entry, 13 August 1950.

[23] Author interview with LGEN Henry E. Emerson, USA Ret.

[24] *Ibid.*

[25] *Pictorial History of the Korean War*, p. 136.

[26] Author interview with MGEN James A. Johnson, USA Ret.

[27] Oral Interview with MGEN James A. Johnson, USA, Ret., conducted by Dr. Charles Hendricks.

[28] All of Sonny's letters quoted in the text are part of the author's personal collection.

[29] Author interview with COL Dick J. Oostenink, Jr., USA, Chaplain Corps, Ret.

[30] Barth, *Tropic Lightning and Taro Leaf*, p. 22; and 25th ID WD entry, 19 August 1950.

[31] 25th ID WD entry, 20 August 1950.

[32] Appleman, *South to the Naktong*, pp. 385-389.

[33] 1st CD WD entry, 7 September 1950.

[34] 5th RCT NL, April 1993; and an undated fragment of *Star and Stripes*.

[35] Author interview with LTC Norman W. Cooper, USA Ret.

[36] *Ibid.*

[37] *Ibid.*

[38] *Ibid.*; and author interview with Dr. D. Randall Beirne, COL, USAR Ret., who stated, "Just before the war I was sent to Coronado, California, to embarkation school. Each battalion sent one officer. Those from the 1st and the 2nd Battalions should not have been on active duty. The 1st Battalion officer had been a prisoner of war in World War II and deserted his company early in Korea. The one from the 2nd Battalion had cracked up in Italy in World War II and lasted for only two days of combat in Korea. The 5th had too many of these. Several other officers who failed in World War II also failed when they got to Korea."

[39] Author interview with Mr. Gerald Pack.

[40] 25th ID WD entry, 21 August 1950.

[41] 25th ID Periodic Intelligence Report # 38, from 211800 to 221800 August 1950. The NKPA's extensive use mines and tunnels, a characteristic of the Sobuk-san mining district, compounded American difficulties.

[42] 25th ID WD entry, 22 August 1950.

[43] Author interview with 1st SGT George Freedman, USA Ret.

[44] 25th ID Quartermaster Letter, "Deceased Personnel," 22 August 1950.

[45] 25th ID G-1 Daily Summary, 22 August 1950. Losses for the 5th Infantry include those incurred by the 72nd Engineers but not those of the 555th FAB. In comparison, the 24th Infantry had incurred 48 KIA, 572 WIA, 82 MIA, and 263 non-battle casualties. The 27th Infantry had incurred 82 KIA, 367 WIA, 61 MIA, and 231 non-battle casualties. The 35th Infantry had incurred 48 KIA, 171 WIA, 62 MIA, and 289 non-battle casualties. The attached 29th Infantry had incurred a shocking 45 KIA, 192 WIA, 478 MIA, and 142 non-battle casualties. With the exception of the 5th and 24th Infantry Regiments, the other regiments possessed just two infantry battalions. The 29th Infantry was soon disbanded, its two battalions being used to form the third battalions of the 27th and 35th Infantry Regiments.

[46] The 1st Battalion never succeeded in gaining the highest peak of Sobuk-san. See Appleman, *South to the Naktong*, p. 483.

[47] Courtesy of Dr. D. Randall Beirne, COL, USAR Ret.

[48] Author interview with Dr. D. Randall Beirne, COL, USAR Ret.

[49] *Ibid.*

[50] Author interview with Mr. Ronald Denton.

[51] 25th ID WD entry, 23 August 1950.

[52] Author interview with Dr. D. Randall Beirne, COL, USAR Ret.

[53] The company administrator billet was filled by a warrant officer whose job was to free the CO, XO, and the first sergeant from paperwork so they could concentrate on leading and fighting their company.

[54] Author interview with LGEN Henry E. Emerson, USA Ret.

[55] *Ibid.* Sergeant Lyons received a battlefield commission on 7 October 1950.

[56] *Ibid.* Lieutenant Emerson attempted to press charges against this officer, but he quickly found out that few people were ever punished for cowardice in Korea.

[57] 25th ID G-1 Daily Summary, for 23-24 August 1950.

[58] Author interview with Mr. Robert H. Middleton.

[59] *Ibid.*

[60] 25th ID WD entry, 25-26 August 1950.

[61] North Korean soldiers often shouted "Manzai" in the assault, which translates loosely as "Hooray." They also shouted "Banzai," a linguistic remnant of the Japanese occupation.

[62] Author interview with COL Claude W. Baker, USA Ret. Captain Hilgard was awarded the Silver Star, posthumously, per General Orders No. 78, Eighth Army, Korea.

[63] Author interview with 1st SGT George Freedman, USA Ret.

[64] *Ibid.*

[65] Author interview with COL Claude W. Baker, USA Ret.

66 *Ibid.*

67 Information concerning this officer was provided by Dr. D. Randall Beirne, COL, USAR Ret.

68 25th ID WD entry, 27 August 1950.

69 *Ibid.*, 28 August 1950.

70 See 25th ID WD entries for details of these actions.

71 Author interview with COL Claude W. Baker, USA Ret.

72 25th ID WD entry, 1 September 1950.

73 25th ID G-1 Daily Summary, 31 August 1950.

74 25th ID Tank Status Report, 31 August 1950.

75 25th ID WD entry, 1 September 1950.

76 This officer walked back up the hill after the attack, and LT Cooper, quite understandably, relieved him on the spot. Lieutenant Cooper appeared before a board in 1951 to testify against the officer, but he does not know what ever happened to the man. Author interview with LTC Norman W. Cooper, USA Ret.

77 Author interview with Mr. Gerald Pack. Having already earned one Purple Heart on Fox Hill, he received a second Purple Heart for the wounds incurred on Sobuk-san. Mr. Pack knew PFC Calhau, and though both men served in different platoons, he recalls that PFC Calhau was a good soldier. Mr. Pack spent the next year in various hospitals. He volunteered to return to Korea and served with the 5th RCT from mid-1951 to early 1953 and attained the rank of SFC. He recently went blind in one eye due to shrapnel wounds incurred on Sobuk-san.

78 25th ID WD entry, 2 September 1950.

79 Author interview with LTC Norman W. Cooper, USA Ret.

80 Author interview with Dr. D. Randall Beirne, COL, USAR Ret.

81 Courtesy of Dr. D. Randall Beirne, COL, USAR Ret.

82 Author interview with Mr. Joseph Gonzales, Sr.

83 25th ID WD entry, 5 September 1950.

84 Author interview with LGEN Henry E. Emerson, USA Ret.

85 *Ibid.* LTC Throckmorton recommended LT Emerson for the Distinguished Service Cross, but it was down graded to the Silver Star.

86 Appleman, *South to the Naktong*, pp. 484-485. The 27th Infantry Regiment "Wolfhounds" relieved the 5th RCT.

87 25th ID G-1 Daily Summary, 9 September 1950.

88 Author interview with Mr. Donald L. Gottschall.

89 This letter is dated 8 September 1950.

90 *Ibid.*

91 Author interview with MAJ Earl J. Law, USA Ret.

92 The note is dated 11 September 1950.

CHAPTER TEN

1 Appleman, *South to the Naktong*, p. 547. The number of MIA reported after nine weeks of fighting was approxi-   mately three hundred less than would be reported after eight years in Vietnam.

2 "War's Top Atrocity! GIs' Beer Cut Off," *The Honolulu Advertiser*, 13 September 1950.

3 *Ibid.*

4 "WCTU Boasts of Prohibition (later Repealed) on Free Brew," *The Honolulu Advertiser*, 13 September 1950.

5 "5 More Hawaii Soldiers Die; 2 are Missing," *The Honolulu Advertiser*, 13 September 1950.

6 1st CD WD entry, 14 September 1950.

7 "Yanks Burned Alive By Captors," *The Honolulu Star-Bulletin*, 15 September 1950.

8 "Ban Beer for Water, Fruit Juice in Korea," *The Honolulu Advertiser*, 17 September 1950.

9 "3 More Hawaii Soldiers Wounded," *The Honolulu Advertiser*, 17 September 1950.

10 1st CD WD entry, 18 September 1950.

11 "Two Breweries Open Taps to Korean GIs," *The Honolulu Advertiser*, 28 September 1950.

12 "Silver Star to Oahu Officer," *The Honolulu Advertiser*, 28 September 1950.

CHAPTER ELEVEN

1 Appleman, *South to the Naktong*, p. 543. The Eighth Army had equipment for just two ponton treadway bridges across the Naktong.

2 Jehuda L. Wallach, *The Dogma of the Battle of Annihilation: The Theories of Clausewitz and Schlieffen and Their Impact on the German Conduct of Two World Wars* (Westport: Greenwood Press, 1986), p. 45.

3 The word "Cavalry" was an honorific. It was an infantry division.

4 Appleman, *South to the Naktong*, p. 553.

5 1st CD WD entry, 13 September 1950.

7 Appleman, *South to the Naktong*, p. 553.

8 Charles and Eugene Jones, *The Face of War* (New York: Prentice-Hall, Inc., 1951), p. 49.

9 Barth, *Tropic Lightning and Taro Leaf*, pp. 91-92.

10 Appleman, *South to the Naktong*, p. 552.

11 1st CD Periodic Report for the period 150600 to 151800 Sep 1950.

12 Author interview with LTC Keith W. Whitham, USA Ret.; 1st CD WD entry, 15 September 1950; and 1st CD Periodic Report for the period 150600 to 151800 Sep 1950.

13 Futrell, *The United States Air Force in Korea*, p. 161.

14 Blair, *The Forgotten War*, p. 285; and 1st CD WD entry, 16 September 1950.

15 Author interview with LTC Norman W. Cooper, USA Ret.

16 Author interview with Mr. Horace Anderson.

17 Author interview with LTC Keith W. Whitham, USA Ret.

18 Author interview with Mr. Frank Valvo.

19 1st CD WD entry, 16 September 1950, confirms that four antitank guns were captured.

20 Author interview with Mr. Frank Valvo and Mr. Horace Anderson.

21 Author correspondence with Mr. Charles Shepherd, and 5th RCT NL, September 1999.

22 Author interview with Mr. Horace Anderson.

23 1st CD WD entry, 17 September 1950.

24 *Ibid.*

25 Information derived from several different letters Sonny wrote his parents over the next couple of months, and an author interview with Mr. Alton Kenawell, Johnnie's brother.

26 "Three Honolulu Soldiers Win Korea Medals," *The Honolulu Advertiser*, 13 June 1951.

27 Author interview with Dr. D. Randall Beirne, COL, USAR Ret.

28 *Ibid.*

29 *Ibid.*; and 5th RCT "Awards and Decorations" letter dated 2 January 1951. Sergeant First Class McCraine was awarded the Silver Star on 2 January 1951.

30 Author interview with Dr. D. Randall Beirne, COL, USAR Ret., and 5th RCT NL, August 1995.

31 *Ibid.*

32 *Ibid.*

33 Captain Hula was awarded the Silver Star, posthumously, on 2 January 1951. See, 5th RCT "Awards and Decorations" letter dated 2 January 1951.

34 Author interview with Dr. D. Randall Beirne, COL, USAR Ret.

35 5th RCT Unit Report from 171800 Sep 50 to 181800 Sep 50. A Unit Report was a comprehensive document that covered the enemy situation, friendly mission, activities of friendly units, personnel strengths, friendly and enemy losses, logistics, morale, etc. There is a gap in the 5th RCT's official records from 9 January to 17 September 1950. A portion of the August 1950 records was recently found at the National Archives.

36 A lieutenant who commanded a rifle or heavy weapons company for thirty days in combat was eligible for promotion to captain. Captain Emerson had recently been promoted, as had CAPT Conger in E Company.

37 Author interview with LGEN Henry E. Emerson, USA Ret. 1st Battalion knocked out 3 T-34s that day.

38 Futrell, *The United States Air Force in Korea*, p. 162.

39 McClure, *Op. Cit.*, pp. 88-89.

40 *Ibid.*

41 Author interview with Dr. D. Randall Beirne, COL, USAR Ret.

42 *Ibid.*

43 *Ibid.*

44 *Ibid.*

45 *Ibid.*

46 *Ibid.*

47 *Ibid.*

48 *Ibid.*

49 *Ibid.*

50 *Ibid.* Though LT Beirne recommended all these men for the Bronze Star, only the ranking sergeant received one. "That's how they gave out awards in those days," LT Beirne informed the author.

51 *Ibid.*

52 Blair, *The Forgotten War*, pp. 285-286. The 1st Battalion, 21st Infantry incurred 120 casualties in an other wise successful crossing of the Naktong on assault boats the next morning.

53 Appleman, *South to the Naktong*, p. 553. The 24th Infantry Division was also known as the "Victory" or "Taro Leaf" division.

54 *Ibid.*, p. 389.

55 1st CD WD entry, 19 September 1950.

56 5th RCT Unit Report from 181800 Sep 50 to 191800 Sep 50.

57 Author interview with MAJ Frank Brooks, USA Ret.

58 Author interview with Dr. D. Randall Beirne, COL, USAR Ret.

59 *Ibid.*

60 *Ibid.* Sergeant First Class Cabral survived his wounds and the doctors saved his arm. COL Beirne believes that SFC Cabral was awarded the Silver Star.

61 Author interview with Mr. Thomas Throckmorton.

62 Author interview with Dr. D. Randall Beirne, COL, USAR Ret.

63 5th RCT Unit Report from 181800 Sep 50 to 191800 Sep 50.

64 5th RCT PW Reports, 19 Sep 50.

65 5th RCT Unit Report from 191800 Sep 50 to 201800 Sep 50.

66 Author interview with LTC Norman W. Cooper, USA Ret.

67 Appleman, *South to the Naktong*, p. 554

68 5th RCT Strength Report 21 Sep 50.
69 Author interview with LTC Keith W. Whitham, USA Ret.
70 "Hawaii's 5th One of Best in Korea: Gay," *The Honolulu Advertiser*, 20 March 1951.

CHAPTER TWELVE

1 Author interview with COL Albert R. Throne, USA Ret.
2 The 3rd Combat Engineer Battalion was organic to the 24th Infantry Division.
3 Author correspondence with 1st SGT Hibbert Manley, USA Ret.
4 Oral Interview with MGEN James A. Johnson, USA, Ret., conducted by Dr. Charles Hendricks. Lieutenant Johnson was experienced enough to recognize that the mines had been hastily laid and were probably not booby-trapped.
5 Author correspondence with 1st SGT Hibbert Manley, USA Ret.
6 5th RCT Unit Report from 201800 Sep 50 to 211800 Sep 50; and Oral Interview with MGEN James A. Johnson, USA, Ret., conducted by Dr. Charles Hendricks.
7 Author interview with LTC Norman W. Cooper, USA Ret.
8 Author correspondence with 1st SGT Hibbert Manley, USA Ret.
9 5th RCT Unit Report from 201800 Sep 50 to 211800 Sep 50.
10 5th RCT Unit Report from 211800 Sep 50 to 221800 Sep 50.
11 Appleman, *South to the Naktong*, pp. 584.
12 Author interview with LTC Keith W. Whitham, USA Ret.
13 24th ID Special Order Number 228, 20 November 1950. Sergeant Pearce was awarded the Silver Star for his actions that night.
14 Author interview with COL Claude W. Baker, USA Ret.
15 Author interview with LTC Keith W. Whitham, USA Ret.
16 "Go for Broke" was the motto of the 442nd Infantry. General Emerson recommended SGT Sylva for the Distinguished Service Cross, but the award was downgraded to a Silver Star. Author interview with LGEN Henry E. Emerson, USA Ret. Master Sergeant Albert Chang, *This Way to War* (Honolulu: Tongg Publishing Company, 1952), pages not numbered, includes a photo of Sylva with the caption that "PFC Adrian J. Silva [sic]" was awarded the Silver Star and killed in action. That Sylva was a sergeant before Sobuk-san is confirmed in an author interview with LTC Keith W. Whitham, USA Ret., who recalls that SGT Sylva's rifle squad escorted his tank platoon at Bloody Gulch on 11 August 1950. The Korean and Vietnam Memorials in Honolulu and his headstone at the Punchbowl state that SGT Adrian J. K. Sylva was KIA on 22 September 1950, the day before the 1st Battalion commenced the attack on Kumchon. A couple of possibilities may account for the discrepancy in dates. The Graves Registration Team may have made a typographical error when they recorded his death, or SGT Sylva may have been KIA in a different firefight the day before the Battle of Kumchon began in earnest. Several witnesses place Doctor Hedberg at the front on 24 September 1950, walking calmly through the 1st Battalion's positions as he treated the wounded, which indicates that SGT Sylva may have been KIA on 24 September 1950.
17 Information on LT Young was acquired in correspondence with LTC Keith W. Whitham, USA Ret. Information on the NKPA defenses was found in the Oral Interview with MGEN James A. Johnson, USA, Ret., conducted by Dr. Charles Hendricks.
18 24th ID Special Order Number 228, 20 November 1950, lists the citation for MSGT Dunn's Bronze Star for Valor.
19 Author interview with LTC Norman W. Cooper, USA Ret.
20 Oral Interview with MGEN James A. Johnson, USA, Ret., conducted by Dr. Charles Hendricks.
21 Author interview with Dr. D. Randall Beirne, COL, USAR Ret.
22 5th RCT Unit Report from 231800 Sep 50 to 241800 Sep 50.
23 Author interview with LTC Keith W. Whitham, USA Ret.
24 "Honolulu Man Commands Group Operating Behind Enemy Lines," *The Honolulu Star-Bulletin*, 27 September 1950.
25 Author interview with 1st SGT Hibbert Manley, USA Ret.
26 The caption of the cover page photo in *The Honolulu Advertiser*, 30 April 1951.
27 Author correspondence with Mr. Herbert Ikeda.
28 24th ID Special Order Number 228, 20 November 1950.
29 5th RCT Unit Report from 241800 Sep 50 to 251800 Sep 50.
30 Author interview with LTC Keith W. Whitham, USA Ret.
31 *Ibid.*
32 5th RCT Unit Reports from 231800 Sep 50 to 251800 Sep 50.
33 Appleman, *South to the Naktong*, pp. 584-585. The 6th Tank Battalion, organic to the 24th Infantry Division, was equipped with the M-46 "Patton" tank armed with a 90-mm main gun and a couple of machine guns.
34 "Silver Star Awarded to 5th RCT Medic," *The Honolulu Advertiser,* 24 October 1950.
35 "Those Unarmed Medics are Among the Heroes of the Battle," *The Honolulu Star-Bulletin*, 29 September 1950.
36 Blair, *The Forgotten War*, pp. 290-291.
37 "5th RCT Commander gets DSC in Korea," *The Honolulu Advertiser*, 3 March 1951.
38 5th RCT Unit report from 251800 Sep 50 to 261800 Sep 50.

[39] 5th RCT PW Reports, 29-30 Sep 50.

[40] Author interview with LTC Keith W. Whitham, USA Ret. Lieutenant Whitham received a second Silver Star for his actions at Kumchon and during the drive on Okchon.

[41] Author interview with LTC William O. Perry, Jr., USA Ret.

[42] 25ID WD Personnel Status Reports, and 5th RCT Unit Reports for the period in question.

[43] The postmark on the envelope is 30 September 1950.

[44] This excerpt is from a letter Sonny wrote on 26 September 1950.

[45] The excerpt is from a letter Sonny wrote on 27 September 1950.

[46] 5th RCT Unit Report from 301800 Sep 50 to 011800 Oct 50; and 5th RCT Patrol Reports, Red Patrol Number 3, 1 Oct 50. The same patrol noted that, "only about 30 to 50 percent have weapons." Note the usage of color code words. The 5th RCT used "Red" for the 1st Battalion, "White" for the 2nd Battalion, and "Blue" for the 3rd Battalion. These simple code words did not fool anyone for long who may have been monitoring the 5th RCT's radio and wire communications. The same codes were in effect at the time of Sonny's death in March 1951.

[47] 5th RCT Unit Reports from 011800 Oct 50 to 071800 Oct 50.

[48] 5th RCT Training Memorandums dated 8 Oct 50 through 12 Oct 50.

[49] Author interview with LGEN Henry E. Emerson, USA Ret.

[50] Author interview with Mr. Horace Anderson.

[51] Oral Interview with MGEN James A. Johnson, USA, Ret., conducted by Dr. Charles Hendricks.

CHAPTER THIRTEEN

[1] 5th RCT Operations Order #20, 15 Oct 50 and 5th RCT Unit Report from 151800 to 161800 Oct 50.

[2] Blair, *The Forgotten War*, p. 349; Russell Spurr, *Enter the Dragon: China's Undeclared War Against the U.S. in Korea*, 1950-1951 (New York: New Market Press, 1988), pp. 115-118; and Alexander L. George, *The Chinese Communist Army in Action: The Korean War and its Aftermath* (New York: Columbia University Press, paperback edition, 1969), p. 6. Captured Chinese soldiers stated during interrogation that the Fourth Field Army had earned the honorific "Iron" troops during the Chinese Civil War.

[3] Author interview with COL Claude W. Baker, USA Ret.

[4] Author interview with LGEN Henry E. Emerson, USA Ret.

[5] Blair, *The Forgotten War*, pp. 332-333, 341-342, and 350-351. See also, Lynn Montross and Captain Nicholas A. Canzona., *U.S. Marine Operations in Korea 1950-1953. Volume III. The Chosin Reservoir Campaign* (Washington, D.C.: Historical Branch, G-3, Headquarters U.S. Marine Corps, 1957), pp. 8-11.

[6] They also favored integrating X Corps into the Eighth Army's command structure. Much to General Walker's dismay, General MacArthur kept X Corps an independent unit reporting directly to him.

[7] Ridgway, *The Korean War*, p. 44.

[8] Blair, *The Forgotten War*, pp. 365-368; and Lynn Montross and Captain Nicholas A. Canzona. *U.S. Marine Operations in Korea 1950-1953. Volume III. The Chosin Reservoir Campaign*, pp. 21-31.

[9] Blair, *The Forgotten War*, p. 319. Blair believes that perhaps 40,000 NKPA troops managed to escape.

[10] 5th RCT Operations Order #23, 21 Oct 50.

[11] 5th RCT Personnel Periodic Report, 211800 Oct 50. These prisoners were captured between 14-21 October 1950.

[12] 5th RCT Unit Report from 211800 Oct 50 to 221800 Oct 1950.

[13] 5th RCT Unit Report from 221800 Oct 50 to 231800 Oct 50.

[14] 5th RCT Unit Report from 241800 Oct 50 to 251800 Oct 50.

CHAPTER FOURTEEN

[1] Author's personal files.

CHAPTER FIFTEEN

[1] Spurr, *Enter the Dragon*, p. 83.

[2] Appleman, *South to the Naktong*, p.673, identifies LT Glenn C. Jones as the KMAG advisor assigned to the ROK 3rd Battalion, 2nd Regiment. *Register of Graduates and Former Cadets, United States Military Academy, West Point, New York*, provided the information on 1st LT Wilber G. Jones, Jr. It is equally possible that the two "Jones" are the same or different individuals.

[3] *Ibid.*, pp. 673-675.

[4] 5th RCT Unit Report from 241800 Oct 50 to 251800 Oct 50. This Unit Report includes a map of CCF locations drawn by a North Korean PW.

[5] Letter courtesy of Dr. D. Randall Beirne, COL, USAR Ret.

[6] 5th RCT Unit Report form 271800 Oct 50 to 281800 Oct 50. The 5th RCT's success was primarily due to two factors. First, the NKPA unit opposing the 5th RCT was not as well trained as those encountered in earlier battles. Second, LTC Throckmorton was a superb tactician who fully integrated his fire support into his scheme of maneuver.

[7] 5th RCT S-2/S-3 Journal entry, 28 Oct 50.

[8] *Ibid.*

[9] Ridgway, *The Korean War*, pp. 51-52.

[10] Blair, *The Forgotten War*, p. 370; and 5th RCT Unit Report from 281800 Oct 50 to 291800 Oct 50, which states that two of the 89 PWs captured on 29 October 1959 may be Chinese.

[11] Blair, *The Forgotten War*, pp. 375-377.

[12] *Ibid.*, p. 369.

[13] Oral Interview with MGEN James A. Johnson, USA, Ret., conducted by Dr. Charles Hendricks.

CHAPTER SIXTEEN

[1] The M-4 A3E8s had a 76-mm gun. This tank probably belonged to the 6th Tank Battalion, 24th Infantry Division, which was equipped with Patton tanks armed with a 90-mm gun.

[2] The excerpts are from a letter Sonny wrote to his parents on 30 October 1950.

[3] Roster of officers in the 5th Infantry Regiment, 31 October 1950. Between 7-16 October, F Company had received a new commanding officer and four lieutenants.

[4] Ridgway, *The Korean War*, p. 53. Ridgway was discussing the entry of the Chinese into the war, but these words might also apply to the NKPA's resurgence on the battlefield.

[5] "Six Survivors of Massacre are Rescued," *The Honolulu Advertiser*, 26 October 1950.

[6] Appleman, *South to the Naktong*, pp. 540, and 587-588; and author interview with COL Dick J. Oostenink, Jr., Chaplain Corps, USA Ret. Appleman describes North Korean atrocities committed in Seoul as "ghastly." The NKPA murdered between 5,000 and 7,000 civilians at Taejon. Colonel Oostenink recalls seeing hundreds of murdered civilians lying in open air mass graves at Taejon during the 5th RCT's advance on Seoul. He discovered scores of murdered civilians lying in a church.

[7] 25th ID G-2 Summary, 22 August 1950.

[8] 1st CD WD entry, 13 September 1950.

[9] 1st CD WD entry, 21 September 1950.

[10] Author interview with Dr. D. Randall Beirne, COL, USAR Ret.

[11] Oral Interview with MGEN James A. Johnson, USA, Ret., conducted by Dr. Charles Hendricks.

[12] Author interview with MGEN James A. Johnson, USA Ret.

[13] 5th RCT Unit Report from 291800 Oct 50 to 3018800 Oct 50; and Oral Interview with MGEN James A. Johnson, USA, Ret., conducted by Dr. Charles Hendricks.

[14] Author interview with 1st SGT George Freedman, USA Ret.

[15] 5th RCT Unit Report from 301800 Oct 50 to 311800 Oct 50.

[16] 5th RCT PW Reports, 31 Oct 50.

[17] 5th RCT Operations Order, 31 Oct 50.

[18] 5th RCT S-2/S-3 Journal entry, 31 October 1950.

[19] 5th RCT Casualty Statistics from 29 Sep 50 to 31 Oct 50; and 5th RCT Unit Report from 301800 Oct 50 to 311800 Oct 50.

[20] Author interview with COL Frank A. Athanason, USA Ret.

[21] Author interview with LTC Keith W. Whitham, USA Ret.

[22] Author interview with LGEN Henry E. Emerson, USA Ret. The Army had a program that provided night school opportunities to men seeking degrees, but General Emerson's point that it is "damn near impossible for a combat arms officer to go to night school" should not be dismissed lightly.

[23] Appleman, *South to the Naktong*, p. 683; and Author interview with LTC Keith W. Whitham, USA Ret. Whitham states that the bodies included Chinese soldiers.

[24] Oral Interview with MGEN James A. Johnson, USA, Ret., conducted by Dr. Charles Hendricks.

[25] Appleman, *South to the Naktong*, p. 684.

[26] How Able was slang for "Haul Ass." Author interview with LTC Keith W. Whitham, USA Ret.

[27] Blair, *The Forgotten War*, pp. 370-371.

CHAPTER SEVENTEEN

[1] Fehrenbach, *This Kind of War*, pp. 194-195, describes the CCF's advance.

[2] A CCF "army" was the rough equivalent in size to an U.S. Army corps.

[3] No more than three regiments of 122-mm howitzers and a handful of multiple rocket launchers accompanied the original CCF units that intervened in Korea. Spurr, *Enter the Dragon*, p. 118. See also, Lynn Montross and Captain Nicholas A. Canzona. *U.S. Marine Operations in Korea 1950-1953. Volume III. The Chosin Reservoir Campaign*, pp. 93-94.

[4] The terms "officer" and "NCO" are used loosely here to represent CCF commanders and small unit leaders, respectfully. For ideological reasons, the CCF did not use the same system of ranks traditionally found in most armies.

[5] George, *The Chinese Communist Army in Action*, pp. 157-161.

[6] *Ibid.*, pp. 30, 37, 51.

[7] English, *On Infantry*, pp. 168-173.

[8] Lynn Montross and Captain Nicholas A. Canzona. *U.S. Marine Operations in Korea 1950-1953. Volume III. The Chosin Reservoir Campaign*, p. 92.

[9] *Ibid.*

[10] Author interview with LTC William O. Perry, Jr., USA Ret.

[11] Fehrenbach, *This Kind of War*, p. 193; and Roy E. Appleman, *Disaster in Korea* (College Station: Texas A&M Press, 1989), p. 18-19. The Changjin Reservoir is the proper Korean name for the area veterans usually describe as the Chosin Reservoir, which is of Japanese origin.

[12] Blair, *The Forgotten War*, pp. 380-384; and Appleman, *South to the Naktong*, pp. 691-708.

[13] Ridgway, *The Korean War*, pp. 53-59. Ridgway blames much of the disaster on the regimental and battalion commanders who failed to take adequate security measures. For the Chinese perspective, read Spurr, *Enter the Dragon*, pp. 138-151.

[14] "U.S. Suffers War's Worst Defeat," *The Honolulu Advertiser*, 3 November 1950.

[15] 5th RCT Unit Report Number 83, from 031800 Nov 50 to 041800 Nov 50. Captain Hubert H. Ellis, the Commanding Officer of C Company, was also involved in stopping the ROK rout.

[16] Author interview with LGEN Henry E. Emerson, USA Ret.

[17] Appleman, *South to the Naktong*, pp. 710-711. Appleman states two ROK regiments fought in this battle, the 3rd and 5th. The 5th RCT Unit Report mentions only the ROK 5th Regiment. Both ROK regiments were probably present.

[18] Gene McClure, *Op. Cit.*, pp. 135-138.

[19] Appleman, *South to the Naktong*, p. 711; and author interviews with LTC Keith W. Whitham, USA Ret., and 1st SGT Hibbert Manley, USA Ret. After the battle, 1st LT Hansel's comrades wrote his actions up in the hope he would be awarded the Medal of Honor, posthumously, but this recommendation was downgraded to the Distinguished Service Cross. Whether the first sergeant received a posthumous decoration is unknown.

[20] Author interview with 1st SGT Hibbert Manley, USA Ret.

[21] Author interview with 1st SGT George Freedman, USA Ret.

[22] Author interview with Dr. D. Randall Beirne, COL, USAR Ret.

[23] Author interview with MSGT Arlen Russell, USAF Ret.

[24] Author interview with 1st SGT Hibbert Manley, USA Ret.

[25] The number of casualties was derived from 5th RCT Unit Reports covering this period of time.

[26] Blair, *The Forgotten War*, p. 399.

[27] *Ibid.*, note on pp. 433-434. General MacArthur made this announcement: "Tell the boys when they reach the Yalu they are going home. I want to make good on my statement that they are going to eat Christmas dinner at home."

[28] McClure, *Op. Cit.*, pp. 143-144.

[29] 5th Infantry Regiment Special Orders, 12 November 50.

CHAPTER EIGHTEEN

[1] Author interview with Mr. James Shaw.

[2] *Ibid.*

[3] *Ibid.*

[4] Corporal Nakamura would attend Sonny's funeral.

[5] *The Senior R.O.T.C. Manual*, p. 266. In 1950 the Army's noncommissioned officer grades were CPL, SGT, SFC and MSGT. Sergeants wore the rank insignia associated with the present day staff sergeant - three chevrons up, one down. First Sergeant was an occupational title; the grade was that of a MSGT. In Korea commanders were authorized to promote enlisted men at their discretion to replace small unit leaders lost in combat. Heavy casualties in the infantry witnessed many young soldiers thrust into positions of immense responsibility with a corresponding meteoric rise in rank.

[6] Author interview with Mr. James Shaw.

CHAPTER NINETEEN

[1] McClure, *Op. Cit.*, pp. 73-76.

[2] "Fifth RCT Mourns a Fearless Sergeant," *The Honolulu Advertiser*, 18 November 1950.

[3] Commanding Officer 5th RCT Letter to CG 24th ID, 18 November 1950. It reads, "On 16 November 1950 during northward advance of this unit a 1/4 ton 4x4 was completely demolished by two mines resulting in death of one man and serious injury to another. Upon investigation a complete minefield was discovered. Minefield had been emplaced for a considerable time. Engineer officer from 3rd Engineers stated it was an American minefield."

[4] "Fifth RCT Mourns a Fearless Sergeant," *The Honolulu Advertiser*, 18 November 1950, attributes this remark to LTC Ward. "Detroit GI Watches a Great Soldier Die," *Detroit Free Press*, 19 November 1950, is an abridged edition of the former article and attributes this statement to LTC Throckmorton. See also LTC Keith Whitham's account in the 5th RCT NL, May 1994.

[5] Private First Class Beste's comments are included in both columns, neither of which released Ranger's real name pending notice of next of kin. Mr. Ray Warner provided Ranger's name in the 5th RCT NL, March 1994.

CHAPTER TWENTY

[1] Casualty figures were compiled from a summary of 5th RCT daily unit reports.

[2] Schnabel, *Policy and Direction*, p. 295.

[3] Appleman, *South to the Naktong*, p. 754.

[4] Toland, *In Mortal Combat*, pp. 282-283.

[5] Appleman, *South to the Naktong*, p. 761.

[6] Author interview with Mr. Horace Anderson.

[7] *The Forgotten War... Remembered* (Paducah: Turner Publishing Company, 1990, revised edition 1993), p. 151.

[8] Letter courtesy of Dr. D. Randall Beirne, COL, USAR Ret.

[9] Author interview with Dr. D. Randall Beirne, COL, USAR Ret.

[10] 5th RCT Operation Order # 37, 23 November 1950.

[11] 24th ID G-1 Strength Report, 9 November 1950.

[12] A 105-mm howitzer-equipped direct support FAB's TO&E authorized strength was 46 officers, 7 warrant officers, and 621 enlisted men. The 24th Infantry Division's third direct support FAB, the 63rd FAB, had been disestablished on 26 August 1950 due to heavy losses. See Appleman, *South to the Naktong, North to the Yalu*, p. 389.

[13] Eliot A. Cohen and John Gooch, *Military Misfortunes: The Anatomy of Failure in War* (New York: The Free Press, 1990), p. 184 and pp. 188-189.

[14] "MacArthur Leads 'Final' Offensive Against Reds," *The Honolulu Advertiser*, 24 November 1950.

[15] "Reds Talk Tough But It's Action by M'Arthur," *The Honolulu Advertiser*, 25 November 1950.

[16] "Return of Troops by Christmas Doubtful," *The Honolulu Advertiser*, 25 November 1950.

[17] Spurr, *Enter the Dragon*, p. 171.

[18] Appleman, *Disaster in Korea*, pp. 77-87.

[19] *Ibid.*, pp. 106-109.

[20] *Ibid.*, pp. 138-139.

[21] *Ibid.*, pp. 98-99.

[22] Blair, *The Forgotten War*, pp. 469.

[23] *Ibid.*, pp. 477-496. The 2nd Infantry Division had suffered 4,940 casualties in two weeks of fighting.

[24] *Ibid.*, p. 485.

[25] Appleman, *Disaster in Korea*, pp. 86-87; and MacArthur, *Reminiscences*, pp. 371-372, 374.

[26] MacArthur, *Reminiscences*, p. 374.

CHAPTER TWENTY-ONE

[1] Author interview with MSGT Arlen S. Russell, USAF Ret.

[2] 24th ID WD entry, 26 November 1950.

[3] 24th ID WD entry, 27 November 1950.

[4] 5th RCT Patrol Report, 27 November 1950.

[5] 24th ID WD entry, 27 November 1950.

[6] 24th ID WD entry, 28 November 1950.

[7] Appleman, *Disaster in Korea*, pp. 145-146.

[8] Dr. D. Randall Beirne, COL, USAR Ret., provided the author a copy of a letter he mailed home that described the engagement that follows in grim detail.

[9] 24th ID WD entry, 28 November 1950, states the enemy assault commenced at this time.

[10] Lieutenant Beirne identified this man as "Mac Clogan" in his letter. A cursory check of MSGT Al Chang's *This Way to War* revealed a photograph of CPL Arthur McClogan eating Poi and laulaus during the fighting at Waegwan. The author suspects "Mac Clogan" is CPL McClogan.

[11] The 5th RCT NL, 1 August 1995, contained Private Armon's full name.

[12] Dr. D. Randall Beirne's letter included the last names of the men mentioned in the text. Mr. Ray Warner's research uncovered their first names. Sergeants Bannister, Cole, and Adams were declared dead on 12 December 1951.

[13] 24th ID WD entry, 28 November 1950.

[14] Chang, *This Way to War*, page not numbered.

[15] Author interview with Dr. D. Randall Beirne, COL, USAR Ret.

[16] Author interview with LGEN Henry E. Emerson, USA Ret.

[17] Appleman, *Disaster in Korea*, p. 222.

[18] Blair, *The Forgotten War*, p. 455.

[19] Author interview with LGEN Henry E. Emerson, USA Ret.

[20] 5th RCT casualties were compiled from daily unit reports.

[21] 5th RCT S-1/S-4 Journal entry, 2 December 1950.

[22] Author interview with LGEN Henry E. Emerson, USA Ret. LGEN Emerson informed the author that the 5th RCT was going to be withdrawn from Korea immediately after the Eighth Army reached the Yalu and revert to its pre-war status as Pacific General Reserve. Consequently, the 5th RCT did not have priority on being supplied with winter clothing.

[23] *Ibid.*

[24] Appleman, *Disaster in Korea*, pp. 308-309.

[25] Author interview with COL Dick J. Oostenink, Jr., USA, Chaplain Corps, Ret.

[26] Author interview with COL Claude W. Baker, USA Ret.

[27] Author interview with 1st SGT Hibbert Manley, USA Ret.

[28] Appleman, *Disaster in Korea*, p. 353.

[29] Blair, *The Forgotten War*, pp. 503-504.

[30] *Ibid.*, pp. 528-529.

[31] 5th RCT Summary for the Period 010001 December 1950 to 312400 December 1950.

[32] 5th RCT S-1/S-4 Journal entry, 0900, 2 December 1950.

[33] Author interview with LTC William O. Perry, Jr., USA Ret. In December Captain Perry was transferred to 2nd Battalion to be the S-3A Assistant Operations Officer.

34 5th RCT Summary for the period 010001 December 1950 to 312400 December 1950.

35 Author interview with COL Frank A. Athanason, USA Ret.

36 Author interview with Judge Samuel L. Lewis.

37 5th RCT Summary for the Period 010001 December 1950 to 312400 December 1950. Elements of Love and Tank Companies counterattacked to relieve the hard-pressed gunners.

38 Author interview with Dr. D. Randall Beirne, COL, USAR Ret.

39 *Ibid.* First Lieutenant Wagonhurst had resigned from the Army in 1949, but he volunteered to return to active duty to serve in the Korean War.

40 Author interviews with COL E.P. Crockett, USA Ret. and LTC Keith W. Whitham, USA Ret. Lieutenant Whitham remained the regimental aerial observer until he rotated out of Korea in April 1951.

41 Author interview with LTC Keith W. Whitham, USA Ret. This brought Tank Company up to a strength of twenty-two M4 A3E8s. The 21st Infantry's Tank Company had never reached full strength in the fierce defensive battles of the Pusan Perimeter, and later, deep in North Korea, the 24th Infantry Division decided to reduce overhead and attached the remnants of the company to the 5th RCT.

42 Author interview with COL E.P. Crockett, USA Ret.

43 *Ibid.*

44 5th RCT Summary for the Period 010001 December 1950 to 312400 December 1950.

45 Author interview with COL Albert R. Throne, USA Ret.

46 24th ID G-1 Strength Report, 12 December 1950.

47 5th RCT Replacement Request, 16 December 1950.

48 5th RCT Request for Shoulder Patch, 18 December 1950; and Stanton, *U.S. Army Uniforms of the Korean War*, p. 220. A phone conversation with the Institute of Heraldry confirmed the authorization date. On 10 August 1960, the 5th RCT patch was rescinded when an Army-wide reorganization abolished the regimental system.

49 Author interview with COL E.P. Crockett, USA Ret.

50 Colonel Throckmorton's Christmas Greetings, 22 December 1950.

CHAPTER TWENTY-TWO

1 5th RCT Summary from 010001 December 1950 to 312400 December 1950.

2 5th RCT S-1/S-4 Journal entry, 28 December 1950.

3 5th Infantry December Casualty Statistics, 4 January 1951.

4 5th RCT Casualty List, December 1950. CAPT Lukitsch was relieved of his command when these men were listed as MIA.

5 Ridgway, *The Korean War*, p. 86.

6 *Ibid.*, p. 88.

7 Blair, *The Forgotten War*, pp. 637-638.

8 *Ibid.*, pp. 576-577.

9 Ridgway, *The Korean War*, pp. 89-90, and 108.

10 Author interview with COL Claude W. Baker, USA Ret.

11 Author interview with COL Robert J. Lamb, USA Ret. First Lieutenant Lamb, West Point Class of 1946, joined E Company as a rifle platoon leader in November during the advance to the Yalu. He was promoted to captain during the retreat and assumed command of F Company in December.

12 Author interview with MSGT Arlen S. Russell, USAF Ret.

13 Blair, *The Forgotten War*, pp. 592-599.

14 Ridgway, *The Korean War*, pp. 93-96.

15 5th RCT Summary for the Period 010001 Jan 51 to 312400 Jan 51.

16 Futrell, *The United States Air Force in Korea*, pp. 276-278.

17 Ridgway, *The Korean War*, p. 82.

18 Blair, *The Forgotten War*, p. 600.

19 5th RCT Summary for the Period 010001 Jan 51 to 312400 Jan 51. A 4 January 1951 entry reads, "The Regimental Commander then ordered the 1st Battalion with support from the 555th FA Battalion to cover the withdrawal of the 3rd Battalion in accordance with previous plans. Forward observers reported many enemy were killed by artillery concentrations in the middle of their formations." See also, Roy E. Appleman, *Ridgway Duels for Korea* (College Station: Texas A&M Press, 1960), p. 57.

20 Author interview with Dr. D. Randall Beirne, COL, USAR Ret. He recalls, "Part of the convoy was left behind because a driver feel asleep at the wheel and officers were late checking."

21 Author interview with COL Dick J. Oostenink, Jr., USA, Chaplain Corps, Ret.

22 Author interview with Dr. D. Randall Beirne, COL, USAR Ret.

23 Author interview with COL Dick J. Oostenink, Jr., USA, Chaplain Corps, Ret.

24 Author interview with Mr. Ronald Denton.

25 5th RCT Summary for the Period 010001 Jan 51 to 312400 Jan 51.

26 Author interview with Mr. Donald L. Gottschall.

27 Information derived from a letter LT Beirne mailed his family on 6 January 1951. Courtesy of Dr. D. Randall Beirne, COL, USAR Ret.

28 24th ID, Assistant Chief of Staff, G-1, Summary of 1-31 December 1950, contains a copy of this memorandum dated 10 December 1950. The 24th Infantry Division had been virtually destroyed at Taejon in July 1950.

29 For example, see: 5th RCT Memorandum [no subject], 18 January 1951. "In view of the known enemy capability of conducting air operations, including paratroop drops, the following precautions will be taken immediately by all units to include rear installations. . ." It includes instructions that directed commanders to camouflage equipment, dig slit trenches, man antiaircraft guns, and prepare contingency plans.

30 5th RCT Memorandum To All Unit Commanders, 8 January 1951. Moreover, the soldiers had been shooting the insulators from telegraph and telephone poles, a practice COL Throckmorton demanded stopped.

31 5th RCT Memorandum on "Use of the Bayonet", 26 January 1951.

32 Captain Kennedy was evacuated just after the "Home-by-Christmas" Offensive for a hemorrhaging perforated ulcer, no doubt aggravated by his incessant abuse of alcohol. Author interview with LTC Keith W. Whitham, USA Ret., and COL E.P. Crockett, USA Ret. Lieutenant Gaylord was promoted to captain on 9 March 1951. 5th RCT S-1 daily summation, 9 March 1951.

33 A photograph exists of the crew of *J. Aku Head Pupule* with their tank . Lieutenant Vance B. McWhorter, who was KIA on 9 November 1950, is sitting on the Sherman's front slope.

34 Author interview with COL E.P. Crockett, USA Ret.

35 Virtually every armored unit in Korea resorted to painting tigers on the frontal hulls of its tanks. See Jim Mesko, *Armor in Korea* (Carrollton: Squadron/Signal Publications, Inc., 1984) for color drawings and photographs.

36 Author interview with Mr. James W. Hart.

37 *Ibid.*

38 5th RCT Summary for the Period 010001 Jan 51 to 312400 Jan 51.

39 Author interview with COL Claude W. Baker, USA Ret.

40 5th RCT S-1/S-4 Journal entry, 21 January 1951.

41 Author interview with Dr. D. Randall Beirne, COL, USAR Ret.

42 5th RCT Summary for the Period 010001 Jan 51 to 312400 Jan 51.

43 5th RCT Summary for the Period 010001 Jan 51 to 312400 Jan 51.

44 5th RCT S-1/S-4 Journal entry, 30 January 1951.

45 Corporal Parks was subsequently awarded the Silver Star. "Three Honolulu Soldiers Win Korea Medals," *The Honolulu Advertiser*, 13 June 1951.

46 5th RCT Summary for the Period of 010001 Jan 51 to 312400 Jan 51.

47 Author interview with Mr. Horace Anderson and Dr. D. Randall Beirne, COL, USAR Ret. Captain Cooper, from Baltimore, Maryland, West Point Class of 1947, lost a kidney as a result of his wound and retired at the rank of major a couple of years later. He was an extremely popular officer who knew his men, weapons and tactics. Captain Conger, also from the Class of 1947, was equally competent and retired from the Army as a colonel.

48 Author interview with Mr. Horace Anderson.

49 *Ibid.*

50 *Ibid.*

51 *Ibid.* The author found photographs in the National Archives taken by MSGT Chang that confirmed he was present during the assault on Hill 256.

52 Author interview with COL Robert J. Lamb, USA Ret.

53 Michael Costello, "The Army Thinks He's Earned A Rest," *The Reader's Digest*, January 1952. This article was condensed from one that originally appeared in V.F.W. Magazine.

54 24th ID, Assistant Chief of Staff, G-1, log book entry, 30 January 1950.

55 5th RCT Summary for the Period of 010001 Jan 51 to 312400 Jan 51. See also 5th RCT Administrative Journal entry, 120001 Feb 51 to 122400 12 Feb 51: "Important engagement this unit participated in was outlined in the military feat accomplished by 1st Lt Carl H. Dodd, Inf, and his 3rd Platoon, Co E, 2nd Bn, 5th RCT, and 1st Lt Arthur E. Mahoney, Inf, and his 1st Platoon, Co F, 2nd Bn, 5th RCT. Lt's Dodd and Mahoney led the bayonet charge over vital key terrain features swiftly capturing the objectives with the least number of casualties while inflicting heavy losses upon the enemy." However, LT Mahoney actually served in G Company. Author interview with Mr. Ray Warner.

56 Blair, *The Forgotten War*, pp. 663-664.

57 5th RCT Summary for the Period of 010001 Jan 51 to 312400 Jan 51.

58 5th RCT General Orders, 23 January 1951. This must have been a second award.

59 5th RCT Casualty Report for January 1951, 2 February 1951. The 5th RCT Casualty Report for February 1951, 3 March 1951, contains an addendum, which provides additional casualty statistics incurred in January 1951 not covered in the previous report.

60 5th RCT NL, 20 June 1991.

61 Author interview with Mr. James W. Hart.

62 5th RCT Summary for the Period of 010001 Feb 51 to 282400 Feb 51; and Appleman, *Ridgway Duels for Korea*, p. 187.

63 24th ID, Assistant Chief of Staff, G-1, Summary for 1-28 February 1951.

64 Author interview with Mr. James W. Hart.

65 5th RCT Memorandum for "All Unit Commanders 5th Infantry Regiment," 8 February 1951.

66 5th RCT Administrative Journal entry, 190001 Feb 51 to 192400 Feb 51.

67 5th RCT Administrative Journal entries, 030001 Feb 51 to 032400 Feb 51, and 040001 Feb 51 and 042400 Feb 51.

68 When the 5th RCT was attached to the 25th Infantry Division, and later to the 24th Infantry Division, its casualties were identified as 5th RCT on the rosters prepared by the respective divisional G-1 sections. During the combat team's brief, yet bloody, attachment to the 1st Cavalry Division at Waegwan, its casualties were listed as 1st Cavalry Division. The rationale for this procedure is debatable. It may have simplified the administrative burden, or it may have ensured that the 1st Cavalry Division, knowing that the 5th RCT would soon be detached, received more than its fair share of replacements. Perhaps it was for a combination of both reasons. One consequence is that it is nearly impossible to tabulate the 5th RCT's casualties incurred at Waegwan, and thus for the war.

69 Author interview with Mr. Horace Anderson.

CHAPTER TWENTY-THREE

1 Blair, *The Forgotten War*, p. 695.

2 5th RCT Summary for the Period of 010001 Feb 51 to 282400 Feb 51.

3 Author interview with LTC William O. Perry, Jr., USA Ret.

4 Blair, *The Forgotten War*, p. 728.

5 Blair, *The Forgotten War*, pp. 751-752; and Ridgway, *The Korean War*, pp. 110-111. Ridgway writes that General J. Lawton Collins, Chief of Staff of the Army, objected loudest, largely because the Republican Party was claiming that President Truman had no Korean strategy other than killing large numbers of Chinese.

6 "Oahu Woman Cited As "Mom of the 5th RCT'," *The Honolulu Advertiser*, 4 March 1951.

7 5th RCT Summary for the Period of 010001 Feb 51 to 282400 Feb 51.

8 Author interview with Dr. D. Randall Beirne, COL, USAR Ret.

9 Author interview with COL Albert R. Throne, USA Ret.

10 Author interview with COL E. P. Crockett, USA Ret.

11 5th RCT Casualty Report for February 1951, 3 March 1951. The 5th RCT Casualty Report for March 1951, 5 April 1951, contains an addendum for the February report.

12 Author interview with Mr. James W. Hart.

13 Ridgway, *The Korean War*, p. 113.

14 Blair, *The Forgotten War*, p. 737.

15 Appleman, *Ridgway Duels for Korea*, p. 354.

16 Author interview with 1st SGT George Freedman, USA Ret.

17 Sergeant Choy was awarded the Bronze Star for this action. "Three Honolulu Soldiers Win Korea Medals," *The Honolulu Advertiser*, 13 June 1951.

18 Blair, *The Forgotten War*, pp. 750-751.

19 Information derived from a letter LT Beirne wrote his family on 13 March 1951. Courtesy of Dr. D. Randall Beirne, COL, USAR Ret.

20 5th RCT Summary for the Period of 010001 Mar 51 to 312400 Mar 51.

21 Author interview with MSGT Arlen Russell, USAF Ret.

CHAPTER TWENTY-FOUR

1 Families in Hawaii often sang this song when a loved one went off to war. Words courtesy of 1st SGT George Freedman, USA Ret. He did not recall the name of the composer.

2 5th RCT Summary for the period of 010001 Mar 51 to 312400 Mar 51.

3 Letter courtesy of Dr. D. Randall Beirne, COL, USAR Ret.

4 Lieutenant Beirne identified this man as "Sergeant Amitanni" in a letter he wrote home shortly after the battle. A cursory check of MSGT Al Chang's *This Way to War* revealed a photograph of SFC Amatuani Faamaile, from Hawaii, who earned the Silver Star and the Purple Heart serving in the 5th RCT. He was positively identified as a member of K Company in a 5th RCT casualty roster compiled in March 1951.

5 5th RCT Summary for the period of 010001 Mar 51 to 312400 Mar 51.

6 5th RCT Unit Report from 201800 Mar 51 to 211800 Mar 51.

7 *Ibid.*

8 Author interview with Mr. Frank Valvo. Master Sergeant Noneman's death is not listed in the 5th RCT casualty reports of the period, another indication that the 5th RCT's losses were higher than officially reported.

9 5th RCT S-2/S-3 Journal entry, 23 March 1951.

10 *Ibid.*

11 Author interview with LTC Keith W. Whitham, USA Ret.

12 Author interview with COL E. P. Crockett, USA Ret., and LTC Keith W. Whitham, USA Ret.

13 Author interview with Mr. James W. Hart.

14 Information derived from a letter LT Beirne wrote his family on 26 March 1951. Courtesy of Dr. D. Randall Beirne, COL, USAR Ret.

15 5th RCT S-2/S-3 Journal entry, 23 March 1951.

16 *Ibid.*

17 The type and location of the Chinese weapon, as well as the description of the terrain, was obtained in an author interview with Mr. James W. Hart.

18 5th RCT Unit Report from 221800 Mar 51 to 231800 Mar 51. The 5th RCT S-2/S-3 Journal is even more specific, clearly identifying F Company as the unit that attempted to seize Objective 43.

[19] 5th RCT Casualty Report for March 1951.

[20] 5th RCT Heavy Mortar Company Summary for the Period 010001 March 1951 to 312400 March 1951.

[21] Author interview with Mr. James W. Hart.

[22] 5th RCT Casualty Report for March 1951. Mr. Hart believes thirteen men were killed or wounded from the tank round alone. Author interview with Mr. James W. Hart.

[23] R. E. Dupuy and T.N. Dupuy, *The Encyclopedia of Military History from 3,500 B.C. to the Present* (New York: Harper and Row, Publishers, 1977), p. 1251. The Communist armies incurred approximately 1,600,000 battle casualties and 400,000 non-battle casualties during the Korean War. Approximately 60 percent of the battle casualties were Chinese.

CHAPTER TWENTY-FIVE

[1] 5th RCT Unit Report from 231800 Mar 51 to 241800 Mar 51. The 5th RCT captured nine PWs from this regiment on 24 March 1951.

[2] George, *The Chinese Communist Army in Action*, p. 6.

[3] 5th RCT Unit Report from 231800 Mar 51 to 241800 Mar 51; 5th RCT S-2/S-3 Journal entry, 24 March 1951; and 5th RCT Casualty Report for March 1951.

[4] 5th RCT Casualty Report for March 1951.

[5] 5th RCT S-2/S-3 Journal entry, 24 March 1951.

[6] Author interview with Mr. James W. Hart; and 5th RCT S-2/S-3 Journal entry, 24 March 1951.

[7] Author interview with Mr. James W. Hart.

[8] 5th RCT Unit Report 241800 Mar 51 to 251800 Mar 51.

CHAPTER TWENTY-SIX

[1] Author interview with Mr. James Shaw.

[2] 5th RCT Summary for the Period of 010001 Mar 51 to 312400 Mar 51.

[3] Headquarters 24th Infantry Division, General Orders Number 509, 17 July 1951; 5th Infantry Report of Casualties, March 1951, dated 5 April 1951; and author interview with Mr. Robert H. Middleton.

[4] Author interview with COL E. P. Crockett, USA Ret.

[5] Second Lieutenant Walls received his commissioned in May 1951. Author interview with COL E.P. Crockett, USA Ret.

[6] 5th RCT S-1 daily summation, 30 March 1951.

[7] 5th RCT Summary for the Period of 010001 Mar 51 to 312400 Mar 51.

[8] Author interview with COL E. P. Crockett, USA Ret.

[9] LTC Owens had assumed command of the 3rd Battalion when LTC Heckemeyer fleeted up to be XO of the combat team. 5th RCT S-1 daily summation, 28 March 1951.

[10] The author does not know the name of the jeep driver, though he probably died in the explosion, too.

[11] Mr. Harold Thralls' account is in the 5th RCT NL, March 1992.

[12] 5th RCT Casualty Report for March 1951, 5 April 1951. See also 5th RCT Casualty Report for April 1951, 7 May 1951, which contains an addendum for the previous month's report.

[13] Information derived from a letter dated 2 April 1951, courtesy of Dr. D. Randall Beirne, COL, USAR Ret.

[14] Author interview with MAJ Earl J. Law, USA Ret., provided details concerning LT Buckner's role at Nuremberg.

[15] Mr. Dan M. Gonzales provided the author an unpublished article he wrote that describes the death of Lieutenant Buckner. The 555th FAB's Command Report for April 1951 recorded that Lieutenant Buckner's death occurred on 5 April, but eyewitnesses said he died on 4 April. See also, 5th RCT NL, May 1994, which includes Mr. Fred T. O'Keefe's description of LT Buckner's heroism as seen from G Company's positions. Mr. O'Keefe believes LT Buckner was George Company's FO that day, but Mr. Gonzales recalls otherwise.

[16] Author interview with MAJ Earl J. Law, USA Ret.

[17] Information derived from a letter LT Beirne wrote his family on 7 April 1951. Courtesy of Dr. D. Randall Beirne, COL, USAR Ret.

[18] Dr. D. Randall Beirne, *Korean War Veterans Memorial: A Tribute to Those Who Served* (Paducah: Turner Publishing Co., 1995), p. 107.

[19] Information derived from a letter LT Beirne wrote his family on 7 April 1951. Courtesy of Dr. D. Randall Beirne, COL, USAR Ret.

[20] Lieutenant Smith is a pseudonym. General Henry E. Emerson, USA Ret., requested that the author use a pseudonym in order to protect the reputation and memory of his former platoon leader.

[21] Author interview with LGEN Henry E. Emerson, USA Ret.

[22] First Lieutenant "Smith" received the Bronze Star for Valor, three Purple Hearts, and the Combat Infantryman's Badge in Korea.

[23] Author interview with Mr. Horace Anderson.

[24] Blair, *The Forgotten War*, pp. 773-774. Colonel Throckmorton continued his illustrious career, and retired with the rank of general. His subsequent duty assignments would include Commandant of Cadets at the United States Military Academy, CG 82nd Airborne Division, CG XVIII Airborne Corps, Deputy MACV in Vietnam, and Commander in Chief, Strike Command.

[25] LGEN E. M. Flanagan, *The Angels: A History of the 11th Airborne Division* (Novato: Presidio Press, 1989) pp. 119, 129, 166-167, 179, 180, 181, 187-189, 227, 232, 234, 242-243, 290 and 328.

[26] Several officers, including West Pointers, all of whom requested to remain anonymous, expressed this view.

Lieutenant Colonel Ward was probably not offered command of the 5th RCT because senior officers in the Eighth Army viewed him as a heavy drinker.

27 Author interview with Dr. D. Randall Beirne, COL, USAR Ret.

28 Author interview with sources who requested to remain anonymous.

29 Author interview with 1st SGT Hibbert Manley, USA Ret.

30 Author interview with LTC William O. Perry, Jr., USA Ret.

31 For details of the personnel turnover, see: 5th RCT Command Report, April 1951.

32 Blair, *The Forgotten War*, pp. 799-800.

33 Author interview with Mr. Donald L. Gottschall.

34 Colonel Throckmorton departed Korea for Oahu on 20 April 1951. Appleman, *Ridgway Duels for Korea*, p. 447. Appleman states that two of the 5th RCT's battalion commanders were new. Actually, all three of the infantry battalion commanders were new.

35 5th RCT Command Report, April 1951.

CHAPTER TWENTY-SEVEN

1 George, *The Chinese Communist Army in Action*, p. 8.

2 5th RCT Command Report, April 1951.

3 Author interview with COL Robert J. Lamb, USA Ret.

4 24th ID Command Report, April 1951.

5 The 24th ID was attached to I Corps at this time. See Appleman, *Ridgway Duels for Korea*, map on p. 454.

6 The ROK 1st Division, on the other hand, was a solid formation that had earned a formidable reputation. Other ROK units, when well led and provided adequate artillery support, performed with distinction, too. For example, the 2nd Platoon, A Company, 31st Regiment, ROK 2nd Division was awarded a Presidential Unit Citation for its extraordinary heroism on 16-17 May 1951 at Chongpyong. See Appleman, *Ridgway Duels for Korea*, p. 461, 468-469, and 528.

7 G-3 HQ 24th ID Journal, 23 April 1951; and 5th RCT Command Report, April 1951.

8 G-3 HQ 24th ID Journal entry, 22 April 1951.

9 Author interview with COL Claude W. Baker, USA Ret.

10 G-2 HQ 24th ID Artillery Journal, 22 April 1951.

11 5th RCT Command Report, April 1951.

12 G-3 HQ 24th ID Journal, 22 April 1951.

13 *Ibid.*

14 Author interview with COL Robert J. Lamb, USA Ret.

15 G-3 HQ 24th ID Journal entry, 22 April 1951.

16 *Ibid.*

17 5th RCT NL, "A Tribute to Arson Easy," by MSGT E.C. Lundquist, April 1994.

18 Author interview with MAJ Earl J. Law, USA Ret.

19 Author interview with Mr. Albert F. Semasko.

20 Author interview with MAJ Earl J. Law, USA Ret.

21 Author interview with CWO Sal Bosco, USA Ret.

22 G-3 HQ 24th ID Journal entry, 23 April 1951.

23 *Ibid.*

24 *Ibid.*

25 The order to withdraw was corroborated in a conversation the author had with COL Robert J. Lamb, USA Ret., who received an order to withdraw Fox Company to the MSR at this time.

26 Department of the Army, General Order No. 18, 18 February 1953.

27 5th RCT NL, "A Tribute to Arson Easy," by MSGT E.C. Lundquist, April 1994.

28 List of 5th RCT Prisoners of War compiled by CSM Timothy F. Casey, USA Ret., and Mr. Dan M. Gonzales.

29 Author interview with COL Robert J. Lamb, USA Ret.

30 Author interview with Mr. James W. Hart.

31 *Ibid.* Though most of the men who accompanied SFC Hart were killed, missing, or captured that night, PFC Gadlin made it back to friendly lines. He subsequently became the supply sergeant for F Company.

32 *Ibid.*

33 G-3 HQ 24th ID Journal entry, 23 April 1951.

34 Author interview with 1st SGT George Freedman, USA Ret.

35 5th RCT Command Report, April 1951.

36 This was the second time PFC Baumgarner was wounded in Korea. "Maverick Garners Heart," *Soldiers Magazine*, April 1983.

37 Author interview with Dr. D. Randall Beirne, COL, USAR Ret.

38 Author interview with Mr. James Shaw.

39 Department of the Army, General Orders No. 64, 30 June 1952. PFC Council's DSC was not awarded posthumously, probably in the hope that he had been taken prisoner by the Chinese. Regrettably, either he was killed in action or he perished in captivity.

40 Author interview with MAJ Earl J. Law, USA Ret.

41 *Ibid.* Sgt. Grey (or possibly "Gray") provided this information to LT Law at a later date, who shared it with the author.

42 Author interview with Mr. James Shaw.

43 "Top Heavy" is the author's opinion.

44 Author interview with COL Frank A. Athanason, USA Ret.

45 *Ibid.* Years later, COL Stuart thanked COL Athanason for saving his life.

46 G-3 HQ 24th ID Journal entry, 23 April 1951.

47 Author interview with MAJ Earl J. Law, USA Ret.

48 List of 5th RCT Prisoners of War compiled by CSM Timothy F. Casey, USA Ret., and Mr. Dan M. Gonzales.

49 Author interview with Mr. James W. Hart. All accounts mention the night of 23 April as being very quiet. The CCF rested in preparation for a major attack planned for the following day.

50 Author interview with COL Robert J. Lamb, USA Ret.

CHAPTER TWENTY-EIGHT

1 The 5th RCT Command Report for April 1951 identifies B Company, 6th Tank Battalion as the tank company attached to the 5th RCT on 25 April 1951. This is an error. Statements from survivors, and Billy C. Mossman, *Ebb and Flow: November 1950 - July 1951* (Washington, D.C.: Center of Military History, United States Army, 1950), p. 421, state that D Company, 6th Tank Battalion was attached instead. Mossman cites the 6th Tank Battalion Command Report for April 1951 as his source. The author located a portion of this unit's command report at the National Archives, but not the critical section that would have identified which company supported the 5th RCT. Elements of C Company, 6th Tank Battalion were operating in the area, too.

2 5th RCT Command Report, April 1951.

3 Walter Booth, "The Pattern that Got Lost (Ranger Units in Korea)," *Army*, April 1981.

4 24th ID Command Report, April 1951.

5 G-3 HQ 24th ID Journal entry, 25 April 1951; and Robert W. Black, *Rangers in Korea* (New York: Ivy Books, 1989), pp. 140-142. Black served in the 8th Ranger Company during this period and is intimately familiar with its combat actions.

6 Black, *Rangers in Korea*, pp. 145-154.

7 *Ibid.*; and, G-3 HQ 24th ID Journal entry, 25 April 1951.

8 Black, *Rangers in Korea*, p. 151.

9 The 5th RCT Command Report, April 1951. Details on Love Company's attempts to reach the Rangers are sketchy.

10 Black, *Rangers in Korea*, p. 149.

11 5th RCT Command Report, April 1951.

12 See footnote number one, this chapter.

13 The April 1951 S-3 Operations portion of the April 1951 5th RCT Command Report was written after 7 June 1951 when LT Crockett became the regimental assistant operations officer (S-3A). "Drafting the S-3 April report was not my first order of business upon reporting to HQ," he recalled. Author interview and correspondence with COL E. P. Crockett, USA Ret.

14 Black, *Rangers in Korea*, p. 151. The 2nd Battalion, 21st Infantry recorded that this incident occurred at 0921.

15 *Ibid*, p. 153. Black makes no mention of the missing Ranger officer. This is an important point in that the 5th RCT Command Report is emphatic that the pick-up of Ranger stragglers was the sole reason the combat team delayed its withdrawal until late afternoon.

16 Mossman, *Ebb and Flow*, pp.491-421.

17 "S-2 Command Report for April," 5th RCT Command Report, April 1951.

18 Author interview with COL E. P. Crockett, USA Ret.

19 Author interview with COL Robert J. Lamb, USA Ret.

20 Author interview with COL Frank A. Athanason, USA Ret.

21 CG 24th ID Artillery message, 241530, April 1951.

22 Black, *Rangers in Korea*, p. 153.

23 Author interview with LTC William O. Perry, Jr., USA Ret.

24 "Delay" is misspelled as "Dealy"; 5th RCT Command Report, April 1951.

25 The author, based on an interview with COL Athanason, believes Polmal best fits the description.

26 5th RCT S-2 Intelligence Summary, April 1951.

27 Author interview with COL Claude W. Baker, USA Ret.

28 Author interview with 1st SGT Hibbert Manley, USA Ret.

29 Author interview with Judge Samuel L. Lewis.

30 Author interview with COL E. P. Crockett, USA Ret.

31 Headquarters, 5th Infantry Regiment Affidavits signed by PFC Davon Heller on 25 August 1951, and Colonel Arthur H. Wilson, 24 August 1951, indicate that MAJ Wells managed to get the column moving, however, testimony from survivors state categorically that B Battery could not possibly have moved due to the wrecked 3/4 ton truck blocking the road in the narrow defile. The affidavits may have been exaggerated out of a desire to secure for MAJ Wells a posthumous award for valor he so richly deserved.

32 Author interview with COL Frank A. Athanason, USA Ret.

33 Author interview with MAJ Earl J. Law, USA Ret.

34 *Ibid.*

[35] G-3 HQ 24th ID Journal entry, 25 April 1951.

[36] Author interview with COL Claude W. Baker, USA Ret.; and Appleman, *Ridgway Duels for Korea*, p. 481.

[37] G-3 HQ 24th ID Journal entry, 25 April 1951.

[38] Author interview with COL Robert J. Lamb, USA Ret.

[39] *Ibid*. Captain Lamb's wounds forced his evacuation from Korea. In addition to his Purple Heart, he received the Silver Star for gallantry in action.

[40] 5th RCT NL, September 1993, contains Mr. Estes Philpott's experiences.

[41] Author interview with Mr. William T. Welch.

[42] *Ibid*. Years later Mr. Welch discovered that Clarence Young survived the ambush.

[43] Author interview with LTC William O. Perry, Jr., USA Ret.

[44] Author interview with COL E. P. Crockett, USA Ret.

[45] Author interview with COL Claude W. Baker, USA Ret.

[46] *Ibid*.

[47] Author interview with COL E. P. Crockett, USA Ret. Three months after Death Valley, when American troops reoccupied Pisi-gol, the 5th RCT dispatched a team of investigators who scoured the battlefield in search of lessons learned. An officer from Tank Company looked over *Hawaii Calls'* extensive battle damage and concluded the HEAT rocket had not knocked out the tank. Rather, fragments from a mortar round had circumvented the exhaust grill on the engine deck and penetrated the radiator, thus causing the engine to overheat. Indeed, several mortar rounds were noted to have detonated on *Hawaii Calls*. LT Crockett was recommended for the DSC, but this award was downgraded to the Silver Star.

[48] The battlefield is the loneliest place on earth, and participants rarely see the same events the same way no matter how close they may be to one another on the firing line. For example, LT Athanason does not recall seeing elements of the 2nd Tank Platoon, which was heavily engaged just a short distance away. Author interview with COL Frank A. Athanason, USA Ret.

[49] *Ibid*.

[50] This was probably the same ambulance LT Crockett observed.

[51] Author interview with COL Frank A. Athanason, USA Ret. Lieutenant Jurden awoke the next morning when a Chinese soldier attempted to cut a ring off his finger. He gave the ring to the enemy soldier who took him prisoner. The Chinese treated him as best they could, but their only medicine was "hot water and salt." They released him with a small number of other badly wounded men thirty days later where the Americans could find them.

[52] Author interview with Judge Samuel L. Lewis.

[53] Author interview with MAJ Earl J. Law, USA Ret.

[54] Author interview with 1st SGT Hibbert Manley, USA Ret.

[55] Author interview with Mr. William T. Welch.

[56] *Ibid*.

[57] 5th RCT Command Report, April 1951.

[58] 5th RCT NL, December 1993.

[59] *Ibid.,* September 1993.

[60] 5th RCT Command Report, April 1951.

[61] Executive Officer's Command Report, April 1951, reads:
"The morale during the month was high. The effect of the rotation policy seems to give new life to many men. This, coupled with successfully taking anything the enemy could throw against them, had the effect of raising morale in the entire regiment. The withdrawal and delaying action had one adverse effect in that many dead and wounded could not be evacuated and had to be listed as missing in action."

[62] Barth, *Tropic Lightning and Taro Leaf*, p. 84.

[63] Author interview with COL Claude W. Baker, USA Ret., provided the casualty percentage. Lieutenant

[64] Appleman, *Ridgway Duels for Korea*, pp. 494-495. First Corps reported its battle casualties as 1,118 in the 25th ID; 823 in the 3rd ID; 208 in the 1st CAV; 1,274 in ROK 1st ID ; 1,182 in British 29th Brigade; 250 in the Turkish Brigade; 42 in the Belgian BN; 81 in the Philippine 10th BCT; and 98 in other corps units.

[65] The 5th Infantry Command Report, S-1 Summary, for April 1951.

[66] 555th FAB Periodic Personnel Report, 1800 15 April 1951 to 1800 30 April 1951. Key 555 FAB casualties were John R. Lindy, the adjutant (WIA); Ralph E. Muntzel, the Liaison Officer assigned to the 1st Battalion (WIA); Delbert A. Jurden, the S-2 (Listed as MIA but subsequently recovered alive); R. Maurice Metzear, a Battery Motor Transport Officer (WIA); William T. Bryan, a Liaison Officer (WIA); Ralph P. Dixon, Jr., an FO (MIA/but actually was captured); William C. Hall, an FO (MIA); Edward M. Krohner, a Unit Administrator (WIA); Roy T. Nakashima (Listed as MIA but actually KIA); Earl J. Law, listed as an FO but Acting XO (WIA); Julius M. Gordon, an FO (WIA).

[67] Author interview with COL E. P. Crockett, USA Ret.

[68] 24th Infantry Division Artillery Command Report for April 1951. Taro Leaf gun crews expended 87,720 105-mm and 33,840 155-mm howitzer rounds in April and claimed to have inflicted 4,050 KIA and 12,150 WIA on the Communists. During the critical period of the Chinese Spring Offensive, 22-29 April, division artillery fired 36,862 105-mm and 14,189 155-mm howitzer rounds and claimed to have inflicted 2,040 KIA and 6,120 WIA on the enemy.

[69] 24th ID G-4 Journal entry, 1500 26 April 1951.

[70] Author interview with COL Frank A. Athanason, USA Ret.

71 In a memorandum for the record on 26 April, 24th Infantry Division reported that the 555th FAB had lost 11 of its 105-mm howitzers on 25 April and had brought out seven, with two of these unserviceable. Appleman, *Ridgway Duels for Korea*, p. 481. Lieutenant Colonel Stuart informed Appleman in an interview conducted on 9 August 1951 that B Battery lost all six howitzers, A Battery three, and C Battery two. It is not clear if LTC Stuart informed Appleman that one of the A Battery howitzers had actually been lost on 23 April.

72 24th ID G-4 Journal entry, 1500 26 April 1951.

73 Author interview with LTC William O. Perry, Jr., USA Ret.

Chapter Twenty-Nine

1 Author interview with MAJ Earl J. Law, USA Ret.

2 S-1 Monthly Summary, April 1951; and the S-1 Summary for April 1951.

3 Blair, *The Forgotten War*, p. 854.

4 George, *The Chinese Communist Army in Action*, p. 175.

5 *Ibid.*, pp. 182-183.

6 Author interview with COL Frank A. Athanason, USA Ret.

7 Author interview with Judge Samuel L. Lewis.

8 Author interview with COL E. P. Crockett, USA Ret.

9 *Ibid.*

10 5th RCT S-1 daily summation, 11 March 1951.

11 Author interview with LTC William O. Perry, Jr., USA Ret.

12 Eighth Army Report of Selected Diseases, 13 April 1951. Thirty-six Black soldiers were serving with the 19th Infantry, seventeen in 24th ID Artillery, twenty-two in the 3rd Engineer Battalion, four in the 24th Medical Battalion, and one in Headquarters Company, 24th ID.

13 Author interview with COL E. P. Crockett, USA Ret.

14 Author interview with COL Frank A. Athanason, USA Ret.

15 Author interview with Mr. William T. Welch. Master Sergeant Welch was promoted from corporal to this rank in less than a month. His personnel records, which had been misplaced, were belatedly found, and he was promoted once his time in service in the pre-war 187th Airborne RCT and combat experience as a rifle platoon sergeant in the 5th RCT was taken into account.

16 5th RCT S-3 Command Report for May 1951.

17 Blair, *The Forgotten War*, p. 870.

18 5th RCT Command Report and S-3 Command Report for May 1951.

19 5th RCT S-3 Command Report for May 1951.

20 *Ibid.*

21 *Ibid.*

22 Blair, *The Forgotten War*, p. 870; and Appleman, *Ridgeway Duels for Korea*, p. 505.

23 5th RCT Command Report for May 1951.

24 G-3 HQ 24th ID Journal entry, 17 May 1951.

25 *Ibid.*

26 *Ibid.*

27 Master Sergeant Johnnie Walls received his commission as a second lieutenant shortly after this engagement. Author interview with COL E. P. Crockett, USA Ret.

28 CO 5th Infantry Regiment letter recommending that Tank Company receive the Distinguished Unit Citation, 24 July 1951. The award was not approved.

29 G-3 HQ 24th ID Journal entry, 17 May 1951.

30 *Ibid.*

31 *Ibid.*

32 CO 5th Infantry Regiment letter recommending that Tank Company receive the Distinguished Unit Citation, 24 July 1951.

33 G-3 HQ 24th ID Journal entry, 17 May 1951.

34 CO 5th Infantry Regiment letter recommending that Tank Company receive the Distinguished Unit Citation, 24 July 1951.

35 G-3 HQ 24th ID Journal entry, 17 May 1951.

36 CO 5th Infantry Regiment letter recommending that Tank Company receive the Distinguished Unit Citation, 24 July 1951.

37 Blair, *The Forgotten War*, pp. 874-877, 883.

38 5th RCT S-3 Command Report for May 1951.

39 Blair, *The Forgotten War*, pp. 890-891.

40 5th RCT S-3 Command Report for May 1951.

41 *Ibid.*

42 5th RCT Command Report for May 1951.

43 Author interview with Mr. William T. Welch.

44 5th RCT Command Report for May 1951.

45 Author interview with COL E. P. Crockett, USA Ret.

46 Author interview with LTC William O. Perry, Jr., USA Ret.

47 Captain Campbell placed the 2nd Tank Platoon in for the Distinguished Unit Citation. The Taro Leaf ap proved the recommendation, but IX Corps rejected it. Author interview with COL E. P. Crockett, USA Ret.

48 A total of 4,411 CCF PWs were captured that day. Boatner, *Army Lore and Customs*, p. 149; and 5th RCT S-3 Command Report for May 1951.

49 "Hawaii's 5th RCT Captures Record Number of Reds," *Honolulu Star-Bulletin*, 2 June 1951.

50 Author interview with LTC William O. Perry, Jr., USA Ret.

51 Correspondence from Mr. James W. Evans, President, Outpost Harry Survivors Association, 28 April 1994; and 5th RCT NL February 1995.

52 5th RCT NL, 1 February 1951, contains a letter written by COL Wendell P. Knowles, USA Ret., on 13 January 1991.

53 *Ibid.* Colonel Knowles commanded the 555th FAB up until just before it was overrun. His letter includes the admission that his information is "hearsay," yet he was briefed shortly after the battle by several of his former officers who survived the overrun.

54 Associated Press story reported by Mr. William C. Barnard, 31 July, in an undated edition of the *St. Louis Globe-Democrat*, found in the June 1992 edition of the 5th RCT NL. For details on PFC Feiner, see *The Forgotten War... Remembered*, p. 123.

55 Laurence Jolidon, *Last Seen Alive: The Search for Missing POWs from the Korean War* (Austin: Ink-Slinger Press, 1995) is an excellent account of the handful of people who have worked hard to discover the fate of the Korean War MIAs.

56 Author correspondence with COL E.P. Crockett, USA Ret., who interviewed Mr. Bleuer at the author's request.

57 Information derived from correspondence with COL E.P. Crockett, USA Ret., and LGEN Henry E. Emerson, USA Ret.

58 Author interview with LGEN Henry E. Emerson, USA Ret.

59 The Distinguished Unit Citation was redesignated the Presidential Unit Citation toward the end of the Korean War. In contrast, various elements of the elite 27th "Wolfhounds," a divisional unit, received a total of three Distinguished Unit Citations in the Korean War.

60 Author interview with LGEN Henry E. Emerson, USA Ret.

61 Author interview with Dr. D. Randall Beirne, COL, USAR Ret.

62 Author interview with LTC William O. Perry, Jr., USA Ret.

63 Author interview with 1st SGT George Freedman, USA Ret.

Infantrymen in Korea carefully disarm a Chinese soldier. (source: NA)

64 Correspondence from 1st SGT Hibbert Manley, USA Ret.,

65 *Ibid.*

66 Casualty statistics were derived from, Harry G. Summers, Jr., *Korean War Almanac* (New York: Facts on File, Inc., 1990), p. 118.

EPILOGUE

1 J. R. Farrington led a successful effort to sway votes in Congress for Hawaiian Statehood based in part on Hawaii's tremendous blood sacrifice in the Forgotten War. He used the meticulous casualty records kept by the local newspapers for his statistics. Thus, SGT Calhau, from Oahu, is included in these statistics, while CPL Kenawell, from Pennsylvania, is not. Hawaii's sons served in every branch of the Armed Forces and were liberally sprinkled throughout every unit of the Army. Nevertheless, the concentration of Hawaiian residents was greater in the 5th RCT than in units of comparable size at least through the first year of the Korean War. Hawaii's two Medal of Honor winners were PFC Herbert K. Pililaau, C Company, 23rd Infantry, 2nd Infantry Division, from Waianae, Oahu; and SGT Leroy A. Mendonca, B Company, 7th Infantry, 3rd Infantry Division, from Honolulu. Their respective awards were posthumous.

2 Ernest had retired from his position as Chief Bailiff in Honolulu and was now a real estate agent.

3 Author interview with Manuel G. Calhau. Rumors of Sonny's death preceded his father's arrival at the school, perhaps inadvertently leaked by shocked school administrators. For all his faults as a teenage rebel, Sonny had been extremely popular with students and faculty alike.

4 Author interview with Manuel G. Calhau.

5 Over 100 letters mailed to Sonny by his family, sweetheart, and friends were eventually returned to sender. Some of these letters had been mailed the previous November, prior to Sonny's evacuation to Japan for medical treatment.

6 Author interview with Manuel G. Calhau. Theresa refused to let Ernest deposit Sonny's death gratuity for several years. She wanted nothing to do with what she derisively termed "blood money."

7 *Honolulu Star-Bulletin*, "Amazing Mail Delays. Delegate to Ask Why Letters are Late in Reaching GIs," 3 July 1951. The Army responded to the article in the *Honolulu Star-Bulletin* with an article the next day. The Commander, U.S. Army Forces Pacific, explained the fault lay in the war zone and not in Hawaii. This answer pleased no one and Delegate Joseph R. Farrington said he would ask for an investigation by the Defense Department. See "Army Explains Mail Delivery in the War Zone," *Honolulu Star-Bulletin*, 4 July 1951.

8 The Honorable Mr. Joseph R. Farrington brought this information to the attention of Congress and to the Secretary of the Army, the Honorable Mr. Frank Pace. Letters and correspondence dealing with this issue are in the author's personal collection. Mr. Farrington's Washington secretary was a friend of the family's.

9 Author interview with Manuel G. Calhau.

10 The resolution is in the author's personal collection.

11 Author's personal collection. Regrettably, Sonny's Purple Heart has disappeared over the years.

12 *Ibid.*

13 *Ibid.*, and author interview with Mr. Alton Kenawell. Corporal John Kenawell rests on the military crest of Birch Hill Cemetery, Burnham, Pennsylvania. Dorothy visited Theresa twice in Lanikai after the war. Her husband, Brady, took the death of his oldest son hard.

14 Author interview with Manual G. Calhau.

15 Joseph C. Goulden, *Korea: The Untold Story of the War* (New York: McGraw-Hill Book Company, 1982), p. 646.

5TH RCT CASUALTY LIST

KILLED IN ACTION UNLESS INDICATED OTHERWISE

Compiled and maintained by Raymond J. Warner

Category I: Verified by Official Documentation

Name	Rank	Unit	Date	Notes (a)
Abbott, Wilbur E.	Cpl	F	4 Apr 51	
Adams, John R .	Sfc	G	13 Oct 51	
Adams, Lloyd E.	Cpl	A	23 Aug 50	
Adams, Troulius	M/Sgt	K	31 Dec 53	DED
Aguinaldo, Benito R.	Cpl	C	12 Aug 50	
Ah Let, Louis	Cpl	B	12 Aug 50	
Aki, Clarence H.	Sgt	Hq/555	23 Feb 54	DED
Albers, Billie D.	Pfc	I	19 Sep 50	
Alexander, George R	Pfc	C	12 Aug 50	
Alexander, James T.	Pvt	G	24 Sep 50	
Allegretto, Angelo	Pvt	G	3 Sep 50	
Alonzo, Francisco Jr.	Pfc	E	10 Dec 50	SSM
Amberger, William D.	Pvt	E	7 Aug 50	
Anderson, Donald E.	Cpl	L	7 Mar 51	
Andrzejewski, Thomas E.	Sfc	G	1 Nov 51	
Arcidiacono, Pangrazio A.	Pvt	K	28 Jul 52	
Ash, Dean M.	Pfc	C	5 Nov 51	
Asuncion, Julian	Pfc	A	23 Aug 50	
Atkins, Leonard H	Cpl	G	28 Jan 53	
Aumack, Edward J.	Cpl	C	20 Oct 51	
Axtell, Everett J.	Sfc	Hq/5	23 Apr 51	
Baduria, Daniel Jr.	Pfc	A	29 Aug 50	
Bae-Jong-Tae	Sgt	72 E	18 Apr 53	ROK/NBC
Bailey, R. V.	Cpl	I	13 Jul 52	
Bair, James R.	Cpl	F	29 Aug 52	
Baker, Alvin D.	Cpl	I	21 Aug 52	BSM
Baker, Arthur L.	Cpl	E	4 Apr 51	BSM
Baker, James M.	Sgt	A	1 May 53	
Ball, Clarence H.	Pfc	L	30 Aug 50	
Ballinger, Jay T.	Pfc	L	7 Mar 51	
Banning, George C.	Pfc	B	11 May 53	
Bannister, Norman L Jr.	M/Sgt	K	28 Nov 50	DED
Barber, Clifford A.	Pvt	F	21 Aug 50	
Bare, Jay T.	M/Sgt	L	23 Apr 51	
Barnes, Donald E.	Pfc	I	3 Aug 51	
Barnett, Frankie L.	Pfc	B	7 Sep 50	
Barnette, Homer E.	Pfc	F	30 Jan 51	
Barrica, Eugene A.	Pvt	Med	31 Dec 53	DED
Barrow, Henry G.	Sfc	F	4 Nov 50	
Barry, Arthur A..	Cpl	H	16 Sep 51	DED
Bartning, Louis E.	Sgt	F	30 Jan 51	
Bason, Lester W.	Pfc	L	3 Sep 50	SSM
Bass, James W.	Sgt	M	1 Sep 50	
Bauer, Philip F. Jr	2nd Lt	C/555	6 Dec 53	DOW
Bauernfiend, Howard H.	Pvt	Tk	11 Aug 52	
Beasley, Carrie L.	Pvt	G	27 Nov 50	
Beck, Jack A.	Cpl	A	3 Jun 51	
Becker, Richard R .	Sfc	Med	13 Jan 52	NBC
Bedoya, Vincent V.	Cpl	C	12 Aug 50	
Beene, Wilson J. Jr.	Cpl	F	27 Jul 52	DOW
Behring, Waiter P.	Pvt	K	29 Mar 53	
Belkom, George P.	Sgt	K	4 Aug 51	
Bellis, Donald P.	Cpl	G	20 Oct 51	
Bender, Robert L.	Pfc	H	31 Dec 53	DED
Bennett, George C.	Cpl	F	17 Sep 50	
Bennett, Granvil L.	Pfc	F	6 Apr 51	
Berhing, Walter P.	Pvt	K	29 Mar 53	
Bertning, Louis E.	Sgt	F	30 Jan 51	
Berube, Joseph P.	Pvt	C	20 Oct 51	
Beskon, John	Pfc	H	21 May 51	DOW
Bierner, Jimmie B.	Pfc	A	25 Jun 52	
Black, Junior	Pfc	G	13 Aug 50	SSM
Bland, David P.	Pfc	A	25 Apr 51	2 PH
Blasczyk, Paul J.	Pfc	A	12 Jul 51	
Blechinger, Ferdina	Pfc	G	17 May 51	
Bly, Richard L.	Cpl	G	16 Nov 50	DOW
Bobbitt, Swanson L.	Pfc	G	31 Jan 51	2 PH
Boisvert, Eugene R.	Pfc	G	4 Sep 50	
Bonas, Herbert F.	Cpl	E	4 Apr 51	
Book, Andrew	Sfc	G	3 Sep 50	SSM
Boone, Charles	Pvt	L	25 Sep 50	
Booth, Robert E.	Cpl	E	15 Mar 54	DED
Bosselli, Jack	Pfc	72 E	3 Aug 50	
Bowen, Robert A.	Cpl	I	5 Oct 52	DOW
Bowers, Harold C.	Cpl	Med	3 Feb 51	2 PH
Boyer, Virgil W. Jr.	Sgt	L	5 Feb51	SSM/2 PH
Bragg, Nicholas M.	Pvt	K	30 Aug 50	
Brannon, Charles E.	1st Lt	B	15 Jun 51	2DSC/SS/POW
Brant, Albert W. Jr.	Cpl	L	17 Oct 52	DED
Brantigan, Henry J.	Pfc	B	24 Mar 51	
Braxton, Charles	Pfc	B/555	5 Sep 50	
Breedlove, William M.	Pvt	C	30 Oct 52	
Brewster, Billy B.	1st Lt	Hq/5	27 Nov 50	BSM
Bridge, Charles E.	Pfc	E	28 Jun 52	
Brindel, Clyde W. Jr.	Sfc	E	31 Dec 53	DED
Britt, Robert E.	Sgt	B/555	15 Jul 54	DED
Broadston, Merle D.	Sfc	Hq/555	12 Aug50	
Bronele, Dominic A.	Pvt	K	12 Jun 53	
Brooks, Raymond	Sgt	Mtr	28 Feb 52	
Brown, Daniel K.	Sgt	A	25 Apr 51	
Brown, Juelynn O.	Pfc	L	3 Sep 50	
Brown, Wallace	Pvt	D	29 Jul 52	NBC
Brown, William R.	Pvt	L	3 Sep 51	NBC
Brunda, Paul	Cpl	K	18 Oct 51	
Bruner, Walter T.	Pfc	G	3 Sep 50	
Bryant, Cecil Jr.	Pvt	Hq/3	11 Aug 50	
Bryant, Emmitt R.	Pfc	5th Inf	12 Jun 53	
Buckner, McKinley C.	1st Lt	B/555	5 Apr 51	BFC
Burd, Joseph C.	Pfc	C	7 Sep 52	
Burke, Harvey W.	Sgt	I	20 Aug 52	
Burkholder, Donald M.	Pfc	A	21 Sep 51	
Burton, Donald K.	Sfc	E	30 Jan 51	
Busby, James E.	Cpl	K	18 Oct 51	
Busch, Charles R.	Pfc	-/555	15 Jul 54	DED
Butler, William E.	Pfc	I	5 Aug 50	
Cadiz, Liberate	Cpl	L	3 Sep 50	2 PH
Calhau, Ernest M.	Sgt	F	23 Mar 51	
Calius, Rosalio	Pfc	5th Inf	30 Jan 51	
Camacho, Louis C. Jr.	Pfc	F	13 Aug 50	
Camillo, Anastacio	Cpl	C	12 Aug 50	
Campomizzi, Arthur E.	Pfc	F	7 Feb 53	
Cantella, Nicholas D.	Cpl	L	5 Feb 51	SSM
Cardenas, Edward C.	Cpl	L	7 Jul 51	NBC
Carlson, Charles E.	Pfc	G	19 Oct 51	

Name	Rank	Unit	Date	Notes (a)	Name	Rank	Unit	Date	Notes (a)
Carol, John W.	Pvt	-/555	15 Jul 54	DED	Cutler, Donald J.	Pfc	M	10 Aug 50	
Carriere, Oscar G.	Pfc	L	25 Sep 50		Cutter, Fred	Pfc	A	14 Oct 51	
Carroll, Charles F.	Sfc	72 E	25 Sep 50		Dale, Douglas	Cpl	H	5 Aug 50	
Carroll, Roland S. Jr.	Pvt	L	5 Feb 51	SSM	David, Clophas J.	Cpl	F	21 May 51	DOW
Carson, Donavan R.	Sgt	E	12 Dec 51		Davidson, Harold J.	Pfc	Med	11 Aug 50	
Carter, Fred C.	Cpl	H	31 Dec 53	DED	Davie, Herbert E.	Pvt	H	23 Apr 51	
Carter, George E.	Pfc	K	5 Apr 51	DOW/2 PH	Davies, Esau E., Jr.	Pfc	A	30 Aug 50	
Cary, Daniel A.	Pfc	F	31 Aug 50		Davies, Everette	Cpl	E	31 Dec 53	DED
Casanova, Herbert V. Jr.	Pfc	A	4 Feb 51		Davies, Max O.	Pfc	Med	13 Aug 50	
Cash, Floyd	Pvt	H	22 Apr 51		Davis, Clark W.	Pvt	C	20 Oct 51	
Casillas, Roberto L.	Pfc	G	27 May 51		Davis, Issac S.	Sgt	M	17 Sep 50	
Cason, James E.	Sgt	K	15 Dec 50		Davis, Madison L.	M/Sgt	C/555	31 Dec 53	DED
Castro, Hector	Pvt	F	26 Oct 51	NBC	Davis, Roscoe M.	Pfc	G	6 Dec 50	DED
Caudill, James A.	Cpl	A	12 Jul 51		Day, Robert W.	Pfc	M	30 Jul 52	
Cave, Charles L.	Pfc	G	9 Oct 51		Dean, Marion V.	Pfc	F	8 Jan 53	
Cayan, Donald C.	Pfc	72 E	18 Apr 53	NBC	De Angelis, Homer G.	Pvt	5th Inf	27 Aug 50	
Chadwick, Richard E.	Cpl	Med	29 Oct 50		DeBenedictus Michael	Pfc	F	9 Sep 50	
Chambers, Leslie D.	Pvt	5th Inf	29 Aug 50		DeMello, Justin M. Jr.	Sfc	I	18 Sep 50	
Champion, Merrill J.	Pfc	L	18 Aug 52	DOW/2 PH	Demello, Stanley C.	Sgt	I	16 Aug 50	
Chan, Clarence	Cpl	A	23 Apr 51	DED/2 PH	Demieri, James J.	Pfc	I	10 Aug 52	
Charnow, Fred	Pfc	C	12 Aug 50		DeNyse, George	Pvt	K	3 Aug 52	
Chatigny, Thomas	Pfc	E	16 Sep 50		Depermentier, Leonard J.	Cpl	I	24 Mar 51	DOW
Chavis, Burnice	Pfc	F	9 Dec 51	2 PH	De Rouen, Adam J.	Pvt	F	19 Oct 51	
Christian, Claibourne	Pfc	Hq /1	22 Jul 51		DeVita, Michael	Pvt	G	27 Jan 52	
Chudo, John	Sgt	Med	Aug 50		Dibble, Clarence	Pfc	F	4 Sep 50	
Chung, Raymond C.S.	Sfc	F	4 Nov 50	2 PH	Di Croce, Louis A.	Cpl	A	23 Aug 50	
Church, Freddie E.	Pfc	F	1 Nov 50		Di Pasquo, Daniel	Pvt	B	25 Aug 50	
Cicchella, Michael	Pfc	B	11 May 53		Dixon, Donald C.	Pfc	Sv/555	15 Sep 50	
Clairmont, Donald J.	Sgt	A/555	25 Apr 51	DED	Dixon, Johnnie E.	Pfc	L	18 May 51	
Clark, Herbert Fletcher	Sgt	G	12 Oct 51		Dobbs, James A.	Pfc	L	4 Apr 51	
Clark, Vern R.	Pfc	B	21 Sep 50		Dodd, John E.	Cpl	G	30 Jan 51	
Clarke, Wilson D.	Pfc	C	12 Oct 52	DOW	Doherty, John C.	Cpl	C	20 Feb 53	
Clyburn, Lesley W.	Pfc	K	13 Jan 53	DED	Doherty, John Cornelius	Cpl	C	12 Oct 51	
Coats, Jessie Jr.	Sgt	B	10 Jan 52		Dollar, James R.	Pvt	M	7 Mar 51	
Cobb, Willard L	Cpl	A/555	12 Aug 50		Donini, Remo	Pfc	Tk	11 Aug 52	
Coghlan, Thomas	Cpl	I	19 Sep 50		Dorrell, Thomas A.	Pvt	E	20 Oct 51	
Colageo, Louis A.	Pfc	C	24 Mar 51		Dorrion, Neil K.	Sgt	Med	4 Nov 50	SSM
Colarusso, James, Jr.	Pfc	K	22 May 51	DOW	Doucet, Joseph	Pvt	B/555	15 Jul 54	DED
Cole, Delmar P.	Sfc	K	28 Nov 50	DED	Duffner, lifford G.	1st Lt	E	5 Apr 51	
Collette, Joseph R.	2nd Lt	L	7 Jun 52		Duke, Roy E.	Pfc	F	4 Nov 50	
Collins, Estle L.	Pfc	D	25 Aug 50		Dukes, Frank	Pfc	E	10 Dec 51	
Colmenares, August	Cpl	I	19 Sep 50		Dupuis, Joseph N.	Sgt	C	25 Apr 51	
Combs, Bobby V.	Sgt	I	10 Jan 52		Dzielski, Michael L.	Pvt	5th Inf	6 Sep 50	
Connelly, Charles K.	-	B	21 Aug 50		Dziura, Edward M.	Pfc	G	27 Nov 50	DOW
Connolly, Mark	Pfc	E	30 Jun 51	DED	Eastwood, Arthur T.	Pfc	A	11 Aug 50	
Conroy, John K.	Pvt	B	30 Jan 51		Eaves, Bobby W.	Cpl	L	18 Oct 51	2 PH
Conway, James A.	Pvt	5th Inf	12 Jun 53		Echols, Tommie L.	Pfc	5th Inf	21 Jul 53	
Cook, William R	Pfc	Tk	17 Sep 50		Eckert, Albert	Pfc	A	24 Oct 52	NBC
Cooke, Albert B.	Pfc	Tk	16 Sep 50		Edgemond, Carl W.	Cpl	A	23 Aug 50	
Cooke, John P.	Sfc	L	18 Sep 50		Edwards, Albert MIA	Cpl	-/555	15 Jul 54	DED
Cooper, David R.	Pfc	B/555	17 Jul 52		Ege, Duane E.	Sfc	B	9 Feb 52	
Cooper, Gilbert R.	Cpl	A	7 Jun 52		Egikruat, Robert C.	Pfc	I	19 Sep 50	
Copas, George W.	Cpl	5th Inf	18 Jul 53		Eiland, Durward S.	Cpl	Hq/3	11 Aug 50	
Coraci, Thomas J.	Pvt	C	23 Apr 51	MIA	Eilers, John F.	Pfc	E	16 Sep 50	
Corley, Freddie C.	Cpl	G	29 Oct 50		Elliot, Jimmie L.	Pvt	D	18 May 51	
Cota, Clarence S. Jr.	Pvt	C	4 Feb 51		Elus, Glen G.	Pfc	C	12 Aug 50	
Council, Darrel D.	Pfc	D	23 Apr 51	DSC/PH	Emerson, Bertram F.	M/Sgt	Sv/555	12 Aug 50	
Cox, Harold E.	Pfc	I	10 Jan 52	2 PH	Emhoff, Roy	Pvt	C	19 May 51	
Crane, Lebanon	Cpl	F	8 Aug 50		Epstein, Louis W.	Pfc	F	7 Aug 50	
Creech, Clayton F.	Pfc	E	12 Jul 51	NBC	Escalante, William C.	Pfc	K	14 Jan 54	DED
Crews, Bryant	Pvt	A	24 Jan 53		Evans, Edward J.	Pfc	L	25 Apr 51	
Crisona, Peter	Pvt	A	28 Jan 53		Evens, William J.	Sfc	C	10 Aug 50	
Crocker, Jerome C.	Pvt	E	7 Aug 50		Fabrizio, Lewis	Pvt	A	19 May 51	
Cromier, Clarence	Pfc	E	7 May 52		Fain, John W. Jr.	Cpl	E	6 Aug 50	
Crosby, Stanley W. Jr.	1st Lt	B	10 Aug 50		Falkowski, Alexander	Pfc	C	3 Feb 51	DED
Cross, Harold R.	Sfc	K	27 Jul 53	(b)	Fancher, Maxie	Pfc	G	28 Jan 53	
Cunningham, Eugene M.	Pvt	B	24 Mar 51		Farina, Nicolo D.	Pfc	A	17 May 51	BSM
Cunningham, Jimmie D.	Pfc	B	29 Mar 51		Farley, Ronald J.	Pfc	B	24 Sep 50	
Curran, Patrick S.	Pfc	H	21 May 51		Farmer, Robert W.	Sfc	F	16 Sep 50	
Curtin, Edward L.	Pfc	C	9 Jun 52		Farrelly, Felix D.	Cpl	5th Inf	12 Jun 53	
Curtis, Robert L.	Pfc	Mtr	19 Dec 51		Fee, Denver	Pfc	I	6 Feb 53	

Name	Rank	Unit	Date	Notes (a)	Name	Rank	Unit	Date	Notes (a)
Feeney, Joseph L., Jr.	Pfc	A	17 May 51		Guyer, Jesse V.	Pfc	A	31 Aug 50	
Ferguson, Andrew C. Jr.	Pfc	F	19 Mar 51		Haigh, Raymond C., Jr.	Pfc	A	23 Apr 51	MIA
Fernandez, Casiano	Cpl	5th Inf	19 Jun 53		Haley, Louis R.	Pfc	K	18 Sep 50	
Ferreira, Gerald J.	Sgt	E	16 Sep 50		Hall, Richard Lee	Cpl	-/555	14 Jul 53	
Ficker, William Jr.	Sgt	I	23 Jul 52		Hall William C.	1st Lt.	-/555	25 Apr 51	MIA
Figueroa, Massas S.	Pvt	G	28 Jan 53		Hamaguchi, Kenichi	Pfc	C	12 Aug 50	
Finnegan, Thomas J. Jr.	Pfc	Hq/5	2 Oct 50		Handrich, Melvin O.	M/Sgt	C	25 Aug 50	CMH
Flanagan, Donald F.	Cpl	I	23 Apr 51	DED	Hansel, Morgan B.	1st Lt	C	4 Nov 50	DSC/SSM
Flanders, John D.	Pfc	Hq/5	5 Sep 50		Hanson, Leroy E.	Sgt	Hq/1	11 Aug 50	
Flowers, Arthur	Cpl	Hq/2	9 Sep 52	DOW	Hardy, Robert J.	Pfc	G	24 Sep 50	
Fondry, Gerald	M/Sgt	I	24 Jul 52	DOW	Harr, Donald F.	Pvt	G	24 Sep 50	
Ford, Ben E.	1st Lt	L	15 Oct 51		Harris, Johnson J.	Cpl	H	14 Oct 51	
Ford, Charles W.	Pfc	F	25 Apr 51		Harrison, Dick	Cpl	A	2 Oct 51	DOW
Forte, Pete R. Jr.	Cpl	F	8 Aug 50		Harrison, Hubert C.	Pvt	F	8 Jan 53	
Foster, Garfield	Pvt	E	23 Jun 52		Hartley, George W.	Cpl	I	1 Sep 50	
Foster, Thomas H.	Cpl	L	9 Aug 50		Hartneck, Clifford J.	Sgt	B	21 Aug 50	
Fouty, Sanford W.	Pvt	F	25 Apr 51		Hastings, Donald W.	Pfc	C	30 Jun 51	DED
Fox, Alfred W.	Pvt	I	8 Oct 52		Hastings, Robert A,	Cpl	K	24 Feb 51	MIA
Fox, Eldon E.	Cpl	C	26 Jul 51	DED	Hatfield, Cecil	Pfc	L	30 Aug 50	
Frazier, Edward M.	Cpl	Sv	13 Apr 53	NBC	Haugtredt, Orvis A.	Pfc	B	24 Sep 50	2 PH
French, Jennings	Pfc	Med	27 Sep 52		Hawley, Clifford R	Cpl	E	13 Feb 51	
Frezzo, Louis B.	Cpl	G	3 Sep 50		Haygood, Freddye L.	Pvt	G	27 Jan 52	
Frisz, Charles D.	Pfc	F	1 Nov 50		Hayslip, Wallace A.	Cpl	F	13 Oct 51	
Frost, Carl D.	Pfc	G	3 Sep 50		Head, Richard G.	Pvt	I	23 Apr 51	MIA/DIC
Fujita, Takeshi	Pfc	A	29 Aug 50		Headley, Clarence M	M/Sgt	B/555	8 Aug 50	
Fukamizu, Haruo	Cpl	C	12 Aug 50		Hearren, Raymond L.	Sgt	A/555	6 Dec 50	DED
Fulk, Lester E.	Cpl	K	18 Feb 54	DED	Heath, Leslie R.	Cpl	A	30 Jun 51	DED
Fulks, Orlan	Pfc	L	5 Oct 52	DED	Heaton, James L.	Pvt	G	3 Sep 50	
Fuller, Donald A.	Pvt	Hq/3	11 Aug 50		Hebb, Leonard	Pfc	72 E	10 Aug 50	
Fuller, Noah D.	Pvt	G	25 Apr 51		Hedgecoth, Bennie J.	Sgt	K	28 Nov 5O	DED
Fulton, Marvin C.	Pvt	C	20 Oct 51		Hedgespeth, Clifton	Pfc	5th Inf	12 Jun 53	
Furman, Cecil A.	Pvt	B	20 Jun 52		Heflin, Robert P.	Cpl	C/555	15 Jul 54	DED
Gaffey, Patrick J.	Pfc	B/555	8 Aug 50		Helton, Orvil	Pfc	B	27 Aug 50	2 PH
Galius, Rosalio	Sfc	C	30 Jan 51	BSM	Hema, Thomas	Cpl	G	4 Sep 50	
Garcia, Serafini R.	Pfc	F	4 Sep 50		Hembree, William C.	Sgt	I	19 Sep 50	
Gardner, Frederick	Pfc	L	25 Apr 51		Henthien, William A.	Sgt	F	21 May 51	
Gardner, Glenn	Sgt	G	9 Aug 50		Herald, Paul G.	Pvt	B	27 Aug 50	
Gaskins, Billie L.	Pfc	Hq/3	11 Aug 50	SSM/PH	Herreira, Gerald J.	Sgt	5th Inf	16 Sep 50	
Gaylord, William A.	Pfc	E	16 Sep 50	SM	Herrmann, Eugene H.	Pfc	E	13 Oct 51	
Gbur, Michael A	Pvt	B/555	12 Aug 50		Herron, Jessie E.	Pfc	B/555	15 Jul 54	DED
Geise, Robert L.	Pfc	F	24 Mar 51		Hess, Edward J.	Pfc	Mtr	24 Mar 51	
Getchell, Maurice S.	Pfc	B	12 Aug 50		Hewett, Francis L.	Cpl	Mtr	30 Oct 50	DOW/SSM
Gettings, Charles E.	Pvt	D	29 Jul52	NBC	Hew Len, Richard D.	Pfc	Hq/1	7 Nov 50	
Gibson, Aubrey L.	Cpl	A/555	12 Aug 50		Hilgard, Carter D.	Capt	C	25 Aug 50	SSM
Gibson, Howard J.	Pvt	5th Inf	9 Oct 51		Hill, Robert L.	Pfc	G	13 Aug 50	
Gilbert, Billy M.	Pvt	L	- Aug 50		Hill, Thomas H.	Sgt	5th Inf	24 Aug 50	DOW
Gilbertson, Francis R.	Cpl	A	8 Aug 52		Him-oo-Jhong	Pfc	K	10 Feb 53	ROK
Gilder, Elbert E. Jr.	2nd Lt	G	22 Jan 51		Hinson, Charles B.	2nd Lt	B/555	12 Aug 50	
Gilley, Billy J.	Pvt	E	22 Apr 51	MIA	Hodapp, Arthur L.	Pfc	A	3 Jul 51	DED
Gillispi, George D. Jr.	WOJG	Tk	7 Aug 50		Hoeflich, Irvin D.	Pfc	Mtr	25 Aug 50	
Gilson, William A.	Cpl	B	30 Oct 50		Hoff, Stanford I	Pfc	K	4 Nov 50	
Gittings, James W. Jr.	Pvt	F	30 Oct 51		Hoffman, Rchard E.	Cpl	F	3 Sep 50	
Gluckman Leroy M	Pvt	A	23 Apr 51		Holmes, Willard B.	Pvt	B	7 Dec 51	
Goldstein Leroy	Pvt	B	23 Oct 52	DOW	Holt, Oliver	Cpl	Mtr	19 Feb 51	DOW
Goiter Arlyn R.	Cpl	F	19 Feb 53	DOW	Holynskyj, Walter	Cpl	L	2 Sep 52	
Gomes John H.	Pfc	G	3 Sep 50		Hooker, Joseph	Pfc	C	26 Aug 50	
Gomes Robert	Pfc	E	20 Sep 50		Hookona, Peter H.	Sfc	B	25 Aug 50	
Gotto, Satoshi	Pfc	A	23 Aug 50		Hopper, Charles T.	1st Lt	A/555	14 Jul 53	
Graham, Alexander	Cpl	5th Inf	13 Jun 53		Houston, Bobby L.	Pfc	F	26 Jan 51	
Graybeal, Donald R.	Pvt	5th Inf	13 Jun 53		Hovel, John	Cpl	F	13 Oct 51	
Green, Billy F.	Pvt	L	5 Feb 51		Howell, Harley D.	Pfc	5th Inf	13 Jun 53	
Greenburg, Jerome E.	Pvt	Med	31 Jul 52		Howze, Frank B.	Maj	-/555	15 Sep 50	
Greene, Ralph H.	1st Lt	I	14 Oct 51		Hugg, John O.	Cpl	Hq/3	18 Oct 51	
Griffin, Glen Wilson	Pfc	E	10 Dec 51		Hughes, Jack W.	Pvt	G	4 Apr 51	
Griffin, Horace A.	Pvt	F	19 Oct 51		Hughes, Michael J	Cpl	A	26 Aug 50	
Griffin, Verbel J.	Pvt	A	14 Oct 51		Hughs, John A. Jr.	Pfc	B	6 Sep 52	
Griffith, Harold W.	Cpl	Mtr	31 Aug 51	DED/POW	Hula, Frank E.	Capt	L	18 Sep 50	SSM
Grine, Lawrence D.	Pfc	A	21 Sep 50		Hunt, Ray D.	Pfc	G	3 Sep 50	
Grundman, Richard A.	Sgt	5th Inf	31 Aug 50		Hunt, Willie R.	Cpl	72 E	10 Aug 50	
Guilford, Howarth I.	Pvt	G	11 Sep 52		Hutchinson, Donald L.	Pvt	E	27 May 51	
Gunns, Marvin L.	Pfc	F	22 Apr 51	MIA	Huth, William P.	Pfc	E	22 Apr 51	MIA

Name	Rank	Unit	Date	Notes (a)	Name	Rank	Unit	Date	Notes (a)
Hutto, Albert C.	Cpl	B	8 Sep 50		Knierien, Howard H.	Sgt	C	27 Jun 51	
Hyre, Jack R.	1st Lt	C/555	25 Apr 51		Knobloch, Carl F	2nd Lt	A/555	11 Aug 50	
Ikeda, Yoshio	Sgt	C	12 Aug 50		Knopp, Roy E.	Pvt	F	1 Nov 50	
Inghram, Samuel D.	Sfc	K	30 Oct 50	2 PH	Kochi, Takashi	Pfc	K	21 May 51	
Ishimoto, Akira A.	Sgt	I	11 Aug 50	2 BSM	Koonce, Charles E.	Pvt	C	22 Jun 52	
Ivy, Emmit M.	M/Sgt	555	12 Aug 50		Kravitz, Leonard M.	Pfc	M	7 Mar 51	DSC
Iwami, Osamu	Pvt	F	9 Aug 50		Kreml, Richard G.	Pfc	-/555	15 Jul 54	DED
Jackson, Chester A.	1st Lt	I	8 Aug 52		Kripoton, John A.	Pvt	C	12 Oct 52	
Jackson, Donovan J.	M/Sgt	Hq/I	10 Jun 53		Krupa, Laddie	Sfc	E	15 Aug 52	
Jackson, James R..	Sfc	K	4 Apr 51	SSM	Kuhns, Homer K.	Cpl	C	24 Sep 50	BSM
Jackson, Robert H.	Pfc	C	13 Oct 51	2 PH	Kuni, Moses E.	Pfc	G	24 Sep 50	
Jacobs, Herman L.	Pfc	E	31 Dec 53	DED	Kuwahara, Shoso	Pfc	E	16 Oct 51	
Jagnow, Arthur C.	M/Sgt	E	11 Jan 52		Kuzminski, Benjaman	Cpl	E	20 Sep 50	
Janssen, Marvin T.	Pfc	D	8 Aug 52	DOW	Labar, Robert	Pfc	72 E	3 Aug 50	
Jarmagin, J. D.	Pfc	E	31 Dec 53	DED	LaBelle, Roland L.	Cpl	K	4 Apr 51	
Jeal, John W.	M/Sgt	C	10 Aug 50	DSC	Lalatovich, Paul	Pvt	F	27 Oct 52	
Jefferson, Loyd	Pvt	5th Inf	13 Jun 53		Lane, James L Jr.	1st Lt	G	23 Jul 53	
Jenkins, Benjamin W.	Pfc	L	25 Apr 51		Lane, Tyler E.	Cpl	Sv/555	12Aug 50	
Jensen, William L.	Cpl	K	25 Sep 50		Lang, Raymond J.	Pvt	E	22 Apr 51	MIA
Jernigan, Vernon	2nd Lt	K	27 Aug 50		Langfitt, Bruce B.	WOJG	Sv/555	12 Aug 50	
Johnson, Charles L.	Pfc	E	10 Aug 50		Langley, Robert G.	Cpl	C	5 Apr 51	
Johnson, Eugene A.	Sgt	D	16 Sep 50		Langlitz, Wallace J.	Pfc	A	6 Sep 50	
Johnson, James N.	Pfc	C	30 Jan 51		Laro, George	Cpl	F	— — 50	
Johnson, John H.	Pvt	K	14 Jun 53		Lasua, Lawrence P.	Sgt	I	29 Nov 50	
Johnson, Joseph E.	Pfc	G	23 Jul 53		Lawrence, Robert T.	Cpl	I	6 Sep 52	
Johnson, Phillip B.	Cpl	K	18 Sep 50		Leathers, Harry F.	Cpl	G	9 Aug 50	DOW
Johnson, Truman E.	Pvt	5th Inf	16 Jul 53		LeBlanc, Oreste I.	Pfc	B/555	12 Aug 50	
Johnson, Victor E.	Pfc	M	13 Oct 51		Lee, Elvin M.	2nd Lt	D	30 Oct 50	
Jones, Andrew W.	Pvt	5th Inf	16 Oct 51		Lenz, Arden J.	Pvt	E	16 Sep 50	
Jones, Connie W.	Cpl	B	- Dec 53	DED	Leshaw, Jerome	Cpl	C	19 Oct 51	
Jones, Dennis M.	Cpl	A	15 Jan 53		Levy, Leo	Pfc	E	31 Dec 53	DED
Jones, Egar D.	Pfc	F	7 Aug 50		Lewis, Daniel H.	Pfc	K	30 Oct 50	
Jones, Jessie L.	Pvt	G	19 Oct 51		Lewis, Johnnie L.	Cpl	H	4 Nov 50	DED
Jones, John W.	Pfc	F	24 Jul 52	DOW	Liggins, Alvin R. Jr.	Pfc	I	5 Dec 51	
Jones, Joseph	Pvt	5th Inf	13 Jun 53		Light, Johnny D.	Pfc	B	21 Aug 50	2 PH
Jones, Samuel L.	1st Lt	C	20 Oct 51		Lindahl, Rune	Pfc	A	29 Aug 52	
Joseph, David J.	Pfc	F	3 Aug 50	SSM	Long, Jac E.	Pfc	F	3 Jan 51	
Joyner, Raymond C.	Sgt	Hq/555	12 Aug 50		Longdale, Paul F.	Pfc	I	2 Sep 52	DOW
Judd, John C.	Sgt	A	19 Oct 51		Looney, Harold W.	Pvt	F	22 Apr 51	MIA
Kaapana, Basil K.	Cpl	5th Inf	18 Sep 50		Lovins, Edward	Pvt	G	22 Aug 52	DOW
Kalama, Clarence L.	Pfc	5th Inf	12 Aug 50		Lucas, Harry R.	Cpl	C	22 Jun 52	
Kamierzia, Wasil M.	Cpl	I	6 Mar 51	DOW	Lujan, Eutiquio J.	M/Sgt	A	31 Dec 53	DED
Kaneshiro, David T	Sfc	B/555	12 Aug 50		Lum, Chew W.	Pvt	B	14 Oct 51	
Karalewicz, Francis A.	Cpl	Sv/555	12 Aug 50	DED	Lundy, Arthur C.	Cpl	A/555	12 Aug 50	
Kauahi, Alexander K.	Pfc	D	1 Sep 50	BSM	Lunt, Lowell Dewitt Jr	Cpl	K	4 Apr 51	BSM
Kauanui, David L.	Cpl	F	8 Aug 50		Luti, Anthony	Pvt	A	23 Apr 51	MIA
Kauno, Herbert K.	-	C	25 Sep 50		Lynch, Dan G	Sgt	A/555	30 Nov 50	DOW
Ke, Hiram V.	M/Sgt	L	28 Nov 50	DED/SSM	Mace, Jackie M.	Pfc	A	29 Aug 50	
Keith, Edward L.	Pfc	K	18 Nov 50		Machinski, Daniel J.	Pfc	B	13 Oct 51	
Kelii, Mathew K.	Cpl	I	18 Sep 50		Mack, Leroy F.	Pvt	A	23 Apr 51	
Keller, John F.	Pvt	C	29 Mar 51	DOW	Mackley, Glenn R	Pfc	Hq/555	7 Jun 53	
Kelly, George A.	Pfc	Mtr	26 Nov 50		Maggi, Anthony J.	Pvt	A	25 Apr 51	
Kenawell, John	Cpl	F	17 Sep 50	DOW	Makaena, Charles K.	Cpl	Hq/555	11 Aug 50	
Kendall, Randolph L.	Pfc	G	8 Aug 50		Mann, Donald W.	Cpl	D	25 Aug 50	BSM
Kenzel, Robert W.	Pfc	A	15 Oct 51		Manning, James E.	Pvt	G	17 May 51	
Keomaka, Samuel	Cpl	I	21 Aug 50		Manton, Beverly S	Pfc	B/555	18 Jan 53	
Ketterman, Andrew R.	Pfc	C	21 Aug 50		Marchant, Glen V.	Cpl	G	24 Sep 52	DOW
Kilar, Robert	Cpl	-	8 Dec 50	DED	Marek, Raymond W.	Cpl	I	26 Jul 53	
Killian, Charles O.	Pfc	F	25 Apr 51		Marks, Kent M.	Pvt	B	25 Apr 51	
Killian, Clarence A.	Pvt	5th Inf	21 Aug 50		Marshal, Ronald D.	Cpl	A	21 Sep 50	
Kim, Yoo Jhong	Pfc	K	10 Feb 53	ROK	Martin, Bobby G.	Cpl	H	13 Aug 50	
King, Joseph R.	Cpl	A	23 Jul 51		Martin, Charles	Sgt	Hq/3	1 Sep 50	
King, Willis G.	Pvt	5th Inf	11 Jun 53		Martin, Claire	Pvt	C	25 Apr 51	
Kingsley, John E.	Capt	B/555	15 Jul 54	DED	Martin, William R.	Pfc	A	23 Aug 50	
Kiriu, Hiroshi	Pvt	E	13 Oct 51		Martinet, John A.	Pfc	A	15 Jan 53	
Kirkpatrick, Charle	Pfc	B	27 Aug 50		Martinet, Xavier P.	Pfc	B	21 Aug 50	
Klein, John Albert	Pvt	B	7 Dec 51	2 PH	Matos-Irizarry, Ramon P.	Cpl	G	23 Feb 53	
Klein, Roy D.	Pvt	G	28 Sep 52	DOW	Matthess, Richard R.	Pfc	K	5 Apr 51	
Klug, Kenneth W.	Pfc	A	19 Oct 51		Mattucci, Anthony M.	Pfc	B	31 Dec 53	DED
Kluss, Joe	Sgt	A	3 Sep 50		Matutino, Gregorio E.	Pfc	A	23 Aug 50	
Klutts, Carl F.	Pvt	B	13 Oct 51		Mauricio, James P.	Pvt	C	20 Oct 51	

Name	Rank	Unit	Date	Notes (a)	Name	Rank	Unit	Date	Notes (a)
Maynard, Norman J.	Pvt	Med	16 Feb 53	NBC	Naranjo, Agapito D.	Pfc	F	31 Aug 50	
Mayo, John M.	Pfc	C/555	13 Oct 51	DOW	Naset, George R.	Cpl	B	24 Sep 50	
Mazalan, George A.	Pvt	K	7 Aug 51	NBC	Nesbit, Cecil E.	Pfc	G	17 Sep 50	
McCarthy, Edward J.	Pvt	G	9 Apr 51		Newman, Leonard H.	Pfc	Sv	6 Apr 51	
McCasland, Wayne W.	Cpl	I	1 Sep 50		Ng, George K. S.	Pfc	M	15 Oct 51	
McClafferty, Cornelius P.	Pfc	I	3 Aug 51	DOW	Nieb, Kenneth W.	Pvt	C	24 Sep 50	
McCleain, Leroy	Pfc	A	31 Dec 53	DED	Niederriter, Henry	Pvt	C	12 Aug 50	
McClure, Kenneth C.	Pfc	G	24 Sep 50		Nishimura, Charles K.	Cpl	C	12 Aug 50	
McCormack, Edward J.	Pvt	F	31 Jul 52		Niwa, Daniel J.	Pfc	G	9 Oct 51	
McCracken, Paul T.	Sgt	L	28 Nov 51	DED	Nix, Victor H., Jr.	Pvt	5th Inf	28 Aug 50	
McCullough, Robert	Pfc	D	23 Aug 50		Noble, William Jr.	Pfc	D	12 Jul 52	
McCullough, Willie J.	Pvt	E	14 Oct 51		Noneman, Robert P.	M/Sgt	E	22 Mar 51	DSC
McDonald, Bobby W.	Pfc	H	7 Aug 50		Norris, Howard G.	Pfc	A	3 Feb 51	
McDowell, Leonard	Cpl	E	24 Jun 52		Nylander, Kenneth R.	Cpl	E	16 Sep 50	SSM
McGovern, John F.	Sgt	L	3 Sep 50		O'Brien, William J.	Pfc	G	3 Sep 50	
McGriff, Grover J.	M/Sgt	C/555	14 Jul 54	DED	O'Connor, John J.	Capt	B/555	30 May 53	DOW
McHenry, Everett E.	Pfc	C/555	14 Jul 54	DED	O'Hara, Paul F.	Cpl	E	4 Apr 51	
McJunkin, William C.	Sgt	F	17 Jan 52	2 PH	Odom, Silly J	Pfc	G	27 Jan 52	
Mckie, Robert J.	Pfc	Hq/-	2 Oct 50		Ogden, Howard D.	Sgt	G	19 Oct 51	
McKinney, Henry C.	Sgt	F	7 Nov 51		Oh-Sang-Choi	Pvt	F	18 Jan 53	ROK
McMorran, William	Cpl	B	16 May 51	DOW	Oiler, William R.	Sgt	I	28 Nov 50	DED
McQuiston, Vance R.	Sgt	A	24 Sep 50		Okamura, Arthur I.	Pfc	A	14 Oct 51	DSC
McWhorter, Vance B.	1st Lt	Tk	9 Nov 50	SSM/BSM	Oleson, Alien K.	Cpl	Med	24 Sep 50	
Medina, Raul C.	Cpl	E	4 Apr 51		Olivas, Albert S.	Pvt	I	3 Aug 50	
Meiggs, Richard W.	Pfc	F	22 Apr 51	MIA	Otagura, Thomas N.	Pfc	G	14 Aug 50	
Meldrum, John H. Jr.	Pfc	Hq/3	11 Jun 53		Otterstrom, Rawland N.	Cpl	C	13 Oct 51	DSC
Melton, William S.	Pfc	5th Inf	13 Jun 53		Owen, Reuben D.	Pfc	C	12 Aug 50	
Mendenhall, Robert E.	Pfc	Med	27 Sep 52		Pangle, James F.	Pfc	H	26 Jan 51	MIA
Mendoza, James J.	Pfc	L	4 Apr 51		Pappapetru, William P.	Pvt	B	13 Oct 51	
Menthien, William A.	Sgt	F	21 May 51		Paradise, John R.	Pfc	E	16 Sep 50	
Mercer, Foster M.	Cpl	Hq/-	5 Sep 50		Park, Wilson	Pfc	L	9 Aug 50	
Mercer, John A. Jr	1st Lt	B/555	8 Aug 50		Parker, Charles E.	1st Lt	F	18 Jan 53	
Merchant, Glen V.	Cpl	G	24 Sep 52	DOW	Parkhurst, Paul O.	2nd Lt	-/555	15 Jul 54	DED
Metzcar, Maurice R,	Capt	-/555	25 Apr 51	DED	Parunago, Tom	Cpl	G	9 Aug 50	DOW
Micele, Raymond A.	Pfc	I	7 Mar 51	2 PH	Patterson, Jerome E.	Pvt	E	15 Oct 51	
Michalak, Leland P.	Pfc	A	13 Jul 51		Patterson, Richard W.	Pvt	G	27 Sep 52	
Michiel, Max R.	Pvt	E	22 Apr 51	MIA	Pearo, Gerald P.	Cpl	D	31 Dec 53	DED/ BSM
Miller, Bobby	Pfc	A	30 Sep 51	DED	Perkins, Jesse L.	Cpl	A	25 Apr 51	
Miller, Earl K.	Pvt	G	3 Sep 50	DSC	Peters, Daniel G.	Pfc	K	5 Mar 51	
Mills, Albert D.	Pfc	G	17 May 51		Peters, Fred H.	Cpl	K	24 Sep 50	
Misemer, Donald O.	Pvt	I	3 Aug 51		Peters, James M.	Cpl	-/555	12 Aug 50	
Misuraco, Jerrome A.	Cpl	D	30 Oct 50		Peters, Richard E.	Pvt	E	22 Apr 51	
Miyahara, Samuel S.	Sgt	H	15 Mar 54	DED	Phelan, William T.	Pvt	F	18 Jan 53	
Miyasato, Wilbert Y.	Cpl	B	14 Oct 51		Phelps, Woodrow W.	Cpl	Med	24 Sep 50	
Miyashiro, Tomayoshi	Cpl	G	2 Oct 50		Phillips, Johnnie E.	Pvt	H	23 Apr 51	
Moccio, Raymond D.	Pfc	L	18 Aug 52	DOW	Phipps, Jeril	Pfc	B	31 Oct 50	DOW
Modena, Willie E.	Sgt	M	18 Oct 51		Piela, Gene L.	Cpl	B	17 Jul 52	
Moeller, Arthur A.	Cpl	5th Inf	11 Jun 53		Pierce, George Jr.	Pvt	C	20 Oct 51	
Mohr, Louis W.	Pfc	G	4 Sep 50		Pierce, Robert A.	Pfc	D	30 Oct 50	BSM
Mokiao, Raymond T.	Cpl	F	8 Sep 50		Pierce, Thomas C. Jr.	Pfc	Med	24 Sep 52	
Montoya, Feles	Pvt	F	17 Sep 50		Pike, Raymond S.	Pfc	C	10 Jul 52	
Moody, John I.	Sfc	A/555	13 Feb 51		Pinckney, Bobbie N.	Pfc	E	21 Jun 52	
Moon-Jong-Doo	Pfc	B	24 Sep 50		Plumber, Paul W.	Sgt	I	13 Jul 52	
Moreno, Gilbert T.	Pfc	I	23 Apr 51	MIA/DIC	Pollard, Aubrey W.	Pfc	I	19 Sep 50	
Morrissey, John A.	Pvt	L	10 Aug 52		Ponciano, Benjamin A.	Sgt	E	16 Sep 50	DSC
Morrow, Henry	Pvt	E	10 Oct 51		Poole, William J.	Sgt	D	23 Aug 50	
Morris, William A.	Pfc	F	22 Apr 51	MIA	Popovich, Michael	Cpl	D	12 Aug 50	
Morse, Dale B.	Pfc	F	31 Aug 50		Porter, James B.	1st Lt	Hq/3	11 Jun 53	
Morton, Raeford L.	Cpl	C/555	14 Jul 54	DED	Porter, Richard E.	Sgt	F	22 Apr 51	MIA
Mullicane, Paul F.	Pfc	Hq/-	6 Sep 50		Potvin, Joseph E.	Cpl	B/555	12 Aug 50	
Mun-Son-Ju	Pvt	G	4 Sep 50	ROK	Powell, Harold L.	Pfc	I	21 Aug 52	
Murphy, Thomas J.	Pfc	B	9 Nov 51		Prestage, Douglas	Sgt	B	31 Dec	DED
Muse, Earl.	Cpl	F	4 Nov 50		Przvbyse, Alexander	Sfc	F	3 Sep 50	
Musick, Lee R.	Sgt	K	28 Nov 50	DED	Pugh, David L.	Pvt	F	23 Mar 51	
Myer, William H.Jr.	Cpl	F	13 Aug 50	2 PH	Pumper, Melvin J.	Pvt	C	25 Apr 51	
Myers, Stephen A.	Cpl	C	25 Aug 50		Pytel, Leon J	Pfc	Hq/555	12 Aug 50	
Nabanjo, Agapito D.	-	F	31 Aug 50		Queja, Edward A.	Pfc	K	18 Sep 50	
Nagy, Paul A.	Cpl	C	12 Aug 50		Quinn, Claude J.	Pfc	C	21 Aug 50	
Nakama, Seiso	Pfc	C	12 Aug 50		Quiroz, John A.	Cpl	L	30 Oct 50	DOW
Nakashima, Roy T.	1st Lt	B/555	22 Apr 51		Ramirez, Ignacio	Pfc	I	15 Aug 50	
Nakatani, Seinojo R.	Pfc	F	31 Aug 50		Ramirez-Lopez, Ramiroo	Pfc	F	4 Aug 52	

Name	Rank	Unit	Date	Notes (a)	Name	Rank	Unit	Date	Notes (a)
Ramos-Echevarria, Pedro	Pvt	F	4 Aug 52		Sewers, Douglas H.	Pvt	G	1 Feb 53	
Ramsey, Donald L.	Cpl	F	1 Sep 50		Shaffer, William E.	Pfc	A	4 Feb 51	
Rasha, Willie	Pfc	G	27 May 51		Shafter, William A.	Pfc	H	31 Dec 53	DED
Reaves, David J.	Cpl	F	21 Apr 51		Shaw, Billy D.	Pvt	M	18 Oct 51	
Redding, Richard F.	Pfc	C/555	8 Aug 50		Shedd, Harold	Cpl	A	25 Apr 51	MIA/DIC
Reed, Richard E.	Pfc	I	28 Nov 50		Shelton, Jim Jr.	Pfc	B	13 Oct 51	
Reihner, John J.	Cpl	L	2 Sep 50		Shields, Mark L.	Pfc	72 E	16 Aug 50	
Reinhard, Marcus	Sfc	F	1 Sep 50		Shimogawa, Kenneth K.	Pvt	E	20 Sep 50	SSM
Renteria, John L.	Pvt	E	22 Apr 51	MIA	Shin, Denk Man	Pvt	K	3 Feb 53	MIA/ROK
Rentz, Barney C.	Pfc	C	9 Jun 53		Shipe, Robert N.	2nd Lt	A	19 Oct 51	
Reynolds, William G.	Sgt	F	5 Aug 52		Short, Thomas L.	Pfc	A	25 Apr 51	
Rhoades, James F.	Cpl	Med	21 Aug 52		Shows, J. M.	Pvt	G	21 Sep 52	
Rhoden, Donis E.	Pfc	5th Inf	13 Jun 53		Shuman, Herbert C.	Cpl	Tk	11 Aug 50	
Rhodes, Charles M.	M/Sgt	-/555	14 Jul53	DED	Shumate, Elmer L.	Pfc	B	13 Aug 50	
Rhodes, Elden P.	Pfc	E	20 Oct 51	DOW	Sibley, John A.	Cpl	G	19 Oct 51	2 PH
Rice, Curtis R.	Pfc	5th Inf	13 Oct 51		Simbre, Rofino	Cpl	5th Inf	12 Aug 50	
Richardson, Orvil C.	Pfc	A	12 Jul 51		Simmons, Ross D.	Pfc	B	6 Nov 51	
Richardson, William	Pfc	E	16 Sep 50		Sis, Albert J.	Cpl	G	4 Sep 51	NBC
Richner, Alfred D.	Sgt	F	4 Nov 50	DED	Sissom, Clyde Ezra	Pfc	E	10 Dec 51	
Rickert, Ernest L.	Pfc	I	17 Jan 53		Sloan, Donald E.	-	F	8 Sep 50	
Riddaugh, Frederick	Pfc	B	27 Aug 50		Smallstay, William A.	Cpl	-/555	15 Sep 50	
Riddle, James W.	Sgt	B	22 Apr 51	DSC	Smarr, Charles F.	Pfc	C	10 Aug 50	
Rigsby, Chester E.	Pvt	B	5 Aug 52		Smith, Bobby J.	Cpl	E	20 Sep 50	DSC
Roach, Wendell E.	Pvt	5th Inf	26 Aug 50		Smith, Bobby L.	Cpl	I	7 Dec 51	DOW
Roberts, Carl W.	Pvt	5th Inf	12 Jun 53		Smith, Denver J.	Cpl	C	25 Aug 50	
Roberts, William J.	Pvt	Med	13 Oct 51		Smith, Frank H.	Cpl	E	25 Jul 51	2 PH
Robertson, Teddy E.	Pvt	L	2 Dec 51		Smith, Ivory V.	Pfc	G	24 Sep 52	
Robichaud, John J.	Cpl	F	7 Aug 50		Smith, James C.	Sgt	Med	24 Sep 50	
Robinson, Stanley E.	Sgt	Tk	11 Aug 52		Smith, John L.	Pvt	F	8 Aug 50	
Robison, Leland W.	Pfc	H	13 Aug 50		Smith, Kenneth L.	Pvt	E	24 Oct 52	DOW
Robison, Malcolm A.	1st Lt	L	5 Oct 52	DED	Smith, Lawrence W.	Pvt	B	30 Jan 51	
Robson, Raymond C.	Pfc	F	4 Nov 50		Smith, Ray W.	Pfc	B/555	12 Aug 50	
Rockenbauch, Robert C.	Pvt	L	3 Apr 51		Smith, Roy E.	Cpl	E	4 Feb 51	
Rocus, Paul Edward	Pvt	F	9 Dec 51		Smith, Sherwin V.	Pfc	C	12 Aug 50	
Rodrigeus, Edward	Sgt	D	29 Aug 50	SSM	Smith, William D.	Cpl	I	19 Sep 50	
Rodriguez, Julio	Pfc	M	19 Sep 50		Smith, William J.	Pfc	H	2 Sep 50	
Rodriquez, Lupes	Cpl	I	2 Sep 50		Smothers, Comer	Sfc	A	25 Apr 51	
Rohanna, Louis J.	Cpl	5th Inf	1 Oct 50	SSM	Snook, Russell L.	Pvt	K	18 Oct 51	
Romero, Manual J.	Cpl	I	3 Aug 51	SSM/PH	Snyder, Charles F	Cpl	B/555	12 Aug 50	
Romero, Humberto	Pvt	B	25 Apr 51		Sommers, Hugh M. Jr.	Pvt	E	22 Apr 51	DSC
Ross, Enoch	Pvt	72 E	18 Apr 53	NBC	Song-Yong-Shik	Pvt	G	3 Sep 50	ROK
Ross, Raymond E.	Pfc	B	25 Apr 51		Sowers, Douglas H.	Pvt	G	1 Feb 53	
Rosser, William T.	Pfc	A	23 Aug 50		Spagnola, Michael	Pvt	5th Inf	14 Jun 53	
Roth, Oscar F.	Pvt	C	27 Jun 51		Sparks, Robert H.	Pfc	G	19 May 51	
Rotramel, Thomas E.	Cpl	I	4 Apr 51		Spertzel, Fred F.	Pfc	G	12 Mar 51	
Roussin, Joseph R.	Pvt	I	19 Oct 51		Spirat, Richard H.	Cpl	A	18 May 51	2 PH
Routt, Howard D.	Pfc	-/555	14 Jul 53	DED	Splittstoesser, Bernard M	Pfc	B/555	14 Jul 53	DED
Rushing, Larry W.	Pfc	I	18 Sep 50		Spoonemore, Herbert	Pfc	E	13 Oct 51	DOW
Russo, Vincent J.	Pfc	Med	3 Jul 52		Spotted Bear, Ignatius	Pfc	E	22 Jun 52	
Rutledge, Fostine R	Sfc	E	14 Aug 52		Sprinkle, Warren H.	Pvt	5th Inf	13 Jun 53	
Sabel, Michael E.	Pvt	5th Inf	18 Oct 51		Spruell, Johnnie H.	Sfc	C	4 Sep 52	DOW
Sakamoto, James N.	Pfc	C	12 Aug 50		Starkey, Jack R	Cpl	F	8 Aug 50	DSC
Sanders, Earl J.	Pvt	E	4 Apr 51		Starnes, Raymond S.	Pfc	E	25 Jul 51	
Savearingen, William F.	Pvt	F	8 Aug 50		Steffen, Daniel F.	Pvt	A	29 Mar 51	
Schaefer, George J.	Pvt	E	14 Oct 51		Sterner, Alton	Pfc	L	19 Jun 53	
Scheffler, Elmer H. Jr.	Pvt	Med	13 Oct 51		Stewart, Bill J.	Pvt	A	6 Jul 52	2 PH
Schifano, Robert J.	Cpl	Mtr	31 Dec 53	DED	Stewart, Harry M.	Cpl	I	20 Sep 50	
Schlegel, Delmond W.	Pvt	E	21 Oct 51		Stewart, Leon S.	Pfc	Mtr	11 Jun 53	
Schlette, Joseph W.	Cpl	M	15 Oct 51		Stoll, James W.	1st Lt	B/555	8 Aug 50	
Schmelzer, Raymond J.	Pvt	Tk	24 Oct 52		Stonestreet, Donald M.	Pvt	Hq/1	12 Jun 52	NBC
Schmidt, Arthur E.	Pfc	5th Inf	22 May 53		Strong, Gordon M.	1st Lt	Co E	15 Aug 50	
Schmitt, Edward C.	Cpl	B	19 Aug 52	DOW	Stroud, Arthur H.	Cpl	Mtr	30 Nov 50	
Schneider, Arley B.	Cpl	A/555	12 Aug 50		Stroup, Jack D.	Pfc	L	5 Feb 51	
Schneider Roger F.	Pfc	A/555	20 Sep 50		Stuhan, George R	Pfc	Hq/555	8 Aug 50	
Schwartz, Dwain E.	Cpl	C/555	14 Jul 53	DED	Stull, Richard D.	Pfc	D	29 Jul 52	NBC
Sciulli, William J.	Cpl	C/555	13 Dec 50		Su-Sang-Kyo	Pvt	I	9 Jan 53	ROK
Seagle, John R.	Cpl	G	9 Apr 51		Summers, John F.	Pfc	B	29 Mar 51	
Sears, Warren	Pvt	I	5 Oct 52		Sun, Celestine H. T.	Cpl	Hq/5	2 Oct 50	
Segobia, Oscar G.	Sfc	A	14 Oct 51		Surber, Earnrest E.	Pfc	A	25 Apr 53	
Sellars, Donald R.	Pfc	K	4 Feb 53	NBC	Sutherland, Kenneth L.	Capt	M	31 Mar 51	SSM
Serrano-Seranno, Anselmo	Pvt	L	5 Sep 52		Sutton, Andrew M.	Cpl	L	30 Oct 50	

Name	Rank	Unit	Date	Notes (a)
Swearingen, William F.	Pvt	F	8 Aug 50	
Sweat, Joseph V.	Pfc	5th Inf	6 Aug 52	DOW
Sweezey, Robert .	M/Sgt	B	12 Aug 50	
Swope, Wallace C.	Cpl	E	30 Jan 51	
Sylva, Adrian J. K.	Cpl	A	22 Sep 50	SSM/2 PH
Tabor, James L.	Sfc	H	10 Aug 50	
Taets, Donald L.	Pfc	G	30 Jun 52	
Tafoya, Elias Barrientos	Pvt	B	7 Dec 51	
Taggart, Robert	Sfc	Med	- Aug 50	
Takeshita, Nobuyuki	Pfc	I	22 Jul 51	NBC
Tallman, George R.	Pfc	L	16 Aug 52	
Taylor, James P.	Pfc	-/555	14 Jul 53	DED
Taylor, John J.	Cpl	Med	23 Apr 51	DED/DIC
Tegay, Aron A.	Pfc	D	16 Sep 50	
Tenn, Francis H.	Cpl	F	30 Jan 51	2 PH
Therrie, David L.	Pfc	L	20 Sep 50	
Thomas, Charles C.	Sgt	E	2 Nov 50	
Thomas, Lloyd	Sgt	-/555	14 Jul 53	DED
Thompson, Ralph L.	Pfc	G	4 Sep 51	NBC
Thomsen, Alien E.	Pfc	L	12 Aug 52	
Tilden II, Henry C.	Pfc	K	4 Apr 51	
Timmons, Robert L.	Capt	A	23 Aug 50	SSM
Tobias, Stanley P.	Pfc	5th Inf	23 Jul 53	
Tomlinson, Carl D.	Pvt	A	7 Apr 53	
Tompkins, Richard A.	Pfc	Med	25 Sep 50	
Toro, George	Cpl	F	15 Aug 50	
Torres, Rosalio J	Sgt	72 E	8 Aug 50	DOW
Torres, Russell G.	Sgt	E	30 Jan 51	
Townsend, Merlyn F.	Cpl	A	10 Feb 53	NBC
Travers, Joseph R.	Pfc	D	22 Apr 51	DED
Travis, Chester B	Pfc	A/555	12 Aug 50	DOW
Trinkaus, Joseph F.	Pvt	K	25 Mar 51	
Trout, Earl M. Jr.	Pfc	B	25 Apr 51	
Tsunoda, Suso	Sgt	Med	19 May 51	
Tucker, John L.	Pfc	72 E	15 Aug 50	
Tumlinson, Carl D.	Pvt	A	7 Apr 53	
Turner, Marvin	Cpl	K	18 Sep 50	
Turovh, David A.	Pvt	C	23 Apr 51	
Tyner, Jake	Cpl	F	8 Sep 50	
Tyrrell, Frederick	Cpl	5th Inf	27 Aug 50	
Uehara, Noboru	Pvt	B	25 Apr 51	
UNKNOWN	X-26	-	22 Aug 50	(c)
Uptegrove, John W.	Pfc	A	23 Apr 51	DED
Uyehara, Alfred S.	Sgt	K	28 Nov 50	DED
Van Alien, Charles	Cpl	G	4 Sep 50	
Van Antwerp, Frank G.	Sgt	Med	16 Sep 50	DSC
Van Arsdale, Edward C.	Pvt	C	19 May 51	
Vanden Bergh, Dona	Cpl	5th Inf	23 Jul 53	
Vandervoot, William A.	Pvt	C	12 Aug 50	
Vanhoesen, Marshal	Cpl	Tk	11 Aug 50	
Van Hook, Joseph J.	Cpl	I	3 Aug 51	DOW
Vannoy, James M.	Cpl	C	25 Apr 51	
Vaughn, Aubrey D.	Pfc	C	7 Jul 51	MIA
Veenstra, Albert W.	Sfc	G	16 Nov 50	BSM/3 PH
Veld, Richard	Pfc	5th Inf	13 Jun 53	
Vertcnik, Steve J.	Pfc	B	23 Aug 50	
Vick, Donald G.	Pvt	A	19 Oct 51	
Vierra, Harold A.	Cpl	G	25 Sep 50	
Viers, Edris A.	Sfc	A/555	12 Aug 50	DED
Vigil, Jose	Pvt	E	24 Sep 50	
Vincent, Frank H.	Pfc	M	18 Sep 50	
Vines, Cecil	Pvt	5th Inf	13 Jun 53	
Vydra, Edward R.	Sgt	K	10 Nov 51	
Wadsworth, Freeman M	Pvt	F	5 Aug 50	SSM
Waligorski, Raymond S.	Sgt	C	19 May 51	
Walk, John H.	Cpl	G	24 Sep 50	
Walker, Guy J.	Pfc	K	31 Dec 53	DED
Walker, Thomas S.	1st Lt	M	15 Oct 51	
Walraven, Martin N.	Pvt	I	3 Aug 51	
Walter, Francis G.	Cpl	H	25 Jun 51	2 PH
Wands, Leroy	Pfc	C	12 Oct 51	

Name	Rank	Unit	Date	Notes (a)
Ward, Jesse	Sgt	Sv	14 Jul 53	
Warner, Leonard K.	1st Lt	H	23 Apr 51	DSC/2 SSM/2 PH
Warp, Harold	Cpl	C	24 Sep 50	
Warren, Robert P.	Sgt	I	7 Aug 50	
Washburn, James F.	Pvt	Med	30 Aug 52	DOW
Waterhouse, Albert	Pvt	A	25 Apr 51	
Watkins, Jack G	M/Sgt	C	4 Nov 50	SSM
Watson, Eugene F.	Pfc	L	30 Aug 50	
Watson, John W.	Pvt	Med	10 Dec 51	DOW
Watt, George W.	Sgt	Hq/555	12 Aug 50	DED
Watts, Franklin H.	Pfc	G	19 Oct 51	
Wax, Robert I.	Cpl	Hq/555	11 Aug 50	
Weaver, Clyde W.	Pvt	B	13 Oct 51	DOW
Weaver, Edward T.	Cpl	-	21 Aug 50	
Webster, Calvin A.	Cpl	E	28 Jan 53	
Weiss, Irving S	Pfc	L	4 Apr 51	2 PH
Wells, Frederick Alven	Maj	Hq/5	25 Apr 51	
Werbe, Alvin F.	Pvt	C	25 Apr 51	
Wheeler, Robert N.	Pfc	G	15 Aug 50	
Whipkey, Howard K.	Pvt	A	25 Sep 50	
Wilkins, Joseph H.	Cpl	72 E	29 Sep 50	DOW
Williams, Alvin G.	Pfc	B	7 Sep 50	
Williams, Charles E.	Pfc	K	4 Apr 51	SSM
Williams, Ellis E.	Sgt	E	19 Jun 52	
Williamson, Charles	Pfc	A	28 Aug 50	
Wilson, Carvin	Sgt	C	22 Jun 52	
Wilson, Leroy W.	Cpl	B	10 Aug 50	
Wilson, Jerry	Pfc	I	6 Feb 53	
Wilson, Sylvester	Pvt	K	18 Oct 51	
Winchell, Otto B.	Pvt	5th Inf	27 Aug 50	
Windham, Wiullie E.	Sfc	-/555	12 Aug 50	DED
Wing, Elmer V.	Pfc	L	5 Oct 52	2 PH/ DED
Wingard, Lewis M.	Pvt	D	30 May 51	DED
Winstead, Henry G.	Sgt	Med	22 May 51	
Wiseman, Paul E.	Pfc	F	18 Jun 53	
Wojonowiak, Frank P.	Pfc	K	17 Oct 52	DED
Wood, Thomas F.	2nd Lt	5th Inf	13 Jun 53	
Woodbury, Harold	Pfc	72 E	3 Aug 50	
Woodward, Cecil V.	Cpl	K	17 Sep 50	
Worden, Arthur J	Pvt	F	1 Nov 50	
Worley, Charles W	2nd Lt	A	23 Aug 50	
Wozniak, Richard	Cpl	A	3 Jan 53	NBC
Wright, Sylvester	Pvt	F	14 Oct 51	
Wyles, Homer H.	Pfc	5th Inf	13 Jun 53	
Yackent, Edward T.	Sfc	A	30 Jan 53	NBC
Yang, Edwin D. S.	Pfc	A/555	4 Oct 50	
Yeager, Lawrence M.	Pvt	I	3 Sep 52	
Yeargle, Raymond E.	Pfc	D	12 Jul 51	
Young, Gerald E.	Cpl	I	31 Jul 51	NBC
Young, John R.	Pvt	5th Inf	12 Jun 53	MIA
Zahm, Eugene C.	Pvt	F	16 Oct 52	
Zatezalo, Nicholas G.	Cpl	I	3 Feb 51	
Zimmer, Raymond J.	Pfc	K	18 Oct 51	
Zimmerman, Luther B.	Pfc	I	15 Aug 50	
Zorn, Darrell W.	Pfc	G	28 Jan 53	

Category II: Based Upon Reliable Research (Must be Verified) (d)

Name	Rank	Unit	Date	Notes (a)
Alien Arthur B.	Pfc	Hq/555	12 Aug 50	
Axtell Everett J.	Sfc	Hq/2	23 Apr 51	
Barnes Carl M.	Pfc	C	25 Apr 51	
Barnett James J. Jr.	Pfc	A	11 Aug 50	
Bass Nova L..	Pvt	Hq/555	12 Aug 50	
Benthien William A.	Sgt	F	21 May 51	
Berneburg Fred W.	Cpl	-/555	25 Apr 51	
Black James E.	Pvt	I	23 Apr 51	DED
Boughter James M.	Pvt	A	24 Sep 50	DOW
Bowling Lawrence	Cpl	K	4 Nov 50	DOW/2PH

Name	Rank	Unit	Date	Notes (a)
Brouillette Neilso	1st Lt	-/555	20 Oct 51	
Bryant Emmitt R.	Pfc	-	12 Jun 53	
Brzycki Norbert A.	Sfc	A	23 Apr 51	
Busier Odell	Pfc	A	27 Aug 50	
Cirulli Samuel J.	Pfc	Hq/555	12 Aug 50	
Condroski Victor J.	Pfc	-/555	25 Apr 51	
Cooke William A. Jr.	Sfc	Hq/555	12 Aug 50	
Cruse Chester A.	Pfc	Sv/555	12 Aug 50	
Davis Nicholas	Cpl	-/555	9 Feb 51	
Dower James A	Cpl	-/555	25 Apr 51	
Falanai Matagisa S	Cpl	Hq/555	12 Aug 50	
Falin Jno E.	Pfc	A/555	12 Aug 50	
Falk Charles A.	Sfc	M	28 Nov 50	DSC
Fuller Wirt C. Jr.	Pfc	Hq/555	12 Aug 50	
Gose Ray V.	Pfc	D	13 Jun 53	
Grisard Thomas E.	M/Sgt	-/555	25 Apr 51	
Head James E.	Cpl	I	28 Nov 50	DED
Heard Richard L.	Cpl	-/555	25 Apr 51	
Hunt Frederic L. Jr.	Pfc	B/555	12 Aug 50	
Kennedy Franklin P.	Cpl	-/555	25 Apr 51	
Knutson Floyd V.	Pvt	-/555	25 Apr 51	
Koehler Frank J. Jr.	Sgt	A/555	12 Aug 50	
Ledford J. T.	Pfc	-/555	9 Feb 51	
Levercom Michael E.	Cpl	Hq/555	12 Aug 50	
Loveland Niles S.	Cpl	Hq/555	12 Aug 50	
Lydon Eugene M.	Cpl	-/555	13 Sep 52	
McCormick Arthur G.	Cpl	Hq/555	12 Aug 50	
McCleod Richard N.	1st Lt	-/555	6 Mar 51	
Memmer Donald J.	Cpl	B/555	22 Apr 51	
Montesinos Jose A.	Sgt	A/555	10 Aug 50	
Motherway James B	M/Sgt	B	12 Jun 53	
Mowery Lewis D.	Cpl	-/555	25 Apr 51	
Pains Jack G.	Pfc	Hq/555	12 Aug 50	
Rasmussen John N.	Pfc	B/555	12 Aug 50	
Ritchie Robert B.	1st Lt	A	24 Mar 51	DOW/BSM
Satterfield Roger	Pfc	-/555	25 Apr 51	DOW
Sheridan William L.	Pfc	Hq/555	12 Aug 50	
Sides William Jr.	Pfc	Hq/555	12 Aug 50	
Silva Eugene W.	Pfc	Hq/555	12 Aug 50	

Name	Rank	Unit	Date	Notes (a)
Smothers Loyd	Sgt	A/555	12 Aug 50	
St Clair David A.	Pfc	B/555	12 Aug 50	

Category III: Verbal Reports (Must be Verified)

Name	Rank	Unit	Date	Notes (a)
Akina Frederick K.	Pvt	-	17 Jun 52	
Berry Cecil D.	-	-	-	
Black William H.	Pfc	B	12 Aug 52	
Burgio Anthony R.	Pvt	-	9 Sep 50	
Cave James E.	Cpl	-	1 Jan 51	
Contiliano Mario	Pvt	-	19 Dec 52	
Cooper	Sgt	K	17 Sep 50	
Davis Howard K.	-	B/555	-	
Franz David	Pfc	D	-	MIA
Gillispie Leroy	-	Svc/555	- 50	
Grizzard James F.	-	A/555	25 Apr 51	
Herb James D.	Pvt	-	-	
Hitchcock -	-	K	28 Nov 50	
Homowan Alfredo C.	Cpl	-	5 Sep 50	
Houston James M.	Pvt	-	8 Aug 50	
Jones Robert H.	-	B/555	-	
Jones William D.	Pvt	G	-	
Lau Hee Walter L.	-	-	30 Nov 50	
Lewis Harold	-	E	-	
Little John M.	-	I	- 52	
Marta Arthur H.	-	H	-	
Miller Donald G.	-	E	-	
Miller John R.	-	-	-	
Ryan John J. Pfc	-		18 Sep 52	
Sealy Hoyt L.	1st Lt	-	3 Dec 50	
Sheridan William L.	Pfc	Hq/555	12 Aug 50	
Shibao Nobumi	Cpl	-	25 Nov 52	
Shimabukuro Robert	Sgt	-	15 Aug 52	
Van Housen -	-	G	- 53	
Walters William F.	SFC	H	-	
Whiteside William	2d Lt	-/555	-	
Workman Charles W.	Pfc	-	27 Sep 50	
Young John R.	Pfc	-	13 Jun 54	DED

Notes:

(a) Abbreviations:

BFC - Battle Field Commission	BSM - Bronze Star Medal	CMH - Congressional Medal of Honor
DED - Missing, Declared Dead	DSC - Distinguished Service Cross	DOW - Dead of Wounds
MIA - Missing in Action	MIA/DIC - Missing in Action/Died in Captivity	NBC - Non-battle Casualty
PH - Purple Heart Medal	ROK - Republic of Korea Army	SSM - Silver Star Medal
SM - Soldier's Medal	POW/DED - Prisoner of War, Declared Dead	

(b) Last KIA in Korea, DOW 27 July 53

(c) Unknown soldier, buried in Masan Cemetery, Korea

(d) Large number of 555FA Bn casualties in Aug 50 from TF Kean/Bloody Gulch and April 51 from CCF Spring Offensive/Death Valley

KOREAN EX-PRISONERS OF WAR (1950-53)

5TH REGIMENTAL COMBAT TEAM OF THE U.S. 8TH ARMY

PARTIAL LIST ONLY

The following released Prisoners of War have been extracted from the National Archives List of Korean War Prisoners and other sources by CSM Timothy F. Casey (USA-Ret).

Additional names provided by United Press International News Service to its affiliated newspapers in 1953 and from various annual membership rosters of the 5th Regimental Combat Team Association were consolidated and compiled in April 1994 by Dan M. Gonzales, member of the 5th Regimental Combat Team Association.

Notes to abbreviations: from Far East Command Letter, dated 1 August 1952, Subject: Returned American Military Personnel. (RET = returned to military control, method unknown (escaped, released, etc); (REL = released by the enemy on lines); (ESC = escaped); (NAT ARCH = National Archives list of Prisoners of War); (N/L = not listed); (UPI = United Press International News Service); (5th RCT AR = 5th Regimental Combat Team Association annual roster).

NAME	CAPTURED	UNIT	BN/REGT	INTERN CAMP	STATE	SOURCE
Aguilera, Vincent	N/L	Hq, 2d	5th RCT	N/L	Fort Worth, TX	UPI News
Balkcom, William M.	25 Apr 51	A Co	5th RCT	N/L	Lindale, GA	NAT ARCH
Beckwith, Harold W.	N/L	F Co	5th RCT	N/L	Meriden, KS	UPI News
Bedrosian, Raymond	22 Apr 51	E Co	5th RCT	N/L	Albany, NY	NAT ARCH
Bemerer, Albert L.	23 Apr 51	C Co	5th RCT	N/L	Cincinnati, OH	NAT ARCH
Bernard, Charles E.	23 Apr 51	A Co	5th RCT	N/L	Atglen, PA	NAT ARCH
Blackburn, William L.	22 Apr 51	E Co	5th RCT	N/L	Monroe, WA	NAT ARCH
Bleuer, Gene	51	B Co	5th RCT	Pyongyang	Rock Island, IL	Interview
Booth, Nathaniel	22 Apr 51	E Co	5th RCT	N/L	Bassfield, MS	NAT ARCH
Borie, Harry E.	23 Apr 51	Med Co	5th RCT	N/L	Philadelphia, PA	NAT ARCH
Bowditch, Arthur J.	N/L	A Co	5th RCT	N/L	N/L	5th RCT AR
Bowling, Vernone E.	23 Apr 51	I Co	5th RCT	1,4	KY	NAT ARCH
Bradely, Horace Jr.	23 Apr 51	I Co	5th RCT	N/L	Lake George, NY	NAT ARCH
Brunelle, Harry E.	N/L	A Co	5th RCT	N/L	Alamo, TX	5th RCT AR
Butler, Frederick Jr.	N/L	D Co	5th RCT	N/L	Martson, MO	UPI News
Campbell, Paul B.	17 May 51	C Co	5th RCT	N/L	Bishop, MD	NAT ARCH
Carter, Menifee G.	25 Apr 51	B Btry	555 FAB	N/L	W. Palm Beach, FL	5th RCT AR
Carvalho, Paul P.	23 Jan 51	E Co	5th RCT	1,3	HI	NAT ARCH
Clay, Jessie W.	23 Apr 51	A Co	5th RCT	N/L	Marketsville, VA	NAT ARCH
Collins, Gene E.	23 Apr 51	C Co	5th RCT	N/L	Paducah, KY	NAT ARCH
Defontes, Earl	23 Apr 51	A Co	5th RCT	N/L	HI	NAT ARCH
Diaz, Lupe	14 Dec 50	K Co	5th RCT	N/L	MI	NAT ARCH
Dixon, Ralph P. Jr.	25 Apr 51(?)	A Btry	555 FAB	N/L	N/L	NAT ARCH
Drange, Julian K.	25 Apr 51	G Co	5th RCT	N/L	Hazel Run, MN	NAT ARCH
Dudley, Robert W.	25 Apr 51	A Btry	555 FAB	N/L	N/L	NAT ARCH
Dylag, Edwin C. (RET)	N/L	Hvy Mtr	5th RCT	N/L	N/L	FEC G2Ltr
Elsburry, Irvin B.	23 Apr 51	C Co	5th RCT	N/L	Sutherland, IA	NAT ARCH
Ends, Frank M. (RET)	23 Apr 51	B Co	5th RCT	N/L	MA	FEC GSLtr
Farrell, Thomas S.	N/L	Med Co	5th RCT	N/L	Trinidad, CO	UPS News
Fenton, Daniel E.	N/L	B Btry	555 FAB	N/L	Terre Haute, IN	5th RCT AR
Field, Maurice E.	25 Apr 51	F Co	5th RCT	N/L	Hoisington, KS	NAT ARCH
Flath, Herman H.	22 Apr 51	E Co	5th RCT	1,4	IN	NAT ARCH
Flower, Gerald M.	22 Apr 51	F Co	5th RCT	N/L	Memphis, TN	NAT ARCH
Fogliano, Luke L. (RET)	N/L	Hvy Mtr	5th RCT	N/L	N/L	FEC G2Ltr
Franz, David	23 Apr 51	D Co	5th RCT	3	MA	NAT ARCH
Gall, Ethan A. (RET)	N/L	I Co	5th RCT	N/L	N/L	FEC G2Ltr
Gaskins, June V.	15 Sep 51	C Btry	555 FAB	N/L	Nashville, GA	NAT ARCH
Gauthier, Joseph A.	23 Apr 51	A Co	5th RCT	N/L	Opelousas, LA	NAT ARCH
Gorski, Raymond A.	22 Apr 51	E Co	5th RCT	1	MI	NAT ARCH
Goodwin, William J.(ESC)	22 Apr 51	F Co	5th RCT	N/L	N/L	FEC G2Ltr
Grussing, Daniel	22 Apr 51	D Co	5th RCT	1	MN	NAT ARCH
Habben, Alvin C.	14 Jul 53	C Btry	555 FAB	6	MN	NAT ARCH
Harden, Chales P.	25 Apr 51	A Btry	555 FAB	N/L	N/L	NAT ARCH
Harrison, Jake	23 Apr 51	Hq 1st	5th RCT	N/L	Lake City, TN	NAT ARCH
Hart, James W.	N/L	F Co	5th RCT	N/L	Tulsa, OK	5th RCT AR
Hart, Robert L.	25 Apr 51	B Btry	555 FAB	N/L	Fairmont, IL	5th RCT AR
Hartman, John R.	23 Apr 51	H Co	5th RCT	N/L	Granite City, NC	NAT ARCH
Hauer, Victor N. Sr.	25 Apr 51	C Btry	555 FAB	N/L	Austin, TX	NAT ARCH

NAME	CAPTURED	UNIT	BN/REGT	INTERN CAMP	STATE	SOURCE
Hawkins, Harold L.	17 May 51	G Co	5th RCT	N/L	Willow Springs, MO	NAT ARCH
Heller, Joseph J.	23 Apr 51	C Co	5th RCT	1,3	PA	NAT ARCH
Hewitt, Roy E.	N/L	G Co	5th RCT	N/L	Council Grove, KS	UPI News
Higo, Koyei (RET)	N/L	G co	5th RCT	N/L	HI	FEC G2Ltr
Hodapp, Arthur L. (RET)	23 Apr 51	A Co	5th RCT	N/L	N/L	FSC G2Ltr
Hope, James R.	N/L	E Co	5th RCT	N/L	N/L	5th RCT AR
Howell, Thomas J.	N/L	C Btry	555 FAB	N/L	Amarillo, TX	UPI News
Hughes, Melvin D. (RET)	N/L	C Co	5th RCT	N/L	MD	FEC G2Ltr
Huffman, Joseph R.	23 Apr 51	A Co	5th RCT	1	MI	NAT ARCH
Inannatuono, Frank D.	N/L	E Co	5th RCT	N/L	Tiffin, OH	5th RCT AR
Ingbino, Gregorio	14 Dec 50	K Co	5th RCT	N/L	HI	NAT ARCH
Itagaki, George J.	23 Apr 51	I Co	5th RCT	1	HI	NAT ARCH
Jarvis, Bobby W.	23 Apr 51	B Btry	555 FAB	N/L	Wichita Falls, TX	UPI News
Jenner, John R.	23 Apr 51	A Co	5th RCT	N/L	Syracuse, NY	NAT ARCH
Keenan, William P.	28 Apr 51	I Co	5th RCT	2,5	ME	NAT ARCH
Kelman, Walter	23 Apr 51	A Co	5th RCT	1	PA	NAT ARCH
Kennedy, Doanld	25 Apr 51	B Btry	555 FAB	N/L	Joplin, MO	NAT ARCH
King, John	25 Apr 51	G Co	5th RCT	N/L	Cochran, GA	5th RCT AR
La Claire, Peter S.	22 Apr 51	F Co	5th RCT	N/L	Fulton, NY	NAT ARCH
Landie, Andre A.	11 Dec 50	K Co	5th RCT	N/L	MA	NAT ARCH
Lang, Henry J.	22 Apr 51	E Co	5th RCT	2,5	NY	NAT ARCH
Larose, Arthur L.	22 Apr 51	D Co	5th RCT	3,4	MA	NAT ARCH
Leipold, James D. (RET)	22 Apr 51	F Co	5th RCT	N/L	N/L	FEC G2Ltr
Linfante, Raymond A.	22 Apr 51	E Co	5th RCT	N/L	Newark, NJ	NAT ARCH
Lionti, Salvatore P.	29 Apr 51	K Co	5th RCT	N/L	OH	NAT ARCH
Livesay, Carl E.	25 Apr 51	B Btry	555 FAB	N/L	Deuniak Springs, FL	UPI News
Long, Jessie L.	N/L	A Co	5th RCT	N/L	Ft Mill, SC	5th RCT AR
Lundquist, Ed	23 Apr 51	E Co	5th RCT	N/L	Hickory, NC	5th RCT AR
Mabiba, William	14 Dec 50	K Co	5th RCT	N/L	CA	NAT ARCH
Mahrenholz, Robert W.	23 Apr 51	I Co	5th RCT	N/L	Mt. Ayr, IA	NAT ARCH
Martin, Joe E. (RET)	N/L	F Co	5th RCT	N/L	TN	FEC G2Ltr
McBride, Jimmie C. (RET)	N/L	I Co	5th RCT	N/L	N/L	FEC G2Ltr
McMurtrie, Thomas H.	23 Apr 51	Med Co	5th RCT	N/L	Pottsville, PA	NAT ARCH
McNeil, John J.	23 Apr 51	C Co	5th RCT	N/L	Brooklyn, NY	NAT ARCH
Miller, Henry L.	23 Apr 51	B Btry	555 FAB	N/L	Magnolia, MS	NAT ARCH
Miller, William E.	17 May 51	A Co	5th RCT	N/L	Bellfountain, OH	NAT ARCH
Millholland, Charles	20 Apr 51	A Co	5th RCT	1	TN	NAT ARCH
Mincey, Harry F.	23 Apr 51	A Co	5th RCT	N/L	Cleveland, OH	NAT ARCH
Mitchell, Lawrence	25 Apr 51	A Btry	555 FAB	N/L	Woodbury, NJ	NAT ARCH
Muntzel, Ralph E. (RET)	N/L	N/L	555 FAB	N/L	N/L	FEC G2Ltr
Nothstein, Edward E.	23 Apr 51	C Co	5th RCT	N/L	Leighton, PA	NAT ARCH
Osborne, Ed	22 Apr 51	E Co	5th RCT	2,5	Wilkesboro, NC	NAT ARCH
Olazabel, Joseph D.	14 Jul 53	C Btry	555 FAB	6	CA	NAT ARCH
Palacio, Marcus F.	25 Apr 51	B Btry	555 FAB	1	Brundage, TX	NAT ARCH
Paul, Frank G.	22 Apr 51	D Co	5th RCT	N/L	Copley, PA	NAT ARCH
Perkins, Marion E.	23 Apr 51	C Co	5th RCT	N/L	Lawrence, IN	NAT ARCH
Pearl, Charles W. (RET)	N/L	C Btry	555 FAB	N/L	OH	FEC G2Ltr
Pendelton, Robert R.	22 Apr 51	E Co	5th RCT	N/L	Los Angeles, CA	NAT ARCH
Perez, Robert	25 Apr 51	G Co	5th RCT	N/L	NY	NAT ARCH
Perry Jackie L.	22 Apr 51	D Co	5th RCT	N/L	Dayton, OH	NAT ARCH
Peasner, Thomas R. Jr.	23 Apr 51	C Co	5th RCT	N/L	Lancaster, TX	UPI News
Phillips, Johnnie E.	23 Apr 51	H Co	5th RCT	N/L	Bakersfield, CA	NAT ARCH
Radcliff, Warner R. (RET)	N/L	G Co	5th RCT	N/L	N/L	FEC G2Ltr
Ramos, Ralph	23 Apr 51	Med Co	5th RCT	N/L	Sugar City, CO	NAT ARCH
Reedy, Doyle L.	N/L	Hq 2d	5th RCT	N/L	Chalsea, OK	UPI News
Reeves, Henry E.	N/L	E Co	5th RCT	N/L	Port Arthur, TX	UPI News
Renouf, Bernard N.	22 Apr 51	E Co	5th RCT	N/L	West Hartford, CT	NAT ARCH
Replog, Phillip M.	15 Jul 53	N/L	555 FAB	6	TN	NAT ARCH
Risley, Paul F.	23 Apr 51	A Co	5th RCT	N/L	OH	NAT ARCH
Robinson, Mendel F.	29 Apr 51	K Co	5th RCT	N/L	SC	NAT ARCH
Robbins, Edward P.	22 Apr 51	D Co	5th RCT	N/L	Fall River, MA	NAT ARCH
Runyon, William R.	25 Apr 51	A Btry	555 FAB	N/L	Indianapolis, IN	NAT ARCH
Ruth, Gerald G.	23 Apr 51	I Co	5th RCT	1,4	OH	NAT ARCH
Ryder, Donald F.	N/L	M Co	5th RCT	N/L	N/L	5th RCT AR
Schultz, Gerald L. (RET)	N/L	A Btry	555 FAB	N/L	N/L	FEC G2Ltr
Shea, Robert T.	14 Dec 50	K Co	5th RCT	N/L	MA	NAT ARCH
Spackman, Thomas M.	23 Apr 51	C Co	5th RCT	N/L	Rochester, NY	NAT ARCH
Stamper, Cecil C.	23 Apr 51	N/L	5th REGT	N/L	Baltimore, MD	NAT ARCH
Stanley, George A.	23 Apr 51	A Co	5th RCT	N/L	Poulsbo, WA	NAT ARCH
Stenson, Keith E.	23 Apr 51	N/L	5th RCT	1	MN	NAT ARCH
Stone, Clovis R.	N/L	A Co	5th RCT	N/L	West, TX	UPI News

NAME	CAPTURED	UNIT	BN/REGT	INTERN CAMP	STATE	SOURCE
Thompson, Elmer L.	25 Apr 51	Med Co	5th RCT	1,4	MS	NAT ARCH
Thrush, Ralph L. Jr.	N/L	C Btry	555 FAB	N/L	N/L	5th RCT AR
Tinker, Estal T.	25 Apr 51	A Co	5th RCT	N/L	OK	NAT ARCH
Tupa, Joseph S.	28 Apr 51	C Co	5th RCT	1,4	HI	NAT ARCH
Umi, Charles M.	N/L	A Btry	555 FAB	N/L	HI	FEC G2Ltr
Varela, Santiago J.	25 Apr 51	B Btry	555 FAB	N/L	St. Louis, MO	5th RCT AR
Velligas, Frank K.	N/L	M Co	5th RCT	N/L	N/L	5th RCT AR
Viscuso, Andrew J.	23 Apr 51	I Co	5th RCT	N/L	Phoenixville, PA	NAT ARCH
Wakehouse, Donald L.	N/L	C Btry	555 FAB	N/L	N/L	5th RCT AR
Watson, Wilburn C.	23 Apr 51	C Co	5th RCT	N/L	Burnsville, MS	NAT ARCH
Whitlinger, John B.	23 Apr 51	A Co	5th RCT	N/L	Zanesville, OH	NAT ARCH
Wilkins, Samuel III (RET)	23 Apr 51	A Co	5th RCT	N/L	N/L	FEC G2Ltr
Windsor, Robert	23 Apr 51	C Co	5th RCT	N/L	Idaho Falls, ID	NAT ARCH
Wolfe, Howard	23 Apr 51	A Co	5th RCT	1	AL	NAT ARCH
Wolfe, William L.	25 Apr 51	Sv Btry	555 FAB	N/L	Fairmount, WV	NAT ARCH
Woods, Gordon H.	25 Apr 51	C Co	5th RCT	1	WV	NAT ARCH
Wright, Eugene P. (REL)	23 Apr 51	C Co	5th RCT	N/L	N/L	FEC G2Ltr
Wright, James N.	23 Apr 51	C Co	5th RCT	N/L	Newport News, VA	NAT ARCH
Yewchyn, Mike	N/L	H & G	5th RCT	N/L	N/L	5th RCT AR

Soldiers of the 5th RCT advancing, 19 March 1951. (source: Chang)

278

BIBLIOGRAPHY

BOOKS

The American Battle Monuments Commission World War II Commemorative Program. Washington, D.C.: American Battle Monuments Commission

Lieutenant Colonel Appleman, Roy E. *Ridgway Duels for Korea.* College Station: Texas A&M Press, 1990.

Lieutenant Colonel Appleman, Roy E. *Disaster in Korea.* College Station: Texas A&M Press, 1989.

Lieutenant Colonel Appleman, Roy E. *South to the Naktong, North to the Yalu.* Washington, D.C.: Office of the Chief of Military History, Department of the Army, 1961.

Balkoski, Joseph. *Beyond the Beachead: The 29th Infantry Division in Normandy.* Harrisburg: Stackpole Books, 1989.

Barker, A.J. and John Walter. *Russian Infantry Weapons of World War II.* New York: Arco Publishing Company, Inc., 1971.

Brigadier General Barth, G. B. *Tropic Lightning and Taro Leaf in Korea: July '50 - May '51.* Athens, Greece: Chief of Public Information, Department of the Army, 1955.

Blair, Clay. *The Forgotten War: America in Korea 1950-1951.* New York: Anchor Books Doubleday, 1989.

Major Boatner, III, Mark M. *Army Lore and Customs of the Service: Regular Regiments of the Korean Conflict.* Tokyo: Pacific Stars and Stripes, 1954.

Bryan, William S., Editor. *Our Islands and Their People.* New York: The Thompson Publishing Co., 1905.

Carlson, Doug. *Punchbowl: The National Memorial Cemetery of the Pacific.* Aiea: Island Heritage Publishing, 1992.

Master Sergeant Chang, Albert. *This Way to War.* Honolulu: Tongg Publishing Company, LTD., 1953.

General Collins, J. Lawton Joe. *Lightning Joe: An Autobiography.* Baton Rouge: Louisiana University Press, 1979.

Captain David, Allan A. and Sergeant Norwin E. Austin, Editors. *Battleground Korea: The Story of the 25th Infantry Division.* Tokyo: 25th Infantry Division History Council, 1951.

Dupuy, R. E. and T. N. Dupuy. *The Encyclopedia of Military History from 3,500 B.C. to the Present.* New York: Harper and Row, Publishers, 1977.

Eisner, Will. *America's Combat Weapons.* New York: Sterling Publishing Co., Inc., 1960.

Major English, John A. *On Infantry.* New York: Praeger, 1984.

Fehrenbach, T. R. *This Kind of War: A Study in Unpreparedness.* New York: Macmillan Company, 1963.

Freitas, J.F. *Portuguese-Hawaiian Memories.* Honolulu: The Print Shop Company, Limited, 1930.

Goncharov, Sergei N., John W. Lewis, and Xue Litai. *Uncertain Partners: Stalin, Mao, and the Korean War.* Stanford: Stanford University Press, 1993.

Goulden, Joseph C. Korea. *The Untold Story of the War.* New York: McGraw-Hill Paperbacks, 1982.

Colonel Hackworth, David H. and Julie Sherman. *About Face: The Odyssey of an American Warrior.* New York: Simon and Schuster, 1989.

Colonel Heinl, Jr., Robert Debs. *Victory at High Tide: The Inchon-Seoul Campaign.* New York: J.B. Lippincott Company, 1968.

Hoyt, Edwin P. *On to the Yalu.* New York: Stein and Day, Inc., 1984

Hoyt, Edwin P. *The Pusan Perimeter.* New York: Military Heritage Press, 1984.

Jolidon, Laurence. *Last Seen Alive: The Search for Missing POWs from the Korean War.* Austin: Ink-Slinger Press, 1995.

Jones, Charles and Eugene. *The Face of War.* New York: Prentice-Hall, Inc., 1951.

Captain Johnson, Melvin M. and Charles T. Haven. *Automatic Weapons of the World.* New York: William Morrow and Company, 1945.

General MacArthur, Douglas. *Reminiscences.* New York: Mcgraw-Hill Book Company, 1964.

McAdoo, Albert J. *The 5th RCT in Korea: The First Fifty Days. Book One.* P.O. Box 878, Acton, MA. 01720-0012, 1990.

McAdoo, Albert J. *The 5th RCT in Korea with the 24th Infantry Division. Book Two.* P.O. Box 878, Acton, MA. 01720-0012, 1990.

McClure, Gene Edwin. *Gene Edwin McClure: An Autobiography.* Unpublished manuscript located in the University of Texas.

Medal of Honor Recipients 1863-1978. Washington, D.C.: U.S. Government Printing Office, 1979.

Montross, Lynn and Captain Nicholas A. Canzona. *U.S. Marine Operations in Korea 1950-1953. Volume I. The Pusan Perimeter.* Washington, D.C.: Historical Branch, G-3, Headquarters U.S. Marine Corps, 1954.

Mossman, Billy C. *Ebb and Flow: November 1950 - July 1951.* Washington, D.C.: Center of Military History, United States Army, 1990.

General Ridgway, Matthew B. *The Korean War.* New York: Doubleday and Company, 1967.

Major Sawyer, Robert K. *Military Advisors in Korea: KMAG in Peace and War.* Washington, D.C.: Office of the Chief of Military History, Department of the Army, 1962.

Register of Graduates and Former Cadets United States Military Academy, West Point, New York. West Point: Association of Graduates, USMA, 1993.

The Senior R.O.T.C. Manuel. Washington, D.C.: Department of the Army, 1950.

Schnabel, James F. *U.S. Army in the Korean War: Policy and Direction: The First Year.* Washington, D.C.: Office of the Chief of Military History, Department of the Army, 1971.

Spurr, Russell. *Enter the Dragon: China's Undeclared War Against the U.S. in Korea 1950-1951.* New York: New Market Press, 1988.

Stanton, Shelby. *U.S. Army Uniforms of the Korean War.* Harrisburg: Stackpole Books, 1992.

Sterling, Elspeth P. and Catherine C. Summers. *Sites of Oahu.* Honolulu: Bishop Museum Press, 1978.

Summers, Jr., Harry G. *Korean War Almanac.* New York: Facts on File, Inc., 1990.

Toland, John. *In Mortal Combat: Korea, 1950-1953.* New York: William Morrow and Company, Inc., 1991.

Veterans of Foreign Wars Memorial Edition Pictorial History of the Korean War: MacArthur Reports. Veterans' Historical Book Service, Inc., 1951.

5th Regimental Combat Team Association

The 5th RCT Association provided copies of their monthly newsletter. Each issue contains a treasure trove of first person accounts of the 5th RCT in Hawaii and Korea from the perspective of both officers and the rank-in-file. The author conducted numerous interviews with men who served in the 5th RCT during the years 1949 - 1951. Most of these conversations were tape recorded and are in the author's personal files.

Honolulu Archives

The Honolulu Archives provided access to the Joseph R. Farrington Papers, a rich trove of material written by a man who was determined to achieve statehood for his beloved Hawaii.

National Archive Material

The National Archives provided access to records dealing with the 5th Regimental Combat Team from January 1949 to March 1951, and the 25th Infantry Division from August 1950 to October 1950. The 5th RCT's records were found in INRG-3 and INRG-5: Record Group 407, Box 4689; and INRG-5: Record Group 407, Boxes 4690-4691, and Boxes 5237-5240. The 25th Infantry Division's records used in this project were the 25th Infantry Division Records: History Book 1. Additionally, the author had access to the files on the 1st Cavalry Division (SEP 50) and the 24th Infantry Division (SEP 50-MAY 51).

Newspapers

Microfilmed copies of the *Honolulu Advertiser* and the *Honolulu Star-Bulletin* were obtained in the Honolulu Public Library.

Personal Letters, Photographs and Associated Documents

Mr. and Mrs. Manuel G. Calhau (Manley) provided unlimited access to Sonny's letters and those written by friends and relatives. Due to the extreme personal nature of these letters, sensitive information was deleted as required to protect the privacy of others. Information of a repetitive nature was deleted in the interest of clarity. Sonny's letters required a little editing, for instance, he would rarely insert a question mark (?) into its proper place at the end of a sentence. Moreover, he probably had but limited access to maps, so most of his Korean place names were misspelled and subsequently corrected by this author. In the main, however, Sonny's letters are in their original form, with but a few changes to assist the reader.

Tropic Lightning Museum

The Tropic Lightning Museum at Schofield Barracks, Oahu, Hawaii, home of the 25th Infantry Division (Light) Tropic Lightning provided access to their rare book collection and files pertaining to the 25th Infantry Division during the Korean War. Moreover, the museum kindly allowed the author to copy a large number of photographs depicting the 5th RCT in action during the first year of the Korean War.

The Windward Oahu War Memorial. This shot was taken on the day the plaque bearing the names of the men who fell in Korea was added. The old Pali Road is in the background. (source: Calhau family)

INDEX

King Company, 5th RCT, opens fire on Chinese Communist Forces.
(sources: NA/Chang)

About the Author

Michael P. Slater is an active duty U.S. Marine. Following Desert Storm he became interested in the history of the 5th RCT when his father-in-law told him about his brother SGT Ernest Malcolm Calhau who was KIA on 23 March 1951 leading 1st Squad, 1st Platoon, Fox Company, 5th RCT up Hill 814 in the ROK.

Slater has interviewed numerous veterans ranging from riflemen to battalion commanders.

Slater is a graduate of The Citadel and American Military University. His passion in life is visiting WWII and Korean War era battlefields.

Printed in the USA
CPSIA information can be obtained
at www.ICGtesting.com
JSHW050438101023
49917JS00016B/743